# The Scriptures of Won Buddhism

CLASSICS IN EAST ASIAN BUDDHISM

# The Scriptures of Won Buddhism

A Translation of the *Wŏnbulgyo kyojŏn*
with Introduction

Bongkil Chung

A KURODA INSTITUTE BOOK

**University of Hawai'i Press**
Honolulu

Printed in the United States of America

24   23   22   21   20   19      6   5   4   3   2   1

**Library of Congress Cataloging-in-Publication Data**
The scriptures of Won Buddhism : a translation of the Wŏnbulgyo
kyŏjon with introduction / Bongkil Chung.
    p.    cm.—(Kuroda Institute Classics in East Asian Buddhism)
Includes bibliographical references and index.
  ISBN 0-8248-2185-8 (hardcover : alk. paper)
  1. Wŏn Pulgyo (Sect).    2. Wŏn Pulgyo (Sect)—Doctrines.
I. Chung, Bongkil.    II. Series.
BQ9222 .S26 2003
294.3'92—dc21                                        2002011186


ISBN  978-0-8248-7933-4  (pbk.)

The Kuroda Institute for the Study of Buddhism and Human Values
is a nonprofit, educational corporation founded in 1976. One of its
primary objectives is to promote scholarship on the his-torical,
philosophical, and cultural ramifications of Buddhism. In association
with the University of Hawai'i Press, the Institute also publishes
Studies in East Asian Buddhism, a series of scholarly investigations
of significant themes and topics in the East Asian Buddhist tradition.

*Designed by Santos Barbasa Jr.*

**Kuroda Institute
Classics in East Asian Buddhism**

**Kuroda Institute**
**Studies in East Asian Buddhism**

# Contents

# TRANSLATION
## *The Canon*

# TRANSLATION

## *The Scripture of Sot'aesan*

# Foreword

Wŏnbulgyo—"Consummate," or "Circle," Buddhism—is a Korean new religion formed in the early twentieth century that purportedly derives from the unique enlightenment experience of its founder, Sot'aesan (1891–1943). After his enlightenment, Sot'aesan researched different religious systems to guide him in framing his insights before finally deciding that his realization had profound affinities with Buddhism. Because of these affinities, Sot'aesan originally called his new religion the *Pulbŏp yŏn'guhoe*, the Society for the Study of the Buddha-dharma, and later his followers came to call their tradition Wŏnbulgyo. In this book, Professor Bongkil Chung, a lifelong student and scholar of this religion, offers the first complete scholarly translation of the core canonical materials of Wŏnbulgyo along with a valuable introduction to Wŏnbulgyo history and thought and the wider milieu of fin-de-siècle indigenous Korean religion.

Despite calling itself Wŏnbulgyo, the religion's connections to the broader Buddhist tradition have rarely been as transparent as the name might imply. The Wŏnbulgyo ecclesiastical leadership has at various points in time been decidedly ambivalent about their religion's associations with mainstream Buddhism. Some later redactions of their canonical materials have even sought to obscure these associations by replacing emblematic Buddhist explanations of religious development in favor of explanations unique to Wŏnbulgyo. After a lifetime of research on these texts, Professor Chung has become an outspoken advocate of the Buddhist underpinnings of Wŏnbulgyo thought and in this translation has restored what he believes to be earlier, more authentic, Buddhistic interpretations that have been expurgated in later church redactions. This decision has not been without its consequences: Professor Chung's attempts to defend his scholarly views have led to a personal estrangement from some church leaders; and even though this translation was promoted by the church itself to serve as a definitive new translation of Wŏnbulgyo texts for overseas proselytization, the church leadership has withdrawn its imprimatur from his activities. Professor Chung details the reasons for his decision to restore these readings in Appendix I; but the detailed analysis he provides there of internal changes in the Wŏnbulgyo canonical recensions provides little

hint of the profound personal ordeal he endured in defending his translation. However one may regard his translation, we must applaud Professor Chung's courage in adhering to the highest standards of scholarly integrity and academic independence in its preparation.

The Western-language translation of Korean Buddhist materials, especially those written in vernacular Korean, is still in its infancy and there are few precursors available to help guide the translator. We therefore are fortunate that, in many respects, Professor Chung has been preparing for much of his adult life for this task of translating Wŏnbulgyo materials. After graduating from Won Kwang College (now University) in Korea, Professor Chung came to the United States to study Western philosophy and to build the background necessary to convey Wŏnbulgyo concepts accurately in English. Much of Professor Chung's scholarly research has also focused on analyzing the contours of Wŏnbulgyo thought. Finally, he has spent years developing a terminology that would make Wŏnbulgyo ideas accessible to readers of English. Professor Chung has drawn on all the tools in his scholarly arsenal to convey the flavor and meaning of the original Korean texts. Written vernacular Korean was still very much a work in progress during the early twentieth century and the meaning of the Korean texts is not always clear-cut, even to the specialist. Professor Chung has taken an important first step in making this material intelligible to a Western audience. Wŏnbulgyo has arguably been the most successful of the Korean new religions and in recent decades has even made substantial strides toward establishing a worldwide presence for itself. The patient reader of Professor Chung's book will be rewarded with a full set of documents on this uniquely Korean innovation in religious thought, which sought creatively to adapt Buddhist ideas and practices in ways better suited to modern, secular society.

Robert E. Buswell, Jr.
*Los Angeles, California*

# Preface

This book is a study of a new form of Buddhism, Won Buddhism (K. Wŏnbulgyo), that started in Korea upon the spiritual awakening of a young man in 1916 and is now deeply entrenched in Korean society. Its founder predicted that Won Buddhism would be a major world religion in four to five hundred years. For now, however, there are some unsettled questions concerning its true identity. The most troublesome is whether it is an offshoot of the grand old Buddhism, as the Korean Buddhist order (*Chogye*) claims, or one of the Korean folk religions. The founder of Won Buddhism made it clear that the essential tenets of the doctrine he was establishing was Buddha-dharma or Buddhism; if Buddha-dharma were deleted from its doctrine, the heart of Won Buddhism would be removed. It must be pointed out, furthermore, that the founder has acknowledged his indebtedness to Buddhism and has noted that many masters in the past founded separate schools and sects of Buddhism to teach sentient beings. Among the numerous folk religions that have arisen in Korea around the turn of the twentieth century, three are prominent: Ch'ŏndogyo (Religion of Heavenly Way), Chŭngsan'gyo (Religion of Chŭngsan), and Wŏnbulgyo (Won Buddhism). Presently, these three are all healthy in Korea and have overseas branch chapters. I have included in the introduction a brief history and theology of Ch'ŏndogyo and Chŭngsan'gyo as a way of identifying Won Buddhism in the context of the Korean religious milieu for the following three reasons. First, the founder of Won Buddhism predicted that the founders of the other two religions would be recognized as eminent prophets with the spreading of Won Buddhism as a world religion. Second, some essential tenets of Won Buddhism were anticipated in either one or both of the other two religions. Third, the polemics of the Chŭngsan'gyo allege that the founders of Won Buddhism grafted the essential tenets of their doctrine with Buddhism to create Won Buddhism. I have also included a brief history of the Korean Buddhist persecution that lasted for five hundred years to help readers understand why the founder of Won Buddhism has established a new form of Buddhism.

The inception of this book goes back to 1960, when I was staying in

the central general headquarters of Won Buddhism upon graduation from Won Kwang College (now University) in Korea. The second patriarch of the Won Buddhist order gave me warnings concerning the translation of the *Canon* in this translation. The warning came when I did not have the slightest idea of going to the United States of America for graduate studies, let alone translating this book. He seemed to have known what was going to happen thirty years later, in 1991, when I got into the project of this translation. Since there was an English version of *The Scripture of Won Buddhism* (1988), a revised version of *The Canonical Textbook of Won Buddhism* (1971) for Won Buddhist church use, this book was meant to be a scholarly translation from its very inception. However, the newly elected fourth patriarch of the order planned to have a new English translation made for Won Buddhist church use. As was requested by the order of Won Buddhism, I submitted the manuscript of this translation to the translation committee appointed by the order, which tried to do a collective editing on my manuscript only to fail to come to agreement on some critical terms. So the committee decided to commission a third translation for Won Buddhist church use.

The Korean original of this translation is the 1962 edition of the *Wŏnbulgyo kyojŏn*, translated here as *The Scriptures of Won Buddhism*, which consists of two books: the *Canon* and the *Scripture of Sot'aesan*. Until this edition (1962) was published, the Won Buddhist order used the *Pulgyo chŏngjŏn* (Correct canon of Buddhism) published in 1943. The *Canon* of the 1962 edition is a redaction of the *Canon* of the 1943 edition. During the redaction process some tenets crucial to the integrity of doctrine were altered with the effect that the light of the original writer's wisdom was significantly dimmed. I have restored in my translation those crucial points and tried to persuade the Supreme Council of the Won Buddhist order to acknowledge the importance of the restoration. Although the current leaders of Won Buddhism are convinced of the importance of restoration, they are unwilling to bear the responsibility of correcting the errors themselves. The second patriarch of the Won Buddhist order had decreed that the 1943 edition be preserved permanently; some external scholars will compare the two editions to see the errors made during the redaction. It is my firm conviction that those altered parts should be restored to the original writings not only in the translation but also in the Korean original, lest its doctrine be like an inefficacious drug. The founder viewed his new form of Buddhism as a medicine to cure the world of illness and save sentient beings from suffering in the bitter seas of misery. The points of restoration can be found in the relevant notes and in appendix 1.

It is with great pleasure that I acknowledge my indebtedness to the

encouragement and beneficence of my mentors, patrons, and friends in Korea and in the United States, without which this work could not have been initiated or completed. I would like to express my gratitude to Professor George C. Kerner, my advisor for the doctoral dissertation at Michigan State University, who advised me to apply Anglo-American analytic philosophy to analyzing a moral system in the Oriental tradition. I would like to thank Dr. Carole Craven, Dr. Bok-in Kim, Dr. Kwang-soo Park, Mr. Sam Chamberlin, Ms. Maxine Cheesman (Wŏn Myŏng-do), and the late Su-ŭn Song for reading the manuscript in its various stages and for numerous valuable suggestions for improvements. I am especially indebted to the Kuroda Institute's two readers for the press, Professor Robert Buswell, Jr., and Professor Jacqueline Stone, each of whom went through the manuscript with great care and offered judicious and constructive criticism on a number of points. I have substantially revised the first half of the introductory essay following their suggestions. I am also grateful to Professor Buswell for his gracious consent to write the foreword to this work. I would like to express my gratitude to Professor Chung-ying Cheng, editor of the *Journal of Chinese Philosophy* (University of Hawai'i) for permitting me to use part of my article published in the journal for the introductory essay in this book. My thanks also go to Joanne Sandstrom for her labor in copyediting the manuscript. Of course, I take full responsibility for whatever errors in facts or interpretations there may be in this book.

Professor Song Chun-eun, a dear friend in the dharma, now president of Won Kwang University, encouraged me in 1991 to produce an academic translation of the Won Buddhist scriptures and helped me be released from teaching for two semesters by arranging half of the necessary financial aid for the nine-month sabbatical leave (1991–1992) at Florida International University; I owe him a great debt of gratitude. I am grateful to Provost James A. Mau and the Committee for Sabbatical Leave of the university for awarding me the sabbatical leave, without which I could never have done the translation. I am ever so grateful to Kim Chi-hyŏn, *pŏpsa* of Won Buddhism, who provided me with half of my stipend for the nine-month sabbatical leave and without whose generous help this translation could not have been completed, and to Kim In-chŏl, *pŏpsa*, then head of the administrative branch of the Order of Won Buddhism, for providing me with the necessary stipend for the 1992 summer term so that I could concentrate on writing the introductory essay. During the writing of the introduction, Hurricane Andrew (August 24, 1992), the effects of which have ever since been felt in completing this book, passed through south Florida. Chang Kyŏng-chin, *pŏpsa* of Won Buddhism, and Mrs. Kim Hyŏn-gang-ok

have provided me with a generous subvention for publication of this book; I am deeply grateful to these patrons, without whose moral and financial support this book would not have seen the sunlight. Last but not least, I would like to thank my wife, Shin-ok, and our two sons, Andrew and Daniel, who have been living with an anachronistic person preoccupied with this humble work.

# Abbreviations and Conventions

| | |
|---|---|
| **C** | Chinese |
| **CCP** | *Chŏngsan chongsa pŏbŏ* |
| **dt** | dharma title |
| **HC** | *Han'guk chonggyo* |
| **HCCS** | *Yŏsan Yu Pyŏng-dŏk paksa hwagap kinyŏm: Han'guk ch'ŏrhak chonggyo sasang* |
| **HCSC** | *Chinsan Han Ki-du paksa hwagap kinyŏm: Han'guk chonggyo sasang ŭi chae chomyŏng* |
| **HH** | Pak Chŏng-hun, comp. *Hanuran hanich'i-e* |
| **HKCS** | *Sungsan Pak Kil-chin paksa kohi kinyŏm: Han'guk kŭndae chonggyo sasangsa* |
| **HMWS** | *Munsan Kim Samnyong paksa hwagap kinyŏm: Han'guk munhwa wa wŏnbulgyo sasang* |
| **HSS** | *Sŏksan Han Chong-man paksa hwagap kinyŏm: Han'guk sasangsa* |
| **ICCY** | Yu Pyŏng-dŏk. *Irwŏnsang chilli ŭi che yŏn'gu* |
| **IMWS** | *Sot'aesan taejongsa t'ansaeng paekchunyŏn kinyŏm nonmunjip: Illyu munmyŏng kwa wŏnbulgyo sasang* |
| **J** | Japanese |
| **JCP** | *Journal of Chinese Philosophy* |
| **K** | Korean |
| **KAZ** | Robert Buswell, trans. *The Korean Approach to Zen: The Collected Works of Chinul* |
| **KC** | *Wŏnbulgyo kyogo ch'onggan* |
| **KJ** | *Korea Journal* |
| **KM** | *Kinyŏm munch'ong* |
| **PC** | *Pojo chŏnsŏ* |
| **PGC** | *Pulgyo chŏngjŏn* |
| **S** | Sanskrit |
| **SS** | *Scripture of Sot'aesan* |
| **T** | *Taishō shinshū daizōkyō* |
| **TCH** | *Taesun chŏn'gyŏng haesŏl* |
| **TJD** | *The Teachings of JeungSanDo* |
| **TSR** | *Taejonggyŏng sŏnoerok* |
| **TT** | *Tonggyŏng taejŏn* |

**WBC**      *Wŏnbulgyo chŏnsŏ*
**WBK**      *Wŏnbulgyo kyojŏn*
**WBS**      *Wŏnbulgyo sasang*
**WBSJ**     *Wŏnbulgyo sajŏn*
**WE**       Won Buddhist era
**WK**       *Wŏnbulgyo kyosa*

I have followed the McCune-Reischauer system for the transliteration of Korean proper names, the Wade-Giles system for Chinese, and the Hepburn system for Japanese. Sanskrit terminology that appears in *Webster's Third New International Dictionary* are left unitalicized: this includes such technical terms as dharmakāya, nirvāṇa, samādhi, prajñā, and dhyāna.

Citations for cross-references within the *Scriptures of Won Buddhism*, which consists of the *Canon* and the *Scripture of Sot'aesan*, are in the following fashion: *Canon*, pt., chap., sec. I, A, 1, a of the *Canon*; *SS* I:1 for the chapter and section of the *Scripture of Sot'aesan*. Citations from the *Taishō* canon are listed in the following way: title and fascicle number (if necessary); *T*[aishō]; *Taishō* serial number; *Taishō* volume number, page, register (a, b, or c) (e.g., *Chin-kang po-jo po-lo-mi ching*, *T*, 235.8.748c–752c).

The Korean full name starts with the family name followed by the first name except those already published in the Western style (first name first followed by family name).

# Study

# Introduction

## *The Foundation and Doctrine of Won Buddhism*

### Part One: Sot'aesan's Life and the Foundation of Won Buddhism

#### I. Background

Won Buddhism is one of the major religions of modern Korea and has been preparing itself to grow to be a world religion ever since it was founded upon the spiritual awakening in 1916 of a young Korean man, Pak Chung-bin (1891–1943), better known in the West as Sot'aesan. According to his biographer, his enlightened vision showed that the world was entering a new era of material civilization, by the formidable power of which sentient beings were about to be enslaved. He felt it urgent to show the sentient beings how they could be delivered from the tormenting seas of misery and realized that the best means lay in Buddha-dharma. Because Buddhism in Korea had been hibernating for five hundred years because of a massive persecution by the Cho-sŏn dynasty's (1392–1910) pro-Confucian national ideology, Sot'aesan could not rely on the Korean Buddhist order for the realization of his goal. Thus, Sot'aesan started to establish a new Buddhist order under the name the Society for the Study of Buddha-dharma (K. Pulbŏp yŏn'guhoe). The order grew under this name until 1947, when its second patriarch, Song Kyu (1900–1962), better known as Chŏngsan, renamed the order Won Buddhism. The term "Won Buddhism" is an English rendering of the Korean *wŏnbulgyo* (circle Buddhism). The order is called Wŏn (circle) Buddhism because it has enshrined a circular symbol called Irwŏnsang (unitary circular symbol) as the sign of Dharmakāya Buddha.[1] Under the former name, no question could have been raised about whether the new order was a sect of Korean Buddhism, for Sot'aesan himself presumed he was establishing a new form of Buddhism relevant to the contemporary secular world.

Its followers go to their temples on Sundays to attend the dharma

---

1. The fact that Dharmakāya Buddha is enshrined instead of the Buddha statue that can be the image of Sambhogakāya or Nirmanakāya Buddha reveals Sot'aesan's spirit of Buddhist renovation. For this reason alone, Won Buddhism can be classified as a new form of Buddhism.

meeting, where they enhance their faith and practice to realize Buddha-dharma in daily life. Like Christian churches, Won Buddhist temples are found in both rural and urban areas; temple buildings are also con-structed more like Christian churches, without a pinnacle, than like traditional Buddhist temples. It is noteworthy that clergywomen, who constitute more than 80 percent of the temple ministers, are all celibate while there are far fewer celibate clergymen than married clergymen. Most of the clergy have been educated in B.A., M.A., or Ph.D. pro-grams in the College of Won Buddhism, one of the colleges of Won Kwang University, a major private university in Korea founded by the Order of Won Buddhism. Besides this university, the order has founded several junior and senior high schools. In addition, the order has been establishing numerous charitable organizations, in pursuit of one of its three goals: the religious edification of people in the Buddha-dharma, education, and charitable works (the first being the primary task of the order).

Won Buddhism's ecclesiastical system is more like that of the Catho-lic Church than that of most Protestant Churches as is spelled out in its constitution. In accordance with it, the head dharma master (*chong-bŏpsa*), elected by the Supreme Council of the Order, represents the Order of Won Buddhism. However, the spirit of this office is Buddhist, as the term "dharma" signifies and implies the "transmission of the dharma from the Buddha through patriarchs" in the Buddhist tradition; its first head dharma master was the founder, Sot'aesan.[2] The order's first religious canon, *Pulgyo chŏngjŏn* (Canon of Buddhism), published a few months after Sot'aesan's death in 1943, contains its doctrine, which reveals the heart of Mahāyāna Buddhist doctrine in a renovated and simplified form. With the new name of the order promulgated in 1947, however, the order declared that Won Buddhism is not a sect of Korean Buddhism but an independent and autonomous new Buddhist order. This proclamation was largely based on the publication of its scripture *Wŏnbulgyo kyojŏn* in 1962, which is translated in this book as *The Scriptures of Won Buddhism*. No Buddhist scripture is included in this volume though some essential elements of Mahāyāna Buddhism are preserved.[3]

To carry out its mission in accordance with its constitution, the order operates through the administrative branch and the inspection branch

---

2. The head dharma masters of the order after Sot'aesan are Chŏngsan Song Kyu (r. 1943–1962), Taesan Kim Tae-gŏ (r. 1962–1994), Chwasan Yi Kwang-jŏng (r. 1994– ).
3. The *Pulcho yogyŏng* is included in the *Wŏnbulgyo chŏnsŏ*, the first book of which is the *Wŏnbulgyo kyojŏn*.

at the central general headquarters in Iksan City, North Chŏlla province, Korea. The order functions through the parish system; the head of each parish of the order reports to the general headquarters, and the temples of each parish follow the order's directions for disseminating the teachings of the doctrine.[4] The clergywoman, her hair in a chignon (hairpin invisible), wears a white blouse (in summer) or a black blouse (in winter) and a long black skirt. The clergyman wears a habit like that of a Catholic priest except his collar is gray on a white shirt and does not stand up like that of the Catholic priest's. The gray of the collar preserves the color of the Korean Buddhist monk's robe. While performing ceremonies including the Sunday service of the dharma meeting, both wear the same type of robe, white in summer and gray in winter. The Sunday dharma meeting is more like a Christian service than a Buddhist one; the order of ceremony includes singing hymns as well as chanting incantations. Included also in the ceremony is the dharma master's sermon, which is sometimes more like that of a Christian minister than a Buddhist priest's dharma talk. The details of faith and practice in Won Buddhism are spelled out in the introduction to this translation.

Chŭngsando[5] claims that Sot'aesan created a new religion by grafting some elements of their essential doctrine onto Buddhism. Some others claim that Sot'aesan borrowed from Ch'ŏndogyo, another Korean indigenous religion.[6] Moreover, the Chogye order of Korean Buddhism tries to persuade the Won Buddhist order to identify itself as a sect of Korean Buddhism, which the latter resists. Thus, there are some unsettled questions concerning the identity of the Order of Won Buddhism, questions whether Won Buddhism is a sect of Korean Buddhism or a mixture of the doctrines of some Korean indigenous folk religions. These questions have forced me to present a brief description of the history of the Buddhist persecution and a brief introduction to Ch'ŏndogyo and Chŭngsan'gyo for contextualizing Won Buddhism against its background. The historical context of the three indigenous religions

---

4. As of now, there are fifteen parishes in Korea, two parishes in the United States, one in Europe, and one in Japan. At present there are more than four hundred branch temples in Korea and more than thirty overseas temples.

5. The Chŭngsan'gyo ecclesia has changed the name of their order to Chŭngsando (The Way of Chŭngsan), claiming that Chŭngsando is not a religion in the conventional sense.

6. Robert Buswell Jr. observed, "Other reform movements designed to present Buddhism in a way that would be more relevant to modern concerns arose with increasing frequency. Among the most prominent of these was Wŏn Buddhism, founded in 1916 by Sot'aesan (1891–1943), which combined Buddhist teachings with a disparate variety of elements drawn from Confucianism, Taoism, Tonghak, and even Christianity." See Buswell, "Buddhism in Korea," in *Buddhism and Asian History*, ed. Kitagawa and Cummings, p. 157.

seems to be tight enough to support the claim that certain essential threads run through them as Sot'aesan indicated.[7]

It is an open question whether a new messiah comes of necessity in a degenerate age, as the founders of the three Korean indigenous religions have claimed. Sot'aesan in particular said, "When the world enters into the degenerate and troublesome era, a great savior-sage comes of necessity with a truthful law potent enough to rule the world, rectifies the world, and harmonizes the spirit of humankind by redirecting the numinous power of Heaven and Earth."[8] Sot'aesan's followers have consolidated this idea as an article of faith in its dogma. However, this idea is not new with Sot'aesan; the idea was expressed by his two predecessors, Ch'oe Che-u (1824–1864) and Kang Il-sun (1871–1909); both used the expression "closing the earlier heaven and opening a later heaven."[9] It was this idea with which Ch'oe Che-u initiated what is now called Ch'ŏndogyo and Kang Il-sun founded Chŭngsan'gyo. Sot'aesan's religious thought can better be understood by clarifying his relationship, if any, to the thought of the founders of these two indigenous religions in Korea. Some elements of the doctrines of the two can be identified in Sot'aesan's religious thought. Moreover, Sot'aesan recognized the two founders as rare prophets, saying that they will be highly respected when Won Buddhism becomes widely and firmly established.[10] This assertion makes it necessary for us to present the essence of their teachings.

What Sot'aesan had in his precognition upon his spiritual awakening in 1916 was the opening of a new era of great scientific and material civilization, which could cause enormous misery to humankind unless spiritual power was also simultaneously strengthened. Thus, for Sot'aesan, "opening the later heaven" meant the opening of a dazzling material civilization. He would have borrowed the tenet of any religion if it were sound and useful for his plan to lay out a blueprint to save sentient beings and cure the world of moral illness. However, he took the Buddha-dharma as the central tenet of the doctrine, with which he synthesized some elements of Confucianism and Taoism, as he him-

---

7. SS, VI:32, "If we compare it [the establishment of Sot'aesan's order] to a year's farming, we can say that Ch'oe Che-u told people to prepare for farming as it thawed, Kang Il-sun showed people the calendar of farming, and you, our Master, directed to farm, can't we?" To this Sot'aesan said, "What you have just said is also plausible."

8. See SS, XIV:1.

9. Choe Che-u's cognomen is "Suun" and Kang Il-sun's cognomen "Chŭngsan"; the former is often referred to as "Choe Suun" and the latter as "Kang Chŭngsan." The name "Chŭngsan'gyo" means the religion of Chŭngsan; "chŭng" is the Korean reading of a Chinese logograph signifying a rice steamer.

10. See SS, VI:31 and 32: "Since our precursors [Choe Che-u and Kang Il-sun] helped the later sages to come, the latter will venerate their precursors."

self declared.[11] There is no written evidence that any of the tenets of Ch'ŏndogyo and Chŭngsan'gyo had been incorporated into the new doctrine. Since he took the Buddha-dharma as the main doctrine, this religious order still carries the name "Buddhism."

## A. Korean Buddhism during the Chosŏn Dynasty: Persecution

Although Korean Buddhism is a vibrant religious force in modern Korea, around the turn of the twentieth century it was barely surviving in remote mountain valleys after five hundred years of ruthless oppression and ostracism by the Chosŏn dynasty's pro-Confucian national ideology. Sot'aesan thought that Buddha-dharma should be revived as a means to saving the world in the future. But why did Sot'aesan need a new form of Buddhism? A glance at a brief history of Buddhist ostracism during the Chosŏn dynasty will help readers understand why Sot'aesan founded a new religious order independent of the Korean Buddhist order.

Buddhism ever since its first introduction into Koguryŏ (37 B.C.–668) in 372 had quite an illustrious history until the end of the Koryŏ dynasty (935–1392).[12] Buddhism during the Koryŏ dynasty enjoyed the status of a state religion and national ideology. However, it suffered a reversal in the Chosŏn dynasty as Neo-Confucianism came to be adopted as the state ideology.

The anti-Buddhist spirit initiated around the end of Koryŏ dynasty began to materialize during the early years of the Chosŏn dynasty. The Neo-Confucians, who had presented anti-Buddhist memorials to the Koryŏ king, plotted to ostracize Buddhism with the founding of the Chosŏn dynasty, and the Chosŏn court started to wield an anti-Buddhist policy, initiating five hundred years of Buddhist oppression.

Yi T'aejo (r. 1392–1398), the founder of the Chosŏn dynasty, was a faithful lay Buddhist around the end of Koryŏ dynasty and set up Muhak Chach'o (1327–1398) as the royal master in 1392. T'aejo made considerable contribution to the Buddhist cause without yielding to the anti-Buddhist fervor of the Neo-Confucians, who tried to enforce the policy to abrogate Buddhist temples and force Buddhist monks to secede from the order. The Chosŏn court's anti-Buddhist policy was put in full force by the second king, Chŏngjong (r. 1399–1400), who usurped the throne from his father. Chŏngjong abolished Buddhist rituals and services in the court. All the lands of the Buddhist order except seventy temples outside of Seoul were taxed for the state's armaments,

---

11. See SS, II:1; Bongkil Chung, "Won Buddhism," 425–448.
12. For a brief but incisive survey of Korean Buddhism, see Buswell, "Buddhism in Korea," pp. 151–158. For Korean Buddhism up to and inclusive of the Koryŏ period, idem, KAZ, pp. 1–95.

and all the male and female servants of the temples were allocated to the government offices. The third king, T'aejong (r. 1401–1418), who also usurped the throne, closed all but 242 Buddhist temples, confiscating the lands and allocating the temple servants to the state. T'aejong abolished the system of royal and national masters and strictly enforced the certificate system for priests, making it difficult for one to become a Buddhist monk.

Sejo (r. 1456–1468), the seventh king, was the great pro-Buddhist sovereign who protected Buddhism against the endless poignant anti-Buddhist memorials presented by the Neo-Confucian cabinet members. Sejo made truly great contributions to the Buddhist cause so that the rights of Buddhist monks were well protected and monks were allowed to enter the castle town freely, an action that had been prohibited by his father, Sejong (r. 1419–1450), the fourth king. However, the anti-Buddhist policy became severe with the enthronement of the ninth king, Sŏngjong (r. 1469–1494). In 1492, for instance, he abolished the monk certificate system and drafted all those monks with no certificate for military service, leaving Buddhist temples virtually deserted. The tenth ruler, Yŏnsan'gun (r. 1495–1506), abolished a Buddhist nunnery, making the nuns into court servants and monks into servants of the government offices. In addition, the government confiscated all the temple land. His son, Chungjong (r. 1506–1544), demonstrated the harshest anti-Buddhist policy of all the kings of the Chosŏn dynasty. Chungjong abolished the dual systems of Korean Buddhism, Sŏn and Kyo, relegating Korean Buddhism to that of no sect or school. In 1509 Chungjong had all the temples in each province closed, making the temple lands the property of the Confucian shrines. In 1512 the great bells of Hŭngch'ŏn-sa and Hŭngdŏk-sa were melted to make weapons, and Wŏn'gak-sa was demolished and the wood of the temples distributed to those whose houses had been demolished during his father's reign. He ordered all copper and bronze Buddha statues melted to make weapons. In 1518 he ordered all the nuns removed from the nunnery and demolished the Buddha statues there.

In 1545, the thirteenth king, Myŏngjong (r. 1546–1567), was enthroned at twelve years of age, and his mother, Queen Dowager Munjŏng, was appointed regent to the young sovereign. She tried to restore Buddhism. In 1550 the Queen Dowager Munjŏng restored the two schools of Buddhism, Sŏn and Kyo, entrusting Po-u (1515–1565) with the responsibility of reviving Buddhism. Po-u helped the Dowager Queen Munjŏng to make Pongŭn-sa the head temple of the Sŏn sect and Pongsŏn-sa the head temple of the Kyo sect; he also enforced the laws for becoming a monk and the national examination for selecting high priests. Thus, many able monks took the examination, including Sŏsan Hyu-jŏng (1520–1604) and his disciple Yujŏng (1544–1610),

who organized the monk-army from all over the country against the Japanese invasion in 1592 which ruined the whole country. During the fifteen years of Queen Dowager Munjŏng's reign Buddhism was revived; however, Buddhism declined again with the death of Queen Dowager Munjŏng and Po-u's murder by fanatic Confucians.

After Hideyoshi's invasion of Korea in 1592, the social status of Korean monks took a favorable turn; however, the unfair persecution by the Chosŏn court and the Confucian administrators continued. The responsibility for the erection and defense of mountain fortress walls on the capital's north and south mountains was put solely on the Buddhist monks. Monks were forced to make paper, oil, and shoes and do other drudgery for the government officials and the Confucian officials. Buddhist monks were still treated as the lowest of all the lowly classes in the society.[13] The eighteenth king, Hyŏnjong (r. 1660–1674), prohibited any good citizen from becoming a Buddhist nun and ordered nuns to return to secular life, closing Chasu-wŏn and Insuwŏn and confiscating their land and legion of servants. In 1749, the twenty-first king, Yŏngjo (r. 1725–1776), prohibited Buddhist monks from entering the capital city (Seoul).

During the Chosŏn court's centuries of rejection and oppression, an enervated Buddhism survived in the remote mountain valleys. Although this Buddhism was not identified with any particular sect, the main current of the Buddhist practice was Sŏn. Eventually the monks practiced either Sŏn, doctrinal study, or chanting, and large temples provided separate halls for Sŏn practice, scriptural studies, and chanting. Monks were divided broadly into "monks scrutinizing phenomena" (sap'an sŭng) and "monks scrutinizing noumena" (ip'an sŭng). The former made great contributions to keep the temples from ruin and keep the order in existence even while bearing all sorts of oppression from the Chosŏn court officials and the Confucian aristocrats, while the latter contributed to the life of Buddha's wisdom.

Thus Buddhist monks were prohibited from entering the capital city in principle for more than five hundred years of the Chosŏn dynasty except when it needed a manual labor force. In April 1895, the ban was lifted as the impotent Chosŏn court was compelled to do so by the re-monstrance of Japanese Nichiren missionaries.[14] Thus ended the five hundred years of the Chosŏn dynasty's oppression of Buddhism. Buddhist monks could again freely engage in Buddhist activities. The Cho-

---

13. The seven classes socially despised during the Chosŏn dynasty: male and female servants, kisaeng (courtesans), musicians and entertainers, cobblers, village officers, errand boys, and Buddhist monks.

14. See Yu Pyŏng-dŏk, "Ilche Sidae ŭi Pulgyo" (Buddhism during the Japanese occupation), PKC, pp. 1159–1187.

sŏn court became conscious of its mistakes and finally put an end to the centuries-old anti-Buddhist policy; it even tried to put all Buddhist temples under governmental supervision. At the same time there arose a Buddhist movement to have a unified autonomous control of all the temples. In 1899, Wŏnhŭng-sa outside of Tongdae-mun (East Gate) in Seoul was designated the head temple, where all the ecclesiastical business of Korean Buddhism was to be administered with one provincial head temple in each of the thirteen provinces, thus unifying all the Buddhist temples in the country. In 1902 the Chosŏn court set up a governmental office to control all the temples in the country. Because of the political chaos of the Chosŏn dynasty, the government's good intention produced nothing propitious to the Buddhist church although there was improvement on the status and the general treatment of Buddhist monks in Korean society.

In 1906 Yi Podam and Hong Wŏlch'o established the Society for the Study of Buddhism (Pulgyo Yŏn'guhoe) at Wŏnhŭng-sa. Influenced as it was by Japanese Pure Land Buddhism (J. Jōdoshu), this society was not representative of Korean Buddhism. However, the society established a new institution for Buddhist education, Myŏngjin Hakkyo, at Wŏnhŭng-sa; this institution was the predecessor of Tongguk University. In March 1908, fifty-two monks representing the Korean Buddhist ecclesia met at Wŏnhŭng-sa and adopted as the name of the order Wŏn-jong (Consummate order) and set up the administrative office there. This was the origin and cradle of a new Buddhist order in Korea. However, right after the Japanese annexation of Korea in 1910, the supreme patriarch of Wŏn-jong, Yi Hoe-gwang, went to Japan to have Wŏn-jong merged with the Japanese Sōto Zen sect. Enraged at this, the monks in the southern four provinces (North and South Kyŏngsang and North and South Chŏlla provinces) held a general meeting at Songgwang-sa in January 1911 and established Imjejong (C. Linchi; J. Rinzai). Imjejong moved its central administrative office from Songgwang-sa to Pŏmŏsa, propagating in opposition to Wŏn-jong in Seoul. Since such movement occurred only after Korea had lost its national identity to Japan and since the colonial government regulated all matters of Korean temples and monks, the conflicts between the two sects disappeared of themselves, and Korean Buddhism together with the Korean national fate fell under the control of the Japanese Government General.

Korean Buddhism had to change its system under the control of the Japanese Government General as it proclaimed new ordinances for Buddhist temples.[15] In compliance with the colonial government's

---

15. See Yun E-heum, "Han'guk Minjok Chonggyo-ŭi Yŏksajŏk Silt'ae" (The historical reality of korean folk religion), *HC* 23:87–120.

temple regulations, the Korean Buddhist order consisted of thirty head temples with the general headquarters established in Seoul, the thirty head temples being the provincial headquarters for thirty parishes. A central general office was placed in Seoul for the purpose of coming up with a unified Buddhist ideology and education with the name, the Order of Sŏn and Kyo (Sŏn Kyo yangjong) of Korean Buddhism. However, this central meeting office had no power to control the thirty head temples as it did only the clerical work. Thus, a central organization was needed for the control of all the Buddhist temples in the country. In January 1922 an office for the general affairs of Korean Buddhism was established at Kakhwang-sa. In January 1929, a nationwide assembly of Buddhist monks was held at Kakhwang-sa, where the constitution of the order and various by-laws were adopted. Not long thereafter the necessity of renovation was so strongly felt that a movement took place for the establishment of a supreme head temple. In spring 1941, T'aego-sa (now Chogye-sa) was built as the general central temple with the new name of the order, Chogye-jong, replacing the old name, the Order of Sŏn and Kyo of Korean Buddhism. On April 23, 1941, the Chogye order set up Chungwŏn as the first supreme patriarch and started the Buddhist ecclesiastical business on June 6, 1941.

In October 1945, a nationwide Buddhist assembly was held to adopt the new constitution of the order, abolishing the Japanese temple regulations, and Pak Han-yŏng was set up as the first supreme patriarch of the new Chogye order. Released from Japanese fetters, Korean Buddhism was promised a bright future. During the past half century, Korean Buddhism has come a long way, recovering its full vitality; now it is very healthy and has significant effect on Korean society.

There remains a question whether Sot'aesan would have established a reformed Buddhist order if Korean Buddhism had been as healthy as it is today. One wonders whether he might have established a Korean folk religion like Ch'ŏndogyo or Chŭngsan'gyo. The three founders of the three Korean indigenous religions, Ch'oe Che-u, Kang Il-sun, and Sot'aesan, had identical soteric plans: "To deliver suffering sentient beings to a paradise on earth." Only the first two religions were active in the world late in the nineteenth century, a time they regarded as the turning point of "closing the earlier heaven and opening the new heaven." Ch'oe Che-u was executed in 1864; hence he saw neither of the two world wars nor the thirty-six years of the Korean people's suffering under Japanese oppression. Kang Il-sun died in 1909, one year before the annexation of Korea by Japan in 1910. Sot'aesan attained his spiritual awakening in 1916, five years after the annexation, and died in 1943, two years before the liberation of Korea at the end of World War II in 1945.

## B. Eastern Learning (Tonghak) and the Religion of Heavenly Way (Ch'ŏndogyo)

The closing period of the Chosŏn dynasty (1392–1910) in which Ch'oe Che-u (1824–1864) lived belongs to the putative degenerate age. The dynasty was plagued with internal corruption and the plundering of the common people by the ruling class; in addition, foreign powers persisted in making demands of the impotent Chosŏn court.[16] Its corrupt government had lost its correct direction as a consequence of the bloody wrangling among the factions of the Confucian ruling class. The common people, especially the peasants, suffered from the exploitation and extortion of the aristocratic class and the wealthy local families. In addition, there were recurrent epidemics, floods, severe cold in the winter, and famine so that the common people suffered great misery. It was during this degenerate age of inequality, plundering, injustice, ignorance, poverty, and disease and the inroads of foreign powers that Ch'oe Che-u[17] tried to "deliver the Korean people from the misery and protect the identity of his nation." Tonghak (Eastern Learning) is the root of Ch'ŏndogyo,[18] which Ch'oe Che-u initiated upon his mysterious religious experience on April 5, 1860.

On that day, Ch'oe unexpectedly felt chill in his heart, and his body trembled, but he could not know or describe the nature of the illness; suddenly, he heard the words of a supernatural power. Rising, he asked,

---

16. As space is limited, the details of the historical facts depicting this period cannot be presented here. See Takahashi, *History of Korea*, pp. 90–111, also chapter 6, "The Intrusion of the Great Powers in Korea in Modern Times"; Han Woo-keun, *History of Korea*, pp. 361–436. See also Ki-baek Lee, *A New History of Korea*, pp. 255–260, 279–288. Ch'oe Che-u's Tonghak (Eastern Learning) movement was the moving force of the Tonghak peasant uprising against the corruption and plundering of the Chosŏn dynasty, which, being threatened thereby, asked Japan for military reinforcement to defend itself from the rebellion. The Chinese government, feeling its interests in Korea being threatened, sent its army to Korea. China's defeat in the Sino-Japanese War gave Japanese imperialists more pretexts to put an end to the Chosŏn dynasty. Threatened by the Japanese presence in Korea, the Chosŏn dynasty turned to Russia for help, but Japan defeated Russia in the Russo-Japanese War. In 1910, Korea (Taehan dynasty) was annexed to Japan, losing its national identity. At the end of WWII, Korea was liberated from Japan but divided into North Korea and South Korea.

17. Ch'oe Che-u was born in 1824 in Kyŏngju. His father was Ch'oe Ok, his mother, Han (no first name known) a concubine. He lost his mother when he was six years old and his father when he was sixteen. The social discrimination against children born of a concubine was severe; they were despised, and had no way of getting a government office. Thus, Ch'oe's frustration and inferiority complex must have begun to develop in him an antagonism to Korean society. See *TT*, pp. 1–2.

18. The Order of Ch'ŏndogyo is impressive in Korea, and scholars within and outside the order have accumulated significant research on its various aspects; the bibliography on the subjects related to Ch'oe Che-u and Ch'ŏndogyo lists 106 items. See Kim Hong-ch'ŏl, "Han'guk Sinhŭng Chonggyo ŭi Hyŏnhang" (Contemporary status of newly risen religions in Korea), *HC* 23:443–515.

"Who are you?" The voice said, "Don't be afraid; people call me Su-preme Lord [K. sangje]."[19] The voice further said, "Since I have no merit, I am begetting you into the world to let you teach this law to the people, hence doubt not." Choe Che-u asked further, "Then, should people be taught the Western Way [Catholicism]?" The answer was, "No! I have a divine amulet with me; its name is 'elixir of life;' its shape is *t'ai-chi*, another shape is *kung-gung* [bow-bow]. Receive this divine amulet and cure the people of their illness; receive my magic formula and teach people with it to make them like me. Then you can also enjoy longevity and spread virtue under Heaven."[20] Ch'oe Che-u regarded the message as a divine revelation from the Supreme Lord. Upon this experience, Ch'oe Che-u declared that his way was the great way of ultimate nonbeing (K. *mugŭk taedo*), claiming that he received it from God.

A great many people gathered to follow him, and he began to propa-gate his way in June 1861; however, the Chosŏn court and the Con-fucians started to oppress them as they hurt Christians. In January 1862, Ch'oe declared, "The way is the heavenly way, but the learning is the Eastern Learning." Tonghak or Eastern Learning stood against Western Learning (Catholicism), which was spreading rapidly in Seoul in the mid-nineteenth century. The religious doctrine of Tonghak is a syncretism of the Eastern religions of Buddhism, Confucianism, and Taoism, which Ch'oe Che-u thought should not be replaced with Western Learning. He lamented, however, that luck had run out for the three ways of Buddhism, Confucianism, and Taoism.[21]

Ch'oe Che-u's Tonghak was both religious and sociological, as a reaction to Western Learning, which was propagating its faith in the capital; Tonghak nurtured the people of the farming villages. The aris-tocratic class (*yangban*) had suppressed the grievances of the peasants against society until the mid-nineteenth century; these grievances came to be expressed in the religious movement of Tonghak. Tonghak as-serted that the era had come when the nation should be strengthened and the livelihood of the people be assured, and it called for reform of the corruption-ridden government. Furthermore, it went on to assert that the time had come when these goals might be achieved. It was this millenarian aspect that led the Chosŏn court to view with alarm the spreading popularity of Tonghak faith. Accordingly, in 1863 Ch'oe Che-u was arrested on charges of misleading the people and sowing

---

19. See *TT*, p. 33.
20. Ibid., pp. 38, 62.
21. *TT*, p. 8; Yang Ŭn-yong, "Han'guk chonggyo sasang esŏ bon shin chonggyo" (New religions viewed in the context of the history of Korean religions), *HC* 23:164.

discord in the society; he was executed the following year.[22] His trial and execution sent many of his followers into hiding in the mountains, and for a time the popularity of Tonghak waned. But under its second patriarch, Ch'oe Si-hyŏng (1829–1898), despite great difficulties the *Canon of Tonghak Doctrine* (*Tonggyong taejŏn*) and *Hymns from Dragon Pool* (*Yongdam yusa*) were compiled, thus systematizing the tenets of the new religion. The movement to bring new converts under Tonghak discipline owed its success to the peasants' deep hostility toward the aristocratic class and Tonghak's resistance to the inroads of foreign powers.

Upon the execution of the second patriarch, Ch'oe Si-hyŏng, on July 20, 1898, Son Pyŏng-hŭi (1861–1922) tried to straighten out the difficult situation. Pursued by the government, Son Pyŏng-hŭi escaped to Japan. He communicated with some of the members of the Enlightenment Party exiled in Japan, enlarging his vision of the new trends of the world. He was able to communicate secretly with his followers in Korea and organize the Tonghak movement while in Japan. In 1905, he renamed Tonghak "Ch'ŏndogyo." Returning to Korea in January 1906, he started to reorganize the order, promulgating its constitution. Thus, Son Pyŏng-hŭi established a new system of the order as Ch'ŏndogyo with its central general headquarters set up in Seoul with seventy-two parishes. Of many significant cultural achievements, Ch'ŏndogyo established an educational institute where the doctrines of Ch'ŏndogyo and Western Learning were taught. By publishing the *Ch'ŏndogyo wŏlbo* (Monthly report), Ch'ŏndogyo made a significant contribution to the enhancement of the spirit of the Korean people; Ch'ŏndogyo played a pivotal role in the independence movement of March 1, 1919, against the Japanese occupation of Korea. For their active participation in the movement, Son Pyŏng-hŭi and many Ch'ŏndogyo members were imprisoned by the Japanese Government General.

The ideological direction of Ch'ŏndogyo was to synthesize the thoughts of Buddhism, Confucianism, and Taoism. Son Pyŏng-hŭi as the third patriarch had several writings on Ch'ŏndogyo, of which the *Kakse chin'gyŏng* (The true scripture for enlightening the world) and the *Togyŏl* (The secret of the way) show well the change of course from Tonghak to Ch'ŏndogyo.[23]

In the *Kakse chin'gyŏng*, heaven, earth, and man are regarded as trinity, and as the creative transformation of unitary energy, which means the creative transformation of heaven. As heaven is the fundamental source of the change of yin and yang and the principle that

---

22. See Ki-baik Lee, *New History of Korea*, pp. 258–259.
23. See Yu Pyŏng-dŏk, *Tonghak-Ch'ŏndogyo*, pp. 330–346. Both *Kakse chin'gyŏng* and *Togyŏl*, very short treatises written in Chinese, are attached as appendixes to the *Ch'ŏndogyo ch'anggŏnsa* (Founding history of Ch'ŏndogyo).

explains the birth and growth of all things in the universe, heaven cannot be the object of respect (religious worship). Thus, Son Pyŏng-hŭi replaced the expression "heavenly lord" with "heaven." This ideological tendency was advanced to the extent that the expression "man is just heaven" was consolidated, replacing Ch'oe Che-u's original expression, "man is heavenly man." It is argued that if one is enlightened to one's own mind, then one's body is heaven, and one's mind is the very heaven. Hence, to worship heaven amounts to worshiping one's own mind. This is very similar to the Mahāyāna Buddhist view that the triple world is nothing but the pure mind, namely, the nature (C. *hsing*), which is related to the principle of the universe. Since heaven can rule all things only through man, man rules them on behalf of heaven; in this sense, too, man is heaven. Thus, the central doctrine of Ch'ŏndogyo lies in the faith in the heavenly way, and man is to realize a heaven on earth by knowing and following the heavenly way. Heaven originates in human mind, and the unitary ultimate principle in the spirit of man. Thus, Ch'ŏndogyo regards man as supreme. Ch'oe Che-u implied this by his view that "man should be attended as heaven," and Son Pyŏng-hŭi that "man is heaven." With this tenet as the essence of Ch'ŏndogyo theology, the following should be mentioned as its central doctrine.

1. God is enshrined in one's body, and human mind is none other than God's mind. This means that man is none other than God. This view, it is argued, overcomes both the view that God transcends the world and the view that God is immanent in the world because God is both transcendent and immanent. God is believed as the absolute and infinite being who presides over the creative transformation of all beings, but he has not finished his plan of human history, thus works through human beings. Though God is beyond any human conceptualization and perception, a deep faith in him will help one attain an insight of God's meaning and understand that the universe is a manifestation of God through his own infinite creative transformation.

2. The fundamental source of the universe is the ultimate energy (K. *chigi*), the numinous emptiness of which fills the universe, directing all affairs to be what they are. This ultimate energy is both material and spiritual, yet it is at the same time God's numinous energy, which connects itself to human mind, being the original source of the evolution of all beings in the universe. Thus, God and the ultimate energy are identical.

3. Ch'ŏndogyo's view of humanity is tied to its religious tenet of "serving the Supreme Lord (God)," which is the relation of man to God. Since man is God as is asserted in its theology, one should honor God enshrined in the human body as one honors one's own parents. Since the human being is born with God enshrined within, it is one's fundamental duty to serve and honor God with utmost sincerity and

respect. Moreover, God's numinous energy is omnipresent, intervening in every human affair; hence one must obey the divine intentions.

4. Ch'ŏndogyo's moral philosophy teaches that God does not choose between good and evil. Since human original nature emanates from God, it cannot be evil. Evil arises when humans cannot correct their energy with their disturbed mind, thus violating the divine mandate. If humans can keep their energy aright with the concentrated mind, the good can be achieved. Hence, Ch'ŏndogyo takes as its central moral practice Protecting the Mind and Correcting the Energy, and takes as its fundamental moral virtues Sincerity, Respect, and Faith.

The salient features of Ch'ŏndogyo's thoughts are implied in its theology, cosmology, humanism, and ethics.

The first salient feature is the thought that Man is Heaven. Ch'ŏndogyo holds the view of "man qua heaven" and the ethics that, therefore, man should be treated as heaven.[24] This tenet aims at restoring the dignity, liberty, and equality of humanity. To this point, only God was regarded highly; humanity was held in lower regard because the two were misunderstood as separate, subjugating the latter to the former. The idea of man qua heaven has changed the point of importance from God to humanity. The humanism of Ch'ŏndogyo has deified the dignity of humanity, realizing its fundamental liberty and equality. This is not equality under God or the equality achieved by abolishing class distinctions; it is the fundamental equality of God and man, which elevates man to the dimension of God. In this humanism, human beings are the center of all values, and the subject of all actions is the human being. Man's subjective decision is the ultimate cause of all social phenomena, and the leading part of the historical creation is also man.

The second salient feature of Ch'ŏndogyo is the thought of "Opening."[25] In Ch'ŏndogyo, however, Opening means the development of a new civilization, culture, and humanity after a great change of the universal energy. Since the world cannot get out of darkness and the established culture has reached its impasse, the deadlock can be broken only through a new great change and renovation. Ch'ŏndogyo divides history into two; the past world is called the "earlier heaven" and the future world the "later heaven." By "opening of the later heaven" Ch'ŏndogyo means that the past culture and civilization have been

---

24. This reminds one of the moral imperative theorized by Immanuel Kant: "Act in such a way that you always treat humanity, whether in your own person or in the person of any other, never simply as a means, but always at the same time as an end." See Kant, *Groundwork of the Metaphysics of Morals*, p. 96. This tenet aims at creating a world where a human being is the end in itself, never a mere means as was the case with the Korean peasants to the ruling class throughout the Chosŏn dynasty.

25. The Korean word "*kaebyŏk*" is used with the meaning of the universe bursting open for the first time, comparable to "genesis."

closed and the new culture of the later heaven has opened. The opening of the later heaven includes spiritual opening, opening of the Korean race, and social opening, through which a universal humanitarian culture will be unfolded.[26]

The third salient feature is its goal to build up the nation and provide for the welfare of the people. While Ch'ŏndogyo aims at delivering sentient beings in general by spreading the virtue of its teaching, Ch'oe Che-u emphasized the good maintenance of the destiny of Korea. In the scripture of Ch'ŏndogyo there are warnings against the invasion of Korea by Japan and the West and a strong denunciation of the Chinese domination of Korea. It was Ch'oe Che-u who started the fresh Korean nationalism by rejecting the foreign invasions and led the Tonghak movement, and later the Tonghak peasant revolution, with the motto: Building up the nation and providing for the welfare of the people. According to Ch'ŏndogyo, Korean nationalism had three strands: (1) the Tonghak revolution, (2) the enlightenment movement, and (3) the rejection of wickedness and protection of justice. During the troubled period (second half of the nineteenth century), the enlightenment movement was progressive; however, it lacked the support of the general populace because its background was the foreign powers. The movement of rejecting the wickedness and protection of justice was autonomous and independent; however, it was confined within the conservatism of the Chosŏn court's ruling class. In contrast, the nationalism of the Tonghak movement was both autonomous and progressive so that it overcame the limitations of the other two movements. Thus, with the ideal to build up the nation and provide for the welfare of the people, the Tonghak movement awakened the awareness of the Korean people to stand up and repel the foreign invasions. It succeeded in awakening the alienated and oppressed class of people to the truth that it is people that are the master and the power to save the country.

The fourth salient feature is the view that everything returns to the unitary source as man and heaven are one based on the unitary ultimate truth. This means that others and I become one; my nation, the whole human race, and I become one; and the thoughts and minds of all people become one, returning to the unitary truth. The new creative unification overcomes all conflicts and contradictions by finding the point of harmony and agreement among diversity. In consequence, all get out of the history of struggle and strife and enter the path of peace and unity. This ideology, based on the principle of unity and totality,

---

26. The idea of "bursting open," "unfolding," or simply "opening" of a new age or a new world initiated in Ch'ŏndogyo was adopted by Chŭngsan'gyo and Won Buddhism. Thus, the founders of the three Korean indigenous religions seem to have discerned their times to be the end of a long age of darkness in human history.

overcomes the polar ideology of individualism and totalitarianism. This ideology seeks liberty and equality simultaneously by overcoming the limits of individualism and totalitarianism.[27]

Ch'ŏndogyo aims at realizing a heavenly world on the earth instead of realizing it in the next life. It claims that, to realize the goal, one must attain "the spiritual opening" for the perfection of one's personality, and that the morally sound society, where all human beings are treated equal, should be realized. This goal can be achieved by religious and moral practice; the following five principles should be observed.

1.  To enshrine the heavenly lord in one's mind. Since man is originally the creature of God, one must have faith in God; however, one must also have faith in one's own divine spirit. Hence, the religious practice lies in being in touch with God by expanding one's own divine spirit.
2.  To unify one's spirit with God's Great Spirit and to apply the great justice of heaven and earth to human beings by expanding the energy of the body.
3.  To eliminate calamity and to increase blessings (the greatest blessing is longevity).
4.  To spread the way of Ch'ŏndogyo to people.
5.  To protect the country and to deliver all the sentient beings.

The religious ritual of Ch'ŏndogyo includes

> chanting of its mantras;
>
> performing the "clear water ritual" at 9:00 every night, when the whole family holds prayers in front of the table with the bowl of clear water;
>
> attending the prayer service on every Sunday; and
>
> offering the "rice of sincere gratitude."

All these practices are called "prayers" and characterized as silent confession, the prayer on Attendance Day (Sunday), and special prayer.

## C.  The Religion of Chŭngsan (Chŭngsan'gyo)
### 1. Origins

As is the case with Ch'ŏndogyo, so is Chŭngsan'gyo a product of a degenerate age. It is a Korean folk religion initiated in 1902 by Kang Il-

---

27. One wonders whether the idea of "returning to the unitary source" theorized in Ch'ŏndogyo is not a reflection of Hua-yen Buddhist metaphysics, which holds that everything is identical with everything else. One of the Zen conundrums is on this theme: The myriad dharmas return to one; where does the one return? See *Pi-yen lu*, case XLV, *T*, 2003.48.181c; Cleary and Cleary, *Blue Cliff Record*, 2:318; *SS*, VII:10.

sun (1871–1909), better known as Chŭngsan.[28] The entire numerous (once, one hundred) orders with different denominations are sects of Chŭngsan'gyo. The origination of Chŭngsan'gyo is closely related with the Tonghak peasant revolution that arose in North Cholla province in 1894. It was a social movement that was launched by the alienated and oppressed peasants during the ending period of the Chosŏn dynasty. However, this revolution ended without achieving its ideal and goal. Thus, those of low class who participated in the rebellion were more frustrated than before the uprising, and those extremists who could not return to their normal life were searching for a new way of social reform. During the rebellion, Kang Il-sun followed the army and observed the course of rebellion without participating in any battle, as he knew the eventual failure of the uprising.[29] Observing the failure of the Tonghak revolution and the resulting social chaos, Kang Il-sun thought such chaos could not be straightened out by any of the existing religions or any human power, but only by a divine magical art. In search of the method to save the world and human beings, Kang Il-sun studied all sorts of things: the doctrines of Confucianism, Buddhism, and Taoism, as well as yin-yang philosophy, geomancy, divination, and medicine on the one hand, and such occult disciplines as calling rain and hail and the magic art of transforming his own body into something else. He even wished to attain omniscience. Thereafter, he wandered about Korea for three years from 1897 to gain a correct comprehension of the social reality.[30] Upon returning to his home village in 1901, he started ascetic practice at Taewŏn-sa in Mt. Moak in North Cholla

---

28. See *TJD*, chaps. 1, IV: "He [Kang Il-sun] was born into this world around midnight on the nineteenth day of the ninth lunar month (November first), 1871.

> Finally I stopped in this eastern land of Korea, where the Buddhist monk Chinp'yo devoted his whole life at Kŭmsan-sa in Moaksan mountain to my incarnation as a human child. I stayed in the Maitreya statue of the Kumsan-sa for thirty years. There I gave Ch'oe Suun the great Heavenly Commandment and Spiritual Teaching for him to rectify humanity's violation and open up Great Enlightenment. Yet he was unable to move beyond the boundaries of Confucianism to bring forth the True Law and direct the ways of spiritual faith and human knowledge to open up the Great Unified Truth. Thus, in the year of Kapcha (the Year of the Rat, 1864) I withdrew my heavenly command and spiritual knowledge from him. And finally I came down to earth on my own accord, as a human child, in the Year of Sinmi (the Year of the Ram, 1871). "Sangje" (the Supreme Lord in person), who emerges from the book of *Tonggyong-taejŏn* and the songs of *Suun kasa*, speaks of Me." (Ibid., chap. 2:19)

29. See *TCH*, I:14 (p. 14).
30. *TCH*, I:27 (p. 15).

province to attain omniscience to deliver the world.[31] While he was carrying out extreme ascetic practice, he was awakened to "the great way of heaven and earth," conquering greed, lust, anger, and delusion. As the rumor spread of Kang Il-sun's awakening to the Way, followers appeared from 1902 on. He taught his followers how to practice chanting spells; when he treated patients, he gave prescriptions to them and made them chant the spells or use amulets while taking the drugs.[32] Those who thought of being cured followed him as a divine man. Moreover, he preached that he had the great authority to rule heaven, earth, and humankind and that he had come to the world to open a new heaven and earth, a paradise into which he would deliver all sentient beings suffering in the bitter seas of misery. Accordingly, his followers came to believe that Kang Il-sun had come to save the world as the incarnation of God. However, Kang Il-sun's establishment of a religious order is related to the chaos after the failure of the Tonghak revolution, together with the Buddhist beliefs in Maitreya Buddha's coming, and the rumor of Ch'oe Che-u's resurrection. Kang Il-sun said, "Those who believe in Jesus Christ wish for the coming of Jesus, those who believe in Buddha wait for the coming of Maitreya Buddha, those who believe in Tonghak wait for the rebirth of Ch'oe Che-u. No matter who comes, as long as the one person comes, all will proclaim that their Teacher has come and follow Him."[33] Kang Il-sun propagated his religion for seven years, from 1902 to 1909. The area of his propagation was the seven districts where the Tonghak rebellion had been most active (Chŏnju, T'aein, Chŏngŭp, Kobu, Puan, Sunch'ang, Hamyŏl); the center of his activities, however, was the vicinity of Mt. Moak, where he had opened his herbal drugstore. His followers were mostly the peasants of North Chŏlla province who participated in the Tonghak rebellion and others of low social class. Kang Il-sun, however, did not use a religious name for his order, nor did he do any work for systematization of his order. He did only what is called "the reconstruction of heaven and earth," which was the essence of his religious planning; he limited his activity to teaching his doctrine to those who were around him.

## 2. Multiple Branches

In 1907, five years after the initiation of the order, Kang Il-sun and most of his followers were arrested by Kobu county's authority for an alleged plot to organize a righteous army. Though they were all released because of insufficient evidence, this event increased their doubts about Kang Il-sun's power. Thus, some of the followers protested against the delay of the promised opening of the new heaven and earth. There was

---

31. *TCH*, II:1 (p. 18).
32. *TCH*, II:27 (p. 36); IV:15 (pp. 218–220).
33. *TCH*, III:44 (p. 170).

frequent pleading to him that the paradise be realized quickly. In the midst of this, Kang Il-sun died (in 1909). Most of his followers were disappointed at his death and dispersed without attending the funeral; only a few remained to hold the funeral. Some, however, still believed in Kang Il-sun's resurrection. Two years after his death (1911), his wife, Head Woman Ko (*kosubu*) (1880–1935),[34] fainted while she was offering a birthday sacrifice to her husband's spirit and revived from the swoon four hours later. Thereupon, Head Woman Ko mimicked Kang Il-sun's words and deeds, saying that the latter's divine spirit was transferred into her own. With this episode known, the old followers of Kang Il-sun gathered around Head Woman Ko and in 1914 formed an order with her as the head. They named the order Sŏndogyo (alternately, T'aeŭlgyo), setting up Kang Il-sun as the founder and Head Woman Ko as the head of the order. As the order's influence grew, however, Ch'a Kyŏng-sŏk (Head Woman Ko's cousin) and some followers split off from Ko and her followers, renaming the order Poch'ŏngyo. In 1919, as Ch'a Kyŏng-sŏk's power consolidated, Head Woman Ko separated her own order with the new name T'aeŭlgyo. While Ch'a Kyŏng-sŏk was having a feud with Head Woman Ko, those who had followed Kang Il-sun either left the order for good or started to establish a new order of their own, claiming that they each had received Kang Il-sun's religious insignia.

As Chŭngsan'gyo branched out into several orders, the number of Chŭngsan'gyo followers increased greatly. Ch'a Kyŏng-sŏk's order, especially, in size and activities aroused a great deal of social interest as well as criticism. Within six months, its members increased to hundreds of thousands. It is said that his order grew to be so powerful it could purchase one-tenth of the territory of Korea. Ch'a Kyŏng-sŏk even presumed to be the son of heaven or new emperor and paraded his power and authority, setting Kang Il-sun's teachings and authority at naught. Consequently, a severe conflict and antagonism began to surface, and some of the officials and believers of Poch'ŏngyo broke away, establishing new orders. During the Japanese occupation, the number of Chŭngsan'gyo sects reached more than a hundred. However, it began to wither or dissolve because of Ch'a Kyŏng-sŏk's failure to enthrone himself as the emperor and the split of his order as its consequence. The decisive blow was the Japanese Government General's ordinance to crack down on pseudo-religions.[35]

---

34. *TCH*, IV:13 (p. 215). Being Kang Il-sun's second wife, she has been deified and worshiped in the Chŭngsando order.

35. See Yun E-heum, "Han'guk Minjok Chonggyo-ŭi yŏksajŏk Silt'ae," *HC* 23:87–120. According to ordinance no. 83, the officially recognized religions were Shinto, Buddhism, and Christianity.

After Korea's liberation in 1945, the various orders of Chŭngsan'gyo tried to reform their stagnant orders and to grow as a Korean folk religion. However, the reunion of all the orders remained difficult because of the differences in their hermeneutics of the Chŭngsan'gyo doctrine. Now, there is one order under the name Chŭngsando with Kang Il-sun as its heavenly supreme lord and Head Woman Ko as the head woman. The order is thriving.[36]

### 3. Fundamental Doctrine

The syncretism in the doctrine of Chŭngsan'gyo resulted from Kang Il-sun's formulation of "opening the later heaven."[37] He preached that in "the earlier heaven," life was small and simple so that any critical situation could be set aright by a single religious thought; the situation of his day was so vast and complicated that it could not be corrected with any single religious ideology. Thus he emphasized that a new synthesis of the merits of all religions had to form the ideological foundation of "later heaven."[38] The doctrine of Chŭngsan'gyo has the characteristics of a grand synthesis of the merits of all religions. For example, the doctrine is based on aspects of traditional shamanism, Taoism, yin-yang philosophy, and geomancy. It regards highly the Confucian cardinal moral virtues of benevolence (*jen*), righteousness (*i*), propriety (*li*), wisdom (*chih*), and faith (*hsin*) and takes Tonghak's moral virtues of sincerity (*sŏng*), respect (*kyŏng*), and faith (*shin*) as the moral discipline. In addition to these tenets are included the Buddhist thought of Maitreya Buddha's descending to the earth, Tonghak's practice of chanting spells and hymns, and Christianity's belief in Christ's second coming. Different sects emphasize different points. However, some central tenets of the doctrine common to all sects can be found in the scriptures *Taesun chŏn'gyŏng* (The canonical scripture of the great itinerancy) and *Chŭngsan chongdan kaeron* (Introduction to the order of Chŭngsan'gyo).[39]

The cosmology in this religion takes as its first cue not the origin of the universe, but the mode of its existence, called "the schedule of the universe" (*undo*), which is regarded as preestablished in accordance with the law of the yin-yang cosmogonic system. It can, however, also be controlled by the authority and power of Kang Il-sun, the supreme heavenly lord.[40] In Chŭngsan'gyo, the "opening of heaven and earth"

---

36. The current (1999) Order of Chŭngsando has discredited the *Taesun chŏngyŏng* (Scripture of great itinerancy) after publishing the *Chŭngsando dojŏn* (Scripture of Chŭngsan's way), which is 1,200 pages long, an expansion of the former.
37. *TCH*, IV:142 (p. 370).
38. *TCH*, V:3 (p. 393).
39. See Yu Pyŏng-dŏk, *Han'guk minjung chonggyo sasangnon*, pp. 47–54; idem, *Han'guk sinhŭng chonggyo*, pp. 306–314.
40. *TCH*, V:4 (pp. 395–396).

is due to this control of the schedule of the universe. In accordance with the law of the schedule of the universe, Chŭngsan'gyo divides the preestablished world into the earlier (prior) and the later (posterior) heavens. The age when the earlier heaven is replaced with the later heaven is regarded as the degenerate age. According to this cosmology, the era of the earlier heaven is characterized by extreme absurdity, inequality, and injustice, while the era of the later heaven is characterized by equality, justice, and prosperity. During the degenerate age, all the facts accumulated in the earlier heaven are clearly exposed and all hidden oppositions and conflicts surface; hence, the social tension, struggles, and chaos become extremely violent. The "reconstruction of heaven and earth" performed by Kang Il-sun, however, adjusted the schedule of the universe toward the opening of the later heaven, and the promised paradise will be constructed in the later heaven with all the conflicts and antagonism dissolved.

In the theology of Chŭngsan'gyo, the realm of divinity is separated from that of humanity when the relationship between gods and man is explained. However, in this religion, such objects of reverence as gods, the soul, angels, and ghosts are regarded as nothing but metamorphoses of human nature confined in the body of man. Thus, the divine nature is a metamorphosis of human nature, and divinity is a metamorphosis of personality. This unique theory of god and man in Chŭngsan'gyo appears more clearly in its tenet that "god and man act simultaneously." In other words, it is believed that if fighting breaks out in the human world, then fighting breaks out among the ancestor spirits in heaven. And the fighting in the human world ends right only upon the end of the fighting in heaven. Believers explain the inseparable relation between the realm of divinity and that of humanity by saying that divinity frequents the human mind. In other words, they think that what happens in the realm of humanity reflects what happens in the realm of divinity; the situation in the divine realm reflects the situation in the human realm. Thus, the theology of Chŭngsan'gyo includes anthropomorphism. Moreover, the supreme heavenly lord and other divine officials are regarded as being elected among the departed spirits just as in the political structure in the human world. Hence the object of their religious worship, Kang Il-sun, is not a monotheistic God, but the presiding god in the realm of heaven (which, in monotheism, is created by God).

The most salient feature of the Chŭngsan'gyo doctrine is "the reconstruction of heaven and earth."[41] The founder, Kang Il-sun, is worshiped as the heavenly supreme lord (the highest of the heavenly gods of

---

41. *TCH*, IV:1–173 (pp. 200–391).

Taoism) or the supreme lord of the nine heavens (the Buddhist nine celestial bodies). Kang Il-sun claimed that he had been the supreme lord with absolute authority in heaven and that Mateo Ricci (1552–1610) in China with all the divine saints, the Buddha, and Bodhisattvas pleaded all the misfortunes in the human and divine realm to the ninth heaven. So he descended to the Canopy Tower in the Country of Great Laws (France)[42] and wandered about the three realms to stop in an Eastern land. He stayed in the statue of Maitreya Buddha at Kŭmsan-sa in Mt. Moak for thirty years, bestowing on Ch'oe Che-u the heavenly mandate and divine directions to establish the great Way. However, Ch'oe Che-u, confined within the Confucian tradition, failed to manifest the true law and to illuminate the true light of the great Way; hence, Kang Il-sun withdrew the heavenly mandate and divine direction in 1864 and descended to the world in 1871.[43] He preached that since the world of great fortune is to open at the end of the degenerate age, one should not incur or commit sin, but must participate in the New World of paradise with pure heart. He said further that he will preside over the three realms (heaven, earth, man) with divine authority to open a paradise of immortality and deliver therein all sentient beings suffering in the bitter seas of misery. Based on sermons like these, Kang Il-sun is worshiped by his followers as the savior of the world with divine authority higher than that of any other god. The religious activities to save the sentient beings in this world are called "the reconstruction of heaven and earth." By this is meant that Kang Il-sun as the supreme lord with absolute divine authority in the ninth heaven has opened a new world by readjusting the course of heaven and earth and has thereby eliminated the calamities and misfortunes of the degenerate age. According to the Chŭngsan'gyo doctrine, all the social discord and chaos as well as political and religious confusions in this world are due to the following three causes: (1) Viewed from the course of the universe, the present age is at the turning point of the earlier heaven being replaced with the later heaven, and hence the necessary course for opening a new heaven (world). (2) While the realm of divinity and that of humanity are inseparably related, the situation in the realm of divinity at the present age is at a total chaos so that there is no cooperation between gods and men, and the chaotic heavenly situation is reflected in the human situation. (3) The established religions, which are apt to quarrel with each other, have lost the ability to open the true path for human beings to take.

The reconstruction of heaven and earth was Kang Il-sun's project to

---

42. Chŭngsan'gyo followers claim that it was the Eiffel Tower in Paris, but it was designed in 1889; he was born in 1871.
43. *TCH*, V:12 (pp. 403–405). See Yu Pyŏng-dŏk, *Han'guk shinhŭng chonggyo*, p. 309.

save the human race by eliminating the three elements of instability. He called together all the divine spirits to form a "government of creative transformation" to "reconstruct heaven and earth." The reconstruction of heaven and earth consisted of (1) readjustment of the schedule of the course of heaven and earth: the plan to open the later heaven where sentient beings can avoid chaos and misfortune and establish unity of government and religion in the degenerate age; (2) reconstruction of the realm of divine spirits: the project to provide the way of cooperation of divinity and humanity by purifying and uniting the realm of divinity; (3) reconstruction of humanity: the project to give directions for the way of personal moral perfection with which to avoid the misfortune of the degenerate age in harmonious cooperation with the divine spirits and to participate in the opening of the later heaven.

The ideology of Chŭngsan'gyo is called "Chŭngsan thought," "Chŭngsan" being Kang Il-sun's cognomen. This thought newly systematized Korean traditional thought. The following points are regarded as the salient features of Chŭngsan thought.

1. *Sanctity of humanity.* A salient feature of the Chŭngsan ideology is the thought that human dignity is more sacred than anything else in the world. Kang Il-sun proclaimed that in the earlier heaven only the celestial beings were venerated, with terrestrial beings humbled; in the later heaven, however, a new world opens where humanity is revered more than anything else. In other words, humanity should take the center of the world since humans are nobler than gods, who were regarded as objects to be feared. Thus, Kang Il-sun reversed the dictum in the earlier heaven "man proposes; god disposes" to that in the later heaven "god proposes; man disposes."[44] In Kang Il-sun's thought of the sanctity of humanity was implied the leveling of social class discrimination and the equality of man and woman.

2. *Resolution of grudges.* Kang Il-sun related the tension, enmity, and fighting of the present age to the grudges characteristic of the earlier heaven. In the earlier heaven the principle of mutual opposition was in charge of human affairs, and human affairs were accordingly off the moral principle. Consequently, the universe was filled with grudges and enmity so that the murderous spirit exploded to cause all the cruelty and calamity in the human world. Kang Il-sun intended to correct the world by mending the blueprint of heaven and earth by straightening the way of divinity so that he could resolve grudges from all antiquity and erect a government of creative transformation to edify all humans with endless governance and silent teaching.[45] Because the calamities of the present age are a result of the grudges accumulated in the earlier

---

44. *TCH*, VI:106 (p. 433).
45. *TCH*, V:4 (p. 394).

heaven, all the grudges must be resolved if the New World of the later heaven is to open. Only then will the paradise of immortality be realized on the earth. Kang Il-sun suggested resolving all the grudges by "returning to the origin,"[46] which means resolving all the grudges accumulated by individuals; in this way, subsequent grudges—among groups, classes, races, and nations—would be resolved.

3. *National sovereignty.* Kang Il-sun put great emphasis on the idea that Korea was the chosen country that received him, the heavenly ruling god, who descended to save the world. Moreover, he expressed a strong Korean nationalism and elitism, saying that Korea would be a first-class nation, where the true law to brighten the whole world would emerge, and that the whole world would be unified as one family around Korea.[47]

### 4. Object of Religious Worship and Rituals

The object of worship in Chŭngsan'gyo is its founder, Kang Il-sun, who claimed to have descended as the heavenly ruling god to save the world. Numerous other spirits are included as the object of religious worship: Tan'gun (the progenitor of the Korean race), the gods of each race, Confucius, Śākyamuni Buddha, Jesus Christ, cultural gods, Ch'oe Che-u, Mateo Ricci, and Chinmuk (a Buddhist monk).[48]

The religious rituals are slightly different from order to order of Chŭngsan'gyo; however, all the different orders use the same mantra and amulet for chanting that Kang Il-sun is said to have used while he was performing the "reconstruction of heaven and earth." The spell is chanted in order to have one's wishes be realized; adherents believe that chanting the spell will help open the third eye with which to attain omniscience. Among the several spells, the *t'aeŭlchu*,[49] which Kang Il-sun got while he was doing ascetic practice, is the most important. The amulet that is burned is a piece of paper where curious characters and phrases are written. Followers believe that this ritual can exorcise demons, cure diseases, or enliven a dead man.

A unique feature of Chŭngsan'gyo is that it still has many separate orders. During the Japanese occupation of Korea, the number of its orders reached one hundred. Even now, Chŭngsan'gyo is known to have about sixty separate orders. Membership during the Japanese occupation was claimed to have reached several million. Now, it is estimated at about a hundred thousand.

---

46. *TCH*, VI:124 (436).
47. *TCH*, V:38 (p. 421).
48. Chinmuk (1562–1633) was an eminent Buddhist monk who did miracles and stayed at Taewŏn-sa, where Kang Il-sun did ascetic practice.
49. The Mantra of New Life *(T'aeŭlchu)* reads: "Heal your mind, body and spirit; enlighten and enrich your spirituality; protect yourself from sudden accidents, disasters or illnesses."

## D. The Society for the Study of Buddha-dharma (Pulbŏp yŏn'guhoe)

We have seen above that Ch'oe Che-u called his order Tonghak and never heard of the name Ch'ŏndogyo and that Kang Il-sun never heard his order called either Chŭngsan'gyo or Chŭngsando. Kang Il-sun's order had no name before his death in 1909; it had been identified as Chŭngsan'gyo until it was renamed Chŭngsando or the Way of Chŭngsan recently by one of its sects. Sot'aesan, who called his order Pulbŏp yŏn'guhoe (Society for the Study of Buddha-dharma), never heard of Wŏnbulgyo (Won Buddhism). Just as Son Pyŏng-hŭi renamed Ch'oe Che-u's order Ch'ŏndogyo in 1905, Song Kyu renamed Sot'aesan's order Wŏnbulgyo in 1947.

A detailed biography of Sot'aesan is given in the next section. Here, a brief reflection focuses on the vestiges of the religious thought of Ch'oe Che-u and Kang Il-sun that might have influenced Sot'aesan's religious thought. Ch'oe Che-u started his Tonghak movement upon the religious experience of a divine revelation from a heavenly spirit in 1860, and Kang Il-sun claimed that he was the very heavenly lord who had given the former the divine command to save the world. Kang Il-sun also said, "I sent Confucius, Buddha, and Jesus to Earth to put them at my service."[50] It should be remembered, however, that Kang Il-sun made up his mind to attain the magic power to save the world only after he followed the Tonghak army and observed the deplorable national and social situation in Korea resulting from the defeat of the Tonghak rebellion.

As the name of Sot'aesan's order shows, it was unquestionably Buddhist in nature. Although some tenets from other religions were synthesized with Buddha-dharma, Sot'aesan made it clear that what should be learned, taught, and practiced was Buddha-dharma.[51] Now, the question is whether the tenets of Ch'ŏndogyo and Chŭngsan'gyo have been grafted with Buddha-dharma in formulating the doctrine of Won Buddhism, as is alleged by Chŭngsando. In spite of Sot'aesan's prediction that Ch'oe Che-u and Kang Il-sun would be recognized and honored as great prophets with the recognition of Won Buddhism as a world religion, he mentioned nothing about the doctrine of Ch'ŏndogyo or Chŭngsan'gyo. He declared that the essence of his religious doctrine was a synthesis of Buddhism, Confucianism, and Taoism.[52]

Thus, some questions linger whether some of the religious tenets of the two earlier indigenous religions might have influenced Sot'aesan in creating the doctrine of Won Buddhism. Both Sot'aesan and Song Kyu

---

50. See *TJD*, 2:32.
51. See *SS*, I:15.
52. See *SS*, II:1.

had some connections with Chŭngsan'gyo prior to the groundwork for establishing the new religious order. When Sot'aesan attained his spiritual awakening in 1916, the followers of Poch'ŏngyo (a sect of Chŭngsan'gyo) were active in his village. He learned from a follower of Poch'ŏngyo a method of sacrificial service to the spirits of heaven and earth. He offered seven days of sacrificial services with some of his villagers in July 1916, attracting about forty followers in a couple of months.[53] Selecting eight serious followers from among them, Sot'aesan formed a ten-member body for the new life movement in July 1917 with the center position vacant; it was filled by Song Kyu in 1918. In 1917 Song Kyu stayed briefly at Kang Il-sun's house after meeting with Ch'a Kyŏng-sŏk while Kang Il-sun's wife, Head Woman Ko, was establishing an order. Later that year Song Kyu moved to Taewŏn-sa to do ascetic practice; this was the same Buddhist temple where Kang Il-sun had attained spiritual awakening while doing ascetic practice in 1901.[54] What Song Kyu, only a seventeen-year-old boy at that time, could have learned from the Head Woman Ko is not known except that some miraculous episodes occurred around him as the result of his concentrated prayers. Thereafter, he moved to Kim Hae-un's house and stayed there offering prayers in 1918. It was during this time that Sot'aesan located him with his clairvoyance and received him as the new order's "mother of dharma" and his successor.

In July 1918, Song Kyu filled the center position of the ten-member body, which was the initial formation of the Supreme Council of the Order of Won Buddhism. Sot'aesan seems to have done what Kang Il-sun called "reconstruction of heaven and earth" in a different way. With his nine disciples, he took a year from 1918 to 1919 to erect an embankment for reclamation of a tidal land for farming. Then he ordered his nine disciples to perform sacrificial services for several months until their sincerity was recognized by the numinous spirit of heaven and earth; this event is called "the dharma authentication" for establishing a new religious order. This event can be taken to be the second stage of Sot'aesan's way of doing what Kang Il-sun called "the reconstruction of heaven and earth." We can surmise that Sot'aesan might have learned the essence of Kang Il-sun's religious doctrine and come to realize that it could not be relied on as the correct way of delivering sentient beings from the tormenting seas of misery, for he sent Song Kyu, still a teenager, to a Buddhist temple, Wolmyŏng-am, as a novice to Zen Master Paek Hang-myŏng. Sot'aesan moved to Mt. Pyŏn where the above temple was; he built a cloister, close to Wŏlmyŏng-am, and spent five

---

53. *WK*, III:3.
54. See *WBS*, XV.

years there drafting the essential tenets of the doctrine of his order. Establishing the general headquarters at Iksan from 1924 to 1943, Sot'aesan trained his followers with the newly formulated doctrine under the name of the order the Society for the Study of Buddha-dharma. The canonical writing *Pulgyo chŏngjŏn* (Correct canon of Buddhism) was published in March 1943, but Sot'aesan did not see it, as he had died two months earlier.

It is hard not to argue that the two founders of the Society for the Study of Buddha-dharma grafted some central tenets of Chŭngsan'gyo onto the Buddha-dharma to create a new form of Buddhism. The question is why Sot'aesan took Buddha-dharma as the heart of the doctrine of his order. After his spiritual awakening at age twenty-five in 1916, Sot'aesan was introduced to the Diamond Sūtra in his dream and borrowed it from a Buddhist temple (Pulgap-sa) for perusal. He also perused the classics of Confucianism, Taoism, and Ch'ŏndogyo. Then he made up his mind to take the Buddha-dharma as the central doctrine of the religious order he was establishing, saying that the Buddha is the sage of all sages. We can surmise that upon his spiritual awakening Sot'aesan might have attained foresight and insight potent enough to fathom the width and depth of the spiritual powers of Ch'oe Che-u and Kang Il-sun.

We have seen above that the significant tenets of the two indigenous religions are "the degenerate age," "opening the later heaven," "opening of spiritual culture," "respect of humanity," "resolving grudges," "beneficence of Heaven," "gratitude," and "realization of an earthly paradise." And these tenets were integrated into the religious doctrine of the Society for the Study of Buddha-dharma, which Sot'aesan established. However, these tenets have been critically synthesized with the Buddha-dharma in such a way as to lose their original meanings. We must examine how those thoughts have been integrated in Sot'aesan's thought.

The motive behind founding the new religious order hints at the thought of "opening the later heaven"; "opening of the later heaven" meant for Sot'aesan unfolding a world of great material civilization, by the formidable power of which human beings could be enslaved. He thought that human beings could not be delivered unless spiritual power were expanded to cope with the harsh consequences of material civilization. He also thought that spiritual power could only be expanded by faith in truthful religion and training in sound morality. By "truthful religion" Sot'aesan originally meant the Buddha-dharma, which excludes anthropomorphism and any form of superstition. By "sound morality" he meant a religious ethics that yields sound moral standards for justice. He was well aware of the criminal acts committed

by the sects of some indigenous religions at that time.[55] The fact that Sot'aesan identified the Buddha-dharma as truthful religion although Korean Buddhism had been alienated and hibernating for five centuries implies that he could not depend on Ch'oe Che-u or Kang Il-sun as the founder of truthful religion and sound morality. Nor could he depend on Korean Buddhism unless it were seriously renovated.

The most significant tenet of Chŭngsan'gyo doctrine is that of "resolving grudges." This tenet is identified in one of the four platforms of the Society for the Study of Buddha-dharma. In Sot'aesan's view, the main moral illness of the world is "resentment," which is the source of grudges and enmities among people; Sot'aesan's ethico-religious teaching highlights the importance of changing "resentment" to "gratitude." This is expounded in the chapter "Fourfold Beneficence,"[56] which is the heart of Won Buddhist religious ethics. The tenet of beneficence requital (gratitude) is stated in "The Essentials of Daily Practice" as follows: "Let us change the life of resentment into the life of gratitude."[57] Thus, it can be argued that one of the salient features of Chŭngsan'gyo doctrine is given a philosophical justification in Sot'aesan's new Buddhism. For Kang Il-sun, the misery of today is the explosion of the grudges of the earlier heaven; the present enmities and conflicts cannot be defused without having the original grudges in the earlier heaven resolved, which he claimed to have done with his "reconstruction of heaven and earth." For Sot'aesan, the world can only be saved from misery by faith in truthful religion and training in sound morality. He systematized the truthful religion and sound morality in the *Pulgyo chŏngjŏn*. The expressions "truthful religion" and "sound morality" implied that the religions of his time were not completely "truthful" and the moral teachings not "sound." For instance, the heart of the religious and moral tenets of Ch'ŏndogyo is to worship and treat humanity as heaven. In Sot'aesan's view, this tenet was unrealistic although it can be argued that "man as heaven" is another way of saying the Mahāyāna Buddhist tenet that all sentient beings are none other than Buddhas. No moral and philosophical justification is provided for one to treat humans as heaven. Sot'aesan's solution to this problem is expressed in a motto: Everywhere is the image of Buddha; do all things as making an offering to Buddha. Sot'aesan has provided both teleological and deontological justification for the injunction that one ought to treat humanity as ends, never merely as means as I have analyzed below.[58] The main religious characteristic of Buddhism is "making

---

55. See *SS*, XIV:10.
56. See *Canon*, pt. 2, chap. 2, "Fourfold Beneficence."
57. See *Canon*, pt. 3, chap. 1, sec. 5.
58. See pt. 2, II, C, 2, e: "Concluding Remarks" of this introduction.

offerings to Buddha" and that of Confucianism is "requiting parental favors" (filial piety). The former is teleological and the latter deontological. Sot'aesan combined the two by proposing that one ought to requite beneficence as making offering to Buddha. And all sentient beings are Buddhas with powers to bless or punish. Thus, the doctrine of Sot'aesan's new Buddhist order is a synthesis of the moral and religious tenets of Buddhism and Confucianism.

The central doctrine as systematized by Sot'aesan and Song Kyu is the tenet of Irwŏnsang or Unitary Circular Form as the symbol of Dharmakāya Buddha. It is the fundamental source of all beings in the universe and the original nature of all buddhas and patriarchs, and the Buddha-nature of all sentient beings. The circle is the symbol of the object of religious worship and the standard of religious practice enshrined in 1935; it is approached through the channels of worship and practice. Religious worship of Dharmakāya Buddha lies in awareness and requital of beneficence; religious practice lies in correct enlightenment and right practice. The former is the way of curing the world of moral illness, the latter the way of delivering sentient beings suffering in the bitter seas of misery. The rest of the doctrine in the *Correct Canon of Buddhism* (1943 edition) is to show how these dual religious goals should be realized. For Sot'aesan, an ideal human being is one who is enlightened to his or her own Buddha-nature, which is the ultimate reality of the universe, and who lives an enlightened life on the one hand and returns the universal beneficence of nature on the other. Thus, Sot'aesan has shown a realistic way of "resolving grudges" by the tenet of fourfold beneficence as is explained below.

Still, the issue of Sot'aesan's originality remains; we must examine in detail the way he established a new religion. According to Thomas F. Hoult, "All religious doctrines are syncretic."[59] According to Radhakrishnan, "The Buddha takes up some of the thoughts of the Upaniṣads and gives to them a new orientation. The Buddha is not so much formulating a new scheme of metaphysics and morals as rediscovering an old norm and adapting it to the new conditions of thought and life."[60] These remarks seem to apply to the foundation of the Society for the Study of Buddha-dharma, for Sot'aesan created a new religious order by taking Buddha-dharma as the central tenets of the doctrine and synthesizing the doctrines of other religions with it. Sot'aesan was

---

59. Quoted by Roland Robertson in *The Sociological Introduction of Religion*, p. 103: "For example Christianity was historically composed of elements from Eastern and Near Eastern religions (e.g., virgin birth, baptism, burial services), from Greek religions (asceticism, cosmology, eschatology), from Judaism (monotheism), and from gnostic religious doctrines."
60. Radhakrishnan and Moore, *Sourcebook in Indian Philosophy*, p. 272.

modest enough to acknowledge that Śākyamuni Buddha was his ancestral master, although he came to begin a new round of the Buddha's game.[61] Sot'aesan renovated some of the inert doctrines of the ancient sages and included them in the doctrine of a fresh new religion.

In 1947, four years after Sot'aesan's death, Song Kyu, the new head dharma master (chongbŏpsa) of the order, renamed the order Wŏnbulgyo or Won Buddhism. He had the *Pulgyo chŏngjŏn* redacted into the *Wŏnbulgyo kyojŏn*, which was published several months after his death in 1962. I have translated it in this book as *The Scriptures of Won Buddhism*.

## II. Sot'aesan's Early Years

Sot'aesan had his spiritual awakening in 1916, six years after the Korean people had lost their independence to the Japanese imperialists. He died in 1943, two years before the liberation of the Korean people from the Japanese occupation. During that whole time, Sot'aesan worked to establish a new religious order. Upon outbreak of the Pacific War in 1941, the Japanese Government General in Korea tried to transform Korean Buddhism into Japanese imperial Buddhism.[62] As Sot'aesan's order appeared lukewarm to that policy, the Japanese governor general took a firmer stance—either to crack down on it or make it a cat's-paw of that policy. The governor general ordered Sot'aesan to go to Japan to pay homage to the Japanese emperor. Sot'aesan had no choice but to comply with the implied threat; but, mysteriously, there came a notice that he did not have to go to Japan after all. Nevertheless he was aware seriousness of the situation. Sot'aesan vowed to die so that his religious order could survive; the Japanese Government General thought that once Sot'aesan died the whole order would die with him. Sot'aesan took ill on May 16 and died at a hospital (with a Japanese physician in attendance) on June 1, 1943; he suddenly dropped his head and passed away on a chair while he was talking to O Ch'ang-gŏn, one of his first nine disciples.[63] The following pages describe Sot'aesan's life and the steps he took to establish a new form of Buddhism. The main source of the biography that follows is the *Wŏnbulgyo kyosa* (History of Won Buddhism) compiled and published by Wŏnbulgyo Chŏnghwasa in 1975. This work was based on the *Pulbŏp yŏn'guhoe ch'anggŏnsa* (History of the Foundation of the Society for the Study of Buddha-dharma), written by Song Kyu in 1938.

---

61. See *SS*, II:9.
62. In 1915 the Japanese Government General promulgated its statute 83, Rules for Propagation, which aimed at putting all religious activities under Japanese control. See Yun E-heum, "Han'guk minjok chonggyo-ŭi yŏksajŏk silt'ae," pp. 87–120.
63. See *TSR*, chap. 21, "Kyodan sunan chang" (The order's suffering).

## A. Birth and Childhood

Sot'aesan's full name was Pak Chung-bin, and "Sot'aesan" was his cognomen. Sot'aesan was born the third son to a peasant family on May 5, 1891, in a village on the southwest coast of the Korean Peninsula.[64] There were no extraordinary signs at his birth. His biographer, however, has recorded some of the extraordinary behaviors while he was still a child. Even in childhood, Sot'aesan was awe-inspiring in appearance, magnanimous in conduct, and fond of asking questions of grown-ups. Once he made a promise, he never broke it, no matter how hard it was to keep it. One can get a glimpse of his character from a few anecdotes told of him.[65]

---

64. *IIII*, pp. 315 316. His father was Pak Hoe-gyŏng (dt Sŏngsam) and his mother's surname Yu (dt: Chŏngch'ŏn). Sot'aesan claims to have been a descendant of Pak Hyŏk-kŏse (57 B.C.–A.D. 3), the progenitor of the Silla kingdom (57 B.C.–A.D. 918). Sot'aesan's seventh great-greatgrandfather moved from Yangju county, Kyŏnggi province, to Yŏng-gwang county, South Cholla province. In 1884, seven years before Sot'aesan's birth, his father moved to Kilyong-ni, where Sot'aesan was born. His biographer writes that even though Sot'aesan's father was poor and unlearned, people respected him for his sagacity. His mother was also respected as a virtuous person for her natural benevolence.

65. See *HH*, pp. 236–238.

> On a late spring day when he was four years old, the child Sot'aesan was having breakfast with his father. Finishing up his rice, he took some rice from his father's bowl and ate it. His father scolded him for being ill mannered and threatened to whip him. The child Sot'aesan warned that, if his father whipped him, he would knock his father's hat off before the sunset. In the afternoon, his father returned home from the work field and was lying on the floor for a short rest. The child suddenly cried out, "Tonghak rebels have turned up on the Norumok road!" The father, startled and flustered, went over the rear fence, hiding himself in the bamboo grove behind his house. After a while he recalled his son's warning at the table and thought much of his child's extraordinariness.
>
> When he was ten years old, Sot'aesan was learning Chinese classics with another boy from a teacher in the village. The teacher was resentful because Sot'aesan had not brought him any fruit from his home. On the winter solstice, the teacher offered a bowl of red-bean gruel to the other boy and did not offer Sot'aesan even a glass of warm water to go with the cold lunch he had brought. Sot'aesan was displeased. Later, the teacher told to his friends that he was so tenacious that he had never been frightened by anyone. Hearing this, the child Sot'aesan, smiling, said that he would terrify him before the sunset. The teacher said, "If you can make me frightened, I will credit an honor to your family. If, however, you fail to do so before the sunset, you will be thrashed on the legs." So the child Sot'aesan set fire to a heap of dried pine leaves beside a huge stack of firewood that was the teacher's main source of income. The teacher was terrified by the fire and in his anger tried to get hold of Sot'aesan. The child said, "I have just kept my promise. Why are you so mad?" Running away, he never went back to the teacher again.

According to the biographer, his career as a founder of a new religious order started when he was still a child. At age seven, he was struck with wonder about the natural phenomena on a fine spring day: "How high and wide is the sky? Why is it so clear and serene? How and why do clouds and storms come out of such a clear sky?"[66] The nature of his query was such that even if scientific explanation had been given of the natural phenomena, he would not have been satisfied, for he was asking a why-question, not a how-question; he wanted to know the source of the natural law that produced such phenomena.[67] Many other questions intrigued him. At age nine, his own existence and that of his parents, brothers, and all things were put into questions whenever he thought of them. The alternation of day and night became the object of doubt when he thought about it. Thus, he was bothered by endless doubts. He was puzzled at why his father and mother became his parents among so many people. Although he was ignorant of Buddhism, he was interested in the affinity relations among human beings. He was puzzled about why some people were born rich, why some were born good-looking. While Śākyamuni Buddha was struck by the problem of human existence, Sot'aesan's quest for truth started with questions of natural phenomena of the universe and moved toward the question of human existence.[68] When he attempted to solve all those doubts, they were like mountains in the clouds and fogs; the harder he thought about them, the vaster they became.[69] While he was inquiring into the nature of the sky, the sky seemed to be attached to the mountain, so he climbed it to investigate the sky.[70] As his mind was concentrated on those questions, he was not concerned with clothes, food, or play. He wondered whether there was someone who knew answers to his questions. Although he was studying Chinese classics as his parents guided him to do, he had little interest in them.

### B. Search for Truth

Young Sot'aesan's aspiration for finding answers to his questions got deeper and deeper. At age eleven, upon returning from the yearly memorial service for the ancestors, his search for solutions started.[71] At the service he observed that a sacrificial rite was performed to the mountain god before the main memorial service was held. He wanted to know why.

---

66. *WK*, pt. 1, chap. 1, sec. 2.
67. Han Chongman, "Sot'aesan ŭi saengae wa sasang" (Sot'aesan's Life and Thought), *IMWS*, p. 12.
68. Ibid., pp. 12–13.
69. *HH*, p. 235.
70. *HH*, p. 236.
71. The tombs were at Maŭm-ni, Kunsŏ-myŏn, Yŏnggwang-gun, Chŏllanam-do.

*Q.* What's the reason for performing the sacrificial rite to the mountain god before holding the memorial service to our ancestors, which is the main purpose of today's rite?

*A.* The mountain is the sovereign land of the tomb and the mountain god rules the mountain. Hence, we must perform a sacrificial rite to the ruler of the mountain before holding the memorial service.

*Q.* Then, what kind of authority and power does the mountain god have?

*A.* The mountain god is so divine that his power of creative transformation is beyond imagination.

*Q.* Is it possible for a human being to see a mountain god?

*A.* He might appear to someone who wishes to see him with utmost sincerity.

After this conversation, the young Sot'aesan thought that if the mountain god were so powerful and divine, he might have the power to answer Sot'aesan's questions. Thereafter, the young Sot'aesan daily climbed Mt. Kusu after breakfast to offer prayers for the mountain god to appear. He collected various wild fruits on the mountain for an offering, which he placed on the flat rock where he prayed.[72] According to the biographer, he did not skip a single day for four years—that is, until he was fifteen years old, when his search for truth changed its course.

When he was fifteen (1906), the young Sot'aesan went to pay New Year's greetings to the family of his wife.[73] There someone was giving a reading of ancient novels, *Choungjŏn* and *Pak T'aebujŏn*, where the hero had his wishes realized by meeting an enlightened master of the Way, under whose guidance he attained an extraordinary spiritual power. Hearing this, there was a great change in the heart of the young Sot'aesan. In spite of his sincere prayer for the past four years, the mountain god had not appeared. Inspired by the hero in the ancient novel, Sot'aesan decided to find an enlightened master of the Way, who

---

72. *HH*, pp. 239–240. This flat rock, being slightly slanted, is called *madang pawi* (yard rock); it is at the summit of the northwestern part of Mt. Kusu, four kilometers from Sot'aesan's birthplace. Mt. Kusu at that time was thick with forest, and fierce wild animals abounded, so even a strong young man would not dare to enter it alone. Thinking that his parents would prohibit him from entering the mountain for fear of danger, the young Sot'aesan climbed it secretly, telling his parents that he was going to school. When the truth was found out, his mother was so moved by his sincerity that she supplied him with white rice cake for the sacrificial offering (and did not tell his father).

73. At fifteen, he was married to Yang Ha-un in accordance with the order of his parents. His in-laws lived at Changji-ri, Kunsŏ-myŏn, Yŏnggwang-gun, South Chŏlla province.

is after all a human being. He thought it likely that there could be one
among so many people. Thus, his resolution to meet the mountain god
was replaced with a new resolution to find an enlightened master of the
Way. He spent the next six years in search of one. If there was a strange-
looking man on a road, he invited that man to his house overnight to
see if he was the one. When he heard of a recluse, he would go to see
him and invite him to his house to find out if he was an enlightened
master.

Once, young Sot'aesan was duped by a wretched beggar. When
Sot'aesan was passing by a tavern, he saw a beggar reading loudly a
verse:

> Who could be awakened to this great dream?
> It is only I who know it throughout my life![74]

The beggar was wearing hundreds of cloth pieces sewn together; his
whole body was covered with pustules, so that no one would sit beside
him. Since there was a saying that an enlightened master of the Way
sometimes disguised himself in such a way to test people, Sot'aesan
thought that this beggar was not an ordinary man. He approached and
greeted the man, buying him wine and food. Sot'aesan invited him to
his house for several days and treated him with utmost hospitality only
to realize that the man was a helpless idiot.[75]

---

74. A verse by Chu-ko Liang (181–234), Chinese soldier, born in Shantung; regarded
by Chinese as a favorite hero. Aided Lin Pei in founding the Shu or Minor Han dynasty
(221–264); chief minister (221–234); known as strategist. The provenance of this quote is
not identified.

75. *HH*, p. 241. On another occasion, young Sot'aesan heard of a hermit residing in a
remote mountain. Sot'aesan sent for him. When he came, he said to Sot'aesan's father,
"It's been a long time since I attained supernatural power upon ascetic practice in the
mountain. If your son is trained under my guidance, he will attain a wondrous power.
Now, if he wishes to initiate the training, you should make me a gift of a farming ox.
Would you do so?" Sot'aesan's father, being credulous, was going to do so and called
young Sot'aesan to come and meet with the hermit. Sot'aesan, however, said, "I would
meet you by paying homage according to the rules of etiquette. However, this is not an
ordinary meeting. If I find the teacher in you, I will take you as my mentor the rest of my
life. I will make a gift and treat you as my mentor only if you demonstrate your principle
and the wondrous power in front of me." The hermit said, "I have mastered the art of
miraculous acts and calling miraculous spirits. Hence, try me." Sot'aesan said, "Then,
bring the miraculous spirit in my presence." The hermit agreed to do so, and, in a clean
room, he chanted his spells throughout the night, but no spirit came. He pleaded that his
failure was due to a death or a birth in the village or to something that had happened in
that room in the past. So he asked for a different room. Sot'aesan knew that the hermit
was making an evil trick and abandoned the project in his mind. However, he granted the
request of the hermit, finding another room, where the hermit again chanted the magic
spell throughout the night only to fail again. The hermit, being embarrassed, fled, creeping over the fence while young Sot'aesan left the room for a while. See *HH*, pp. 241–243.

## C. Entering into Meditation

According to the biographer of Sot'aesan, the child Sot'aesan had little interest in learning at school or in household management; he concentrated his effort wholly on the search for truth. At the beginning his father did not understand him; however, he was so moved by his son's sincere devotion that he wholeheartedly supported his son's search for truth. He even built a small hut near a flat rock on top of a mountain peak where Sot'aesan could accumulate spiritual concentration. However, Sot'aesan's father passed away in October 1910, six years before Sot'aesan's enlightenment.[76] Sot'aesan had to assume the responsibility of the head of the household since his oldest brother had left to be the heir of his uncle's family and his immediate elder brother had died young. The family was deeply in debt. Sot'aesan's mother and wife were unable to handle the family affairs, and Sot'aesan was not interested in maintaining household affairs. The household became destitute.

Sot'aesan became discouraged. All those alleged wizards were none other than ordinary people of falsehood and sorcery; there was nowhere to go to learn the truth. At age of twenty-two, he gave up his hope to find an enlightened master of the Way. After that he spent quite a long time with his mind undecided except on one thought, "What should I do with this doubt?"[77] At the beginning he had certain ideas on household affairs and felt it troublesome to live on. With days and months passing by, he gradually forgot everything except the same question. Sometimes, he passed a whole day with only that question, from morning till night, and sometimes from evening to morning. At about twenty-four, he even forgot the question, gradually falling into the state of trance. He was not aware of walking, sitting, speaking, or eating, reaching the state of utter quiescence like a statue.

As his house had not been taken care of for many years, the walls and doors were falling apart and rain leaked through the roof so that when there was a storm, the water drenched his seat. Twice, the family had to move. His morning and evening meals were coarse food, and often there was not enough of it. To make matters worse, a tumor grew large in his abdomen, and his body became covered with blotches; he suffered from asthma; he was so emaciated that his family became worried about him. Some neighbors in the village had pity on him; others regarded him as a lost soul. Sot'aesan, however, was in the state of trance.[78] His mental state was such that he seemed to be aware of things for a while only to be oblivious of them again and seemed to re-

---

76. *WK*, p. 25.
77. *HH*, p. 244.
78. *HH*, p. 245.

member something only to fall into mental blank. For several years, his wife continued offering prayers for his spiritual recovery.

### D. Awakening from Trance and Enlightenment

On April 28, 1916, at age twenty-five, Sot'aesan was sitting in absorption at early dawn as usual in his dilapidated house at the village of Norumok. Suddenly, with the first gray of dawn, his spirit became refreshed and brighter. Feeling strange, he looked around the four directions; the weather was serene; bright stars lit the sky. He breathed the fresh air, wandering about in the yard. Ideas arose in his mind one after another; he wondered whether he had not undergone hardships until then, and what he should do to be relieved from suffering. It came to his mind that he would comb his hair, clip his fingernails, and wash his face and hands first of all.[79]

As the day broke, he looked for a washbasin; his family was startled on the one hand and pleased on the other by the sudden change in his behavior and watched him very carefully. It was the initial stage of awakening from the deep absorption. After breakfast on that day, a few men from the neighboring village dropped by his house. They discussed the meaning of some passages in the *Tonggyŏng taejŏn*[80] they had brought: "I have a divine spell; its name is a mysterious medicine; its shape is a circle [two bows put together] or the Great Ultimate."[81] After a while, a couple of Confucian followers dropped by his house to take a brief rest and argued on the meaning of a passage in the *I Ching*: "The great man is he who is in harmony in his attributes with heaven and earth; in his brightness, with the sun and moon; in his orderly procedure, with the four seasons; and in his relation to what is fortunate and what is calamitous, in harmony with the spirit-like operations [of Providence]."[82] Hearing the discussion, Sot'aesan discerned the meaning of the passage. He wondered if this clarity was a symptom of his mind's being brightened. Afterward he examined one after another all the questions he had had in the past and realized that all of them were resolved in one thought; thus, he attained supreme enlightenment.

According to the biographer, it was on this day that the light of the great Way (truth) illuminated the ten directions and Sot'aesan's great aspiration was fulfilled and his new religious order came into being. Thereafter, Sot'aesan's mental and physical condition improved day

---

79. *HH*, p. 247.
80. *The Great Canon of Eastern Scripture*, the scripture of Ch'ŏndogyo.
81. Two bows put together forming a circle and bent, making the inner twisted line of *t'ai chi*. See *SS*, VI:29.
82. See *Book of Changes*, commentary on hexagram no. 1, *ch'ien* (heaven); James Legge, trans., *Yi King*, p. 417.

after day; the emaciated body recovered quickly without medical treatment, and his complexion and body were full of extraordinary perfection.[83]

Because Kilyong-ni where Sot'aesan grew up is a poor village in a remote mountain valley, his common knowledge was extremely limited. Since he had studied Chinese classics from the village teacher for barely two years, he had had no opportunity to learn the doctrine and history of any of the religions of the world. Thus, writes his biographer, he attained the great enlightenment and pierced the central doctrines of all religions with the principle of Irwŏn (unitary circle) after eighteen years of search for truth and ascetic practice not through learning, but through his eternal sagely nature.

## III. Preparation for the Establishment of a Religious Order

### A. Sot'aesan's Decision on Buddha-dharma

According to Sot'aesan's biographer, Sot'aesan was full of joy and self-confidence upon his enlightenment. Reflecting how he attained the supreme enlightenment, he said, "Though it is difficult to figure out how I have reached this stage, I can see that I was helped by the four-fold beneficence [heaven and earth, parents, brethren, and laws] while I was seeking the truth for myself."[84] He became aware of there having been Confucianism, Buddhism, and Taoism from the ancient times and newly risen indigenous religious orders in the East and religions in the West. Since he had had no opportunity to learn any of them, he made up his mind to peruse those religious doctrines to check their main tenets. He obtained some of the basic scriptures of the various religions through the courtesy of his neighbors and studied some of the basic scriptures of Confucianism, Buddhism, Taoism, Ch'ŏndogyo, and Christianity.[85] Upon doing so, he sighed, saying, "Ancient sages had known what I have come to know." He said that although the central tenets of the basic scriptures of all religions were in general proper and there were few principles to discard, some religious doctrines were more profound than others; Buddha-dharma was the best if the fundamental

---

83. *HH*, p. 247.
84. *WK*, pp. 29–30; *HH*, p. 248.
85. *WK*, pt. 1, chap. 3, sec. 1. The scriptures he perused include the four classics and the *Hsiao-ching* (Filial piety) of Confucianism; the *Chin-kang ching* (Diamond Sūtra), *Sŏnyo* (Essentials of Zen), *Pulgyo taejŏn* (Compendium of Buddhism), and *P'alsangjŏn* (Eight aspects of the Buddha's Life) of Buddhism; the *Yin-fu ching* (Secret planning) and *Yü-shu ching* (Jade hinge) of Taoism; the *Tonggyŏng taejŏn* (Canon of Eastern learning) and *Yong-dam yusa* (Hymns from Dragon Pool) of *Tonghak*; and the Old and New Testaments of Christianity.

truth was to be explicated.[86] He said further that, upon reflection on the motive of his aspiration for truth and the course of his search for it, he realized that many things he did coincided with the words of the Buddha. He said, "When I open a religious order in the future, therefore, I will take Buddha-dharma as the central tenet of the doctrine and incorporate other religious doctrines into it if they are proper, and establish a perfect religious order."[87] Thus, from the very beginning of this religion, the founder put Buddha-dharma as the foundation stone.

## B. First Sermon

After perusing the basic scriptures for reference and examining the times, he felt it urgent to revive the morality of man. Thus, he put forward a slogan: "As material power is unfolding, let us unfold the spiritual power accordingly." This became the founding motto of the new religion, and the main point is stated in the founding motive.[88] Sot'aesan then crafted his first sermon; it includes his thoughts on how to cultivate one's own life, how to regulate one's family, how the strong and the weak can both make progress, and what a leader should prepare.[89] In this first sermon, Sot'aesan lays out the most fundamental moral norms for the New World.

The main points of these four moral injunctions are as follows:

1. One must receive sufficient education in order to extend one's learning necessary for good life in the new world and train oneself in spiritual cultivation, inquiry into facts and principles, and mindful choice in karmic action.
2. As the head of a household one must have a solid occupation, practice thrift and saving, educate one's children, abide by the moral and civil laws, and learn good household management from others.
3. To realize a harmonious world, the strong ought to help improve the weak on the principle of mutual benefit, and the weak ought to regard the strong as a benevolent guide so that the two make mutual progress without enmity.
4. A leader should have more knowledge than those who are led, should be trustworthy, should never look after his or her own self-interest, and should check his or her deeds against his or her moral knowledge.

---

86. *HH*, p. 249.
87. *HH*, p. 249; *WK*, pt. 1, chap. 3, sec. 1; *SS*, I:15–19.
88. See *Canon*, pt. 1, chap. 1.
89. See *Canon*, pt. 3, chap. 13.

## C. Initial Skillful Means and Nine Disciples

Upon expressing the motto and the first sermon, Sot'aesan had a thought concerning his future steps. "What I have attained to is the essence of the Way and its virtue, and what I am to achieve is to deliver sentient beings to a paradise by establishing a religious order. However, I have been regarded as an invalid until recently; I have never visited any religious institution; and the general populace is interested in falsehood and superstitions without any true knowledge of the good life. So, what should I do from now on?"[90] With these thoughts in mind Sot'aesan waited for the right time to begin edifying people.

At that time Poch'ŏngyo, a sect of Chŭngsan'gyo, was proselytizing among the general populace; in the villages near Kilyong-ni, too, it was quite active. Sot'aesan made up his mind to make use of the situation to gather people, whom he could edify with truthful laws later when they were ready to receive his message. In July 1916 Sot'aesan talked with a Chŭngsan'gyo follower[91] and learned the procedure of sacrificial rites from him. Devoutly praying with some of the villagers over seven days, Sot'aesan fascinated them with words and bearing that ordinary people like them could not have imagined. In a couple of months, his followers numbered forty. Sot'aesan postponed his plan to give systematic instructions to those who communicated with him for five months because most of them had no experience of disciplined life and had gathered around him with false hope. Sot'aesan selected eight followers with firm faith and sincerity.[92] Sot'aesan organized the ten-member body of male adherents in July 1917 (2 w.e.).[93] He assigned the position of leader (heaven) to himself and eight others (north, south, east, west, northeast, southeast, northwest, southwest), leaving the center position (earth) empty for a year. (It was later filled by Song Kyu, who succeeded Sot'aesan upon his death in 1943.)

---

90. *WK*, p. 33.

91. According to Chŭngsan'gyo polemics, it was Pak Kong-u, Sot'aesan's second cousin.

92. They were Kim Sŏng-sŏp, Kim Sŏng-gu, Pak Han-sŏk, O Ch'ang-gŏn, Yi In-myŏng, Pak Kyŏng-mun, Yu Sŏng-guk, and Yi Chae-p'ung. With Song Tog-gun, who joined two years later, they were the first nine disciples in Sot'aesan's new order.

93. *WK*, p. 36; *SS*, I:6. Sot'aesan devised a ruling system whereby many human beings can be included in the edification plan. The unique feature of the method is that under the guidance of only one member, all people in various districts can be trained in the teaching. First, one body (group) of nine members is formed; to it is added a leader, who guides the practice of the nine members. Each of the members then forms a nine-person group. Then the leaders of the nine bodies form a body to which is added a leader, who guides the practice of the nine members of this leaders' body. This tree can grow indefinitely, including millions of people, and yet one has to exert one's effort to only nine members. Sot'aesan decided to make different categories of those bodies; under the Supreme Council (*suwidan*) there are Bodies of Devotees (*chŏnmu ch'ulsin*), Bodies of At-home Devotees, and Common Bodies depending on one's aspiration, circumstance, and practice.

The members of the first group showed some improvement in their faith and devotion. However, what they wanted was a certain incomprehensible secret access to the occult, and quick success in enlightenment. They did not want to work at learning and comprehending the ultimate truth and the principle of justice. Seeing this, Sot'aesan directed them to the correct Way with words that he said were the injunctions of the Lord of Heaven. He formulated certain ways of monthly service, three times a month, on the first, eleventh, and twenty-first day each month. He also ordered each member to keep a diary to check the ups and downs of his faith and devotion and facts of his practice.[94]

## D. An Inchoate Canon and the Period of Foundation

From 1917 (2 w.e.) on Sot'aesan dictated many aphorisms and poetical compositions to Kim Sŏngsŏp, a collection of which was edited with the title *Pŏbŭi taejŏn* (The great canon of the essence of laws). According to the biographer, its import was so profound that the ordinary intelligence of his disciples could not fully figure out its meaning. However, its gist was that the vein of true law (dharma), which had disappeared for a while, was appearing again; the general trend of the world is such that when unreasonable times are gone, reasonable times are sure to come;[95] and Sot'aesan would establish a new religious order.[96] The members rejoiced in reciting the aphorisms; the recitation was a great help in strengthening faith in his teaching. After he finished drafting the doctrine of the order, however, Sot'aesan instructed his disciples to burn it because he didn't believe it suitable as the definite doctrine for delivering countless sentient beings. The first section of the introduction and eleven stanzas were memorized by some of his disciples and recorded.[97]

In 1918 (3 w.e.) Sot'aesan proclaimed his timetable for establishing the new religious order. The history of the order was to be marked by the number of generations starting with 1916, the year of his enlightenment, as the first year of the order's era, each generation consisting of thirty-six years. The first generation of establishment would consist of three periods of twelve years each. The first twelve years would be for establishing the spiritual and financial foundation of the order and for meeting people who had affinity with the order's foundation. The second twelve years would be for formulating the doctrine and editing the teaching materials. The third twelve years would be for cultivating men and women of ability who would spread the law and propagate the law.

---

94. See *Canon*, pt. 3, chap. 6 for the details of keeping a diary.
95. This seems to reflect the thought of "opening the later heaven" advocated by both Ch'oe Che-u and Kang Il-sun.
96. *WK*, p. 37; *SS*, XIV:2.
97. *SS*, XIV:2.

## IV. Groundwork for Founding the Order

### A. Savings Union and the Embankment Project

With his nine disciples, Sot'aesan began to do the groundwork for the establishment of a new religious order. The groundwork consisted of the establishment of a savings union, the embankment project, and prayer and authentication from the dharma realm.

Sometime in August 1917 (2 w.e.), Sot'aesan established a savings union.[98] At that time, almost all the peasants were in a deplorable state of poverty, ignorance, and laziness. For the members of the savings union, Sot'aesan set up such precepts as diligence and frugality, abolition of empty formalities, doing away with superstitions, abstinence from alcoholic drink and smoking, and group work. It was a movement for new life and life renovation. Only a few months later, the members of the union had saved a large sum of money (Japanese currency). With this fund, the union ran a charcoal business and ended with a large profit as the charcoal price rose steadily because of the great demand for charcoal during World War I. In March 1918 (3 w.e.), Sot'aesan collected the funds so far saved. Pointing to the riverside tidal land in front of Kilyong-ni (his birthplace), Sot'aesan said, "Look at that tidal land! That is a piece of land deserted for thousands of years. Why don't we reclaim it for farmland?" The construction work for an embankment commenced. The villagers, who had never seen any undertaking like that, expressed cynicism and ridicule. The members of the union paid no attention to the criticisms, silently concentrating on the embankment work. Under Sot'aesan's direct supervision and spiritual guidance, the nine disciples as one body cooperated to carry out the project through the hot summer and the cold winter, struggling hard against difficulties. The project was completed in the third month of 1919 (4 w.e.) after one year of labor. About twenty-five acres of tidal land was reclaimed for farming. Upon completion of the embankment, Sot'aesan explained to his nine disciples that there was much preparatory work to be done for a new grand religious order for the new era.[99] The new life movement and the embankment project provided the financial ground for the founding of the new religious order. Sot'aesan named the farmland "the farmland reclaimed with toiling and moiling" (chŏnggwan p'yŏng). Through this achievement Sot'aesan demonstrated a model of new life; the balanced improvement of mental and physical life was made possible by his leadership and the selfless cooperation of the nine members as one body. The principles of thrift and saving, gradual growth from small to great, cooperation as one body, and selfless ser-

---

98. For the reason, see *SS*, I:7.
99. See *SS*, I:8.

vice for the public well-being became the moral norms and spiritual foundation of the order.

At the foot of Ongnyŏ peak, Sot'aesan had a nine-room house built, starting it in October 1918 and finishing it in December. This was the first temple of the new order. (Before this new house, the nine members had to meet at a Confucian shrine, and later at an inn on the bank of the river nearby.) On the ridge beam of the newly built house, Sot'aesan wrote:

> With Irwŏn (unitary circle) as the loom,
>> the sun and the moon as the weaving shuttle,
> The great doctrine of spring and autumn
>> shall be woven.

To this he added:

> The pine is standing
>> having gathered the remaining spring
>>> from all other trees;
> The brook is roaring,
>> having gathered the drizzles
>>> from a thousand mountain peaks.[100]

Upon the completion of the temple, Sot'aesan had little leisure, as he supervised the embankment project during the day and often preached sermons to his disciples in the evening at the temple. The members of the union rejoiced in listening to their master's sermon at night in spite of their hard labor during the day. According to the biographer, they were making gradual improvement on both public service and moral cultivation; they were becoming trustworthy and independent, and their superstitious attitude was being supplanted by faith in the truth. These visible improvements signified that the day for the opening of a new religious order was approaching.

### B. Prayer and Numinous Authentication

In March 1919 (4 w.e.) when the Korean independence movement was spreading all over the country, the embankment project was almost completed. The disciples asked, "Master, the movement against Japanese imperialism is now spreading everywhere in the country. At this critical moment, what is the right thing to do?" To this Sot'aesan answered that the independence movement was not simply an outcry for the autonomy of the Korean people but the prelude to the dawn of a new era. He said, "We have no time to waste, and there are urgent

---

100. See *SS*, I:12.

things to be done. All the great individuals and great organizations have their historical missions, which the divine truth endows at the right time. Let us hurry up to complete the embankment project and pray to the numinous spirits of Heaven and Earth so that the destructive energy of enmity under Heaven can be harmoniously resolved."[101]

Sot'aesan ordered his disciples to offer a special prayer to transform themselves from egoistic beings into altruistic ones so that they could serve the public well-being; he preached a sermon to them.[102] The nine disciples asked Sot'aesan for guidance. Beginning in April 1919 they offered prayers three days of every month with ten days of ablutions in between the prayer days as directed by their master. Each of the nine disciples was assigned a mountaintop as the site of prayer with the one in the center surrounded by eight others. Prayer consisted of each member setting up a flag of the union on the mountain assigned to him, preparing incense and a bowl of clear water, bowing and confessing, reading the prayer, and reciting an incantation. On August 21, 1919 (4 w.e.), Sot'aesan said to the members,

> The devotion with which you have been offering prayers is truly praiseworthy. To reflect it on my own experience, however, it is not sincere enough to move the will of Heaven. It is because there is some egoistic element left in your mind. If annihilating your ego can propagate the correct law [truthful religion], would you carry it out?[103]

To this, the nine disciples said in unison, "Yes, we will do it." Sot'aesan continued:

> There is an old saying, "One sacrifices oneself in order to preserve one's integrity." There were some who performed miracles by following this principle. Why wouldn't the numinous spirits of Heaven and Earth be affected if you would not mind sacrificing your life for the well-being of all sentient beings? In the near future, a great Way [religion] with correct doctrine will be established in the world and the disturbed mind of mankind will be corrected thereby, contributing to the blessings of sentient beings. If so, you will be the savior of the world, and the hidden merit of yours will be eternal. Hence, you must show your views on this matter from your true hearts.[104]

101. *CCP*, III:3. This seems to have reflected Kang Il-sun's thought of "resolving grudges and bitterness."
102. *SS*, I:13, for the sermon.
103. *WK*, pp. 46–47.
104. *WK*, p. 47.

The nine disciples were downcast for a while but agreed that they would gladly sacrifice their lives. With great admiration, Sot'aesan told them to carry out the sacrifice at each prayer site on the next prayer day[105] after ten days of ablutions. On August 21, the nine disciples gathered in the dharma hall, and the Master ordered them to arrange a bowl of clear water and daggers on the table. He ordered them to press their bare thumbs under their names as a form of signature on the sheet of white paper on which was written "Sacrifice with no Regret" and then had them prostrate themselves and offer a silent confession of their determination to sacrifice. Sot'aesan examined the paper and saw nine fingerprints in blood where they had pressed their bare thumbs. Showing the paper to them, Sot'aesan said, "This is the evidence of your single heart." He burnt the paper and consecrated it to heaven, ordering them to go to the prayer sites. Soon after they stepped out Sot'aesan called them back to the dharma hall, saying that he had needed to tell them one more thing.[106] He said, "The numinous spirits of heaven and earth have already responded to your mind, and a planning in the realm of dharma has been completed; hence success of our plan has been assured by this. You have consecrated yourselves to the world."[107] Although the disciples understood what Sot'aesan said, their excited mental condition was not easily calmed down. After 11:00 P.M. Sot'aesan ordered the nine members to go together to the top of the center mountain and return after offering prayers. Upon saying this, Sot'aesan gave dharma names and dharma titles to his nine disciples, saying, "The individual with the secular name has died. Now I give you a new name, a universal dharma name, for making a new start in your life. Deliver many sentient beings therewith."[108]

The nine disciples continued their prayer even after the event until Sot'aesan ordered them to stop in October of that year. The prayers of the nine members and the holy event of law (dharma) authentication were the spiritual foundation of selfless service for the public well-being, which strengthened the followers' faith, solidarity, and public spirit for the founding of the new religious order.

In November 1919, Sot'aesan changed the name of the order from Savings Union to The Association for the Establishment of the Society for the Study of Buddha-dharma and had all the documents recorded in the designatory name Buddha-dharma. Sot'aesan explained the rea-

---

105. This day (August 21) is observed as the Day of Dharma Authentication in Won Buddhism.
106. See SS, I:14.
107. Ibid.
108. Ibid.

son for adopting Buddha-dharma as the heart of the doctrine of the new religious order:

> What we are going to learn is the teachings of the Buddha and what we should teach our descendants is also what the Buddha taught. Hence you should exert a great effort to the inquiry into the heart of Buddha-dharma so that you may be enlightened to its truth.... Buddhism has been treated contemptuously in this country for several hundred years so that no one would respect anything carrying the word "Buddhism." If the fundamental truth is to be discovered and if sentient beings are to be led to the gate to blessings and wisdom through correct moral cultivation, no other teaching than Buddha-dharma should be taken as the main doctrine. Moreover, Buddhism will be the main religion of the world.... The worship of the Buddha shall not be limited to taking refuge in the statue of the Buddha. One will realize that all things in the universe and the dharma realm of the empty space are none other than the manifestation of the Dharmakāya Buddha. The Buddha-dharma will not be separated from daily work.[109]

## V. Drafting the Doctrine

### A. Dharma Meeting at Mt. Pongnae

Sot'aesan searched for a place for retreat and rest where he could prepare for founding the new religious order in his mind. Thus in March 1919 (4 w.e.) he, accompanied by O Ch'ang-gŏn, visited Wolmyŏngam at Mt. Pongnae, where he stayed for ten days before he returned to Kilyong-ni. In July, he sent Song Kyu there to find a place to stay. In October, Sot'aesan entrusted the matters of the association to several members and left for Wolmyŏngam with a plan to do spiritual cultivation for a few years. Song Kyu, who had been waiting for him, was delighted at his arrival, and Paek Hang-myŏng, abbot of Wolmyŏngam, received him warmly. The motive behind Sot'aesan's entering the mountain was to take a spiritual rest after several years of hard work, to draft the doctrine for the religious order to be opened, and to shield his enlightened mind, avoiding attention from the public in the turbulent times.

While staying there, Sot'aesan had a cloister, called Sŏktuam, built near Wŏlmyŏngam; there he gave sermons to his visiting followers. During this time Sot'aesan visited Kŭmsan-sa in Kimje county and stayed there for a while. He drew a circle on the door lintel of the room

---

109. See *WK*, p. 52; *SS*, I:15.

where he stayed. It was the first expression of his thought on Irwŏnsang as the central tenet of the doctrine. Irwŏnsang was enshrined as the symbol of the object of religious worship and the standard of moral discipline later in 1935 at Taegakchŏn (Great Enlightenment Hall) in the headquarters of Won Buddhism.

## B.  Drafting the Doctrine at Pongnae Cloister

While Sot'aesan was staying at Wŏlmyŏngam, Song Chŏk-pyŏk and others came and expressed their wish to wait on him. In December 1919 (4 w.e.), Sot'aesan moved to a thatched hut next to Silsangsa, in the center of Mt. Pongnae, where he devoted himself to mental and physical repose while living in poverty with a few disciples (Song Kyu, Song To-sŏng, and O Ch'ang-gŏn). With the turn of the New Year (5 w.e.) the number of his followers coming from several districts (Yŏnggwang, Kimje, Chŏnju) increased, and Sot'aesan, moved by their devotion, welcomed them and preached sermons to them morning and evening. The main point of his sermons at that time was on the method of spiritual concentration by observing the mind and the method of seeing into one's own nature and realizing buddhahood.[110]

In April 1920 (5 w.e.) at Sŏktuam, Sot'aesan announced the outline of the doctrine for the new religious order. Its contents consisted of two ways: the essential way that each individual as an individual ought to follow and the essential way of practice. The essential way to follow was the fourfold beneficence (saŭn) and four essentials; the essential way of practice was the threefold practice (samhak) and eight articles (for threefold practice).[111]

The tenet of fourfold beneficence expounds the indebtedness, gratitude, and ingratitude to heaven and earth, parents, brethren, and laws. The four essentials are the equal rights of man and woman, discrimination of the wise from the fool, the education of the children of others, and respect (as for one's own father) toward those who devote themselves to the public. The threefold practice includes spiritual cultivation, inquiry into facts and principles, and mindful choice in karmic action, which should be followed as the way of moral cultivation. The threefold practice is a reformed and expanded form of the triple discipline of śīla, samādhi, and prajñā in Buddhism. The eight articles consist of four articles to keep—faith, zeal, doubt, sincerity—and four articles to forsake—disbelief, avarice, laziness, delusion.

---

110. Note that the the last two lines of Bodhidharma's four-line gāthā are reflected here: "Pointing directly to the human mind, seeing into the self-nature, and attaining buddhahood."

111. WK, pt. 1, chap. 5, sec. 3.

According to the biographer, the central tenets of the doctrine are simple and clear; the structure of the doctrine is complete; and, therefore, all the followers of the doctrine can attain to the great Way without falling into delusion and partiality. This is the basic doctrine of the new religious order.

While staying at Pongnae Cloister, Sot'aesan exchanged his ideas for Buddhist renovation with Buddhist monks. Eventually, he wrote *On the Renovation of Korean Buddhism* (*Chosŏn pulgyo hyŏksillon*) and *Essentials of Culture and Inquiry* (*Suyang yŏn'gu yoron*). The main point of the former was that the outmoded and obsolete Buddhist practice should be modernized and renovated to be useful for the general salvation. The latter contains the correct method of mental cultivation and articles of inquiry as the correct ways of discipline.

## C. Rallying the Founding Members

Seeing that the number of followers was increasing at Pongnae Cloister, Sot'aesan tried to test his method of edification via the ten-member body, in which the leader of the unit edifies the nine other members, and each of those nine members becomes in turn the leader of a new body of ten members. In June 1921 (6 w.e.), he organized a unit of male members in Yŏnggwang and, in August, two units, one male and one female, pulling together the members from the districts of Yŏnggwang, Kimje, and Chŏnju. However, it was not easy to manage them because of the uneven attendance of the members. Hence Sot'aesan resumed teaching them directly. Sot'aesan's teaching went through three stages. Upon the enlightenment, his main concern was to lead his followers to aspiration and faith in the new religious order. For the next three years (1917–1919) he took as the main concern of his edification the faith and devotion, solidarity, and public spirit of his followers. After the announcement of the outline of the new doctrine in 1920 (5 w.e.) his main concern was to train his followers with the new doctrine.

A few years after his entrance into the mountain, Sot'aesan, feeling that the conditions were growing in favor of opening the new religious order, prepared to leave the mountain. In 1922 (7 w.e.), Sot'aesan gained about twenty new followers who played indispensable roles in the founding of the new religion.[112]

---

112. In September 1922 (7 w.e.) Sot'aesan sent Song Kyu to Chinan district, where he met Ch'oe To-hwa at Mirŭk-sa in Mt. Mandŏk. In December Sot'aesan took O Ch'anggŏn and Song To-sŏng there and met Ch'oe To-hwa, Chŏn Sam-sam, Chŏn Ŭm-gwang, and Ro Tŏksongok. In March 1923 (8 w.e.) Sot'aesan returned to Mt. Pongnae and met Sŏ Tong-p'ung and Sŏ Chung-an at Kimje. Besides these, he met Ku Nam-su, Yi Mangap, Chang Chŏng-su, and Chang Chŏk-cho at Wŏnp'yŏng; Pak Ho-jang from Chŏnju; and Pak Wŏn-sŏk from Iri.

## VI. Founding of the New Religious Order

### A. The Inaugural Meeting of the Society for the Study of Buddha-dharma

Sŏ Chung-an and his wife Chŏng Se-wŏl came to Pongnae Cloister and suggested that Sot'aesan move to a place where his teachings could be available to the general public.[113] While Sot'aesan was discussing the plan for opening the order with them, he was informed of his mother's illness in Yŏnggwang. Promising to meet with his disciples in winter, Sot'aesan returned home; his mother passed away in July 1923. At that time his followers from various districts gathered at the temple at Ong-nyŏ peak to offer their condolences. The hall was too small to accommodate all of them, however, and the building site was not adequate for a permanent monastery. Thus Sot'aesan proposed to build a temple elsewhere. He decided to build three thatched houses (one house with ten rooms and two houses of eight rooms each) at the foot of Pŏmhyŏn-dong in October. This was the first construction of Yŏngsan Monastery.

In November 1923, Sot'aesan went to Chŏnju, where he set up a temporary branch in the house provided by Pak Ho-jang and Yi Ch'ŏng-ch'un. Sot'aesan entrusted Sŏ Chung-an with laying down the prospectus and regulations for opening the new order, then returned to Pongnae Cloister. When Sot'aesan told Paek Hang-myŏng of his plan for the development of the new order, the latter was deeply moved and said that he would let Sot'aesan use part of the temple at Naejang-sa, where Pak had been appointed abbot, for propagation. To this Sot'ae-san responded, "Since the Buddhist temple is public property, the matter cannot be handled by one or two persons' accord; however, it will be a ray of hope for the bright future of Buddhism if it can be done."[114] In February 1924 (9 w.e.) Sot'aesan went to Naejang-sa to find out that Paek Hak-myŏng's intention had been thwarted by the opposition of the monks there. Sot'aesan offered solace to Paek Hang-myŏng, who was sorry about the embarrassing situation. Sot'aesan went to Seoul with a few disciples and set up a temporary branch office in a house provided by Sŏ Chung-an. He stayed there for a month, gaining several new disciples.[115]

In March 1924, Sot'aesan left Seoul for Chŏnju, North Cholla province, where he met with several followers. Sŏ Chung-an and others proposed to prepare for the founding of the new order, which was named the Society for the Study of Buddha-dharma. For the site of the

---

113. See *WK*, pt. 1, chap. 5, sec. 5.

114. *WK*, pt. 1, chap. 5, sec. 5. Sot'aesan sent Song Kyu, Kim Kwang-sŏn, O Ch'ang-gŏn, Yi Tong-an, and Yi Chun-gyŏng to Naejang-sa.

115. Sot'aesan met Pak Sa-si-hwa, Song Sŏng-wŏn, Yi Tong-jin-hwa, Kim Sam-mae-hwa, and Yi Kong-ju, who made a great contribution to the founding at the early stage.

society Sot'aesan chose Iri (now renamed Iksan) and its vicinity because it was thought that this vast area could provide poor people with a good place to live and because there was convenient transportation for followers from across the country. The members of the steering committee unanimously agreed with his decision. On April 29, 1924, the new religious order, tentatively named the Society for the Study of Buddhadharma, held its inaugural meeting at Pogwang-sa, a small temple in Iri City. At the meeting, the constitution for the organization of the order was adopted. After the inaugural meeting, Sot'aesan, together with his followers, searched for a site for constructing the general headquarters of the order in various districts of Iri and its vicinity and chose the current site of the headquarters in August 1924.[116]

### B. The Communal Life of Devotees

Although the initial construction of the general headquarters was finished by the unified efforts of the devotees and laity, it was unclear how it would be maintained and supported. In December 1924, Song Chŏkpyŏk and others proposed starting a taffy-peddling business. It was not a profitable business, however, so they brought it to an end in July 1925. Thereafter, they started tenant farming for a Japanese colonial company in Mansŏng-ni to earn the money for Zen retreats. The expenses of the general headquarters were paid from the membership fees and the income from the tenant farming. The communal life of the devotees began there. As they were mostly poor peasants, they had to labor to earn their livelihood. Besides the taffy-peddling business and tenant farming, they even tried such businesses as raising silkworms, managing orchards, and raising stock. According to Sot'aesan's biographer, they did all sorts of menial work without complaint or hesitation as they found it a great joy to work as founding members of a new religious order.

### C. Announcement of a New Method of Training

In May 1924, Sot'aesan held a month-long Sŏn (Zen) retreat at Mt. Mandŏk, where he met Kim Tae-gŏ.[117] In March 1925 (10 w.e.), Sot'aesan announced the new method of training: regular-term training and daily training to train his followers in the new doctrine of the or-

---

116. Sŏ Chung-an donated the cost for the whole site (2.43 acre) and part of the construction cost (600 yen). Some members from various districts also raised funds (800 yen). The membership of the inaugural year was more than sixty male and seventy female members, and the number of devotees was thirteen. About ten devotees constructed two thatched houses, where the sign Pulbŏp yŏn'gu hoe was put up for the first time.

117. Kim Tae-gŏ (1914–1998) was inaugurated *chongbŏpsa* (head Dharma master of the order) in 1962, succeeding Song Kyu (1900–1962).

der.[118] On May 6, 1925, Sot'aesan held the first regular-term training for ten people with Song Kyu as their instructor. In November, the winter regular-term training was held for more than twenty participants with Yi Ch'un-p'ung as the instructor. These were the beginnings of the training in the dharma of the order. The regular-term training was aimed at training the members periodically in two sessions of Sŏn retreat: a winter session (from November 2 to February 6) and a summer session (from May 6 to August 6). The training course consisted of eleven subjects: chanting, seated meditation, scripture study, lecture, discussion, *kongan* ("meditative case"; C. *kung-an*; J. *kōan*), principles of nature, regular-term diary, carefulness, deportment, and occasional sermon. The daily training was aimed at constantly training the members with the things to heed for daily application and the things to heed while attending the temple.[119] To enforce these practices, the method of checking one's actions against the rules of mindful action and writing in the daily diary were used. In the daily diary one is not only to write down the progress in one's practice but also to record one's spiritual, physical, and material giving and taking, and one's observance of the thirty precepts.[120] To enforce this practice, a provision was made for the group leader to check diaries monthly and evaluate them yearly; in addition, a rule was set up that one make a yearly report of one's practice to the Department of Edification.[121] This method was so simple and systematic that people of all walks of life could be trained to enter the correct way toward the realization of enlightenment.

## VII. Molding the Structure of the Order

### A. Publication of Periodicals for Edification

One of the important projects launched after the general meeting in March 1928 (13 w.e.) was the publication of a periodical for edification. In May 1928 a monthly periodical, *Wŏlmal t'ongsin* (Monthly communication), was issued in carbon copies until its thirty-fourth issue (December 1930); it resumed in April 1932 with the new title *Wŏlbo* (Monthly report) in mimeograph copies until its forty-eighth issue (June 1933). Japanese authorities confiscated the copies of the forty-eighth issue for alleged violation of their publication laws. In September 1933 a permit for publication of the periodical *Hoebo* (Report of the society) was obtained from the office of the Japanese governor-general. The periodical was published in mimeograph copies and in December 1934 in printed issues. In 1940 (25 w.e.), as World War II intensified, it was published quarterly; it was stopped with the sixty-fifth

---

118. See *Canon*, pt. 3, chap. 2.
119. Ibid.
120. Ibid., chap. 11.
121. One of the administrative offices in the order.

issue in January 1941. *Wŏlmal t'ongsin* carried the gist of Sot'aesan's sermons, notices, and news of the order to the branch temples. In addition to these items, *Wŏlbo* and *Hoebo* carried an exchange of ideas in the order. *Hoebo*'s printed issues played the role of edification and cultural function under Japanese oppression. *Hoebo* remains an important resource for Won Buddism because it carries sermons, reports of spiritual awakenings, subjects for contemplation, opinions, and questions dating from the early years of the order.[122]

## B. Publication of Early Scriptures

In March 1928 the order also undertook the publication of the early scriptures and the new regulations of the order. These publications, however, the *Prospectus and Rules of the Order* and the *Essentials of Cultivation and Inquiry*, fell short of expressing the central doctrine of the order, and the system and the structure of the order were too jejune to support its development. In 1930 (15 w.e.), Sot'aesan ordered a few of his disciples[123] to edit and publish the main points of the doctrine and systems that he had formulated and announced by that time.[124]

## C. Enshrinement of Irwŏnsang and Training of the Priests

In April 1935 (20 w.e.) the construction of the Great Enlightenment Hall (Taegakchŏn) was completed in the central general headquarters and the Mind Buddha, Irwŏnsang, was enshrined at the altar in the hall. By this event the new order's system of religious faith was established. Upon his enlightenment Sot'aesan had expressed his view of the ultimate truth in terms of the great Way of Irwŏn and had drawn the circular form, formulating the plan to identify Irwŏn as the essence of the fourfold beneficence. At this time he decided to expand his view and enshrine it as the object of religious faith.[125] Sot'aesan kept expounding the doctrine of Irwŏn in his sermons and discourses. Dur-

122. *WK*, pt. 2, chap. 3, sec. 1.

123. Song Kyu, Song To-sŏng, Chŏn Ŭm-gwang, Yu Hŏ-il.

124. The publications are as follows: in July 1931 (16 W.E.), *Pulbŏp yŏn'guhoe chodan kyuyak* (By-laws for founding the Society for the Study of Buddha-dharma); in April 1932 (17 W.E.), *Pogyŏng yuktae yoryŏng* (Six general principles of treasure scripture); in May 1934 (19 W.E.), edited version of the *Pulbŏp yŏn'guhoe hoegyu* (Constitution of the Society for the Study of Buddha-dharma); in December 1934, *Pogyŏng samdae yoryŏng* (Three general principles of treasure scripture); in April 1935 (20 W.E.), *Chosŏn pulgyo hyŏkshillon* (On renovation of Korean Buddhism), which had been drafted at Pongnae Cloister in 1920 (5 W.E.); in August 1936 (21 W.E.), *Yejŏn* (Book of rites); *Hoewŏn suji* (What the members should know) and *Pulbŏp yŏn'guhoe yakpo* (Manual of the Society for the Study of Buddha-dharma); and in 1939 (24 W.E.), *Pulbŏp yŏn'guhoe kŭnhaengbŏp* (How to practice diligently in the Society for the Study of Buddha-dharma).

125. Following this, Sot'aesan had Irwŏnsang enshrined in the enlightenment hall of Ch'oryang Temple in September 1936 (21 W.E.), Yŏngsan Temple and Shinhŭng Temple in March 1937 (22 W.E.), and all the new branch temples thereafter.

ing the winter Sŏn retreat started in November 1938 (23 w.e.) Sot'aesan formulated and promulgated how to enshrine the mind Buddha Irwŏnsang and wrote "The Provenance of and Vow to the Mind Buddha Irwŏnsang."[126] Thus, the tenet of Irwŏnsang became the heart of the new order's doctrine, being the object of religious worship and the standard of religious practice. Irwŏnsang was enshrined not only in the branch temples but also in the houses of all the lay followers so that in 1940 (25 w.e.), 180 families in thirteen districts enshrined it in their houses. In November 1938 Sot'aesan held the winter retreat for training the priests from all branch temples in the doctrine with Yu Hŏ-il as the monitor. This became the beginning of the yearly training of the priests (kyomu).

## VIII.  Sot'aesan's Last Years

### A.  Critical Situation

In April 1940, the order was entering the third twelve-year cycle of the first generation. During this critical moment of the Sino-Japanese War, the surveillance and interference of the Japanese police intensified. Being aware of the difficulty of holding on much longer, Sot'aesan tried to carry out a few projects. However, his plans all miscarried as a result of the interference of the Japanese colonial government.

When the Pacific War broke out in 1941, the Japanese authority forced the order to insert the Japanese national pledge into the order's service programs and exacted for the Japanese national defense the income from the performance of rituals. A police detective, stationed in the central general headquarters to keep watch on the order, arrested staff members several times. *Hoebo* ceased publication. With the outbreak of the Great East Asian War (WWII) in December 1941 (26 w.e.), the Temporary National Security Act was announced, and the order was required to submit the report of its continuity, whereby the establishment of any new branch temple was restricted. The order was forced to join the League of Buddhists, a Buddhist monks' organization led by Japanese Buddhist monks; league members were often called out to work for the Japanese national cause at critical times. The number of winter and summer Sŏn retreats and the regular dharma meetings were curtailed so that the time and energy could be used for teaching the Japanese language and mobilizing labor. Sometimes the temple precinct was used as a military training site.

In such a seemingly hopeless situation, however, Sot'aesan was able to pacify the Japanese with passive cooperation. In January 1940, Sot'aesan had submitted to the Japanese authority an application form

---

126. See *Canon*, pt. 2, chap. 1, sec. 4; the title was changed to "The Vow to Irwŏnsang" in the 1962 edition of the *Canon*.

for permission to establish an academy (*yuil hagwŏn*) where the devotees of the order could be educated, but it was turned down in the following year. In April 1942, his application for establishment of an orphanage (*chayugwŏn*) was also rejected. As the situation became more critical, even those organizations already established were at a standstill. The Japanese colonial government did not allow any Korean organization, large or small, to survive except the pro-Japanese groups. Because Japan was a pro-Buddhist nation, any order that supported Buddhism was permitted, although any matter of importance was inspected by the Japanese authority in advance and reported to them afterward. Sot'aesan thus had to put all his new plans on hold. In May 1942 (27 w.e.), he had the total assets of the order, which had previously been registered under the names of some prominent disciples, notarized as the property of the order. From October 1942, Sot'aesan managed to find opportunities to make a final visit to the branch temples in various districts, consolidating the laity's faith in the order. In April 1942, a new regulation of the order was adopted and put into effect; it defined the head dharma master (*chongbŏpsa*) of the order, the secretary-general, and five departments, replacing the old regulation, in which there were two branches (administration and inspection) and twelve departments.

## B. Last Enforcement of the Order's Regulations and the Verse of Dharma Transmission

The Hoegyu (Regulations of the society) that Sot'aesan had Pak Chang-sik draft in 1941 consists of 250 articles in twelve chapters. One of the articles set the term of the head dharma master of the order at six years; the old article had no term limit. Another article provided for a supreme council of nine male and nine female members under one leader. This council was to assist the head dharma master.

From this time on, Sot'aesan pressed his elite disciples to finish compilation of the *Pulgyo chŏngjŏn* as if he felt the time of his death approaching. On January 28, 1941, he promulgated the verse (gāthā) of the dharma transmission[127] and how to practice Sŏn in motion and at rest to the assembly of the winter Sŏn retreat. He said:

> It was customary for the masters in the past to deliver the gāthā of the transmission of the dharma in a hurry at the moment of death. However, I deliver it to you in advance and

---

127. *Canon*, pt. 2, chap. 1, sec. 6:

> Being turns into Nonbeing and Nonbeing into Being
> Turning and turning eternally;
> Then, ultimately, Being and Nonbeing are both void,
> Yet, the Void is also complete.

to everybody equally while in the past they delivered it to a
few secretly. Whether you will receive the dharma completely
or not depends on the status of your practice. Hence, exert
yourselves to the practice lest you should regret later.[128]

Thereafter Sot'aesan's sermon at regular dharma meetings, evening
meetings, and Sŏn sessions were focused on the problem of birth and
death and the causal law of karmic retribution. He often enjoined his
disciples to take good care of themselves, saying, "I am about to leave
for a remote and deep place to rest. Examine yourselves to see that you
not regress when I am gone, and make a firm resolution."[129] Releasing
the doctrinal chart to be inserted as a frontispiece of the *Pulgyo chŏngjŏn*
in January 1943, Sot'aesan said, "The quintessence of my teaching is
contained herein; but how many can understand the true essence of my
intentions?"[130] He said further, "A master's creation of a new dharma,
the disciples' reception and transmission of it to their posterity, and the
general public's reception and practice of it with pleasure in the future
form a trinity; their merits are equal."[131]

## C. Compilation and Publication of *Pulgyo chŏngjŏn*

In September 1940 (25 w.e.), Sot'aesan ordered some handpicked disciples of his[132] to unify and edit the works so far published. In 1942 (27
w.e.), he often urged them to finish the compilation, giving his decision
for the final version. When the final draft was completed, he had it sent
to the press, saying that, as he did not have much time, he had to have it
published even though the work was not to his complete satisfaction.
Still, he said, the volume contained the gist of his lifetime aspiration
and planning. He pleaded with his disciples to learn by words, practice
with body, and be enlightened to it, so that the teaching should be
transmitted to tens of thousands of generations. He said that in the
future people all over the world would recognize this teaching, would
be deeply moved by it, and would hold it in deep respect. The publication was delayed because the Japanese authority did not give permission to publish it. In March 1943, the work was approved for
printing with Kim T'ae-hŭp, president of the *Pulgyo sibo* (Buddhist
times) as the publisher. It was published in August, two months after
Sot'aesan's death. The *Pulgyo chŏngjŏn*[133] was the main scripture of this

---

128. See *SS*, XV:2.
129. Ibid., 4.
130. Ibid., 7.
131. Ibid., 19.
132. Song Kyu, Song To-sŏng, Sŏ Tae-wŏn, Yi Kong-ju, and Pak Chang-shik.
133. The 1962 edition of the *Canon (chŏngjŏn)* is nearly identical to that of the 1943 edition; the main difference is that Part One (Renovation of Buddhism) of the latter was
redacted in *SS* I of the former.

order for nineteen years, until the publication of *Wŏnbulgyo kyojŏn* in 1962.

## D. Sot'aesan's Entrance into Nirvāṇa

When in January 1941 Sot'aesan presented the gāthā of the dharma transmission and the method of practicing Sŏn meditation in motion and at rest, he said that he was transmitting the dharma to the public instead of a chosen few and not at the time of one's last breath, but sufficiently prior to death. He did this because he was aware of his impending death. After that, Sot'aesan's sermons were mainly about birth and death and the causal law of karmic retribution. One day he said to Song Kyu, "Try to lead the order for yourself. It seems difficult for me to stay much longer."[134]

At the regular dharma meeting on May 16, 1943, Sot'aesan said, "Birth and death are like the cycle of the four seasons or the repetition of day and night. This is the principle whereby all things in the universe are being operated and the truth whereby heaven and earth operate. Buddhas and bodhisattvas are free and not deluded when they come and go, while ordinary human beings and other sentient beings are bound and deluded when they go through birth and death."[135] In the afternoon of that day, Sot'aesan suddenly fell ill; he passed away on June 1, after twenty-eight years of teaching. According to the biographer, his disciples' grief over his death was beyond description, and the lament of the general public seemed endless; the empty dharma realm and the phenomenal things in the world showed sadness.

His funeral service was held at 10 A.M. on June 6, 1943, at Taegakchŏn. Thousands of mourners from various districts attended with the Buddhist monks from Iri. His body was cremated at the Iri crematorium and the remains were preserved at the public cemetery at Kŭmgang-ni after the seventh-week mass, on July 19. Kim T'ae-hŭp presided over the mass.[136] At the mass, the eminent Japanese Buddhist monk Ueno, highly respected by the high officials of the Japanese Government General, expressed his condolences between sobs.

Upon completion of the funeral services, the Supreme Council of the Order met at Taegakchŏn on June 7 and elected Song Kyu the next head dharma master on June 8. At the end of World War II, two years after Sot'aesan's nirvāṇa, Korea was liberated. His successor, Song Kyu, better known by his cognomen "Chŏngsan," renamed the order Wŏnbulgyo in 1947. Chŏngsan played the central role in systematizing the doctrine of the order before and after Sot'aesan's death. It should be

---

134. *SS*, XV:5.
135. Ibid., 14.
136. Without him the *Pulgyo chŏngjŏn* could not have been published.

noted that Sot'aesan accepted Chŏngsan as the "mother of the law" of
the new religious order.

## E.  Chŏngsan, the New Head Dharma Master

Song Kyu, the new head dharma master of the order, was born on the
fourth day of the eighth month in 1900.[137] He was the eldest son to
his father, Song Pyŏk-cho, and mother, Yi Un-oe. According to his
biographer, he was endowed with unusual natural gifts and with magnanimity. From childhood on, his serene appearance gave a sacred impression to whoever saw him.[138] In accordance with Confucian family
tradition, Song Kyu read the Confucian classics from the time he was
eight years old, but he was not much interested in the Confucian
learning. While reading historical records of ancient sages, he had an
aspiration to cultivate the great Way to become a great master under the
heaven. Accordingly, he tried to find a wizard or a recluse in mountain
valleys and in remote districts. Sometimes he sat in spiritual concentration in a one-room thatched house for several days; there followed some
sort of miracles, which surprised his neighbors. With his aspiration
growing stronger, Song Kyu moved to North Chŏlla province when
he was seventeen years old, visiting several religious orders. While staying in a village called Hwahae-ri, he was visited by Sot'aesan in 1917,
a year after the latter's enlightenment. In July 1918 (3 w.e.) he went
to Sot'aesan and was appointed the center position of the first ten-
member body at age eighteen. With the other eight members, he completed the task of prayer and dharma authentication with the miraculous fingerprints in blood.[139] Thereafter Chŏngsan spent five years
at Pongnae Cloister, helping Sot'aesan draft the new doctrine. From
1924 (9 w.e.) on, he shared all the troubles of constructing the central
general headquarters with other adherents; for twelve years he exerted
himself mainly to provide materials for instruction and to educate
the able young devotees. For six years from 1936 (21 w.e.) Song Kyu
exerted himself to develop the holy place at Yŏngsan and to rear the
younger generation, drafting the *Pulbŏp yŏn'guhoe ch'anggŏnsa* (History
of founding the Society for the Study of Buddha-dharma). From 1942
(27 w.e.) he helped Sot'aesan compile the *Pulgyo chŏngjŏn*, assisting him
with managing all the important matters of the order. In 1943 (28 w.e.)
he was elected the head dharma master of the order upon Sot'aesan's
entrance into nirvāṇa. In 1947 Chŏngsan renamed the order Wŏnbulgyo or Won Buddhism. It should be noted here that Chŏngsan's

---

137. His birthplace: Sosŏng-dong, Ch'ojŏn-myŏn, Sŏngju-gun, North Kyŏngsang province, Korea.
138. *WK*, p. 103.
139. See *WK*, p. 105; *SS*, I:14.

analects, the *Chŏngsan chongsa pŏbŏ* (The dharma words of Master Chŏngsan), is one of the two holy scriptures of the Won Buddhist order. Song Kyu died in January 1962, and the *Wŏnbulgyo kyojŏn* (Scriptures of Won Buddhism) was published in September 1962. Because of his illness, he had appointed a committee of five members to compile the new scripture. Thus, Chŏngsan fulfilled Sot'aesan's prediction that the young Chŏngsan was the "mother of the law" of the new order.

## Part Two: Sot'aesan's Religious Thought

### I. The Intention to Save the World

**A. The Founding Motive**

To understand the nature of Sot'aesan's religious thought, we must ask why he established a new religion carrying the name "Buddhism." Sot'aesan compared the religion he was establishing to a medical institution, his teachings to medicine, and the priests of his order to physicians.[1] Moreover, he compared his new religious order to a medical center, and Buddhism, Confucianism, and Taoism to specialty hospitals. However, he took Buddha-dharma as the central tenet of the doctrine and synthesized it with some useful tenets of Confucianism and Taoism, hence the name Won *Buddhism*.[2]

If no one were ever ill, no medicine, physicians, or hospitals would be necessary; and if the world were a paradise, no religion would be necessary. What was wrong with the world and the three traditional religions in Korea? The world was at the turning point of old and new eras where the lights of the ancient sages were dimmed for a long time and the light of a new sage for the new era was not yet lit.[3] The moral world especially was dark, and sentient beings were suffering deep in the tormenting seas of misery. Sot'aesan's enlightened view reflected the fact that the world was about to enter a dangerous era, aggravated by the formidable power of material civilization. Material power has dual harmful effects. Material conveniences cause enormous harm to living beings as is seen with nuclear accidents, ozone layer depletion, radiation, highway fatalities, and the pollution of air, water, and earth, to name but a few. In addition, material conveniences fan the fire of avarice for wealth, enfeebling the moral sense of humankind and deepening the bitter seas of misery. In Sot'aesan's view, the only way to save sentient beings themselves lies in unfolding the spiritual power and

---

1. See *SS*, III:56.
2. See *SS*, II:1, for Sot'aesan's intention for the synthesis of the three Asian religious doctrines.
3. See above pt. 1, "Background."

strengthening the wisdom and moral sense of humankind. This task can only be carried out by edification in truthful religion and training in sound morality. This idea is expressed in the founding motive.[4] Sot'ae-san, however, did not have a totally negative view of material civilization. The ideal world, which he called "a limitless paradise," cannot be realized without advancing both material civilization and spiritual culture. Unfortunately, humankind was being enslaved to the formidable power of material civilization; thus Sot'aesan expressed his idea for building a paradise as follows: As material power is unfolding, let us unfold the spiritual power accordingly.[5] By comparing the society materially advanced but spiritually backward to a person physically healthy but mentally ill and a society spiritually advanced but materially backward to a person mentally healthy but physically ill, Sot'aesan has corrected the prejudice of the traditional religions against the value of the mundane world. This world is not something to be cursed. On the contrary, it could be a paradise if its ills are cured. Thus, the goal of the new religious order was to deliver all sentient beings suffering in the bitter seas of misery and to cure the world of illness. This goal was to be achieved by religious edification of the world, and the religion Sot'aesan relied on was Buddhism. However, as we have seen above, Buddhism as practiced in Korea at that time could not be relied on; it had to be reformed and renovated to be applicable to the ailing world.

## B. Sot'aesan's Renovation of the Korean Buddhist System

Sot'aesan declared categorically that Buddha-dharma is superior to any other ethico-religious system.[6] He made it clear to his disciples in the inchoate stage of the order that what should be learned, taught, and practiced was Buddha-dharma. He made this declaration when most Koreans had been following Confucian morals for five centuries and when any Buddhist idea was a taboo in Korean society. However, he was clearly aware of the necessity to reform Korean Buddhism if it was to be used as a means to deliver sentient beings, and that was why he wrote the essay "On the Renovation of Korean Buddhism" (Chosŏn pulgyo hyŏksillon).[7] The spirit of renovation of the Buddhist practice is expressed in four sets of mottoes in the *Canon*. It is necessary to analyze the mottoes for a proper understanding of Sot'aesan's religious thought.

---

4. See *Canon*, pt. 1, chap. 1.
5. See "Mottoes," which follows the frontispiece of the *Canon* below.
6. See *Canon*, pt. 1, chap. 2.
7. Published in 1935 (20 W.E.) and inserted as part 1 of book 1, *Pulgyo chŏngjŏn* in 1943. In the *Wŏnbulgyo kyojŏn*, the Korean original of this translation is summarized as part of the introductory chapter of the *Taejonggyŏng* (Scripture of Sot'aesan). See *SS*, I:15–19.

1. *Everywhere is the Buddha-image; do all things as making an offering to Buddha.* Here Buddha does not mean the Buddha Śākyamuni; it refers to the cosmic body of Buddha (Dharmakāya Buddha), which is omnipresent. In the metaphysics of Hua-yen Buddhism it is referred to as Vairocana Buddha, which is identified with the universe itself.[8] Thus, by this motto, the traditional Buddhist ritual of making an offering to the Buddha statue for blessings is abolished, and a new way of receiving Buddha's blessing is suggested as, in Sot'aesan's view, everything in the universe is the manifestation of the cosmic body of Buddha, which has the power and authority to bless or punish. More realistic and practical ways of making an offering to living buddhas are spelled out in terms of awareness of and requital of beneficence (to heaven and earth, parents, brethren, and laws), which is the heart of Won Buddhist religious life. This idea is highlighted as one of the four fundamental principles of the order, as the doctrinal chart of the *Canon* shows. Since the essence of the fourfold beneficence is identified with Buddha's cosmic body, symbolized in Irwŏnsang, the symbol of the object of religious worship, there is an ongoing question whether Won Buddhism is truly Buddhism. Sot'aesan's answer is that the Buddha statue has been worshiped for more than two thousand years and proven to be ineffective.[9] In his view the new era needs a new form of Buddhism, one that can be of true service to the realization of a limitless paradise in the mundane world.

2. *Timeless Zen and placeless Zen.* While the tenet of beneficence spells out the way of religious life epitomized in terms of requital of beneficence as a Buddha offering, the second motto, maintaining the Zen mind anytime and anywhere, aims at helping one realize enlightenment in daily mundane life. What is assumed in this practice is that in one's mind is hidden the original enlightenment covered up with defilement. Hence, by practice of Zen, one is to see in one's own nature the original enlightenment, or what Chinul called "the mind-essence of void and calm, numinous awareness."[10] If Zen without enlightenment is like the sun without heat and light, as D. T. Suzuki claims, and if Zen monks

---

8. See "Hua-yen Wu Chiao chi-kuan" (Cessation and contemplation in the five teachings of the Hua-yen), *T*, 1867.45.513; Cleary and Cleary, *Entry into the Inconceivable*, p. 68: "The reality body of the Buddha is inconceivable; formless, signless, without comparison, it manifests material forms for the sake of beings. In the ten directions they receive its teachings. Nowhere is it not manifested." See also *Mo-ho chi-kuan*, *T*, 1911.46.75b: "Vairocana Buddha is ubiquitous; how can you say that objects of vision and thought are not true dharmas? This is the truth of neither being nor nonbeing."
9. See *SS*, II:13.
10. *T*, 2020.48.1007ab; Buswell, *KAZ*, p. 147. The terms in question are used in the *Canon*, pt. 2, chap. 1, sec. 1. I owe the English rendering of "*kong chŏk yŏng chi*" to Buswell.

spend years in remote mountain valleys to attain enlightenment, a host of questions arise concerning Sot'aesan's way of Zen practice. For one thing, one can keep the Zen mind or the true mind in daily life only if one is awakened to one's own nature. If not, one will be unable to disperse the thick clouds of greed, anger, and hatred and the delusions that create the bitter seas of misery. For another, controversies remain over whether enlightenment comes gradually or suddenly, whether one can finish cultivation of mind suddenly or gradually after enlightenment, and whether one can ever experience enlightenment without years of strenuous Zen practice.[11] Sot'aesan's view on this issue is as drastic as his view on the object of Buddhist worship: he said that enlightenment to one's own nature should be done at home during one's youth. Moreover, awakening to one's own nature is only a necessary condition for realizing buddhahood; being enlightened is like mastering the alphabet of a language or knowing how to use a carpenter's chalk and square. It is totally another matter whether one can write Shakespeare's *Hamlet* or build a mansion. Whether one practices Zen anytime and everywhere can be known, in Sot'aesan's view, by reflecting on whether one can cultivate the One Mind when one's six senses are free from work and whether one can do justice and forsake injustice when the six senses are at work.[12] This is a way of demythologizing the secret content of the Zen monk's enlightenment (some Zen masters said that the essence of Zen lies in eating when hungry, drinking water when thirsty, and taking a nap when tired).

3. *Maintain one mind in motion and at rest; perfect both soul and body.* An extension of the reformative spirit of the above mottoes is Sot'aesan's operation on the ills of the traditional religious mind. Maintaining one mind in motion and at rest and perfecting both soul and body require that Buddhists maintain Buddha's enlightened mind not only in quiet mountain valleys but in the hustle and bustle of urban life. It also requires the practitioner to improve both spiritual and physical life in good balance. This requirement implies a sharp criticism of the century-old Buddhist sangha system, reminding one of Paichang's rule, "A day without work—a day without eating."[13] In Sot'aesan's view this rule should be applied in the secular world, which suffers from the moral defilement of greed, hatred, and delusions. He encouraged his followers to eliminate poverty, ignorance, and disease by having a sound

---

11. Buswell, *Zen Monastic Experience*, pp. 220–222: "But when Korean meditation monks who are training in the kanhwa technique routinely admit that they expect it will take upwards of twenty years of full-time practice to make substantive progress in their practice, there seem to be valid grounds for questioning how subitist *in practice* the Sŏn tradition really is" (p. 220).
12. See *Canon*, pt. 3, chap. 7, "Timeless Meditation."
13. See Dumoulin, *Zen Buddhism*, p. 172.

occupation while putting the doctrine into practice in daily life. He exemplified the spirit of these mottoes by spending a year in hard labor working on the embankment to reclaim the tidal land even before he mentioned anything about Buddhism to his disciples. With this example Sot'aesan aimed at correcting the wrong view of the past that the practitioner of the Way—whether Buddhist, Confucian, or Taoist—should only exert himself or herself to improve his or her soul or mind, ignoring or despising anything material, including the body. Sot'aesan thus put utmost importance on the balanced perfection of the mental and physical life by having his followers take a daily vow to maintain and use their minds and bodies perfectly.[14]

4. *Buddha-dharma is living itself; living is Buddha-dharma itself.* In this last set of mottoes Sot'aesan shows his intention to help his followers deliver themselves from the misery of the world by practicing Buddha-dharma in their daily lives. This set of mottoes questions the relevance of Buddhism isolated in remote mountain valleys. In Sot'aesan's view, Buddhism contained effective cures for the ills of the world in general and Korean society in particular. The cause of the human predicament, individual or collective, ultimately lies in the three poisonous elements of the human mind—greed, anger, and delusion—, which can best be removed by Buddha-dharma. One's knowledge of Buddha-dharma, no matter how extensive it may be, will be of no use unless one can realize its goals in daily life as an individual, a member of a family, a society, a state, and the world. While Confucianism was concerned exclusively with the importance of the secular world of human affairs, Buddhism was concerned with teaching its unimportance. Sot'aesan was as much concerned with the importance of the mundane world as Confucius, saying that benevolence and righteousness are the main principles of morality.[15] Inasmuch as Korean society was based on Confucian social norms, traditional Buddhism could not be suggested. Thus, the set of mottoes in question does not mean that the general populace should practice the kind of Buddhism practiced by Buddhist monks in remote mountain valleys. The Buddha-dharma that is to be followed in the secular world is the doctrine expounded in the *Canon* of this translation. One can say that Sot'aesan's teaching responds to both Nāgārjuna (second century c.e.) and Chu Hsi (1130–1200).

Nāgārjuna said:

> If one, keeping the precepts for laymen, can be born in the celestial world, attain the way of bodhisattva, and realize nirvāṇa, why does one need the precepts for monks? He

---

14. See *Canon*, pt. 2, chap. 1, sec. 4 for "The Vow to Irwŏnsang."
15. See *SS*, I:5.

answered: Although both ways lead to emancipation, there are differences of difficulty and easiness. Laymen have to make a living, which requires various toilsome works. Hence, if one wishes to devote oneself to Buddha-dharma, one's family life will be ruined. However, if one devotes oneself to one's family, the way of Buddha-dharma will be neglected. One can neither take nor discard the Way; to follow the Way properly is difficult. However, if one becomes a monk, one frees oneself from worldly responsibility, anger, and disturbance, finding it easy to devote oneself to the practice of the Way.[16]

A different argument was expressed by Hyu-jŏng (1520–1604):

How could it be a trivial matter for one to leave home and become a monk? It is neither for seeking for physical comfort, nor for wearing warm [clothing] and eating to be full, nor seeking for fame and wealth. It is for the Buddha's wisdom to continue and to deliver sentient beings by transcending the triple world.[17]

Chu Hsi wrote:

The mere fact that they discard the three bonds (between ruler and minister, father and son, and husband and wife) and the five constant virtues (righteousness on the part of the father, deep love on the part of the mother, friendliness on the part of the elder brother, respect on the part of the younger brother, and filial piety on the part of the son) is already a crime of the greatest magnitude. Nothing more need be said about the rest.[18]

The grand plan Sot'aesan had for establishing a new religion through a synthesis of the two religious traditions can be seen in his answer to an avid Confucian who had just converted to his teaching. He said, "To practice the perfect and great Way, one should be able to apply the truth to all human affairs, taking the way of emptiness and quiescence [Buddhist nirvāṇa] as the substance of the Way and benevolence (jen),

---

16. See Terada Toru and Mizuno Yaoko, eds., Dōgen, p. 307. Dōgen (1200–1253) quotes Nāgārjuna in the Shōbō genzō (Treasure chamber of the eye of true dharma). Since Dōgen does not provide the provenance of the quotation, I am not sure whether the quotation is his interpretation of Nāgāradian's thought. The quotation is my translation from the Chinese original in the Japanese text. For another translation, see Yūho Yokoi, Zen Master Dōgen, p. 69.
17. See Sŏsan Hyujŏng, Sŏn'ga kwigam (Paragon of Zen tradition), p. 143.
18. Wing-tsit Chan, Sourcebook in Chinese Philosophy, p. 646.

righteousness (*i*), propriety (*li*), and wisdom (*chih*) as its function."[19] It is probable that neither Nāgārjuna nor Chu Hsi would agree with Sot'aesan on this matter; consequently, Won Buddhism can be called a new religion. Since Buddha-dharma is the heart of the doctrine Sot'aesan established, however, Won Buddhism is a form of Buddhism, a religion of enlightenment.

## C. Epitome of Sot'aesan's Religious Thought

The soteriology of Sot'aesan's new religion lies in deliverance of sentient beings and curing the world of the moral ills. The whole doctrine of Won Buddhism is structured as a means to the realization of these two goals. Sot'aesan adopted some elements of Buddha-dharma and Taoist practice for the former and of Confucianism for the latter; through creative synthesis, he formed a new religion in accordance with his grand plan.[20] Since Buddha-dharma is the heart of the doctrine, however, this religion is more Buddhist than Confucian, and thus carries the name Won *Buddhism*.

Sot'acsan's attempt to bring Buddha-dharma from the mountain valleys to the general populace in urban and rural areas needed a clear doctrinal structure simple but potent enough to transform the sick world into a paradise. By the "sick world" Sot'aesan means the world where people suffer from being deluded, resentful, and egoistic, where neither Buddhism, Confucianism, Taoism, nor the indigenous religions provided effective remedies. The new religious order aimed at two goals: delivering the sentient beings and curing the world of illness. The first goal is to be achieved by self-reliance, the second by tapping the other-power. The essence of the former is correct enlightenment and right practice and that of the latter, awareness of and requital of beneficence. If one is enlightened to one's own nature and lives in accordance with its light on the one hand, and is aware of the universal beneficence of nature to which one owes one's existence and requites it on the other, then one will realize a paradise. The whole doctrine of Won Buddhism is structured to provide ways to realize these goals. The doctrine is epitomized in the doctrinal chart, which shows two ways: the way of religious faith and the way of religious practice.[21] The object of religious faith and the standard of practice are symbolized by Irwŏnsang,

---

19. See below *SS*, VI:20, for the full text of the conversation.
20. See *SS*, II:1, for Sot'aesan's intention to synthesize the three religions.
21. See the doctrinal chart in the *Canon*. Sot'aesan compared the profile of the chart to that of a turtle: The object of religious faith and the standard of practice, symbolized as Irwŏnsang, is the head; the four fundamental principles (awareness and requital of beneficence, correct enlightenment and right practice, practical application of Buddha-dharma, selfless service for the public) are like the four limbs.

which represents the ultimate reality of the universe. The general direction of Won Buddhist religious faith and practice is outlined in the four fundamental principles.[22]

The first of the four fundamental principles requires one to be enlightened to one's own nature or Buddha-nature as symbolized in the circular form, Irwŏnsang, so that one can practice the dharma right in using one's body, mouth, and mind. It is also the mind-seal that buddhas and patriarchs correctly transmit from one to another. It is presupposed in this injunction that one's mind creates a paradise or a hell depending on whether or not one is enlightened to one's own Buddha-nature. Sot'aesan accepts the *Yogācāra* tenet that the whole world is the creation of one's own mind.[23] In his view, the cause of suffering lies in the deluded mind of sentient beings. Thus correct enlightenment and right practice are necessary for delivering sentient beings from suffering. Correct enlightenment and right practice are spelled out in the tenets of Irwŏnsang and the threefold practice.[24]

The second of the four fundamental principles requires one to be aware of and requite the fourfold beneficence (heaven and earth, parents, brethren, and laws), to which one owes one's existence. This reflects Sot'aesan's prescription to cure the world of illness and is the essence of the Won Buddhist religious faith. In Sot'aesan's view, the main cause of social ills is resentment among individuals, families, societies, and nations. The cause of resentment in turn lies in the unawareness of one's indebtedness to the sources of one's existence, the universal beneficence of the Dharmakāya Buddha. Since a world full of resentment is a hell and one full of gratitude a paradise, Sot'aesan expounded the doctrine of beneficence, in which is explained how one is indebted to the fourfold beneficence and how one should requite them. Since the cosmic Buddha body is the essence and the fundamental source of the fourfold beneficence, one should requite that beneficence by offering to the Buddha. This is the heart of the Won Buddhist religious worship.[25]

The third of the four fundamental principles requires one to make practical applications of Buddha-dharma in daily life so that the goal of Buddhist renovation can be achieved. This principle is expressed in the motto Buddha-dharma is living itself; living is Buddha-dharma itself. Sot'aesan's central idea of Buddhist practice lies in the dictum that

---

22. See *Canon*, pt. 1, chap. 3, for the full text.
23. See *SS*, II:27.
24. See *Canon*, pt. 2, chap. 1, "Irwŏnsang"; and chap. 4: "Threefold Practice." These two chapters spell out the ways of correct enlightenment and right practice.
25. See *Canon*, pt. 2, chap. 2, "Fourfold Beneficence"; pt. 3, chap. 10, "How to Make an Offering to Buddha."

one should peruse myriad teachings only to enlighten the One Mind in one's own nature.[26] For this purpose such Buddhist practices as Zen meditation, chanting, and studying some basic Buddhist scriptures and treatises have been adopted with modifications, as can be seen in part 3 of the *Canon*.[27] Implied in this guideline is Sot'aesan's intention to make the Buddha-dharma available to the general populace so that sentient beings could be delivered from suffering.

The last of the four fundamental principles requires one to be altruistic. This is the ideal of the bodhisattva, who finds the true meaning of existence only in delivering sentient beings from suffering. Sot'aesan's enlightened vision revealed that the unfolding power of material civilization was enfeebling the moral sense of humankind and fanning the fires of greed, hatred, and delusions, aggravating the suffering. To reform the world into a paradise, egoism should be replaced with altruism in the world, for, in Sot'aesan's view, as long as human beings remain egoistic, the world can never be reformed for the better no matter how much material wealth is accumulated. Sot'aesan's enlightened view revealed that in the near future the world will be a paradise full of altruistic beings. Sot'aesan has suggested four essentials for social ethics. To be of any service to the public well-being, one should not be a burden to anyone; one should be self-reliant. Thus, the first of the four essentials requires one to cultivate self-reliance. For the well-being of the general public one should be ready to follow the lead of the wise, for the society as a whole will suffer if the deluded lead the society. Thus, the second of the four essentials requires one to follow the lead of the wise ones. This is a way of serving the public selflessly. The third requires one to practice the spirit of universal education, encouraging one, if possible, to educate the children of others who are without resources for education. The necessity of this injunction was deeply felt by Sot'aesan, who deplored the lack of education in Korean society. The last of the four essentials requires the society to develop public spirit by duly honoring those who selflessly dedicate themselves to the public well-being. For the general well-being, it is not enough for the state and law to punish those who cause pain to the general public; it should produce as many altruists as possible in order to change the world of greed, hatred, and delusions into a paradise. Thus the four essentials for social ethics are prerequisite for the realization of the ideal to serve the public well-being selflessly.[28]

---

26. See *SS*, VII:5.
27. See above, pt. 1, VIII, C, "Compilation and Publication of the *Pulgyo chŏngjŏn*."
28. See *Canon*, pt. 2, chap. 3, "Four Essentials."

The central doctrine of Won Buddhism lies in the tenet of Irwŏnsang. *Irwŏn* consists of two Chinese characters: *il* (one, unitary) and *wŏn* (circle), which together are pronounced *irwŏn*, meaning one or unitary circle. Here "one" does not mean number one but "unitary," undivided. *Sang*, the Korean pronunciation of the Chinese character *hsiang*, means a form or symbol; thus *irwŏnsang* is a unitary circular symbol. Irwŏn, the unitary circle itself, cannot be seen, any more than the geometrical circle can. In Won Buddhism Irwŏn refers to Dharmakāya Buddha, which can only be seen to the Tathāgata, the Buddha; thus Irwŏn is the Won Buddhist epithet for Dharmakāya Buddha as symbolized in the unitary circular symbol. Sot'aesan has made it absolutely clear that the circular form, Irwŏnsang, is a model used to let the true Irwŏn be known, just as a finger is used to point at the moon. Unlike the finger, however, which is never a symbol of the moon, Irwŏnsang is the symbol of the object of religious worship and the standard of religious practice, namely, Dharmakāya Buddha, as can be seen in the doctrinal chart.

One enters the religion of Irwŏnsang through religious faith and religious practice. The way of faith is based on the causal law of karmic reward, showing how one is indebted for one's existence to the fourfold beneficence and how one should requite each: the beneficence of heaven and earth is requited when one renders favors to others without harboring any idea of having rendered beneficence, that of parents by protecting the helpless, that of brethren by practicing the principle of mutual benefit, and that of laws by doing justice and doing away with injustice. The heart of Won Buddhist religious worship lies in these ways of beneficence requital as is expressed in the motto Requital of Beneficence as Making of an Offering to Buddha.

The way of practice is based on the principle of true emptiness cum marvelous existence. By this is meant the dual aspects of one's own nature, namely, its substance and its function. Although the substance of one's own nature is truly empty of any differentiation and attachment, it functions marvelously as concentration (samādhi), wisdom (prajñā) and morality (śīla), which are its three attributes. Won Buddhist training in the dharma lies in perfecting these three attributes. To perfect them one carries out the threefold practice: spiritual cultivation for concentration, inquiry into facts and principles for wisdom, and mindful karmic action for morality.

## II. Analysis of the Doctrine

The heart of Won Buddhist doctrine is stated in the tenets of Irwŏnsang, the fourfold beneficence, and the threefold practice. The rest of the *Canon* provides either detailed contents of these three tenets or instructions related to the realization of the dual goals of Won Bud-

dhism—delivering sentient beings and curing the world of illness—spelled out in the four fundamental principles. The fifteen chapters in the *Taejonggyŏng* (Scripture of Sot'aesan) are records of Sot'aesan's interpretations, explanations, and exemplary applications of the central tenets of the doctrine. Summaries of the central themes of each chapter are provided at the end of this introduction.

## A. Irwŏnsang
### 1. The Place of Irwŏnsang in Won Buddhism

What distinguishes Won Buddhism from other religions in general and from Korean Buddhism in particular is the circular symbol called Irwŏnsang enshrined at the altar in the dharma hall. The symbol can also be seen posted high above Won Buddhist temples, like the cross on Christian churches. Because the circular symbol is enshrined instead of the statue of the Buddha Śākyamuni, Won Buddhism is constantly criticized for being unfaithful to the founding father of Buddhism while carrying his name. But the Irwŏnsang is an important element of Sot'aesan's renovation of Buddhism; according to Sot'aesan, the worship of the Buddha statue in the modern era would be a hindrance to propagating the teachings of the Buddha.[29] Thus, Sot'aesan had Irwŏnsang enshrined in 1935 (20 w.e.) as the Mind Buddha, contrasting it with the Buddha statue, which symbolizes the body of the Buddha. Since Irwŏnsang is the symbol of Dharmakāya Buddha or the cosmic Buddha body, the object of religious faith in Won Buddhism, there is no doubt that Won Buddhism is a form of Buddhism.[30]

The circular symbol is well known because it was used as the mind-seal in the Kuei-yang sect of Ch'an Buddhism. Nan-yang Hui-chung (675–775), one of the five chief disciples of the sixth patriarch, Hui-neng (638–713), is said to have used the perfect sign for the first time as the sign of the nature of the enlightened mind.[31] In Korea, the circular symbols were introduced by Sunji (fl. 858), who studied in China under Yang-shan Hui-chi (803–887), cofounder of the Kuei-yang school of the classical Chinese Ch'an tradition.[32]

However, the Irwŏnsang doctrine in Won Buddhism has its root in Sot'aesan's enlightenment in 1916. Sot'aesan asked Chŏngsan to com-

---

29. See *SS*, II:13.

30. See *SS*, I:15–19, for Sot'aesan's unmistakable categorical statements that Buddha-dharma is the heart of the doctrine of Won Buddhism.

31. *T*, 2076.51:244c: "Hui-chung, seeing a monk coming, draws a circle with his hand, and writes the character 'sun' in it; the monk gives no response"; see Heinrich Dumoulin and Ruth Fuller Sasaki, *Development of Chinese Zen*, p. 19.

32. For a detailed history of the origination and development of the circular symbol, see Robert E. Buswell Jr., "Ch'an Hermeneutics: Korean View," in Donald S. Lopez Jr., ed., *Buddhist Hermeneutics*, pp. 248–250.

pose a verse using two Chinese characters meaning "one" and "circle." Chŏngsan composed two lines: "The noumenal essence of all things is unitary; the whole universe is an immense circle."[33] In August 1919 (4 W.E.), Sot'aesan drew a circle on the door lintel in a room of Kŭmsan-sa as the symbol of the truth to which he was enlightened. The circular symbol was enshrined as the sign of the object of religious worship in 1935 when he published the essay "On the Renovation of Korean Buddhism" (Chosŏn pulgyo hyŏksillon). Since this order's name was the Society for the Study of Buddha-dharma (Pulbŏp Yŏn'guhoe) until 1947 (32 W.E.), four years after Sot'aesan's death in 1943 (28 W.E.), there was no question of the identity of the order as a reformed Buddhist order. The question of the relationship of this order to the Korean Buddhism has persisted, however, since the order was renamed Wŏnbulgyo (Won Buddhism) in 1947 by Chŏngsan. To a guest who asked for the meaning of *wŏn* (circle), Chŏngsan answered as follows:

> The noumenal essence of *wŏn* is ineffable because it is the realm where linguistic, audible, and visible characteristics are cut off; the phenomenal characteristics of all things are the appearance of this *wŏn*. Thus, *wŏn* is the fundamental source of all dharmas (truth) and the reality of all dharmas (existence). Therefore, all the religious doctrines, though they are expressed in various ways, are nothing but the truth of *wŏn*, and there is no other dharma.[34]

In this brief reply is expressed the view that the ultimate truth of the universe is unitary. To a further question whether the word "Buddhism" (*pulgyo*) should better be dropped, Chŏngsan replied:

> The term "Buddha" means enlightenment and mind. The truth of *wŏn* may be so perfect as to include all dharmas (truth); however, it will be just an empty principle if there is no mind which is enlightened to it. Thus, the two terms "*wŏn*" and "*pul*" (buddha) are so related to each other as to be inseparable, referring to the unitary truth.[35]

To the question whether Won Buddhism is Buddhism only in name as there is no Buddha statue enshrined, Sot'aesan replied:

> What is referred to by Irwŏnsang is called *t'aegŭk* (the great ultimate) or *mugŭk* (the ultimate of nonbeing) in Confucianism, Nature or To (the Way) in Taoism, and pure Dharma-

---

33. *CCP*, I:2.
34. *CCP*, IV:1.
35. Ibid.

kaya Buddha in Buddhism; however, one and the same reality is called by these different names. No matter which of these directions one takes, one will eventually return to the realm of Irwŏn. Any religion that is not based on this truth is a wrong way.[36]

In Sot'aesan's view, T'ai-chi, Tao, Dharmakāya Buddha, and Irwŏn are different names of one and the same ultimate reality, providing different conceptual frameworks through which it appears differently to each viewpoint. In his view, the original nature is like the moon high up in the sky while the phenomenal world is like the thousands of moons being reflected on thousands of rivers.[37] Moreover, Sot'aesan made it clear that Irwŏnsang is a sign used to refer to the true Irwŏn, Dharmakāya, just as a finger is a pointer used to point at the moon. As was noted above, Irwŏnsang is also used as the mind-seal transmitted by buddhas and patriarchs as the sign of their enlightenment that is beyond words and letters. To the unenlightened, then, the true Irwŏn, Dharmakāya Buddha, is incomprehensible, just as the moon behind the clouds is invisible. The unenlightened cannot understand the statement that Dharmakāya is the noumenal essence of all things in the universe. To see this we have only to examine some of the statements concerning the identity of reality and appearance. For instance, T. R. V. Murti writes:

> As the Dharmakāya, Buddha fully realizes his identity with the "Absolute" (dharmata, sunyata) and unity (samata) with all beings. It is the oneness with the "absolute" that enables Buddha to intuit the "truth," which it is his sacred function to reveal to phenomenal beings. This is the fountain-source of his implicit strength which he consecrates in the finite sphere. . . . Dharmakāya is the essence, the reality of the universe. It is completely free from every trace of duality. It is the very nature of the universe and is there called *Svabhāvikakāya* (the essential body of the Buddha).[38]

---

36. See *SS*, II:3. This idea is not new with Sot'aesan; Yeh-fu's (1127–1130) *Wŏnsang song* (Eulogy to the circular form) includes the same idea: "Of all the dharmas, pure or impure, in the four dharma realms of three worlds, not a single dharma arises outside of this circle. In Ch'an it is called the first phrase; in Chiao (scriptural teaching) it is called the pure dharma realm. Among the Confucians it is called T'ai-chi, the one pervading substance; in Taoism the mother of all things under heaven. In truth, all these names refer to this. So someone in the past said of this: 'Before the birth of past Buddhas existed one circle; even Śākyamuni could not understand it, how could Kāśyapa transmit it?'" See Mubi Sŭnim, *Kŭmganggyŏng ogahae*, p. 65.

37. See *SS*, IX:5.

38. T. R. V. Murti, *Central Philosophy of Buddhism*, pp. 284–285.

The identity in question is not clear to the unenlightened. Let us look at another statement of the same view. Th. Stcherbatski writes:

> The Buddha must be regarded as the "cosmical order" (dharmatah), his body is the "cosmos" (dharmata).... The reality of Buddha is the reality of the universe, and as far as the Buddha has no separate reality (nihsvabhava), neither has the universe any, apart from him.... All the elements of existence, when sifted through the principle of relativity, become resplendent. All the millions of existence (bhutakoti) must be regarded as the body of the Buddha manifested in them.[39]

In Sot'aesan's view, however, the deluded cannot see the body of the Buddha manifested in all the myriad things, so he uses the circular symbol as the sign of the truth that all things are nothing but the body of the Buddha manifested in them. What is stated in "The Truth of Irwŏnsang" is a brief elaboration of this truth.

Throughout the history of philosophy, East and West, philosophers have tried to grasp the ultimate truth hidden behind the phenomenal world in terms of reality and appearance or noumenon and phenomenon.[40] Sot'aesan's view expressed in "The Vow to Irwŏnsang"[41] does not ignore the transforming aspects of Irwŏn while Chŏngsan's view emphasizes aspects of how Irwŏn appears as the phenomenal world. Sot'aesan writes:

> Irwŏn is the ineffable realm of samādhi, the way of birth and death, which transcends being and nonbeing; the original source of heaven and earth, parents, brethren, and laws; the original nature of all buddhas, patriarchs, ordinary human beings, and all sentient beings. Irwŏn can form permanence and impermanence. Viewed as permanent, it, being ever thus and spontaneous, has unfolded itself into an immeasurable

---

39. Th. Stcherbatsky, *Conception of Buddhist Nirvana*, p. 45.

40. One of the most interesting of worldviews and the most comforting, I believe, is given in Brahmanism. We are well aware of the controversy between Śankara's (788–820) nondualism (*advaita*) and Rāmānuja's (1055–1137) qualified nondualism (*viśistadvaita*) on the relationship between the ultimate reality, Brahman, and the phenomenal world on one hand, and that between Ātman and Brahman on the other. Śankara holds that the phenomenal world is a mere illusory appearance of Brahman to the deluded (*Brahma-vivarta*) just as a piece of rope can appear to be a snake, while Rāmānuja holds that the phenomenal world is a transformation of Brahman (*Brahma-parinama*) like milk curd transformed from milk. See Radhakrishnan and Moore, *Sourcebook in Indian Philosophy*, pp. 509–521.

41. See *Canon*, pt. 2, chap. 1, sec. 4. This is the only treatise written by Sot'aesan himself, in November 1938 (23 W.E.).

world. Viewed as impermanent, it has unfolded itself into an immeasurable world as the formation, endurance, decay, and emptiness of the universe; as the birth, aging, illness, and death of all things; and as the transformation of the four forms of birth through the six realms of existence, letting them be promoted or demoted with favors arising from harm or harm arising from favors in accordance with the functions of their minds and bodies.[42]

It should be noticed that Irwŏn is not only the ineffable realm of samādhi but also the noumenal nature of all things in the universe. This implies idealistic monism since the whole universe is none other than Irwŏn, Dharmakāya Buddha, transforming through the endless world viewed as impermanent. With this general conceptual framework behind, we may better understand the worldview formulated in "The Truth of Irwŏnsang."

### 2. The Truth of Irwŏnsang

Sot'aesan is said to have expressed the most comprehensive truth of the universe as follows:

> All beings are of unitary noumenal nature and all dharmas originate from the unitary fundamental source; amongst which the way of neither arising nor ceasing and the principle of causal retribution, being mutually grounded on each other, have formed a round framework.[43]

In this brief statement Sot'aesan reveals his view of the relation between the noumenal world and the phenomenal world: the noumenal world devoid of arising and ceasing and the phenomenal world arising and ceasing therefrom by the laws of causality. We can detect Sot'aesan's view of nonduality of nirvāṇa and saṃsāra in the idea that the way of neither arising nor ceasing and the principle of causality are each the basis of the other, forming a round framework.

Chŏngsan has expressed the truth of Irwŏnsang in a compressed statement, which is analyzed here.[44] The brief and highly condensed discourse "The Truth of Irwŏnsang"[45] states the ultimate truth of

---

42. Ibid.

43. See *SS*, I:1.

44. In his article "Irwŏnsang-e taehayŏ" (On Irwŏnsang), written in 1937 (see *HH*, pp. 212–219), is formulated the essence of the central doctrine of Won Buddhism including the tenets of Irwŏnsang, the fourfold beneficence, and the threefold practice, which are restructured into the three chapters respectively. Section 4, "The Vow to Irwŏnsang," was written by Sot'aesan himself in 1938, one year after Chŏngsan's writing. See *Kŭmgangsan ŭi chuin*, p. 357.

45. See the *Canon*, pt. 1, chap. 1, sec. 1.

the universe as reflected in the enlightened view of the author. We can quickly point out that this is Chŏngsan's view on the question of reality and appearance, or nirvāṇa and saṃsāra. As stated, this does not imply any religious import; it is mainly concerned with the ultimate metaphysical truth of the universe. I would like to analyze the section "The Truth of Irwŏnsang" by reflecting on several models for interpreting the ultimate truth of the universe. The whole section can be restated as follows:

> Chŏngsan first states that Dharmakāya Buddha, referred to as Irwŏn (unitary circle without the circumference), is the noumenal essence of all things in the universe, the original nature of all buddhas and patriarchs, the Buddha-nature of all sentient beings. This reflects the Mahāyāna Buddhist tenet that all things are nothing but Dharmakāya Buddha. Chŏngsan then states that the realm of Dharmakāya Buddha is devoid of such characteristics as the differentiation of noumenon from phenomenon, being from nonbeing, the change of arising and ceasing, or going and coming, the retribution of good and evil karma, and the linguistic, audible, and visible phenomena. Chŏngsan then writes that it is because of the light of the mind-essence of empty and calm, numinous awareness[46] that the differentiation of noumenon from phenomenon and being from nonbeing appears. And thereby the distinction between good and evil karmic retribution comes into being, and the linguistic, audible, and visible characteristics become clear and distinct so that the three worlds of desire, form, and formless world of pure spirit in the ten directions appear like a jewel on one's own palm. Chŏngsan then adds that the creative wonder of true emptiness cum marvelous existence freely conceals and reveals through all things in the universe throughout the incalculable aeons without beginning.

Irwŏn is another name of the Dharmakāya Buddha in Won Buddhism; it will help us better understand "The Truth of Irwŏnsang" if we analyze the key terms used to express it. Since "The Truth of Irwŏnsang" is expressed in a few technical terms of Mahāyāna Buddhist metaphysics, I will interpret it by examining the central concepts used therein. The first statement refers to the noumenal realm.

---

46. Chinul says that one's own nature is true Dharmakāya and numinous awareness is true Buddha. See *Susim kyŏl*, *T*, 2020.48.1006c; Buswell, *KAZ*, p. 165. The rendering of *yŏngji* (C. *ling-chih*) as "numinous awareness" is Buswell's. See Gregory, *Inquiry into the Origin of Humanity*, p. 179.

> Irwŏn is the noumenal nature of all things in the universe, the
> original nature of all buddhas and patriarchs, the Buddha-
> nature of the ordinary people and sentient beings.

This tenet is prevalent in Mahāyāna Buddhist literature, as can be seen
in the following quotation from the *Ta-sheng chih-kuan fa-men*:

> The buddhas of the three ages together with sentient beings
> all equally have this one pure mind as their substance. All
> things, both ordinary and sagely, each have their own dif-
> ference and diverse appearances, whereas the genuine mind
> is devoid of either diversity or appearance. That is why it is
> termed "Thusness."[47]

Irwŏn refers to the one pure mind called Thusness. In the *Ta-sheng chi-
hsin lun* (The awakening of faith in Mahāyāna) the ultimate reality of
the universe is identified with Mind and given interpretations "in terms
of the Absolute" and "in terms of phenomena." The Mind in terms of
the Absolute is the one world of reality (*dharmadhātu*) and the essence
of all phases of existence in their totality.[48] Thus, "The Truth of
Irwŏnsang" reflects the Mahāyāna Buddhist notion of the ultimate
reality ubiquitous throughout the universe. The characterization of the
noumenal nature of Irwŏn is as follows:

> It is the realm where there is no differentiation of noumenon
> from phenomenon or being from nonbeing; the realm where
> there is no change of arising and ceasing, or going and com-
> ing; the realm where the karmic retribution of good and evil
> has ceased, and linguistic, audible, and visible characteristics
> are utterly void.

This description of the characteristics of Irwŏn also reflects that of the
nature of the Mind in the *Awakening of Faith*.

> That which is called "the essential nature of the mind" is
> unborn and imperishable. It is only through illusions that
> all things come to be differentiated. If one is freed from illu-
> sions, then to him there will be no appearances (*laksana*)
> of objects [regarded as absolutely independent existence];
> therefore all things from the beginning transcend all forms of
> verbalization, description, and conceptualization and are, in
> the final analysis, undifferentiated, free from alteration and
> indestructible.[49]

---

47. *Ta-sheng chih-kuan fa-men*, *T*, 1924.46.642b.
48. *T*, 1665.32.575c; Hakeda's translation, *Awakening of Faith*, p. 32.
49. Hakeda, *Awakening of Faith*, p. 33.

Thus, in "The Truth of Irwŏnsang" is reflected the metaphysical framework of the *Awakening of Faith*. The main difference between the two is that, while the condition for appearance is the light of numinous awareness for Chŏngsan, it is illusions through which the noumenon appears as phenomenon. Thus Chŏngsan attributes the appearance of the phenomenal world to the light of numinous awareness:

> In accordance with the light of void and of calm, numinous awareness, there appears the differentiation of noumenon from phenomenon, and being from nonbeing; wherewith the distinction between good and evil karmic retribution comes into being; and the linguistic, audible, and visible characteristics become clear and distinct so that the three worlds in ten directions appear like a jewel on the palm; and the creative wonders of true emptiness cum marvelous existence freely conceal and reveal through all things in the universe throughout incalculable aeons.

Thus, for Chŏngsan, the phenomenal world is none other than the wonderful manifestation of Dharmakāya Buddha, Irwŏn, for he says that the three worlds in the ten directions appear like a jewel on the palm in accordance with the light of numinous awareness, which is the true Buddha-nature.

Chŏngsan's view of the phenomenal world exemplifies the principles of metaphysical idealism: that reality is somehow mind-correlated or mind-coordinated, that real objects composing the "external world" are not independent of perceiving minds, but have an existence correlative to mental operations. The differentiation of the phenomenal world is in accordance with the light of the mind-essence of void and calm, numinous awareness. Of course, Sot'aesan himself once held the idealist worldview: everything is a creation of the mind.[50] Chŏngsan's view is strikingly similar to that of Immanuel Kant in this sense. Just as the phenomenal world appears in accordance with the light of numinous awareness, the phenomenal world, according to Kant, depends for its appearance on the a priori forms of intuition, viz., space and time, and a priori forms of understanding, viz., the twelve concepts.[51] For Kant

---

50. See *SS*, II:27: "'If someone asked me what is taught in this order, how should I answer?' The Master said, 'Buddhism is a religion that teaches one to be enlightened to the truth that 'all things are nothing but creations of the mind.'"
51. Kant, *Critique of Pure Reason*, pp. 111–114. Notice that, just as the concept of existence and nonexistence and that of causality belong to the phenomenal self as the forms of understanding for Kant, the differentiation of noumenon from phenomenon, being from nonbeing and causality appear in accordance with the light of numinous awareness.

the phenomenal world is totally dependent on the mind.[52] Kant further says: "[E]xternal objects (bodies), however, are mere appearances, and therefore nothing but a species of my representations, the objects of which are something only through these representations. Apart from them they are nothing."[53]

In "The Truth of Irwŏnsang" the dynamism of noumenon and phenomenon is expressed in terms of "the creative wonders of the true emptiness cum marvelous existence." The term "true emptiness cum marvelous existence" can also be expressed as "marvelous existence of true emptiness" or "true emptiness of marvelous existence"; "marvelous existence" and "true emptiness" are not two realities but two modes of one and the same reality, Dharmakāya Buddha. This term expresses the principle in the Heart Sūtra that "form does not differ from emptiness; emptiness does not differ from form. Form is just emptiness; emptiness is just form."[54] Ho-tse Shen-hui (670–762) takes true emptiness as the substance and marvelous existence as the function of True Thusness.[55] This interpretation of the term is used in Won Buddhism, as can be seen in the principle of Zen practice described in the *Canon*: "The true Zen can only be practiced if one takes true emptiness as the substance and marvelous existence as the function."[56] This may give us the impression that we can separate true emptiness from marvelous existence. However, we should understand the two expressions as referring to the two aspects of the True Thusness of One Mind, just as samādhi is the substance of prajñā and prajñā the function of samādhi for Hui-neng.[57] It is Tung-shan Liang-chieh (807–869) in the "Five Ranks" who uses true void as the absolute and marvelous existence as the relative phenomenal.

> But the two, Absolute and relative phenomenal, are not separate, are not two, but one. The Absolute is the Absolute with regard to the relative. The relative, however, is rela-

52. Ibid., p. 82: "All our intuition is nothing but the representation of appearance; that the things which we intuit are not in themselves what we intuit them as being, nor their relations so constituted in themselves as they appear to us, and that if the subject, or even only the subjective constitution of the sense in general, be removed, the whole constitution and all the relation of objects in space and time, nay space and time themselves, would vanish. As appearances, they cannot exist in themselves, but only in us."

53. Ibid., p. 346.

54. See Buswell, *Zen Monastic Experience*, p. 23; *Po-jo po-lo-mi-t'o hsin ching*, *T*, 251.8.848c.

55. See *Hsien-tsung chi*, 30, *T*, 2076.51.458c.

56. See *Canon*, pt. 3, chap. 7.

57. *Liu-tsu-tan-ching*, *T*, 2007.48.338b. Hui-neng also says, "True Thusness is the substance of thought and thought is the function of True Thusness." Ibid., 338c.

tive with reference to the Absolute. Therefore, the relative phenomenal in Buddhist philosophical terminology is "marvelous existence" which is inseparable from True Emptiness. Thus, the expression is *chin-kung miao-yu*.[58]

Thus, the oneness of the Absolute and the relative phenomenal is the fundamental concept of the "Five Ranks" of Liang-chieh. This view can be found in the expression of Sot'aesan's view of nonduality.

> The great way [the ultimate truth] is characteristic of mutual identification, mutual implication and mutual penetration so that existence is identical with non-existence, principle [noumenon] is identical with fact [phenomenon], birth is identical with death and motion is identical with rest. In this way of nonduality there is nothing wanting.[59]

The tenet of nonduality is not new with Sot'aesan; it was expressed by Nāgārjuna (second or third century).[60] The reality of Irwŏn, Dharmakāya Buddha, is conceived as the interaction of true emptiness (absolute) and marvelous existence (phenomenal); therefore, it contains in itself both true emptiness and marvelous existence. The true emptiness is thought to be transcendental and yet is conceived as not being outside of marvelous existence. The difference between the two is not ontological but epistemological.

From this conceptual analysis of "The Truth of Irwŏnsang" we can see that there is nothing particularly religious in the statement of the truth; it is basically a statement of the author's worldview expressed in terms of Mahāyāna Buddhist idealism. The faith in Irwŏnsang lies in believing in each of the propositions that are stated in "The Truth of Irwŏnsang."[61] There is nothing particularly religious in believing, for instance, that Irwŏn, Dharmakāya Buddha, is the noumenal essence of all things in the universe, the original nature of all buddhas and patriarchs, and the Buddha-nature of all sentient beings. This is rather an expression of the truth to which one is to be enlightened. What makes the faith in Irwŏnsang religious is the latter's being the fundamental source of the fourfold beneficence to which one owes one's life.

---

58. See Dumoulin and Sasaki, *Development of Chinese Zen*, p. 26.
59. See *SS*, VII:4.
60. See *Chung-lun*, *T*, 1564.30.36a; Kenneth Inada, *Nāgārjuna*, p. 158, verse 19: "Saṃsāra (i.e., the empirical life-death cycle) is nothing essentially different from nirvāṇa. Nirvāṇa is nothing essentially different from saṃsāra." Verse 20: "The limits (i.e., realm) of nirvāṇa are the limits of saṃsāra. Between the two, also, there is not the slightest difference whatsoever."
61. See *Canon*, pt. 1, chap. 1, sec. 2.

## B. Irwŏnsang and Threefold Practice

### 1. Practice of Irwŏnsang

The heart of Won Buddhist practice lies in being enlightened to the truth of Irwŏn, the mind-seal, correctly transmitted from buddhas and patriarchs, and thereby acting perfectly without being excessive or deficient when one uses one's eyes, ears, nose, tongue, body, and mind. One's most important task is to be enlightened to the truth of Irwŏn. In this fundamental principle, the arteries of Mahāyāna Buddhist practice are extended in Won Buddhism. The practice in question assumes that all sentient beings are endowed with the original enlightenment symbolized in the form of a circle and enshrined as the sign of the object of faith and the standard of practice. To the unenlightened, Irwŏn is like the moon behind the clouds or a jewel hidden in the mud.[62] Thus, Irwŏnsang plays the role of a finger pointing at the moon. But what if clouds cover the moon? Just as it is necessary for one to have a firm faith in the existence of the moon behind the clouds, it is of utmost importance for the practitioner to have a firm faith in the Buddha-nature, Dharmakāya Buddha, as the essence of one's mind although one is not aware of it.

Chŏngsan explained the practice of Irwŏnsang under the title "How to Model Oneself on Irwŏnsang" (here he means by Irwŏnsang the mind devoid of delusive thoughts):

> It lies in turning the light back and illuminating inwardly one's own nature [*dharmakāya*]. Although our mind is originally devoid of arising and ceasing, going and coming, or differentiation and attachment, its true nature is obscured with numberless delusive thoughts when the six roots give rise to six consciousnesses, which meet the six qualities produced by the objects and organs of sense [i.e., color, sound, smell, taste, touch, and idea]. Hence, the practitioner should have a firm conviction that one is endowed with the true nature and take this conviction as the highest standard (directive) of practice, so that one should always moderate and subdue the passions (of the six roots), annihilate delusive thoughts, and exert oneself to have the true state of Irwŏn. For this, one practices daily the recitation of the sacred name of Amitābha or the seated meditation. If one intends to do

---

62. This simile is found in Chinul, *Chinsim chiksŏl*, *T*, 2019.48.1000c; Buswell, *KAZ*, p. 168: "Therefore we know that even amid the troubles of the dusty world, the true mind remains unaffected by those troubles. Like a piece of white jade which has been thrown in the mud, its color remains unchanged."

rigorous practice in the dharma, one must reflect on the mind of Irwŏn [the realm devoid of delusive thought] without forgetting even for a moment. For instance, one must remove greed from one's mind as soon as it moves by reminding oneself of the Irwŏn mind that one has forgotten. Or in any situation where anger, foolishness, or any other delusive thoughts arise in the mind, one should thus exert oneself to trace back the radiance of the mind of Irwŏn, checking day and night, and in motion and at rest. This will be the way of modeling oneself after Irwŏnsang. If one continues this practice for a long time, one will eventually realize the realm of no discrimination, devoid of truth and falsity, and no distinction between subject and object so that one can transcend birth and death, residing in the realm of no characteristics. Such a one will recover the reality of Irwŏn and attain the *dharma-kāya* of Tathāgata.[63]

The idea elaborated here by Chŏngsan is expressed in a highly compressed single sentence in Korean in the section "The Practice of Irwŏnsang" in the *Pulgyo chŏngjŏn*. The main point can be paraphrased as follows. How can one practice the truth of Irwŏnsang? The first step is for one to have a firm faith, as the model or standard of practice, that one is endowed with the Buddha-nature, prajñā-wisdom; the next step is to be enlightened to the truth of Irwŏnsang; the third step is to know, nourish, and use one's own mind which is as perfect, complete, utterly fair, and unselfish as Irwŏn, namely, prajñā-wisdom. The section on the practice of Irwŏnsang in the *Canon* (1962) is different from that in the *Pulgyo chŏngjŏn* (1943).[64] The original writing in the *Pulgyo chŏngjŏn* of the section in question by Chŏngsan is as follows:

One is to establish the model of practice by having faith in the truth of Irwŏnsang. The method of practice is for one, being enlightened to the truth of Irwŏnsang, to know one's own mind which is as perfect, complete, utterly fair, and unselfish as Irwŏn, namely, prajñā-wisdom; to foster one's own mind which is as perfect, complete, utterly fair and unselfish as Irwŏn, namely, prajñā-wisdom; and to use one's own mind which is as perfect, complete, utterly fair and unselfish as Irwŏn, namely prajñā-wisdom. Herein lies the practice of Irwŏn.[65]

---

63. See Chŏngsan, "Irwŏnsang e taehayŏ," *KC*, 3:127.
64. The *Pulgyo chŏngjŏn* was the official canonical text used from 1943 until the *Wŏnbulgyo kyojŏn* was published in 1962. The *Canon* in the latter is a redaction of book 1 in the former.
65. See *PGC*, pt. 2, chap. 2, sec. 3.

The altered section in the *Canon* is translated as follows:

> Having faith in the truth of Irwŏnsang as well as taking it as
> the standard of practice, one is to know one's own mind
> which is as perfect, complete, utterly fair and impartial as
> Irŏnsang; to nourish one's own mind which is as perfect,
> complete, utterly fair and impartial as Irwŏnsang; to use
> one's own mind which is as perfect, complete, utterly fair and
> impartial as Irwŏnsang. To do this is to practice Irwŏnsang.

The crucial question is whether one's own mind (the functioning
Buddha-nature) is as perfect, complete, utterly fair, and impartial as
Irwŏn as in old version or as Irwŏnsang as in the new version. For those
of inferior spiritual capacity, the latter is indispensable; for those of
superior capacity, the Irwŏnsang plays the role of a finger pointing at
the moon (Buddha-nature). Notice further that the phrase "awakening
to the truth of Irwŏnsang," which is necessary for one to keep oneself
from falling into corrupt practice, is deleted in the new version (1962
edition). Deleted also from the new version is the important term
"prajñā-wisdom" in the old version. Beings of lower capacity may mistake Irwŏnsang, the circular symbol, for Dharmakāya Buddha just
as they mistake the finger for the moon when the moon is behind the
clouds. The practitioner must start the practice with a firm faith that
the Dharmakāya Buddha is hidden in one's mind. With this faith as the
standard of practice one is to be enlightened to the truth of Irwŏnsang
so that one can know, nourish, and use one's own mind, namely prajñā-
wisdom, which is as perfect, complete, utterly fair, and impartial as
Irwŏn, namely, Dharmakāya Buddha. What is of utmost importance in
this practice is the requirement that one should be awakened to one's
own nature, Dharmakāya, in order to make any progress in the practice
of Irwŏn. This clearly reflects one of the central tenets of the Ch'an
tradition running through Shen-hui, Tsung-mi, and Chinul: that only
one who is awakened to the fact that the mind-nature is fundamentally
pure and the defilement fundamentally empty can avoid falling into the
corrupt practice of those of inferior faculties in the gradual school.
Thus, Chinul quotes from Tsung-mi, "Cultivation prior to awakening
is not true cultivation."[66] For those of inferior faculties who are not yet
awakened to their original nature, the circular symbol, Irwŏnsang, plays
the role of the finger pointing at the moon, reminding them of their
Buddha-nature, Irwŏn. Sot'aesan himself warns his followers against

---

66. See *Koryŏguk pojo sŏnsa susim kyŏl*, *T*, 2020.48.1008c; Buswell, *KAZ*, p. 154. For the
provenance of the quotation in Chinul's writing, see Buswell's endnote 30. Kuei-feng
Tsung-mi, *Ch'an-yüan chu-ch'üan chi tou-hsü*, *T*, 2015.48.407c.

possible misunderstanding of the role the circular symbol, Irwŏnsang, plays. He says:

> However, I do not mean that the senseless Irwŏnsang drawn on the wood-board owns such truth, power, and the method of practice. Irwŏnsang is a model that is used to let you know the true Irwŏn; this is analogous to when you point at the moon with your finger, the latter is not the former. Hence, the practitioner must discover the true Irwŏn by means of Irwŏnsang.[67]

Thus, it is against Sot'aesan's teaching to model our mind after Irwŏnsang, the circular symbol, although we are tempted to do so before awakening to what it refers to.[68] For, certainly, the Buddha-nature, or Dharmakāya Buddha, has nothing whatsoever to do with the circular form drawn on a wood board any more than the moon has anything to do with the finger. Moreover, Sot'aesan made it clear that we should use the circular form, Irwŏnsang, as a *hwadu*, or "critical phrase," for awakening to what it refers to, namely, Dharmakāya Buddha.[69] Finally, notice the difference between the last sentences of the two versions. The old version (1943) ends by saying "Herein lies the practice of Irwŏn," while the new version (1962) ends by saying "Herein lies the practice of Irwŏnsang." The former is for those of high capacity, the latter for those of low capacity. The latter has a danger of blocking the deluded permanently from being enlightened to his or her own prajñā-wisdom. Why, then, did Chŏngsan call the section "Practice of Irwŏnsang" instead of "Practice of Irwŏn"? It is Chŏngsan's skillful means to lead all those deluded beings to the realm of prajñā-wisdom with Irwŏnsang as a pointer or a finger.

The triple practice of Irwŏn—knowing, nourishing, and using one's own nature—reflects morality (*śīla*), concentration (samādhi), and wisdom (prajñā), the three aspects of *dharmakāya* of one's own mind taught in the Buddhist order in general and in Ch'an/Zen tradition in particular. Hui-neng (638–713), the sixth patriarch of Ch'an Buddhism, said:

---

67. *Kŭmgangsan ŭi chuin*, p. 345. When *Wŏnbulgyo kyojŏn* was compiled, the word "senseless" was deleted and the sentence was made smoother, as can be seen in *SS*, II:6.
68. This view reflects Chinul's view on sudden enlightenment and gradual cultivation. See Chinul, *Susim kyŏl*, *T*, 2020.48.1006c; Buswell, *KAZ*, p. 144: "Although he has awakened to the fact that his original nature is no different from that of the Buddhas, the beginningless habit-energies are extremely difficult to remove suddenly and so he must continue to cultivate while relying on his awakening."
69. *SS*, II:8.

When the mind is free from evil, that is morality (*śīla*) of one's own nature. When the mind is free from disturbance, that is the concentration (samādhi) of one's own nature. When the mind is free from delusions, that is the wisdom (prajñā) of one's own nature.[70]

The triple discipline is highlighted as the first three articles of "The Essentials of Daily Practice."[71] The three articles state that our mind-ground[72] is originally free from disturbances, delusions, and defilement, which arise in sense spheres; hence, we should restore our self-nature's concentration, wisdom, and morality by keeping disturbances, delusions, and defilement from arising. By reciting these articles daily, practitioners, whether awakened or not awakened to the mind-ground, remind themselves of the Buddha-nature or *dharmakāya* of their own mind. For the perfect actualization of the three aspects of Irwŏn in daily life, Sot'aesan has tied the triple discipline to religious vows:

> We, deluded beings, vow to keep our mind and body perfectly, to know facts and principles perfectly, and to use our mind and body perfectly by modeling ourselves after Dharmakāya Buddha, Irwŏnsang, so that we may attain the great power of Irwŏn and become unified with the noumenal nature of Irwŏn.[73]

Here Sot'aesan distinguishes Irwŏn from Irwŏnsang just as he distinguished the moon from the finger pointing at it. One who is already enlightened to the Buddha-nature, which he called "Mind Buddha," need not take this vow to model oneself after Irwŏnsang; certainly the enlightened will not mistake the finger for the moon. Only the deluded beings who do not see their own Irwŏn need to model themselves after Irwŏnsang until they can identify themselves with their Mind Buddha, Irwŏn. The ultimate aim of this vow is to attain the three great powers of emancipation, enlightenment, and the Mean through the threefold

---

70. *Liu-tsu t'an ching, T*, 2008.48.342b; Wing-tsit Chan, *Platform Scripture*, p. 59.
71. See *Canon*, pt. 3, chap. 1.
72. The term "mind-ground" is one of several appellations of "true mind." See *Chinsim chiksŏl, T*, 2019.48.999c; Buswell, *KAZ*, pp. 163–164. It is called in different scriptures *bodhi, dharmadhātu, tathāgata*, nirvāna, Suchness, dharma-body, True Suchness, Buddha-nature, *tathāgatagarbha*, and complete enlightenment.
73. See *Canon*, pt. 2, chap. 1, sec. 4. Here the problem remains of the ambiguity whether it is Irwŏn or Irwŏnsang that one should model after, for Irwŏnsang is not Dharmakāya Buddha, but a sign pointing at it like a finger pointing at the moon. It should be "Dharmakāya Buddha, Irwŏn"; then, the unenlightened has nothing to model after. That's why the section "Practice of Irwŏnsang" begins with "One should take the faith in the truth of Irwŏnsang as the model of Practice" in the old *Canon* (1943 edition).

practice of spiritual cultivation, inquiry into facts and principles, and mindful choice in karmic action. In Sot'aesan's view, these powers are emphasized as their final goals of practice by Taoism, Buddhism, and Confucianism.

## 2. Threefold Practice

Concentration, wisdom, and morality are to be perfected by the threefold practice. In "The Practice of Irwŏnsang" is suggested that one is to know, nourish, and use one's mind, which is perfect, complete, utterly fair, and impartial upon being enlightened to the truth of Irwŏnsang. We can see here that one should practice the three aspects of the Buddha mind in daily living, changing the possible bitter seas of misery to a paradise. However, such practice is easier said than done. A baby, though a perfect human being, cannot be expected to do things adults can do. Although all sentient beings are endowed with the Buddha-nature, they suffer because their Buddha-nature does not function properly. Thus, Sot'aesan formulated the way of perfecting the Buddha-nature in the mundane world before he had the doctrine of Irwŏnsang canonized. The actual steps for the practice of Irwŏnsang are spelled out in the chapter "Threefold Practice."[74] The threefold practice consists of spiritual cultivation for mental calmness or concentration (samādhi), inquiry into facts and principles for wisdom (prajñā), and mindful choice in karmic action for morality (śīla).

Sot'aesan identified the threefold practice with the Buddhist triple discipline,[75] which was a threefold classification of the Buddha's Eightfold Path, viz., wisdom (prajñā) from right view and right thought; morality (śīla) from right speech, right action, right livelihood, and right effort; and concentration (samādhi) from right mindfulness and right concentration. Chŏngsan, however, warned that the threefold practice should not be regarded as the repetition of the Buddhist triple discipline.

> You find the triple discipline in traditional Buddhism; but our threefold practice is different from it in scope. While śīla, emphasizing precepts, focused on one's keeping them, mindful choice in karmic action is an essential discipline necessary for individual moral cultivation, regulating the family, ruling a nation, and putting the world at peace. While prajñā emphasized the wisdom emanating from one's self-nature, inquiry into facts and principles is the way of attaining well-rounded knowledge and wisdom on all facts and principles. While samādhi emphasized calmness in meditation, spiritual

---

74. See *Canon*, pt. 2, chap. 4, "The Threefold Practice."
75. See *SS*, II:5.

cultivation is the discipline of keeping One Mind without
going astray from the self-nature in motion and at rest. Success in anything that one does lies in following this threefold
practice, thus no other way can be more perfect than this.[76]

Thus one can see both continuation and discontinuation of the Buddhist triple discipline in the threefold practice. This point can be made
clearer if we analyze the latter.

a. *Spiritual Cultivation* **(Chŏngshin Suyang)**  We can easily
see that cultivation of spirit or spiritual cultivation is a means to attain
the great spiritual calmness in motion and at rest. In Won Buddhism,
spiritual cultivation aims at maintaining the mental state of serene
reflection or quiet illumination in the hustle and bustle of daily life.
By "spirit" is meant the mental state that is clear and calm, devoid of
differentiation or attachment to anything. This is the state one aims at
while sitting in meditation or chanting "Namo Amitābha." However,
sitting in meditation or chanting is not the main course of spiritual cultivation; timeless meditation,[77] viz., maintaining the suchness of One
Mind in motion and at rest, is the essential practice for spiritual cultivation. When Sot'aesan was formulating the doctrine of threefold
practice, he had in mind ordinary people. Zen monks in deep mountain valleys do not need as much spiritual cultivation as those ordinary
people struggling to survive in the mundane world where they constantly face the adverse conditions that arouse and fan the fire of the
three poisons of greed, anger, and delusion. If one is disturbed by
greed, anger, or delusion, one loses the dignity and integrity of one's
personality and ends up ruining one's family and disgracing oneself.
Suffering from agony and delusion or from vexation and anxiety, one may
end up feeling sick of life, falling into despair, having a nervous breakdown, becoming mentally deranged, or even committing suicide. Thus,
the purpose of spiritual cultivation is to attain the spiritual power so that
one's mental poise in any kind of adverse condition be as immovable as a
huge mountain and as serene and calm as the empty sky.[78] The spiritual
cultivation Sot'aesan suggests here is quite different from the kind of
meditation practiced by Buddhist monks in deep mountain valleys. This
is the difference Chŏngsan makes between the two systems.

b. *Inquiry into Facts and Principles*  Wisdom (prajñā) is the
main and essential element of the path of the Buddhist triple discipline.[79] Mental concentration alone cannot completely purify the mind;

---

76. See *CCP*, p. 129; *KJ* 24, 5 (1984):26.
77. See *Canon*, pt. 3, chap. 7, "How to Practice Timeless Zen."
78. See *Canon*, pt. 2, chap. 4, sec. 1.
79. Etinne Lamotte, "The Buddha, His Teachings and His Sangha," in *The World of
Buddhism*, ed. Heinz Bechert and Richard Gombrich, p. 53.

to ensure quiescence, peace, and nirvāṇa, wisdom is also necessary. One should have clear and precise vision, embracing the four noble truths and penetrating in depth the general characteristics of things— impermanence, suffering, and the impersonality of phenomena—as well as the peace of nirvāṇa.[80]

In Won Buddhism the conception of wisdom has undergone a change even though Sot'aesan said that inquiry into facts and principles leads to wisdom and enlightenment (*bodhi*). The term "inquiry into facts and principles" reflects the Confucian notion of "investigation of things and extension of knowledge."[81] Here we can see that Sot'aesan's reformed Buddhism is as much this-worldly as Confucianism is; wisdom attained from awakening to one's own nature may not be sufficient to cope with the problems arising in the complexity of the mundane world. In Sot'aesan's view, the Zen practiced for sudden or gradual enlightenment by Zen monks cannot be suggested for the general public, for it was evident that very few succeeded in attaining supreme enlightenment. The Won Buddhist path for wisdom is formulated from traditional Buddhist paths (hence the Lin-chi tradition of *kanhwa Sŏn*, the Sŏn of "observing the critical phrase," is a small part of the daily meditation in Won Buddhism) and the needs of the contemporary world. While emphasis for the traditional Buddhist monk was put on wisdom for the final enlightenment into the ultimate truth of oneself and the world, Sot'aesan put more emphasis on showing how, upon awakening to the truth of Irwŏnsang, one can realize a good life in the mundane world. This requires one to have a clear understanding of what Sot'aesan calls facts and principles. By facts are meant right, wrong, gain, and loss in all human affairs; by principles are meant the fundamental metaphysical principles of the universe, viz., the difference between noumenon and phenomenon and the change of existence and nonexistence. By existence and nonexistence are meant the cycle of the four seasons, the atmospheric phenomena of winds, clouds, rain, dew, frost, and snow; birth, aging, illness, and death of all things; and the evanescence of rising and falling, prosperity and decline. To steer away from the perilous stream of suffering, one must understand right from wrong and gain from loss in human affairs, and such fundamental principles of all things in the world as the difference between noumenon and phenomenon, existence and nonexistence. Thus, inquiry into facts and principles is a philosophical investigation to figure out the first

---

80. Ibid.
81. See Legge, *Confucius*, pp. 357–358: "Wishing to cultivate their persons, they first rectified their hearts. Wishing to rectify their hearts, they first sought to be sincere in their thoughts. Wishing to be sincere in their thoughts, they first extended to the utmost their knowledge. Such extension of knowledge lay in the investigation of things."

metaphysical principle of the universe; figuring this out may help one understand the meaning of one's existence in the universe—but only if one is enlightened to the truth of Irwŏnsang, which is none other than a summary of the Mahāyāna Buddhist worldview as I have argued above. Sot'aesan explains the purpose of inquiry into facts and principles as follows.

If one acts as one pleases without knowing right, wrong, gain, and loss in human affairs, whatever one does can lead to offense and suffering. If one lives without knowing the principle of the ultimate reality and its phenomenal appearances and the vicissitudes of existence and nonexistence, one will suffer because one will not know the cause of unexpected suffering and happiness, and one's thoughts will be hurried and narrowminded. Nor will one understand the principle of birth, aging, illness, and death, and the causal law of karmic retribution. One will be unable to distinguish truth from falsehood, falling into falsehood and eventually ruining one's family and disgracing oneself. The purpose of inquiring into the unfathomable principle of the universe and complicated human affairs is to attain the ability to analyze and pass prompt judgment on practical daily affairs.

Thus, the Won Buddhist way of attaining wisdom by inquiring into facts and principles is different from the traditional Zen Buddhist way of attaining wisdom, which aims at awakening into one's self-nature through rigorous practice.[82] One is to study scriptures,[83] give lectures, exchange ideas in discussions, sit in meditations with ŭidu, the "topic of doubt," inquire into the principles of nature and the metaphysical first principle of the universe.

*c. Mindful Choice in Karmic Action*    Morality (*śīla*) in the Buddhist triple discipline consists of conscious and willed abstention from misconduct of body (taking the life of living beings, theft, sexual misconduct), of speech (falsehood, slander, harsh and useless speech), and of mind (covetousness, animosity, and wrong view). Its aim is to avoid any action that might harm someone else.[84] For Hui-neng, the morality (precept) of self-nature simply means the absence of evil in the mind-ground.

Since the self-nature referred to by the circular symbol Irwŏnsang in Won Buddhism is none other than Dharmakāya Buddha, the precept

---

82. See Buswell, *Zen Monastic Experience*, pp. 220–222.

83. The scriptures are included in the *Wŏnbulgyo chŏnsŏ* (Compendium of the scriptures of Won Buddhism): *Wŏnbulgyo kyojŏn* (Scriptures of Won Buddhism), *Pulcho yogyŏng* (Essential scriptures of the Buddha and patriarchs), *Yejŏn* (Book of rites), *Chŏngsan chongsa pŏbŏ* (Master Chŏngsan's dharma words), *Wŏnbulgyo kyosa* (History of Won Buddhism), *Wŏnbulgyo kyohŏn* (Constitution of Won Buddhism), *Wŏnbulgyo sŏngga* (Hymns of Won Buddhism).

84. Lamotte, "The Buddha," p. 52.

of self-nature can be kept intact only if no evil is committed by body, speech, or mind. In other words, the practice of Irwŏnsang is to follow one's self-nature—namely, prajñā-wisdom, which is perfect, complete, and strictly fair and impartial—while using one's six senses. Being enlightened to one's self-nature is a necessary but not a sufficient condition for realizing buddhahood, for force of habit may keep one from following prajñā-wisdom even after one has an experience of awakening to one's self-nature.[85] Thus, most people need to engage in gradual cultivation even after sudden awakening. This requires one to train oneself in choosing justice and forsaking injustice while creating karma by body, mouth, and mind. Thus, this practice is called mindful choice in karmic action.[86]

The powers of spiritual cultivation and inquiry into facts and principles will be complete only if one attains the power or the ability to create right karma, which needs the practice of mindful choice in karmic action. Otherwise, one's practice will be like a fruit tree that has healthy roots, branches, leaves, and flowers but bears no fruit.[87] Depending on the kind of karma one creates, one creates a heavenly paradise or a hell no matter where one finds oneself. Evil or good karma follows one wherever one goes, like a shadow.

Sot'aesan notes that we humans do not always do good even though we know it is preferable and cannot always avoid evil though we know

---

85. For sudden enlightenment and gradual cultivation, see Chinul, *Susim kyŏl, T,* 2020.48.1006c; Buswell, *KAZ,* p. 144: "Although he has awakened to the fact that his original nature is no different from that of the Buddhas, the beginningless habit-energies are extremely difficult to remove suddenly and so he must continue to cultivate while relying on his awakening."

86. Sot'aesan defines *"chagŏp,"* literally "karma production," as the function of the six sense organs, viz., eyes, ears, nose, tongue, body, and mind. Since "karma" means "action," *"chagŏp"* can be translated as "action." However, *"chagŏp"* means more than an action; it carries the meaning of the law of karmic retribution, according to which the fruits of one's action accrue to oneself sooner or later wherever one goes until they are worn out. This translation has a strong support in the tenet of repentance, which warns against accumulating evil karma. See *Canon,* pt. 3, chap. 8.

87. This analogy implies Sot'aesan's emphasis on right action, for which concentration and wisdom are necessary, thus spiritual cultivation precedes and wisdom follows in the path of cultivation. This is different from mainstream Buddhist tradition. In Buddhism, *śīla* comes first, with samādhi and prajñā following. The analogy in Buddhism is the moon (prajñā) reflected on the water (samādhi) in an unbroken bowl (*śīla*). Since no water can be contained in a broken bowl (precepts broken) the practitioner starts with right action (*śīla*), for there cannot be samādhi while committing evil actions. Thus, there cannot be prajñā without samādhi, which in turn cannot exist without *śīla*. Thus, in the doctrinal chart of the old version, the order is *śīla,* samādhi, prajñā, as was the original intention of Sot'aesan's formulation of the doctrine, while in the new version the order is concentration, enquiry, mindful choice. The question remains whether one can attain samādhi while breaking precepts or one can keep *śīla* without sufficient spiritual cultivation.

we should, so that we often discard a tranquil paradise and enter a perilous sea of misery. We do so because we cannot always control the burning greed or we are pulled by the powerful force of habit. Thus, we aim at changing the detestable sea of misery into a paradise by training ourselves to create good karma and keep evil karma from being produced. For this purpose, the practice includes keeping a daily diary, which involves checking the thirty precepts of prohibitions.[88] In addition to this, one is required to practice carefulness and deportment while creating karma.

The way of training leading to the practice of Irwŏnsang thus lies in being enlightened to one's own Buddha-nature and applying it to daily living, which one can realize through the threefold practice. The essence of the latter is summarized in the conclusion of "Timeless Zen":

> When the six sense organs are free from work, eliminate delusive thoughts and cultivate One Mind; when the six sense organs are at work, eliminate injustice and cultivate justice.[89]

This is another way of saying that Buddha-dharma should be practiced in daily living, and daily living is none other than Buddha-dharma. In this way Sot'aesan has brought Buddha-dharma out of the deep mountain valleys and into the mundane world.

## C. Fourfold Beneficence as the Essence of Dharmakāya Buddha

### 1. The Way of Religious Worship

Faith in the truth of Irwŏnsang is the first necessary step toward enlightenment. The purpose of enlightenment is to know, nourish, and use the enlightened mind. Thus, the faith in the truth of Irwŏnsang is the belief in the purely metaphysical principle of the universe expounded in "The Truth of Irwŏnsang." In other words, there is nothing particularly religious or devotional commanded in the truth, faith, and practice of Irwŏnsang, Dharmakāya Buddha; these are expounded as the details of one of the four fundamental principles of Won Buddhism, viz., correct enlightenment and right practice. In this fundamental principle are contained the essentials of the Buddhist practice renovated and relevant to the need of the secular world. This part of the doctrine is mainly concerned with the way of realizing a self-reliant person. This way is not much different in principle from that of traditional Buddhist practice.

---

88. See *Canon*, pt. 3, chap. 11.
89. Ibid., chap. 7.

What makes an important difference in the doctrine of Won Buddhism is the emphasis on religious ethics based on the principle of the fundamental sources of human existence. While one endeavors to realize buddhahood through the threefold practice, one must ask whether one can succeed in realizing such a goal without help from other sources than one's own Buddha-nature. It was Sot'aesan's realization upon his great enlightenment that he could not have attained it without help from heaven and earth, parents, brethren, and laws. Later, Sot'aesan developed the idea of beneficence into a central tenet of the religious doctrine, viz., awareness of beneficence and its requital, which is the second of the four fundamental principles of the order. When Irwŏnsang was enshrined as the symbol of Dharmakāya Buddha, it was regarded as the fundamental source of the fourfold beneficence and as the Buddha-nature of the Tathāgata (Thus Come One, the Buddha). Since the phenomenal world is none other than the manifestation of Dharmakāya Buddha, Irwŏn, there is nothing that is not the image of Buddha. The fourfold beneficence is the essence of Dharmakāya Buddha.[90] Thus, one's existence depends on the fourfold beneficence, which, in Sot'aesan's view, is the manifestation of Dharmakāya Buddha. The religious worship in Won Buddhism lies in awareness of beneficence and its requital. The requital of beneficence is done as a way of making offerings to Dharmakāya Buddha—hence, the motto: since everywhere is the image of Buddha, do all things as making an offering to Buddha. The essence of the Won Buddhist religious life, however, lies in the ways of requiting the beneficence.[91] Thus, the meaning of the Buddhist expression "making offerings to the Buddha" has undergone a drastic change in Won Buddhism. Spelling out the fourfold beneficence as the essence of Dharmakāya Buddha, viz., heaven and earth, parents, brethren, laws, which are the fundamental sources of human existence, the essence of recompensing them for their beneficence is added. One can recompense heaven and earth for their beneficence by harboring no idea of having rendered favors, parents by protecting those who cannot protect themselves, brethren by practicing the principle of mutual benefit, and laws by forsaking injustice and doing justice. The Won Buddhist religious life will be empty if this practice is not carried out. The

---

90. Reynold Niebuhr used the expression "the universal beneficence of nature" quoted in the *Shorter Oxford English Dictionary* under the entry "beneficence." It is self-evident that we human beings cannot exist without the universal beneficence of nature such as the beneficence of the sun, the moon, water, air, and so on.

91. This is summarized as the essence of the requital of beneficence in the doctrinal chart in the *Pulgyo chŏngjŏn* (1943), which has been replaced with the four essentials in the *Wŏnbulgyo kyojŏn* by the editor. It was one of the mistakes committed by the editor of the 1962 edition. See appendix 1.

following is an analysis of the tenet of awareness of beneficence and its requital expounded in the chapter "Fourfold Beneficence."[92]

## 2. Fourfold Beneficence as the Source of Moral Duties

Sot'aesan means by "beneficence" (*ŭn*) that without which one cannot exist. In this sense of the term "beneficence," one is indebted to the fourfold beneficence. As a proof of this truth, Sot'aesan asks us to think, in order to know our indebtedness to the fourfold beneficence, whether we could preserve our existence without them. He challenges us to think whether we could preserve our existence without heaven and earth,[93] whether we could have brought ourselves into this world and nourished ourselves without our parents,[94] whether we could survive alone if there were no other human beings, animals and plants,[95] or whether peace and order could be maintained without laws of moral cultivation for individuals, of managing a household, of regulating a society, of ruling a nation, and of keeping the world in peace.[96] Even an imbecile will understand that one's life is an impossibility without these things, and nothing can be a greater beneficence than that without which one cannot exist. Thus one owes one's life to the fourfold beneficence, and no further argument is necessary for the proof of our indebtedness to the fourfold beneficence.

Once it is proven that one is indebted to the fourfold beneficence, no further argument is necessary to prove that it is one's prima facie duty to requite it. Sot'aesan thinks it a matter of necessary course to requite the beneficence to which one owes one's life. Requital of beneficence is thus a general moral duty in Won Buddhism. From the religious aspect of the doctrine, the fourfold beneficence is the incarnation of Dharmakāya Buddha with the power to bless or punish. From the moral point of view it is the foundation of moral duty: our moral duties are derived from the fact that without it our life is an impossibility and that therefore it must be requited.

The two principles, religious and moral, are conjoined by the imperative that one ought to requite beneficence as a way of making a reverent offering to Buddha.[97] If, for instance, I treat other human beings on the basis of fairness as required by the rule of requital of the beneficence of brethren, I will be treating them as buddhas and thus be blessed as they have the power to bless or punish. If, however, I treat them unfairly, violating the moral principle of fairness, they, the living bud-

---

92. See *Canon*, pt. 2, chap. 2.
93. Ibid., sec. 1.
94. Ibid., sec. 2, I.
95. Ibid., sec. 3, I.
96. Ibid., sec. 4, I.
97. See *Canon*, doctrinal chart.

dhas, will punish me. In what follows Sot'aesan's views on how one is indebted to and how one ought to requite the fourfold beneficence as moral duties will be explained.

**a. The Beneficence of Heaven and Earth**    Sot'aesan's metaphysical view of heaven and earth is that the automatic rotation of the grand framework of the universe is in accordance with the ways of heaven and earth and that the result of their rotation is their virtue.[98] The virtues of heaven and earth are exemplified in the brightness of the sun and moon and the favors of the wind, clouds, rain, and dew. Because of the former we can discern and know myriad things, and because of the latter myriad living beings are nurtured and we are able to survive off their products.[99]

In the ways of heaven and earth Sot'aesan finds eight beneficent characteristics, from which he derives eight moral maxims for humankind. The ways of heaven and earth are extremely bright, extremely sincere, extremely fair, natural, vast and limitless, eternal, without good or ill fortunes, and ubiquitously responsive without harboring the idea of having done favors. Finding a moral standard in the ways of heaven and earth is not new with Sot'aesan; we can find the same view in the Confucian tradition. Chou Tun-i (1017–1073), who quotes from the *I Ching* (Book of changes),[100] says, "Thus [the sage] establishes himself as the ultimate standard for man. Hence, the character of the sage is identical with that of heaven and earth; his brilliance is identical with that of the sun and the moon; his order is identical with that of the seasons; and his good and evil fortunes are identical with those of spiritual beings."[101] Thus the ancient sages found their moral standards in what they thought were the characteristics of heaven and earth. Sot'aesan does the same thing; his originality lies in deriving moral duties from the fact that we are indebted to the beneficence of heaven and earth.

The way to requite the beneficence of heaven and earth is to model oneself after their ways. This is like requiting the beneficence of one's teacher by practicing her or his teaching.[102] Thus, one is to improve one's moral virtues by following the moral rules derived from the eight characteristics of the ways of heaven and earth and modeling oneself after those eight characteristics.

The first maxim requires one to model oneself on the brightness of

---

98. *Canon*, pt. 2, chap. 2, sec. 1, I.
99. Ibid., II. It is assumed, for instance, that without the sun no living being can exist on the earth.
100. Legge, *The Yi King*, p. 417.
101. Wing-tsit Chan, *Reflections on Things at Hand*, p. 6.
102. *SS*, IV:24.

the ways of heaven and earth when one investigates facts and principles.[103] One must understand such principles because one's moral conduct will be based on one's view of the world and one's self. In Sot'aesan's view, moral problems arise from foolishness and lack of knowledge of right or wrong and gain or loss. No one in that state can be a reliable moral agent. Hence, one must learn facts and principles to attain such wisdom and knowledge, modeling oneself on the brightness of heaven and earth.

The second maxim requires one to model oneself on their way of sincerity and be consistent in sincerity when one tries to accomplish anything good. The term "sincerity" is used not only with its usual meaning of truthfulness and honesty, but also with the meaning of wholehearted devotion. According to Sot'aesan, nothing is more sincere in this sense than heaven and earth. This idea can be found in the Confucian tradition. "Sincerity is the Way of Heaven and the attainment of sincerity, or [the] attempt to be sincere, is the way of man."[104] Mencius (c. 371–c. 289 B.C.) says, "Sincerity is the way of Heaven. To think how to be sincere is the way of man. Never has there been one possessed of complete sincerity who did not move others. Never has there been one who had not sincerity who was able to move others."[105] Sot'aesan suggests that everyone ought to model himself or herself on the way of sincerity as a way of requiting the beneficence of heaven and earth.

The third maxim requires one to model oneself on the way of fairness of heaven and earth and to follow the Mean without being affected by remoteness or closeness or by feelings of joy or sorrow, anger or pleasure, when one handles myriad things.[106] In Sot'aesan's view heaven and earth are fair to all when they rear living beings. The sun shines for all without discrimination against anyone. When we humans handle our affairs, however, we are often unfair because we are affected by remoteness or closeness or by joy or anger. Unfairness is one of the moral evils that aggravate the human predicament. Sot'aesan suggests that we ought to emulate the way of fairness as a way of requiting the beneficence of heaven and earth.

The fourth maxim requires one to do what is reasonable and to forsake what is unreasonable, modeling oneself on the way of reason-

103. By "facts" are meant rightness and wrongness, gain and loss in human affairs; and by "principle" such metaphysical first principles of the universe as noumena and phenomena, being and nonbeing. The latter includes the rising, abiding, decaying, and ending of the universe; the rotation of the four seasons; and the birth, aging, illness, and death of all things.
104. Legge, *Confucius*, p. 413.
105. Legge, *Works of Mencius*, 303.
106. *Canon*, pt. 2, chap. 2, sec. 1, IV.

ableness and naturalness of heaven and earth. There is orderliness in the succession of the four seasons and in the rotation of day and night. Seasons for sowing and harvesting are not disorderly. To the way of reasonableness belongs the course of birth, aging, illness, and death of all sentient beings. The purpose of this maxim is to help one be free from sufferings caused by unreasonable and unnatural actions. In the mundane world unreasonable desires, decisions, programs, and plans often aggravate the human predicament.

The fifth maxim requires that one model oneself after the vastness of heaven and earth and practice impartiality.[107] Impartiality in thought and deeds is often used as a criterion of moral integrity. Moreover, partiality in handling human affairs causes unnecessary suffering for others. Impartiality is a necessary condition for the most important moral virtue in the Neo-Confucian tradition, namely, *jen* (humanity, benevolence). According to Chu Hsi, "A man originally possesses *jen*. It comes with him from the very beginning. Simply because he is partial, his *jen* is obstructed and cannot be expressed. Therefore, if he is impartial, his *jen* will operate."[108] Sot'aesan's ideal is that everyone realize this virtue.

The sixth maxim requires one to emancipate herself or himself from the vicissitudes of all things and from the cycle of birth, old age, illness, and death. Things on the earth are like transient waves whereas heaven and earth are like permanent ocean. Sot'aesan suggests that one ought to realize the cosmic body of Buddha (Dharmakāya), which is free from bodily birth and death, modeling oneself on the eternity of heaven and earth.

The seventh maxim requires one to detect misfortune in good fortune and good fortune in misfortune, modeling oneself on the way of there being no good or bad fortune in heaven and earth lest one should be caught by either of them.[109] The point of this maxim is that one ought not to be blinded or carried away by either good or bad fortune inasmuch as "favor or beneficence sometimes arises in harm and harm in favor."[110]

The eighth maxim requires that one, following the way of heaven and earth, expect no reward from others for rendering favors to them. Further, one ought not to make an enemy out of one who is ungrateful to one's favor. The same virtue is taught in the Bible: "But when you give alms, do not let your left hand know what your right hand is doing" (Matthew 6:3). The moral virtue of "harboring no idea of self-praising"

---

107. Ibid.
108. Wing-tsit Chan, *Reflections on Things at Hand*, p. 62.
109. *Canon*, pt. 2, chap. 2, sec. 1, IV.
110. Ibid., sec. 4.

is one of the moral ideals for both Buddhists and Confucians. D. T. Suzuki points out that the notion of "nonabiding" or "harboring no false idea" is central to the philosophy of Mahāyāna Buddhism.[111] We find in the Diamond Sūtra the noted advice, "One should develop a mind which does not abide in anything."[112] The attempt to find a model of this moral virtue in the ways of heaven and earth was made by Neo-Confucian philosophers. Cheng-i (1033–1107) said, "Heaven and Earth create and transform without having any idea of their own. The sage has a mind of his own but does not take any [unnatural] action."[113] The moral virtue suggested in this maxim is a lofty ideal, as it requires one to keep from self-praise, from self-conceit, or from assuming a patronizing air.

If one practices the eight articles for cultivating the eight moral virtues, one can form one body with heaven and earth in virtue: wisdom (rightness), sincerity, fairness, reasonableness and naturalness, magnanimity (vastness), immortality (eternity), imperturbability in the face of one's good or ill fortunes, and benevolence. Once one has perfected one's moral character with these virtues, one's moral influence on other sentient beings will be like that of heaven and earth, and hence they will warmly receive one.[114] This idea is not so exorbitant as it seems; it was quite prevalent in the morals of Neo-Confucianism. Cheng-hao (1032–1085), for instance, said, "The man of *jen* regards Heaven and Earth and all things as one body. To him there is nothing that is not himself. Since he has recognized all things as himself, can there be any limit to *jen*?"[115] Chu Hsi reiterates Cheng-hao's point, and Wang Yang-ming does the same.[116] Sot'aesan has not only revived the Confucian moral ideals in Won Buddhism but also provided a way of realizing them through the eight articles of the requital of the beneficence of heaven and earth.

If one does not requite the beneficence of heaven and earth, one will suffer the consequences, for ingratitude to heaven and earth incurs heavenly punishment.[117] Although heaven and earth are empty and silent to one's deeds, unexpected hardships and sufferings in life and sufferings caused by one's deeds can be attributed to one's ingratitude to heaven and earth[118]—for example, being ignorant of facts and principles, insincere, either excessive or deficient, irrational, partial, igno-

---

111. Suzuki, *Studies in the Laṅkāvatāra Sūtra*, p. 95.
112. *Chin-kang po-jo po-lo-mi ching, T,* 235.8.749c.
113. Chan, *Sourcebook*, p. 643.
114. *Canon*, pt. 2, chap. 2, sec. 1, VI.
115. Chan, *Sourcebook*, p. 530.
116. Chan, *Reflections*, p. 63; idem, *Instructions for Practical Living*, p. 272.
117. *Canon*, pt. 2, chap. 2, sec. 1, VII.
118. Ibid., sec. 2, I.

rant of the transformation of the phenomenal world, ignorant of good and bad fortune and the ups and downs of the world, and attached to the idea of having rendered favors to others, covertly praising oneself and overtly boasting.

   **b. The Beneficence of Parents**   Sot'aesan notes that one is indebted to one's parents for life, nurturing, and instruction in one's duties and responsibilities to human society.[119]

   Neo-Confucian moralists used the filial duty to criticize the Buddhist monks who had left their parents for the monastery life.[120] According to the Neo-Confucians, Buddhist monks were egoists afraid of the difficulties arising in the mundane world. In the Confucian tradition one's filial duty to one's parents is the fundamental principle of morality. It is important, therefore, to see how the moral duty of filial piety is reinterpreted in the religious ethics of Won Buddhism.

   According to Confucius, filial duty is the foundation of virtues and the root of civilization.[121] Tseng Tzu, one of his disciples, asked what surpasses filial piety as the virtue of a sage. To this Confucius replied, "Man excels all the beings in heaven and earth. Of all man's acts, none is greater than filial piety. In the practice of filial piety, nothing is greater than to reverence one's father."[122] He says also, "He who loves his parents does not dare to act contemptuously toward others."[123] In Won Buddhism, the concept of filial piety undergoes a drastic change.

   The central principle for the requital of the beneficence of parents lies in protecting the helpless, as parents protect their helpless children.[124] Sot'aesan thinks that one should follow four maxims as a way of requiting the beneficence of parents: One ought to follow the way of practice and the way man qua man ought to follow.[125] One ought to support one's parents faithfully as much as one can when they lack the ability to help themselves, and help them have spiritual comfort. In accordance with one's ability, one ought to protect the helpless parents of others as one's own as much as one can, during and after the lifetime of one's parents. After one's parents are deceased, one ought to enshrine their pictures and biographical records and remem-

119. Ibid., II.

120. Chan, *Sourcebook*, p. 646.

121. Mary Lelia Makra, *The Hsiao Ching*, p. 3.

122. Ibid., p. 19.

123. Ibid., p. 5.

124. *Canon*, pt. 2, chap. 2, sec. 2, III.

125. The threefold practice includes spiritual cultivation, enquiry into facts and principles, and mindful choice in karmic action; the Way man qua man ought to follow is the requital of the fourfold beneficence and the practice of the four essentials. See *Canon*, pt. 2, chap. 6.

ber them.[126] The main principle of the requital of the beneficence of parents, formulated as a moral imperative, is contained in the second and third maxims. They prohibit one from harming, exploiting, or being inhumane to the weak (individual, family, or nation). One's filial duty is given a new meaning by the first maxim, as it requires one to be a moral being who has attained the three great powers of emancipation (Taoist), enlightenment (Buddhist), and the Mean (Confucian) and is capable of requiting the fourfold beneficence. Thus, in Sot'aesan's moral system, the moral duty of filial piety requires one to improve one's moral character to the level of a sage since one must be a sage if one follows the first maxim.

Sot'aesan's view on the consequence of ingratitude to the beneficence of parents reflects the Confucian view on being unfilial. "So it is that, from the Son of Heaven to the commoners, if filial piety is not pursued from the beginning to the end, disasters are sure to follow."[127] Sot'aesan interprets the consequence of being unfilial in the Buddhist concept of karma. One's offspring follows one's examples, and this is an inevitable course. Thus, if one is filial, one's offspring will be. In accordance with the law of karma, one will be helped and protected whenever necessary since one protects and helps those in need.[128]

If one does not requite the beneficence of parents, one's own offspring will follow one's example. Those who believe in the morality of filial duty will also condemn one. Moreover, throughout many lives, one will be deserted by other people when in need of help, in accordance with the law of karma. This is one of the examples of synthesis Sot'aesan has made of Confucianism and Buddhism.

**c. The Beneficence of Brethren**    The term "brethren" here designates all people, birds, beasts, and plants as well as one's own siblings.[129] But what beneficence does one receive from other people? Did Thomas Hobbes not say that people in the state of nature are at war with one another? Did David Hume not say that the worst enemy of man is man?

In Sot'aesan's view, humans are capable of either harming or blessing others; however, life is an impossibility without help from others. People of different occupations help one another by exchanging products on the principle of "mutual benefit" and thus are indebted to one another. Sot'aesan does not say that there are no crooks and other morally despicable ones. By the principle that we are indebted to the beneficence of brethren, Sot'aesan means that people in general, some-

---

126. *Canon*, pt. 2, chap. 2, sec. 2, IV.
127. Makra, *Hsiao Ching*, p. 3.
128. *Canon*, pt. 2, chap. 2, sec. 2, VI.
129. Ibid., sec. 3, I.

times including crooks, are helped by one another and that without depending on others, life is an impossibility.

Pointing out the way we are indebted to the beneficence of brethren, Sot'aesan spells out the way of requiting it: "Act in accordance with the principle of mutual benefit based on fairness by which you are indebted to brethren, and conduct the exchange among people of various occupations on the principle of mutual benefit based on fairness."[130] With this general principle of justice[131] Sot'aesan spells out five maxims that require people of various occupations to exchange what they can offer with others on the principle of mutual benefit based on fairness.[132] Thus people of all walks of life (scholars, civil service employees, farmers, artisans, tradesmen) ought to follow the principle of mutual benefit when they exchange what they have with others.

As a way of justifying the principle of fairness, Sot'aesan considers the consequences of gratitude and ingratitude to the beneficence of brethren. If grateful, people will be blessed in a paradise. If we requite the beneficence of brethren, fellow humans will be influenced by the virtue of mutual benefit and will bear goodwill to one another. In such a society one will be protected and respected, individuals will be endeared one to another, families will promote mutual friendships, and there will be mutual understanding among societies and peace among nations.[133] This end is the guiding force of Won Buddhism, the founding motive of which was to deliver all sentient beings suffering in the bitter seas of misery to an earthly paradise.

Ingratitude to the beneficence of brethren will drive all brethren to hate, and they will abhor one another and make mutual enemies, causing quarrels among individuals, ill will among families, antagonism among societies, and war among nations.[134] Hence, people should realize the beneficence of brethren and honor the rule of mutual benefit based on the principle of fairness.

*d. The Beneficence of Laws*    It may sound unnatural to say that we are indebted to the beneficence of laws. However, this idea is not new with Sot'aesan, and it will seem much less unnatural if we recall what Socrates said in the *Crito*:

> What charge do you bring against us [the laws] and the state, that you are trying to destroy us? Did we not give you life in the first place?... Are you not grateful to those laws which

---

130. Ibid., III.
131. Sot'aesan seems to have anticipated John Rawls's theory of justice as fairness.
132. *Canon*, pt. 2, chap. 2, sec. 3, IV.
133. Ibid., VI.
134. Ibid., VII.

are instituted for this end, for requiring your father to give a
cultural and physical education?[135]

By "laws" Sot'aesan means the religious and moral teachings that
sages show us to follow, the laws with which scholar-officials, farmers,
artisans, and tradesmen direct and encourage us to preserve our life and
advance our knowledge, and the judicial institutions that help serve
justice and punish injustice and help discriminate right from wrong
and gain from loss.[136] Thus, the term "laws" covers religious and moral
principles, social institutions, legislation, and civil and criminal laws.
The connotation that Sot'aesan assigns to the term is "the principle of
fairness for human justice." This principle can benefit individuals,
families, societies, nations, and the whole world when applied.[137]

Upon showing how we are indebted to the beneficence of laws,
Sot'aesan formulates the general rule for requiting it and then derives
five moral duties. The basic moral principle that we ought to follow to
requite the beneficence of laws is as follows: "If we are indebted to the
prohibition of certain things by the laws, we ought not to do them; and
if we are indebted to the things encouraged by the laws, then we ought
to do them."[138] Simple chastisement of injustice is like cutting the top
off a noxious plant but leaving its roots intact. In Sot'aesan's view, a
moral agent needs a much wider moral education than being instructed
simply in the rightness or wrongness of an action. The moral education must include, as a preparation for the requital of the beneficence
of laws, learning and practicing the way of individual moral cultivation,
the way of regulating one's family, the way of harmonizing society, the
way of governing the state, and the way of putting the world at peace as
an individual person and as a member of a family, society, nation, and
the world respectively.[139]

Sot'aesan does not specify in the five articles the method of cultivating individual morality, of regulating a family, of social harmony, of
statecraft, or of obtaining world peace. All those methods, however,
must be based on the principle of justice and must provide a way of
realizing justice in individuals, families, societies, states, and the world.
Sot'aesan's idea here reflects the moral, educational and political programs of the Confucian tradition summarized in the *Great Learning*.[140]
The main aim of the *Great Learning* is to show that illustrious virtue

---

135. F. Hamilton and H. Cairns, eds., *The Collected Dialogues of Plato*, pp. 35–36.
136. *Canon*, pt. 2, chap. 2, sec. 4, II.
137. Ibid., I.
138. Ibid., III.
139. Ibid., IV.
140. Legge, *Confucius*, pp. 357–358.

starts with individual moral cultivation. Sot'aesan does not mention illustrious virtue; his ideal is that everyone realizes human justice. It is not the time for the world to rely for its well-being on the manifestation of the ruler's illustrious virtue; it is time for the mass of people to realize justice for the sake of their own well-being. Otherwise the bitter seas of misery will get deeper.

Sot'aesan answers the question why we should requite the beneficence of laws in terms of blessings and punishment. If we are grateful to laws, we will be protected by them; if not, we will be punished, bound, and restrained. Further, the requital of the beneficence of laws improves our personal dignity since we cultivate our moral character with the teachings of the sages. A world composed of people who do not requite the beneficence of laws would be disordered and would drive itself into shambles.[141]

**e. Concluding Remarks**    When Sot'aesan established a new religious order, he synthesized the two moral systems of Buddhism and Confucianism by reforming and renovating some of the central tenets of both so that their religious and moral teachings could be made relevant to the new era. In Sot'aesan's view the ills of the world could be cured only if people felt indebted and grateful to the fourfold beneficence. He explains how we are indebted to each of the four beneficences and why we should requite them. He derives moral duties from the way we are indebted to them and uses the religious force to help us put our hearts into the moral duties, saying that a reverent offering to Buddha is none other than requiting the fourfold beneficence. Since the moral duties to requite the fourfold beneficence are mostly Confucian and thus this-worldly, and since the fourfold beneficence is identified with the cosmic body of Buddha, Sot'aesan is suggesting that we practice the two teachings in our daily life. In this way Sot'aesan has synthesized the two apparently opposing moral systems into a new ethico-religious system of Won Buddhism.

The synthesis is shown in the doctrinal chart of the 1943 edition. The essence of the Confucian moral teaching is *jen* (benevolence, human-heartedness) and *i* (righteousness), which Sot'aesan acknowledged as the leading moral principle.[142] The essential principles of the requital of the beneficence of heaven and earth and that of parents are "harboring no false idea upon rendering favors to others" and "protecting the helpless" respectively. And these two moral virtues cannot be practiced unless one genuinely loves others or "cannot witness the suffering of others" or "does not do to others what one does not like oneself," which is the essence of the Confucian moral virtue of *jen*. The essential

---

141. *Canon*, pt. 2, chap. 2, sec. 4, VII.
142. See *SS*, I:5.

principles of the requital of the beneficence of brethren and that of laws are "the way of mutual benefit" and "the way of eradicating injustice and maintaining justice" respectively. The Confucian moral virtue of righteousness is reflected in these two ways. Since the fourfold benefi-cence is the essence of Dharmakāya Buddha, one's requital of benefi-cence is making an offering to the Buddha.[143] The central moral principles of the Confucian ethics are synthesized as the essential ways of beneficence requital, which in turn is none other than worshiping Dharmakāya Buddha. Thus, the two ethico-religious principles of Con-fucianism and Buddhism have been synthesized in the doctrine of Won Buddhism.

## III.  A Summary of the *Taejonggyŏng* (Scripture of Sot'aesan)

*The Scripture of Sot'aesan* is book 2 of the *Scriptures of Won Buddhism* (*Wŏnbulgyo kyojŏn*); it is the analects of Sot'aesan recorded by his dis-ciples, which was published by Chŏnghwasa in 1962. It is divided into fifteen chapters in accordance with the nature of the topics Sot'aesan covered. Because some sections could easily have been entered into different chapters, there is a danger of oversimplifying the contents of a given chapter. This summary of each chapter attempts to give an over-view of the contents of Sot'aesan's sayings. It should be noted here that the source of much of the *Scripture of Sot'aesan* is an earlier collection of Sot'aesan's sayings called the *Kŭmgangsan ŭi chuin* (The owner of Mt. Kŭmgang), which has undergone severe editing in the process of its canonization as the *Scripture of Sot'aesan*.

The first chapter, the Introduction, has nineteen sections. Collected in this chapter are Sot'aesan's sayings on the Buddha Śākyamuni as the origin of his enlightenment and introductory remarks on his plan to open a new religious order; his enlightenment and the state of his mind upon the enlightenment; his intention to take the Buddha Śākyamuni as the source of his enlightenment and Buddha-dharma as the central doctrine of the new religious order to be established; and his thoughts after the enlightenment on the society of that time and the necessity to open a new religious order. Sot'aesan expresses the realm of his enlightenment as "a clear framework," a sign of the truth of Irwŏn-sang,[144] the realm that is the ground of the Way or Truth of neither arising nor ceasing and the causal law of karmic retribution. Irwŏnsang is the sign of the noumenal nature of all beings of the universe and the

---

143. This is the crux of Sot'aesan's synthetic renovation of the two ethico-religious sys-tems; unfortunately the essential principles of beneficence requital in the doctrinal chart in the 1943 edition has been replaced by four essentials in the 1962 edition.
144. *Canon*, pt. 2, chap. 1.

fundamental source of all dharmas. Since he found similarities between his aspiration, his search after truth, and the realm of his enlightenment and those of the Buddha Śākyamuni, he decided to take the latter as the origin of his enlightenment and Buddha-dharma as the central doctrine of the new order. He recognizes Buddha-dharma as the supreme Way because it elucidates the principles of human nature, the great truth of birth and death, the law of causality, and the method of practicing the great Way. Included also is the explanation of the founding motive:[145] "Since material power is unfolding, let us unfold spiritual power accordingly," a motto that emphasizes the importance of spiritual autonomy. Disclosed also is the formation of a unit of ten members, which established the dual foundations of the order: the financial foundation by the embankment project to reclaim tidal land and the spiritual foundation by the numinous authentication of the prayer from the dharma realm. Recorded also are his views that Buddhism would be the main religion in the future (with the qualification that Buddha-dharma applicable to the new world should be Buddha-dharma practiced in daily life); that its object of religious worship is the truth of Dharmakāya Buddha; that its practice should be useful to daily living; and that the Buddha-dharma can unify the making of an offering to Buddha and daily work. Emphasized also is the necessity of the integrated practice of the threefold practice: morality (śīla), concentration (samādhi), and wisdom (prajñā).[146]

The second chapter, "On the Doctrine," consists of thirty-nine sections. Explicated in this chapter are the central tenet of the doctrine of the order, Irwŏnsang, together with the ways of its faith, its practice, and the merits thereof; the unitary source of all dharmas; the relationship between Irwŏnsang and human beings; the contents of faith and practice of Irwŏnsang; and the method of practical applications of its faith and practice and their merits. Included also is the view that the ultimate truth of all religions is identical and agrees with the truth of Irwŏnsang; hence the religious doctrine should show how the truth can be realized in daily living. The religious faith in Irwŏnsang lies in believing in the truth of Dharmakāya Buddha, the fourfold beneficence,[147] namely, that all beings of the universe have the authority to bestow blessings or punishment and that the practice of Irwŏnsang lies in nurturing, awakening to, and following the Buddha-nature modeling on the truth of Irwŏn: emptiness, roundness, and rightness. This is approached with the threefold practice: spiritual cultivation, inquiry into facts and principles, and mindful choice in karmic action. Ex-

---

145. Ibid., pt. 1, chap. 1.
146. Ibid., pt. 2, chap. 4.
147. Ibid., chap. 2.

plained is the inseparable relationship between the threefold practice and the life of clothing, food, and shelter. Emphasized is the importance of an integrated practice of the threefold practice and mindfulness in choosing actions. By emphasizing the necessity of a balanced improvement of material civilization and spiritual culture, statecraft and religion, an ideology is proposed for the realization of a utopia.

The third chapter, "On Practice," consists of sixty-three sections. Explicated in this chapter are the method of integrated practice of the threefold practice (spiritual cultivation, inquiry into facts and principles, and mindful choice in karmic action); distinctions of what is essential and what is secondary, right and wrong in the practice of this order; and various precepts for practice. It is shown that the central doctrine of the order is summarized in the nine articles of practice spelled out in the essentials of daily practice,[148] a complete practice of which is necessary and sufficient for one to realize buddhahood in this world. The way of attaining the three great powers (cultivation, inquiry, and mindful choice) in motion and at rest is elucidated as the fundamentals of the integrated practice of the threefold practice. Emphasis is put on the necessity of Buddhist practice in daily living. The three great powers should be attained by Zen practice;[149] one should not fall into the practice of senseless emptiness or hasty practice; and one should cultivate a balance between mind-nature and temperament. If one is to do more than one thing at a time, spiritual cultivation can be done only if all the tasks at hand are carried out flawlessly. The great scripture is not one of words but of all the principles and facts of the world; hence, one should not be attached to one's own fixed narrow views. Warned against are the desire to attain supernatural powers and the attachment to pursuing the exclusive learning external to the practice of the order. It is also taught that one should attain liberation by freeing oneself from holding to one thought. By training oneself in Zen retreats, one should learn to subdue the disturbances of the world. Explicated also are the mental precepts for those who are on the dharma stage of subjugation of *mārā* by dharma power.[150]

The fourth chapter, "The Way of Humanity," consists of fifty-nine sections. In this chapter are explicated what is primary and what is secondary in the Way and its virtue, the main principles of the Way of humanity, the essential rules of conduct in life, and the essentials of what the leader should be endowed with. The Way is defined as whatever ought to be done right; the ways of heaven and earth and of humans are used as examples. Virtue (C. *te*, K. *tŏk*) is defined as

---

148. Ibid., pt. 3, chap. 1.
149. Ibid., chap. 7.
150. Ibid., chap. 17.

beneficence produced by doing what ought to be done. There are virtues of heaven, earth, and human beings as the result of these following
their ways. If all people followed the way of humanity,[151] there would
be harmony among individuals, families, societies, nations, and the
world. To follow the way of humanity, one should know what is primary
from what is secondary and what is reasonable from what is unreasonable, putting into practice what is primary and reasonable. One should
also practice the virtue of detached giving. The strong and the weak
should learn from each other, and in any situation one should be able
to attain stability in keeping one's sphere in life. What is essential in
protecting one's mind and body is the sense of reverence and awe. A
householder should maintain the spiritual harmony of the family and
try to have a sound occupation. Children should be taught through
spiritual influence, exemplary actions, catechism, and strict discipline.
The expenditure for the rituals of coming of age, wedding, funeral, and
memorial service should be curtailed; however, the funeral service
should not slight the merit of the deceased. One should learn from the
good and evil of one's predecessors. True morality (the Way and its
virtue) does not exist in making wonders; the true way of humanity lies
in doing what a human being ought to do.

The fifth chapter, "On Cause and Effect," consists of thirty-three
sections. The main point of this chapter is to expound the brightness
and numinousness of the principle of causality. Expounded also is the
view that the law of causality is like the principle of yin-yang's mutual
advancement. Hence, it is suggested that one should apply this principle to the production of mutually beneficent karma. The principle of
causality is explained in terms of reciprocity of giving and receiving,
viz., giving is receiving. In other words, good and evil karmic retribution occurs in accordance with mutual reciprocity between yin and
yang. This is so because the circular recurrence in the truth of Irwŏnsang is none other than the principle of yin-yang's reciprocity; hence, in
accordance with the way of yin-yang's reciprocity, whatever one does
results in karmic retribution in accordance with it. Since animals live
with their roots in heaven, their physical and mental functions sow the
seeds of karma in the dharma realm of empty space; karmic retribution
results when the seeds of action meet the conditions appropriate for
their fruition. Emphasized is the reward and punishment of heaven and
earth brought about in accordance with truth, so is one to live without
deceiving oneself, others, and heaven and earth. Emphasized also is the
necessity to produce mutually productive causes and conditions without
producing mutually destructive ones. Meeting with a malefic karmic

---

151. Ibid., pt. 2, chap. 6.

cause and condition, one should resolve the karmic affinity (cause and condition) by dropping any thought of revenge; one should be heedful not to create evil karma with body, mouth, and mind. Without being intoxicated with temporary pleasures, one should prepare for eternal happiness; without being discouraged by temporary unhappiness, one should continue creating good karma in order to improve the living. Two of the most evil karmic actions are to mislead the public and to judge people to be guilty without clear evidence.

The sixth chapter, "Clarification of Doubtful Points," consists of forty sections. Recorded in this chapter are Sot'aesan's answers to doubtful points on the metaphysical principles of the universe, major and minor issues of human affairs, and the meanings of the sayings and teachings of various ancient sages in various scriptures. The numinous and bright awareness of heaven and earth makes clear distinctions for karmic actions. Recorded also is the principle that the formation, endurance, decay, and disintegration of the universe is realized at every moment. The world of perfect bliss depends on the transcendence of the mind, and hells on the shackle of the mind. Sot'aesan's interpretation is given to "the four perceptions of self, a being, a soul, and a person" in the Diamond Sūtra[152] for an easy and practical application in daily living. The true meaning of the Buddhist emptiness illumines the fundamental source of the ultimate truth. Doubtful points in the tenet of the four-fold beneficence[153] and things to heed for daily application[154] are clarified. Warning against his disciples' reckless criticism of his predecessors is recorded; legendary prophecy is interpreted in accordance with the correct Way; a great practitioner of the Way does not perform any supernormal deed. Sudden awakening and sudden cultivation are compared to darkness retreating without its being noticed and the brightness of dawn coming without its being noticed. Hence, earnest and endless effort on awakening and in practice are emphasized.

The seventh chapter, "On the Principle of Nature,"[155] consists of thirty-one sections. This chapter contains explanations of the essential meaning of and answers to the questions concerning the metaphysical principles of nature. By "the principles of nature" is meant the fundamental principles of all things in the universe and of original human nature. The realm of perfect adaptability of the great Way is defined as the unity of being and nonbeing, noumenon and phenomenon, birth and death, and motion and rest. Hence, the right practice of the principle of nature lies in a great, perfect, and correct enlightenment to the

152. Edward Conze, *Perfect Wisdom*, p. 129.
153. *Canon*, pt. 2, chap. 2.
154. Ibid., pt. 3, chap. 2, sec. 2.
155. Ibid., sec. 1.

realm of the perfect adaptability of the great Way. To understand the
noumenal realm of original nature, which is ineffable and devoid of
an iota of thought, is incomplete; a complete enlightenment should
include an awakening to the bright and numinous function of the original nature. The noumenal essence of original nature is devoid of good
and evil in its substance but can be either good or evil in its function.
Seeing into original nature is important for right practice, but is not
the final phase of practice; a perfect practice of original nature lies in a
perfect accord with it upon seeing into it. Though it rarely happens,
there were some who attained buddhahood immediately upon seeing
into the original nature; generally, however, realizing buddhahood requires more effort than seeing into the original nature. Thus, an emphasis is put on the earnest effort to attain buddhahood after seeing into
the original nature. Knowing the substance of the original nature lies
in showing how the ultimate reality (noumenon) of all things appears as
the phenomenal world of diversity and showing that the phenomenal
world of diversity is the ultimate reality of unity. Knowing the function
of the original nature lies in knowing how to reduce being into nonbeing and nonbeing into being so that, as a universal truth, there is
immutability in change and change in immutability. Thus, a perfect
mastery of the substance and function of the original nature is viewed as
the practice of the original nature.

The eighth chapter, "On the Buddha-stage," consists of twenty-three
sections. Recorded in this chapter are the teachings on the ability and
the realm of the great mercy and pity of the omnipotent Buddha. The
great mercy is defined as the state of mind the Buddha has when he is
pleased to see anyone who exerts efforts toward attaining wisdom
(prajñā) and accumulates merits of detached giving. The great pity is
defined as the Buddha's mind of sadness when he sees and guides out
of an evil path anyone who resents heaven and earth, ancestors, brethren, and laws. Buddhas and bodhisattvas have the ability to be great
or small at will, to be great beings on and above the dharma stage of
transcendence (ch'ulga),[156] and to formulate a new dharma by manip-
ulating all dharmas and correcting the obsolete ones. If one's practice
reaches the ultimate stage, one will attain the threefold mastery of spirit
(numinousness), the Way, and dharma, of which the mastery of dharma
can be attained only by one who has attained the great, perfect, and
correct enlightenment. One who masters the fundamental truth of the
universe and applies it to the functions of the six senses is a great sage.
Buddhas and bodhisattvas employ heavenly beatitude to be free of
human pleasures; the Buddha has the power to overcome the karma

---

156. Ibid., chap. 17, 5.

of heaven (the natural inevitable law of cause and effect), freely to go or come, and freely to promote or demote on the six realms of existence. The Buddha regards the triple world in the ten directions as his own possession and makes use of them freely; if one is enlightened to the grand homestead, one will see that it is replete with infinite and wondrous principles, treasures, and creative wonders.

The ninth chapter, "On Deliverance," consists of thirty-eight sections. Explicated in this chapter are the principle of human birth and death, going and coming; the meaning and method of deliverance of the soul after death; and the way of preparing for death. The ultimate reality of all things in the universe is the noumenal nature that is originally clear and pure with no name, form, going and coming, or birth and death. Since the final goal is to attain emancipation from the ills of birth and death by awakening to the principle of birth and death, one is advised to transcend the attachment of love and greed by a firm spiritual concentration. Sermons are to help one who has not been emancipated from birth and death to follow a good path without falling into an evil path. Because of the wondrous principle of mutual response in the universe, a mind responds to another mind and an anima to another anima. The soul of the deceased can thus be delivered if, for the sake of the numinous consciousness of the deceased, many people offer silent prayers, make donations, and have a high priest give sermons.

The tenth chapter, "On Faith and Devotion," consists of nineteen sections. Explained in this chapter are the meaning and merit of faith and devotion, correct and incorrect faith, and examples of these. Faith and devotion are the root for attaining supreme enlightenment, the foundation for solving all the Zen conundrums (*Kongan*) and thereby attaining the great, perfect, and correct enlightenment, and the basis of doing myriad good deeds by observing all the precepts. Faith and devotion help one have no doubt in one's mentor, follow the mentor's guidance, have no complaints about anything, report one's faults without hiding anything, and transcend favorable and adverse conditions in practice of the dharma. Correct faith lies in perfecting faith in other-power and in self-power. Since firm faith lies in the mind, only one whose mind will not waver (even when facing death) can inherit the lineage of the order.

The eleventh chapter, "Aphoristic Sayings," consists of forty-five sections. Recorded in this chapter are short aphoristic sayings on following original nature,[157] virtuous deeds, and public service. The good and wisdom are preferable; however, one should not be bound to a minor good or petty wisdom lest they hinder one from doing a greater

---

157. Ibid., chap. 12.

good and attaining a greater wisdom. Thus, one should do the detached good and brighten wisdom without leaving any trace of it. Here lies the way of doing a magnanimous goodness and brightening wisdom. Self-conceit hinders one's spiritual growth; hence, concession and humility should be practiced as virtues. When there is not an iota of self in one's mind, the triple world in ten directions becomes one's own property.

The twelfth chapter, "Exemplary Practice," consists of forty-seven sections. Recorded in this chapter are the magnitude of Sot'aesan's omnibenevolence, his magnanimous handling of daily affairs, and his application of truth in actual life. One of his disciples was so ill tempered that the congregation tried to expel him from the order, but Sot'aesan advised that the essence of Buddha-dharma is to edify deluded beings by myriad skillful means and, therefore, they should do their best to help edify him. The congregation was trying to expel another of his disciples who committed an offense, but Sot'aesan showed the way of penitence by saying that he would never give him up even though he leave the order. To keep watch over the order the Japanese government placed a police detective in the headquarters; Sot'aesan took care of him with the same love he showed to his disciples. The detective was struck with admiration for Sot'aesan, making a considerable contribution to the viability of the order during the Japanese oppression. Sot'aesan directed the congregation by doing such exemplary deeds as weeding the courtyard himself and putting tools back in the right place. He warned against luxury. One should not dispute with others in matters of minor importance; one should make a sharp distinction between public and private matters for fear of infringing on any matter of public concern. Religion and morality are meant to cure spiritual illness, not physical illness.

The thirteenth chapter, "On the Order," consists of forty-two sections. Explained in this chapter are the ways of unity, harmony, maintenance, and development of the order; the relationship between seniors and juniors in the order; that between public and private matters; and the duties of the priest. For the development of the order, there should be genuine camaraderie between mentor and disciple and between fellow devotees. To keep eternally good affinity in the dharma, one should not force another to do anything the latter does not want, nor should one attempt to defeat others. One should correct oneself by reflecting rightness and wrongness of someone else's deed without mentioning them. Propriety and respect should be maintained as camaraderie deepens among fellow devotees: juniors should hold seniors in reverence and gratitude; seniors should welcome juniors with gratitude. Private affairs should be sharply separated from public affairs (duty); one should not be negligent of public affairs no matter how trifling. The devotee should always know of his or her duty to be altruistic;

he or she should not surrender to any adverse condition or owe anything to the public. The devotee should not hesitate to do any lowly menial work, nor should he or she be attached to anyone's private household.

The fourteenth chapter, "On Prospects," consists of thirty sections. Recorded in this chapter are Sot'aesan's views on the future of the order and the world, the changing phenomena of the world in the future, and other prophesies. After the first generation there will be increasing numbers of people who hunger after this teaching; several decades after that, over a period of four to five hundred years, this teaching will be demanded everywhere in Korea and all over the world. In the future only truthful religions will survive; teachings of trickery and injustice will find no place to stand. Just as material conveniences and technologies are adopted after they are proven to be useful, all the religious teachings will spread widely after they prove to be useful. Thus, the religious doctrine in the future should be useful to daily living. All sound religions will be harmonious and adaptable to one another by understanding the unitary source of all the doctrines. In a world of material abundance, people will realize the importance of spiritual culture, exerting themselves to moral cultivation.

The last chapter, "On Entrusting," consists of nineteen sections. Recorded in this chapter are Sot'aesan's special and earnest teachings to his disciples given near his death. While supervising the compilation of the *Pulgyo chŏngjŏn*, Sot'aesan said that the essentials of his lifetime ambition, principles, and morals were expressed in that one volume, which his disciples should learn, practice, and be enlightened to, so that the teachings could be transmitted through tens of thousands of generations. The verse of dharma transmission[158] should be given to the general public rather than to a single disciple. He told his disciples to have firm faith and devotion so that they could learn and practice the heart of the doctrine summarized in the doctrinal chart in the *Pulgyo chŏngjŏn*. In the order one should reach the true realm of practice by putting into practice what one knows; one should have one's mind's eye open and see Dharmakāya Buddha clearly. Sot'aesan compared the cycle of birth and death to the circulation of the seasons and the repetition of day and night. He taught by this analogy that one should attain the spiritual power to keep oneself free from being deluded during the path of birth and death and to be emancipated from the cycle of birth and death.

---

158. Ibid., pt. 2, chap. 1, sec. 6.

# Translation

*The Canon*

*As material power is unfolding,*
*Let us unfold our spiritual power accordingly.*

*Everywhere is the Buddha-image;*
*Do everything as making an offering to Buddha.*

*Timeless Zen and placeless Zen.*

*Maintain one mind in motion and at rest.*
*Perfect both soul and flesh.*

*Buddha-dharma is living itself;*
*Living is Buddha-dharma itself.*

## Doctrinal Chart

**Correct enlightenment and right practice**

The way of practice, based on true emptiness cum marvelous existence

*Threefold practice*

Mindful karmic action (*śīla*—follow the Nature)
Spiritual cultivation (*samādhi*—nourish nature)
Inquiry into facts and principles (*prajñā*—see into the Nature)

*Eight articles*

*To keep*: faith, zeal, doubt, sincerity
*To forsake*: disbelief, greed, laziness, delusion

*How to practice Zen in motion and at rest*

When the six sense organs are free from work, eliminate worldly thoughts and cultivate One Mind; when the six sense organs are at work, eliminate injustice and cultivate justice

Timeless Zen, placeless Zen

**Practical application of Buddha-dharma**

*Truth of Irwŏnsang*

*Irwŏn* is Dharmakāya Buddha; it is the noumenal nature of all things in the universe, the mind-seal of all buddhas and sages, the Buddha-nature of all sentient beings.

*The Verse on Irwŏnsang*

Being turns into Nonbeing and Nonbeing into Being, Turning and turning;
Then, ultimately, Being and Nonbeing are both void; yet the void is also complete.

**Awareness and requital of beneficence**

The way of faith, based on cause-effect response

*Fourfold beneficence*

Beneficence of heaven and earth
Beneficence of parents
Beneficence of brethren
Beneficence of laws

*Essential principles of beneficence requital*

The way of harboring no false idea after rendering favors
The way of protecting the helpless
The way of mutual benefit
The way of doing justice and eradicating injustice

Requital of beneficence as making an offering to Buddha

Everywhere is Buddha image; do all things as an offering to Buddha.

**Selfless service for the public**

# Part One

## *General Introduction*

### Chapter One: The Founding Motive

As a result of scientific advancement, the ability of the human spirit to make use of material things has gradually weakened while the power of the material things that human beings make use of has daily grown stronger, conquering the weakened spirit of humankind and thereby bringing the latter under its rule. With human beings enslaved to material things, how can they avoid suffering in the bitter seas of misery?

The founding motive of this religious order is to lead all sentient beings suffering in the bitter seas of misery to a vast, immeasurable paradise by expanding spiritual power and thereby subjugating the material power through faith in truthful religion and training in sound morality.

### Chapter Two: An Outline of the Doctrine

The teachings of the Buddha embody supreme truth. As the truth and expediencies of his teachings are boundless, numerous Buddhist priests of high virtue have taken them as the basis of their schools and sects of Buddhism, thereby opening the gates of propagation and teaching countless people. The fundamental principles of all religions of the world originate from a unitary source. However, as different religions have been established with different systems and methods for propagation for a long time, there has been discordance among them and among different sects of a religion. This discordance is due to ignorance of the fundamental principles that underlie all religions and their sects: how could such discordance be the original intention of all buddhas and sages?

The Buddhist system in particular was mainly intended to guide the life of monks in a monastic order and was not suitable for people living in the secular world. Anyone who wished to be a true Buddhist under such a system had to ignore his or her duties and obligations to the secular life and give up his or her occupation. Under such a system, the Buddha-grace, no matter how good Buddha-dharma may be, cannot reach the numberless sentient beings of the world. How could such a system be the great and perfect Way?

Therefore, we have enshrined Dharmakāya[1] Buddha, Irwŏnsang,[2] which is the noumenal essence of all things in the universe and the mind-seal of all Buddhas and sages, as the object of religious faith and the standard of practice. We have laid down the fourfold beneficence (*ŭn*)[3] of heaven and earth, parents, brethren, and laws as the main principle of religious faith; and the threefold practice (*samhak*)[4] of spiritual cultivation, inquiry into facts and principles, and mindful choice in karmic action as the main principle of practice. We have also decided to synthesize the central doctrines of all the religions of the world for practical use so that we can have faith in a grand and perfect religion.

## Chapter Three: Four Fundamental Principles

The four fundamental principles are correct enlightenment and right practice, awareness and requital of beneficence, practical applications of Buddha-dharma, and selfless service for the public.

*Correct enlightenment and right practice* means that one should be enlightened to and model oneself on the truth of Irwŏn, namely, the mind-seal, which buddhas and patriarchs correctly transmit from one to the other so that one can act perfectly without partiality, attachment, excessiveness, or deficiency when one uses the six sense organs: eyes, ears, nose, tongue, body, and mind.[5]

*Awareness and requital of beneficence* means that one should know how one is indebted to heaven and earth, parents, brethren, and laws and feel grateful to them for their beneficence and requite their beneficence, modeling on the way one is indebted to them. Even if one has something to resent, one ought to find out how one is indebted to the beneficence and thereby be grateful rather than resentful so that one can requite the beneficence.[6]

*Practical application of Buddha-dharma* means that the follower of Buddha-dharma should not be shackled to or disabled from managing worldly affairs as in the past but be able to manage worldly affairs better by being a Buddhist. In other words, one should not become useless to the world by being a Buddhist; making a lively application of Buddha-

---

1. The essence-body of a Buddha, one of the three aspects of a Buddha, the other two being reward-body (*sambhogakāya*) and transformation-body (*nirmānakāya*), the last being the body of the historical buddhas expediently taken on to instruct beings. See below, *SS* II:2.
2. Unitary circular symbol; see below, pt. 2, chap. 1.
3. The source of benefaction to which one owes one's life. See below, pt. 2, chap. 2.
4. See ibid.
5. For the realization of this goal the tenets of Irwŏnsang and the threefold practice are formulated. See below, pt. 2, chaps. 1 and 4. See also the doctrinal chart.
6. The tenet of fourfold beneficence is expounded for this goal. See below, pt. 2, chap. 2.

dharma, one should be a valuable person to oneself, one's family, one's society, and one's country.[7]

*Selfless service for the public* means that one should forsake egoism as well as self-indulgent conduct for oneself or one's own family and do one's best to devote oneself to the grand task of delivering all sentient beings, following the way of Mahāyāna altruism.[8]

---

7. How some of Buddha-dharma can be practiced is expounded in part 3 below.

8. The tenet of four essentials (pt. 2, chap. 3) shows how this ideal can be realized.

# Part Two

## *Doctrine*

### Chapter One: Irwŏnsang (Unitary Circular Symbol)

#### Section One: The Truth of Irwŏnsang

Irwŏn[9] is the noumenal nature[10] of all beings in the universe, the original nature[11] of all buddhas and patriarchs, and the Buddha-nature[12] of all sentient beings. It is the realm where there is no differentiation of noumenon from phenomenon or being from nonbeing, the realm where there is no change of arising and ceasing or going and coming, the realm where the karmic retribution of good and evil has ceased, and the realm where the verbal, audible, and visible characteristics are utterly void.[13] In accordance with the light of [the mind-essence of] empty and calm, numinous awareness,[14] the differentiation of noumenon from

---

9. Unitary circle without circumference used to refer to Dharmakāya Buddha; Irwŏnsang, unitary circular symbol, is used as the sign of Irwŏn. See below, *SS* II:6.

10. In the doctrinal chart of the 1943 edition, Irwŏnsang is referred to as "this circular emptiness" implying the noumenal nature, which is devoid of the phenomenal characteristics; in this section of the same edition you read "the noumenal nature" rather than "original source" of all beings. What could be the original source of all beings unless it is like the anthropomorphic deity, which has no place in the metaphysics of Buddhism?

11. The Korean original has "mind-seal"; however, this translation follows the 1943 edition, where "original nature" was used.

12. In *WBK* (the 1962 edition), "original nature" is used; this translation follows *PGC* (the 1943 edition). See also *Fohsing lun* 1, *T*, 1610.31.787a: "All sentient beings are endowed with Buddha nature." Sot'aesan and Chŏngsan used "Buddha-nature" in the sense that all sentient beings are endowed with the Buddha-nature as taught in several Mahāyāna Buddhist scriptures like the Lotus Sūtra and the Nirvāṇa Sūtra. When the question whether human original nature is good or evil is not yet settled, the term "original nature" should not replace the term "Buddha-nature" when applied to sentient beings against the intention of the two original authors.

13. This proposition reflects the Mahāyāna Buddhist view of the ultimate reality and appearance—for instance the *Ta-sheng-chi-kuan-fa-men*, *T*, 1924.46.642b: "The Buddhas of all the three ages together with sentient beings, all equally have this one mind as their substance. All things, both ordinary and sagely, each have their own differences and diverse appearances, whereas this genuine mind is devoid of either diversity or appearance."

14. "Mind-essence," being the original nature of the enlightened being, is added in the translation. Chinul says, "This is your pure mind-essence of void and calm, numinous awareness." *Susim kyŏl*, *PC*, pp. 36–37; *T*, 2020.48.1007ab; Buswell, *KAZ*, p. 147.

phenomenon, and being from nonbeing appears; wherewith the distinction between good and evil karmic retribution comes into being; and the verbal, audible, and visible characteristics become clear and distinct so that the three worlds[15] in the ten directions appear like a jewel on one's own palm, and the creative wonder of true emptiness cum marvelous existence[16] freely conceals and reveals through all beings in the universe throughout incalculable aeons without beginning. This is the truth of Irwŏnsang.

### Section Two: Faith in Irwŏnsang

To have faith in Irwŏnsang[17] is to believe in Irwŏn[18] as the noumenal nature of all beings in the universe, as the original nature of all buddhas and patriarchs, as the Buddha-nature of all sentient beings, as the realm where there is no differentiation of noumenon from phenomenon or being from nonbeing, as the realm where there is no change of arising and ceasing or going and coming, as the realm where the karmic retribution of good and evil has ceased, and as the realm where the verbal, audible, and visible characteristics are utterly void; and to believe that, in accordance with the light of the empty and calm, numinous awareness, the differentiation of noumenon from phenomenon and being from nonbeing appears in the realm of no differentiations, that the difference between good and evil karmic retribution comes into being, that owing to the verbal, audible, and visible characteristics becoming clear and distinct, the three worlds in the ten directions appear like a jewel on one's own palm, and that the creative wonder of true emptiness cum marvelous existence conceals and reveals through all things in the universe throughout the incalculable aeons without beginning.

### Section Three: The Practice of Irwŏnsang

One is to establish the model of practice by having faith in the truth of Irwŏnsang. The method of practice is for one, being enlightened to the

---

15. The Buddhist three worlds are the world of sensuous desire, the world of form, and the formless world of pure spirit.

16. The true void is the mysteriously existing: truly void, or immaterial, yet transcendently existing. Ho-tse Shen-hui (670–762) in *Hsien-tsung chi* 30, *T*, 2076.51.458c, explains, "True void is the substance and marvelous existence is the function." Tung-shan liang-chieh (807–869), in "Five Ranks" uses true void as the absolute and marvelous existence as the relative-phenomenal. Dumoulin, *The Development of Chinese Zen*, p. 26.

17. See below, *SS* II:4 for explanations.

18. The 1943 edition has the "truth of Irwŏnsang" as the noumenal nature, and the 1962 edition has "the truth of Irwŏnsang" as the original source. Since the original wording comes from Master Chŏngsan, I had to consult Master Taesan (1914–), head dharma master of the Order of Wŏn Buddhism, who advised me to use "Irwŏn" instead of "the truth of Irwŏnsang" to avoid incoherence between sections 1 and 2.

truth of Irwŏnsang, to know one's own mind, which is as perfect, complete, utterly fair, and unselfish as Irwŏn, namely, prajñā-wisdom; to foster one's own mind, which is as perfect, complete, utterly fair, and unselfish as Irwŏn, namely prajñā-wisdom; and to use one's own mind, which is as perfect, complete, utterly fair, and unselfish as Irwŏn, namely, prajñā-wisdom. Herein lies the practice of Irwŏn.[19]

### Section Four: The Vow to Irwŏnsang

Irwŏn is the ineffable realm of samādhi, the way of birth and death, which transcends being and nonbeing; the original source of heaven and earth, parents, brethren, and laws; the original nature of all buddhas, patriarchs, ordinary human beings, and all sentient beings. Irwŏn can form permanence and impermanence. Viewed as permanent, it, being ever thus and spontaneous, has unfolded itself into an immeasurable world. Viewed as impermanent, it has unfolded itself into an immeasurable world as the formation, endurance, decay, and emptiness of the universe; as the birth, aging, illness, and death of all things; and as the transformation of the four forms of birth[20] through the six realms

---

19. This section in *PGC* (the 1943 edition) has undergone a significant alteration in the corresponding section in *WBK* (the 1962 edition) thereby cutting the main artery of Buddhist faith and practice. Thus, the translation of the full text of the section in *PGC* replaces that of the section in *WBK* which is as follows: "Believing in and modeling oneself on the truth of Irwŏnsang, one is to know one's own mind which is as perfect and complete, and most fair and impartial as Irwŏnsang; to nourish one's own mind which is as perfect and complete, and most fair and impartial as Irwŏnsang; and to use one's own mind which is as perfect and complete, and most fair and impartial as Irwŏnsang. In this lies the practice of Irwŏnsang."

See "Practice of Irwŏnsang" in the Introduction for an analysis of this section. Chinul wrote that cultivation prior to awakening is not true but corrupt cultivation; Hyu-jŏng (1520–1604) wrote that the cultivation of the way with deluded mind only helps defilements (*Sŏn'ga kwigam* [Paragon of Zen tradition], para. no. 28). Thus, the all-important prerequisite of true practice, "awakening," has been deleted in the new *Canon*. Secondly, the all-important term "*panyaji*," prajñā-wisdom has been deleted; thirdly, one is advised to model one's mind on Irwŏnsang, the sign of Irwŏn. As Sot'aesan has warned, one should not take the finger for the moon (*SS* II:6).

It is seemingly contradictory to title this section "The Practice of Irwŏnsang" and end it with "herein lies the practice of Irwŏn." However, the unsurpassed skillful means of Chŏngsan, the author of this chapter, lies in the idea that for the unenlightened, Irwŏnsang should be used as a sign of Irwŏn because they cannot see the Dharmakāya of their own mind; in this way Chŏngsan lets them know that Irwŏnsang is the sign of the true Irwŏn and hence one should be enlightened to it before one can make any progress in the right practice. Thus, before the enlightenment one should take Irwŏnsang as a pointer to Irwŏn, and upon enlightenment, know, foster, and use one's enlightened mind, wisdom, as perfect as Dharmakāya, Irwŏn, in which lies the practice of Irwŏn after enlightenment.

20. Viviparous, as with Mammalia; oviparous, as with birds; moisture- or water-born, as with worms and fishes; metamorphic, as with moths from chrysalis, or with devas, or in hells, or the first beings in a newly evolved world.

of existence,[21] letting them be promoted or demoted with favors arising from harm or harm arising from favors in accordance with the functions of their minds and bodies. To be promoted and favored rather than demoted or harmed, we, deluded beings, vow that we shall sincerely discipline ourselves to keep our mind and body perfectly, to know facts and principles perfectly, and to use our mind and body perfectly by modeling ourselves on this Dharmakāya Buddha, Irwŏnsang, until we are endowed with the great power of Irwŏn and unified with the nou-menal nature of Irwŏn.

### Section Five: The Dharma Words of Irwŏnsang

If one is enlightened to the truth of this *wŏnsang* (circular symbol) one will know that the triple world in ten directions is one's own property; that all things in the universe are unitary in their noumenal nature despite their phenomenal differences; that Irwŏn is the original nature of all buddhas, patriarchs, ordinary human beings, and sentient beings; that the principle of birth, aging, illness, and death is analogous to the rotation of spring, summer, autumn, and winter; that the causal law of karmic retribution is analogous to the mutual overcoming of yin and yang[22]; and that it is perfect and complete, and utterly fair and unselfish.

This *wŏnsang* is to be used when one uses one's eyes; it is perfect and complete, and utterly fair and unselfish.

This *wŏnsang* is to be used when one uses one's ears; it is perfect and complete, and utterly fair and unselfish.

This *wŏnsang* is to be used when one uses one's nose; it is perfect and complete, and utterly fair and unselfish.

This *wŏnsang* is to be used when one uses one's mouth; it is perfect and complete, and utterly fair and unselfish.

This *wŏnsang* is to be used when one uses one's body; it is perfect and complete, and utterly fair and unselfish.

This *wŏnsang* is to be used when one uses one's mind; it is perfect and complete, and utterly fair and unselfish.

### Section Six: The Verse on Irwŏnsang

Being turns into nonbeing and nonbeing into being,
Turning and turning,

---

21. Hells, hungry ghosts, animals, malevolent nature spirits, human existence, and deva existence.
22. The cosmic dual (positive and negative; male and female) force. See below, SS V:2 for Sot'aesan's view on yin and yang.

Then, ultimately, being and nonbeing are both void,
Yet the void is complete.[23]

## Chapter Two: Fourfold Beneficence (*Saŭn*)

### Section One: The Beneficence of Heaven and Earth (*Ch'ŏnjiŭn*)

*I.    The Principle of Indebtedness to Heaven and Earth*

The easiest way to understand how one is indebted to heaven and earth is to think whether one can preserve one's existence and live without heaven and earth. Then, even an imbecile will admit that one cannot live without heaven and earth. What could be a greater beneficence than that without which one cannot exist?

Heaven and earth have their ways and virtues. The automatic movement of the heavenly bodies is in accordance with the way of heaven and earth; what results from following the way is the virtue of heaven and earth. The way of heaven and earth is exceedingly bright; exceedingly sincere; exceedingly fair, reasonable, and natural; vast and limitless; eternal and immortal; with no good or evil fortune, and harboring no idea of return upon bestowing favors. All beings maintain their lives and preserve their bodies owing to the great virtues that result from heaven and earth following their ways.

*II.    The Details of Indebtedness to Heaven and Earth*

1.   It is owing to air in the sky that one can breathe.
2.   It is owing to the ground of the earth that one can support one's body to live.
3.   It is owing to the brightness of the sun and the moon that one can discern and know the things in nature.
4.   It is owing to the favor of winds, clouds, rain, and dew that myriad things can grow and one can live off their products.
5.   It is owing to the principle of no birth and no death of heaven and earth that one can attain eternal life following the way of no birth and no death.

*III.    The Principle of Requiting the Beneficence of Heaven and Earth*

The proper way for one to recompense heaven and earth for their beneficence lies in modeling oneself on and practicing the way of heaven and earth.[24]

---

23. See below, *SS* VII:31 for comments on this verse.
24. See *SS* VI:24.

IV.  *The Details of Requiting the Beneficence of Heaven and Earth*

1.  Modeling oneself after the exceeding brightness of the sun and the moon, one ought to inquire into and attain thorough knowledge of facts and principles.[25]
2.  Modeling oneself on the exceeding sincerity of heaven and earth, one ought to be consistent in carrying out whatever one has to do until one attains the goal.[26]
3.  Modeling oneself on the extreme fairness of heaven and earth, one ought to keep the Mean in handling all affairs without being attached to remoteness, closeness, intimacy, or estrangement; or to such feelings as pleasure, anger, sorrow, and joy.
4.  Modeling oneself on the reasonableness and naturalness of heaven and earth, one ought to take what is reasonable and forsake what is unreasonable by separating reasonableness from unreasonableness.
5.  Modeling oneself on heaven and earth's being vast, great, and limitless, one ought to do away with partiality and attachment.
6.  Modeling oneself on the eternity and immortality of heaven and earth, one ought to emancipate oneself from the transformation of all things and birth, aging, illness, and death.
7.  Modeling oneself on heaven and earth's having neither good nor evil fortunes, one ought to be detached from good or evil fortunes, finding good fortune in ill fortune and ill fortune in good fortune.
8.  Modeling oneself on heaven and earth's harboring no idea of bestowing favors, one ought to cultivate the way of no false idea in motion and at rest; one ought to keep one's mind free from false thoughts and ideas after rendering spiritual, physical, or material favors; and one ought not to hate, or make a foe out of, anyone who is indebted but, perchance, ungrateful.[27]

V.  *The Ingratitude to Heaven and Earth*

If one does not know indebtedness to, requital of beneficence of, and ingratitude to heaven and earth, or if one does not practice the details of requiting the beneficence even if one knows them, then one is ungrateful to heaven and earth.

---

25. See below, chap. 4, sec. 2, I, for definitions of "facts" and "principles" or refer to the Glossary for these terms.

26. This moral maxim reflects the Confucian moral ideal: "Sincerity is the way of Heaven and the attainment of sincerity is the way of man." See *Chung-yung*, chap. 18; Legge, *Confucius*, p. 413.

27. Cf. Hakeda, *The Awakening of Faith*, p. 93.

*VI.    The Effect of Requiting the Beneficence of Heaven and Earth*
If one practices the details of requiting the beneficence of heaven and earth, one's virtue will be unified with that of heaven and earth so that one will be none other than heaven and earth. Although the sky is empty and the earth silent without directly bestowing any blessings or reward of virtue, one will attain heavenly power, heavenly life, and the brightness of the sun and the moon so that one will be venerated by people, heavenly beings, and the world as if one were heaven and earth.[28]

*VII.    The Consequence of Ingratitude to Heaven and Earth*
If one is ungrateful to heaven and earth, one will incur heavenly punishment. This can be explained plainly. Since one does not model oneself on the way of heaven, one will, of necessity, be ignorant of facts and principles, insincere in whatever one does, either excessive or deficient in whatever one does, irrational in handling various affairs, and partial and biased in many situations. One will also be ignorant of the transformation of all things in the universe; human birth, aging, illness, and death; good or ill fortune and calamity or blessings. One will further harbor the idea of bestowing favor on others, being conceited covertly and boasting overtly. How could there be no sin and retribution for such a person? Although heaven and earth are empty and calm, unexpected suffering or the suffering one has caused is the punishment as a consequence of ingratitude to heaven and earth.

**Section Two: The Beneficence of Parents (*Pumoŭn*)**

*I.    The Principle of Indebtedness to Parents*
The easiest way to understand how one is indebted to one's parents is to consider whether one could have brought oneself into this world and whether, even if one could, one could have grown up all by oneself. Anyone would admit that one could not. If one could not have brought oneself into this world or grown up without one's parents, what could be a greater beneficence than that of parents?

Although the birth and death of a human being is due to the creative transformation of natural law, one is indebted to one's parents for the great beneficence of giving birth, rearing at a time of helplessness, and teaching the general moral principles of humanity.

---

28. This reflects the *Book of Changes*, commentary on hexagram no. 1, *ch'ien* (Heaven). See Legge, *Yi King*, p. 417: "The great man is he who is in harmony, in his attributes, with heaven and earth; in his brightness, with the sun and moon; in his orderly procedure, with the four seasons; and in his relation to what is fortunate and what is calamitous, in harmony with the spirit-like operations (of Providence)."

*II.   The Details of Indebtedness to Parents*
1. It is owing to one's own parents that one receives one's body, which is the fundamental source of myriad facts and principles.
2. One's parents raise and protect one with compassion, without minding any kind of trouble, until one can be independent.
3. One's parents teach one the duties and obligations of humanity and then guide one into human society.

*III.   The Principle of Requiting the Beneficence of Parents*
Realizing that one was indebted to one's parents when one was not self-reliant, one ought to provide protection to the helpless as best as one can.

*IV.   The Details of Requiting the Beneficence of Parents*
1. One ought to follow the essential ways of practice, namely, threefold practice and eight articles,[29] and the essential ways of humanity, namely, fourfold beneficence and four essentials.[30]
2. When one's parents become helpless, one ought to serve them faithfully to ensure their mental and physical comfort.
3. While one's parents are alive or after they have passed away, one ought to protect even the helpless parents of others to the best of one's ability as if they were one's own parents.
4. After one's parents have passed away, one ought to enshrine their biographical chronicles and their portraits to commemorate them for a long time.

*V.   The Ingratitude to Parents*
If one does not know indebtedness to, requital of beneficence of, and ingratitude to one's own parents, or if one does not practice the details of requiting the beneficence even if one knows them, then one is ungrateful to one's own parents.

*VI.   The Effect of Requiting the Beneficence of Parents*
If one requites the beneficence of one's own parents, the world will naturally respond with benefits for oneself and will regard one nobly though one is grateful only to one's own parents. As it is a necessary principle for offspring to model on their parents, the filial patterns of one's own children will surely reflect the way one requites the beneficence of one's own parents. As an effect of protecting the helpless, one will be helped by people if and when one becomes helpless throughout numberless reincarnations.

---

29. See below, pt. 2, chaps. 4 and 5.
30. See below, pt. 2, chaps. 2 and 3.

*VII.   The Consequence of Ingratitude to Parents*
If one is ungrateful to one's own parents, one will be hated and rejected by the world even though one is ungrateful only to one's own parents. One's own offspring will surely pattern themselves on what one does, bringing calamities upon oneself. One will also be neglected by the public when one becomes helpless throughout numberless reincarnations.

### Section Three: The Beneficence of Brethren (*Tongp'oŭn*)

*I.   The Principle of Indebtedness to Brethren*
The easiest way to know how one is indebted to brethren[31] is to consider whether one could live where there are no other human beings, birds, beasts, grass, or trees. Anyone would admit that one cannot live without them. What could be a greater beneficence than that of brethren if one cannot live without depending on their help and on things they provide?

In general, there are four classes of occupation: scholar-official, farmer, artisan, and merchant. People work according to their occupations, helping and being indebted to one another on the basis of mutual benefit when they exchange their products with one another.

*II.   The Details of Indebtedness to Brethren*
1. Scholars educate and direct us after learning and doing research; civil servants and government officials manage administrative business for us.
2. Farmers provide us with materials for clothing and food by planting and raising farm products.
3. Artisans provide us with shelter and commodities by manufacturing various goods.
4. Merchants provide us with conveniences for living by exchanging myriad goods.
5. Birds and beasts, and grass and trees, too, are of help to us.

*III.   The Principle of Requiting the Beneficence of Brethren*
Since one is indebted to brethren through the principle of mutual benefit, one ought, either as a scholar, farmer, artisan, or merchant, to honor the principle of mutual benefit, to requite the beneficence; this one does when one exchanges myriad types of learning and goods with others, modeling oneself on the principle.

---

31. The term "*tongp'o*" in this work means fellow human beings or fellow creatures including animals, and even plants; hence the term "brethren" should be understood in this inclusive sense.

*IV.   The Details of Requiting the Beneficence of Brethren*
1. A scholar-official ought to follow the principle of fairness for mutual benefit while educating others with myriad types of learning and managing administrative affairs.
2. A farmer ought to follow the principle of fairness for mutual benefit while providing materials for clothing and food.
3. An artisan ought to follow the principle of fairness for mutual benefit while providing shelter and commodities.
4. A merchant ought to follow the principle of fairness for mutual benefit while exchanging myriad goods.
5. One ought not to destroy grass or trees or take the life of birds or beasts without justifiable reason.

*V.   Ingratitude to Brethren*
If one does not know indebtedness to, requital of beneficence of, and ingratitude to brethren and if one does not practice the details of requiting the beneficence even if one knows them, then one is ungrateful to brethren.

*VI.   The Effect of Requiting the Beneficence of Brethren*
If we are grateful to brethren, the following will be the effect. All the brethren influenced by mutual benefit will love and rejoice in one another. One will be protected and received with honor by brethren; individuals will love one another. There will be friendship between families, mutual understanding between societies, and peace between nations so that, eventually, an unimaginable utopia will be realized.

*VII.   The Consequence of Ingratitude to Brethren*
If people are ungrateful to their brethren, all brethren will hate and dislike one another, becoming enemies. There will be quarrels among individuals, hatred between families, antagonism between societies, and no peace between nations so that the world will be at war.

    If all the people in the world are not grateful to their brethren and if all brethren fall into the seas of misery as a result of mischievous actions of ingratitude, then the savior sage, with compassion and expedient means, is to deliver the sentient beings of ingratitude by means of morality, political power, or the sword.[32]

### Section Four: The Beneficence of Laws (*Pŏmnyurŭn*)

*I.   The Principle of Indebtedness to Laws*
The easiest way to understand indebtedness to laws is to consider whether one could live in peace and order without the principle of

---

32. This paragraph in the *Kyojŏn* is in the previous section (VI), which is a mistake in the original. It has been moved to the right place in this translation.

moral cultivation in individuals, the principle of regulating a family, the laws to put a society in order, the laws to rule over a country, and the laws to maintain peace in the world. One will admit that one could not. If one cannot live without them, what could be a greater beneficence?[33]

Generally, by laws is meant the principle of fairness for the sake of morality and justice, which can help an individual if reflected on one, a family if reflected on it, a society if reflected on it, a nation if reflected on it, or the world if reflected on it.

*II.    The Details of Indebtedness to Laws*
  1. Sages come to the world to meet the needs of the times and to show with religious and moral teachings the right path for one to follow.
  2. The facilities and institutions of scholars, farmers, artisans, and merchants are established whereby one is guided and encouraged for the sake of preserving one's life and the extension of knowledge.
  3. Laws preserve the public peace and order by distinguishing right from wrong, gain from loss; and by punishing the unjust and protecting the just so that one can live in peace.

*III.    The Principle of Requiting the Beneficence of Laws*
If one is indebted to the law's prohibition, then one ought to comply with the prohibition; if one is indebted to the law's permission and encouragement, then one ought to comply with the permission and encouragement.

*IV.    The Details of Requiting the Beneficence of Laws*
  1. As an individual, one ought to learn and practice the principle of moral cultivation.
  2. As a member of the family, one ought to learn and practice the principle of regulating the family.
  3. In a society, one ought to learn and practice the principle of social regulations.
  4. In a country, one ought to learn and practice the laws governing the country.
  5. In the world, one ought to learn and follow the laws for realizing peace in the world.[34]

---

33. The term "*pŏmnyul*" (law) includes civil and penal laws as well as religious and moral teachings.
34. This resembles the educational and political programs of Confucianism summarized in the *Ta-hsüeh* (The Great Learning), sec. 5: "Their hearts being rectified, their persons were cultivated. Their persons being cultivated, their families were regulated. Their families being regulated, their States were rightly governed. Their States being rightly governed, the whole kingdom was made tranquil and happy" ( Legge, *Confucius*, p. 359).

*V.   Ingratitude to Laws*

If one does not know indebtedness to, requital of beneficence of, and ingratitude to laws and if one does not practice the Details of Requiting the Beneficence even if one knows them, then one is ungrateful to laws.

*VI.   The Effect of Requiting the Beneficence of Laws*

If one practices the details of requiting the beneficence of laws, then one will be protected by laws; one will feel restrictions diminish gradually and freedom increase; one's personality will improve; and the world will be in good order. Facilities and institutions for scholars, farmers, artisans, and merchants will be improved to a great extent for helping to build a comfortable world. In this way, one will be requiting the beneficence of legislative and administrative laws, too.

*VII.   The Consequence of Ingratitude to Laws*

If one is ungrateful to laws, then the following will be the consequence: one will not be forgiven by the laws; one will lose freedom and be restricted by laws; one's personality will be depraved; and the world will be disordered and turned into a shambles.

## Chapter Three: The Four Essentials

### Section One: Cultivation of Self-reliance

*I.   The Principle*

Unless one is a helpless infant, suffers from the infirmities of old age, or lies on a sickbed, one ought to cultivate self-reliance as a moral discipline so that one can fulfill the duties and obligations that one cannot avoid as a human being. Furthermore, one ought to render protection to those who are helpless.

*II.   Details of Reliance on Others in the Past*
  1. One lived in idleness depending on parents, sibling, spouse, children, or other relatives if their means of living was higher than one's own. If the kindred did not grant such demands, then one lived in the same house with them. If one got into debt and could not repay it, then one's whole family, trying to repay it, was ruined.
  2. A woman depended on her parents when young, on her husband after marriage, and on her children when old. As a result of unequal rights, she did not receive an education like a man. She did not have rights in society, nor did she have the right to inherit property. She could not avoid restrictions on everything she did with her own mind and body.

*III.   What the Self-reliant Should Do for Those Relying on Others*
  1. One should not grant the request of dependence by anyone who can be self-reliant.
  2. At the time of inheritance, a parent should distribute the property equally among the first son, second son, and daughters except those who are unable to keep it.
  3. After marriage, each spouse should be economically independent; the primary concern in married life should not be confined to love but extended to one's duties and obligations.
  4. All other matters should be managed in accordance with circumstances and laws; all should be treated duly in accordance with what they do, regardless of their sex.

*IV.   The Details of the Cultivation of Self-reliance*
  1. One should not depend on someone else for a living as in the past unless one cannot help it because of infancy, senility, or illness.
  2. Women should be educated sufficiently to work in society like men.
  3. Both husband and wife should engage diligently in their occupations for a comfortable life; they should share equally their duties and obligations to the family and to the nation.
  4. The second son ought to fulfill his filial duty to his parents during their lifetime and after their deaths as the first son did in the past.

**Section Two: The Wise One as the Standard**

*I.   The Principle*
It is natural in principle that the wise teach the foolish and that the foolish learn from the wise. If one wishes to learn in any circumstance, therefore, one should attain one's goal without being hindered by an unreasonable system of discrimination.

*II.   The Details of the Unreasonable System of Discrimination in the Past*
  1. There was discrimination between nobles and commoners.
  2. There was discrimination between a legitimate child and an illegitimate one.
  3. There was discrimination between the aged and the young.
  4. There was discrimination between man and woman.
  5. There was discrimination between races.

*III.   The Details of Regarding the Wise One as the Standard*
  1. Anyone whose discipline in following the original nature[35] and moral conduct is superior to one's own should be regarded as one's own teacher.

---

35. See below, pt. 3, chap. 12, for the meaning of "following the original nature."

2. Anyone who manages administrative business more efficiently than oneself should be regarded as one's own teacher.
3. Anyone whose knowledge of life is above one's own should be regarded as one's own teacher.
4. Anyone whose learning and particular skills are above one's own should be regarded as one's own teacher.
5. Anyone whose common knowledge is above one's own should be regarded as one's own teacher.

Any of the persons mentioned above need not always be regarded with such distinctions; such a person should be regarded as one's own teacher only when one seeks to learn.

### Section Three: The Education of the Children of Others

*I.   The Reason for Educating the Children of Others*
If educational institutions are limited or the spirit of education is confined by selfish motives, world civilization will be delayed. Hence, the educational spirit should transcend the boundary of self-interest and the educational institutions should be expanded for the general education of all of the younger generation. Only then will world civilization be advanced so that all brethren will be able to live together in a paradise.

*II.   The Defects of Education in the Past*
1. Governments and societies did not encourage education.
2. The educational system was restricted to upper-class males.
3. Few educated people returned the benefit of their education to the public.
4. Because there was no free press and few other methods of communication, there was little exchange of opinions on education.
5. As educational spirit was confined by self-interest, the rich, if they had no children, tried, sometimes in vain, to have them, while the poor, though they were eager to educate their children, were unable to do so for lack of funds.

*III.   What Should be Done for the Education of the Children of Others*
1. As we have entered an era when the defects of education are removed, we ought to educate the children of others as if they were our own children whether or not we have our own children. For the realization of this ideal, we must support educational institutions as far as we can and educate as many children as we can as if they were our own children.
2. The state and society should establish many educational institutions and vigorously carry out the educational plan.
3. Those who carry out the ideal of educating the children of others—whether in a religious order, a society, a state, or the world—should be recognized and rewarded for their merit.

**Section Four: Veneration for Those Dedicated to the Public**

*I.   The Purport*

If the world venerates those who dedicate themselves to the world, there will be many who will dedicate themselves to the world. If a nation venerates those who dedicate themselves to the nation, there will be many who will dedicate themselves to the nation. If a religious order or a society venerates those who dedicate themselves to the religious order or the society, there will be many who will dedicate themselves to the religious order or the society. Hence, we must venerate those who dedicate themselves in various ways to the world, the nation, a religious order, or a society. In accordance with a spirit of dedication to the public, each of us ought to render service to the public appropriately.

*II.   The Deficiency in Work for the Public in the Past*

1.  There was deficiency in the professional education for the scholarly, agricultural, industrial, and mercantile classes, which provide the main resources for living and the foundation of public well-being.
2.  There were few institutions and facilities for the scholarly, agricultural, industrial, and mercantile classes.
3.  Religious doctrines and systems were not suited for the general public.
4.  The government and society rarely commended those who dedicated themselves to the public well-being.
5.  Education in general was not self-sufficient; it was dependent on outside forces.
6.  Self-interest at the expense of others' well-being and partiality in close, distant, intimate, or estranged relationships was extreme.
7.  General learning and common knowledge were deficient.
8.  Few knew the difference between public veneration for those who dedicated themselves to the public and family affection for those who dedicated themselves only to their own families.

*III.   The Details of Veneration for Those Dedicated to the Public*

1.  Living in an era when deficiencies in work for the public are being removed, we ought to distinguish between devotion to family affairs and dedication to the public and prefer the latter to the former, other things being equal.
2.  Those who have dedicated themselves to the public well-being ought to be supported when old according to the degree of their merits; after their death, the public ought to take responsibility for an honorable funeral; their pictures and biographical records ought to be kept and commemorated for a long time.

# Chapter Four: The Threefold Practice (*Samhak*)

## Section One: Spiritual Cultivation (*Chŏngsin Suyang*)

*I.  The Purport*

By "spirit" (*chŏngsin*) is meant the mental state that, being clear and calm, is devoid of mental differentiation or dwelling on anything. By "cultivation" (*suyang*) is meant the nourishment of a clear and calm spirit by the removal of internal differentiation or dwelling on anything, and by keeping the mind from external distraction.

*II.  The Purpose*

Sentient creatures have an innate knowledge of, and a desire to do, certain things. Human beings, the lords of all creatures, by seeing, hearing, and learning, know and desire many more things than other animals. If one is blinded by the desire to obtain what one knows and do what one wishes to do, one has no time to think about the sense of shame or the rules of justice but instead spends time trying to satisfy one's greed by means of power, skill, or the sword. As a consequence, one ends up ruining one's family and disgracing oneself. Suffering from agony and delusion or from vexation and anxiety, one ends up feeling sick of life, even falling into despair, having a nervous breakdown, becoming mentally deranged, or committing suicide in extreme cases. Thus, the purpose of Spiritual Cultivation is to attain a sound spirit and thereby to nourish the power of spiritual autonomy by removing the greed that spreads through a thousand branches and ten thousand leaves.

*III.  The Result*

If one continues training oneself in Spiritual Cultivation for a long time, one's spirit becomes as impregnable as iron and rock, giving rise to spiritual autonomy under myriad conditions and eventually endowing oneself with the power of cultivation.

## Section Two: Inquiry into Facts and Principles (*Sari yŏn'gu*)

*I.  The Purport*

By "facts" (*sa*) is meant rightness and wrongness, gain and loss in human affairs. By "principles" (*ri*) is meant the absolute and the phenomenal and the being and nonbeing of all things in the universe. The absolute is the noumenon of all beings in the universe; the phenomenal is the phenomenal world diversely differentiated in the universe. Being and nonbeing are (1) the cycle of four seasons of heaven and earth, namely, spring, summer, autumn, and winter; (2) the atmospheric phenomena of winds, clouds, rain, dew, frost, and snow; (3) the birth, aging, illness, and death of all things; and (4) the transformation of

rising and falling, of prosperity and decline. By "inquiry" (*yŏn'gu*) is meant study and investigations of facts and principles.

## II.   *The Purpose*

The most basic principles to which all things in the universe are amenable are those of the absolute and the phenomenal, being and nonbeing; the fundamental laws that govern human affairs are rightness and wrongness, gain and loss. As the world is vast, its principles are innumerable; as there are so many people, the variety of human affairs is limitless. However, suffering and happiness which fall upon oneself accidentally or as the fruit of one's deeds are the effect of what one causes by the operation of one's six sense organs.[36] If one acts as one pleases without knowledge of rightness or wrongness and gain or loss in human affairs, whatever one does every moment by the operation of one's six sense organs will lead to an offense and suffering, creating the immense sea of misery. If one lives without knowing the principles of the absolute and the phenomenal and being and nonbeing, the following will be the consequence: one will not know the cause of the unexpected suffering and happiness falling on oneself; one's thought being hurried and narrowminded, one will not know the principle of birth, aging, illness, and death, and the causal law of karmic retribution; and, unable to distinguish truth from falsity, one will fall into falsity and rely on false hope, eventually facing the ruin of one's family and disgracing one's own person. Thus, the purpose of inquiring into and investigating in advance the unfathomable principles of the universe and of complicated human affairs lies in attaining the ability to clearly analyze and pass a prompt judgment on practical daily affairs.

## III.   *The Effect*

If one continues training oneself in inquiry into facts and principles (*sari yŏn'gu*) for a long time, one will develop the power of wisdom to analyze and judge without obstruction on myriad facts and principles so that one will eventually attain the power of inquiry.

### Section Three: Mindful Choice in Karmic Action (*Chagŏp Ch'wisa*)

## I.   *The Purport*

By "karmic action" (*chagŏp*) is meant the operation of the six sense organs: eyes, ears, nose, tongue, body, and volition.[37] By "mindful choice" (*ch'wisa*) is meant choosing what is just and forsaking what is unjust.

---

36. Or six roots, viz., eye, ear, nose, tongue, body, and mind.
37. Choose (the right) and forsake (the wrong) when you create karma by body, mouth, and mind. The term "*chagŏp*" has two Chinese characters meaning "production" and "karma"; thus it should be translated as "production of karma," which does not simply mean producing action. Sot'aesan has used the term in question in the sense of "karma production" in this book. See below, pt. 3, chap. 8; *SS* V:26, 27, 29, 31.

*II.    The Purpose*

Even if one has attained the power of cultivation as the result of spiritual cultivation and the power of inquiry as the result of inquiry into facts and principles, the cultivation and inquiry will be in vain with no practical effect if these are not put into practice when one deals with actual matters of daily life, like a healthy fruit tree that bears no fruit.

In general, we human beings cannot always do good even though we know it is preferable and cannot always sever evil even though we know we should, so that we discard a tranquil paradise and enter a perilous sea of misery. What is the cause of this? It is this: either we do not do good because we do not know right from wrong in adverse conditions; or we do not do good because, even if we know right from wrong, we cannot control our burning greed or we are pulled by the force of habit, which is as unyielding as iron and rock. Thus, the purpose of mindful choice in karmic action lies in creating a paradise and avoiding the detestable sea of misery by training ourselves to do justice and forsake injustice without fail.

*III.    The Effect*

If one continues training oneself in mindful choice in karmic action for a long time, one will attain the power of practice to do courageously what is just and to forsake courageously what is unjust while dealing with all sorts of affairs, eventually attaining the power of mindful choice.

### Chapter Five: The Eight Articles Necessary for Carrying Out the Threefold Practice

#### Section One: Four Articles to Keep

*I.    Faith*

By "faith" is meant a firm belief, which is the motivating power for making up one's mind when one attempts to accomplish anything.

*II.    Zeal*

By "zeal" is meant a disposition of valiant progress, which is the motive power for encouragement and acceleration when one attempts to accomplish anything.

*III.    Doubt*[38]

By "doubt" is meant a sense of searching inquiry into what one does not know concerning facts and principles, which is the motive power

---

38. "Doubt," a Zen technical term, does not mean skeptical perplexity but a spirit of inquiry into the full significance of what one has not yet experienced.

for understanding what one does not yet know when one attempts to accomplish anything.

*IV.  Sincerity*

By "sincerity" is meant an unremitting state of mind, which is the motive power for achieving the goal when one attempts to accomplish anything.

## Section Two: Four Articles to Forsake

*I.  Disbelief*

By "disbelief" is meant the opposite of belief, which is the cause of indecision when one attempts to accomplish anything.

*II.  Greed*

By "greed" is meant the vehement desire to take things excessively.

*III.  Laziness*

By "laziness" is meant a dislike of activity when one attempts to accomplish anything.

*IV.  Delusion*

By "delusion" is meant acting as one pleases without knowing anything about the absolute and the phenomenal, being and nonbeing, rightness and wrongness, and gain and loss.

## Chapter Six: The Essential Ways of Humanity and the Essential Ways of Practice

The fourfold beneficence and the four essentials are the essential ways of humanity; and the threefold practice and the eight articles are the essential ways of practice. One cannot follow the essential ways of humanity without following the essential ways of practice, and one will be unable to manifest the virtue of following the essential ways of practice without following the essential ways of humanity. To give an analogy, the essential ways of practice are like the medical art of a physician and the essential ways of humanity are like the medicine used to cure the patient.

# Part Three

## *Practice*

### Chapter One: The Essentials of Daily Practice[39]

1. The mind-ground[40] is originally devoid of disturbances, but they arise in response to the mental spheres;[41] hence, let us maintain the concentration (samādhi) of the self-nature by keeping disturbances from arising.
2. The mind-ground is originally devoid of delusions, but they arise in response to the mental spheres; hence, let us maintain the wisdom (prajñā) of the self-nature by keeping delusions from arising.
3. The mind-ground is originally devoid of errors,[42] but they arise in response to the mental spheres; hence, let us maintain the precepts (*śīla*) of the self-nature by keeping errors from arising.
4. Let us remove disbelief, greed, laziness, and delusions by means of faith, zeal, doubt, and devotion.
5. Let us change the life of resentment into the life of gratitude.
6. Let us change the life of dependency into the life of self-reliance.
7. Let us change those unwilling to learn into those who learn well.
8. Let us change those unwilling to teach into those who teach well.
9. Let us change those who do not have public spirit into those who have it.

---

39. In the following nine articles, which are to be recited daily, the whole doctrine is spelled out for practice in the imperative form. Articles 1, 2, and 3 reflect the threefold practice; 4, the eight articles; 5, the fourfold beneficence; 6, 7, 8, 9, the four essentials. Since the term "mind-ground" refers to what Irwŏn or Dharmakāya does, the tenet of Irwŏnsang is put into practice in articles 1, 2, and 3. Chŏngsan said, "Reading and practicing the essentials of daily practice throughout one's life will be sufficient for the realization of buddhahood" (*CCP*, bk. 2, XI:7; see below, *SS* II:34 and 35 for comments).
40. The fundamental basis of the mind from which all things spring. An English rendering of the Chinese *hsin-ti* is defined in the *Tsu-t'ang chi* under the biography of Nan-yüeh Huai-jang. See Yampolsky, *Platform Sutra*: "You should understand the doctrine of the mind-ground, which teaches that this mind-ground is as if planted with seeds" (p. 164).
41. The sphere of form for the eye, of sound for the ear, of smell for the nose, of taste for the tongue, of touch for the body, of thought for the mind.
42. An English rendering of the Chinese *fei*, which Wing-tsit Chan translated in *The Platform Scripture* (p. 109) as "evil," Yampolsky, as "error"; I follow the latter.

## Chapter Two: Regular-term Training and Daily Training

### Section One: Regular-term Training

To train the practitioner in the teachings, the following subjects are scheduled: (1) intoning the name of a buddha,[43] (2) sitting in meditation, (3) studying scriptures, (4) giving lectures, (5) discussing, (6) observing *ŭidu* (topic of doubt),[44] (7) investigating the principle of nature,[45] (8) keeping a regular-term diary,[46] (9) keeping a daily diary,[47] (10) being heedful, and (11) behaving well.

Intoning the name of a buddha and sitting in meditation are the training subjects for spiritual cultivation; studying scriptures, giving lectures, discussing, observing *ŭidu*, investigating the principle of nature, and keeping a regular-term diary are the training subjects for inquiry into facts and principles; and keeping a daily diary, being heedful, and behaving well are the training subjects for mindful choice in karmic action.

*Intoning the name of a buddha.* One intones repeatedly a phrase of incantation chosen by the order.[48] The purpose of this practice is to concentrate the spirit, which is dispersed into a thousand branches and ten thousand leaves, on the phrase of incantation and to unify thousands and tens of thousands of thoughts into a concentrated thought.

*Sitting in meditation.*[49] One concentrates one's physical and mental forces at the elixir field (*tanjŏn*)[50] to correct the physical force and to protect the mind. Without dwelling on the idea of one thought, one stays in the true realm of perfect rest[51] and nondiscrimination. This is the method of nourishing the pure and fundamental spirit of humanity.

*Studying scriptures.* One studies the scriptures assigned by the order and other scriptures for reference. The purpose of studying scriptures is to let the practitioner know the direction and way of the practice.

*Giving lectures.* One elucidates the meaning of a topic chosen from

---

43. Invocation "Namo Amitābha." See below, chap. 3.

44. A topic of meditation, normally problems set by Zen masters, upon which thought is concentrated as a means to attain inner unity and illumination. See below, chap. 5, for twenty essential test cases of *ŭidu*.

45. The study of the principle of human nature and natural law, or metaphysics, reflects the Sung Neo-Confucian philosophy of human nature (*hsing-li hsüeh*). See below, *SS* VII.

46. See below, pt. 3, chap. 6.

47. Ibid.

48. Normally "Namo Amitābha," the meaning of which is "I take refuge in the boundless life and enlightenment" in Won Buddhism. "Amitābha" in Mahāyāna Buddhism means "boundless light."

49. See below, pt. 3, chap. 4.

50. Two and a half inches below the navel.

51. *Parinirvāṇa*; the perfection of all virtue and the elimination of all evil, release from the miseries of transmigration and entrance into the fullest joy.

facts and principles. The purpose of having the practitioner give lectures is for him or her to sharpen the capacity of wisdom by exchanging views and opinions formally in front of an audience.

*Discussing.* In a group discussion, one talks freely about the point of one's awakening from what one has seen or heard. The purpose of discussions is to have the practitioner sharpen the capacity of wisdom by exchanging opinions and views in a lively manner without any restrictions of formality.

*Observing ŭidu.* One investigates a doubtful issue or topic one may face while practicing Inquiry into Facts and Principles. Or one may investigate one of the test cases of *ŭidu* that ancient buddhas and patriarchs composed. One may then submit one's comprehension of the meaning of the topic to an expert opinion. The purpose of *ŭidu* practice is to help the practitioner attain the ability to analyze clearly problems in facts and principles.

*Investigating the principle of nature.* One solves all the problems involved in the fundamental principles of all beings in the universe and one's original nature and is thereby enlightened.

*Keeping a regular-term diary.* One records the number of daily working hours, income and expenditures, number of mindful choices in mental and physical functions, one's awakening, and one's thoughts.

*Keeping a daily diary.* One records the number of mindful and mindless actions,[52] the phases of learning, and the violation of any of the precepts.

*Being heedful.* One remembers what one has resolved to do and not to do in accord with the situations when one acts (uses one's six sense organs).

*Behaving well.* One lives a life worthy of humankind. The purpose of right conduct is to help the trainee achieve the practical effect of the training by constantly checking one's conduct and putting into practice what one has learned.[53]

## Section Two: Daily Training

To be trained daily in the dharma, the practitioner must practice the following articles of observation: the six articles of heedfulness for daily application and the six articles to heed while attending the temple.

*I.  The Things to Heed for Daily Application*
1. In handling daily affairs, one should be heedful to choose the right and forsake the wrong upon a sound thinking.

---

52. Watchfulness over one's action, speech, and thought for right conduct is *yunyŏm*; heedlessness in one's action, speech, and thought is *munyŏm*.
53. This last statement does not exist in the old *Canon*.

2. Prior to handling a state of affairs, one should be heedful to prepare and train oneself for it in accordance with the situation.
3. One should be heedful to review the scriptures and laws of the order in one's leisure hours.
4. Upon perusing the scriptures and laws, one should be heedful to exercise oneself in *ŭidu*.[54]
5. One should be heedful to practice intoning the name of a buddha or sitting in meditation at dawn or before retiring upon finishing the daily household affairs after supper.
6. Upon dealing with any matter of importance, one should be heedful to check whether or not one has practiced what one had resolved to do and what not to do.

II.  *The Things to Heed while Attending the Temple*
1. Whenever one comes to the temple, one should be heedful to exchange questions and answers on how one has done while practicing the things to heed for daily application.
2. If one has had an awakening on a matter, one should be heedful to report it to one's mentor for an expert opinion.
3. If a point in a state of affairs is unusually doubtful, one should be heedful to submit the doubtful point to one's mentor for clarification.
4. One should be heedful to set aside the funds to pay one's expenses prior to the yearly Zen sessions and to receive training in specialized courses of the dharma at a Zen monastery.
5. One should be heedful to concentrate on the practice in the dharma at the temple on the day of the regular dharma meeting by having all other matters settled in advance.
6. Upon returning from the temple, one should be heedful to check whether one has learned anything, or awakened to some truth, or been enlightened out of any doubt, or gained anything, so that one can apply to daily life whatever one has learned.

### Section Three: The Relationship between Regular-term Training and Daily Training

Regular-term training, being the training done in quietude, is the method of preparing the material for daily practice, taking spiritual cultivation and inquiry into facts and principles as the main subjects. Daily training, being the training when one is engaged in daily activities, prepares material for regular-term training, taking mindful choice in karmic action as the main subject. These two ways of training, being

---

54. See below, chap. 5.

complementary, provide both priesthood and laity with a way of cultivation that can be followed constantly.

### Chapter Three: Intoning the Name of a Buddha

*I.   The Purport*

The repeated intoning of the name of a Buddha is a method of producing a single thought in one's spirit when it is scattered into many delusive thoughts; it is also the method of calming the spirit, which is disturbed in both favorable and adverse conditions. The phrase of incantation, "Namo Amitābha,"[55] means "I take refuge in the boundless life and enlightenment." In the past, this phrase was intoned in the hope of being born into the Paradise of the Western Pure Land by the divine power of Amitābha. In this order, however, we aim at discovering the Amitābha of our own minds and returning to the paradise of our own original nature. Since there is neither arising nor ceasing in the mind-ground, it can be said to be eternal life; and since it is clear and numinous without any delusion, it is none other than enlightenment. Therefore, this mind is called the Amitābha of one's own mind. Our self-nature, being clear and pure, is utterly devoid of sin and blessing, suffering having been extinguished eternally. Thus, this is the immutable paradise of the original nature.

For a correct practice of intoning the name of a buddha, therefore, its practitioner, understanding this principle first of all, must let the spirit that is scattered into tens of thousands of branches rest in one thought of *amita* and let the mind that is disturbed in favorable and adverse conditions return to the realm of eternal peace, by taking one's own mind free from arising and ceasing as the foundation and by watching the one thought that is free from going and coming.

*II.   The Method*

The method of intoning the name of a buddha is so simple and easy that anyone can do it. When one practices intoning the name of a buddha

1. One should keep one's posture upright and set the physical and spiritual energy at ease; one should not swing or shake the body.
2. One should not make the voice too loud or too soft, keeping it suitable to one's physical and spiritual energy.
3. One should concentrate the spirit on the unitary sound of intoning the name of a buddha, collecting the unitary mind

---

55. The Sanskrit *"namo"* means "submitting oneself to"; *"amita"* means boundless, infinite, or immeasurable. *"Amitābha,"* meaning boundless light, refers to the presiding Buddha in the Western Paradise, whose mercy and wisdom are perfect. In Won Buddhism, Amitābha is identified with one's own original nature, which neither arises nor ceases.

along with the phrase "Namo Amitābha" so that the one thought and the intoning voice continue together.

4. One should release the mind from any thought and keep the mental state of leisure and inaction; one should not imagine the figure of Amitābha as a way of seeking a buddha from outside; and one should not have any other delusive thoughts.

5. To get hold of the mind, it may be helpful to intone the name of a buddha by the counting of beads or beating a "wooden fish" (J. *mokugyo*; K. *mokt'ak*) or a drum.

6. If one is annoyed by delusive thoughts while attending to any matter or while one is walking, standing, sitting, or reclining, they can be cleared up by intoning the name of a buddha; however, the intoning should be stopped if it distracts the mind from concentrating on the work one is doing.

7. As intoning the name of a buddha helps one look back on the radiance of one's mind and original nature, it can maintain the calmness of one's mind when one is confronted with occasions for vexation, greed, or attraction to favorable or adverse conditions.[56] Thus, if one knows the principle of intoning the name of a buddha, its unitary sound can subdue hundreds and thousands of evil demons and spirits. Mere verbal intoning without the concentration of one thought will be of little effect; however, the voiceless repetition of the name of a buddha can help one attain to samādhi if one can keep the unitary concentration of one's mind.

*III.   The Merits*

If one practices intoning the name of a buddha for a long time, one will naturally attain to samādhi and enjoy supreme bliss, the goal of the practice. The articles of its merits are identical with those of sitting in meditation.[57]

Intoning the name of a buddha and sitting in meditation are the two halves of the same course of spiritual cultivation. If the defilements of greed, anger, and delusions are excessive, then the practitioner must first replace them with intoning the name of a buddha and then enter the realm of the True Thusness of one's original nature through sitting in meditation. Intoning the name of a buddha is essential during the day and any time of disturbing conditions around one; and sitting in meditation is essential for the night or dawn and any time when the disturbing conditions are remote. If one applies intoning the name of a

---

56. Favorable conditions can be worse than adverse conditions since the former can make one lazy, conceited, or insincere while the latter can make one grow.
57. See below, chap. 4, III.

buddha and sitting in meditation in a timely fashion and connects the two practices by checking one's surrounding and mental state, one will attain the great power of calmness.

## Chapter Four: Sitting in Meditation

*I.   The Purport*

Sitting in meditation is a practice the purpose of which is to calm delusive thoughts and allow the true nature of one's mind to manifest. It is also a practice to make the fiery energy descend and the watery energy ascend in one's body. As delusive thoughts calm down, the watery energy will ascend in the body; as the watery energy ascends, delusive thoughts calm down. Consequently, one's mental and physical functioning will be consistent, and one will feel both the spirit and the vital force refreshed.

If, however, delusive thoughts persist in one's mind, the fiery energy will constantly ascend, burning up the watery energy in the body and covering up the light of the spirit. The human body functions like a steam engine; not even a finger can be moved without the dual force of fire and water. Since the six sense organs are all controlled by the brain and hence the fiery energy of the whole body is contracted there when one uses the six roots to see, hear, or think, the watery energy of the whole body is dried and burned there as the oil in the lamp is burned when it is lit. One's face flushes and one's mouth dries out if one racks one's brain, looks minutely at a thing, or talks loudly; this is the phenomenon of the ascending fiery energy. One should use one's six sense organs with frugality even for rightful things; why should one let useless delusive thoughts burn the flame of the brain day and night? Thus, sitting in meditation is a practice to remove all delusive thoughts, to let the original nature of True Thusness[58] manifest, to have all the fiery energy descend, and to let the clear and pure watery energy ascend.

*II.   The Method*

The method of sitting in meditation is very simple and easy; anyone can practice it.

1.  Sit on a mat comfortably; hold your head and back straight in an upright, seated posture.[59]
2.  Loosen the tension of the body and gather it at the elixir field

---

58. *Bhūtatathatā* (S) is reality as contrasted with unreality or appearance, unchanging or immutable as contrasted with form and phenomena. It is also called self-existent pure Mind, Buddha-nature, Dharmakāya, and dharma-nature.

59. The Buddha's sitting posture with legs crossed and soles upward, left over right being the attitude for subduing demons, right over left for blessing, the hands being placed one above the other in similar order.

(*tanjŏn*); be aware only of the physical energy concentrated at the elixir field with no thought dwelling anywhere. If your mind is unguarded, the energy loses concentration. If that happens, do not forget to check the concentration of energy.

3. Keep your breathing uniform, inhaling a little longer and stronger than exhaling.

4. To keep the demon of drowsiness away, keep your eyes open; however, you may try with your eyes closed if you feel refreshed as long as there is no danger of drowsiness.

5. Keep your mouth always closed. If the ascent of the watery energy and the descent of the fiery energy go well as the practice matures, clear and smooth saliva will flow from the salivary gland, which you may gather in the mouth and swallow once in a while.

6. Let your spirit be wakeful in calmness and calm in wakefulness; if you become drowsy, collect your mind to freshen the spirit; if your mind turns to delusive thoughts, replace them with right thought; then stay in the realm of the True Thusness of your original nature.

7. The beginner at sitting in meditation sometimes suffers from pain in the legs and the invasion of delusive thoughts. If your legs ache, you may change their positions, one upon the other. If delusive thoughts invade your mind, recognize them only as delusive thoughts; then they will disappear of themselves. Do not be vexed with or discouraged by them.

8. If you sit in meditation for the first time, your face and body may feel itchy occasionally as if ants were crawling over them. Be sure not to touch or scratch. This is the symptom of the blood passing through the blood vessels.

9. While sitting in meditation, do not search for any extraordinary pivotal point or any miraculous traces; should you notice such phenomena, recognize them as wicked and pass over them as nothing worthy of attention.

If you practice sitting in meditation for a long time as described above, you will eventually forget the distinction between subject and object, time and place, remaining in the realm of the True Thusness of your original nature and rejoicing in unparalleled spiritual bliss.

### III.   *The Merits*
If one attains the power of sitting in meditation after a long period of practice, one will reap the following ten benefits.

1. Rash and thoughtless behavior gradually diminish.
2. The operation of the six sense organs becomes orderly.

3. Suffering from illness diminishes and one's complexion brightens up.
4. One's memory improves.
5. One's patience grows.
6. Attachment lessens.
7. Vicious dispositions change into right ones.
8. The wisdom of one's original nature shines.
9. One will enjoy supreme bliss.
10. One will gain liberty from birth and death.

*IV. The Necessity of Concentrating at Elixir Field (Tanjŏn)*
It is a common practice since ancient times that, sitting in meditation, one is to eliminate all thoughts by concentrating one's mind on the unitary mental sphere. Thus, there are various methods of concentration in accordance with each advocacy and expedient; however, if the mind is concentrated on the head or an external mental sphere, thoughts are stirred and the fiery energy ascends, making it difficult to calm the mind. If, however, the mind is concentrated at the elixir field (*tanjŏn*),[60] thoughts are not easily stirred and the fiery energy descends, making it easy to calm the mind.

Concentration at the elixir field is not only necessary for sitting in meditation; it is of vital importance to the preservation of health.[61] If one concentrates one's mind on the elixir field and swallows the water (saliva) springing from the jade-pond (salivary duct) plentifully, the watery and fiery energies will be balanced and suffering from physical illness will diminish. One's complexion will become lustrous; one's vital force will be replete and one will attain to the mental decoction (*simdan*) that secures longevity. Thus, the concentration at the elixir field serves two purposes, the calmness of Zen (*sŏnjŏng*)[62] and health.

The advocates of *kanhwa-Sŏn*[63] denounce the concentration at the elixir field, alleging that the practice leads one to a dead meditation of senselessness. *Kanhwa-Sŏn*, however, can be adopted as a provisional expedient only for certain people; it cannot be practiced by the general

---

60. See below, *SS* III:14, for comments.
61. "The elixir field, being the field of the vital force, wards off all diseases. If the mind stops at the elixir field, the vital force and breathing harmonize and thereby cure illness" (*Maha chigwan, T*, 1911,46.108a).
62. Korean pronunciation of the Chinese *ch'an-ting*, being the Chinese rendering of the Sanskrit dhyāna samādhi. Zen, being dhyāna as an element of samādhi, covers the whole ground of meditation, concentration, abstraction, reaching the ultimate beyond emotion or thinking. The main characteristic of *sŏnjŏng* is serene reflection or clear awareness in the tranquility of no thought.
63. Meditation practiced with *hwadu*; the same as holding *ŭidu* (topic of doubt) in meditation. See below, *SS* III:14 for comments.

public. If one concentrates on *hwadu* for a long time, one can easily become ill because of the rush of blood to the head. Furthermore, those who cannot by nature become caught up in *hwadu* will lose interest in meditation.

Therefore, we set the time for sitting in meditation and the time for the inquiry into *hwadu* separately so that one can devote oneself to one of them at a time. In this way the perfect calmness and wisdom can both be brought to completion. In this way one can be safeguarded against losing oneself in emptiness and calmness and against exhausting mental discriminations. In this way, one can attain to the essence of True Thusness devoid of motion and rest.

## Chapter Five: Essential Test Cases of *Ŭidu*

1. The World Honored One[64] is said to have descended to his royal home without leaving the Tuṣita[65] heaven and to have delivered all sentient beings while he was still in the womb of his mother. What is the meaning of this?
2. The World Honored One is said to have declared after his first seven steps when born from his mother's right side, "In the heavens above and (earth) beneath I alone am the honored one." What is the meaning of this?
3. Once at the Spirit Vulture Peak (Gṛdhrakūṭa), the World Honored One held up a flower to the assembly, which was silent; only Mahākasyapa wore a smile. The World Honored One then declared, "I hereby pass the eye of the true law to Mahākasyapa."[66] What is the meaning of this?
4. The World Honored One, entering into nirvāṇa, said that he had not uttered a single dharma in his life starting from Magadava[67] and reaching the river Hiranyavati.[68] What is the meaning of this?

---

64. Śākyamuni, the sage of Śākya clan, the Buddha.

65. The Tuṣita heaven, the fourth *devaloka* in the passion realm, or desire realm, lies between the Yama and Nirmānarati heavens. Its inner department is the Pure Land of Maitreya who, like Śākyamuni and all buddhas, is reborn there before descending to earth as the next Buddha; his life there is 4,000 Tuṣita years, or (each day there being equal to 400 earth-years) 584 million earth years.

66. *Wu-men-kuan*, case VI, *T*, 2005.48.293c. Blyth, *Zen Classics*, p. 76: "I have the eye of the True Law, the Secret Essence of *Nirvāṇa*, the Formless Form, the Mysterious Law Gate. Without relying upon words and letters, beyond all teachings as a special transmission, I pass this all on to Mahākasyapa."

67. The modern Sārnāth near Benares. Here he is reputed to have preached his first sermon and converted his first five disciples.

68. Otherwise said to be *nairanjñāna* (groves of staves), said to have grown from the staff with which a heretic measured the Buddha and which he threw away because the more he measured, the higher the Buddha grew.

5. The myriad dharmas return to the One. Where does the One return?[69]

6. There is one thing with which none of the myriad dharmas can be associated. What is it?

7. Investigate myriad dharmas and thereby get enlightened to the One Mind.[70] What is the meaning of this?

8. Even before the ancient buddhas[71] were born, there was a unitary circle. What is the meaning of this?

9. What sort of a body is it that you had before you received your body from your parents?

10. When one is in a sound sleep without dreaming, where is one's numinous awareness?

11. All things are nothing but the mind's creation.[72] What is the meaning of this?

12. This very mind, just this is Buddha.[73] What is the meaning of this?

13. Why are all sentient beings dragged into the cycle of rebirth through the six realms of existence while all buddhas are released from this cycle?

14. It is said that one who practices well is not separated from the self-nature. What sort of a practice is it that is not separated from the self-nature?

15. In what sense are mind, nature, principle, and vital force identical and how are they differentiated from the unity?[74]

16. Do all things in the universe have arising and ceasing or do they have neither arising nor ceasing?

17. The karmic retribution of cause and effect among all things takes place in this life because the parties recognize each other. How could the karmic retribution take place in their next lives when they have no remembrance of their previous lives to recognize each other?

---

69. *Pi-yen lu*, case XLV, *T*, 2003.48.181c; Cleary and Cleary, *Blue Cliff Record*, 2:318: "A monk asked Chao-chou, 'The Ten Thousand Dharmas return to the One. Where does the One return?' The master replied: 'While I was staying at Ching-chou I made a hemp that weighed seven pounds.'" See below, *SS* VII:10.

70. Here "One Mind" means "True Thusness" (*bhūtatathatā*), or the universe as one mind.

71. The seven buddhas are Vipaśyin, Śikhin, Viśvabhū, Krakucchanda, Kanakamuni, Kāśapa, and Śākyamuni.

72. The *Ta-cheng-chi-shin lun*, *T*, 1666.32.577b; Hakeda, *Awakening of Faith*, p. 32: "The triple world [the world of desire, form, formless], therefore, is unreal and is of mind only. Apart from it there are no objects of the five senses and of the mind."

73. *Ching-te ch'uan-teng lu*, *T*, 2076.51.309b. Shi-tou (700–790) said, "If you realize the Buddha's knowledge, then the mind is the Buddha."

74. This question reflects Sung Neo-Confucian metaphysics.

18. It is said that heaven and earth do not seem to know anything but they know everything. What is the meaning of this?

19. When one enters nirvāṇa, one's numinous awareness is unified with Dharmakāya. How can an individual soul be separated from it and what makes the distinction between past and present lives?

20. I have a volume of scripture that is not made of paper and ink. It always sheds light though it does not contain a word. What is the meaning of this?

### Chapter Six: Keeping a Diary

*I.    The Purport*

The purpose of requiring the practitioner, laity and priesthood alike, learned or ignorant, to keep a daily diary is for one to reflect whether one has been mindful (*yunyŏm*) or mindless (*munyŏm*),[75] how the study of subjects was, and whether one has kept or violated any of the precepts. The purpose of requiring a diary of the practitioner at a learning institute or at a Zen monastery is for one to record daily the hours of work, the income and expenditure for the day, how one has used one's mind and body, and awakening or reflective thoughts.

*II.    How to Record in the Daily Diary*

1. One should check and record how many times one has acted mindfully and how many times mindlessly. One must put in "mindful" on the actions that one has done bearing in mind the resolution to do or not to do certain things and "mindless" on the actions that one has done without bearing the resolution in mind. In the beginning, one should only record how many times one was mindful or mindless as defined here regardless of success or failure of the resolution to do or not to do certain things. As the practice deepens, one must calculate mindfulness and mindlessness by the number of successes or failures.

2. For the subjects of spiritual cultivation and inquiry into facts and principles in the category of learning, the hour of study should be recorded; regular dharma meetings and Zen sessions should be recorded whether or not one has attended them.

3. One must record whether one has violated any of the precepts; if violated, one should record the number of violations of a particular article of the precepts.

4. Anyone who is illiterate or poor at filling out forms can check

---

75. See below for the definition of "mindful" and "mindless"; "mindless" is used here in the sense of careless absentmindedness; it does not mean absence of false thoughts that one may harbor after rendering a favor to others.

the practice of mindfulness and mindlessness by means of the bean investigation. Such a person can calculate the frequency of mindfulness by white beans and mindlessness by red beans.

*III.   How to Record in a Regular-term Diary*
1. The reason for requiring one to record the number of working hours is for one to check whether one has spent the time valuably or wasted it so that, if any was wasted, one should remind oneself not to waste any time in the future.
2. The reason for requiring one to record one's daily income and expenditure is that, if one has no income, one should find a way to earn it by working diligently; and if expenditure is more than it should be, one should cut it down so that one can prevent poverty and make one's life comfortable. This recordkeeping also aims at breaking down the bad habit of living in idleness though one may be affluent.
3. The reason for requiring one to record how one has used one's mind and body is to let one examine and know the balance of offenses and blessings of the day. It also aims at letting one attain the power of mindful choice,[76] examining right from wrong.
4. The reason for requiring one to record any episode of awakening and reflective thoughts is to check the level of one's enlightenment to the principles in terms of the absolute and the phenomenal, and being and nonbeing.

## Chapter Seven: How to Practice Timeless Zen

Generally speaking, Zen is a practice for attaining mental freedom[77] by awakening to one's original nature, which is devoid of mental differentiation or dwelling on anything. From ancient times, there has been no one who has not practiced Zen with the aspiration to attain to the great Way.

The true Zen can be practiced only if one takes true emptiness as the substance and marvelous existence as the function.[78] When one confronts myriad external mental spheres, one must keep the mind as immovable as a great mountain and as clear and pure as an empty space. One's mind must function freely without adhering to motion in

---

76. The power to do the right and to forsake the wrong, which one attains as the result of practicing mindful choice in karmic action; see pt. 2, chap. 4, sec. 3.

77. See pt. 2, chap. 4, sec. 1.

78. Ho-tse Shen-hui (670–762) in *Hsien-tsung chi* 30, *T*, 2076.51.458c, explains, "True void is the substance and marvelous existence is the function." Here true void and marvelous existence should be understood as synonymous with "meditative calmness and concentration" (*śamatha*) and "insight contemplation" (*vipaśyanā*), respectively. See Donner and Stevenson, *Great Calming*, p. 82.

motion or rest at rest. If one does so, all of one's mental differentiation will at no time be separated from the calmness, and the operations of the six sense organs will always be in accordance with the self-nature of empty and calm, numinous awareness. This is the so-called Mahāyāna Zen and the method of practicing the threefold practice simultaneously.

It is said in a sūtra, "You should develop a mind that does not abide in anything."[79] This is the great way of cultivating the undisturbed actions in myriad mental spheres. This way may seem very difficult to follow. However, if the details of the way are properly understood, Zen can be practiced even by a farmer working with a hoe, an artisan working with a hammer, a store clerk working at a cash register, a public official doing administrative business, or a person toiling at home.[80] What is the use of choosing a particular place and insisting on rest against motion?

One who is practicing Zen for the first time, however, will experience a great deal of difficulty in controlling the mind. This is analogous to ox herding in that when the rein of the mind is slackened even for a moment, one's moral sense is immediately damaged. Hence, one should not lose the spirit to fight to the last any conditions that arouse vehement desire in one's mind. One's mind will gradually attain harmony and maturity so that one's mental functions will eventually be as one wills them to be. Whenever one confronts adverse conditions, therefore, one should remind oneself of the opportunity to cultivate one's mind, checking only whether one's mind is being attracted to the conditions. If the occasions in which one's mind is under control in any conditions increase, one may test one's mind against such conditions that one usually loves and, also, conditions one abhors. If the mind is still disturbed in such situations, one's moral sense is immature. If the mind is not disturbed in such conditions, one may regard it as the sign of one's mind becoming mature.[81] One should not be off guard, however, as soon as one feels that one's mind is not disturbed. The mind is undisturbed because of strenuous effort; it is not undisturbed of

---

79. *Chin-kang po-jo po-lo-mi ching*, *T*, 235.8.749c; Conze, *Perfect Wisdom*, pp. 126–127: "Therefore, then, Subhuti, the Bodhisattva, the great being, should produce an unsupported thought, i.e., a thought which is nowhere supported, a thought unsupported by sights, sounds, smells, tastes, touchables or mind-objects."

80. Cf. Yung-chia, *Ch'eng-tao ko*, *T*, 2014.48.396a; Buswell, *KAZ*, p. 174: "Walking is *Sŏn*, sitting is *Sŏn*. During speech, silence, action, and silliness, the essence is at peace."

81. For testing the mind's maturity, see Chinul, *Chin-sim chiksŏl*, *T*, 2019.48.1003a–b; Buswell, *KAZ*, p. 179: "If there comes a time when you want to test true mind, you should take all the hateful and lustful situations you have encountered throughout your whole life and imagine that they are right before you. If a hateful or lustful state of mind arises as before, your mind of the path is immature. If hateful or lustful thoughts do not arise, your mind of the path is mature."

itself. The mind will be tamed if it is undisturbed even when it is off guard.

If one practices Zen for a long time cutting off all afflictions and attains the freedom of the mind, one's mind will be as firm as a steel pillar and will be as impregnable as a granite wall. Such a mind cannot be coaxed by wealth and prosperity nor can it be bent by the sword and power. With such a mind, one can do everything without being entangled or being driven to one's wit's end. While living in the world of defilements, one will attain to hundreds and thousands of samādhi in the world of defilement. If one reaches this realm, the whole world will change into one true dharma realm, where all things, right or wrong, good or evil, or pure and impure have the taste of ghee.[82] This is what is called the teaching of nonduality, from which arise freedom from birth and death, emancipation from the cycle of rebirth, and the paradise of the Pure Land.

Recently, there have been many who, thinking Zen to be very difficult, have the opinion that no one with a family and occupation can practice it, and therefore, Zen can be cultivated only by sitting on a mountain. This opinion is based on ignorance of the great truth that everything is of unitary nature. If Zen can be practiced only when one is seated, it may not be practiced when one is standing. The Zen that can be practiced only when one is seated but not while one is standing is a crippled Zen; how can it be the great way to deliver sentient beings?

Moreover, the self-nature is not limited in its emptiness and calmness. If one practices Zen like a lifeless log, it is not the practice of Zen to train one's nature but a production of useless invalids. Therefore, the true Zen is practiced and samādhi is attained if one's mind is neither disturbed in adverse conditions nor affected by conditions that arouse strong desire. The general principle of timeless Zen can be expressed as follows: "When the six sense organs are free of work, eliminate delusive thoughts and cultivate One Mind; when the six sense organs are at work, eliminate injustice and cultivate justice."

## Chapter Eight: The Discourse on Repentance

Though it is necessarily true that, in accordance with the principle of yin-yang's mutual advancement,[83] one who does good will be repaid by reciprocal production and the evildoer will be repaid by reciprocal

---

82. A rich liquor skimmed from boiled butter used as a symbol for the Perfect Buddha-truth.

83. The dual force of negative/positive, female/male, and darkness/brightness as expounded in the yin-yang school of Chinese philosophy. This principle of the universe is interpreted here as the fundamental principle of the Buddhist causal law of karmic retribution.

destruction, one who is always repentant and reforms oneself can free oneself from the retributive force of reciprocal production and destruction, controlling sins and blessings for oneself. That is why all buddhas and patriarchs have unanimously taught the necessity of repentance.

Repentance in general is the first step in discarding an old lifestyle and cultivating a new life; it is the first step one takes on the good path, leaving the evil one. If one keeps doing good, repenting of one's past faults, one's old evil karma will gradually diminish, and no new karma will be produced; thus the good path will come closer and the evil one will move further away of itself. Thus, it is said in a Buddhist treatise, "The earlier mind producing evil is like clouds covering the sun, and the later mind doing good is like the bright light dispelling the darkness."[84] As sin originates in the mind, it will disappear when the mental dispositions that cause sins perish. Evil karma is produced by ignorance (*avidyā*); it will be extinguished by the light of wisdom (prajñā) of one's original nature. Why, then, should not those people moaning with sin and suffering enter the gate of repentance?

The roots of sinful karma are greed, anger, and delusions. Even if one repents of past faults seriously, sins will never cease if one commits offenses again later. Even if one who committed a grave offense deserving of falling into the evil path (of beasts, hungry ghosts, hell) does some meritorious deeds as a temporary repentance, one will receive blessings as much as one deserves, leaving sinful karma intact as long as greed, anger, and delusions remain. This is analogous to the attempt to cool the water boiling in a cauldron by adding a little bit of cold water, leaving the fire burning hot under the cauldron. As the power of fire is strong and the power of the cold water weak, the water in the cauldron will never be cooled down.

There are many in the world who repent of their previous offenses but few who do not repeat them afterwards. There are some who do a few meritorious deeds as a temporary repentance leaving the roots of greed, anger, and delusions intact in their mind; how could they expect to have their sinful karma cleared away?

There are two kinds of repentance: repentance by action, and noumenal repentance. Repentance by action is done by sincerely repenting of one's previous offenses in front of the Three Precious Ones (Triratna)[85] and by doing good of all sorts. Noumenal repentance is done by getting enlightened to the realm that is originally devoid of sinful nature and thereby eliminating all defilements and delusions in one's mind. If

---

84. *Fo-shuo wei-tseng-yu ching*, *T*, 688.16 (page number unidentified).
85. This should have been changed to "Dharmakāya Buddha, the fourfold beneficence" in the new *Canon*, for Won Buddhists do not worship the Buddhist Three Precious Ones.

one wishes to extricate oneself from sins once and for all, one should do both forms of repentance, thus doing all good actions and eliminating the roots of greed, anger, and delusions at the same time. In this way, the evil karma accumulated for thousands of kalpas will be cleared away just as one who wishes to cool the water in the cauldron adds a great amount of cold water to the boiling water and extinguishes the burning fire underneath.

If, by sincere repentance and practice, one is enlightened to one's Buddha nature, which is calm and wakeful, and thereby attains freedom of the mind, one can choose one's natural karma as one pleases and free oneself from birth and death. For such a one, there will be nothing to take or forsake and nothing to hate or love, so that the triple world and the six realms of existence will be of one equal flavor. For such a one, motion and rest, favorable and adverse conditions are equally nothing but samādhi. For such a one, myriad sin and suffering will vanish as ice melts away in hot water so that sin and suffering will no longer be sin and suffering. As the light of the wisdom of one's own self-nature radiates, the whole world is none other than a Buddhist monastery and the whole world is none other than the Pure Land,[86] where not one sinful characteristic can be found. This is the so-called repentance of the buddhas and patriarchs, and the Mahāyāna repentance. Only on this stage can it be said that the sinful karma has been completely cleared up.

Recently, there have been groups of self-styled Buddhist priests who, not knowing the importance of precepts and the causal law of karmic retribution, acted as they pleased under the pretext of "unhindered action," thus occasionally defiling the teachings of the Buddha. This is because they know only that the self-nature is devoid of discrimination but do not know that it can discriminate when it functions. How can one say that they know the true way, which transcends being and non-being? There are also many who regard the enlightenment to one's self-nature as the completion of practice, thinking that neither repentance nor practice is necessary after enlightenment. The truth is that defilements and attachments are not all annihilated at the same time with the enlightenment to one's self-nature. Even if one has attained to buddhahood by attaining the three great powers,[87] one cannot avoid one's own fixed karma. One should bear this point in mind in order not to develop a wicked view and misunderstand the words of the Buddha and patriarchs; one should not make light of sinful karma.

---

86. Sukhāvatī, the western paradise, presided over by Amitābha.
87. The powers of spiritual cultivation, inquiry into facts and principles, mindful choice in karmic action. See pt. 2, chap. 4: "Threefold Practice."

*Verses of Repentance*

> *For Repentance by Action*

All the evil karma ever committed by me since of old,
As a result of my beginningless greed, anger, and delusion,
Produced by my body, mouth, and volition—
I now repent of it all.

> *For Noumenal Repentance*

Sins have no self-nature; they arise from mental functions.
If and when the mental functions are extinguished, sins are
    also dead.
Sins are dead, the mental functions extinguished, and both
    void.
This then is called true repentance.[88]

## Chapter Nine: Silent Confession and Prayer

As soon as one is born into this world, one needs help from without as well as one's own effort in order to lead a life. One's own effort and help from without are the fundamental source of one's life, the two being the mutual basis of each other. Hence, one who has acquired an unquestionable power from without is like a tree the roots of which are secure in the soil. We have learned of the unquestionable beneficence and power of Dharmakāya Buddha, which is the source of the fourfold beneficence. Taking the perfect fourfold beneficence as the root of our religious faith, we offer prayers of gratitude when we lead a happy life; we beg for forgiveness when we suffer; we offer a silent confession or say an explanatory prayer for a right decision when it is difficult to make a right one; we offer a silent confession or say an explanatory prayer for a favorable condition when we confront a difficult one; and we offer a silent confession or say an explanatory prayer for a guard against becoming wicked and foolish when we find ourselves in a favorable situation. If one continues silent confession and prayer, understanding their principles well, one will receive great power from the fourfold beneficence. Because sincerity moves heaven, one's wishes will be fulfilled and one will lead a joyful life.

Since anyone who does things contrary to the vow will instead be punished by the great power of the fourfold beneficence, one can be said to know the original purpose of silent confession and prayer only if

---

88. These verses in the old *Canon* are restored in this translation because they are regularly chanted at certain prayers in Won Buddhism, as can be found in the *Yŏmsongjip* (Collection of liturgical verses).

one, bearing this point in mind, does not offer any false confession or prayer.

When one offers a silent confession or a prayer, one starts it with the following words:

> May Heaven and Earth watch over me!
> May Parents watch over me!
> May Brethren respond to me!
> May Laws respond to me!
> I, who am indebted to thee, hereby confess in front of
>     Dharmakāya Buddha, the original source of the
>     fourfold beneficence!

Upon addressing the fourfold beneficence in this way, one may pray for the realization of one's wishes within the limits outlined above. If there is a direct counterpart to one's prayer, one can offer a silent prayer, a direct prayer, or an explanatory prayer; if there is no direct counterpart to one's prayer, a silent confession or an explanatory prayer can be offered. Silent confession is a form of prayer done silently in one's heart; an actual or direct prayer is a form of prayer performed directly to the recipient, if there is any, of one's prayer; an explanatory prayer is a form of prayer performed for an audience to listen to, to be influenced by, and to arouse awakening by.

## Chapter Ten: How to Make an Offering to Buddha

In the Buddhist tradition, it has been only the Buddha statue to which people make offerings to the Buddha in supplication for pardon of sins or bestowal of blessings, which are in reality the concerns of heaven and earth, parents, brethren, or laws. This practice should be changed. All things in the universe are the manifestations of Dharmakāya Buddha; hence one meets Buddha everywhere and, therefore, ought to do everything as making an offering to Buddha. To make a realistic and successful offering to Buddha, one ought to make it to heaven and earth if sins or blessings are related to them, and to parents, brethren, and laws if sins or blessings are related to them, respectively.

The period of making an offering to Buddha should not be indefinite as in the past. Success in certain things requires one to make offerings to Buddha for myriad reincarnations; in certain other things, several hundreds or scores of reincarnations. Certain things require one to make offering to Buddha for one or two reincarnations. Certain things may require scores of years, several months, several days, or only a moment; hence making an offering to Buddha will be a realistic and successful one only if it is made for the right period of time depending on the nature of things for which it is made.

## Chapter Eleven: The Precepts

*I.   The Ten Precepts for the Grade of Elementary Faith*
1. Do not take life without justifiable reason.
2. Do not steal.
3. Do not commit adultery.
4. Do not drink alcoholic beverages without justifiable reason.
5. Do not gamble.
6. Do not speak evil.
7. Do not quarrel without justifiable reason.
8. Do not embezzle public funds.
9. Do not borrow or lend money to a close friend without justifiable reason.
10. Do not smoke without justifiable reason.

*II.   The Ten Precepts for the Grade of Unwavering Faith*
1. Do not handle public affairs by yourself.
2. Do not speak of the faults of others.
3. Do not lose your mind in search of gold, silver, and other jewels.
4. Do not wear luxurious clothes.
5. Do not associate yourself with unjust people.
6. Do not talk while someone else is talking.
7. Do not be untrustworthy.
8. Do not say artful and flattering words .
9. Do not sleep at an improper time without justifiable reason.
10. Do not join in a singing and dancing party of impropriety.

*III.   The Ten Precepts for the Grade of Struggle between Dharma and Māra*
1. Do not be conceited.
2. Do not have more than one spouse.
3. Do not eat the flesh of a four-legged animal without justifiable reason.
4. Do not be lazy.
5. Do not be double-tongued.
6. Do not make absurd remarks.
7. Do not be jealous.
8. Do not be greedy.[89]

---

89. *Rāga* (S), vehement longing or desire; one of the three poisons; tainted by and in bondage to the five desires arising from the objects of the five senses, things seen, heard, smelt, tasted, or touched. The five desires of wealth, sex, food and drink, fame, and sleep.

9. Do not be angry.[90]
10. Do not be deluded.[91]

## Chapter Twelve: The Essential Discourse on Following the Original Nature

1. One should not confine one's faith to one's mentor; one must have faith in the dharma as well.
2. One should choose the best of all dharmas proposed by ten people and have faith in it.
3. Being the lord of the four forms of birth, one should love to learn.
4. One should not neglect learning because one is already knowledgeable.
5. One should not pass one's time in wine and dalliance but use it in searching for the truth.
6. One should not be attached to one side.
7. In dealing with all things, one should not lose the sense of reverence at any time; and one should fear greed as if it were a fierce lion.
8. One should teach oneself daily and hourly.
9. If something goes wrong, one should examine oneself and should not bear a grudge against others.[92]
10. Observing the fault of others, one should not reveal it but correct one's own faults.
11. Observing the good of others, one should make it known to the world without forgetting it.
12. One should listen to another's entreaty, if it is a righteous one, putting oneself in that person's shoes.
13. One should exert oneself to do the right even at the risk of one's life, though one may abhor doing it.
14. One should exert oneself to refrain from doing the wrong even at the risk of one's own life, though one may love doing it.
15. One should not urge others to do what they do not want to, but mind one's own business.
16. If one has a wish and wants it to be fulfilled, one must cultivate it by reflecting it on whatever one sees and hears.

---

90. *Dvesa* (S), hate, dislike, enmity; one of the three poisons.
91. *Moha* (S), illusion, delusion, infatuation, foolishness, ignorance, and stupidity.
92. This reflects a Confucian moral virtue: "The Master said, 'In archery we have something like the way of the superior man. When the archer misses the center of the target, he turns round and seeks for the cause of his failure in himself.'" *Doctrine of the Mean*, chap. 14, sec. 5; Legge, *Confucius*, p. 396.

## Chapter Thirteen: The First Religious Discourses

*I.    The Essentials of Self-cultivation*[93]

1. One must engage oneself in studies in order to prepare oneself with sufficient learning in accordance with the times.

2. One will be able to attain stability in keeping one's sphere in life and maintain justice in such conditions as joy, anger, sorrow, and pleasure only if one becomes proficient in the power of spiritual cultivation.

3. One will be able to analyze truth from falsity and thereby judge quickly right from wrong and gain from loss only if one becomes proficient in the power of inquiry into facts and principles.

4. While dealing with daily affairs, one should maintain carefulness in choosing karmic actions and check one's conduct against one's knowledge.

*II.    The Essentials for Regulating the Family*

1. One should take up an occupation in order to secure clothing, food, and shelter. One should check the balance of earnings and expenditure, advocating thrift and saving.

2. The head of a family should not forget to extend one's knowledge by learning, neglect the education of one's children, or forget the obligations to serve elders and guide juniors.

3. The members of a family should encourage each other to live in concord and should exchange opinions among themselves.

4. The whole family must have teachers and friends who can help enlighten the mind and should obey the government, which illuminates laws.

5. One should be heedful to refer to various homes of the present and the past to learn with what sort of hopes and means one could make a happy home or ruin it.

*III.    The Way of Progress for the Strong and the Weak*

1. Generally, by the strong is meant the one who wins in any situation; and by the weak, the one who is defeated. Since there cannot be the strong unless there is the weak and since the weak becomes the strong by depending on the strong, there is mutual dependence on each other and there is friendliness as well as estrangement.

2. The strong can remain strong forever by helping the weak grow strong on the principle of mutual benefit when the strong treat the weak. The weak can grow strong, improving themselves from

---

93. Articles 2 and 3 are translations of the original in *PGC* (the 1943 edition), which are garbled in *WBK* (the 1962 edition).

the position of the weak to the position of the strong, by taking the strong as their guide and patiently coping with hardships of any kind. The strong will degenerate into the weak if the strong abuse power in behalf of selfish interests, harming the weak. The strong must understand how they can remain strong and they can degenerate into the weak. The weak will never become the strong if they simply confront the strong without considering how the strong and the weak can reverse their lots. The weak must understand the principle of how the weak can become the strong.

*IV.  What a Leader Should Prepare*
1.  The leader should be more knowledgeable than those who are led.
2.  The leader should not lose the confidence of those who are led.
3.  The leader should not exploit those under guidance for personal profit.
4.  Confronting any matter, the leader should square conduct with knowledge.

## Chapter Fourteen: The Sermon on Suffering and Happiness

*I.  An Explanation of Suffering and Happiness*
Generally, a human being, upon birth, finds two things: suffering, which one abhors, and happiness, which one enjoys. One may have suffering that seems accidental or suffering caused by oneself. One may enjoy unexpected happiness or happiness one has earned. Though people love happiness and abhor suffering, there are few who try to examine the causes of suffering and happiness. Few examine whether momentary suffering will be everlasting or will bring about happiness, or whether momentary happiness will be everlasting or will change into suffering. However, one should live as ever eternally with deserved happiness and suffering by thoroughly discerning the difference between deserved and undeserved happiness and suffering; and, to keep undeserved suffering and happiness away, one should be heedful to practice mindful choice based on sound thinking while we make applications by walking, standing, sitting, reclining, speaking, keeping silent, moving, or resting.

*II.  Causes of Discarding Happiness and Embracing Suffering*
1.  One is ignorant of the causes of suffering and happiness.
2.  Even if one knows the causes of suffering and happiness, one does not put into practice what is right.
3.  One has formed the energy of habit as firm as steel and rock by acting, seeing, hearing, and thinking as one pleases without any mental and physical discipline.

4. One has not perfected practice until one has removed evil habit and transformed one's temperament by disciplining one's mind and body in the dharma.

5. One is eager to achieve whatever one does without taking the least pain.

## Chapter Fifteen: Ailing Family and Its Remedies

Just as an ailing person can be crippled, disabled, or even die if left untreated,[94] so can an ailing family be deformed, corrupted, or even ruined if, for a long time, the householder is unaware of the ills of the family or lacks the sincere effort necessary to cure them. The following are some indications showing how a family becomes ailing: everyone tends to expose the faults of others without being aware of his or her own; everyone intends to live a life of unjustifiable dependence; those in need of proper guidance are unwilling to follow it; the one in the position to edify others with proper guidance does not do it; everyone lacks a moral sense of public spirit such as commending good people while having pity on bad ones, granting others what is profitable while taking over losses, and granting others what is comfortable while taking over what is uncomfortable.

To remedy these ailments, each member of the family should always check his or her own faults; everyone should do away with a life of unjustifiable dependence; those in need of proper guidance should follow it; the one in the position to edify others should do so with rightful guidance; and everyone should forsake egoism and practice altruism. Then the family will be cured of these ailments and become an exemplary one.

## Chapter Sixteen: How to Perfect Both Soul and Flesh

In the past, no one living in the secular world was regarded as a follower of the Way. As a consequence, an evil custom of living in idleness was prevalent among those who alleged to be followers of the Way, doing much harm to the individual, the family, the society, and the state. From now on, as the world is transformed into a fresh new world, the religion for such a new world should be a living religion in which religious practice and daily secular life should not be separated from each other. Therefore, we should obtain clothing, food, and shelter with the truth of Dharmakāya Buddha, Irwŏnsang, the mind-seal transmitted correctly through buddhas and patriarchs together with the threefold practice, viz., cultivation, inquiry, and mindful choice. We should also try to attain to the truth with clothing, food, and shelter together with

---

94. The title of this chapter in *WBK* is "Ailing Society and Its Remedies"; this translation restores the title of the chapter in *PGC*, the old *Canon*; the restoration is explained in the translator's note.

the threefold practice. In this way, we intend to perfect soul and flesh and thereby contribute to the individual, the family, the society, and the nation.

### Chapter Seventeen: Ranks of Dharma Stages

In accordance with the practitioner's level of practice, there are the following six dharma stages: the three grades of elementary faith, unwavering faith, struggle between dharma and *māra*; and the three positions of dharma subjugating *māra*,[95] transcendence (*ch'ulga*),[96] and the supremely enlightened Tathāgata (Thus-come).

1. Elementary faith: One is at this stage if one, learned or ignorant, male or female, old or young, good or evil, high or low, has for the first time accepted the Buddhist teaching in this order, receiving the ten precepts for the elementary faith.

2. Unwavering faith: One is at this stage if one keeps every one of the ten precepts for the grade of elementary faith and has advanced to the preparatory level of the grade of unwavering faith, receiving and keeping the ten precepts for unwavering faith with a general understanding of the doctrine and regulations of this order. One at this stage is not lured to give up this dharma in one's business, thoughts, faith, and sincerity.

3. Dharma-*māra* struggle: One at this stage, receiving and keeping every one of the ten precepts for the grade of elementary faith and every one of the ten precepts for the grade of unwavering faith, has advanced to the preparatory level for the grade of dharma-*māra* struggle and receives and keeps every one of the ten precepts for the grade of dharma-*māra* struggle. One at this stage has the following qualifications: (a) One minutely analyzes dharma and *māra* and makes no serious errors in interpreting the scriptures of this order. (b) One amuses oneself in eliminating delusive thoughts in myriad situations and does not meddle with what is none of one's own business. (c) One confronts *māra* with dharma, understanding the nature of the struggle between dharma and *māra* without committing any of the major offenses against the essential ways of humanity and the essential ways of

---

95. The personification of any defilement or negative tendency that hinders one from practicing the dharma. The destroyer, evil one, devil; he sends his daughters or assumes monstrous forms or inspires wicked men to seduce or frighten the sage. In Won Buddhism, *māra* consists of the three poisons, viz., greed (for wealth, sex, fame, and profit), anger (hatred, detestation, ill will), and delusions (stupidity, jealousy, conceit, false thought).

96. Literally, "leaving home" means transcending the boundary of concern to one's own self, family, clan and state, taking all sentient beings as one's own body and the whole universe as one's own home.

practice.[97] (d) One subdues *māra* with dharma more than half of the time even in cases of minute affairs.

4. Dharma power's subjugation of *māra*: (a) One is promoted to the preparatory level for the position of *māra*-subjugation by the power of dharma upon passing every one of the requirements for the promotion to the grade of dharma-*māra* struggle. (b) Dharma is ever victorious over *māra* in the struggle between the two. (c) One interprets in detail the doctrine of the scriptures of this order and has a complete mastery of the principles of the absolute and the phenomenal, and being and nonbeing. (d) One has attained emancipation from the ills of birth, aging, illness, and death.

5. Transcendence (ch'ulga): (a) One is promoted to the preparatory level for the position of transcendence after fulfilling every one of the requirements for the promotion to the position of *māra*-subjugation by the power of dharma. (b) One can formulate the moral laws concerning right and wrong and gain and loss in human existence on reflection of the principles of the universe, namely, the absolute and the phenomenal, and the vicissitudes of being and nonbeing. (c) One is well versed in the essentials of the doctrines of the extant world religions. (d) Freeing oneself from the boundary of estrangement and closeness, and oneself and others, one would have no regret even if one should undergo any kind of hardships and deadly circumstances on behalf of all sentient beings.

6. Tathāgata of supreme enlightenment: (a) One is advanced to the preparatory level of the position of the Tathāgata of supreme enlightenment upon satisfying every one of the requirements for promotion to the position of transcendence. (b) One, being merciful and compassionate, saves all sentient beings by all-powerful expediencies. (c) With countless skillful means, one delivers sentient beings by acting as circumstances dictate, yet without straying from justice and without letting one's skillful means become known to the delivered. (d) When one acts (the six sense organs are in motion), one's discriminations are free from partiality and attachment;[98] when one does not act (the six sense organs are at rest), one's discriminations are in accordance with the law.

---

97. See above pt. 2, chap. 6.
98. This reflects what Hui-neng (638–713) taught: "We ought to so purify the mind that the six aspects of consciousness (sight, sound, smell, taste, touch, mentation) in passing through their six sense-gates will neither be defiled by nor attached to their six sense objects. When our mind works freely without any hindrance and is at liberty to come and to go, then we have attained the intuitive insight of prajñā, which is emancipation." *Lu-tzu ta-shih fa-pao tan-ching*, *T*, 2008.48.351ab. See below, *SS* IX:38 for Sot'aesan's comments.

# Translation

*The Scripture of Sot'aesan*

# I. Introduction

1. Upon his great enlightenment on the twenty-eighth day of April, in the first year of Won Buddhism (A.D. 1916), the Master said, "All things in the universe are of unitary noumenal nature and all dharmas are of unitary source, amongst which the way of neither arising nor ceasing and the principle of cause-effect response, being mutually grounded on each other, have formed a round framework."[1]

2. Sometime after his great enlightenment, the Master perused the basic scriptures of various religions.[2] Upon reading the Diamond Sūtra, he said, "The Buddha Śākyamuni is truly the sage of all sages. Though I have attained to the Way [supreme enlightenment] without any teacher's guidance, my aspiration and the course of ascetic practice for attaining to the Way coincide, upon reflection in many points, with what the Buddha Śākyamuni did and said. Hence, I choose the Buddha Śākyamuni as the origin of my enlightenment. When I open a religious order in the future, I will establish a perfect and complete one with Buddha-dharma as the main tenets of the doctrine."

3. The Master said, "Buddha-dharma embodies the supreme truth. It elucidates the principle of true noumenal nature, solves the grave matter of birth and death, brings the causal law to light, and provides the method of practice. Thus, it is superior to all other religious doctrines."

4. Examining the turbulent times, the Master expressed the fundamental guideline in a motto: As material power is unfolding, let us unfold spiritual power accordingly.[3]

---

1. This is a summary expression of the truth of Irwŏnsang. The principle of neither arising (birth) nor ceasing (death) pertains to the realm of nirvāna and dharmakāya; and the causal law of karmic retribution pertains to saṃsāra.

2. *WK*, pt. I, chap. 3, sec. 1: "Sot'aesan surveyed the Four Classics and the *Hsiao-ching* [Filial piety] of Confucianism; the *Chin-kang ching* [Diamond Sūtra], the *Sŏnyo* [Essentials of Zen], the *Pulgyo taejŏn* [Compendium of Buddhism], and the *P'alsangjŏn* [Eight Aspects of the Buddha's life] of Buddhism; the *Yin-fu ching* [Secret planning] and *Yü-shu ching* [Jade hinge] of Taoism; the *Tonggyŏng taejŏn* [Compendium of Eastern learning] and the *Kasa* [Hymns] of Ch'ŏndogyo; and the Old and New Testaments of Christianity.

3. See above, *Canon*, note to the founding motto.

5. In only a few months of his edification, the Master had more than forty followers, of whom he selected nine who were sincere and firm in faith. He decided that they would be the main disciples for the establishment of a new religious order. He said to them, "Humankind is the lord of all things, and all things are to be used by humankind. Benevolence (C. *jen*) and righteousness (C. *i*) are the main principles of morality; trickery is not. It is a matter of necessary course, therefore, that human spirit should rule over all material things and that the moral principles of benevolence and righteousness should rule human conduct. Recently, however, the main moral principles have been ignored, and trickery is rampant. Thus, the supreme morality has been abnegated. At this critical time, we ought to act in concert and agreement in order to rectify the public morality, which is declining daily. You should understand this point and thereby prepare to be the founders of a great new religious order."

6. As a way of edifying the people of the world, the Master devised a method of organizing ten people as a unit and said, "By this simple method all people can be efficiently trained by only one mentor, who can exert his or her effort only to nine members, though billions of people can be guided by this method." He organized the first unit of this order with the nine disciples he had earlier chosen and said, "This unit is formed responding to the ten directions: the leader corresponds to heaven, the center to the earth, and the eight members of the unit to the eight directions. Unfolded, it corresponds to the ten directions; folded, the ten directions are joined in one body." Sot'aesan was the leader of the unit, Song Kyu, the center; the remaining eight members were Yi Chae-ch'ŏl, Yi Sun-sun, Kim Ki-ch'ŏn, O Ch'ang-gŏn, Pak Se-ch'ŏl, Pak Tong-guk, Yu Kŏn, and Kim Kwang-sŏn.[4]

7. In preparation for founding the new religious order, the Master established a savings association and said to the members, "The task we are about to embark upon is something that not everyone can do. What cannot be done by everyone requires unusual patience and effort. As we are poor, we will be unable to lay the foundation for the task without unusual thrift and labor. Hence we ought to observe the articles of the association with utmost sincerity, and thereby set an example of the founding spirit for our younger generation." Sot'aesan then ordered the members of the association to refrain from smoking and drinking, to save *poŭnmi*,[5] and to participate in cooperative labor.

---

4. These are the dharma names that Sot'aesan conferred on the nine disciples on August 21, 1919. See below, sec. 14.

5. *Poŭnmi* literally means "rice for requital of beneficence." A small portion of one's daily portion of rice was saved and donated for the public well-being. This practice is one of the four general duties of a Won Buddhist, the remaining three duties being praying at dawn and evening, proselytizing at least nine people into this order, and observing the laws and regulations of the order.

8. The Master started an embankment project to reclaim the tidal land in front of Kilyong-ni [in March 1918 (3 w.e.)]. He supervised, saying, "You, nine members, are undergoing a great deal of hardship with this project, especially because you have no experience of labor. However, your happiness will be great since you have come to the world to meet the opportunity to establish a great religious order. It is much more significant for one to be a progenitor by establishing something with a great deal of trouble than to be a keeper of something that someone else has toiled to establish. The order we are about to establish was unheard of in the past, and there will rarely be anything like it in the future. The doctrine of such an order should be formulated with the following considerations. Morality and science should be improved side by side for the realization of a truly civilized world. One's religious practice and public service should be carried out together by maintaining the balance of action and rest. Various religious doctrines should be synthesized for the realization of unity and harmony among them. Naturally, much work awaits us because we plan to establish a perfect order."

9. While the embankment project was being carried out by the members of the unit, a wealthy man in a neighboring village had a dispute with the association concerning the ownership of the tidal land. He also submitted an application to the county authority for permission to reclaim the tidal land and frequented the county office, thus raising issues on the ownership of the land. Seeing this, the members detested him. The Master said to the members, "The occurrence of this dispute in the process of the project seems to be the will of heaven to test the sincerity of our hearts; hence you should not be distracted by this dispute. You should not detest or bear a grudge against him. Right prevails in the end. Even if all our hard work ends up in his private property, we would have nothing to be ashamed of. Although it may not be used for the public as it was originally planned, he is at least one of the members of the society. Since our intention is always to work for the public well-being and since a considerable piece of farmland is to be cultivated for the villagers of this poor riverside, our work brings benefits to the general public. If you continue exerting yourselves with the original intention to work only for the public well-being, transcending the boundary of egoism, matters will be resolved aright."

10. One day Yi Ch'un-p'ung came and paid homage to the Master. Pointing to the nine members who were working at the site of the embankment project, the Master asked Ch'un-p'ung, "They follow me to learn the supreme Way. Do you know why I have ordered them to build the embankment instead of teaching the supreme Way?" Ch'un-p'ung answered, "Although my shallow opinion cannot fathom the depth of your intention, there seem to be two reasons. First, you intend to have them prepare for the expenses necessary for learning by em-

banking the tidal land. Secondly, you intend to prove to them that if they work together in perfect accord, there is nothing that they cannot do." The Master said, "Though you are right in general terms, listen to me for my further intentions. Since they have come to learn the Way, the teacher must know the depth of their faith. If you try to create farmland out of tidal land that has been deserted for tens of thousands of years, the villagers will laugh at you. The members had no experience of hard labor. Hence, you can discern the depth and sincerity of their faith by observing how they carry out the project embracing such ridicule and hard labor. Further, if you examine the completion of this project from start to finish, you will be able to measure their ability to accomplish many other projects in the future. They will learn that the source of blessings and prosperity lies in self-sufficiency, which is based on thrift, savings, and diligence. They will have a golden opportunity to train themselves in the practice of following the original nature[6] while they undergo all sorts of hardships and strengthen their patience in overcoming suffering. With these points in mind, I have embarked upon this project."

11. Upon completion of the embankment project (1919), the members of the association talked among themselves: "At the beginning, the task ahead of us seemed as difficult as if we were going to create a mountain on flat land. Now that the project is completed, the embankment was rather an easy one. How difficult could it be to attain to the Way?" Listening to the conversation, the Master said, "You ask this because you don't yet know how to attain to the Way; however, if you knew the Way, you would realize that it is easier than having a meal. Why should this frame of mind, which is magnanimous and placid, be like the labor needed to build the embankment? If the point is not clear to you, just keep in mind what I have said and think it over when you are enlightened to the Way of practice."

12. When the first temple of the order was under construction at the foot of the Ongnyŏ peak in Kilyong-ni, the Master wrote on the ridgebeam:

> With Irwŏn as the loom,
> The sun and the moon as the weaving shuttle,
> The great doctrine of spring and autumn
> shall be woven.

To this he added:

> The pine is standing,
>     having gathered the remaining spring
>         from all other trees;

---

6. See above, *Canon*, pt. 3, chap. 12.

The brook is roaring,
  having gathered the drizzles
    from a thousand mountain peaks.

13. The Master said to his nine disciples, "Now, material civilization is daily flourishing with immense power while the spirit of humankind, making use of material conveniences, is growing weaker so that individuals, families, societies, and the nation will lose stability, and all sentient beings will suffer greatly in the seas of misery. How could we, who aspire to deliver the world from misery, not care about the situation? Some sages in the past who wished to deliver sentient beings moved the will of heaven by prayers of utmost sincerity. Why don't you prove the truthfulness of your intention by moving the will of heaven with prayers of utmost sincerity so that the spirit of humankind may be the master of material things instead of being enslaved to them? Your mind is none other than that of heaven; hence, if your mind is concentrated in purity unstained by selfishness, the power of your mind will be united with the virtue of heaven and earth so that your mind will lead everything you do to success. Therefore, you must bear in mind that your mind contains an element able to move the will of heaven and that you have the responsibility to deliver all sentient beings." He then selected dates and prayer sites for each member and had them offer prayers at the same time.

14. On August 21, 1919 [4 w.e.], the nine disciples' utmost sincerity and devotion, which transcended the limits of life and death, produced a miraculous event: the seal of blood on white paper.[7] Seeing this, the Master said, "The divine spirits of heaven and earth have already been moved by your sincerity and devotion and a planning in the dharma realm has been completed; hence the success of our plan has been assured by this. Now that you have consecrated yourselves to the good cause of the world, do not lose this mind whenever you confront diffi-

---

7. See *WK*, pt. 1, chap. 4, sec. 5. The prayers (held three times a month) continued for four months until August 21, 1919, but nothing particular happened. Sot'aesan pointed out to his disciples that the divine spirits of heaven and earth had not been moved by their prayers because they had not eliminated selfishness from their hearts. Sot'aesan asked whether, as a candle lights others and consumes itself, they would sacrifice their lives if that were the only way to carry out the good cause. The disciples expressed willingness to do so with much enthusiasm. So they prepared to sacrifice their lives at their prayer sites at the same time. Before departing for the prayer sites, they had a prayer together in the dharma hall, where they put their daggers on the altar table beside the white paper on which was written: We will die with no regret. They prostrated themselves before the table after pressing their thumbs under their names on the paper. There appeared fingerprints of blood. Taking that as the evidence of authentication from the dharma realm, Sot'aesan stopped them from going to the prayer sites and gave this sermon, then ordered them to go to the prayer sites to conclude the prayer. Even after the event, the prayers continued until Sot'aesan stopped them in November.

culties and hardships while working for the public well-being. When you feel attached to your family or five desires,[8] just recall what has happened today so that you can detach yourselves from such adverse conditions. With this pure mind of no attachment exert yourselves in practice and public service." The Master then conferred dharma titles and dharma names on them, saying, "Your names of the past are the names of the secular world and private names. Those with the secular names have already died. With these dharma names, you are born again; keep the dharma name and deliver therewith countless sentient beings."[9]

15. The Master said, "From now on, what we should learn is Buddha-dharma and what we should teach our followers is also Buddha-dharma. Exert yourselves to be enlightened to the fundamental truth by inquiring into the gist of Buddha-dharma. Though I already knew the truth of Buddha-dharma, I have only instructed you so as to arouse your faith by an unsystematic teaching in accordance with the capacity of the followers without mentioning whether Buddha-dharma is true or false, or right or wrong. I did so for the following reasons. Your spiritual capacity was not quite ready to analyze the truth of Buddha-dharma. Buddhism has been treated contemptuously in this country for several hundred years so that no one would respect anything carrying the name 'Buddhism,' and thus I was reluctant to introduce Buddha-dharma lest it would not be respected by the world.

"If the fundamental truth is to be discovered and if sentient beings are to be led to the gate of blessings and wisdom through correct practice, then no other religion than Buddha-dharma should be taken as the main doctrine. Moreover, Buddhism will be the major religion of the world. However, Buddha-dharma of the future will be different from that of the past. Buddha-dharma of the future will be practiced by all walks of life, namely, by scholar-officials, farmers, artisans, and tradesmen, and by the laity as well as the priesthood. The worship of the Buddha shall not be limited to taking refuge in the statue of the Buddha. One will realize that all things in the universe and the dharma realm of empty space are none other than the Buddha. Buddha-dharma will not be separated from daily work. The one who handles worldly affairs well will be the one who practices Buddha-dharma well; and one who does not do well with worldly affairs cannot be said to know Buddha-dharma. The ritual of making offerings to Buddha for blessing should be reformed so that Buddha and place for making offerings are not set aside in a particular place; they are wherever one works and

---

8. Desires for wealth, sex, food and drink, fame, and sleep.
9. The names of the nine disciples appearing in *SS* I:6 above are the dharma names that Sot'aesan gave them.

wishes for blessings. In this way there will be no place where the dharma hall and the Buddha [image] are not found; and the blessings of the Buddha will reach even grasses and trees and his virtue will be felt everywhere, creating the Buddha land of blessings. Listen! This is a rare opportunity you have met, and you have made yourselves founders of a new religious order when people in general do not know what is happening. Though what I am saying cannot be proven at this point, do not take my words as groundless; you will see the truth of my words in the near future if you follow my guidance."

16. The Master said, "Buddhism, being a religion with close affinity to Korea, has received both welcome and rejection to a great extent. It had been well received until five hundred years ago; since then, it has been rejected, up until recent times. Subject to political changes and pushed out by the power of the Confucian national ideology of the Chosŏn dynasty, Buddhists hid themselves in deep mountain valleys, where they led ascetic lives. There were few in the secular world who understood Buddha-dharma. Accordingly, the superficial opinions of the few who alleged to know of Buddhism ran as follows.

> In a place rich in the scenic beauty of hills and waters there are Buddhist temples with monks and Buddha statues. As there are monks and Buddha statues, people go to the temples to make offering to the Buddha statues for blessings and forgiveness of evils committed. The monks, being disciples of the Buddha statues, remain unmarried, with heads shaven, clad in humble clothes, intoning the name of a buddha with beads in hand or reciting the Buddhist scriptures, going around begging with knapsacks on their backs, paying respects even to the lowest people in the secular world, refraining from eating fish and meat, and from drinking, smoking, and killing living beings. No one of noble birth, with wealth, or who is fortune's favorite is supposed to become a Buddhist monk; only an ill-fated person, or a person who has failed in the secular world, or who has fallen behind the times is to become a Buddhist monk. If a monk attains enlightenment after strenuous cultivation of the Way, he becomes a geomancer who chooses auspicious sites for graves and houses. An enlightened monk has the power to call winds and summon rains, or to play such magic as moving across mountains and crossing lakes and rivers on foot,[10] though such a prodigious monk can rarely be found out of thousands or tens of thousands of monks. Therefore, Buddha-dharma is a futile

---

10. The original Chinese phrase is Casting away mountains and upsetting the sea.

way, which ordinary people in the secular world cannot follow. Though it is all right for one to go to such scenic sites
for a picnic, anyone who goes to the temple to worship the
Buddha or who leaves home to become a monk will have his
home ruined. Since the Buddhists practice cremation, their
descendants will receive no help from the spirits of their
ancestors.

"Thus monks who believed in Buddha-dharma were regarded as
extraordinary human beings. The real life of most monks, however, was
not correctly known to the secular world. They had the Buddha statues
enshrined in clean temples built in deep mountain valleys of beautiful
scenery away from the troubled secular world. Alone without any relatives around, they lived, appreciating the breeze passing through pine
leaves, and the moon through creeping vines, and the natural orchestra
of birds singing, and the brooks murmuring in all directions. They lived
carefree on the food and clothing the laity provided, intoning the name
of a buddha, or reciting certain Buddhist scriptures, or strolling out of a
stately temple building into a wood. Though not all Buddhist monks
lived like this, most of them led a life of leisure, purity, and taste. While
the Buddhist monks lived like that, however, the supreme Buddha-
dharma remained unknown to the secular world, and the monks fell
into a self-complacent Hīnayāna egoism. How could this be the original
intention of the Buddha? Therefore, we intend to reform some part
of the doctrine and the system without altering the central tenets of
Buddha-dharma so that the Buddhism of a few should be that of the
general populace, and so that partial practice should become complete
practice."

17. The Master continued, "The supreme Way of the Buddha is
limitless in its loftiness, profundity, and immensity; and the penetrating
power of the Buddha's wisdom is beyond verbal or literary description.
However, the following points are in general true of the penetrating
power of the Buddha's wisdom. While ordinary people are aware only
of birth and death and are ignorant of the cycle of birth and death, the
Buddha knew the principle of neither birth nor death [in the realm of
nirvāṇa] and of limitless life through endless reincarnations. While we
do not know the fundamental principle of our being, the Buddha knew
even the fundamental principles of all things in the universe. We,
unclear about good paths and evil paths, are apt to fall into evil paths
[the destinies of the beast, the hungry ghost, and hell]; after he had
delivered himself, the Buddha had the ability to deliver all sentient
beings from evil paths to good paths. While we do not know how we
cause happiness and suffering for ourselves, the Buddha knew how
sentient beings cause these for themselves as well as the causes of the
happiness and suffering that unexpectedly fall on sentient beings. While

we are at the end of a tether when we exhaust the resources of blessings, the Buddha has the ability to have blessings return when they are dried out. While we do not care whether our wisdom is shining or dimmed, the Buddha has the ability to brighten wisdom when it gets dimmed and the ability to keep it from getting dim. While we commit wrong-doing as a result of being distracted by the three poisons of greed, anger, and delusions, the Buddha is never distracted by them. While we do not know the emptiness of all things in the universe because we are attached to the phenomenal existence of all things in the universe, the Buddha knows that all things in the phenomenal world are empty of reality and that being comes out of nonbeing. While we do not know the six realms of existence, namely, deva, human existence, *asura* [malevolent natural spirits], beasts, hungry ghosts, and hells, and the four forms of rebirth, namely, viviparous as with Mammalia, oviparous as with birds, moisture- or water-born as with worms and fishes, metamorphic as with moths from chrysalis, the Buddha knows how sentient beings transform themselves through these paths. While sentient beings try to take advantage of others in order to make themselves happy, the Buddha, in dealing with any matter, follows the principle of mutual benefit or makes it his blessing and happiness to benefit others regardless of gain or loss, even at the risk of his own life. While we regard nothing other than what we actually possess as our property, nothing other than the actual house we live in as our own house, and no people as our own family other than our own family, the Buddha regards all things in the universe as his own property, the whole universe as his own house, and all sentient beings as his own family. It is our aspiration, therefore, to devote ourselves with such wisdom and ability as the Buddha's to delivering sentient beings."

18. The Master continued, "The doctrine and system of traditional Buddhism were structured mainly for the livelihood of the bonze priests and, hence, were unsuitable for those people living in the secular world. Accordingly, the laity was not of primary but of secondary importance so that none of the laity could stand in the lineage of the direct disciples of the Buddha or enter as a patriarch except those who made an unusual material contribution or attained extraordinary spiritual culti-vation. The aim of a religion lies in delivering sentient beings; however, the Buddhist temples are located in deep mountain valleys remote from the secular world. How could people, busy with secular life, leave the mundane life behind to find the leisure for learning Buddha-dharma? The Buddhist scriptures are written in Chinese compound words that are too difficult to understand and learn and too difficult to teach to the general public, learned or ignorant, men or women, old or young. As the Buddhist monks, having no occupation either as scholar-officials, farmers, artisans, or tradesmen, depended on the laity's offerings to the Buddha statue, donations, and alms for food and clothing, this lifestyle

could not be for the general public. Monks were strictly prohibited from marrying. They articulated various forms for Buddhist offering, but did not provide the rules of rite and propriety for the secular world. Thus, the livelihood of the monks cannot be followed by the general public. In this order, therefore, these matters shall be reformed.

a. There shall be no discrimination between priesthood and laity as to the question of primary and secondary status; distinctions will only be recognized in the degrees of practice and public service.

b. There will be no discrimination between priesthood and laity in the lineage of dharma succession.

c. The temples for Buddhist practice shall be established wherever the laity reside.

d. Scriptures shall include only the most essential ones and shall be written in an easy language that the general public can learn.

e. Priests shall be allowed to have suitable occupations in accordance with circumstances.

f. A priest shall be free to marry if he wishes.

g. Complicated and useless formalities shall be abolished from the rituals of Buddhist offering, and the new rules of rite shall be formulated with emphasis on realistic rituals appropriate and useful to the secular life.

h. As to the course of a priest's life, one shall acquire, except for special circumstances, general education during childhood, train oneself in practice, and exert oneself for the work of deliverance during the prime of life. During senescence one will stay in a scenic and quiet place, severing the worldly attachments of love and desire and meditating and training oneself to become emancipated from the grave matter of birth and death. In spring and autumn, the old priest will visit temples, one after another, and in the secular world render help in the task of deliverance. In winter and summer one will concentrate on spiritual cultivation [sitting in meditation and intoning the name of a Buddha]. In this way the life of the priest can be well-rounded, lacking nothing.

The order that will execute this doctrine and system shall be made perfect for the times and the public morals."

19. The Master continued, "The subjects taught in the traditional Buddhist sects were not comprehensive. Different sects taught exclusively one of the following: scriptures, *kanhwa* meditation,[11] intoning the name of a buddha, incantation, or Buddhist offering.

---

11. *Kanhwa Sŏn* (J. *kanna Zen*) is a meditation practiced with an essential point in a *kongan* story.

The purpose of studying scriptures lies in having the believer learn the doctrine, system, and history of Buddhism. The purpose of sitting in *kanhwa* meditation is to help one become enlightened to the profound truth, which is difficult to teach by scriptures or verbal explanations. Intoning the name of a buddha and incantation are practiced for spiritual concentration by those who enter the Buddhist order for the first time and have difficulty in entering the correct way of Buddhadharma because of their desires. The method of making an offering to Buddha image is taught for the fulfillment of the believer's wishes and for contributions to Buddhist work.

The laity must learn all of these subjects; however, different sects[12] attached themselves to one or two of them with partial practice, arguing against one another and thereby impeding the faith and practice of the believer. Our intention is to integrate all these practices under one soteriological principle after we examine all *kongan*s [public documents] of the Zen school and all scriptures of the doctrinal schools. Leaving out the complicated *kongan*s and scriptures, we will choose the following: Those *kongan*s and scriptures that explicate the most essential principles of Buddha-dharma, as the training subjects for attaining the power of inquiry into facts and principles; intoning the name of a buddha, sitting in meditation, and incantation, as the training courses for spiritual cultivation; and a number of precepts, explanations of the principle of karmic retribution, and the moral duties to the fourfold beneficence,[13] as the training subjects for mindful choice in karmic action, which are suitable for secular living.

It is our plan that all these three areas of training shall be practiced together in balance by all believers of Buddha-dharma. The purpose of training in the subjects of inquiry is to attain the Buddha's power of inquiry, which creates a thorough comprehension of facts and principles; the purpose of training in the subjects of cultivation is to attain the Buddha's power of cultivation, which keeps one from attaching oneself to worldly things; and the purpose of training in the subjects of mindful choice is to attain the Buddha's power of mindful choice, which lets one analyze right from wrong and do what is right. If the believer takes the threefold great power to be the ground for the Buddhist offering in daily life and to be the moving power to realize all aspirations [to attain Buddhahood and deliver all sentient beings from the seas of misery], then all the doctrines will be unified and the believer's practice will be well-rounded.

---

12. See *PGC*, bk. 1, pt. 1, chap. 6, for the original writing, which was revised as this section; there one reads "those with little understanding of Buddha-dharma."

13. See above, *Canon* pt. 2, chap. 2.

## II. On Doctrine

1. The Master said, "In the past, the founders of various religions came in accordance with the call of the times and taught what humankind ought to do. However, the doctrines with which they edified people varied depending on the times and districts. This is analogous to there being different areas of specialty in medical science. Buddhism takes as its central tenet the emptiness of the ultimate reality of all things in the universe and teaches the truth of neither arising nor ceasing and the causal law of karmic retribution. Thereby, Buddhism mainly explicates the path for changing the deluded into the enlightened. Confucianism takes as its main tenet the reality of all things in the universe and teaches the three duties [the duties of a prince, father, and husband] and the five human relationships [between prince and minister, father and son, husband and wife, brothers, and friends] and the four constant virtues, namely, benevolence [C. *jen*], righteousness [C. *i*], propriety [C. *li*], and wisdom [C. *chih*]. Thereby, it mainly explicates the ways of personal moral cultivation, regulation of household affairs, governing a country, and realizing peace in the world. Taoism takes as its main tenet the way of naturalness manifested in all things in the universe and teaches how to nourish one's nature. It thereby explicates the path of purity, tranquility, and doing nothing unnatural. Now, these three paths are different from one another in what they take as the essence of their doctrines; however, they agree in their purposes, namely, to correct the ills of the world and help all sentient beings. In the past the three religions, namely, Confucianism, Buddhism, and Taoism, taught their specialties exclusively; however, in the future the world cannot be delivered by any one of them; hence, we intend to unify the three doctrines so that all courses of practice shall be designed on the following principles: (a) The threefold practice, namely, the cultivation [of spirit], inquiry [into facts and principles], and mindful choice [in karmic action] shall be unified in the truth of Irwŏn.[14] (b) Spiritual and physical life shall be improved together in complete balance. (c) Principle and fact shall be pursued together.[15] Anyone who sincerely practices in this way will not only master the essences of the three religions but also comprehend the essences of the doctrines of other religions of the world as well as all the truths of the universe, attaining to the supreme enlightenment."

2. One of the Master's disciples asked, "What do you call the great

---

14. See above, *Canon*, pt. 2, chap. 4, sec. 7.

15. Enlightenment into the principle of noumenon and phenomenon, being and non-being, and the construction of affairs of right and wrong, good and evil should be pursued together. Practice and public service should be carried out together. Wisdom and blessedness should be cultivated together.

Way?" The Master said, "What all people can do is the great Way and what only a few can do is the small Way. The consummate essence of Irwŏn, fourfold beneficence, four essentials, threefold practice, and eight articles in our doctrine are what all people can know and practice. Hence the doctrine of this order is the great Way for the world."

3. Pak Kwang-jŏn asked, "How is Irwŏnsang [unitary circular symbol] related to humankind?" The Master answered, "You have raised a question that is concerned with the fundamental truth. Irwŏnsang is enshrined in this order in a similar way as the statue of the Buddha is enshrined in the traditional Buddhist order. However, the statue of the Buddha is the symbol of the Buddha's bodily appearance, whereas Irwŏnsang is the symbol of the essence of the Buddha's mind. The bodily appearance is merely a doll, whereas the essence of mind, being vast, great, and infinite, includes both being and nonbeing and penetrates the three periods of past, present, and future. It is the fundamental source of all things in the universe and the realm of samādhi, which cannot be expressed in words. It is called T'ai-chi [the Great Ultimate] or Wu-chi [the Ultimate of Nonbeing] in Confucianism, Nature or Tao [the Way] in Taoism, and pure Dharmakāya Buddha in Buddhism; however, one and the same principle is called by these different names. No matter which of these directions one takes, one will eventually return to the truth of Irwŏn. Any religion that is not based on this truth is the wrong way. Therefore, we have enshrined Irwŏnsang as the standard for relating our daily life to the essence of the Buddha's mind, and we are related to Dharmakāya Buddha through the two ways of religious faith and practice."[16]

4. Kwang-jŏn asked again, "What is the way of religious faith in the truth of Irwŏnsang?" The Master answered, "To have faith in the truth of Irwŏnsang, one should take it as the object of religious faith and believe in its truth, pursuing blessings and happiness thereby. It stands, as a symbol, for the origin of the fourfold beneficence, which, in turn, is a fourfold categorization of all things in the universe. Heaven and earth, all things, the dharma realm of empty space—all these are none other than the universal Buddha. Therefore, we should always treat all things everywhere with the same sense of respect and awe and a pure heart and pious attitude as we have when we respect the Buddha. We should also treat all things as a way of making an offering to Buddha and thereby create blessedness and happiness realistically. In this way we have reformed the religious faith from a partial faith to a complete one and from a superstitious faith to a realistic one."[17]

5. Kwang-jŏn asked again, "How should one practice Irwŏnsang?"

---

16. See above, *Canon*, pt. 2, chap. 1, sec. 4.
17. Ibid., sec. 2.

The Master answered, "One should take Irwŏnsang as the standard of practice and model oneself after its truth, cultivating one's personality in the following three aspects. First, by being enlightened to the truth of Irwŏnsang, one is to know the beginning and end of all things and the root and branches of all things,[18] the birth, old age, illness, and death of all human beings, and the causal law of karmic retribution. Secondly, one is to nourish one's clear nature, by keeping one's mind, like Irwŏn, from selfishness, or from leaning toward attachment and desire. Thirdly, one is to do all things right and fair, like Irwŏn, without being distracted by such feelings as joy, anger, sorrow, or pleasure, or by the consideration of remoteness, closeness, friendliness, and estrangement. Awakening to the truth of Irwŏn is none other than seeing into one's own original nature; keeping the noumenal nature of Irwŏn is none other than nourishing one's own original nature;[19] and acting as perfect as Irwŏn is none other than following one's original nature.[20] The essential ways of practice in our order, namely, spiritual cultivation, inquiry into facts and principles, and mindful choice in karmic action are these; and threefold practice that the Buddha taught, namely, precept (*śīla*), concentration (samādhi), and wisdom (prajñā), is none other than these. Cultivation is concentration and nourishment of one's nature, inquiry leads to wisdom and seeing into one's nature, and mindful choice is keeping precepts and following one's nature. If one exerts sincere efforts in this threefold practice, one will attain to buddhahood, no matter whether one is learned or illiterate, intelligent or dull, man or woman, or old or young."[21]

6. Kwang-jŏn asked further, "Are you saying then that the circular figure drawn on the wooden board contains in itself such truth, potency, and the way of practice?" The Master answered, "That circular figure is a model that is adopted to make the true Irwŏn known. This is analogous to the fact that the finger used to point at the moon is not itself the moon. Therefore, the cultivator of the Way should discover the true Irwŏn through its symbol, Irwŏnsang, keep the true nature of

---

18. This reflects the Confucian approach to the extension of knowledge: "Things have their root and their branches. Affairs have their end and their beginning. To know what is first and what is last will lead near to what is taught in the Great Learning." See *Ta-hsüeh*, sec. 3; Legge, *Confucius*, p. 357.

19. A synthesis of the Buddhist notion, Dharmakāya, of which Irwŏnsang is the symbol, and the Confucian notion, of nourishing the nature, as can be seen in the *Meng-tzu* VII:1, 2: "To preserve one's mental constitution, and nourish one's nature, is the Way to serve Heaven." See Legge, *Works of Mencius*, p. 449.

20. To act as perfectly as Irwŏn is to follow one's original nature, which is another Confucian notion as is found in the *Chung-yung* (Doctrine of the Mean), I, 1: "What Heaven has conferred is called THE NATURE; an accordance with this nature is called THE PATH *of duty*." See Legge, *Confucius*, p. 383.

21. See above, *Canon*, pt. 2, chap. 1, sec. 3.

Irwŏn, and apply the perfect mind of Irwŏn to daily affairs so that the truth of Irwŏnsang can be realized in our daily life."[22]

7. The Master said, "The truth of Irwŏn can be summarized in terms of emptiness (*kong*), roundness (*wŏn*), and correctness (*chŏng*).[23]

"In nourishing one's nature, to intuit the state of mind which transcends existence and nonexistence is emptiness; the state of mind where nothing comes or goes is roundness; and the mind which does not lean toward anything is correctness.

"In seeing into one's nature,[24] to know, owing to thorough knowledge of the truth of Irwŏn, the realm that is ineffable and devoid of mental phenomena is emptiness; to be free from being stuck as a result of the vast scope of knowledge is roundness; and to see and judge all matters correctly with sure knowledge is correctness.

"In following one's nature, to do all things in *munyŏm* [no thought] is emptiness; to do all things with no attachment is roundness; and to do all things in accordance with the Mean is correctness."[25]

8. The Master said, "The purpose the practitioners of the Way have for enlightenment into the abstruse truth is to make use of it in actual life; it will be of no use if it is left unused. I will tell you how the truth of Irwŏnsang [which is the symbol of] Dharmakāya Buddha can be applied in daily life. First, you must take Irwŏnsang as a *hwadu* for seeing into your original nature and attaining to buddhahood whenever you see it. Secondly, you must take it as the standard of practice so that your moral practice in daily life may be as perfect as Irwŏnsang.[26] Thirdly, realizing that all things in the universe have the actual authority to bless or punish you, it should be taken as [the symbol of] that which you believe as the truth [of karmic retribution]. If you understand this truth, it will be worshiped whenever you see it as if it were the picture of your parents."

---

22. Ibid., secs. 4 and 5.
23. See below, *SS* VII:9.
24. See below *SS* VII:7, 8.
25. This is a grand synthesis of the Confucian moral tenet of the Mean and the Buddhist practice of no thought (*munyŏm*) and no attachment in following the nature, which is a Confucian moral duty, which in turn is synthesized into the realization of the truth of Irwŏn, Dharmakāya Buddha in one's own mind. In the *Chung-yung* II, 1, "Confucius said, 'The superior man *embodies* the course of the Mean, the mean man acts contrary to the course of the Mean'" (Legge, *Confucius*, p. 386). Similarly (IX), "The Master said, 'The kingdom, its States, and its families, may be ruled; dignities and emoluments may be declined; naked weapons may be trampled under the feet; but the course of the Mean cannot be attained to'" (Legge, *Confucius*, p. 389). For the Buddhist practice of absence of thought and no attachment, see *Liu-tzu t'an ching*, *T.* 2007.48.340c: "By absence of thought is meant to see all dharmas but not to be attached to them, and for the mind to be everywhere but not to be attached anywhere."
26. See above, *Canon*, pt. 2, chap. 1, secs. 4 and 5 for "Dharma Words of Irwŏnsang" and "Vow to Irwŏnsang" respectively.

9. Someone asked the Master, "Which Buddha is worshiped as the principal master in your order?" The Master answered, "Śākyamuni Buddha is worshiped as the principal master." The man asked again, "If Śākyamuni Buddha is the ancestral master, shouldn't the Buddha statue be enshrined instead of Irwŏnsang in your dharma hall?" The Master said, "It is hard to teach people the evidence of how the Buddha statue blesses or punishes us. Irwŏnsang is the symbol of the pure and clear Dharmakāya Buddha. Heaven and earth, parents, and brethren are the transformed bodies (*nirmanakāya*) of Dharmakāya Buddha. Law is also what Dharmakāya Buddha gives us. We have enshrined Irwŏnsang as the object of religious faith because we can teach people ample evidence of how heaven and earth, parents, brethren, and law bless or punish us. That is why Irwŏnsang is enshrined as the object of religious faith." The man asked again, "Then it is only in words that Śākyamuni Buddha is worshiped as the original master, and there is no act of worship." The Master answered, "Although no Buddha statue is enshrined in the dharma hall, we direct the laity's faith so that they venerate the Buddha most sincerely and we teach that the true worship of the Buddha lies in transmitting and developing the Buddha's dharma lineage and his work of salvation by accepting the true spirit of his teaching and practicing it whenever the six sense organs are at work. The truthful worship of the Buddha should not be limited to the Buddhist rites performed in front of the Buddha statue every morning and evening."

10. The man asked again, "It seems most adequate to teach the wise people of this intellectually advanced age by explaining the source of blessings and misery by enshrining Irwŏnsang. However, few are the wise in any age, and the world abounds in the deluded. Wouldn't it be more beneficial, therefore, to enshrine the Buddha statue for awakening faith in the general populace?" The Master said, "Even the least intelligent can understand and believe the evidence, if explained in some detail, of how Dharmakāya Buddha, [the fundamental source of] the fourfold beneficence, confers blessings or punishment; however, those who cannot have faith without the statue of the Buddha can very well be delivered where it is enshrined. Then, believers of the statue of the Buddha and those of Irwŏnsang can both be delivered."

11. The man asked further, "Is there any relationship between Irwŏnsang and Śākyamuni Buddha?" The Master said, "Irwŏn is the fundamental source of all truth, and Śākyamuni Buddha is the master who was enlightened to the truth of Irwŏn and taught it to us. Even if the truth subsists in the universe, it will be of no use to us if there is no one who discovers and teaches it to us. On the other hand, Śākyamuni could not become the Buddha when he came to the world if there were no truth of Irwŏnsang. Nor could he have had any material for preaching for forty-nine years but for the truth of Irwŏnsang. Therefore, we

take Irwŏnsang as the symbol of the truth, Dharmakāya Buddha, and Śākyamuni Buddha as the original teacher. In this way we can worship *dharmakāya-tathāgata* [immortal buddhahood] and *rūpakāya-tathāgata* [physical buddha] at the same time. However, this differentiation of Irwŏnsang from Śākyamuni Buddha is made from the point of phenomenal differences; Irwŏn and Śākyamuni are nondual, be it known, from the point of noumenal unity."

12. A disciple asked, "What is the difference between the worship of the statue of the Buddha and that of Irwŏnsang?" The Master said, "The worship of the statue of the Buddha, being limited to his personality, has no more significance than the commemoration and veneration that we, as late disciples, pay to him; whereas the worship of Irwŏnsang has a great significance. Instead of limiting the object of worship to the personality of the Buddha, we treat and worship all things in the universe as the Buddha and seek thereby the source of blessings and punishment in them. Furthermore, one should cultivate one's personality to be as perfect as Irwŏnsang by taking it as the standard of practice. In general these are the differences."

13. The Master said, "The worship of the statue of the Buddha has so far performed some service in the teaching and development of Buddha-dharma; however, it will not from now on. People will be disillusioned about the potency of the Buddha statue after having worshiped it for thousands of years. Being disillusioned about what is only a means, they will have no faith in the dharma. Thus, the worship of the statue of the Buddha will be a hindrance to the teaching and development of Buddha-dharma. Regrettably, there will even be quite a few people who enshrine the Buddha statue as a means of livelihood. For these reasons, we have decided to enshrine Irwŏnsang, the symbol of Dharmakāya Buddha."

14. The Master said, "This is the era when the human race is gradually reaching spiritual maturity with the expansion of knowledge. People will understand the principles of transgression and blessedness when they experience them. Understanding the principle, they will search for the sources of transgression and blessedness. The sources being found, the meaning of transgression and blessedness will be made clear. The meaning being made clear, they will believe in the principle. If people find and worship the object of worship that can easily be understood, then, they, wise or deluded, will attain peace of mind and emancipation. As to the method of making offerings to the Buddha, one must do it for oneself rather than having someone else perform the Buddhist offering on behalf of oneself as in the past. All those who have faith in Buddha-dharma must know how to perform the Buddhist offering, and the doctrine and system of this order can be taken as the method of the Buddhist offering. Whether the worship of the Buddhist offering, done correctly, be answered or not will depend on the sincere

and continued effort proper to each state of affairs. Therefore, whether one has a good or bad affinity with others, whether one can produce good or bad karma, whether one is born rich, poor, high, or low in this lifetime all depends on how well one has made the offering to the Buddha[27] throughout many incarnations. The one who is wise and blessed will have all one's wishes realized because one, being enlightened to the truth of Irwŏnsang, worships all things in the universe and the dharma realm of empty space as the Buddha, and because one does the Buddhist offering with a clear knowledge of the time limit required and with a clear knowledge of the sources of misery and blessedness. For these reasons we have decided to enshrine and worship Irwŏnsang, the symbol of Dharmakāya Buddha, in order to treat as the Buddha all things in the universe and the dharma realm of empty space."

15. One day, while the Master was residing at Pongnae Cloister, an old couple was passing by and said that they were on their way to Silsang-sa to make an offering to the Buddha statue in the temple so that their daughter-in-law, ill-natured and extremely unfilial to them, might be changed thereby for the better. Hearing this, the Master said, "You know that you will be helped if you make an offering to the Buddha statue, but you don't know that you will be better helped by making offerings to a living buddha." The couple asked, "Where is the living Buddha?" The Master said, "Your daughter-in-law in your home is a living buddha. She is the one who has the authority to be filial or unfilial to you. So, why don't you try to make an offering of worship to her first?" The couple asked, "What is the way of making an offering of worship to her?" The Master said, "Buy for her something she might like with the money you would have spent for making an offering of worship to the Buddha statue, for instance. Try to treat her as you would respect the Buddha. Then you will see the result of your making an offering of worship depending on your sincerity." The couple returned home and did as was advised. Their daughter-in-law changed herself to be very filial to them. So the old couple paid a visit to the Master and expressed heartfelt appreciation. The Master said to his disciples beside him, "This is an example of the realistic worship of Buddha offered directly to the actual source of misery and blessedness."

16. Kim Yŏng-shin asked, "Is the making of an offering to the direct agents of the fourfold beneficence the only way of making an offering to the Buddha? Isn't there any other way?" The Master said, "There are two ways of making an offering to the Buddha: one is the offering to the agents of the fourfold beneficence and the other is the offering

27. See above, *Canon*, pt. 3, chap. 10, for the method of making an offering to Buddha. Buddha here means all things in the universe as the manifestation of Dharmakāya Buddha.

to Dharmakāya Buddha through the formless dharma realm of empty space.[28] You make either of the two offerings depending on the time, location, and state of affairs. If you continue exerting sincere effort until you succeed in it, all those things you wish, as long as they are reasonable, will be achieved, though certain things take a longer period of time than others." She asked further, "How do you make an offering to the Truth [Dharmakāya Buddha]?" The Master answered, "If, after setting up your wish toward Dharmakāya Buddha and upon purifying your mind and body, you offer your sincere heart by either entering into the meditation of samādhi, intoning the name of a Buddha, reciting a scripture, or uttering an incantation, eventually your wish will be realized with a great spiritual power with which you can deliver sentient beings suffering in the evil paths and convert hundreds and thousands of *māra*s. To attain such a great power you have to exert strenuous effort and utmost sincerity."

17. Asked by one of his disciples about how silent confessions are answered,[29] the Master said, "It is hard to prove in words the efficacy of a silent confession because one attains its unimaginable potency in a spontaneous and natural way in proportion to one's sincerity. However, let me give you a few examples. Whenever one has difficulty in getting rid of the evil thoughts that arise so often, they will turn to benevolent ones if one offers silent confessions with utmost sincerity. Whenever one repeats doing evil because of the force of past habit, though one tries hard not to, one will be endowed with the power to steer oneself away from it if one offers a silent confession, sincerely repenting the offenses and pledging to do good. In these examples, one will find evidence of how silent confessions are responded to. The erstwhile legends of 'a filial son and the bamboo shoots,' 'a loyal subject and the blood-colored bamboo shoots,' and the incident of 'the fingerprints in blood of the nine disciples' in our order are all examples of how silent confessions are answered.[30] You should bear in mind, however, that one will attain the great power only if one continues one's aspiration wholeheartedly without committing any evil contrary to it. If one attains firm spiritual power in this way, one can even attain a limitless heavenly power which one may display as heaven and earth do."

18. The Master said, "The threefold practice, being the essential way

---

28. See ibid.

29. Ibid., chap. 9.

30. Legend has it that a gravely ill old woman expressed to her son a wish to have bamboo shoots in winter when they are not to be found. Her son, being genuinely filial to his mother, went to a bamboo grove in search of them and found them in the snow. Another legend has it that a loyal subject committed suicide in honor of the moral principle that a subject should be loyal to the sovereign, and bamboos grew where he shed blood. For the fingerprints in blood, see above, *SS* I:14.

of practice in this order, is indispensable for the perfection of one's personality; we cannot do without it even for a moment in spiritual training. This is analogous to the necessity of clothing, food, and shelter for the physical life. Just as clothing, food, and shelter are necessary once one is born into the world and just as one's physical life will be deficient if any one of these three things is missing, so the power of cultivation [of spirit], inquiry [into facts and principles], and mindful choice [in karmic action] are necessary for one's spiritual life. Whatever one attempts to do will not be achieved perfectly if any part of the threefold practice is deficient. Therefore, from the viewpoint of balanced improvement of spiritual and physical life, the items of clothing, food, and shelter for the physical life and the items of One Mind, know-how, and putting into practice[31] for the spiritual life are put together and called the six grand necessities. These are so closely related to each other that none of them can be left out since they are one's lifeline. While people know the importance of the three necessities for the physical life, they do not know the importance of the three necessities for the spiritual life. They are certainly deluded. One should know that the three necessities for one's physical life can better be obtained if one cultivates oneself in the three necessities for the spiritual life. In this lies the law of acting with knowledge of what is essential and what is incidental."

19. The Master said, "People in general exert great effort to procure the daily commodities of clothing, food, and shelter, but they do not search for a more fundamental principle necessary for obtaining them. This is pitiable. If clothing, food, and shelter are necessary for physical life, then, surely, one mind, know-how, and putting into action, which control the physical life, should be pursued even more. Sufficient cultivation of the threefold spiritual power is necessary not only for securing the three physical commodities, but also for cultivating a well-rounded personality. Only if one is awakened to the original nature of one's mind, so that one's mind can function right as one intends, will one's conduct be in accordance with the principle of justice while procuring the three physical commodities. In this way one will pursue wisdom and blessing with knowledge of the causal law of karmic retribution. Only then can one be emancipated from the affliction of birth, old age, illness, and death, thereby attaining eternal life. Herein lies the correct path for procuring the three commodities; hence, the threefold funda-

---

31. One Mind, know-how, and putting into practice are the inchoate ideas for concentration, wisdom, and morality, for the realization of which is taught the threefold practice: spiritual cultivation, inquiry into facts and principles, and mindful choice in karmic action.

mental principle for spiritual training is the foundation of the threefold necessities of clothing, food, and shelter."

20. The Master addressed an assembly at a Zen monastery, "Different sects of Buddhism have practiced different parts of Buddhadharma. The Pure Land sect limits its practice to repetition of intoning "Namo Amitābha," the Doctrinal sect to reading scriptures, the Meditation sect to sitting in meditation, and the Vinaya [observance of rules] sect to keeping precepts, each arguing against the others in favor of the superiority of one practice to the others. While they are practicing just one part of the threefold practice, namely, precepts (*śīla*), concentration (samādhi), and wisdom (prajñā), we intend to have them all practiced together. At dawn Zen [meditation] will be practiced; during the day and night the practitioner will be trained in scriptures, lectures, discussions, *ŭidu*,[32] principles of human nature, diary, and intoning the name of a buddha.[33] Whoever exerts oneself through these courses will achieve much greater results than were achieved through the traditional method."

21. The Master continued, "The threefold practice has three separate subjects when one learns them in the scripture; however, they are closely related to each other like the three legs of a tripod when one trains oneself in them. One cannot train oneself in spiritual cultivation without training in inquiry into facts and principles and mindful choice in karmic action, nor can one train in inquiry without training in cultivation and mindful choice, nor can one train in mindful choice without training in cultivation and inquiry. Therefore, the purpose of having the threefold practice pursued together lies in uniting the powers of the three subjects for speedy progress in practice. The purpose of having the assembly exchange opinions on practice in the Zen monastery is to cultivate the capacity for wisdom thereby so that the practitioner can attain great knowledge, which one cannot otherwise attain by oneself without strenuous exertion."

22. The Master said, "The one who follows the path of practice should always bear the threefold practice in mind against myriad mental spheres in the world. The threefold practice is like the compass and steersman of a ship, without which a ship cannot cross the sea; and humankind cannot lead a good life without the standard of the threefold practice."

23. The Master said, "The method of my edification can be compared to the way a tree is looked at. One can start from leaves and branches and reach the root, or from the root to branches and leaves.

32. See above, *Canon*, pt. 3, chap. 5.
33. Ibid., chap. 2, sec. 1.

Likewise, I teach people in the dharma in accordance with their spiritual capacity."

24. Song To-sŏng said to the Master, "In the past I read some scriptures of ancient sages and listened to someone explaining them. At that time I did not comprehend the true meaning of the scriptures though I read them until I had memorized them. Ever since I followed your teaching, facts and principles have become clearer to me; however, upon reflection, they are the same scriptures and the same explanations. I wonder why I feel that I understand them anew." The Master said, "The scriptures of ancient sages are like ready-made garments, which not everyone can fit into. Learning what is imparted from lips and heart is like having one's garments tailored to one's size and thus helps one cultivate one's spiritual capacity in the dharma in a manner that is right for each individual's capacity and condition. How could practice by reading the fixed scriptures be compared with this method?"

25. A Christian minister said to the Master, "Since ancient times all religions have had their followers observe precepts. In my view, precepts oppress pure human nature and restrain free spirit, impeding the wide spread of the teaching to people." The Master said, "What are the reasons for your view?" The minister said, "Some people reject religion simply because they do not understand the truth it teaches. There are quite a number of people who are hesitant to believe in a religion because they dislike precepts while approving the sacredness of its doctrine. Wouldn't those people also be included in the category of salvation if there were no precepts?" The Master said, "You feel sorry for those who may not be saved; but you don't see the grave consequence of abolishing precepts. In our order, we have thirty precepts,[34] which we keep because none of them should be omitted. They are divided into three sets, ten each, and given in accordance with the level of moral maturity of the follower. Whoever enters the membership in this order receives the first set of ten precepts, which can easily be observed by those who may have difficulty in severing their old habits formed in the secular world. Then, the remaining two sets are given gradually as one makes progress in keeping them. When one is free from the thirty precepts, one is not given any further precept and one does as one pleases because one who is on such a level knows right from wrong and does only what is right. However, anyone who hasn't reached this level of moral perfection should not be left alone without precepts. The way to teach the beginner cannot be the same as the way to treat someone who is awakened to the moral sense. There are more deluded ones in the world than there are enlightened. What you have just said can only be

---

34. Ibid., chap. 11.

good for one or two out of tens of thousands of people. How could anyone, following your suggestion, take care of only one or two and ignore tens of thousands of people? If one were to live alone, it would not matter whether one did as one pleased; however, the world is controlled by the net of laws and the general public is watching, so that one will not find a place to stand if one commits evil. In my view, therefore, one should live in the world as carefully as if one were walking on thin ice lest one deviate from the right path. For this reason, precepts are set up for those who aspire to follow the Way."

26. Once the Master went to the district of Pusan, where a few followers paid a visit to him, saying, "We think highly of your teaching, but we are ashamed and discouraged because we fear we violate the first precept [do not kill without justifiable reason] as we make a living by fishery." The Master said, "Do not worry. It is not easy for one to change one's occupation abruptly. Although you violate one of the thirty precepts you receive, you will be doing twenty-nine kinds of good with a great deal of meritorious contribution to the general public if you keep the remaining twenty-nine precepts with utmost sincerity. Why should one sink into the depth of misery by violating the remaining precepts just because one cannot help but violate one? If you can keep the rest of the precepts, there will be a way to keep the one in question. Bear this in mind and do not hesitate to exert yourselves to practice."

27. The Master once attended a session at a Zen monastery and said, "Yi Inŭihwa has a great resolution to embrace the teaching of this order, which is shown by attending the regular dharma meetings and receiving training at a Zen monastery while neglecting her own business. Instead of recognizing her merit with a prize, I will allow this particular hour to her so that she may ask me any question she wishes." Inŭihwa asked, "If someone asked me what is taught in this order, how should I answer?" The Master said, "Since Buddhism is a religion that teaches one to be enlightened to the truth that 'all things are nothing but creations of the mind,' you may say that we are teaching and learning this truth. If you are enlightened to this truth, you will also comprehend the principle of neither arising nor ceasing and the causal law of karmic retribution." She asked further, "How should one pursue the practice after awakening to such a principle?" The Master answered, "One keeps one's mind from being disturbed, deluded, or defiled by the mental spheres."

28. The Master asked Kim Yŏng-shin, "What do you think is the most indispensable for human life in this world?" Yŏng-shin answered, "I think that things for clothing, food, and shelter are most indispensable." The Master asked further, "Which is the most important of the subjects you learn at school?" Yŏng-shin answered, "I think that the subject of moral culture is the most important." The Master said, "You

are right. Clothing, food, and shelter are indispensable for the physical life, and the subject of morals is important for moral cultivation. This is because clothing, food, and shelter on the one hand and the subject for moral culture [on the other] are the fundamentals for living and moral cultivation respectively. However, the subject of morals taught at school will be insufficient. Only in a religious order where the practice is systematically carried out can practice be developed successfully. Bear in mind, therefore, that moral cultivation comes ahead of all other subjects in importance and, thus, it should be learned prior to any other subjects."

29. The Master raised a question to the assembly at a Zen monastery: "If someone asked you what you are learning here, what would you say?" One of the assembly said, "I would say we are learning the way to attain the three great powers [of spiritual cultivation, inquiry into facts and principles, and mindful choice in karmic action]." Another said, "I would say we are learning the essential ways of humanity [the fourfold beneficence and the four essentials]." There were various answers, to which the Master listened and said, "Your answers are all fair. I will add an elaboration to your answers. So, listen carefully. Though you should give an adequate answer to a question in accord with the personality and attitude of the questioner, I would say that I teach people how one should have one's mind function in general and then detail this answer. I would say I teach (a) to a knowledgeable person, how to apply knowledge; (b) to a powerful person, how to use power; (c) to a wealthy person, how to use wealth; (d) to a resentful person, how to be grateful; (e) to an unfortunate person, how to create blessings; (f) to a dependent person, how to be independent; (g) to a person unwilling to learn, how to learn; (h) to a person unwilling to teach, how to teach; and (i) to an egoist, how to be public-spirited. In a word, I teach that one should make righteous use of one's talents, tangible wealth, and environment."[35]

30. The Master said further, "As material civilization develops, the world today is marked with advanced learning and technology in all walks of life [of scholars-officials, farmers, artisans, and tradesmen]. As a consequence, dazzling instruments and commodities have been produced, fascinating the eyes and spirits of humankind. On the other hand, the spirit making use of the material things has become so weak that it is enslaved to them.[36] Now, this is a matter of great concern. A material thing of great value can be the cause of misery if it is used by a vicious person. The great talent and learning of a bad person can cause

---

35. Items d, f, g, h, and i are respectively articles 5, 6, 7, 8, and 9 of the essentials of daily practice. See above, *Canon*, pt. 3, chap. 1.
36. Ibid.

harm to the public. A good home environment can be misused to create evil karma if a person uses it wrong. Therefore, the products of material civilization will be used to make the world better or worse depending on the application of the laws that show how to use the mind. These products will help build a paradise if the people making use of them use their mind right; they will be like a lethal weapon held by a burglar if people making use of them use their mind wrong. Therefore, you must open your eyes and learn diligently the laws of how to use the mind, which are the heart of all laws, and thereby be a pilot of the mind to make good use of all things on the principle of mutual benefit in all situations. You should exert yourselves to teach the art of mind-application to people so that a truly civilized world shall be realized."

31. The Master said, "The rapid progress of material civilization alone is not sufficient for realizing a perfect world. It needs the advancement of spiritual culture. The core of spiritual culture lies in the morality of humankind. Thus, the world will be a perfect one if material civilization and spiritual culture are advanced in good balance. Scientific knowledge helps improve material civilization, and moral cultivation helps strengthen spiritual culture. Hence, the perfect world needs moral cultivation in humanity as well as scientific advancement. If the world leans toward material civilization, neglecting spiritual culture as is the case with today's world, the world will be like an infant holding a sharp knife in its hand. No one knows when and where humankind will be harmed by the power of material civilization. This world is like a man who is physically healthy but mentally ill. The world, morally advanced but materially backward, however, is like a man who is mentally healthy but physically crippled. Thus, the world cannot be a perfect one if either of the two is deficient; a paradise can only be realized when material civilization and spiritual culture advance in balance."[37]

32. The Master said, "Because of the advancement of material civilization and moral culture, people [nowadays] enjoy [many] material products and conveniences. Hence, they ought to be grateful to inventors and those who help cultivate morality in humankind. Although material civilization, which provides conveniences for physical life, yields its phenomenal results quickly, its merit is limited. Moral culture, being an art of training the formless human mind, yields its results slowly; however, its merit has no limit. The power of moral culture to deliver sentient beings and cure the ills of the world cannot be compared with that of material civilization, and its light cannot be limited to one world. It is regrettable, however, that many people today seek only the fruit of material civilization and few people search for the formless moral culture."

---

37. This is an explanation of the motive behind founding a new religious order. See ibid.

33. The Master said, "In the past the Buddha strictly prohibited the ascetic followers of the Way from wearing good clothes, eating good food, dwelling in a good shelter, and enjoying worldly pleasures. He encouraged them to find pleasure only in keeping their minds and bodies at rest. However, I am teaching that you should work diligently and use clothes, food, and shelter suitable to your means, and use recreation for relief from fatigue. The dharma that was valid in the past may not work for teaching people of high intelligence and an advanced living standard. It is one of the main points of my teaching that Buddha-dharma should be made perfect and versatile so that it can be applied to individuals, families, societies, nations, and the world."

34. The Master addressed an assembly at Yŏngsan Zen Monastery: "They say that the world today is marked by highly developed civilizations. However, we should not be carried away by the brilliance and convenience of material civilization; we should rather take a moment to consider carefully the defects thereof and its future consequences. The further material civilization progresses in today's world, the deeper the roots of moral illness spread so that, if left uncured, the world will reach a critical condition. This brings great worries to those who are concerned about the public well-being. What are the ills of the world today? First, people are ill with money. For those who feel it necessary to have money to satisfy all their desires for pleasure, money is more precious than integrity and honor so that they lose their moral sense and friendliness. This is indeed a serious moral illness. Secondly, people are afflicted with the moral illness of resentment. People—as individuals or as members of a family, a society, or a nation—find fault with others without recognizing their own faults. They forget indebtedness to others without forgetting their favors to others, hating and resenting each other with no end to minor and serious conflicts. This is indeed a serious illness. Thirdly, people are afflicted with the inclination to depend on others for their living. This moral illness is more serious with people in this country [Korea] than others because of the harmful effect of effeminacy for hundreds of years. Those born to a wealthy family would live in idleness, without doing any work; if any of one's relatives, or even friends, was affluent, one would depend on that person for a living. It was deplorable that, in some cases, one hand had to feed ten mouths. Fourthly, people are closed to learning. Nine-tenths of the personality is formed by learning; hence, one must humbly acquire the necessary learning from almost anyone, like honeybees collecting honey. However, many people lose the opportunity to learn because they are conceited. The fifth illness is the lack of interest in education. A person with great learning can be the same as a total ignoramus if he or she does not make use of it or teach it to the next generation. However, some people who are conceited about their learning will not asso-

ciate themselves with those of no learning. The sixth illness is that people have no public spirit. Few people work for the public well-being because of selfishness, which has been hardened as hard as a silver mountain and iron walls for the past thousands of years. Those who, moved by the incentive of fame, pretend to work for the public good, bring failure to the work because of their selfishness. Consequently, almost all institutions and organizations for the public well-being are impoverished. This is a serious illness.

35. The Master continued, "If people are to be cured of these ailments, they should be morally transformed by learning (a) how to be content with one's lot, (b) how to discover beneficence, (c) how to be independent, (d) how to learn, (e) how to teach, and (f) how to work for the public well-being. This moral reformation starts with everyone's self-examination to cure the moral illness. As an old saying goes, one who suffers and is cured from a disease prior to others knows the remedy. You should cure your own moral illness first and then cooperate to cure the world of illness. Now, the prescription to do so lies in our main doctrine, namely, the essential ways of humanity, consisting of the fourfold beneficence and the four essentials, and the essential ways of practice, consisting of the threefold practice and the eight articles.[38] When this doctrine pervades the world, the world will naturally be cured of those ills; and people, men and women, old and young, all will rejoice in a paradise like buddhas and bodhisattvas."

36. The Master said, "The roles of religion and statecraft are like those of a loving mother and a strict father in a family. Religion, being based on supernatural and moral principles, trains people in morality to prevent them from doing evil and to direct them to do good, whereas statecraft, being based on law, metes out reward and punishment to citizens in accordance with what they do. If mother and father do what they ought to do, then their children rejoice in happiness; if they do not know what they, as mother and father, ought to do, their children suffer in misery. Just as the happiness and misery of children depend on what their parents do, the happiness and misery of all people depend on what religion and statecraft do. Thus, our responsibility to deliver all sentient beings and cure the world of illness is heavy. First of all, therefore, we ought to have a thorough knowledge of our doctrine, and then apply it throughout the world. Our responsibility will be left undone until all sentient beings are delivered into a paradise by good statecraft and benevolent administration based on principles of sound morality."

37. The Master addressed an assembly at the closing ceremony of a Zen retreat: "What I have taught for the past three months of Zen

---

38. The central tenets of the whole doctrine consist in these two ways and Irwŏnsang. See above, *Canon*, pt. 2.

retreat can be called 'how to bring forth the southeast wind.' Do you know what I mean by 'wind'? There are two opposing winds in nature, namely, winds blowing from the southeast and those blowing from the northwest, and there are winds of morality and the national law in the world of humankind. Morality is the southeast wind, and the national law is the northwest wind. These two winds are the main principles governing the world. The northwest wind is assigned to the judiciary system of the government, which metes out reward and punishment; the southeast wind refers to the religious order, which assumes the responsibility to edify people. Therefore, you should learn how to bring forth the southeast wind and apply nature's way of reciprocal production and harmony.[39]

"Now, what is the way of producing the southeast wind? The teachings of all buddhas and sages from ancient times are none other than the southeast wind, and our doctrine is also the way of producing the southeast wind. The courses in which you have been trained during this Zen retreat are also the way of producing the southeast wind. Which wind will you produce when you return to your home? Just as many living beings frozen in the heart of the severe winter revive with the arrival of the warm southeast wind, all sentient beings suffering in the seas of misery will be delivered by [faith in truthful religion and training in sound morality]. Wouldn't it be sacred and laudable if, consequently, the sentient beings seized with fear feel relieved, sentient beings afflicted with resentment find gratitude in their hearts, sentient beings afflicted by reciprocal destructive forces can find reciprocal productive forces, sentient beings entangled in the trap of evil conduct and punishment get released, the fallen are rehabilitated, and you can harmonize with whomever you meet in a family, a society, a country, or the world? This is the real motive behind my teaching and what you ought to do."

"However, the influence of such a southeast wind cannot be produced by mere preaching or verbal persuasion; it is brought forth by one's actual practice with the southeast wind provided in one's heart and by influencing others in one's mental and dispositional peace. Hence, you should cultivate and apply what you have learned during this Zen retreat and be the master of the southeast wind wherever you may go."[40]

---

39. The notion of reciprocal production comes from the yin-yang philosophy, the permutation of the five primary elements as they successively produce and destroy each other. Earth generates metal, which generates water, which generates wood, which generates fire, which generates earth; earth destroys water, which destroys fire, which destroys metal, which destroys wood, which destroys earth.

40. It should be noted here that Sot'aesan managed his new religious order in such a way that it was able to survive the harsh oppression of the Japanese Government General in Korea until his sudden death in 1943 (two years before Korea was liberated). It is understandable that he compared statecraft to the chilling northwest wind.

38. The Master said, "The way religion and statecraft should cooperate to contribute to the public well-being can be compared to the two wheels of a carriage. If one or both of the wheels are broken, or if its coachman is a poor driver, it cannot be driven correctly. What should be done to make the carriage run properly? Two things are needed. One is to repair it whenever necessary to prevent it from breakdown; the other is for the coachman to know the roads and drive carefully. Religion and statecraft, likewise, should check themselves against obsolescence and corruption in order to direct the world correctly, and the leaders of both sides should apply moral norms and policies properly reflecting the drift of public sentiments."

39. The Master asked, "Now that we have opened the gate of a religious order, what should be done to correct the corrupt practice of the past and enlighten the world with this new religion?" Pak Tae-wan replied, "Since the success of whatever one does depends on what is nearest to oneself, that is, one's own mind, our own mind should first be renovated if we are to renovate the world." Song Man-gyŏng replied, "Now that our doctrine and system have already been established to respond to the call of the times, the world will naturally be improved if we apply and practice the doctrine and system." Cho Song-gwang[41] replied, "The profound intention of the Great Master is beyond my comprehension; however, I believe that the teaching of the Great Master is perfect and impartial so that the whole human race will be transformed for the better, spontaneously and naturally in accordance with the grand trends of the world."

The Master said, "What you have said is all correct. If one wishes to correct the ills of the world, one must correct one's own mind first; and if one wishes to correct one's mind, one must have the correct way to do so. Since you have already learned the way of practice with the new doctrine, exert yourselves to put into practice what we have learned. If each religion is improved, people will have their minds corrected; if the human mind is renovated, statecraft will be corrected accordingly. Although religion and statecraft have different roles to play, they are closely related in the background, having an influence on good and evil in the world."

## III. On Practice

1. The Master said, "The purpose of having you recite the essentials of daily practice[42] in the morning and evening does not lie in simply letting you recite the nine articles verbally but in checking your mind against the injunctions of the articles. You must check your mind

---

41. See below, *SS* XIV:14.
42. See above, *Canon*, pt. 3, chap. 1.

against them once a day in general and whenever you confront adverse mental spheres. In other words, you check (1) whether there was disturbance in the mind-ground, (2) whether there were delusions in the mind-ground, (3) whether there was error in the mind-ground, (4) whether you carried out the threefold practice with faith, zeal, doubt and sincerity, (5) whether you were grateful or not, (6) whether you were independent or not, (7) whether you learned in sincerity, (8) whether you taught in all sincerity, and (9) whether you did anything for the benefit of others. You must keep checking and contrasting until you reach the stage of moral perfection wherein the goals of these nine articles are accomplished spontaneously even when you do not check. It is said that the human mind is so subtle that it comes into being if you get hold of it and disappears if you let it go. If so, how could the mind be cultivated without checking it constantly? So that you can carry out the practice of mind checking, I have set up the things to heed for daily application and the things to heed while attending the temple;[43] and to check them, I have set keeping a diary.[44] In this way I have made the way of practice watertight. You should be able to achieve the great task of entering into sageness by following this path diligently."

2. The Master said, "The effective way of attaining the power of cultivation in motion and at rest lies in (i) not doing anything that will disturb or carry away your mind and in keeping away from such matters, (ii) responding to all matters without attachment to love or greed and in cultivating a tranquil state of mind, (iii) concentrating your mind on what you do without being carried away to any other matter, and (iv) being heedful to practice intoning the name of a buddha or sitting in meditation whenever you find leisure. The effective way of attaining the power of inquiry in motion and at rest lies in (i) exerting yourself to have a clear understanding of any matter you handle, (ii) exerting yourself to exchange opinions with your mentor or comrades, (iii) exerting yourself to get any doubtful point resolved in accordance with the correct procedure of inquiry if it comes across your mind while seeing, hearing, or thinking, (iv) exerting yourself to understand and practice our scriptures, and (v) expanding your knowledge by reference to the scriptures of ancient religions after you master our scriptures. The effective way of attaining the power of mindful choice in motion and at rest lies in (i) carrying out the right thing once you know it is the right thing for you to do even at the risk of your life, no matter whether it is a matter of grave importance or triviality; (ii) forsaking the wrong even at the risk of your life once you know it is wrong for you to do, no matter whether it is a matter of grave importance or a triviality; and (iii)

43. Ibid., chap. 2, sec. 2, I and II.
44. Ibid., chap. 6.

exerting yourself continuously to practice without being discouraged even if you do not succeed in handling myriad things right away."

3. The Master said, "The religious practice in the past laid disproportionate emphasis on making earnest effort for practice at rest. Because the daily work in the world and following the Buddha path interfere with each other, some spent their whole life on the mountain, leaving their parents, wife, and children behind.[45] In some cases one was lost in reading scriptures, unaware of the rain washing away the grain in the yard. How could this be the right way of practice? Therefore, we do not regard the earnest effort for practice and daily work in the world incompatible; you get your daily work well done through the earnest effort for practice and make practice advance by getting the daily mundane work done well. In this way you attain the threefold great power [of cultivation, inquiry, and mindful choice]. You should exert yourselves for the ceaseless great practice in motion and at rest."

4. The Master said to an assembly at a Zen monastery, "If you have entered the Zen monastery for the first time for intensive Zen training, you will find it onerous or think it uncomfortable to follow the rigorous schedule. If, however, you become proficient at the religious practice and well-trained mentally and physically, you will realize that there is no other life more comfortable and enjoyable than this. Hence, you had better check whether you find it hard or joyous to follow the daily required courses. If you find it hard, it is because of the condition resulting from the remaining karma in the defiled world. If you find it joyous, the gate for attaining buddhahood is opening for you."

5. The Master said, "Whether one would be sincere in whatever one does depends on whether one knows what it has to do with oneself. If one is sincerely in search of clothing and food, it is because one knows that they are indispensable for maintaining one's life. If one is sincere in curing oneself of a disease, it is because one is aware of the importance of the cure in maintaining one's health. If one is sincere in practice, it is because one knows the importance of sincerity for one's own future. If one understands the importance of practice, one can overcome all sorts of difficulties without finding faults with one's mentor or friends in the dharma who are inattentive to oneself. One who does not understand the importance will be impatient in practice, feeling easily discontented with the mentor or friends in the dharma. Such a one will feel that one's

---

45. Cf. Sŏsan's (1520–1604) justification for monks leaving home (S. āraṇyaka): "To become a monk and leave one's family behind is not a trivial matter. The purpose is not to seek for physical ease, nor is it to eat and to be clad luxuriously, nor is it to seek for fame and wealth. It is to avoid birth and death, to sever worldly passions, to succeed to the wisdom of the Buddha, and to deliver all sentient beings by transcending the triple world." Sŏsan's *Sŏn'ga kuigam*, proposition 56.

own practice and the public service are simply for someone else. You should make sure what this training for practice has to do with yourselves."

6. The Master said, "The hunter who aims at a lion or a tiger does not shoot at a pheasant or a rabbit for fear of missing the lion or tiger by shooting at such trivial game. The one who aspires to attain moral perfection, likewise, does not allow desires for trivial things to arise for fear of harming the great aspiration. Therefore, the one who aims at attaining buddhahood will be successful only if one ignores all worldly desires and passions. It will be a great pity if one cannot cut off the trivial desires and passions and thereby hampers one's great aspiration [to attain buddhahood]; this will be like shooting at pheasants and rabbits, and thereby losing the lion or the tiger. That is why I advise that one with great aspiration should sever small desires."

7. The Master said to an assembly at a Zen monastery, "I have heard that a lay person at Yŏnggwang Temple was working for wages near the temple on the day of regular dharma meeting. What do you think of him?" One of his disciples said, "It was wrong of him to put money ahead of practice. If, however, his parents, wife, and children had to starve but for the day's wage, wouldn't it have been right for him to relieve his family from hunger and cold even if he had to miss a regular dharma meeting?" The Master said, "What you say is plausible. However, if he had a true aspiration for practice and knew the value of the dharma, he would have prepared foodstuffs for the day of the regular dharma meeting, which is not held every day. The fact that he searched for foodstuffs on the day of regular dharma meeting proves that he is negligent of practice and lacks sincerity in the dharma. This is guarded against in the things to heed while attending the temple.[46] There is a principle that if one exerts oneself to practice without an iota of selfishness in one's heart, one will be endowed with foodstuffs when one does not have enough in spite of serious preparation in advance. For instance, as soon as a baby is born, its mother is in milk, which is the heavenly stipend."

8. The Master said at a regular dharma meeting, "Today I will tell you how to make money. Listen carefully and try to live in abundance. The method of making money I am going to talk about lies not in any concrete skill but in the way your mind functions. Thus, the whole doctrine of this order can be applied as a method of earning money. Look! How much do some people waste on wine, woman, and gambling in the ordinary life in the secular world? How much do they lose on vanity and foppery and how much do they lose because of laziness

---

46. See above, *Canon*, pt. 3, chap. 2, sec. 2, II, 5.

and falling into discredit? If one who used to live without any correct standard learns the ways of humanity and the ways of practice and does a few things as encouraged or prohibited, one will stop wasting and losing money and will have property increased by being thrifty and trusted. This is a way of earning money. However, people in the world think that practice has nothing to do with earning money and say that they cannot pursue the way of practice for lack of money, and therefore that they cannot attend the regular dharma meeting because they have to earn money. They certainly are narrow-minded. Therefore, one who understands this principle will be convinced that one must exert oneself for practice in order to get out of poverty and that one must attend the regular dharma meeting to find the right way to earn money. Consequently, one will find the way to improve practice and daily life together."

9. The Master said, "People in general take sitting in meditation, intoning the name of a buddha, and reading scriptures in a quiet place as the only courses of practice, without knowing that one can practice in the daily life of the mundane world. They do not know the perfect way of practice through internal concentration and calmness (samādhi) and external concentration and calmness. Generally speaking, the path of practice lies in inquiry into the principles of human nature; thereby one gets enlightened to the original nature, which is devoid of attachment, and acts with no attachment in actual daily life. Anyone who is on this path will surely attain great power of practice. If you, cultivator of the Way, are not attracted to *that* thing while doing *this* thing and not to *this* thing while doing *that* thing in daily execution of your business, then you are cultivating One Mind [concentration]. If you inquire into *this* matter for knowledge while doing *this* thing and into *that* matter for knowledge while doing *that* thing and do all things in orderly manner, then you are cultivating the path of inquiry [into facts and principles]. If you are free from injustice while doing *this* thing and free from injustice while doing *that* thing, then you are cultivating the path of mindful choice [in karmic action]. If you devote yourself to mental concentration by intoning the name of a buddha and sitting in meditation at leisure, devote yourself to inquiry by exercise in the scriptures, and devote yourself to doing the right in motion and at rest, you will accumulate the powers of spiritual cultivation, inquiry into facts and principles, and mindful choice in karmic action.[47] Behold Song Kyu! He has not received even one regular term training of three months since his entrance into the order as he had to attend to the business of the order, either at headquarters or at branch temples; however, to examine his actual ability in practice, his power of spiritual cultivation has reached

---

47. See above, *Canon*, pt. 2, chap. 4.

the level that, having rooted out almost all sources of the passions of love and greed, he is seldom attracted to the feelings of pleasure, anger, sorrow, or joy or to the consideration of remoteness, closeness, friendliness, and estrangement. His power of inquiry into facts and principles has reached the level that he correctly analyzes right from wrong and gain from loss in human affairs and the principles of noumenon and phenomenon and being and nonbeing of all things in the universe. His power of mindful choice in karmic action has reached the level that he can analyze justice from injustice and does the right in nine out of ten cases. In the essays he wrote and sent to me while he was busy with his duties of the office, I have found his understanding of truth profound, his style easy for the general public to read, and his reasoning clear and bright, so that there is little to be corrected. It won't be long before he attains the threefold great power perfectly and becomes an invaluable person who will benefit a great many people wherever he goes. This is the merit of the effort he exerted on practice in motion and at rest. You, too, ought to attain the threefold great power by devoting yourselves to timeless Zen of maintaining one suchness in motion and at rest."

10. The Master said, "When you are free from work, you must always prepare for what you will do when you confront work to be done; when you have things to do, you must always preserve the serene state of mind you are in when you are free from work. If you do not prepare for what you will do when you confront work to be done, you will be unable to avoid being thrown into confusion; and if you cannot preserve the serene state of mind you are in when there was nothing to be done, you will be enslaved to the situation."

11. In a discussion session, Chŏn Ŭm-gwang was making a point on the difference between the one who exerts oneself for practice and the one who does not and said, "Anyone who does not follow the teaching of this order for practice applies the threefold practice in certain situations; however such a one becomes remiss as soon as he is out of the situation, making no progress in the threefold practice throughout his or her life because he or she has no interest in practice. We, practitioners, however, exert ourselves to pursue the threefold practice incessantly in motion as well as at rest and at work as well as at leisure; therefore, we will be endowed with great character if we continue our effort in accordance with the doctrine." The Master listened to this and said, "What Ŭm-gwang has said makes sense; however, I will make his point clearer with an illustration. Suppose three people were sitting here, one designing machinery, the second performing meditation, and the third doing nothing. Looked at from outside, there is nothing different among them; however, there will appear a big difference among them after a long period of time [if they continue what they are doing]. The one who studies machinery will invent a machine; the one who

exerts oneself in meditation will attain the power of spiritual cultivation; and the one who spends all his time doing nothing will have no accomplishment. Thus, if one exerts oneself in one thing for a long time, one will bring about a great result. To give a concrete example, there was a boy with whom I learned Chinese classics together for a while when we were children. He had little interest in learning; he enjoyed imitating an opera singer so much that he played at being one when he opened his book for study and sometimes while he was walking. He continued his habit until his hair turned gray, and had secretly become an amateur singer when I saw him a few years ago. As for me, I began to have interest in the truth in my childhood and had little interest in reading books; what I thought about day and night was the wondrous principle of the universe; because of this, I often fell into deep contemplation without sleeping or eating; and as the result of my sincere effort without pause ever since that time, I have been living a life that is concerned with the truth. From these illustrations, it is clear that the choice of direction in life is most important. Once the right direction is chosen, the foundation of success lies in exerting sincere effort for what one aims at."

12. The Master said, "Many patriarchs of Zen sects have expounded myriad skillful means and ways to Zen; however, the essence of Zen can be summarized as follows: Zen is to realize the [True Thusness of] empty and calm, numinous awareness[48] by eliminating delusions and nourishing true nature. Therefore, the following proposition expresses the general principle of Zen: 'The alertness of calmness is correct, while the blankness[49] of calmness is wrong; the calmness of alertness is correct, while the delusive thought of alertness is wrong.'"[50]

13. The Master attended a session of sitting in meditation and asked the participants, "Now that you are exerting yourselves for sitting in meditation against sleepiness, what is the purpose of this practice?" Kwŏn Tong-hwa replied, "The human spirit is originally perfect and bright, but it is scattered into myriad branches, losing the perfection and dimming the light of its wisdom in adverse conditions of greed. Therefore, the purpose of sitting in meditation lies in attaining the power of spiritual cultivation and the light of wisdom by subduing defilements and gathering the scattered spirit into the concentration of one mind." The Master said, "If you really understand the merit of

---

48. See ibid., chap. 1, sec. 1.
49. Unrecordable (S. *avyākṛta* or *avyākhyāta*) as good or as bad; neutral, neither good nor bad. Here it means absence of numinous awareness in meditation.
50. Cf. *Ch'an-tsung Yung-chia chi, T,* 2013.48.389b–c; Buswell, *KAZ,* p. 172: "The alertness of calmness is correct; the alertness of deluded thoughts is wrong. The calmness of alertness is correct; the calmness of blankness is wrong."

spiritual cultivation, you will continue exerting yourselves for it even if no one else encourages you to do so. However, there is one thing you should be cautious of in its method. If you do not know the details of correct practice of meditation and do not follow its right path, feeling anxious for speedy progress or searching for strange traces, you may get ill or get into a wicked way, or have more defilements arise. Therefore, you must check your practice against the method of sitting in meditation[51] or learn the correct path from your seniors so that you may be on the right track. If you are diligent at the correct practice of meditation, you will easily attain mental and physical freedom as buddhas, sages, and all great masters have attained, mental power of such a great magnitude through this method of Zen."

14. The Master said to an assembly at a Zen monastery, "In recent years, proponents of various sects of Zen Buddhism argue with each other on the correctness of each method. In this order I have adopted the method of concentration at the elixir field[52] so that one should exclusively practice mental concentration for spiritual cultivation while practicing the seated meditation; and the exercise with *hwadu* should be done only once in a while at a proper time. The reason is that the awakening does not occur only at the end of a long mental wrestling with *ŭidu* in a depressed frame of mind; the power of *ŭidu* exercise in a clear spirit at the right moment is superior."

15. One of his disciples asked about the ascending watery energy and the descending fiery energy,[53] and the Master answered, "Water by its nature is cool and clear and has the tendency to descend, while fire by its nature is hot and turbid and has the tendency to ascend. When you are involved in a complicated thought, you feel a rush of blood to the head. When this happens, the sap of life gets dried up and your head feels hot and your spirit becomes turbid. This is because the fiery energy ascends and the watery energy descends. If your mind is cleared of the complicated thought and the vital force is calmed down, your head feels cool and your spirit becomes clear with clear saliva circulating in the mouth. This is because the watery energy ascends and the fiery energy descends."

16. The Master said, "There are two ways to attain the power of spiritual cultivation: one is the cultivation of temperament and the other cultivation of the nature of mind. To illustrate the point, the imperturbability of mind in a critical situation that a soldier cultivates in combat is an example of the cultivation of temperament. If a religious practitioner is not disturbed in any favorable or adverse conditions

---

51. See above, *Canon*, pt. 3, chap. 4.
52. Ibid., IV.
53. Ibid., I.

because he or she has conquered the army of evil [*māra*] in the mental spheres of five desires, this is an example of the cultivation of the nature of mind. Even if a soldier has attained the power of temperamental cultivation, his practice cannot be complete unless he attains the power of the cultivation of the nature of mind. Even if a practitioner has attained the power of the cultivation of the nature of mind internally, his or her practice cannot be complete unless he or she attains the power of temperamental cultivation in actual mental spheres."

17. Yang To-shin said to the Master, "You used to teach us that one should calmly concentrate oneself on what one does without being distracted by any other thing while one is doing one thing. I have tried to follow your teaching. However, this practice led me into trouble. Recently, I was assigned to boil a potion of herb medicine while doing needlework. Because I was concentrating on the needlework, I burned the herb medicine. If I were to pay attention to the medicine while doing needlework, I would be distracted by another thing while doing one thing; if I were to concentrate on the needlework ignoring the medicine, the medicine would be burned. What is the right way to follow in this case?" The Master said, "If you were assigned to boil the herb medicine and do the needlework at the same time, then it was your duty to do both at the same time. Hence, the sound concentration and right practice in that case lay in fulfilling the duty wholeheartedly. If you made a mistake by focusing your attention on one thing only, it was not a sound concentration; it was carelessness. Even if you pay attention to ten or twenty things, you can still cultivate sound mental concentration as long as they are within the scope of your duty, and this practice is an essential way of discipline you take while you work. What you should guard yourself against is the endless delusions caused by thinking what you need not, trying to hear what you need not, trying to see what you need not, and meddling in what is none of your concern, thus your attention being distracted by another thing while doing one thing! Even if thousands of things are taken care of in a day, mental concentration will not be disturbed as long as they are what you ought to do."

18. The Master said, "When you cultivate One Mind, sometimes you do it easily and sometimes you find it difficult to do it. Do you know why? It depends on whether you do right or wrong. Those who do what is right may find it complicated and difficult to do at the beginning; however, the more one does righteous things, the more one will feel magnanimous and calm, so that their future will be wide open and the cultivation of One Mind will be successful. Those who do what is not right may find it pleasurable and easy to do it at the beginning; however, the more they do it, the more painful and complicated they will feel, so that their future will be closed and their cultivation of One Mind will be unsuccessful. Therefore, if one wishes to cultivate One

Mind, one ought to eliminate from one's heart unrighteous wishes and stop doing what is wrong."

19. The Master asked Yi Sun-sun, "How do you pursue the practice at home?" Sun-Sun answered, "I try to cultivate peace and serenity of mind." The Master asked again, "What is your method of keeping the mind peaceful and serene?" Sun-sun replied, "I am merely trying to keep my mind peaceful and serene without really knowing how to do it." The Master said, "In general, a human being lives either in a state of motion or at rest, and there are two aspects of mental calmness, external concentration and calmness and internal concentration and calmness.[54] By external concentration and calmness is meant that you remove the source of *māra* [evil], which would disturb your mind by refraining from foolish and disturbing things. This requires you to make mindful choice of right from wrong in accordance with the moral standard of righteousness in any adverse condition. By internal concentration and calmness is meant that you cultivate mental calmness by keeping defilement from arising; for this you may practice intoning the name of a buddha or sitting in meditation when you are free from work. You will be able to attain mental imperturbability by practicing both external and internal calmness as each is the basis of the other."

20. Song To-sŏng was so fond of reading the newspaper that he would leave his work in progress to read it as soon as it was delivered, and he would at least look at the headlines before resuming his work, even if the work was urgent. Seeing this, the Master warned him, "Now that you are taken up with such a trivial matter as reading the newspaper, I am concerned whether you will be with other matters, too. Everyone has things one loves to do and things one hates to do. Deluded beings are attached to those things they love when they meet them, losing sound spirit; and when they face matters they hate to do, they have an abhorrence of them and ignore what they ought to do, thus failing to fulfill their duties. Such people force themselves to embrace agony and suffering, and they will be deprived of mental peace and the light of wisdom. I am warning you against such a trivial matter as this to call your attention to a vivid example of how one can be carried away. You should always do what is right without being attached to what you love to do or abhorring what you hate to do; you should be a man who can use all circumstances, not one who is dragged by myriad circumstances. Then you will maintain your own nature of True Thusness forever."

21. Yi Ch'ŏng-ch'un asked, "Does attachment remain in the great master who is enlightened to the Way?" The Master answered, "No one

---

54. See above, sec. 9.

who still harbors attachment is enlightened to the Way." Ch'ŏng-ch'un asked again, "Chŏngsan seems to love his children. Isn't it an attachment of love?" The Master said, "Ch'ŏng-ch'un would call a piece of senseless log or rock an enlightened master. If one has a strong attachment of love, one cannot leave the loved ones, or one misses the loved ones when separated so much that one cannot make progress in practice or cannot devote oneself to the public service. Such a thing does not happen to Chŏngsan."

22. The Master said, "People in general do not regard a person as an enlightened spiritual guide unless he or she has read the scriptures extensively. If a certain point of the dharma is explained with reference to some ancient scriptures, people are attentive to it; they do not regard the same point as important if its fundamental principle is expounded in plain words. What a deplorable state of affairs it is! Scriptures are what ancient sages and wise men explicated of principles and ways to enlighten people; however, with the lapse of time, expatiations and annotations have been added to them until they have increased to an enormous number of volumes called 'a five loads of books' and the eighty thousand treasures of scriptures of Buddhism.[55] Even if you devote your whole life to them, that will be insufficient to read them all. How, with so little time to spare, can you become a preeminent and extraordinary figure by attaining the threefold great power of cultivation, inquiry, and mindful choice? The Buddha in the past divided the three periods of his teaching following his entering nirvāṇa, namely, correct (or the period of orthodoxy and vigor), semblance (or the period of scholastics), and decline and termination, predicting how Buddha-dharma would be weakened through the change of times. The main cause of losing vigor lies in having the scriptures complicated with the consequence that sentient beings lose self-sufficiency and become deluded. Therefore, when the period of correct dharma returns, all people are trained in a newly simplified doctrine and convenient way, so that everyone may experience supreme enlightenment by the dharma imparted through lips and heart. So, what is the use of learning the five loads of books and reading the eighty thousand treasures of scriptures? You should not be attracted to such a great collection of complicated ancient scriptures. You should rather train yourselves in the simple doctrine and convenient way until you attain great spiritual ability. Only then may you peruse some of the ancient scriptures and examine theories for reference. You will realize, then, that a quick reference in one morning will be better than ten years of reading."

---

55. Consisting of eighty thousand woodblocks, the wooden printing blocks of the Tripitaka Koreana kept at Haein-sa.

23. The Master said, "Has any of you found a scripture that can be read without end? People in general regard as the only religious scriptures the four books and three classics of Confucianism[56] and the eighty thousand scriptures of Buddhism or other religious scriptures. They do not see a grand scripture, which is wide open in the real world. How regrettable it is! If you look at the world with a truthful frame of mind, everything is a living scripture. When you open your eyes, you will see the scripture; when you listen, you will hear the scripture; when you talk, you will expound the scripture; when you move, you will be applying the scripture. In this way, the living scripture will always open up everywhere. Generally speaking, a scripture consists of explications on facts and principles.[57] Explication of facts is concerned with the analysis of rightness and wrongness and gain and loss in human affairs; the explication of principles is concerned with bringing to light the [metaphysical] principles of noumenon and phenomenon and existence and nonexistence [of all things in the universe]. If you examine all the scriptures of Buddhism and canons of Confucianism and the sacred writings of other religions, you will find that all the myriad discourses will not fall outside the scope of these two [facts and principles], directing humankind to the right path with correct principles. However, facts and principles are not confined in the written scriptures; the whole world consists of facts and principles. We human beings are born, live, die, and are born again in facts and principles. Thus, we cannot be separated from facts and principles, and the world is a scripture that comprises them. In this living scripture, we must learn myriad facts, namely, rightness, wrongness, gain or loss in human affairs, so that we do what is right and beneficial and forsake what is wrong and harmful. In this living scripture, we must learn the principles of noumenon and phenomenon and existence and nonexistence, so that we may be enlightened to the fundamental principle [of the universe]. What could this world be if it is not a living scripture? I suggest, therefore, that you read this living scripture of the world prior to reading so many complicated scriptures."

24. One of the disciples asked, "I am very inefficient in doing things. How can I improve my ability to know and handle things efficiently?" The Master answered, "Train yourself in the dharma before confronting any matter; make a mindful choice when you confront a matter; examine how you did it upon completion of the matter; extend this reflection on any matter even if it is someone else's business. Then you will become proficient in doing things without any difficulty in handling matters of human life."[58]

---

56. *Lun-yü, Chung-yung, Ta-hsüeh, Meng-tzu, Shih-ching, Shu-ching,* and *I-ching.*
57. See above, *Canon,* pt. 2, chap. 4, sec. 2, I.
58. See above, *Canon,* pt. 3, chap. 2, sec. 2, I.

25. The Master said to an assembly at a regular dharma meeting, "When you listen to a sermon or an expounding of the scriptures, you should be attentive to it as if you were receiving a great treasure. No matter how beneficial and edifying the words of the dharma master or the expounder may be, they will be of no consequence if you just listen carelessly without comprehending the essential message. If you listen to any preaching or expounding of the doctrine with a sound frame of mind, checking what you hear against your practice and circumstances, then you will learn a great deal, which will be reflected in your daily life. Only then will the merit of attending the regular dharma meeting be brought to light."

26. At Pongnae Cloister the Master asked, pointing at a lamplight, "Why is it so dark underneath the lamplight, which brightens all around?" Kim Nam-ch'on expressed his opinion, "It is just like me; although I have closely attended the Master for several years, what I know and do is not as good as what the brethren know and do who visit you from afar only once in a while." The Master, smiling, asked Song Kyu, who said, "The lamplight emanates upward, illuminating distant places; the lamp stand, being right underneath the oil cup, is not illuminated. This can be compared to someone who is well aware of the faults of others but is not aware of his or her own faults. This is because one can clearly discern merits and demerits, high and low, of other people because nothing blocks one's view of them. However, when one reflects on oneself, one cannot see correctly whether one is right or wrong because the perception of one's own ego covers up the light of wisdom." The Master asked, "What should such a person of partiality do to illuminate oneself as well as others without bias?" Song Kyu answered, "If one keeps oneself from being moved by pleasure, anger, sorrow, or joy and annihilates all delusive thoughts of ego, then one's knowledge of oneself will be free from partiality."

27. The Master said, "If you wish to attain a perfect personality and expand knowledge, you should not be biased. Today, people in general cling to one side, failing to attain the perfect Way. Confucian scholars cling to the Confucian tradition and Buddhist monks to the Buddhist tradition, and the workers of other religions and societies to what they each know and do, failing to attain the perfect personality. This is because they, being biased, fail to have a clear view [and therefore cannot tell] what is right from what is wrong and what is beneficial from what is harmful, nor do they know how to make application of someone else's useful ideas." One of the disciples said, "If one is off the track of one's own tradition and advocacy, wouldn't one lose one's identity?" The Master said, "What I am saying is not that you should syncretize whatever doctrines there are, losing your own view, but that you should make a wide application of the tenets of other traditions after you have

firmly set up your own point of view. This point should not be misunderstood."

28. The Master said, "There are two causes for an ordinary person to have his or her wisdom dimmed while dealing with matters of daily life. One is vehement desire, which makes one lose the middle path, causing one's wisdom to be dimmed. The other is clinging to one's aptitude, causing one's intelligence outside of one's own specialty to be dimmed. The practitioner of the Way should guard oneself against these two conditions."

29. A follower of Tonghak came to see the Master and said, "I have heard much of you and come to see you from afar. May you take good care of me!" The Master said, "If so, you must have something you are seeking. Tell me what it is." The visitor said, "How can I be an erudite person?" The Master said, "Your coming and asking questions is a good way of extending knowledge, and my listening to what you say is another way of extending it. Let me illustrate the point. If one needs appliances and tools for maintaining one's household, one goes to a store to buy them. If you are in business with insufficient knowledge about business, you gain it in the world. Thus, my knowledge is not gained solely by my inquiry; I gain it from various people I meet. When I meet you, I learn about Tonghak; and when I meet a follower of another religion, I gain knowledge about that religion, too."

30. The Master said, "Human nature is originally neither good nor evil; however, good or evil character is formed through habit, which in turn is formed when one's initial thought responds repeatedly to certain causes and conditions nearby. This point can be illustrated. When you enter this order for the first time with a great aspiration for practice, meet with a mentor and friends in the dharma, and observe the rules and regulations, you find it awkward and unfit to follow them at the beginning. However, if you keep training yourselves in the dharma without giving up the aspiration, you mature in mind and conduct, so that eventually whatever you think and do will be right with little effort to be so. This will be the case because of the power of habit formation. The way one forms habits by responding to causes and conditions is the same for good and evil habits; however, it is easier to form an evil habit than a good one. Furthermore, it is easy to be attracted, unbeknownst to oneself, to evil conditions at an unguarded moment while training oneself to form a good habit; thus, it is easy for one to end up with the opposite of one's initial aspiration. You should bear this point in mind so that you may cultivate good character."

31. The Master said, "I have been guiding many male and female disciples and found some characteristics common to male disciples and some to female disciples. Men in general are more generous but less reliable than women, while women are more scrupulous but less toler-

ant than men. To build up a perfect character, men, being generous, must exert themselves to be reliable and truthful; women, being scrupulous, must exert themselves to be impartial and generous."

32. Seeing one of his disciples eating his meal rapidly and talking endlessly, the Master said, "Even in eating a meal and saying a word, one should not be off the path of practice. If one eats hurriedly or too much, one can get ill; if one says what one should not or what is excessive, one will easily be accompanied by calamity. How can one be off guard against eating a meal or saying a word, saying that they are trivial matters? Therefore, the practitioner of the Way regards whatever one confronts as an opportunity for practice and takes pleasure in handling each matter. You, too, ought to set an aim in this discipline."

33. Mun Chŏng-gyu asked, "What shall I take as the standard for choosing right from wrong in adverse mental spheres?" The Master said, "One should take three reflections as the standard of choosing right from wrong. One must reflect on first, one's initial vow; second, the original purpose of the mentor's teaching; and third, whether one is one-sided in the circumstance concerned. If you take these three reflections as the standard, the path of practice will never be obscured, and whatever you do will turn out right."

34. The Master, accompanied by Yi Ch'un-p'ung, was going over a steep mountain pass behind Ch'ŏngryŏn-am and said, "On a precipitous mountain pass like this, my mental concentration becomes focused! It is because of this that one rarely stumbles on a precipitous road while one can easily stumble on a level road. When you handle a matter, you make fewer mistakes with a difficult matter than with easy ones. Hence, one who pursues practice can attain samādhi of oneness[59] only if one can apply an identical heedfulness to a precipitous or a level place, and a difficult or an easy matter."

35. The Master said, "Have you seen heavenly people? Heavenly people are not those who reside in heaven. The infants over there are heavenly people; they are provided with heavenly stipends through their mothers because they are unselfish. However, the heavenly stipend is cut off as selfishness gradually grows in their hearts. Likewise, the practitioner of the Way will be provided with a heavenly stipend as selfishness is eliminated from his or her heart; and it will be cut off as soon as selfishness arises in his or her heart."

36. One of the disciples said, "By what method of spiritual discipline can I eliminate the five vehement desires[60] and devote myself to prac-

---

59. *Irhaeng sammae* (C. *I-hsing san-mei*; S. *Ekavyūa samādhi*) is "having a straightforward mind at all times, whether walking, staying, sitting, or lying" according to Hui-neng. See *Liu-tsu t'an ching*, *T*, 2007.48.338b.

60. Of wealth, sex, food and drink, fame, and sleep.

tice so that I can live life as serenely as the Buddha?" The Master said, "The best method to free yourself from the defilements of desires is not to eliminate desires but to augment them, turning the petty desires to the great vows. If you apply yourself closely to the great vow, the five desires will calm down; and then you will be able to live life as serenely as the Buddha."

37. The Master said, "I am not teaching that you should suppress the natural feelings of pleasure, anger, sorrow, and joy by force; I am saying that you apply them to various situations in accordance with the Mean.[61] I am saying also that you should not condemn petty talent and desires but should worry about the talent and aspiration being petty. Thus, what I am teaching is only to change what is small to what is great and to switch the devotion a learner has had to petty things to things of great importance. This is a great way of attaining what is great."

38. The Master said, "On the path of practice and public service there is a critical moment, which you should be aware of in advance. The critical moment for one who pursues practice comes when the gate of wisdom is gradually opening; and for one who pursues the path of public service, the critical moment comes when one's accomplishment brings powers to oneself. When petty wisdom brightens, one with low intellectual capacity, being satisfied with it, becomes negligent with practice. When one becomes influential because of the accomplishment, one makes no further progress because one is moved by self-interest and becomes arrogant. Thus, anyone who, on the path of practice or public service, does not guard against such critical moments will eventually sink into the depths of misery."

39. A devout believer[62] in the Master devoted herself to sitting in meditation for several decades and, as a result, became gradually clairvoyant; she could foresee someone's visit or predict when it would start to rain and when it would stop. Seeing this, the Master said, "It is nothing but a hallucination, like the glow of a firefly, which can occur while one devotes one's energy to spiritual cultivation. You should be awakened to get rid of the wicked spirit. If you become fond of it, you will not be enlightened to the supreme Way and will be led astray, becoming a sort of *asura*. It cannot be permitted in the order of correct dharma."

40. Song Pyŏk-cho devoted himself exclusively to sitting in medita-

---

61. See *Chung yung*, chap. 1, sec. 4; Legge, *Confucius*, p. 348: "While there are no stirrings of pleasure, anger, sorrow, or joy, the mind may be said to be in the state of EQUILIBRIUM. When those feelings have been stirred, and they act in their due degree, there ensues what may be called the state of HARMONY."
62. Yi Man-gap (1879–1960).

tion, trying to have the watery energy ascend and the fiery energy descend;[63] however, he ended up with a severe headache. Seeing this, the Master said, "This is what happens if one does not know the correct way of practice. Generally speaking, one's practice cannot be perfect unless it is pursued both in motion and at rest. In motion, one should be heedful mainly to mindful choice [in karmic action] in all circumstances, attaining the threefold great power; at rest one should devote oneself mainly to spiritual cultivation and inquiry [into facts and principles], attaining the threefold great power. One who understands and practices this way will experience little pain in practice, feeling leisurely and wanting nothing like the great seas with no wind. Watery energy will ascend and fiery energy descend naturally as one's mind attains calmness. If one does not understand this way, one can get ill and suffer the rest of one's life. Thus, you should bear this in mind."

41. The Master said, "To show what humankind ought to do is the fundamental principle of my teaching. This principle requires the renovation of the imperfect doctrines of the past to perfection and to make difficult doctrines easy to understand so that everyone can learn the supreme Way. Although my teaching is based on this principle, those who do not understand this and do not forsake the obsolete views do not follow my teaching correctly, arguing that one must enter a quiet mountain to practice, or that one must attain the supernatural power of casting mountains away and upsetting the sea at will. Some claim that reading scriptures, lectures, and discussions are not necessary, and hence one must devote oneself to intoning the name of a buddha and sitting in meditation. Thus, my teaching is not correctly practiced by some. This is regrettable. There are quite a few people in temples and Zen monasteries in all provinces who roam about for their whole life without any occupation, hoping to attain the supernatural power[64] of 'being anywhere or doing anything at will'[65] and the power of enlightenment to the fundamental principles of the universe. Anyone who seeks Buddha-dharma outside of the secular world and tries to attain such supernatural power is practicing the wicked way. Therefore, you ought to pursue the practice within the secular world, following what I teach about the essential way of humanity and the essential way of practice.[66] If you do so, you will be endowed with blessing and wisdom,

---

63. See above, *Canon*, pt. 3, chap. 4, IV.

64. The five supernatural powers are (1) instantaneous view of anything anywhere in the form realm, (2) ability to hear any sound anywhere, (3) ability to know the thoughts of all other minds, (4) knowledge of all former existence of self and others, and (5) power to be anywhere or do anything at will.

65. Literally, "removing mountains and upsetting the sea" and "calling for wind and rain."

66. See above, *Canon*, pt. 2, chap. 6.

and the supernatural power and the power of samādhi may also be attained. This is the right order of practice and is the great Way with sound foundation."

42. The Master said, "Paranormal power is not valued in the order of correct doctrine because it does not help deliver sentient beings; rather, it hampers such deliverance. It is harmful because most of those who try to attain paranormal power enter mountains, leaving the secular world behind; they attach themselves to ultimate quiescence[67] apart from the way of humanity, chanting spells and 'true words'[68] throughout their whole life. If the whole world respects this practice, all walks of life, namely, scholar-officials, farmers, artisans, and tradesmen, will collapse, and morality and law and order will be neglected. As they, being ignorant of the foundation of morality, hope to gain extraordinary talent with preposterous thoughts and wrong desire, they will deceive the world and harm people by abusing some miracle that may occur from hallucination. That's why an old sage said, 'Paranormal power is an episode in the decadent period of Buddha-dharma; and paranormal power which arises in someone with no sound moral foundation is at best a kind of sorcery.'[69] If, however, vehement desires are extinguished in your heart and your conduct is devoid of defilements as the result of sincere practice in the correct doctrine, mysterious traces can occasionally appear in accordance with the light of self-nature. However, this is attained even though it is not sought. This cannot be conjectured by common mortals with wicked thoughts."

43. The Master said, "There are some who, not knowing one's own spiritual capacity, try to be enlightened to the most profound principle of the universe through momentary, unremitting exertions at the first aspiration for cultivating the Way. With such hasty temperament, one can easily get ill or be estranged from the life of practice as a result of desperation at a failure. You should bear this in mind. There do exist exceptional cases in which one reaches the buddha stage at a leap; however, one who would achieve such supreme enlightenment comes with the highest spiritual capacity as the result of continuous effort through reincarnations of many kalpas. One with medium or low

---

67. A translation of *vyupaśama*, referring to the realm that transcends birth and death; it also refers to the stage of the dhyāna of the cessation of feelings and thoughts. Furthermore, it refers to the nature of nirvāṇa, which is no other than the nature of all dharmas.

68. *Chinŏn* (C. *Chen-yen*; J. *Shingon*) is used for mantra and dhāraṇi, indicating magical formulae, spells, charms, esoteric words. Buddhas and bodhisattvas have each an esoteric sound represented by a Sanskrit letter, the primary Vairocana letter, the alpha of all sounds being "a," which is also styled the True Word that saves the world.

69. See *Susim kyŏl*, *T*, 2020.48.1006b–c; Buswell, *KAZ*, pp. 143–144: "Moreover, in the case of accomplished men, phenomenal spiritual powers are like eerie apparitions; they are only a minor concern of the saints."

capacity must devote serious effort to the cultivation of the Way for a long time in the following order. First, one should develop a great aspiration. Only after a great aspiration does a great faith arise. Only after a great faith arises a great zeal. Only after a great zeal arises a great doubt. Only after the great doubt arises sincere effort. And only after a sincere effort follows a great awakening. Coming to know the ultimate truth is not completed with one awakening; it will be followed by thousands or tens of thousands of awakenings."

44. The Master said, "It is foolish for anyone to attempt to attain the supreme wisdom of sages as soon as he or she gets a glimpse of the profound truth; it is a gravely wrong idea. The great sea is tiny water droplets aggregated; the great earth of mountains and fields is tiny clods of dirt aggregated. The great achievements of all buddhas and sages are the fruit of many years of spiritual effort, which is formless and invisible. Those who aspire to attain supreme enlightenment and make a great contribution must begin to accumulate effort with minor tasks first."

45. The Master said, "Of those who have entered the order in search of the Way, leaving their homes behind, some forget their original aspiration and devote themselves to external learning and external knowledge. Such a one may gain extensive knowledge; however, one's spiritual power is weakened thereby, and one will have difficulty in attaining true wisdom. Therefore, those in search of the true Way should check their original aspiration and keep their minds from being distracted in many directions. If one devotes oneself to the cultivation of the threefold great power, one will naturally be endowed with the ability to gain external learning and knowledge as well."

46. The Master said, "Before I attained One Thought [enlightenment], sometimes I offered prayers, sometimes chanted spells that came into my mind, sometimes fell unawares into the calmness of no thought. After I attained One Thought upon the awakening of numinous spirit, there were fluctuations of brightness and darkness between night and day and before and after the fifteenth of each lunar month. When the gate of wisdom was open during these fluctuations, there seemed nothing I could not know or do; when it was closed, I did not even know what to do with my own body; I worried about my own future and wondered whether I was not possessed by something. However, the fluctuations disappeared eventually and the awakened state of mind has continued without fluctuations to this day."

47. The Master suffered from coughing every winter, and his preaching used to be interrupted by coughing. The Master said to a congregation, "Fortunately, I searched for the Way with utmost sincerity since my childhood in accordance with the habit I had formed in my former lives. As you know, however, Kilyong-ni, where I grew up, is a

place of unusual poverty and ignorance. There was no one I could ask
for help or guidance; thus I thought out a plan for ascetic practice,
sometimes sitting up overnight in a mountain, sometimes sitting by a
roadside the whole day, sometimes sitting up in a room overnight,
sometimes bathing in icy water, sometimes fasting, and sometimes
dwelling in a cold room until I became unconscious. At last my doubt
was resolved; however, the ailment was set deep in my body, and my
suffering from the ailment got worse as my vital force got weaker. I
had no choice because I did not know the right path; you are fortunate enough to learn from my experience, so that you came to know
the perfect path of Mahāyāna practice without self-mortification and
ascetic practice. In this way you are blessed. Generally speaking, the
practice of timeless Zen and placeless Zen[70] is the shortcut to follow the
Mahāyāna practice. If you follow this path of practice, you can achieve
great results with little effort, and succeed without getting ill. You
should never follow in my footsteps of useless ascetic practice lest you
hurt yourself."

48. The Master said, "Just as students are given examinations at the
end of each semester, one who goes through the path of practice is
tested in various favorable and adverse conditions when one ascends to
a higher dharma stage[71] or reaches the buddha stage. Thus, it is said
that, when the Buddha was about to attain the Buddhahood, he was
attacked by Pāpiyān,[72] leading an eighty-four-thousand-*māra* army.
Many practitioners thereafter also underwent such tests. Some of you
are trapped in the trial and are fighting against heavy odds; some sur-
rendered, thereby ruining your eternal life; and some have passed the
tests with flying colors and have a rosy future before you. I hope that all
of you examine your level of dharma stage so that you may not fail the
trial."

49. The Master said, "If you learn a skill, you must have your
knowledge checked by your teacher. If you receive moral training, you
must have the rightness and wrongness of your acts checked by your
mentor. Otherwise, your skill will be incorrect, and your practice will be
beside the point. To help you follow the correct path and avoid the
wrong one, therefore, I constantly check the rightness and wrongness of
your conduct and the correctness and incorrectness of your understanding of facts and principles. If you dislike being checked or are dis-
pleased with my reminding you of rightness and wrongness, you must
ask yourselves what was the purpose of your coming to me and how
you can improve your practice. Correct criticisms and advice from me

70. See above, *Canon*, pt. 3, chap. 7.
71. Ibid., chap. 17.
72. The king of evil ones or *māra*, who strives to kill all goodness.

and from other people provide a model for your future and help you open your future. If you resent such benefactors, you will be acting ungratefully. Thus, you ought to exert yourselves to find the correct path of practice, being receptive to my or other people's criticisms on the rightness and wrongness of what you do."

50. The Master said, "A practitioner who trains his or her mind only in a quiet place, avoiding all adverse conditions, is like a fisherman who tries to catch fish, avoiding water. It will not lead to any practical result. Thus, one must train one's mind in adverse conditions of all sorts if one wishes to cultivate the Way correctly; for one can attain the great spiritual power that will not be disturbed in any adverse conditions only if one trains one's mind in such conditions. If one trains one's mind only in a quiet place, one will lose mental composure as soon as one confronts adverse conditions. This is like a mushroom growing in the shade; it will fade away as soon as it is exposed to the sun's light. Therefore, it is said in the *Vimalakīrtinirdeśa Sūtra*, 'A bodhisattva's mind is calm in a noisy place; while a heretic's mind is disturbed in a quiet place.'[73] This teaches that practice depends on what you do with your mind, not on the external mental spheres."

51. The Master said to several disciples, "Turn Buddha-dharma to practical use so that daily life may be improved; do not be enslaved to it lest you waste your life. Generally speaking, Buddha-dharma is a great doctrine with which the world can be saved. If, however, one leaves the secular world behind and enters the mountain, where one spends one's whole life intoning the name of a buddha, reading scriptures, or sitting in meditation with no meritorious deeds of salvation resulting from these practices, one is enslaved to Buddha-dharma. Such a life will neither bring much success to oneself nor any benefit to the world."

52. The Master said to a congregation, "The purpose of knowing the Way lies in making use of it at a right place and at a right time. If you cannot use it when it is needed, it is as good as not knowing of it, let alone gaining any benefit of it." The Master then raised his fan and said, "If you don't know how to use this fan when it is hot, what good is it to own one?"

53. The Master said, "One who does practice in the dharma should be able to sever attachments to all external affinities and drop the internal clinging to One Mind; clinging to One Mind is called the 'bondage of dharma.'[74] If one is bound by the dharma, one will even lose freedom to blink one's eyelid or make a minor bodily movement. One will then be unable to attain the great emancipation. Therefore, one who cultivates the Way should nourish his or her original nature so

---

73. Unidentified.

74. Holding to things (dharmas) as realities, i.e., the tenet that things are real.

as to be spontaneous and natural, letting it function in a lively manner. When the six sense organs [eyes, ears, nose, mouth, body, and mind] are free from work, one should only eliminate delusive thoughts; when the six sense organs are at work, one should steer them away from injustice.[75] One should not cling to One Mind while one is in the state of One Mind. This can be compared to a baby-sitter. A good baby-sitter would let the baby be free to go and come and play as it pleases, stopping it from getting into dangerous places and removing anything that can hurt the baby. It would be foolish of the baby-sitter to hold the baby tightly for the whole day, without letting it go free, for the baby would be distressed by the confinement. The evil of clinging to One Mind is not different from this."

54. The Master said to Kim Nam-ch'ŏn, "The other day, I saw a man riding on an ox's back. As he could not control the ox, he, instead of leading it, went wherever the ox went; he was taken to a thorny path, to a pit, to a mountain, to a field, sometimes falling backward and sometimes forward; his clothes were torn and his body injured. It was a pitiful scene. Watching him, I asked him why he did not get hold of the reins and save himself from such mishap. The man said that he would have been blessed if he had been able to do so, but, because of his ignorance, he had let the ox do whatever it wanted to do. As a consequence, he said, as he grew older and the ox got wilder, it was beyond his control. Today, I see you coming on the back of an ox. Where is the ox?" Nam-ch'ŏn said, "I am on its back now." The Master asked, "What does it look like?" Nam-ch'ŏn answered, "Its height is one fathom, its color is yellow, it wears hempen shoes, its beard is an assortment of gray and black." The Master said, smiling, "You seem to know the shape of the ox you are riding. Is your ox obedient to you or are you, too, taken anywhere it goes?" Nam-ch'ŏn said, "The ox generally does what I want it to do. If it slacks at its work, I give an order to do it; if it is moved to do what is unjust, then I order it not to do it." The Master said, "Since you have clearly discovered the ox and learned how to tame it and since it generally follows your command, tame it so that you can do all things freely."

55. The Master said to an assembly at a Zen monastery, "The Zen training you receive at this intensive Zen session can be compared to the taming of an ox. One who lacks moral training, who deviates from the right path of humanity, who acts licentiously, is like a calf before weaning, which runs about loosely anywhere it pleases. One who leaves home and enters Zen training makes one's mentor worried about the future of one's practice and public service because one has great diffi-

---

75. See *Canon*, pt. 3, chap. 7.

culty in severing the old habit while observing rules and keeping pre
cepts and because such a one suffers from burning passions and worldly
thoughts. Such a one is like a weanling tethered to a stake, calling for its
mother and writhing in agony. After a while, one gradually improves
from pursuing the required courses, understanding directions and what
is taught; wicked and worldly thoughts are silenced in one's mind; and
one gets interested in coming to understand what one did not know
before. One at this stage is like the ox that, though not quite tamed, is
gradually contented with the given conditions. At the next stage, one
interprets the doctrine correctly and does not deviate from the right
path of practice, maturing in the threefold great power of cultivation,
inquiry, and mindful choice. One makes spiritual, physical, and material contribution to the public well-being, thus benefiting the public.
Such a one is like a well-tamed ox, which does whatever the master
makes it do, benefiting him wherever it goes. Thus, the purpose of a
peasant's taming his ox is to have it till the soil at the right time; the
purpose of one's training in an intensive course at a Zen monastery is
to make one able to make a good application of the training in human
society. I hope you exert yourselves to practice without wasting any
moment of this opportunity so that you may, as apostles, make great
contributions with the 'well-tamed spiritual ox' for the great task of
delivering sentient beings and curing the world of illness."

56. The Master said at the opening ceremony of a Zen retreat at a
Zen monastery, "Your admission into the intensive Zen retreat can be
compared to a person entering into a hospital. A physically ill person is
treated with medicine at the hospital; a morally ill person[76] is treated
with moral teachings in a religious order. Hence, the Buddha is called
King of Medicine; his teachings, medicine; and his temples, hospitals.
People, however, know only physical disease and spend money and time
to cure it, while they do not regard moral illness as an illness, let alone
minding to cure it. Anyone who is concerned about the well-being of
the world cannot but deplore this state of affairs. Physical illness, no
matter how critical it may be, will be limited to one life span, and can
be cured in a short time if it is not so critical. Moral illnesses, however,
if left untreated, becomes the seeds of evil and suffering for the endless
future. If one is morally ill, one loses freedom of mind. Being attached
to external temptations, one says what should not be said, does what
shouldn't be done, and thinks what one should not think, driving oneself into fatality, inviting contemptuous treatment from others, or creating sufferings to oneself. In this way, one will be unable to get out of
the endless vicious cycle of wrongdoing and suffering. If one is free

---

76. A person suffering from greed, hatred, delusion.

from moral illness, one can transcend suffering and happiness throughout the universe, being free to come into being and go out of being with
blessings and joy at one's disposal. Listen! You should try to detect
moral illness in your mind and do your best to cure your mind of moral
illness."

57. The Master continued, "If one who follows the path of practice
wishes to diagnose and cure moral illness, one must first of all know
how to cure it. First, just as a patient must describe the symptom of illness to the doctor correctly, you must confess the symptom of moral
illness to your mentor truthfully. Secondly, just as a patient must con-
form to the doctor's directions, you ought to follow the teaching of your
mentor. Thirdly, just as a patient must devote sincere effort to the
treatment until he or she is completely cured, you ought to devote
yourselves to the treatment of moral illness until you are completely
cured of it. If you carry out this practice sincerely, you will not only
recover moral health but attain the medical art of curing people who
suffer from moral illness, thus accomplishing the great task of delivering
sentient beings and curing the world of illness."

58. The Master said to an assembly at a Zen monastery, "Our doctrine for practice is similar to the art of war for restoring peace in a
disturbed country, and you are similar to the fresh recruits who are
learning tactics in an army recruit center. By disturbance I mean the
disturbance that continues in the mental realm of people. The mental
realm of humankind is originally calm, peaceful, bright, and clean;
however, it becomes dark, impure, complicated, and disturbed by the
evil army of selfish desires. Such living circumstances of sentient beings
are called 'the war in the world of mind.' By the art of war I mean the
tactics to conquer all the evil army in the world of mind; the central
military maxim lies in the cultivation of concentration (samādhi), wisdom (prajñā), and precepts (*śīla*) and in differentiating dharma from
*māra*. This is the best tactic to quell the disturbance in the world. People in the world, however, do not regard disturbance in the mind as
disturbance; they are putting the cart before the horse. If you inquire
into the causes of individual, familial, societal, and national disturbances, you will find them in the mental disturbance of humankind.
Thus, the mental disturbance is the origin of all disturbances and the
most critical disturbance; and the tactics to subdue the disturbance in
human mind is the zenith of all doctrines and the most important of all
military arts. Therefore, you should understand this point and cultivate
diligently both concentration and wisdom, observing all the precepts[77]
with utmost effort. If you devote yourselves to practice continuously,

---

77. See above, *Canon*, pt. 3, chap. 11.

you will eventually subjugate all the evil army; and you will be promoted to the dharma stage of the subjugation of *māra* by the power of dharma.[78] It is my conviction that you will, then, be the general commander in subduing the mental disturbance of the whole world where sentient beings are suffering endlessly."

59. The Master said, "From our original nature, which is devoid of discrimination and attachment, arises the mind of good and evil. This is illustrated by comparison to the growth of crops and weeds in the field. Thus, our mind-ground is also called 'the field of the mind.' Just as a fallow field is cultivated into fertile soil, our mind-ground should be cultivated so that we may attain wisdom and blessings. In this way, the expression 'cultivating the field of mind' was coined. Therefore, just as a good farmer keeps weeding the field and grows only the crops, gathering in an abundant harvest in the autumn, the cultivator of the field of mind ought to keep checking the rising of good and evil in the mind and eliminate evil intention, nourishing only conscience so that wisdom and blessing will always be in abundance. A poor cultivator of the field of mind is like a poor farmer. Just as the poor farmer leaves both weeds and crops to grow and leaves the field to be ruined, then has nothing to harvest in autumn, so a poor cultivator of the field of mind acts as he or she pleases undiscriminatingly, following both the good and evil intentions that arise in the mind. Such a one confronts nothing but suffering, with the gate of wisdom and blessing getting farther and farther away. Thus, the causes of suffering and blessing consist in whether or not one does well on the cultivation of the field of mind. How could we be negligent in this matter?"

60. The Master continued, "In the traditional religious orders from ancient times what we call discovery of the field of mind is called seeing into one's own nature and what we call cultivation of the field of mind is called cultivation of and following one's own nature.[79] The cultivation of the field of the mind was taken by all buddhas and sages as their mission, and it is the ground for directing the world properly. Thus, in our order, we have decided that the specialized courses for the cultivation of the field of the mind are spiritual cultivation, inquiry into facts and principles, and mindful choice in karmic action, and we give various directions for the practice of them.[80] Spiritual cultivation is the course for preparing the ground for tilling and farming the field of the mind; inquiry [into facts and principles] is the course for the knowledge of farming and of distinguishing the crops from the weeds; and mindful choice [in karmic action] is the course for putting into practice what

---

78. Ibid., chap. 17, no. 4.
79. See above, II:7.
80. See above, *Canon*, pt. 2, chap. 4; pt. 3, chap. 2.

one knows, gathering in the harvest successfully. Today, greed in humankind is rising as scientific civilization develops; greed cannot be subdued without moral training in the cultivation of the field of mind. There will be no peace unless greed is subdued. Therefore, cultivation of the field of mind will be needed by people. When cultivation of the field of mind is desired, people will look for the true religion, which provides specialized courses for the cultivation. Anyone whose practice is sound will be held in high esteem by the public. Take this opportunity to renew your resolution to be the model farmers of successful cultivation in the field of mind."

61. The Master said to an assembly at a Zen monastery, "As I have talked a great deal during this Zen retreat and today I have to talk again, some of you may feel tired of this. However, those who have little understanding of practice and its virtue will better understand facts and principles and practice them only if enough explanation is given. Thus, I have tried to explain the Way. When sages in the past edified beginners, they endeavored to explain facts and principles to them first and then helped them practice the dharma gradually. You should not be impatient or depressed when your knowledge is not accompanied by deeds after you have been trained at one or two Zen retreats. You should neither look down upon nor blame yourself or another such a one. When you hear a tenet of the doctrine you have already heard several times, you should not disregard it, nor should you be depressed when you find it difficult to practice as you wish. If you hear the same dharma many times and try to practice it over and over again, you will eventually develop a perfect personality whose knowledge and conduct are both perfect."

62. The Master said to an assembly at the closing ceremony of a Zen retreat, "This closing ceremony releases you from a small Zen monastery; however, this is an opening ceremony of a grand Zen monastery [the world]. One who thinks of this event only as the closing ceremony does not know the great way of practice."

63. Kim Tae-gŏ asked, "Since there are no precepts for those who are at and above the dharma stage of subjugation of *māra* by the power of dharma,[81] are they done with the practice in mindful choice in karmic action?" The Master answered, "One at the dharma stage of subjugation of *māra* by the dharma power has ascended to the first level of sageness; hence such a one does not have to discipline oneself in such training as binding with precepts or checking against precepts. However, such a one has inner precepts. First, one should guard oneself against being concerned only with one's own practice and living in

---

81. See above, *Canon*, pt. 3, chap. 17, no. 4.

idleness lest one degrade oneself into Hīnayānistic egoism. Second, one should guard oneself against indulging in enjoyment of riches and honors lest one's original vow be obscured. Third, one should guard oneself against manifesting paranormal power to the eyes of sentient beings lest it interfere with the correct dharma. Besides these, one must devote oneself to the threefold practice of cultivation, inquiry, and mindful choice, making progress toward the buddha stage and nourishing compassion toward the salvation of sentient beings."

## IV. On the Principles of Humanity

1. A new follower asked the Master, "As I live in the valley of Mt. Kyeryong, I often converse with the adherents of various religious orders in the valley. Each of them always admires the merits of his own doctrine, each mentioning *todŏk* [the Way and its virtue; viz., morality] whenever he talks. However, I haven't attained a clear understanding of its meaning. Can you kindly explain its meaning to me?" The Master answered, "It is admirable of you to be interested in learning the Way and its virtue; however, it cannot be explained in a short time since its meaning is quite profound and extensive. Thus, you will be able to understand it only after you receive a considerable training in this dharma; however, I will explain the Way and its virtue to gratify your curiosity. So, listen carefully.

"*To* (way) in general terms means what should be followed. Hence, what heaven follows is called the way of heaven; what the earth follows is called the way of earth; and what humankind follows is called the way of humanity. The way of humanity consists of the way of body and that of mind. Though the fundamental principle of these ways is unitary, their details are innumerable. Thus, if we talk about the way of humanity, which is one of so many details, there are still two branches, physical and spiritual. Analogous to there being roads for the body to travel through the network of highways connecting districts to districts, with countless routes around mountains, on waters, through fields and villages, there are countless major and minor principles for what the mind does for an individual, a family, a society, and a state. To give a few examples, there are moral rules that ought to be followed by parents and offspring, by seniors and juniors, by spouses, by friends, and by brethren. If you know the right course to be followed in whatever you confront, then you know the Way. The greatest among all these ways is our original nature, the truth of which lies in neither arising nor ceasing and the causal law of karmic retribution.[82] This principle unifies all dharmas, on which Heaven and Earth and humankind are all

---

82. See above, I:1.

grounded; thus, anyone who knows this Way knows the greatest of all ways."

2. The Master continued, "*Tŏk* (virtue) means, in plain language, beneficence being brought about in anything and anywhere. When heaven follows the way of heaven, the virtue of heaven is brought about; when the earth follows its way, the virtue of the earth is brought about; when humankind follows the way of humankind, the virtue of humankind is brought about. Thus, myriad virtues are brought about when myriad ways are followed. If you choose to explain human virtues out of so many virtues, you will see that they have countless ramifications. If the ways parents and children ought to follow are followed, then the virtue (beneficence) between them will be brought about; if the ways young and old ought to follow are followed, then beneficence between them will be brought forth; if the ways spouses ought to follow are followed, then beneficence between them will be brought forth; if the ways friends ought to follow are followed, then beneficence between them will be brought forth; if the ways brethren ought to follow are followed, then the beneficence between them will be brought forth. Thus, an individual, a family, a society, a nation, and the world will be harmonized if the respective ways they ought to follow are followed. The greatest virtue is brought about by one who, attaining the supreme enlightenment, ably transcends being and nonbeing, attains emancipation from birth and death, masters the causal law of karmic retribution, and delivers all sentient beings suffering in 'the burning house in the triple world'[83] into a paradise. Such a person can be said to have attained the greatest virtue."

3. The Master continued, "Anyone who advocates *todŏk* only in words with no understanding of its principle, searching for wicked and weird things, and doing absurd and immoral things, is vicious and evil. Of course, such a person has nothing to do with the true Way and the harmonious influence of virtue (beneficence). Hence, one who wishes to practice *todŏk* must first of all know the principle of the Way and, having learned it, must always cultivate virtue sincerely. Anyone who cultivates this path will gradually be enlightened to the Way and become virtuous. Since ordinary people do not understand the fundamental principle of *todŏk*, however, they regard anyone who can do some strange trickery as enlightened to the Way regardless of whether the person is enlightened to the principle of noumenon and phenomenon and being and nonbeing of all things in the universe.[84] They also regard anyone who is of meek mentality as a person of virtue, regardless

---

83. Sot'aesan is alluding here to the famous parable of the burning house from the Lotus Sūtra. See *Miao-fa lien-hua ching* 2, *T*, 262.9.12c–13c; Hurvitz, *Lotus*, pp. 58–62.
84. See above, *Canon*, pt. 2, chap. 4, sec. 2, I.

of whether such a person knows how to make mindful choice in karmic action[85] on what is right, wrong, gain, or loss. Isn't it ludicrous? As it is a right thing for you, as a new follower of this teaching, to wish to know what *todŏk* is all about, you should, bearing in mind what I have said, have a thorough understanding of its principle so that you may not stray from the right path."

4. The Master said, "If one wishes to follow the way of humanity, one should not be careless even a moment; for one cannot follow it unless one is attentive to the ways (duties) that pertain to the relationships between parents and children, teachers and disciples, old and young, husband and wife, friends, all brethren, and any other human situations. Thus, all the sages since ancient times came in accordance with the call of the times and formulated doctrines to explicate the ways [moral laws] humankind ought to follow. Those who make light of such ways and act as they please will not realize the value and dignity of humankind in their lifetime and will not avoid the suffering of the evil path in their next incarnations."

5. The Master said, "All human affairs have roots and branches, and principal and the subordinate parts. If the roots are well taken care of, the branches will also be improved; if only the branches are taken care of, the roots will suffer. If the principal is taken care of, the subordinate will also be improved; if, however, only the subordinate is given all the care, then the principal will suffer. Take humankind and the world for example. Of humankind, the mind is the root, and the body the branch; of the world, morality is the root and science the branch. One knows the Way only if one clearly knows the root and branch and the principal and subordinate; only such a one can correct the affairs of the world."

6. The Master said to Yi Tongjinhwa, "There are two great things for a human being to accomplish in a lifetime. The first is to find a mentor of the correct dharma and to attain buddhahood (supreme enlightenment).[86] The second is, upon attaining supreme enlightenment, to deliver sentient beings. These two are the most essential and greatest of all tasks."

7. The Master read and complimented Tung Chung-shu's writing, which says, "One should practice righteousness without contriving profit and explicate the Way without calculating the merit." The Master then added a line to each sentence: If one practices righteousness without contriving profit, a great profit accrues to oneself; if one explicates the Way without calculating merit, a great merit accrues to oneself.

8. Seeing a horse pulling a cart, the Master asked one of his disciples, "What is going, the horse or the cart?" The disciple answered, "The

---

85. Ibid., sec. 3.
86. Ibid., pt. 3, chap. 17, no. 6.

horse is pulling the cart." The Master asked again, "If it is not going, which should be whipped, the horse or the cart?" The disciple answered, "The horse should be whipped." The Master said, "You are right. To whip the horse is to take care of the essential. To succeed in whatever one does, one must find out the essential and take care of it."

9. Kim Ki-ch'ŏn asked, "How can one know what is reasonable from what is unreasonable?" The Master answered, "Just as the cycle of the four seasons of spring, summer, autumn, and winter follows the orderly path, reasonableness lies in doing all things in accordance with their right order. One acts against reasonableness if one acts without knowing the right order of things, forces oneself to do what is beyond one's capacity, forces others to do what they do not want, or hurts the feelings of others. If one always does what is reasonable, knowing reasonableness from unreasonableness, one will succeed in almost anything."

10. The Master said, "It is a common disposition of humankind to try to do oneself good. However, one succeeds or fails to do so depending on whether one is reasonable or unreasonable, realistic or unrealistic, while one tries to obtain what one wants using one's knowledge and ability. Those who pursue their blessings and happiness reasonably make themselves happy by doing others good, thus cultivating immeasurable paradise; those who pursue blessings and happiness unreasonably do so selfishly by harming others, thus creating immeasurable misery for themselves. Those who pursue blessings and happiness realistically do so from the real source of blessings, obtaining excellent results. Those who pursue them unrealistically try to obtain them from superstitions, obtaining no results. Now, there are few who pursue blessings and happiness reasonably and realistically, while there are many who pursue them unreasonably and unrealistically. It is because the correct dharma has not been spread wide in the world and hence the spirit of the human race is not yet awakened evenly. When reasonable and realistic ways for pursuing blessings and happiness are made widely known, everyone will be influenced thereby as when the sun is high up in the sky."

11. The Master said, "Few who are filial to their parents and fraternal to their brothers do evil to others; few who are not filial to their parents or fraternal to their brothers do good to others. That's why it is said in Confucianism, 'Filial piety is the foundation of all [virtuous] actions.'[87] It is also said that a loyal vassal is to be sought in a family famed for filial piety. These are all truthful words."

---

87. *Analects*, bk. 1, chap. 2, sec. 2. Legge, *Confucius*, pp. 138–139: "The superior man bends his attention to what is radical. This being established, all practical courses naturally grow up. Filial piety and fraternal submission!—are they not the root of all benevolent actions?"

12. The Master said, "What is unbearable to oneself is also unbearable to others; what is pleasurable to oneself is also pleasurable to others. Do not do unto others what you do not like, and do unto others what you are pleased with. This is the way of understanding the minds of others analogically, by reflecting upon one's own mind. If you continue practice like this for a long time, the distance between you and others will disappear, and many will be spiritually influenced by you."

13. The Master said, "Those with wonderful skill know how to regard someone else's skill as their own. Such people can bring prosperity to their family, country, and world."

14. The Master said, "One's intention to render benefit to another person sometimes inadvertently results in causing harm to that person. Thus one should take full precautions when one does good for others. On the other hand, those who are harmed in spite of the good intention should rather be grateful for the goodwill and should not just be resentful about the harm done."

15. While the Master was staying at Yŏngsan Monastery, a new follower offered him food and gifts. The Master received them and said, "I should thank you for paying me homage. However, the friendly feelings you have for me may change depending on your mind. Do you know why?" The follower asked, "How could my respect for you change for nothing?" The Master said, "It depends on what you are seeking. If what you seek can be found in me while you are around me, our friendship will be an everlasting one. If not, then our friendship will not last long."

16. The Master said, "Two factors keep one's being on friendly terms with others while associating with them from being long-lasting. First, one is not mindful (yunyŏm) where one should be. Second, one does not practice 'no thought' (munyŏm) where one should. One is not mindful where one should be if one forgets that one is indebted to someone's favor and if one treats the benefactor with no sense of duty when the benefactor makes one feel regretful. One fails to practice 'no thought' where one should if one wishes the beneficiary to recompense one for the favor after one has done it and if one hates the beneficiary so much more for having received a favor when the beneficiary is ungrateful. In this way, good affinity does not last long; it rather changes to resentment and hatred. Understanding this principle, you should be mindful or practice 'no thought' as the case may dictate so that good affinity may last long. You should be especially careful not to create a bad affinity out of a good one."

17. Yi Kong-ju said to the Master, "Some time ago I gave alms to a poor neighbor, and he has been helping me with my household chores with an unsparing hand ever since. From this I have learned that one should be benevolent to others and that one is repaid with blessings if

one does good to others." The Master said, "Now you have learned the principle that if you give to others benevolently, you will be repaid with blessings. However, do you know, also, that the good deed can be a cause of transgression?" Kong-ju asked, "How could blessings change to transgressions?" The Master said, "I do not mean that the good deed itself becomes a transgression, but that the mind that makes you do good can change to a mind that makes you do evil. Ordinary people, having done favors to others, cannot drop the false thoughts associated with the favor, and their resentments and hatred are increased many times over if the favored one does not recognize the indebtedness or is ungrateful. They produce extreme hatred out of extreme love, and create an enormous enemy out of a small favor. Thus, it is uncertain whether the good they cultivate will really turn out to be good since they often cause transgression out of their attempts to do good. Therefore Bodhidharma said, 'Being devoid of false thoughts in application is called virtuous,' and Lao Tzu said, 'The man of superior virtue is not conscious of his virtue, and in this way he really possesses virtue.'[88] One who pursues practice should understand this principle and apply this mind in order to make favors everlasting ones and blessings eternal ones, so that 'one will be in harmony in one's attributes with heaven and earth.'[89] You should exert yourself to do good without harboring any false thought of virtue and do favors which will not change."

18. Yi Chŏng-wŏn asked, "How can I cultivate a perfect mind not moved by hatred or love?" The Master said, "The way to keep one's mind from being moved by hatred or love lies in changing one's mind from one state to another. For instance, if someone hates you, do not simply hate that person in return. Instead, take the cause of hatred into consideration. If you are the cause of that person's hatred, exert yourself to correct it. Even if you do not deserve hatred, submit yourself to it with equanimity, regarding it as the karma from your former lives. On the other hand, you should resolve not to hate anyone, reflecting on how painful it was even for a moment when you were hated by someone. If you do so, then the person who hates you will turn out to be one who teaches you how to use your mind. Once you regard that person as your teacher, how could hatred arise in your mind? This is a way of keeping your mind from being moved by hatred. If a person loves you, you should not simply rejoice in that love thoughtlessly; you should take the cause of love into consideration. If you deserve to be loved, make a resolution to keep it that way forever. If, however, you do not deserve

---

88. *Tao Tê Ching*, chap. 38.
89. See *Book of Changes*, commentary on hexagram no. 1, *chien* (heaven). Cf. Legge, *Yi King*, p. 417: "The great man is he who is in harmony, in his attributes, with heaven and earth."

such love, you should understand that you are indebted to that person. Moreover, love can be proper or improper. Unless it is a proper love, you should be able to sever it. Even if it is a proper one, you should not be attached to it if you feel it is likely to disturb other important matters; you should take a resolute step to carry out your duties without being disturbed by it. This is a way of keeping yourself from the attachment of love. If you pursue the practice of not being moved by these two ways continuously, you will soon attain a perfect mind."

19. The Master, having seen one of his disciples reprimanding his subordinate, said to him later, "If you admonished him without being moved by hatred or love, what you said will be a lawful sermon; if you were moved by hatred or love, what you said cannot be one. It is a principle of heaven and earth that when heat or cold reaches its extreme, it turns to its opposite; likewise, one's extreme action is sure to languish later."

20. The Master, hearing one of his disciples speak frivolously to a child, said, "There are ways to serve one's seniors when one meets them and ways to be kind to one's juniors when one meets them. Depending on the situation, the formalities of the two may be different, but there is no difference in the spirit of respecting and honoring others. How could you treat a human being in such a rough manner simply because it is a child?"

21. The Master said, "As the proverb 'A tattler is a trumpeter' goes, everyone has a trumpet. When it is played, one melody produces peace in the hearer's mind; another melody creates a feeling of uneasiness; another makes someone sad; another produces pleasure; another makes people live in harmony; and another makes people quarrel. Accordingly, the path of blessings and that of suffering are divided. Such being the case, when you play the trumpet in whatever situation you may be, produce only good melodies making all people live in harmony and making public and private affairs prosperous. Do not produce any tune that makes people quarrel or ruin themselves. If you follow these admonitions, the trumpet will create innumerable blessings. Otherwise, the trumpet will be the cause of unlimited transgression."

22. The Master said, "Though there is hardly any other relationship that is more intimate and closer than that between parents and their children, the children will not readily follow the guidance that the parents themselves cannot follow. Though there is no other relationship kindlier than that between spouses, one's spouse will not do what one encourages him or her to do if one cannot do it oneself. Thus, the best way to teach something to others lies in doing it oneself first."

23. One night, the watchdog at the door of the room for the head dharma master started barking as someone approached, and one of the disciples rose to his feet, rebuking the dog. Seeing this, the Master said,

"The dog is supposed to bark at such a time. Why do you deter it from doing what it is supposed to do? Everyone and everything in the world has its own role to play. Human eyes, ears, nose, tongue, body, and mind all have their functions. If all people of different ranks and classes fulfill their duties, the world will be in order and make progress. Thus, you should fulfill your duties faithfully without interfering with others fulfilling their duties. Among those various agents with duties, there is a central agent that rules over those various agents. For humankind, the agent with primary duty is the mind. For society and the state, the agents with primary duties are the leaders, who manage and control all organizations. Hence, if the one invested with the primary duty neglects that duty, all other duties thereunder will also be neglected, and the organization will become disorderly. You should examine your position carefully and exert yourselves to fulfill your duties. Especially, you should make careful use of your mind, which is in charge of all duties, lest your fate and the future of the public be hindered."

24. The Master said to his disciples, "Generally, the world consists of the strong and the weak. If the strong and the weak cooperate in harmony and do what they each ought to do, the world will realize eternal peace; otherwise, the two will bring calamities upon themselves and there will be no peace in the world for a long time.[90] Thus, an ancient sage said that if the lord treats the servants like his own sons, the servants respect the lord like their own parents; however, if the lord treats the servants like worthless straws, the latter regard the former as an enemy."[91]

25. The Master said, "Though all people want to be respected by others, they do things for which they will be held in disrespect rather than respect. How can they get what they want? The best way for one to be respected by others is for one to respect others first. If you respect and do good for other people, then they will also respect and do good for you."

26. The Master said, "I always feel sorry for the strong who do not know the role of the strong. If one is already strong, one can be so forever, but he or she will be respected as a pioneer and a leader only by rendering assistance and guidance to the weak so that the weak can attain strength. Nowadays, however, the strong try to stay strong by oppressing and deceiving the weak. How can the strong remain strong that way? The weak are not destined to remain weak. If their spirit is gradually enlightened and their vital force recovered, the weak will someday become the strong. Then, the position of the strong who used to bully the weak will naturally be degraded. Thus, a truly wise person

---

90. See above, *Canon*, pt. 3, chap. 13, III.
91. Ibid.

always renders help to the poor and takes care of the weak, retaining his or her strength forever."

27. The Master once visited the order's farming center and, noticing some emaciated pigs in a pigpen, asked for an explanation. Yi Tong-an explained, "While they were fed on the barley that was partly damaged during the rainy season, they were getting fat. Since we started feeding them chaff a few days ago, they do not eat it, getting emaciated like that. They seem to have contracted a habit of eating barley so that they cannot suddenly readjust their appetite for the chaff." The Master said, "We find a living scripture in this. The suffering one experiences when one is suddenly impoverished or when one has suddenly lost power is not different from this. That's why all sages ever since ancient times have regarded riches and honors as no more than the weeds by the roadside, neither rejoicing themselves in wealth and honor when they came nor worrying when they were gone. The emperor Shun[92] never overstepped his authority as the ruler, to which position he had ascended from such mean services as farming and firing pottery. Śākyamuni gave up the throne and passed over the wall in search of truth without attaching himself to anything left behind. How indifferent were they to riches and honors and how admirable were their spiritual powers to transcend suffering and happiness! Hence, if you wish to follow the Way and learn the way of the sage, don't be blinded by momentary comfort, pleasure, and power. Rather, decline them in favor of another. Regardless of your situation, do not attach yourself to riches or honors or be seduced by them. Then, you will be able to rejoice in truly everlasting comfort, fame, and power."

28. The Master explained the meaning of "contentment with poverty and delight in the Way" as follows. "In general, poverty is the state of one who lacks a usual or socially acceptable number of material goods. However, this definition can be extended. One whose face is defective has a facial poverty. One who lacks learning is in poverty of knowledge. One who lacks an acceptable number of goods lives in material poverty. 'To be content within one's bounds' means to be at peace with one's lot in whatever situation one is placed. If one does not know how to feel easy about one's poverty and tries to avoid it by force, one will become more vexed, increasing one's suffering. Thus, one should be contented with the poverty one cannot avoid and should create happiness by preparing for future blessings and wisdom. One who disciplines oneself in the dharma, being contented with his or her lot, finds delight in poverty, knowing that poverty and suffering will help create blessings and happiness in the future. One does so, further,

---

92. Name of a legendary Chinese ruler, said to have ruled from 2255 B.C. to 2205 B.C., who was a farmer before becoming emperor.

because the functioning of one's mind always accords with the truth [the Buddha-nature] and one rejoices oneself in the true realm into which one enters, transcending suffering and pleasure with the power of practice. All sages and enlightened ones from ancient times, having mastered such principles as these and applied such a frame of mind as this, lived the life of 'contentment with poverty and delight in the way.'"

29. The Master said, "One who tries to have all things in the world one's own way is like the fool who, building a house on sand, wishes to live there in splendor for millions of years. The wise one feels grateful and is satisfied with six-tenths of all the things he or she desires. Even if one gets all that one desires, one shares those things with others instead of enjoying them all by oneself; in this way one prevents calamity from falling on oneself and can attain blessings endlessly."

30. The Master said, "A heinous transgression often grows out of a minor offense in the beginning. Hence, you ought to check often what you do and exert yourselves to correct even the smallest faults as soon as they are detected. The orangutan in southern countries is so strong and agile that capturing it is beyond human strength; however, it is caught because it loves wine. People there fill a big jar with wine and place it in a place that orangutans frequent. The orangutan first passes it by, laughing at it, then it comes back to take only a draft. It turns its way back again to take another draft. The orangutan repeats this until it carelessly finishes the whole jar of wine, and eventually it is drunk. Then, it is said, the people come out of their hiding places to catch it. It is captured or killed because it cannot keep up with its initial resolution to drink just a little, ending by drinking the whole jar of wine. Human beings, too, end up committing serious offenses as a result of accumulating a few minor faults that they leave uncorrected. In that way they ruin their future. How could one be off guard against minor offenses?"

31. The Master, worrying about a few young disciples, male and female, who were still off the right track of practice, said, "Some among you start well with practice but go wrong later; others start poorly but do well later. I have been giving you directions that are right for each of you. If you do not mature in practice by the age of thirty, by which time one's personality takes a concrete shape, it will be a matter of great concern of yours, though I am also solicitous about it."

32. While the Master was staying at Pongnae Cloister, there was once a rainy spell in summer, and a dry pool in front of the cloister was full of water. Many frogs from all directions gathered there, producing countless tadpoles. After a while, the rainy spell ended, and the water in the pool was gradually drying up in the hot weather. In only a few more days it would be completely dry. The tadpoles, however, were wiggling their tails, unaware of what was happening. Seeing that, the Master said, "What a pitiful sight it is! They are enjoying themselves with vigor

without knowing that their lives are coming to an end minute by minute. Is it only the tadpoles that face such a fate? The same fate is shared by some people. To the eyes of the wise, those whose expenditures are more than their incomes and those who abuse their power are not different from the tadpoles in the drying pool."

33. The Master said, "Today I will tell you what is the most essential to guarding your mind and protecting your body. Listen to me carefully so that you may use it as a motto for practice in all mental spheres. The motto is Veneration and Awe! In other words, you ought to treat every person and everything with a sense of veneration and awe at all times and places. If one acts without a sense of veneration and awe, complaints and resentments are sure to arise in such kind and intimate relationships as those between parents and children, brethren, and spouses. Trifling circumstances and trivial things can be the cause of restrictions and harm when one acts rashly without any sense of veneration and awe under the pretext of the intimacy of the relationship and the triviality of the matters. Suppose, for example, that while one was stealing a box of matches at a store, one was caught by the storekeeper. Would the storekeeper let one go just because a box of matches is a trifle? Even an extremely generous storekeeper would scold or insult the thief. The direct cause of such scolding and insult seems to be a box of matches, but the real cause of such scolding and insult lies in the desire to take the box of matches; and the desire arose because one did not hold it in veneration and awe. Thus, such a senseless and valueless trifle as a box of matches can hold authority over one who does not hold a thing in veneration and awe. What would happen if one did not hold a valuable thing or a human being with almighty power in veneration and awe? Therefore, I am suggesting that we should always hold everything in veneration and awe. If we live righteously holding everything in veneration and awe, the deep blue sky, the boundless earth, and all the things in the universe are for our use, and all the laws being in force in the world are our guardians. If, however, we act rashly with no sense of veneration and awe, then all things in the universe may harm us, and all the laws being in force in the world will be a policeman's rope to bind us up. How wouldn't they be feared? Therefore, if you, who will be buffeted by the waves of adversity, wish to guard your minds and protect your bodies, bear this motto in mind and apply it in whatever you do."

34. On a New Year's Day, the Master said, "I have received New Year's greetings from many people; were I to follow the custom of the secular world, I would return the courtesies with food or gifts. However, I am giving you a secret with which you can survive the forthcoming turbulent times. Take it as a model." The Master then introduced a poem by an ancient sage that reads:

Gentleness is the most precious of all the arts of life;
>toughness and not yielding are the source of calamity.

Speak carefully as if you had impediment in speech.

If you have an urgent affair at hand,
>handle it as carefully as if you were an idiot.

The more urgent a situation is, the more slowly you should
>think.

When you are in peace, forget not the hidden danger.

If you live in accordance with this plan, you will be a good
>person.

To this, the Master added a line:

Anyone who acts following this plan will always live in ease
>and pleasure.

35. One day, the Master, hearing his disciples arguing for and against a current issue carried in a newspaper article, said, "You should not make rash comments on what is none of your business. One with truthful views does not criticize someone else's affairs so lightly. While reading a newspaper, you should examine the causes and effects of good and evil, so that you can draw a model from them for your future and benefit from them. This is a way of illuminating One Mind by mastering myriad affairs. If you read newspapers in this spirit, the newspapers will turn out to be a living scripture and the source of wisdom and blessings. Otherwise, you will only become opinionated and glib and, as a consequence, you will develop only the skill to criticize people. Anyone who acts like this will easily fall into the valley of offense and suffering. You should guard yourselves against this."

36. The Master, after reproaching Kim Nam-ch'ŏn for certain matters, said to Mun Chŏng-gyu, "I have just scolded Nam-ch'ŏn; however, it was not Nam-ch'ŏn alone who was scolded. What do you think of this matter? No matter whom I reprove, you ought to check your own conduct to correct it if you are liable to such reproach and bear in mind not to do it in the future if you are not at fault at the moment. Never speak ill of or laugh at the person scolded. A foolish person is so busy illuminating the faults of others that his or her own fault is unregarded; the wise is so busy checking his or her own faults that there is no time to find fault with others."

37. The Master said, "When you exert yourself to accomplish something in the world, you are sometimes praised and sometimes criticized by others. If you are simply elated by the praise and dejected by adverse criticisms, you are childish. When people are critical of you, you should check yourself. If there is nothing to be ashamed of in what

you do according to your conscience, you should carry out the work indomitably against the adverse criticisms of myriad people. If what you do is against your conscience, you should throw it up as one would throw away an old hat even if people laud you with praise. This is what an able practitioner does."

38. The Master said, "It is often the case that one exerts oneself to accomplish what one has begun as long as one has made no mistake; but once one has made one or two mistakes, resolve weakens, and one leaves the matter to take its own course. This is like the case in which one is careful to keep one's new clothes clean as long as they are clean, but becomes careless about them as soon as they become dirty or wrinkled. How can one succeed in anything if one does things like that? One with a firm conviction and strong principles and morals may fall into an error while carrying out a plan; however, such a one makes the error a model for the improvement of his or her future, without his or her original resolution being frustrated thereby. For such a one a minor fault becomes the basis for a greater success."

39. The Master said, "People in general prefer benefit to harm but often do more things that are harmful, wish to be rich but do things that cause poverty, and wish to be praised but do things that cause ridicule. Thus it is often the case that people do things that are against what they wish to get. This is because they do not know the cause of suffering and happiness[93] and because they do not practice what they know. You ought to thoroughly investigate this cause and carry out what is right so that there is no contradiction between what you wish and what you do. Then, all of your purposes will be accomplished as you wish."

40. The Master said, "Of various occupations, some cause people to do good and some cause them to do evil. The good-causing occupation is the one through which one can benefit the world and through which one's own mind becomes good naturally. The evil-causing occupation is the one through which one harms the world and through which one's own mind also becomes vicious. Therefore, one should be directed when one chooses an occupation. And the best of all occupations is the Buddha's task, which is to deliver all sentient beings suffering in the sea of misery into a paradise by correcting their minds."

41. The Master said, "The success or failure of a household depends partly on the correct understanding of the head of the household. The following points should be observed if one wants one's household to be prosperous. First, the head of the household should be diligent and sincere. Second, the family members should be in harmony and coop-erate in family matters. Third, one should get started on any business

---

93. See above, *Canon*, pt. 3, chap. 14, II.

only after one has gained enough knowledge and experience. Fourth, one should grow one's business in an orderly manner following the maxim that a journey of a thousand miles starts with but a single step. Fifth, one should make good use of waste material. Sixth, one should have a regular job and a side job, which should be coordinated for a productive business. Seventh, one should not divert the funds to some other purpose before the goal of the productive business has been reached. Eighth, even after the goal has been reached, one should make a sound investment without plotting for profiteering. Ninth, one should regularly examine income and expenditures, spending for the right cause without stint and preventing waste. If one exerts oneself in managing one's household in this way, one's fortune will increase and one's practice will also be helped thereby."[94]

42. The Master said, "A household is a state in miniature, and a state is a conglomeration of many households. Thus, a household is a small state and the foundation of a state. Hence, one who regulates his household well will govern a society and a state well. If every head of household regulates his own household well, the state will be governed well accordingly. Hence, one should know that the obligation of a head of household is heavy and grave."

43. The Master said, "To establish an exemplary household, one must do the following things. First, one should institute a religion in which the whole family can have faith, and the whole family should develop a new life with a new spirit. Second, the head of the household should be virtuous, dignified, wise, and sincere enough to regulate the household. Third, the head of the household should educate the family members; for this, one must become the mirror of the household virtue, acquiring sufficient learning and experience in advance. Fourth, no family member should live in idleness; daily income and expenditures should be balanced; and some savings should be set aside. Fifth, one should not have an occupation that is related to killing or producing intoxication. One should not threaten someone else's life or property or cause anyone to suffer by abusing one's rights. Sixth, spouses should be financially independent of each other as far as possible, endeavoring to help build a prosperous household, society, and nation. Seventh, one should fulfill one's obligations and duties to society and the nation and cooperate with charitable, educational, and religious organizations as much as one can. Eighth, children should be given a balanced education in science and morality; upon completion of the education, they should be directed to serve society, the nation, and a religious order for a considerable period. Ninth, when one divides one's property among

---

94. See above, *Canon*, pt. 3, chap. 13, II.

one's children, the bequest should not be more than the necessary foundation of their livelihood; the rest of the bequest should be donated to social, national, and religious organizations for public well-being. Tenth, for mental and physical rejuvenation, which is necessary for human life in a complicated world, one must have spiritual cultivation and build up one's physical strength by taking a vacation a few times a month or several times a year."[95]

44. The Master, coming across a pregnant woman, used to say, "Refrain from being hard-hearted, speaking evil, and acting ruthlessly." He especially prohibited her from killing any living being, saying, "As the numinous consciousness coalesces while the fetus stays in the mother's womb, what its mother thinks, says, and does easily influences the future character of the fetus. Thus, the pregnant woman's self-restraint is of extreme importance."[96]

45. The Master said, "There are four ways to teach one's children. The first is teaching with one's mind. Having faith in truthful religion, one must cultivate a mind that is upright, virtuous, and calm so that one's children may model themselves after it. The second is teaching by exemplary conduct. One must practice what one teaches, and one's conduct should be in accordance with moral laws, so that one's children may model themselves after it. The third is teaching by words. One must have one's children learn the good words and virtuous deeds of the Buddha, bodhisattvas, sages, great men and women, and other intelligent ones, so that they may model themselves after them. This teaching includes reasoning with one's children on facts and principles.[97] The fourth is teaching by authoritative admonition. This is a teaching used when children have not yet reached the age of discretion; this method should not be used often. Family education from fetus to adulthood can be perfected if one follows these four ways."[98]

46. The Master said, "When one teaches one's children, the following should be observed. First, one cannot teach one's children effectively unless one practices the rules of honoring one's seniors and guiding one's juniors. One will lose the authority and confidence to guide one's family members if it is known to one's children that one is unfaithful and disrespectful to one's parents or does things wrong. Second, one's words and acts should be dignified and serious, for it will be difficult to guide one's children once they become irreverent toward their parents. Third, one should show affection for one's children, for one cannot have a good influence upon them if one is only dignified and

---

95. Ibid., chaps. 13 and 15.
96. See *CCP, Sejŏn*, chap. 2, 2.
97. For the meaning of facts and principles, see above, *Canon*, pt. 2, chap. 4, sec. 2.
98. See *CCP, Sejŏn*, chap. 2, 3.

serious without having affection for them. Fourth, one should keep one's word and should not lose confidence in one's parents; otherwise one's children will not follow one's orders. Fifth, one should be discretionary in one's rewards and punishments; otherwise one will be unable to bring one's children to their senses. Sixth, one should inspire one's children with faith in truthful religion in their childhood; without a firm faith in truthful religion, they will be easily overcome by temptations from external conditions while growing up. Seventh, one should encourage one's children to cultivate public spirit from early childhood; otherwise the bud of selfishness will grow in their hearts. Eighth, one should prohibit one's children from speaking ill of or slandering others; otherwise they will develop a frivolous character and cause calamity to themselves by misuse of the tongue. Ninth, one should keep one's children from taking what is not theirs, however trifling it may be; otherwise they will develop shamelessness in their character."

47. The Master said, "During one's childhood, one can easily partake of the spirit of one's parents by observing what one's parents do. As a parent, therefore, one should choose one's occupation carefully, endeavor to pursue a rightful business, and follow the right path for the sake of one's children."

48. At a memorial ceremony for a benefactor,[99] the Master said, "To honor the merits of the parents who raised and consecrated their precious children to the founding of this order, we give the honorific title *hŭisawi* (benefactor) and offer memorial services. The hearts of the people in general, past and present, are filled with selfishness; hence, there are few who benefit the public with spiritual, physical, and material assets. People with children are preoccupied with the idea of depending on their children and often force them to be confined within their households in spite of their superb natural talent. You, benefactors, on the other hand, rose above the mundane world and consecrated your precious children to this great universal task, disregarding your own prosperity and a life of ease. This is truly a deed of a compassionate bodhisattva. Cherishing the spirit and merit of these *hŭisawi* and honoring their virtues forever, we should become truly public-spirited and altruistic, benefiting the public wherever we may go."

49. While staying at Pongnae Cloister, the Master was informed of his mother's illness; he hurried to his house at Yŏnggwang and waited on his sick mother. After a while the Master said to his younger brother, Tong-guk, "How could I, bringing morality to light, neglect our mother's illness? At present, however, I cannot wait on our sick

---

99. One who has given to this order one's son or daughter or who has risen in the dharma stage to the position of the subjugation of *māra* by the power of dharma or above. See above, *Canon*, pt. 3, chap. 17, nos. 4–6.

mother. The people who follow my teaching have increased to a considerable number. If I do not take care of them, their future will be uncertain, and what I have so far worked on will also be stopped midway. Hence, wait on our sick mother with your whole heart on behalf of me. Then, I might be forgiven for my want of filial piety and you will be one of the founders of this order." The Master then consoled his mother, saying, "The life and death of humankind depends on heaven's decree. Take it easy and always concentrate your mind on the True Thusness of purity." Having said so, he resolutely left home and returned to the cloister, concentrating on his mission to deliver sentient beings.

50. A disciple asked the Master, "Will it be all right to take economy as the main concern in such ceremonies as coming of age, wedding, funeral, and ancestral worship?" The Master said, "One should restrain from extravagance in all ceremonies; however, it is not the intention of the rules of the reformed rites that one does not spend enough, being stingy and making no donation to the public well-being. As the wedding marks the beginning of a new life, what is saved from an economized wedding should be used to help establish funds for the couple's livelihood. As the funeral marks the end of a life, it should be conducted properly in accordance with the merits of the deceased and the duties of the posterity to the deceased."

51. One day the Master was watching some children of the village playing. Two of them started quarreling over the ownership of a trifling thing and came to the Master for solution of the problem, presenting a third child as the witness. The witness, upon pondering a while and realizing that it was nothing of his interests, said that he did not know to whom it belonged. The Master, upon solving the problem, said to his disciples, "Even youngsters quarrel over those things in which they are directly interested, but do not care a straw about things that are none of their interests. So, how could there be many who would work for the benefit of others regardless of their own benefit? Therefore, those who work for the benefit of the public at the sacrifice of their own benefit and power deserve the veneration of the general public. Moreover, those who are thoroughly open-minded cannot but work for the benefit of the general public."

52. The Master said, "Admiral Yi Sun-shin (1545–1598) was a soldier with the moral virtue of a great sage. Although he was a high-ranking officer, he was never conceited, sharing the moments of life and death and joy and suffering with his common soldiers in wartime. When he was deprived of power and demoted to the rank of steed keeper, he devoted himself to rearing the steed without resentment or going astray, sometimes counseling the steed, 'Although you are merely an animal, you ought to do your best in this time of national crisis inasmuch as you

have grown on the national stipend.' He also conceded to other generals easy jobs and honorific matters, taking for himself difficult jobs and unattractive work. He was extremely loyal to his superiors and benevolent to his inferiors. He was thus a sage general with wisdom and virtue combined in him. Those who intend to serve their nation or the world should model themselves after him."

53. The Master had Yu Hŏ-il read the Introduction to the *Shuching* (Book of history). When he reached the passage "The two emperors [Yao and Shun] and the Three Kings [Fu-shi, Shen-nung, and Huang-ti] were those who preserved their minds, but King Chieh of Hsia and King Chou of Shang were those who lost their minds," the Master said, "This passage will be a great secret for survival in the world to come. If one, being covetous of wealth and power, loses conscience, one will ruin both oneself and one's family. If the leader of a nation or the world does the same, the calamity will spread over the nation or the world. You should keep to your sphere in life with respect to clothing, food, and shelter, without being attracted to wealth and power, and without losing conscience. If you do so, you will be safe from dangers in any turbulent times, and you will be the first to be blessed by good fortune from heaven and earth."

54. A wealthy man once relieved his poor villagers from starvation with money and grain in a year of famine. He then wished to be eulogized for his virtuous deed. So the villagers, upon holding a meeting, erected a stele in honor of him. He, however, being dissatisfied with it, erected another stele and built a magnificent pavilion for it, spending a large sum of money. The villagers thought it ludicrous, speaking ill of and laughing at him. Kim Kwang-sŏn, having heard of this, presented the story at a discussion session.[100] The Master, listening to Kwang-sŏn, said, "This is a living scripture, which warns those who seek after fame. That man who tried to glorify his reputation by such work only destroyed his earlier fame. Thus, the foolish one disgraces his or her reputation by seeking after it while the wise one fulfills his or her duty without seeking after reputation, but a great reputation accompanies such a wise one naturally."

55. Yi Ch'un-p'ung asked, "The other day my son entered a mountain and was startled by a hunter's misfire. If my son had been fatally wounded, how should I have handled the incident?" The Master said, "Tell me what you would have done." Ch'un-p'ung said, "As there are laws to solve such problems, I would report the incident to the proper authority and express my feelings as his father." The Master asked Song Chŏk-pyŏk, who said, "As everything happens in accordance with the

---

100. See above, *Canon*, pt. 3, chap. 2, sec. 1, no. 5.

causal law of karmic retribution, I would regard the incident as the consequence of causal retribution, taking no further action." The Master asked O Ch'ang-gŏn, who answered, "If I did not practice Buddha-dharma, I would appeal to the legal authority; I would take no action, accepting the incident as karma." The Master said, "None of what you three have said hits the mean. The laws today require everyone to report any birth or death to the authority. Moreover, one who discovers an unexpected disaster or death is required by the law to report it to the authority. Therefore, I would, as a citizen and as the father, report the incident to the authority right away, entrusting the rest of the matter to the judgment of the legal authority."

56. Listening to someone reading a historical novel one day, the Master said, "When novelists write novels, they often create heinous villains by excessively describing the vicious mentality and devilish actions of a man of small caliber or a scoundrel in order to make the story interesting. However, this can be the seed of an evil karmic affinity. Therefore, you should be careful not to exaggerate reality when you talk about the history of an ancient person or criticize a contemporary person."

57. One day the Master was reading the *Nan-hua ching*[101] and, coming to the passage where it is said that Confucius went to convert Tao Chih[102] only to return in vain after being insulted and humiliated, said, "Being a great sage, Confucius tried to convince him of his fault at the risk of danger and insult, showing the original purpose of delivering sentient beings to be modeled for thousands of years to come. However, the expedient for deliverance can be different for different times. To deliver today's people one should first of all prove one's own moral perfection to the world so that people can naturally be influenced thereby for the better. Because many people try to encourage others to do good while they are not practicing what they preach, people are no longer credulous of mere admonition and encouragement. What I am suggesting is different from the expedient Confucius used to deliver Tao Chih by encouragement. Then, the way one delivers the world by direct encouragement is different in skillful means from the way one delivers the world by practicing oneself first what one preaches. Thus, expedients can be different in different times; however, the fundamental purpose is identical throughout different times."

---

101. The honorific title given by Tang Hsuan Tzung (r. 713–756) to the *Chuang tzu* (Works of Chuang Chou [365–290 B.C.]).

102. A contemporary of Confucius during China's Spring and Autumn period. Tao Chih, the younger brother of the wise man Lo Hsia-hui, was an extremely evil person, roaming over the whole of China at the head of nine thousand bandits.

58. One day the Master, commenting on King Wu of Chou,[103] who dethroned Chou of Shang,[104] subjugated the whole country, and became the emperor himself, said, "If I were in the shoes of King Wu, I would reluctantly strike King Chou of Shang in accord with the people's plea; however, I would decline the throne in favor of a benevolent one. If, however, there is no other benevolent one, and if the people would not accept my declination, I would have to assume the responsibility reluctantly."

59. A man who had returned from a sightseeing tour to Mt. Kŭmgang said to the Master, "While I was going sightseeing, I saw a man who called in or sent away crows and snakes at will. I believe he was a truly enlightened sage." The Master said, "A crow flocks together with crows and a snake keeps company with snakes. How could an enlightened sage keep company with crows and snakes?" The man asked, "Then, what kind of a person is a truly enlightened sage?" The Master answered, "One who is truly enlightened to the truth practices only what a human being ought to do among human beings." The man asked, "Isn't there, then, any particular sign of one who is enlightened to the truth?" The Master answered, "No, there isn't." The man asked, "Then, how can one recognize one who is enlightened to the truth?" The Master answered, "Unless you are enlightened to the Way, you cannot recognize the enlightened one even if you meet one. You can tell whether someone's foreign language is good only if you are good at it; and you can tell whether someone plays a musical instrument well or poorly only if you are an expert in music. Therefore it is said that one can recognize another's expertise only if one has attained to an equal expertise."

## V. On Cause and Effect[105]

1. The Master said, "The principle of turning eternally without arising or ceasing[106] is a truth of the universe; hence going is the basis of coming and coming is the basis of going, and giver becomes receiver and receiver becomes giver. This is an immutable truth through eternity."

2. The Master said, "In accordance with the principle of the cycle of the four seasons in heaven and earth, there is the change of birth, old age, illness, and death of all things. In accordance with the principle of reciprocal overcoming of yin and yang in the universe, there exists the causal law of karmic retribution for the good and evil deeds of human

---

103. Accession in 1122 B.C.
104. Accession in 1154 B.C.
105. The law of causality in this chapter is concerned mainly with the causal law of karmic retribution in the Buddhist religious faith.
106. Origination and annihilation; birth and death.

beings.[107] Winter is the season in which yin is active; however, the yang contained in yin gradually gains in strength, eventually changing into spring and summer. Summer is the season in which yang is active; however, the yin contained in yang gradually gains in strength and changes into autumn and eventually into winter. Human affairs are subject to the relationship of the strong and the weak and the consequence of good and evil karma so that they are on the path of promotion or demotion and face the karmic retribution of reciprocally producing or destroying each other. In this lies the causal law of karmic retribution."

3. The Master said, "As plants live with their roots in the earth, their seeds, sown in the earth, come up and grow in accord with the conditions of right season. Animals, living with their roots in heaven, sow the fundamental causes of good and evil karma in the empty dharma realm whenever they produce karma by thought, speech, and deeds, and the retribution for good or evil deeds is each brought about with the help of the conditions.[108] How could one dare to deceive human beings or heaven?"

4. The Master said, "The fairest rewards and punishments administered by human beings can still be unfair as they are affected by human thought (*yusim*). The rewards and punishments given by heaven and earth are fairest as they are given truthfully and clearly without any prejudice (*musim*) in accordance with the good or evil deeds. As the law of retribution is omnipotent and omnipresent, how can one dare to cheat on it and not be afraid of retribution? Therefore, the sensible one regards the rewards and punishments from the Truth to be more important than those meted out by human beings."

5. The Master said, "Do not hate or speak ill of a person even when he or she does not see or hear you. As spirits and vital force are connected immanently within heaven and earth, the seeds of reciprocal destruction are buried as the spirits and the vital forces are immediately connected if you hate or speak ill of somebody behind his or her back, while the seeds of reciprocal production are immediately buried by the connection of spirits and vital force when you think well of or praise someone even when unbeknownst to that person. As a consequence, the seeds of reciprocal production bear good fruit and the seeds of

107. See above, *Canon*, pt. 3, chap. 8. The dual force of negative and positive as expounded in the yin-yang school of Chinese philosophy is interpreted here as the fundamental principle of the Buddhist causal law of karmic retribution.

108. Here the causal law of karmic retribution is explained in terms of causes and conditions. "Conditions" (S. *pratyaya*) means a cooperating cause, the concurrent occasion of an event as distinguished from its proximate cause. It is the circumstantial, conditioning, or secondary cause in contrast with the direct or fundamental cause (S. *hetu*). The seed is the cause; the soil, rain, sunshine, etc., are the conditions.

reciprocal destruction evil fruit when the seeds meet the appropriate conditions. Worms and centipedes have reciprocally destroying energies, so that, when their skins are burned together, it can be seen that their two opposing energies resist each other until one fades away. From this it can be seen that reciprocally producing energies correspond to each other while reciprocally destroying energies oppose each other."

6. The Master said, "As the weather is fine at times and gloomy at other times, so is human spirit refreshed at times and gloomy at other times; and the mental spheres around oneself are agreeable at times and disagreeable at other times. These are the natural changes brought about in accordance with the principle of cause and effect. The one who understands this principle, abiding in spiritual cultivation, is as calm as heaven and earth when one experiences such changes; the one who does not understand it has one's mind disturbed along with such changes and thus cannot always keep the Mean in pleasure, anger, sorrow, and joy, creating an endless sea of misery."

7. The Master said, "What you give to others out of kindness will return to you in kindly terms; what you snatch from others in malice will be taken away from you in malice. The retributive gain and loss can be multiplied or diminished tens of thousands of times more or less than the original amount, depending on whether the others are on the path of promotion or demotion;[109] however, the retribution is never nullified. Even when the other party does not make any direct retribution, blessings and punishments return to one naturally. Therefore one cannot receive blessings or punishment on behalf of someone else, nor can anyone else take away one's own blessings or punishments."

8. Cho Chŏn-gwŏn asked the Master, "Since buddhas must have done nothing for harmful retribution throughout many kalpas of reincarnation, there should be nothing from which they must suffer. However, Śākyamuni Buddha suffered from various hardships of that time, and you, Master, too, have been suffering from the surveillance of the [Japanese] authority and difficulty in guiding the minds of people ever since you established this order. I do not understand why. Can you tell me why?" The Master answered, "For a long time I have tried to abstain from knowingly doing any wrong; however, my hardships seem to be the consequences of having unknowingly suppressed the malice and spite of obstinate sentient beings while delivering numberless people during many kalpas of reincarnation." He said further, "Even the compassionate Buddha who delivered sentient beings by correct dharma cannot offset the fixed karma with his ability, and the merit for blessedness of the lowliest mortals cannot be offset by their evil karma.

---

109. See above, *Canon*, pt. 2, chap. 1, sec. 4.

However, buddhas and bodhisattvas with extraordinary ability can satisfy within one life span the karma they are supposed to suffer from for
many rebirths, though they cannot eradicate the karma completely."[110]

9. Someone asked the Master, "Can one escape even the fixed karma
if one cultivates oneself in the right practice with utmost sincerity?" The
Master answered, "Though it is difficult to escape the fixed karma at
once, there is a way of mitigating it gradually. If the practitioner,
understanding the principle that a sentient being changes its destiny
through the six realms of existence and the four forms of birth, does not
produce evil karma but produces only good ones daily, the evil path will
go away of itself and the good path will come closer. Even if an evil
affinity retaliates against you for an old debt, the karma will ease of itself
if you treat the other party with a mind that is enlightened to the Way
without harboring any intention to retaliate. When you suffer retribution of an evil karma, reflect on your self-nature, which is devoid of evil
karma and resolves all karmas; reflect that you are paying off an old
debt; then the myriad evil karmas will be like snow melting on a brazier.
This is the way you can resolve the fixed karma with your mind. Moreover, if your religious practice is good, you can always be on the progressive path of the six realms of existence, and you will be on a higher
level than the evil affinity, so that the evil retribution you suffer will
be minimal. If you render meritorious services to the public, you will
always be protected wherever you may go, and, hence, the evil karmic
agent will not be able to find an opportunity easily to invade. In this way
you can mitigate the fixed karma with the power of good karma."[111]

10. Seeing one of his disciples losing his temper after being insulted
by another, the Master said, "Pocket the insult when it is your turn to
take revenge. If you do so, the karma will stop from rolling. If, however,
you revenge yourself on the other party now, he will revenge himself on
you again. If both do not keep from retaliating, the karma of reciprocal
destruction will never cease."

11. A follower of this order, having marital trouble with her husband,
hated him, saying that she would not marry him in their next rebirths.
Hearing this, the Master said, "If you wish to avoid any affinity with
him, you should neither love nor hate him, but treat him with no
thought."

12. While the Master was at Pongnae Cloister, he heard the sad
shriek of a wild boar a hunter had shot and said, "When one thing
gains, another thing suffers a loss." He said further, "From the wild

---

110. The Buddha is said to be unable to do three things: annihilate his fixed karma;
deliver sentient beings with whom he had no prior affinities; deliver all sentient beings into
nirvāṇa at once. See *Ching-te ch'uan-teng lu, chüan* 4, *T,* 2076.51.233c.
111. See *Canon,* pt. 3, chap. 8.

boar's death, I can infer what it did in its former life; and from the hunter's killing the wild boar, I can infer what he will encounter in the future."

13. The Master said, "Though there are countless ways in which one may receive the karmic retribution for various transgressions one commits with one's body, mouth, and mind, I will show you only part of them with a few familiar examples. If one hurts another's feelings by a false charge, one will suffer from cardialgia in one's next life. If one is apt to eavesdrop or cast a furtive glance at another's secret, one will be born as an illegitimate child, suffering from contemptuous treatment and humiliation. If one is apt to expose another's secret and humiliate another, causing him or her to blush for shame, one will live an uneasy life with an ugly birthmark or facial scar in one's next rebirth."

14. One of his disciples asked, "For what kind of evil karma might one be struck dead by lightning?" The Master said, "The karmic cause of one's being struck dead by lightning is that one must have struck many people like lightning. For instance, if one killed a great many people by abuse of one's official authority or sword or caused a great harm to many people by enforcing bad laws, one might be struck dead by lightning."

15. While supervising the construction of a temple building at a Seoul temple of this order, the Master heard the laborers saying that one cannot prosper no matter how hard one may try unless one is helped by some unknown power. The Master said later to his disciples, "People do receive some unknown help or unknown harm. The deluded believe that God, the Buddha, an ancestor, or a spirit administers such unknown help or harm, while the enlightened regard them as the effect of what one has thought and done. One receives the effect in the present of what one caused in the past; and one is to receive the effect in the future of what one causes in the present. The enlightened one thus knows that one receives nothing that one does not cause. The deluded ones unreasonably seek wealth, honors, and prosperity and struggle to avoid poverty and hardships, while the wise peacefully accept blessedness and suffering as things they have already caused, and exert themselves to prepare for future blessedness and happiness. When they do things that result in blessedness, they accumulate merits by virtuous deeds for the public well-being so that the fountain of blessedness will never dry up."

16. The Master said, "What is most urgent is not to teach people myriad scriptures and encourage them to do good, but to help them believe in and be enlightened to the truth of neither arising nor ceasing and the causal law of karmic retribution."[112]

---

112. See above, *SS* I:1.

17. The Master said, "The deluded are envious and covetous when they see others being blessed; however, they are lazy when they should sow the seeds of blessedness. They are like a farmer who wishes to harvest without farming. If a farmer does not sow seeds in spring, he will have nothing to harvest in autumn. This is the causal law of karmic retribution; why should this be true only of farming?"

18. The Master said, "One may badly wish to be blessed and happy but be frustrated in one's next rebirth unless one accumulates the cause of merit in this life. This can be compared to one who cannot live in a luxurious house, though badly wishing to do so, because it is not one's own house. Look at Kong-ch'il. Though one finds Western-style houses standing in a row when one gets off the train at Iri [now Iksan] Railway Station, he or she cannot dare enter any of them but must enter only his or her own humble dwelling. This is a living example of the principle that one can enjoy only those things that one creates."

19. The Master said, "Only the deserving person can enjoy great blessedness for a long time; and the undeserving person will only spoil it or create disaster out of it. Thus, only the wise know how to create, keep, and enjoy blessedness, and can keep it eternally no matter how great it is."

20. The Master said, "The deluded consider fame to be valuable and thus endeavor to create even a false reputation, not knowing that a false reputation can cause calamity. It is inevitable that true merit is revealed to the world though one tries hard to hide it and that false merit will not redound to one's credit no matter how hard one tries to make that happen. Thus, the empty reputation one gains without true merit does not withstand defamation; and the reputation one gains by trickery will be destroyed by trickery, causing even one's deserving credit to be damaged and, in extreme cases, causing loss of one's property and even life. How could one be careless about this matter?"

21. A beggar asked Kim Ki-ch'ŏn to sow the seed of blessedness and Ki-ch'ŏn asked him, "If I sow the seeds of blessedness, do you have the ability to bestow blessedness on me?" As the beggar could not answer, Ki-ch'ŏn said, "The deluded often ask others to sow the seed of blessedness only for their own sake; however, they will be sowing the seeds of sin with such words." Listening to this, the Master said, "What Ki-ch'ŏn has just said is truthful. People in the world wish to be blessed, but few do things that will bring blessedness; no one wishes to suffer from calamity, but there are many who do things that will bring it. That's why there are many who suffer from miseries and few who are blessed."

22. The Master said, "Other people will use sanctions against one who keeps on committing evil and does not refrain from it. If people cannot use sanctions against such a person, then the numinous truth

will. Therefore, the wise abstain from doing evil before other people prohibit them and accept other people's advice before the numinous truth brings sanctions against them; and since there are no secret evils they fear exposed, they can live with peace of mind."

23. The Master said, "Those of you who, being clever, abuse your petty power—do not cheat or harm the mass of people, thinking that they are childish. Collect the minds of the mass of people and you will have the heavenly mind! Collect the eyes of the mass of people and you will have the heavenly eye! Collect the ears of the mass of people and you will have the heavenly ear! And collect the mouths of the mass of people and you will have the Heavenly mouth! How can you cheat and harm the mass of people, thinking they are childish?"

24. A fierce dog that lived near the headquarters of this order was dying, fatally bitten by one of its kind. Seeing this, the Master said, "When the dog was young, it, being ill-natured, bossed other dogs in the vicinity, did all sorts of fierce deeds to them as it pleased. Now, it is to die a wretched death as the karmic effect for that. This is a warning against anyone who abuses power. How could this be looked on as a mere dog's case?" The Master said further, "You can tell, examining the way one's mind functions, whether one is on the path of promotion or on the path of demotion.[113] One on the path of promotion toward buddhahood reveals the following characteristics: (a) One's mind is gentle and virtuous so that one does not harm anyone else. (b) One is modest, respectful, and fond of learning. (c) One believes in truth and exerts oneself in practice. (d) One is pleased to see the success of others. (e) One helps and encourages the weak in various ways. One on the path of demotion [to the evil destinies] is marked with the following characteristics: (a) One has a violent temper, being in conflict with others one meets instead of benefiting them. (b) One is conceited and fond of despising others and does not like learning. (c) One does not believe in the causal law of karmic retribution and has no interest in practice. (d) One is jealous of others successful in life, trying to debase others superior to oneself."

25. The Master said, "If one indulges in committing evil as one pleases and is on everybody's lips for that, one's future becomes gloomy. There was a man who, being appointed magistrate of a county, took the properties and lives of many people by abusing his power. Villagers kept cursing him in chorus whenever they gathered together sitting in the village. As the words of the villagers went, the magistrate was reduced to a miserable lot, showing to many people how he was being punished for his evil deeds. Thus the lips of people are truly to be feared."

---

113. See *Canon*, pt. 2, chap. 1, sec. 4.

26. The Master said, "Among so many evils sentient beings commit senselessly are the following five grave transgressions. The first is for one to mislead the spirit of many people without a sound comprehension of truth. The second is for one to make people disbelieve in the causal law of karmic retribution, thus keeping them from creating good karma. The third is for one to speak ill of and be jealous of a benevolent one. The fourth is for one to mingle with a group of wicked people and help them. The fifth is for one to obstruct people from having faith in truthful religion and hinder its progress. Anyone who does not abstain from committing these five transgressions will never be released from the three evil paths of transmigration [the hells, hungry ghosts, beasts]."

27. The Master said, "There are three kinds of evil karma that should be dreaded. The first is to prejudge and intrigue against another for doing evil from mere appearances. The second is to be jealous of the friendly relationships of other people and come between them. The third is to use one's vicious cleverness and mislead therewith innocent people. One who commits these three evils will be born blind, mute, or insane as a retribution in one's next rebirth."

28. The Master said, "A Zen master in ancient times, though affluent as he had many disciples and donors, supported one of his disciples separately with the income from fruit he harvested from a few fruit trees he had planted and raised. His other disciples asked why, and the Zen master is said to have answered, 'Speaking of him, he had not accumulated any merit in his previous lives nor is he a person capable of benefiting others in the present life. If we feed him with the money and grain we receive for praying for the blessings of the multitude, we will be making his debt much heavier. Since he will have to requite his debt as oxen and horses in his many rebirths, I am trying to lighten his debt out of my affection for him as his mentor by supporting him with the extra income I earn in my spare moments.' Now what the Zen master did is a great admonition to people who live a communal life. If you, bearing this anecdote in mind, do good to others by spiritual, physical, and material contributions, you may consume the offerings from the multitude. If one who can serve only him- or herself receives the offerings from the multitude, that person will be getting into heavy debt, and hence should be prepared for labors for many reincarnations. In general, an altruist is reluctant to receive offerings while an egoist loves to receive them. You ought to carefully inspect yourselves daily and hourly lest you run into debt to the multitude."

29. One day Ch'oe Nae-sŏn treated the members of the order with a dinner. After finishing the meal together with them, the Master said, "Upon rendering the same number of favors, one can be recompensed with different numbers of rewards, depending on the material merit rendered, the mental attitude of the donor, and the ability of the bene-

ficiary. A peasant in Yŏnggwang had helped three officials cross a river during a summer rainy season, becoming acquaintances with them thereafter. It is said that, when he was later rewarded by the three officials for his good deed, there were considerable differences in their rewards, depending on their powers and abilities. Although this is nothing but a trivial example, the principle hidden therein is true of doing good and being recompensed through past, present, and future."

30. While the Master was at Yŏngsan, a dissipated young man in his neighborhood became pious by himself, repenting all evil deeds of his past. He became a disciple of the Master and swore to be worthy of the name of man. When the Master returned to Yŏngsan after making the rounds of several districts for several months, the young man had become dissipated again, squandering his fortune through wine, woman, and gambling. Being ashamed of having sworn before the Master, the young man, while trying to avoid the Master, was confronted by him on a path. The Master then said, "Why is it that you have never come to see me recently?" The young man replied, "I am simply sorry." The Master asked, "What are you sorry about?" The young man said, "How could I not be sorry since what I swore in the past has turned out to be nothing but lying to a sage? Please forgive me!" The Master said, "Since it was you who were careless, dissipated your fortune, and suffer from difficulties, you need not beg for forgiveness from me. If I were to receive retribution for your evil deeds, you might justly feel sorry for me and try to avoid seeing me. Since only you will be recompensed in accord with what you do, either good or evil, it is only yourself that you deceived, though you think you deceived me. Hence, you should not try to avoid me from now on; you have only to rectify your mind."

31. One day while the Master was staying at Yŏngsan, he went out to take a look at a vegetable field nearby. In the manure pit filled to the brim with manure were many worms; a rat, coming along, ate them. The disciples who were weeding the field said, "The rat often comes and eats them like that and returns." The Master said, "Now it is the rat that eats the worms as it pleases; however, it will be the rat that the worms will feed on in a few days." The disciples, without understanding what the Master meant, said, "How could the causal law of karmic retribution of the three periods work so swiftly?" A few days later, the rat, being drowned, started decomposing in the manure pit, and the worms were feeding on it. Seeing that, the Master said, "A few days ago, you seemed to think what I said was strange; however, what I said was based on a circumstantial judgment. At that time, the manure pit was full of manure so that the rat walked on it, feeding on the worms. I surmised that, since the manure would be bailed out of the pit to the vegetable field when you finished weeding it and the pit would be

empty, the rat, which carelessly frequented the pit, could not but be drowned and become food for the worms." The Master then said, "The causal law of karmic retribution for human beings is not much different from this, so that one necessarily receives retribution for good or evil karma either in the present life or in the future, depending on the nature of the karma."

32. When Kim Sammaehwa was slicing meat in the kitchen, the Master asked her, "Have you seen the hill of swords [one of the hells]?" Sammaehwa answered, "No, I have never seen it." The Master said, "The meat on the chopping board was on the sword hill as it was axed, and when it had been killed and knifed into thousands of pieces, it was sliced into tens of thousands of pieces on the chopping boards of many households. Isn't it terrifying?"

33. The Master said, "There were quite a few people who, in spite of deceitful and evil character, lived in prosperity during their lifetimes. In the future, however, it will be difficult for the vicious ones to live well during their lifetimes, because people will exhaust almost all of their blessed or damned retribution before their deaths and there will remain little karmic retribution for their next rebirth. Therefore, as the world enters the era of enlightenment, everything will be truthful and good for those whose minds are truthful and good, and their future will be bright and wide open, while everything will be deceitful and vicious for those whose minds are deceitful and vicious, and their future will be dark and closed."

## VI. Clarification of Doubtful Points

1. The Master attended a session of lectures on scriptures,[114] where his disciples were discussing the issue of whether heaven and earth are numinously bright. Upon listening to the discussion, the Master asked, "Do you or don't you think that heaven and earth are conscious?" Yi Kong-ju said, "I firmly believe that heaven and earth are conscious." The Master asked, "How do you know they are?" Kong-ju answered, "I think that there is discriminating consciousness immanent in the universe." The Master asked, "How do you know there is?" Kong-ju answered, "One is unexpectedly recompensed with blessings after one has done good, and unexpectedly suffers retributive calamity if one does evil. Since there is no error in response, how could it be possible to distinguish good from evil if there is no discriminating consciousness in the universe?" The Master said, "Then present an evidence of such clear distinction so that everyone can understand." Kong-ju said, "I have just expressed an article of my faith based on your teaching in the past; however, I find it difficult to demonstrate the principle by analyz-

---

114. See above, *Canon*, pt. 3, chap. 2, sec. 1, no. 4.

ing it with evidence." The Master said, "It is difficult to comprehend the mysterious realm, and, even if you comprehend it, it is difficult to elucidate it by proof. I will elucidate one end of the realm with a simple example; you should attain an insight from this to reflect upon the unexplainable mysterious realm. In general, the earth is quiet without words or deeds; hence, people regard it as insensate. In reality, however, it is evident that the consciousness of the earth is clear and numinous. Take farming for example. If seeds are sowed, the soil helps the seed grow. Where a red bean is sowed, it is only the red bean that is made to grow. Where a soybean is sowed, it is only the soybean that is made to grow. If one labors for the crop, one is helped to reap an abundant harvest, and where one labors less, one reaps less harvest. If it is tended incorrectly, one is made to suffer loss. Thus, the earth makes due distinctions without any confusion in accordance with the nature of the seeds and what one does. Hearing this, one might say, 'It is because the seed has the element of life in itself and humankind takes trouble for its growth. The earth is nothing but the ground.' But how could the seed bud and grow all by itself without receiving the numinous response of the earth, and what effect could there be if one sowed a seed and fertilized it where it could not receive the response of the earth? This is only one small example. Actually, all living beings that depend on the earth cannot come into being without being numinously influenced by the earth. Therefore, there is no living being that is not controlled by the earth, and there is no living being on which the earth does not apply the power of life and death and prosperity and decline. It is not only the earth that has such wondrous response; in fact, heaven and earth are identical in their noumenal nature. Furthermore, the sun and the moon, stars, winds and clouds, rain and dew, and frost and snow are all of unitary energy and principle, so that every one of them is wondrously efficacious. Therefore, one cannot hide the good or evil deed, no matter how secret it is, from this numinous consciousness, nor can one resist its retribution. This is because of the bright awareness and power of heaven and earth. However, the consciousness of heaven and earth is not like the human feelings of pleasure, anger, sorrow, or joy; it works without any thought or any false idea, being just, impartial, and selfless. One who knows this principle is awed by the brightness of heaven and earth and cannot deceive his or her conscience to do evil in any adverse condition. Furthermore, one who has modeled him- or herself after the numinous awareness of heaven and earth can even attain the unlimited awareness of purity and can exercise the great power of heaven and earth at will."

2. The Master asked his disciples, "Why is it that one feels ashamed to see anything in the universe after one has an evil inclination or commits an evil in secret?" Yi Wŏn-hwa said, "I think that all things in the

universe are aware of one's secret act just as one is aware of a small biting insect creeping on a small part of one's body. One is ashamed of seeing all things after committing evil in secret because all things in the universe are aware of even a trivial matter of humankind." The Master said, "What Wŏn-hwa says is plausible enough; however, I will add a few words. Though one would think that no one can know of one's intention to do something in secret, what one has resolved to do will be carried out in the world sooner or later. When one carries it out in the world, the world will soon know of it. That's why one feels ashamed of even a minor transgression. Thus, if you want to know what another person did in secret, you have only to see what has been exposed. There are people, however, who make vain attempts to dig into someone else's secret in advance."

3. Someone asked the Master, "According to an Eastern theory, the earth is motionless while the heaven moves; and according to the Western theory, the earth moves while the heaven is motionless. Thus, the two theories are confusing. Could you tell me which theory is correct?" The Master said, "It's been a long time since these theories were proffered, and arguments for each are various. To express my opinion briefly, heaven and earth are not different from each other [in their noumenal nature]; hence, heaven and earth are both in motion from the viewpoint of motion, and they are motionless from the viewpoint of quiescence. This is analogous to the vital force and the body of a human being in that the two are inseparable from each other in motion and at rest. The creative transformation [in the universe] is due to the endless circulation of the combination of the heavenly energy and the earth's ground. If the distinction is made of the principal and the subordinate, however, the heavenly energy is the principal and the earth's ground the subordinate in such a way that when the energy moves, the ground follows it. This is the immutable principle in eternity."

4. Sŏ Tae-wŏn asked, "According to the words of the Buddha, this world will be destroyed through the burning of heaven and earth during the kalpa of destruction.[115] Will this happen?" The Master answered, "That's right." Tae-wŏn asked again, "If heaven and earth are both burned down, then will a new universe be framed after this heaven and

---

115. One of the four kalpas, namely, the kalpas of formation, abiding, destruction, and annihilation. The kalpa of formation (*vivarta kalpa*) consists of twenty small kalpas (16,800,000 years) during which worlds and the beings on them are formed. The kalpa of abiding (*vivarta-siddha kalpa*) is the kalpa in which sun and moon rise, sexes are differentiated, heroes arise, and social life evolves. The kalpa of destruction (*saṁvarta-kalpa*) consists of sixty-four small kalpas when fire, water, and wind destroy everything except the fourth *dhyāna*. The kalpa of annihilation (*saṁvarta-siddha kalpa*) is the period from the complete destruction of the world to the beginning of the new kalpa of formation.

this earth are extinguished?" The Master said, "The burning of heaven and earth does not mean the extinction of both; it is analogous to the change of birth, aging, illness, and death of a human being. Just as, in the human world, human beings are born in one part of the world, getting old in another part, getting ill in some part, and dying in some other part without ending, so in the universe, the principles of the four kalpas, namely, the kalpas of formation, abiding, destruction, and annihilation, are in full force in myriad ways. At this very moment, the universe is undergoing the burning of heaven and earth as there are parts of formation, abiding, destruction and annihilation."

5. Tae-wŏn asked another question: "According to the words of Śākyamuni Buddha, there is a major chilicosm of 3,000 great chilicosms (S. *trisahasra*).[116] Is there truly such a world?" The Master said, "Yes, there is. However, the major chilicosm of 3,000 great chilicosms is not what is built outside of this world. It only refers to myriad different worlds differentiated within this world, which exceeds in number a major chilicosm of 3,000 great chilicosms." Tae-wŏn asked further, "According to today's astronomy, there are in the universe many greater worlds than the one where we live. What do you think of that view?" The Master said, "The words of the Buddha can mean different things to different interpretations; and the astronomical theories of today are diverse. However, in the near future, a scholar who is enlightened to the ultimate truth of the universe will prove what I have just said. Do not doubt my words if you have faith in me."

6. Tae-wŏn asked another question: "It is said that the universe has a cycle of promotion and demotion. In which period is Korea?" The Master said, "Korea is in the period of promotion." Tae-wŏn asked, "How long is the period of cycle of promotion and demotion?" The Master said, "The Buddha estimated one great kalpa[117] as the period of the cycle."

7. Tae-wŏn asked further, "When the universe undergoes the transformation of formation, abiding, destruction, and annihilation, what is the process of transformation?" The Master answered, "As the Buddha said, it is destroyed by the three wheels of water, fire, and wind."

---

116. A major chilicosm, or universe, of 3,000 great chilicosms. Mt. Sumeru and its seven surrounding continents, eight seas, and ring of iron mountains form one small world; 1,000 of these form a small chilicosm; 1,000 of these small chilicosms form a medium chilicosm; 1,000 of these form a great chilicosm, which thus consists of 1,000,000,000 small worlds. The "three great" indicates the above three kinds of thousands; therefore 3,000 great chilicosms is the same as a major chilicosm, which is one Buddha world.

117. *Mahākalpa* (S), from the beginning of a universe until it is destroyed and another begins in its place. It has four kalpas or periods, known as the period of formation, the period of existence, the period of destruction, and the period of annihilation. A great kalpa is calculated as eighty small kalpas and to last 1,347,000,000 years.

8. Tae-wŏn asked, "According to a sage in the past, the sun, the moon, and all stars are the spirits of all beings in the universe. Is this view correct?" The Master said, "Yes, it is."

9. A follower in the Chŏnju Temple of this order was once asked by a Catholic whether he knew the creator of the universe. The follower could not answer the question. The Catholic then said, "The Lord of Heaven, who is omniscient and omnipotent, is the creator of the universe." Later, hearing the follower's report on the conversation, the Master said, smiling, "Go to the Catholic and ask him whether he has seen the Lord of Heaven who, he said, is the creator. If he says he hasn't, then tell him that he does not really know the Lord of Heaven. Thereupon tell him that, upon second thought, the creator is not anywhere else than in everyone, so that his creator is his own self and your creator is yourself. Tell him that you have realized that all sentient beings are, each, their own creators. This is the most appropriate view; and hence, if he has a clear understanding of this, it will be a great gospel for him."

10. A disciple asked, "Where is paradise and where is hell?" The Master said, "Paradise is in your mind when your mind transcends both transgression and blessedness, and suffering and happiness; and hell is also in your mind when your mind is shackled to transgression and blessedness, and suffering and happiness." The disciple asked further, "How can I stay in paradise eternally without falling into hell? The Master said, "If you are enlightened to the principle of your own original nature and if the functioning of your mind is always in accordance with original nature, then you will rejoice in paradise without falling into hell."

11. One of his disciples asked the Master, "According to the words of the Buddha, there are thirty-three heavens.[118] Are they arranged layer upon layer in the sky?" The Master answered, "The heavenly worlds are nothing but a gradation of ascetic practice for the attainment of buddhahood. Heaven is where the ascetic with great spiritual power resides either high up in the sky or on the earth." The disciple asked again, "It is also said that the higher one ascends into the heavens, the taller the height of the heavenly beings grows and the lighter their clothing becomes. What's the meaning of these words?" The

---

118. The "Heaven of the Thirty-Three Devas," or "Indra's Heaven," is the second of the six heavens of the desire realm (the realm of sensual desire being one of the three realms, the other two being the form and formless realms). Its capital is on the summit of Mt. Sumeru, where Indra rules over his thirty-two devas, who reside on thirty-two peaks of Sumeru, eight in each of the four directions. Indra's capital is called Sudarśana (Joy View City). Its people are a *yojana* in height, each one's clothing weighs a quarter ounce, and they live 1,000 years, a day and night being equal to 100 earthly years.

Master said, "By 'the height growing taller' is meant the phenomenon of the spiritual power ascending high as one's power of enlightenment improves, and by 'clothing getting lighter' is meant that the spirit becomes lighter as the turbid energy calms down when one's power of enlightenment improves. However, even the deva being who has reached the zenith of the thirty-three heavens can degrade when his good karma is exhausted unless one has attained the great, perfect, and correct enlightenment."

12. Cho Chŏn-gwŏn asked, "I saw somebody suffer punishment upon cutting down and mistreating an old tree in my village. Was it because he was involved in the causal law of karmic retribution with such an insentient thing?" The Master answered, "It was not because he was involved with the tree by the causal law of karmic retribution. In the past dark era there were countless spirits[119] of the rivers and the hills that failed to receive bodies, that dwelt at such trees, in the shrines for a tutelary deity, or in splendid mountains and rivers, enjoying the offerings of foolish people. When they were bothered by human beings whose spiritual power was weaker than theirs, they occasionally gave diseases to them or punished them. However, in this era, which is changing into the era of brightness (*yang*), such spirits will not harm human beings."

13. One of his disciples asked, "Which magic formula should I chant and what method should I use to have my numinous spirit opened so that I may be enlightened to the Way quickly?" The Master said, "The correct path toward the supreme enlightenment has nothing to do with magic formulas; it depends on how sincerely one exerts oneself to practice. This point can be illustrated with the following anecdotes. An illiterate peddler of straw sandals, inspired to follow the path toward buddhahood, asked a practitioner about the meaning of the Way, to which the practitioner answered, *Chŭk-sim-si-pul* (Your mind is Buddha).[120] The illiterate peddler took it for *chip-shin se-bŏl* (three pairs of straw sandals) and recited it for many years, having his mind suddenly opened to realize that his own mind was Buddha. There was once a practitioner who went to buy meat, saying to the butcher, 'Make a cut from the clean part.' The butcher, thrusting his knife into the meat, exclaimed, 'Which part is clean and which part dirty?' It is said that the practitioner was enlightened thereby. These anecdotes prove that enlightenment to the Way does not depend on any particular place or

---

119. Hobgoblins produced from the weird emanations of the trees and rocks on the hills and spirits, the spirits of the waters and the rivers.
120. See *Ching-te ch'uan-teng lu*, *T*, 2076.51.309b. Shih-t'ou (700–790) said, "If you realize the Buddha's knowledge, then the mind is the Buddha."

time, or upon a magic formula. Since we have our own incantations in our order,[121] exerting yourself with them will be much more effective."

14. A laywoman asked the Master, "I wish I could perform purification and offer prayers like the ordained devotees in this order; however, my wish is not fulfilled because I am shackled to household affairs. What should I do?" The Master answered, "The purification of mind makes no distinction between lay followers and the ordained devotees. Hence, purify your mind and offer prayers with utmost sincerity and you will be endowed with great power in accordance with your sincerity."

15. Someone asked Yi Chae-ch'ŏl, "I have heard that your teacher is a sage. Does he know everything, both facts and principles?"[122] Chae-ch'ŏl replied, "Yes, he does." The man asked, "Does he know how to make airplanes and trains?" Chae-ch'ŏl said, "A sage knows the principal parts of facts and principles; technical parts are subjects for the relevant professionals." The man said, "Doesn't this contradict the claim that he knows everything about facts and principles?" Chae-ch'ŏl said, "By principal facts is meant the root; if the root is known, its branches and leaves can easily be understood. Let me illustrate the point with an example. A local governor or the head of a nation may not know what a clerk or a technician knows at a low-echelon administration unit. If, however, he knows the fundamental parts of administration and thereby directs each department well, shouldn't we say that he knows how to govern? The sage's knowledge and wisdom is like this, being well versed in the general principle of noumenon and phenomenon, being and nonbeing, and the facts of right and wrong, and gain and loss.[123] For this, we say he knows everything about facts and principles, though he may not have the knowledge of minute technology. Since he is well versed in the general principles, myriad knowledge is contained therein." Upon returning, Chae-ch'ŏl reported the conversation to the Master, who said, "On the whole, what you said is correct."

16. While the Master was staying in Seoul, Min Chayŏnhwa used to provide the Master with food, and the Master noticed that she delightedly ate the remaining food in his bowl and asked for the reason. Chayŏnhwa said, "I do this because I have learned in a Buddhist scripture that if one provides the Buddha with food and eats the remaining food in the Buddha's bowl, then one is to be delivered and to attain buddhahood." The Master said, "I see that you think so because you firmly believe in and respect me. However, I wonder whether you

---

121. See above, *Canon*, pt. 3, chap. 3; below, *SS* IX:4.
122. See above, *Canon*, pt. 2, chap. 4, sec. 2.
123. Ibid.

believe in those words with a clear understanding or superstitiously without understanding the implications of the words." Chayŏnhwa said, "I simply believe in the words; I haven't tried to analyze their meaning." The Master said, "By the time one provides the Buddha with food and delightedly eats the leftover food, one must have become very intimate with the Buddha. One will naturally see what the Buddha does, hear what the Buddha says, be enlightened to the correct dharma of the Buddha, and will be imbued with the Buddha's habits. Accordingly, one will have a good opportunity to be delivered and to attain buddhahood easily. This is the implication of those words."

17. One of his disciples asked, "There are people who walk around pagodas in Buddhist temples with the belief that, if they do, they will be reborn in the world of utmost joy (*sukhāvati*) [the Pure Land of Amitābha in the West]. Is what they believe true?" The Master said, "The teaching means not only that one's body should go around the stone pagoda but one's mind should go around one's body made from earth, water, fire, and air, and, if so, one can rejoice in the world of utmost joy. If one can only go around the stone pagoda but does not know how one's mind should go around the pagoda of one's body, one certainly does not know the true meaning of going around the pagoda."

18. One of his disciples asked, "According to the words of the Buddha, one will attain the three paranormal insights and six paranormal powers when one's ascetic practice matures.[124] How high should one ascend in the dharma stages[125] to attain them?" The Master answered, "Insight into the mental conditions of self and others in previous lives, insight into future mortal conditions of the three insights, and the paranormal powers of deva-vision, deva-ear, knowing others' thoughts, knowing the former existence of self and others, and being anywhere and doing anything at will of the six paranormal powers can be partially attained by one who has not reached the dharma stage of the subjugation of *māra* by the power of dharma but may not be attained by one who has reached that dharma stage or even above that stage. However, the nirvāṇa insight into present mortal sufferings so as to overcome all passions or temptations and the power to totally eradicate defilements

---

124. The three paranormal insights are (1) insight into the mortal conditions of self and others in previous lives; (2) supernatural insight into future mortal conditions; and (3) nirvāṇa insight, i.e., into present mortal sufferings so that one can overcome all passions or temptations. The six paranormal powers are (4) the instantaneous view of anything anywhere in the form-realm (deva-vision); (5) the ability to hear any sound anywhere (deva-ear); (6) the ability to know the thoughts of all other minds; (7) the ability to know of all former existence of one's self and others; (8) the power to be anywhere or do anything at will; (9) the supernatural consciousness of the waning of vicious propensities. See Lu, *The Vimalakirti Nirdesa Sūtra*, p. 19, n. 1.

125. See above, *Canon*, pt. 3, chap. 17.

can only be attained by buddhas and bodhisattvas who have attained to the supreme enlightenment."

19. One of his disciples requested, "I would like to know the meaning of the four false notions [of an ego, a person, a (deluded) being, and a life]."[126] The Master said, "I am aware that there have been various interpretations by many scholars. However, I will give an interpretation for practical application in daily life. By the false notion of an ego is meant a sense of egotism, namely, thinking of oneself and what one owns as the most important; by the false notion of a person, human-centered thinking, regarding humankind as the lord of all sentient beings and all other things as created for the sake of humankind, and thinking therefore that one can treat all animals as one pleases; by the false notion of a deluded being, one who differentiates deluded beings from buddhas, regarding oneself as worthless and degrading oneself without making any improvement toward buddhahood; and by the false notion of life, one who has the notion of seniority, if one puts in place of justice seniority of age or length of time and position in the work place. If one does not get rid of the four false notions, one cannot attain buddhahood." The disciple asked, "How can I eradicate the four false notions"? The Master answered, "To eradicate the false notion of ego, one must understand the principle of impermanence, namely, one's beloved body, property, position, and power are not really one's own possessions since these will be of no use when one dies. To eradicate the false notion of a person, one must understand the principle that sentient beings exchange their bodies through the endless cycle of the six realms of existence. To eradicate the false notion of a being, one must understand that the Buddha and the deluded beings are not different from one another [in their original nature] such that a buddha is a deluded being when deluded and a deluded being is a buddha when enlightened. To eradicate the false notion of a life, one must understand that, though there is difference of old and young, the noble and the mean in the physical realm, there are no such differences in the noumenal nature. A practitioner of the Way becomes a buddha as soon as these false notions are eradicated."

20. Yi Ch'un-p'ung was a devout Confucianist until he was introduced to the Master. Seeing the Master he broke with the Confucian tradition, entered this order, and said, "I am thrown into ecstasy to see you as if I saw Confucius accompanied by his three thousand disciples. It weighs on my mind, however, that the Confucian sages in the past did not assent to certain tenets of Buddhism." The Master asked,

---

126. *Chin-kang po-jo po-lo-mi ching*, *T*, 235.8.749a: "If a bodhisattva still clings to the false notion (*lakṣana*) of an ego, a personality, a being, and a life, he is not [a true] bodhisattva."

"What were those tenets?" Ch'un-p'ung answered, "It is said that, since Buddhism is based on emptiness and ultimate quiescence, Buddhists abnegate their duties to their fathers and sovereignty." The Master said, "It was the Buddha's original intention to open the gate of deliverance for numberless parents and children throughout his many incarnations for many kalpas. It has occasionally happened, however, that his later disciples did things against his original intentions. You do not have to worry about abnegation of parents and sovereignties since the future doctrine will be made suitable for the times so that faith in Buddha-dharma will improve family life as well as social and national affairs. However, Wu-chi (the Ultimate of Nonbeing) and T'ai-chi (the Great Ultimate) in the *Chou-i* are the true essence of nirvāṇa (emptiness and ultimate quiescence with no selfish desires); the moral virtue of *jen* (benevolence) Confucius taught in the *Lun-yü* is emptiness and ultimate quiescence [nirvāṇa] with no selfish desire; the mental state of equilibrium Tzu-ssu taught in the *Chung-yung*[127] cannot be the silent and unstirred state of equilibrium unless it is emptiness and ultimate quiescence; the illustrious virtue in the *Ta-hsüeh*[128] cannot be manifested without emptiness and ultimate quiescence. Thus, various religions use different words and names, but the fundamental source of all truths is identical. However, if you end up with emptiness and ultimate quiescence, you cannot become a superior man of the way. To practice the perfect and great Way, you should be able to apply the truth to all human affairs, taking emptiness and ultimate quiescence as the substance of the Way, and *jen* (benevolence), *i* (righteousness), *li* (propriety), and *chih* (wisdom) as its function."[129]

21. One of his disciples said to the Master, "A stranger came and asked me who your mentor was. I said, 'Since the Great Master attained the supreme enlightenment all by himself, he had no mentor.'" The Master said, "If there is anyone who asks about my teacher, tell him or her that my teacher is you, disciples, and your teacher is I." Another disciple asked, "Which of the traditional buddhas in the line of

---

127. *The Doctrine of the Mean*, chap. 1, sec. 4; Legge, *Confucius*, p. 384: "While there are no stirrings of pleasure, anger, sorrow, or joy, the mind may be said to be in the state of equilibrium."

128. *The Great Learning*, sec. 1; Legge, *Confucius*, p. 356: "What the Great Learning teaches is—to illustrate illustrious virtue; to renovate the people; and to rest in the highest excellence."

129. The four cardinal virtues in Confucian ethics have their ground in human nature, which is good according to Mencius. See *Meng-tzu*, bk. 2, pt. 1, chap. 5; Legge, *Mencius*, pp. 202–203: "The feeling of commiseration is the principle of benevolence [*jen*]. The feeling of shame and dislike is the principle of righteousness [*i*]. The feeling of modesty and complaisance is the principle of propriety [*li*]. The feeling of approving and disapproving is the principle of knowledge [*chih*]."

the dharma transmission is your ancestral master?" The Master replied, "Though we are at the juncture of transition from the old to a new era, Śākyamuni Buddha is my ancestral master."

22. One of the disciples asked, "As we have abolished the practice of worshiping Buddha statues as part of the Buddhist reformation, should we never erect memorial statues to you, the founder of this order, and your succeeding dharma masters?" The Master answered, "For the purpose of commemorating their contributions, you may erect memorial statues to them, but they should never be the object of religious worship."

23. One of the disciples asked, "Is it because of the degrees of importance among the fourfold beneficence that we pray by saying 'watch over me' to heaven and earth and to parents while we say 'respond to me' to brethren and to laws?"[130] The Master answered, "There is no need to distinguish the degree of importance; however, to speak of the degree of kin relationship, heaven and earth and parents belong to the paternal generation and brethren and laws to the generation of brothers and sisters. That's why I have distinguished them by 'watch over me' and 'respond to me.'"

24. One of the disciples asked, "In 'The Principle of Requiting the Beneficence of Heaven and Earth' in the *Canon*, we read, 'The way for one to recompense heaven and earth for the beneficence lies in modeling oneself after the way of heaven and earth and practicing it.'[131] How could it be enough for us to act by simply modeling ourselves after their ways in order to recompense them for their beneficence when they have bestowed on us such a great beneficence?" The Master answered, "To explain the point by an illustration, suppose that the disciples in the orders of buddhas and bodhisattvas or of other sages and superior men, upon being bestowed with great beneficence, inherit and develop the holy enterprise by learning what their masters knew and practicing what their masters did though they were not recompensed with material rewards. Should we say that they recompense their teachers for the beneficence? Or should we say that they acted ungratefully? From this we can infer that acting by modeling oneself after the way of heaven and earth amounts to recompensing them for their beneficence."

25. One of the disciples asked, "In 'The Details of Requiting the Beneficence of Parents' in the *Canon*, it is required that one ought to complete the essential ways of practice, namely, the threefold practice and the eight articles, and the essential ways of humanity, namely, the fourfold beneficence and the four essentials.[132] How could this be the

---

130. See above, *Canon*, pt. 3, chap. 9.
131. See above, *Canon*, pt. 2, chap. 2, sec. 1, III.
132. Ibid., sec. 2, IV, 1.

way of recompensing one's parents for their beneficence?" The Master answered, "If one completes the essential ways of practice, one will attain the Buddha's wisdom; and if one follows the essential ways of humanity, then one practices the Buddha's deeds. If one, as a son or a daughter, accomplishes Buddha's task by attaining Buddha's wisdom and deeds, one will have one's honorable name widely known, letting one's parents' beneficence be known therewith. If so, one's parents will win an immortal name and they will be respected by all people. How could this be compared with providing one's parents with comforts during their lifetime? This is an excellent way of recompensing one's parents for their beneficence." The disciple asked again, "One reads also, 'One ought to protect the helpless parents of others to the best of one's ability as if they were one's own parents.'[133] How could this be the way of recompensing one's parents for their beneficence?" The Master answered, "If we infer from what the Buddha said about the principle of rebirth, there will be countless parents whom one had in one's rebirths for the past thousands of kalpas and whom one will have in one's rebirths in the future. How can we say that one has recompensed all those parents for their beneficence by limiting the recompense only to one's parents in the present life? Therefore, if one protects the helpless parents of others while one's parents are alive or after their passing away, this is the way of recompensing all the parents of the three periods of time."

26. One of the disciples asked, "How are the things to heed for daily application related to the threefold practice?"[134] The Master answered, "The things to heed for daily application are formulated as the ways of practical application of the threefold practice. The fifth article[135] is the way of putting into practice spiritual cultivation; the second, third, and fourth articles[136] are the ways of carrying out inquiry into facts and principles; the first article[137] is the way of carrying out mindful choice in karmic action; and the sixth article[138] is the way of checking whether

---

133. Ibid., III, 3.

134. See above, *Canon*, pt. 2, chap. 4, for the threefold practice and pt. 3, chap. 2, sec. 2, I, for the things to heed for daily application.

135. "One should be heedful to practice the repetition of the name of a buddha or sitting in meditation at dawn or before retiring upon finishing daily household affairs after supper."

136. "2. Observing the state of affairs, one should be heedful to prepare and train oneself for it prior to handling it. 3. One should be heedful to exercise oneself in the scriptures and laws of the order. 4. Upon mastering the scriptures and laws, one should be heedful to exercise oneself in *ŭidu* (test case)."

137. "1. In handling daily affairs, one should be heedful to choose the right and forsake the wrong upon a sound thinking."

138. "6. Upon dealing with any matter of importance, one should be heedful to reflect on it in order to check whether or not one did what one ought to do or ought not to do."

or not one is carrying out the threefold practice." The disciple asked further, "Can the article of the things to heed for daily application be divided for training in motion and training at rest?" The Master answered, "The third, fourth, and fifth articles are the things to be practiced when one is at rest and the ways of preparing for practice while one is in motion. The first, second, and sixth articles are the things to be practiced while one is at work and the ways of preparing for practice while one is at rest. These two ways are complementary to each other and the ways to keep one from neglecting practice for even a short moment." The disciple asked again, "How are the things to heed for daily application related to the things to heed while attending the temple?"[139] The Master answered, "The things to heed for daily application are the efficient way, to be pursued daily for practice by the learned and the ignorant, men and women, old and young, good and bad, and high and low, while the things to heed while attending the temple are the way to help one practice the things to heed for daily application."

27. Once his disciples of Zen practice had a discussion session.[140] One of the participants said, "The merit of dividing a bowl of rice and offering equally to ten people must be greater than that of offering it to one person." Another participant said, "To offer it for one person to be satisfied has greater merit than to give it for none of the ten people to be satisfied." Seeing that the participants could not reach a solution, the Master judged the matter as follows: "If one gives something to only one person, only one person will gladly recompense one for it; if it is given to a village or a country, a village or a country will gladly recompense one for it; if it is given for the well-being of the world, the world will gladly recompense one for it. Therefore, the merit one has from using a thing for the greater and unlimited public will be much greater than the merit that one may have from using it for a limited number of people."

28. One of the disciples asked, "What is the difference between the merit that derives from practicing charity with one's mind abiding in it and that in which one's mind is not abiding in it?"[141] The Master said, "Practicing charity is like fertilizing a fruit tree. Practicing charity with one's mind abiding in it is like spreading fertilizer on the ground and that with one's mind not abiding in it is like covering the fertilizer with soil after it is spread. The fertilizer spread on the ground will evaporate

---

139. See above, *Canon*, pt. 3, chap. 2, sec. 2, II.
140. Ibid., sec. 1, V.
141. Cf. "Subhuti, thus a bodhisattva should give charity without a mind abiding in false notions of form. Why? Because, if a bodhisattva's mind does not abide in forms when practicing charity, his merit will be inconceivable and immeasurable." See *Chin-kang po-jo po-lo ching*, *T*, 235.8.749a.

easily while the fertilizer covered with soil will stay long in the ground, being absorbed by the tree. The difference between practicing charity with one's mind abiding in it and that with one's mind not abiding in it is like fertilizing a fruit tree in these two different ways."

29. Cho Wŏn-sŏn asked, "A line in the *Tonghak kasa* [Hymns of Eastern Learning][142] reads, 'Benefit lies in *kunggung ŭrŭl* [double bows and a line twisted and tortuous].' What does this mean?" The Master answered, "Though there are various interpretations of this line, I interpret it this way. *Kunggung*, being two bows, refers to Wu-chi [the Ultimate of Nonbeing], making a circle, Irwŏn; *ŭl-ŭl* [twisted and tortuous] becomes T'ai-chi [the Great Ultimate]. This illustrates the foundation of *todŏk* [the Way and its virtue]. The implication of the line is that one will be benefited a lot if one lives without any grudge following such morality." The disciple asked further, "It is said that the gate of fortune will be open if one sings the hymn *Kung-ŭl* [bow-twisted]. What is the meaning of this claim?" The Master answered, "The implication is that if one, having faith in such morality, keeps repeating the name of a buddha or chanting incantations, one's mind will naturally be purified, and resentment and malice will all be resolved in one's mind, thus causing the dharma realm of the universe to be purified and pacified. If so, what could be a better hymn than this? Sing it often!"

30. Before Ch'oe Suinhwa became a follower of this order, she was a devout believer in the teachings of Tonghak as she was from a family of that faith for several generations. One day she said to the Master, "When I was a believer in the Tonghak, I used to believe and expect the rebirth of Ch'oe Su-un, the founder of Tonghak. As soon as I saw you, I felt as if I saw him. This makes me so happy that I cannot control my feeling of joy." The Master said, smiling, "Great sages like him have the liberty to die and to be born as they wish; hence he can freely be born, in accordance with his work plan, either in the land where he dies or anywhere in the East or West. Many masters were born in this country in the past, and there will be many unequaled sages coming from everywhere in the future, establishing an unprecedented religious order. When you follow me, you may believe in me for the *todŏk* (the Way and its virtue) I teach, but do not look to anything else in me to depend on."

31. One of the disciples had a habit of criticizing others recklessly. One day he said that Kang Chŭngsan[143] was a madman. Hearing this, the Master said, "How dare you criticize our precursors so recklessly? It

---

142. Tonghak (Eastern Learning) is a Korean indigenous religion founded in 1860 by Ch'oe Che-u (1824–1864); it was renamed Ch'ŏndogyo in 1905 by Son Pyŏng-hŭi (1861–1922). See Introduction.

143. His name was Kang Il-sun (1871–1909), Chŭng-san being his title. He founded Chŭngsan'gyo, a Korean indigenous religion.

is not right to pass judgment on the teacher for the faults of his disciples. Since one cannot understand a person of great caliber unless one is that person's equal, one should not criticize others unless one is a spiritual master oneself." The disciple asked, "Then, what kind of a person was he?" The Master said, "Chŭngsan was a rare prophet and a divine person. He together with Ch'oe Su-un will be respected and commemorated eternally once our order is widely known to the world."

32. Kim Ki-ch'ŏn asked, "If we compare the 'unfolding of latter heaven,' which our precursors mentioned, to the process of daybreak, we can say that what Ch'oe Su-un did is like announcing the peep of dawn when the world is sound asleep, what Kang Chŭngsan did is like announcing the next phase, and what you, our Master, have been doing is like commencing the day's work as the day is getting bright gradually, can't we?" The Master said, "What you have said seems plausible." Yi Ho-ch'un asked, "If we compare it to a year's farming, we can say that Ch'oe Che-u told people to prepare for farming as it thawed, Kang Chŭngsan showed people the calendar of farming, and you, our Master, directed people to farm, can't we?" The Master said, "What you have just said is also plausible." Song To-sŏng asked, "Although they were such divine persons, Ch'oe Che-u and Kang Chŭngsan are unfairly criticized by people because of the faults of their disciples. What will become of them in the future?" The Master said, "If a good thing is authenticated as good by a true authority, it is to be recognized as good by the public. Hence, our precursors will be recognized because we have authenticated them as the teaching of this order is widely known to the world. Since our precursors helped the sages to come later, the later sages will venerate their precursors."

33. Someone asked, "According to a traditional esoteric legend in this country, a youth named Chŏng will ascend to the throne in Mt. Kyeryong and restore peace in the whole country. Will that really happen?" The Master answered, "The term *kyeryong-san* (Cock-Dragon Mountain) alludes to a world that is about to be brightened or civilized and the expression *Chŏng toryŏng* [the youth, Chŏng] alludes to a righteous leader. Thus, the secret adumbrates the truth that in the bright world to come only righteous people will lead families, societies, nations, and the whole world."

34. Kim Ki-ch'ŏn asked, "Can one ascend to the dharma stage of the subjugation of *māra* by the power of dharma[144] without having seen into one's own self-nature?" The Master replied, "No, one cannot."

35. Ki-Ch'ŏn asked further, "Which takes more austere effort, for one to ascend from the dharma stage of elementary faith to that of the subjugation of *māra* by the power of dharma, or from that of the latter

---

144. See above, *Canon*, pt. 3, chap. 17, no. 4.

to that of the Tathāgata of supreme enlightenment?"[145] The Master answered, "It depends on one's inborn capacity. One with high capacity can leap to the Tathāgata of supreme enlightenment as soon as one ascends to the dharma stage of the subjugation of *māra* by the power of dharma, and others without such exceptional capacity delay at the dharma stage of the latter for a long period of time."

36. Ki-ch'ŏn asked further, "It is said that if a practitioner of the Way makes progress in the practice of the Way, the practitioner can reach a stage of practice where he or she becomes an immortal by separating the spirit from the corpse at death. At which dharma stage in our order can one do it?" The Master answered, "Even someone who has ascended to the dharma stage of the Tathāgata of supreme enlightenment may not be able to do it, while one who has not seen into his or her own self-nature and hence has not ascended to the dharma stage of the subjugation of *māra* by the power of dharma may be able to do it by intensive practice in spiritual cultivation. However, acquiring this ability is not the same as attaining the perfect and supreme enlightenment. Therefore, from now on, one cannot be said to have attained the perfection of the Way if one is ignorant of the facts and principles[146] of humanity no matter how good one is at astrology and topography, how well one can separate one's flesh from bones, or how well one can penetrate into someone else's mind. Therefore, you, followers of the Way, ought to discipline yourselves in the threefold practice[147] in balance in order to cultivate the perfect personality."

37. Ki Ch'ŏn asked further, "One of the requirements to satisfy for one to ascend to the dharma stage of the subjugation of *māra* by the power of dharma states that 'one has attained emancipation from the ills of birth, old age, illness, and death.'[148] Does this mean that one should be able to pass away while sitting or standing as the eminent Buddhist masters did in the past?" The Master answered, "It means that as one has mastered the principle of neither arising nor ceasing,[149] one is not moved by birth and death."

38. Ki-ch'ŏn asked further, "At which dharma stage should one be elected *chongbŏpsa* (head dharma master of the order) in the future?" The Master answered, "Even during the period of degeneration,[150] one will not be qualified to be the *chongbŏpsa* unless one has ascended

145. Ibid., no. 6.
146. Ibid., pt. 2, chap. 4, sec. 2.
147. See above, *Canon*, pt. 2, chap. 4.
148. See above, *Canon*, pt. 3, chap. 17, no. 4, d.
149. See above *SS*, I:1.
150. The third and last period of a Buddhist kalpa. The first is the first 500 years of correct doctrine; the second is the 1,000 years of semblance law, or approximation to the doctrine; and the third is myriad years of decline and end.

at least to the dharma stage of the subjugation of *māra* by the power of dharma." Ki-ch'ŏn asked further, "If there appears a follower of the way whose dharma power is superior to that of the *chongbŏpsa*, how should he be promoted to a higher dharma stage?" The Master answered, "It will be decided by an impartial opinion of the general public in the order."

39. A disciple asked, "How high should one ascend through the dharma stages to be assured of nonregression?"[151] The Master answered, "One should ascend at least to the dharma stage of *ch'ulga* (transcendence)[152] to be so assured. However, 'nonregression' does not mean that one will never regress from the stage of nonregression even if one relaxes one's attention to the goal of attaining buddhahood. As it is a natural law that nothing stays unchanged in the universe, even the buddha who is also called 'nonregressing' should keep his aspiration to supreme enlightenment concentrated in his heart so that he can protect his mind from favorable and adverse conditions of any kind and thousands of *māra*s and heretics. In this sense should 'nonregression' be understood."

40. The disciple asked again, "It is said that one with high spiritual capacity obtains sudden enlightenment and sudden cultivation.[153] Can one with such a high capacity suddenly finish enlightenment and cultivation at the same time?" The Master said, "Of ancient buddhas and patriarchs, some were known to have achieved sudden enlightenment and sudden cultivation. In reality, however, one must go through thousands of steps of enlightenment and cultivation before one attains sudden enlightenment and sudden cultivation. This can be compared to daybreak; darkness retreats without its retreat being noticed and brightness approaches without its approaching being noticed."

## VII. On the Principle of Human Nature

1. The Master, upon attaining supreme enlightenment, expressed his state of mind in a verse:

> When the moon rises through a clear breeze,
> All things are manifested clearly.

2. The Master said, "Human nature is neither good nor evil in its quiescence; however, it can be good or evil when it is stirred."

---

151. The level of *avaivartika* (never regressing, always progressing, not backsliding, or losing ground); never retreating but going straight to nirvāṇa.
152. See above, *Canon*, pt. 3, chap. 17, no. 5.
153. Chinul (1158–1210) taught that even one who attains sudden enlightenment should pursue gradual cultivation because the habit force is not done away with by enlightenment. See *Susim kyŏl* [Secrets on cultivating the mind], *T*, 2020.48.1006b; Buswell, *KAZ*, p. 143.

3. The Master said, "What transcends good and evil is called the highest excellence, and what transcends suffering and happiness is called the perfect bliss (nirvāṇa)."

4. The Master said, "The great Way is of perfect harmony among all differences so that being is identical with nonbeing, principle is identical with fact, birth is identical with death, and motion is identical with rest. In this Way of nonduality, there is nothing wanting."

5. The Master said, "Though there is no barrier in the great Way, which is ubiquitous, human beings do not know this and build barriers between themselves and others. Hence, whoever knows how to illuminate the One Mind by seeing through all things and thereby cultivating it will attain the supreme enlightenment."[154]

6. The Master said, "If one insists that the mind cannot be seen because it has no shape and that the original nature cannot be elucidated because it is ineffable, one has not seen into one's original nature. Only if one can have the form of mind and the reality of the original nature clearly in front of the mind's eye, so that one can see them without rolling one's eyeballs and explain them clearly as soon as one opens one's mouth, can one be said to have seen the Buddha-nature clearly."

7. The Master said, "The purpose a practitioner of the Way has for seeing into one's original nature lies in attaining buddhahood by using one's mind and body as perfectly as one's original nature with the knowledge of it. If one, upon seeing into one's original nature, does not exert oneself to attain buddhahood, one will be like a nice looking lead-axe, producing no merit."

8. The Master said, "Seeing into one's original nature can be compared to a millionaire's recognizing his or her wealth as his or her own for the first time while living with no knowledge of that wealth, and following one's original nature can be compared to the millionaire's recovering from others the right to the property he or she was deprived of while living with no knowledge of it."

9. The Master said, "If the principle of human nature is not explicated in the doctrine of a religion, the doctrine is not complete; for

---

154. Cf. the *Hsin-hsin-ming* [Inscribed on the believing mind], attributed by tradition to the putative third patriarch Seng-ts'an (d. 606):

> In the higher realm of True Suchness
> There is neither "other" nor "self";
> When a direct identification is asked for,
> We can only say, "Not Two."
> In being not two all is the same,
> All that is comprehended in it;
> The wise in the ten quarters,
> They all enter into this absolute faith. (*T*, 2010.48.377a)

the principle of human nature is the origin of all dharmas and the ground of all principles."

10. There was once a downpour of rain while the Master was staying at Pongnae Cloister. Water was falling in torrents off a rocky cliff and rushing through brooks from several mountain valleys. Watching the sight for a while, the Master said, "The waters from mountain valleys are now running through various brooks; however, they will finally converge at one place. The Zen conundrum 'The myriad dharmas return to the One. [Where does the One return?]'[155] implies what this does."

11. The Master wrote a verse for his disciples at Pongnae Cloister:

> Alongside the winding path in Mt. Pyŏn,
> Rocks stand hearing the sound of running water;
> Naught!, naught!; yet, naught!, naught!,
> Nay!, nay!; yet, nay!, nay![156]

12. Upon returning to Pongnae Cloister from Yŏngsan, the Master said to one of his disciples, "When I was coming here by a steamship from Yŏngsan, the sea was deep and vast. I measured the water and counted all the fish. Can you perchance know the amount of water and the number of fish?" The disciple could not guess the meaning of his words.

13. The Master said to his disciples at Pongnae Cloister, "In ancient times, a neophyte asked his mentor about the Way (truth), and the mentor said, 'The Way will be missed if I tell you what it is and it will also be missed if I do not tell you what it is. So, what should I do?' Can you tell me the meaning of his answer?" Those present were silent and made no response. As the yard was covered with a deep layer of snow, the Master went out of the room and started shoveling the snow. One of the disciples went out and took the shovel from him and requested him to enter the room. The Master said, "What I did just now was not simply to shovel the snow; I meant to allude to a profound truth for you."

14. The Master asked Mun Chŏng-gyu at Pongnae Cloister, "Can you make the image of Bodhidharma walk out of the scroll hanging on the wall?" Chŏng-gyu said, "Yes, I can." The Master said, "Then, make him walk." Chŏng-gyu rose from his seat and walked himself. Seeing this, the Master said, "It is Chŏng-gyu that walked. How can

---

155. See above, *Canon*, pt. 3, chap. 5, no. 5, for this *kong-an*.

156. The last two lines remind one of the Mādhyamika spirit of endless negation to help transcend any dualistic ratiocination. Thus the two lines can be reformulated as "There is neither being, nor nonbeing, nor both, nor neither; it neither is, nor is-not, nor both, nor neither." See Inada, *Nāgārjuna*, chap. 1.

you say you made the image of Bodhidharma walk?" Chŏng-gyu said, "A wild goose flying from the eastern sky has changed its direction, flying toward the southern sky."

15. When the Master was staying at Pongnae Cloister, a Zen monk came from Mt. Kŭmgang to pay homage to the Master. The Master asked, "Now that you have troubled yourself to come such a long way, isn't there something you seek from me?" The monk said, "I wish to hear about the Way. Tell me please where the Way is." The Master said, "The Way is where you ask the question." The Zen monk bowed and left.

16. A Zen monk came to Pongnae Cloister to see the Master and asked, "The World Honored One is said to have descended to his royal home without leaving the Tushita Heaven and to have delivered all sentient beings while he was still in the womb of his mother.[157] What is the meaning of this?" The Master said, "Your body is at Sŏktu-am though you haven't left Silsang-sa; and you have finally finished delivering all sentient beings though you are at Sŏktu-am."

17. While the Master was staying at Pongnae Cloister, a man, having been introduced by Sŏ Chung-an, came to pay homage to the Master, who asked, "What have you heard about me, troubling yourself to come up this steep path?" The man said, "I have heard about your supreme excellence of virtue and wished to see you in person." The Master said, "Now that you have seen me, is there anything you seek from me?" The man said, "Living with worldly cares and being disturbed by evil passions and delusions, I cannot rectify my mind. Thus, it is my wish to have my mind rectified." The Master said, "To rectify your mind, you must first of all be enlightened to the original nature of your mind and exert yourself to be impartial in applying your mind. If you want to know the original nature of your mind, inquire into the meaning of this *ŭidu*: 'The myriad dharmas return to the One. Where does the One return?'"[158] The Master wrote this *ŭidu* for him.

18. When the Master was at Pongnae Cloister, Zen monk Paek Hang-myŏng frequented the cloister, occasionally amusing himself with discussing the principle of original nature by extraordinary Zen conundrums. One day, the Master told the novice Yi Ch'ŏng-p'ung a few words. The next day, the Zen monk came to the cloister from Wŏlmyŏng-am and the Master welcomed him, saying, "Ch'ŏng-p'ung over there hulling rice in the mortar seems to be maturing with the Way." The Zen monk, having approached her, said in a loud voice, "Show me the Way without moving your feet!" Ch'ŏng-p'ung held up the pestle, standing solemnly. The Zen monk silently went into the house, Ch'ŏng-p'ung following him. The Zen monk said, "Can you

---

157. See above, *Canon*, pt. 3, chap. 5, no. 1.
158. Ibid., no. 5.

make the Bodhidharma walk out of the scroll hanging on the wall?" Ch'ŏng-p'ung said, "Yes, I can." The Zen monk said, "Then, make him walk." Ch'ŏng-p'ung stood up and walked a few steps. The Zen monk, slapping his lap with admiration, approved her enlightenment, exclaiming, "Enlightenment at the age of thirteen!" The Master observed this scene and said, smiling, "Though seeing into the original nature consists neither in words nor in no words, the approval of seeing into the original nature should not be done in the way you did from now on."

19. One day, Zen monk Paek Hang-myŏng wrote a verse and sent it to the Master. It reads as follows:

> The mountain peaks about to pierce into the sky,
> Return to the sea to form billows.
> Not knowing which way to turn the body,
> You lean toward the peak of a rock to build a house.

The Master responded with the following verse:

> Truly thus is the eminence of the mountain peaks,
> The vast sea rolls through innocent waves of True
>         Thusness;[159]
> Awakening again to the way to turn the body,
> Revealed aloft at the house on the peak of rock.

20. Kim Kwang-sŏn asked, "Before all things in the universe were created, what was the reality of the universe?" The Master said, "Reflect on the state of your mind, which you had before you asked this question." Kwang-sŏn asked again, "What is the use of seeing into one's original nature for practice?" The Master answered, "It is like mastering the alphabet of a language."

21. One of the disciples asked, "What happens to one who has seen into the original nature of one's mind?" The Master said, "One will comprehend the fundamental principle of all things in the universe, and be analogous to a carpenter who has obtained a ruler and a carpenter's chalk line."

22. Listening to Kim Ki-ch'ŏn expounding on the principle of the original nature at a Zen monastery, the Master said, "Today, between being asleep and being awake, I obtained a *cintāmaṇi*[160] and gave it to Samsan.[161] I saw him transform himself into a different person as soon

---

159. True Thusness (S. *bhūtatathatā*), the permanent reality underlying all phenomena, pure and unchanging, e.g., the sea in contrast with the waves.
160. The gem that is capable of responding to every wish, said variously to be obtained from the dragon-king of the sea, or the head of the great fish Makara, or to derive from the relics of the Buddha.
161. Kim Ki-ch'ŏn's dharma title.

as he swallowed it. I am truly refreshed to listen to Samsan's discourse on the principle of the original nature." He continued, "The dharma insignia should be transmitted without the master's being swayed by personal affections; one can only receive it if one's wisdom eye is opened. A dragon can work wonders only if it obtains a *cintāmaṇi*, and a practitioner of the Way cannot attain a great ability without seeing into one's original nature and without knowing how to train one's mind thereby." Mun Chŏng-gyu said, "For a long time we have respected Chŏngsan.[162] Has he also seen into the original nature?" The Master said, "You may start building several houses at the same time, but one house can be finished within a month, and others may need a year or several years to be finished. Chŏngsan will take more time to be enlightened to his original nature."

23. One of the disciples asked, "There is a cliché 'seeing into the original nature and becoming a buddha.' Does one attain buddhahood as soon as one has seen into one's original nature?" The Master said, "Though it rarely happens, there were some who, depending on their high capacity, attained buddhahood directly after seeing into the original nature. However, you will have to exert more effort toward attaining buddhahood than toward seeing into the original nature. Because people were unintelligent in the past, one who had seen into the original nature was regarded as a sage; however, in the world to come, seeing into the original nature will be insufficient for one to be qualified as a sage. Most of the practitioners of the Way will have easily finished seeing into the original nature at their homes during their youths and will search for great masters, exerting themselves to the attainment of buddhahood under them."

24. The Master said to an assembly at a Zen monastery, "It is said that the principle of the original nature cannot be completely explained in words. However, one should be able to explain it clearly in words, too. If any of you think that you are enlightened to it, answer my question. Since it is said that 'The myriad dharmas return to the One,' explain how they return to the One; and since it is asked 'Where does the One return?' tell me where the One returns."[163] One after another of the assembly answered the question; however, none of them received his approval of enlightenment. Then one of the disciples rose from his seat, bowed and said, "Master, ask me the question again." The Master asked the question again, and the disciple said, "Since all dharmas are clearly as they really are and have not returned to anywhere, what is the need for returning to the One?" The Master only smiled in silence.

---

162. Song Kyu's dharma title.
163. See *Canon*, pt. 3, chap. 5, no. 5.

25. The Master said, "Recently one often finds those who, claiming to be experts on the principle of the original nature, try to allude to the ineffable realm by silence. However, this is a fault. One who is truly well versed in the principle of the original nature should be able to separate its beginning from its end; though it is without head or tail, one should be able to elucidate in words what is beyond verbal expression. One who really knows it reveals true knowledge of it in whatever he or she does; one who is ignorant of it reveals ignorance of it in whatever he or she does. However, one should not regard verbal expressions as the only correct method of training in the principle of the original nature. A thousand sūtras and ten thousand treatises on them by patriarchs are like the fingers pointing at the moon."

26. The Master said to an assembly at a Zen monastery, "Is there anyone here who has come into a complete possession of the empty dharma realm and the certificate of its ownership?" As the assembly was silent and made no response, the Master said again, "As all buddhas and bodhisattvas of the three periods of time took pains to obtain the empty dharma realm, which is formless and invisible, they can enjoy all phenomenal things in the universe. As ordinary people and sentient beings attach themselves to the phenomenal things in order to own them, however, without realizing that they cannot own them forever, they end up with wasting invaluable time. What a pitiful state of affairs! Therefore, you should take more trouble to own the formless and empty dharma realm instead of struggling to possess the phenomenal things."

27. The Master said to an assembly at a Zen monastery, "To know the substance of the principle of nature lies in knowing how to divide the great (noumenon) into the small (phenomena) of multitudinous and diverse things and in knowing how to coagulate the small of the multitudinous and diverse things into the great.[164] Knowing the function of the original nature lies in knowing how to reduce being into nonbeing and nonbeing into being so that as a universal truth, there is immutability in change and change in immutability. There are quite a few who, claiming to have been enlightened to the principle of the original nature, can guess the great [noumenon] and nonbeing but cannot comprehend the principle of the small of the phenomenal world and being. How could they claim that they are perfectly awakened to the principle of the original nature?"

28. The Master said to an assembly at a Zen monastery, "Tell me right here how you can divide a human being into mind, nature, prin-

---

164. Knowing the substance of the original nature lies in showing how the ultimate reality (noumenon) of all things appears as the phenomenal world of diversity and showing that the phenomenal world of diversity is none other than the ultimate reality of unity.

ciple, and the vital force; and how you can unify a human being into a single mind, into nature, into principle, or into vital force." There were various answers from the assembly, but the Master did not approve any of them, saying, "When one raises a goat, one does not overfeed her in order to make her grow at once; rather, one follows the correct procedure, feeding her properly. Then the goat will grow to be a fully grown one, bear kids, and produce milk, benefiting human beings. Similar to this is the way the practitioners in a religious order are led to be enlightened to the Way."

29. When the Master was in the room of the head dharma master, a group of inspectors visited him and one of them asked, "Where is the buddha enshrined in your order?" The Master said, "The buddha in our order has gone out of the precinct. If you wish to see him, wait here for a moment." The group did not understand the Master's words and were thus puzzled. Moments later, as it was lunch time, several workers were returning with farming tools from the farm. The Master, pointing at them, said, "They are all buddhas in this order." The visitors were even more puzzled about the Master's words.

30. The Master asked Song To-sŏng to interpret the gāthās that the seven ancient buddhas had left as the insignias of the dharma transmission. To-sŏng interpreted the gāthās of the seven ancient buddhas[165] one after another until he reached the gāthā by Śākyamuni Buddha, which reads

> Dharma is originally patterned after no dharma,
> No dharma is also a dharma.
> When no dharma is to be entrusted,
> Dharma should be patterned after something,
> What should it [dharma] be patterned after?

Hearing this, the Master said, "Stop the interpretation." The Master then said, "Though there is originally not a thing that can be named as dharma, the Buddha taught a dharma for the people of low capacity. The dharma is not a true dharma. If one is enlightened to the real meaning of this gāthā, one need not read tens of thousands of scriptures."

31. In January of the 26th year of this order, the Master gave his gāthā of the dharma transmission[166] and said, "Being is what changes and nonbeing is what does not change. *This* realm is what cannot be said to exist or not to exist. Though it is said 'turning and turning' and 'ultimately,' all these are nothing but verbal semblance used to teach *this* realm. What is the need to say 'both void' or 'complete'? Since *this*

---

165. The seven ancient buddhas, viz., Vipaśyin, Śikhin, Viśvabhū, Krakucchanda, Kanakamuni, Kāśyapa, and Śākyamuni. The last four are said to be of the present kalpa.
166. See above, *Canon*, pt. 2, chap. 1, sec. 6, for the gāthā "Verse on Irwŏnsang."

realm is the quintessence of the original nature, attain it by enlightening to it through intuitive reflection; do not try to understand it by ratiocination."

## VIII. On Buddha-stage

1. The Master said, "Though there are many mountains, high and low, only the highest and deepest mountains with thick forests among them can provide a home for many animals to depend on and live in; though there are many rivers of various sizes, only the widest and deepest sea can provide a home for numberless fish to live in. Likewise, though there are many who claim to be the leader of the world, only the most virtuous and compassionate sage can be the one whom numberless sentient beings can rely on and thereby live comfortable lives."

2. The Master said, "The Buddha's great mercy and compassion are warmer and brighter than the sun. Therefore, wherever his mercy and compassion can reach, delusions of sentient beings are changed into wisdom, cruelty to mercy, stinginess and greed to generosity, and the discrimination of the four false notions[167] to a perfect mind; thus, his power and light cannot be compared to anything."

3. The Master said, "The Buddha's great compassion and great pity are analogous to parents' love and sorrow. Just as the parents of a child are pleased and affectionate when it is healthy and well without troubling them and, being good-natured, behaves well, so, when the Buddha sees one who, being good-natured, is loyal to his or her country, observes the filial duty, is brotherly, venerates his or her teacher, is in harmony with his or her neighbors, relieves the poor and the sick, makes progress in perfecting wisdom by practicing the great Way, and does purely meritorious work by not abiding in any false idea after doing good, then he is very pleased and loves that person, guiding him or her to the way of blessings. This is the Buddha's great compassion. Just as the parents of a child commiserate with it and take care of it when it hurts its eyes with its own finger or grabs a sharp knife and cuts its hand, crying without knowing what it is doing, so the Buddha is saddened by, commiserates with, takes pity on sentient beings, and delivers them by myriad skillful means when they burn their hearts with greed, anger, and delusions, ruin their own lives, do things for which they fall into the evil path,[168] and receive retribution according to their evil karmas, but resent heaven and earth, ancestors, fellow beings, and laws. This is the Buddha's great pity. Though sentient beings live in the Buddha's great compassion and pity, they do not know how they are indebted to the Buddha for the great compassion and pity. However,

167. See above, *SS* VI:19.
168. Hells, hungry ghosts, and animals.

the Buddha does not mind their ingratitude, exerting himself to deliver all sentient beings for tens of thousands of kalpas. That's why the Buddha is called the great guide of the triple world[169] and the loving father of the four forms of birth."[170]

4. The Master said, "As buddhas and bodhisattvas know how to be completely free in going, staying, sitting, reclining, speaking, being silent, moving, and being at rest, they know when to be quiet and when to move, when to be great and when to be small, when to be bright and when to be dull, and when to live and when to die. In this way, they never infringe any rule or regulation no matter what they do or where they are."

5. The Master said, "Just as a good cook can prepare a delicious meal if foodstuff is provided and a tailor can make nice dresses if dress material is provided or alter them if they are poorly made, so a great sage who is well versed in all dharmas can formulate new dharmas out of all dormant ones or renovate obsolete dharmas. However, the practitioners of the Way without such capacity, being unable to create new dharmas or renovate obsolete ones, can only make use of and spread the dharmas created by other sages." One of the disciples asked, "At what dharma stage can one attain such ability?" The Master said, "One should be at the dharma stage of *ch'ulga* (transcendence)[171] or higher to do so; the function of the six sense organs of such a sage manifests correct dharmas that are looked up to as the models for eternity."

6. The Master asked Song Pyŏk-cho to interpret 'the way of accordance with nature' in the *Chung-yung*.[172] Pyŏk-cho said, "In Confucianism, to adapt oneself well with the heavenly principle and the way of nature is called 'accordance with nature.' The Master said, "If one can only follow the heavenly principle, one is at the stage of bodhisattva; one should be able to apply the way of heaven to be at the stage of Tathāgata, the Buddha. This is analogous to an expert horseman who can manage both a tamed and an unbroken horse. Thus, while ordinary people and sentient beings are dragged into the cycle of the six realms of existence and the twelvefold dependent origination,[173] bud-

---

169. The worlds of desire, form, and formlessness.

170. Viviparous, as with Mammalia; oviparous, as with birds; moisture- or water-born, as with worms and fishes; metamorphic, as with moths from chrysalises, or with devas, or in hells, or the first beings in a newly evolved world.

171. See above, *Canon*, pt. 3, chap. 17, 5.

172. Cf. "What Heaven has conferred is called THE NATURE; an accordance with this nature is called THE PATH of duty; the regulation of this path is called INSTRUCTION." Chap. 1, sec. 1; Legge, *Confucius*, p. 383.

173. *Pratītya-samutpāda* (S): ignorance (*avidyā*); action, disposition (*saṃskāra*); consciousness (*vijñāna*); name and form (*nāmarūpa*); the six sense organs (*saḍāyatana*); contact (*sparśa*); sensation, feeling (*vedanā*); desire, craving (*tṛṣṇā*); grasping (*upādāna*); existing (*bhava*); birth (*jāti*); old age, death (*jarāmarana*).

dhas, overcoming fixed karmas, are free to come and go, and to ascend or descend [in the cycle of rebirth and in the dharma stage]."

7. One of the disciples asked, "It is said that Master Chinmuk[174] was attracted to wine and women. Was he?" The Master said, "To my knowledge of Master Chinmuk, one day he, being fond of wine, mistook a bowl of brine for wine and drank it, but nothing happened to him. One day, while he was under a persimmon tree, a woman came to seduce him. No sooner was he going to grant her request than a mellow persimmon fell to the ground, so he was going to pick it up, ignoring her. The woman, being ashamed of herself, withdrew from his presence. To judge from these anecdotes, how could wine and women have been in his heart? Being a great sage, he found no wine in wine and no woman in a woman; he was a Tathāgata."

8. The Master said, "Deluded beings are swayed by pleasure, anger, sorrow, or joy when their minds function, harming themselves and others, while bodhisattvas transcend pleasure, anger, sorrow, and joy when they use their minds, causing no harm to themselves or others. Buddhas use pleasure, anger, sorrow, and joy as if they were their servants, benefiting themselves and others."

9. The Master said, "As soon as one ascends to the dharma stage of the subjugation of *māra* by the dharma power, one is recognized and venerated by devas, men, and *asuras*. However, if the one who has entered the Way intends to hide his or her trace, his or her whereabouts can only be discerned by one at the dharma stage superior to that of the one hiding."

10. The Master said, "When one reaches the ultimate stage of the practice of the Way, one attains the threefold mastery. The first is the mastery of spirit (numinousness), by which one knows clearly, without seeing, hearing, or thinking, the principle of transformation of all things in the universe and the causal law of karmic retribution for the three time periods [past, present, and future]. The second is the mastery of the Way, by which one attains a full knowledge of noumenon and phenomenon and of being and nonbeing of all things in the universe, and a thorough knowledge of right and wrong and gain and loss in all human affairs.[175] The third is the mastery of dharma, by which one can elucidate the principle of right and wrong and gain and loss in human affairs by applying the principle of noumenon and phenomenon and being and nonbeing of all things in the universe. Of the threefold mastery, the mastery of dharma can be attained only by one who has attained the great, perfect, and correct enlightenment."

---

174. See Han Ki-du, *Han'guk sŏnsasang yŏn'gu*, pp. 610–623, for information about Chinmuk (1562–1633).

175. See above, *Canon*, pt. 2, chap. 4, sec. 2, for the definitions of "facts" and "principles."

11. The Master said, "No matter how large a household may be, it can never be as large as the household that is made into one with that of heaven; no matter how great a person may be, he or she can never be as great as one whose vital force is united with that of heaven."

12. The Master said, "One who grasps the fundamental truth of the universe and applies it to the functions of the six sense organs is none other than a heavenly being (deva), a sage, or a buddha."

13. The Master said, "Though infinite principles and powers are immanent in heaven and earth, heaven and earth will be an empty shell if those principles are not recognized and applied by humankind. Humankind is called the owner of heaven and earth and the lord of all sentient beings because it is humankind that is enlightened to them and makes use of them as if they were tools. Humankind cannot do what heaven and earth do, nor can heaven and earth do what humankind does; however, it is the way of heaven and earth that is being applied by humankind for principles [noumenon and phenomenon, being and nonbeing of all things in the universe] and facts [rightness and wrongness, gain and loss in human affairs].[176] Therefore, buddhas and bodhisattvas exercise the great authority of the triple world as they are perfectly enlightened to the principles of noumenon and phenomenon and existence and nonexistence and make use of the way of heaven and earth as they please. In the future, therefore, human authority will be respected more than that of heaven, and the great authority of buddhas and bodhisattvas will be venerated by all people."

14. The Master said, "As deluded beings are of small capacity, they become overly complacent when they obtain something they did not have or learn something that they did not know. Sometimes their lives are imperiled because they act rashly because of it. Buddhas and bodhisattvas, however, are of unlimited capacity so that they are not affected by an increase or decrease in their possessions. As no one can peep into the extent of their possessions, they can keep their possessions intact and preserve their lives peacefully."

15. The Master said to an assembly at a Zen monastery, "Deluded beings care only about the pleasures of human life, which do not last long, while buddhas and bodhisattvas, enjoying the heavenly pleasures, which are formless, can enjoy the pleasures of human life as well. By the heavenly pleasure is meant the spiritual beatitude that buddhas and bodhisattvas relish while practicing the Way. By the pleasures of human life are meant the pleasures human beings enjoy when the five desires[177]

---

176. Ibid.
177. The five desires, arising from the objects of the five senses, are things seen, heard, smelled, tasted, or touched. Also, the five desires of wealth, sex, food and drink, fame, and sleep.

are satisfied in the mundane world, namely, being satisfied with one's wife and children, property, position, or any sense object or environment. The two kinds of pleasures are best illustrated by the life of Śākyamuni Buddha. The prince Siddharta, being the heir to the throne, enjoyed all the worldly pleasures by satisfying his eyes, ears, and the desires of his mind as he pleased. But those were the pleasures of human life. The heavenly pleasure on the other hand was the blissful life the Buddha enjoyed after enlightenment, transcending tangible things and environment and emancipating himself from birth and death and suffering and happiness and from the causal law of good and evil karmic retribution. Confucius is said to have expressed his heart: 'Although I am lying on my elbow as a pillow after having greens as food and drinking a glass of water, I find pleasure in it; unrighteous riches and honors are like floating clouds to me.' These are the words of a heavenly being who enjoyed the heavenly pleasure with his human body.

"The pleasures of human life eventually come to an end. What has come will leave; what has been prosperous will decline; and what is born will die—these are the laws of nature. One with unequaled wealth, rank, and fame in the world will be helpless in face of old age, illness, and death. In the face of one's death, one's spouse and children, property and rank, to which one has devoted one's whole life with all sorts of trouble and greed, will disappear like floating clouds. The heavenly beatitude, however, is the creation of the formless mind; hence the beatitude will be immutable even though one changes one's body. This is analogous to someone with a great talent who will not lose that talent when he or she moves to a new house."

16. The Master continued, "Therefore, an ancient sage said, 'Cultivation of mind for three days will be a treasure of a thousand years, but the thing one has coveted for a hundred years is nothing but dust in one morning.' However, a deluded being, not understanding this principle, regards the body as precious but does not care about the mind, while one who cultivates the Way, understanding this principle, forgets the body in search of the mind. You should detach yourselves from these evanescent beings and exert yourselves to search for the heavenly beatitude. If you maintain the heavenly beatitude for a long period, you will eventually gain the freedom to control mind and body, take the great power to rule the triple world, transcend being and nonbeing of all things and the rebirth through the cycle of six realms of existence. The liberated spirit of yourself, without being embodied, can tour the universe or enter and exit even the world of birds and beasts or insects without any hindrances in the coming and going of birth and death. You can enjoy the heavenly beatitude forever in any world where you may be embodied without being contaminated in that world. This is

the perfect bliss. Once desire for worldly pleasures arises in your heart and you start enjoying it, the heavenly beatitude is lost. If one who enjoys the heavenly beatitude only desires to enjoy pleasures without working for what can maintain the heavenly beatitude, one will become depraved and lose the freedom to control mind and body and be unable to avoid once again the cycle of birth and death through the six realms of existence, being dragged by the rolling wheel of the great nature."

17. A man paid homage to the Master and conversed with him, saying, "The railway between Chŏnju and Iri is managed by investment in stocks of wealthy people in various districts of Chŏlla province; hence they use the train free of charge all the time." As the man seemed to be envious of them, the Master said, "You are really a poor man. Haven't you regarded that train as yours yet?" The man was puzzled, saying, "One needs a great deal of money to own a train. How could a proletarian like me own it?" The Master said, "That's why I called you a poor man, and even if you owned that train, I would not call you a rich man for that. Let me tell you how I manage my household affairs. I have already regarded as mine not only the train between Ch'ŏnju and Iri, but all other vehicles in the country, nay, all the vehicles in the world. Don't you understand what I mean?" The man was bewildered even more, saying, "What you have just said is beyond my comprehension." The Master said, "To own a train, one must pay an enormous amount of money all at once and take responsibility to manage it with a great deal of trouble. The way I own it is rather different. I do not spend an enormous amount of money all at once, nor do I take the responsibility to manage it. When I must take a train for a long trip, I have only to pay for the ticket, enjoying the convenience. Isn't the railroad fare cheap considering the salaries and other expenses paid to its operators, mechanics, and managers? To give another example, a few days ago I went to Seoul and had an opportunity to go to a public park. I strolled here and there, breathing the clean air as much as I could and enjoying the park. Nobody told me to leave it or not to visit the park again. If you have a few pavilions in a summer resort, the yearly expenses for their maintenance will be a considerable amount. I enjoyed such a good park as mine without paying so much money, didn't I? The purpose people have for owning a thing lies in the convenience it provides for them. If I can enjoy the conveniences a train or a park provide in this way, what could be a better way of owning them? For this reason, I said that I owned them all. Moreover, you can regard as yours all things including the earth with mountains and rivers and make use of them properly as they are needed. Nobody will prohibit you from doing so. If you can do so, wouldn't it be a grand household affair? However, the common people of small caliber in the world, being eager to possess whatever they can, are bent on taking those things that cause them a great deal of

work, worry, and responsibility. This is because they haven't discovered the way of managing boundless household affairs."

18. The Master, upon closing a winter Zen retreat, was going on foot to Pongsŏ-sa with a few of his disciples. One of the disciples said, deploring, "It is regrettable that because we have no money, the Master must walk a long distance." Hearing this, the Master said, "If one makes good use of one's six sense organs in this world, everything one does turns out right accordingly, and one can make money thereby. Hence, one's mind and body are the organs for earning money, and everything in the world can become money depending on how they are used. Why should one lament for want of money? As followers of the Way, however, you should not be moved by money. It is the duty of the practitioner of the Way to take it easy whether one has or does not have money. If one does so, one is a truly rich person."

19. One of the disciples said, "They say that there is a grand exhibition being held in Seoul. I wonder whether you might go there to see it." The Master said, "The purpose of holding an exhibition lies in making it known how much development humankind has made in all areas of human life, namely, the works of scholar-officials, farmers, artisans, and tradesmen compared with those of the past. Another purpose lies in helping improve the public intellect by exchanging common knowledge among people. Hence, one will gain a great deal from it if one views it with a right frame of mind. Today, however, I will tell you of a truly grand exhibition. Listen carefully. In general, this exhibition is boundless so that the whole universe, viz., east, west, south, and north, northwest, northeast, southwest, southeast, zenith, and nadir, is the exhibition ground, and everything there is has been exhibited for millions of years. Compared with this grand exhibition, the one being held in Seoul is nothing. Though countless things may be displayed at the exhibition, Mt. Pae and Lake Hwangdŭng, which we can see here, cannot be moved to the exhibition for display, let alone the world famous Mt. Kŭmgang. In the museum various antiques are displayed, but the mountains, rivers, and the earth, which are the most antique of all antiques, cannot be displayed there. In the aquarium the finny tribes are displayed and in the rice granary section grains of various sorts are displayed; however, the finny tribes there are less than a billionth of all the finny tribes in the five oceans, and the grains there compared with the grains of the six continents are no more than a grain of sand of a mountain. Considered in this way, all those things displayed and the grand exhibition itself would look artificial and small to one who has an unlimited view and understanding. Therefore, those who, being magnanimous, discover and observe this limitless exhibition ground will gain immensely from whatever they see or hear. From ancient times, therefore, all buddhas and sages, observing this limitless exhibition,

formulated the laws of right and wrong, gain and loss for humanity by applying the principles of noumenon and phenomenon and existence and nonexistence displayed in this exhibition ground. In this way, they were never poor."

20. One day the Master went for a walk, accompanied by Cho Song-gwang and Chŏn Ŭm-gwang, in Namjung-ni, suburb of Iri City. Song-gwang, seeing a few exceptionally picturesque pine trees at the road-side, said, "How pretty those pine trees are! I wish I could transplant them to my temple." Hearing this, the Master said, "You haven't got out of narrow-mindedness and narrow confinement. The temple has not left the old pine tree, nor has the old pine tree left the temple. The two are both within one fence. Why should the trees be transplanted so that only those in the temple can appreciate them? It is because you haven't freed yourself from partiality and discrimination to discover the grand household of the universe." Song-gwang asked, "Where is the grand household of the universe?" The Master said, "It is right in front of your eyes, but you don't recognize it; hence I will allude to it for you by a symbol." The Master then drew a circle on the ground, saying, "This is the symbol of the grand household of the universe, which is complete with infinitely wondrous principles, infinite treasures, and infinitely creative transformation." Ŭm-gwang asked, "How can one enter the household to be its owner?" The Master said, "You can only enter the grand household if you obtain a key, which is made of the threefold great power,[178] and you cannot make the key without the prerequisites for them, namely, faith, zeal, doubt, and sincerity."[179]

21. The Master asked a Christian minister who came to see him, "What has made you visit with me?" The Minister answered, "I have come to hear some truthful words from you." The Master asked, "Then, have you seen the vast world beyond the boundary of Christianity?" The minister asked, "Where is the vast world?" The Master said, "You will find the vast world if you shift your attention to make a wider observation. Those who do not make wider observations, being used to their own customs and insisting on what they are concerned with, slander others and reject other customs. In this way, they cannot slough off their own rules and old customs, and consequently they fall into prejudice, erecting an impregnable fortress between themselves and others. Antagonism and conflicts between nations, churches, families, and individuals are caused by this prejudice. Why should we divide the originally perfect and great household and the limitlessly great truth [dharma] into pieces by this prejudice? We should destroy these walls

---

178. See above, *Canon*, pt. 2, chap. 4, for the threefold great power.
179. Ibid., chap. 5, sec. 1.

for better communication and harmony, realizing a better world. Then there will be nothing to throw away in the world."

22. The Master said further, "If you can use anything properly at a right place and a right time, all things in the world can be of great service to you, and all laws—penal, civil, and moral—will be your protector. For example, there are all sorts of goods, high or low in value, in a marketplace; we do not buy only rare and precious goods, throwing away things of little value. Depending on situations, the most precious thing can be of no use while the thing of little value can be of great use. Gold and jade are regarded as priceless treasures; however, they cannot take the role of a bowl of rice for a starving person. Lye is very noxious to the human body; however, it is a good detergent for laundry. Thus, each article has a different nature and use. One who does not understand this principle and who regards all goods in the marketplace as useless except those he or she wishes to have is narrow-minded and stupid." Being moved, the minister said, "What a magnanimous master you are!"

23. The Master said, "Buddhas and bodhisattvas regard this world sometimes as a resting place where they live comfortable lives, sometimes as a work site where they work, and sometimes as an amusement park where they pass time leisurely and freely throughout their lives."

## IX. On Deliverance

1. The Master said, "Those who are enlightened to the truth take the matter of dying to be as important as that of living while ordinary people take only the matter of living in the present life to be of great importance. The enlightened ones understand that only those who can die a good death can get a good birth and live a good life, and only those who get a good birth and live a good life can die a good death, and they understand the principle that birth is the fundamental source of death and death is the fundamental source of birth. There is no fixed time for solving this problem; therefore one should prepare for the approach of death when one is over forty years of age lest one meet death hurriedly and unprepared."

2. The Master said, "Since every human being, once born into this world, will die, I will tell you what a close relative should do to help the spirit[180] of the dying person leave and what the dying person should do for him- or herself. So, listen carefully. If one dies suddenly from a sudden attack of illness or if one has no faith in the dharma, the following requirements may not easily be satisfied. However, if the death is not a sudden one or if the dying person has some faith in the dharma,

---

180. This term is used in the sense of "self," the main attribute of which is numinous consciousness.

following these requirements will help strengthen the dying person's spirit and aid its salvation. If one is near death, one's close relative must observe the following points. First, the sickroom should be kept clean with incense often burnt; if the sickroom is not clean, the spirit of the dying patient will be impure. Second, the sickroom should always be kept quiet; if not, the patient will be unable to concentrate his or her spirit. Third, the patient should be told many stories of virtuous persons and be consoled with compliments for his or her virtuous and meritorious conduct; the virtuous thoughts will impress the spirit of the dying patient, which will form the root habit of goodness for the next life. Fourth, no evil or cunning words or lechery or debauchery should be mentioned in front of the patient; otherwise, such bad impressions on the spirit will easily become the habit force of the next life. Fifth, no worries concerning the family property and the family members should be shown in front of the patient; otherwise, attachment and greed in the patient will be furthered so that the spirit cannot leave the place. If the spirit has no opportunity to be reincarnated into a human being in that place, it will easily fall into the evil path [animal, hungry ghost, or hells]. Sixth, if possible, repetition of the name of a buddha,[181] reading scriptures, or sermons on the dharma should be provided in the presence of the patient. If, however, the patient wishes quiet, meditation should be practiced; the spirit of the patient can attain calmness by depending on it. Seventh, when the patient is breathing his or her final breaths, no noise should be made of crying, shaking the body, or calling out to the dying patient. Such behavior only disturbs the spirit of the leaving spirit. Even if one is overcome with sorrow, the deathbed area should be kept quiet for several hours after death."

3. The Master continued, "If one on the deathbed is aware of the approaching final moment, [the following should be done]. First, one should free one's mind from any thought and exert oneself to maintain spiritual concentration. Second, if one must make a will, one should have it made in advance lest it disturb one's spiritual concentration on the deathbed, for nothing is more important for a dying person than spiritual concentration. Third, if, on reflection, one had a grudge against someone for a long time or became an enemy of someone, one should, if possible, invite the concerned person so that the old grudge can be dissolved. If the concerned person is not available, then one must exert oneself to drop the grudge unilaterally. If the grudge in one's mind is not dissolved, it becomes the seed of evil karma in one's next life. Fourth, if, on reflection, one had an attachment to someone and could not be detached, one should let that mind go; for if one cannot do away with an attachment, one cannot enter true nirvāṇa and will

---

181. See above, *Canon*, pt. 3, chap. 3, for the method of intoning the name of a buddha.

instead fall into the cycle of the evil path. Fifth, one who has observed these provisions and has reached the final moment should collect the pure spirit and clear the mind of any worldly thoughts, letting the spirit leave in the state of concentration (samādhi) or repetition of the name of a buddha. Then a person who has no thorough understanding of the truth of birth and death can be born in the world of buddhas and bodhisattvas, avoiding the evil path. These instructions are not meant to be applied simply to anyone on the deathbed. They will be very effective to those who have had faith in the dharma at ordinary times, but one with no faith or training in the dharma will find it difficult to apply them. Hence, you, followers of the Way, should understand this point in advance lest you have cause to regret your unpreparedness, and you should never forget these instructions lest your spirit have attachment during the passage. The matter of birth and death is so important that you cannot be too careful about it."

4. The Master wrote four sentences and had Yi Kong-ju and Sŏng Song-wŏn recite them:

> Together with the eternal Heaven and Earth,
>     Preserve the eternal life.
> Attaining nirvāṇa throughout myriad worlds,
>     Let the true self be manifested clearly.
> Be enlightened to supreme truth throughout endless
>     reincarnations,
>     Having the everlasting flower in bloom.
> Let every step and every thing
>     Be the holy scriptures.

This became the sacred incantation for the deliverance of the spirit of the deceased.

5. The Master composed the "Sermon for Guiding the Spirit before and after Death," which is to be delivered at the funeral service and the deliverance service.[182] The text of the sermon is as follows:

[Addressing the *yŏngga* (spirit of the dying or the deceased)]: Collect your mind and listen carefully to my words. All the things, good or evil, you received in this life are the effects of what you caused in your previous lives, and what you have done in this life is what you will receive in your next life. This is in accordance with the heavenly mandate of great nature. Buddhas and patriarchs, being enlightened to their original nature and thereby having attained freedom of mind, transcend this law of karma and freely choose the six realms of existence and the four forms of birth at will, while ordinary people and sentient beings, being

---

182. To be held seven times on every seventh day after death.

deluded in their original nature and not having attained freedom of mind, are dragged by the natural law of karma into the endless bitter seas of misery. Thus, whether you will be a buddha, a patriarch, an ordinary human being, or a sentient being, whether you will be noble or mean, fortunate or unfortunate, and whether you will enjoy longevity or suffer short life—all depend on what you do. Do you know clearly that whatever you receive in your life is the karmic effect of what you do? Listen again! The natural law of birth and death applies uniformly to buddhas, you, and all other sentient beings; and the original nature of buddhas, you, and all other sentient beings are identical, being originally pure, perfect, and complete. The original nature is like the moon in the empty sky, which, being alone in the sky, is reflected on a thousand rivers. Likewise, the fundamental source of all things in the universe is also the realm of the original nature, which is essentially pure. In the realm of the original nature exists neither name nor form, neither going nor coming, neither birth nor death, neither the Buddha nor a deluded being, neither void nor nirvāṇa, nor this word of negation. It is neither being nor nonbeing, amongst which a being is brought about spontaneously, transforming through formation, abiding, decay, and void; all things go through the process of arising, abiding, decaying, and ceasing; and all sentient beings change through the cycle of the six realms of existence and the four forms of birth. The sun and the moon rotate, changing the day and the night. Thus, the birth and death of your body goes through transformation, which is not truly birth and death. Are you listening? Are you clearly awakened to the realm of the original nature? Listen again! When you discard your body and receive a new one, you will receive it in accordance with what you have loved to do and what you have been attached to most. If you loved the world of buddhas and bodhisattvas more than any other world, then you will receive a body in the world of buddhas and bodhisattvas, rejoicing in the infinite beatitude. If, however, you let greed, hatred, and delusion bind your life all the time, you will receive your body in the realm of the evil path, suffering endless misery for countless kalpas. Are you listening? Listen again. Have an adamantine determination at this moment. If you have the slightest attachment of love and desire, you will fall into the evil path. Once you fall into the evil path, it will be very difficult to receive a human body. If you are not reincarnated into the human world, how can you find the order of a great sage where you achieve the great task of attaining buddhahood and delivering all sentient beings and cultivate wisdom and blessings? Have you listened carefully?

6. The Master said that he had got an idea from the advertisement of a fire insurance company at an exhibition in Seoul, saying, "Although we always say that we should be emancipated from the ills of birth and death, we will be unable to be emancipated from them if we do not

understand the principle of birth and death. If one is convinced that there is no reincarnation when one dies, there will be increased sadness and sorrow at the approach of death. This is comparable to someone without fire insurance who has lost all his or her property to a sudden fire all at once. To the one who knows the principle of reincarnation, however, the birth and death of this life is like changing clothes. Though the body, which is subject to change, dies, the numinous consciousness, being immortal, will receive a new body. Thus, the numinous consciousness guarantees immortal life just as an insurance policy guarantees a new building. If you understand this principle, you will take birth and death with ease; if not, you will be anxious and terrified. If you understand the principle of suffering and happiness, you will accept due suffering and happiness, preparing for eternal pleasure. If you do not understand this principle, however, you will have neither hope nor preparation, so that there is no chance to be delivered from the sea of misery. How could one who knows this principle not worry about and feel pity for such people?"

7. The Master said, "Though there are many ways one should follow, they can be summarized as the ways of life and death. If one does not know the way of life when one lives, one cannot realize the value of life; and one cannot avoid the evil path at the time of death if one does not know the way of death."

8. The Master said, "The birth and death of a human being is likened to the opening and closing of one's eyes, to the inhalation and exhalation of the breath, and to falling asleep and awakening. Except for the difference of length of time, the principle is the same. Since birth and death are nondual and there originally is neither arising nor ceasing, the enlightened regard it as change while the unenlightened regard it as birth and death."

9. The Master said, "Just as the sun rises in the east tomorrow although it sets in the west today, the numinous consciousness leaving the dying body will return into this world with a new body although all sentient beings are subject to death."

10. The Master said, "The world where we live now is called 'this world' and the world where people go after death is called 'the other world.' Thus people believe that the world beyond is different from this world. However, the only difference lies in changing the body and place; there is no world other than this one."

11. The Master said, "When the numinous consciousness leaves this body at death, it first follows what it is attached to and then gets the body in accordance with the person's karma, entering the endless cycle of reincarnation. Now, the way to free oneself from the transmigration through the six realms of existence lies in having no attachment and transcending karma."

12. Chŏng Il-sŏng asked, "When I reach the last moment of my life, how should I keep the one thought[183] of the last moment?" The Master answered, "End it in clear awareness." Il-sŏng asked further, "What is the path of death and rebirth like?" The Master said, "It is like awakening from sleep. Though you seem to have gone in your sound sleep, you are the same Il-sŏng when you wake up. Thus, the identical being called Il-sŏng goes through the endless transmigration of birth and death in accordance with his karma."

13. A disciple asked, "I would like to know what process the spirit takes and what state it is in when it leaves this body and receives a new one." The Master said, "The spirit, at the time of separation from the body, normally leaves it after the vital force and respiration have completely ceased; however, certain spirits leave the body before the vital force and respiration have completely ceased. Upon leaving the body, the spirit stays in the intermediate state of existence[184] for forty-nine days before it is reincarnated. However, certain spirits enter the new wombs as soon as they leave the dying body; some other spirits enter the new wombs after floating around in the intermediate state of existence like wind for several months or several years. Normally, a spirit floats around, being aware of having its body, as in a dream experience. Once it enters a new womb, the previous consciousness is lost, and the spirit regards the new conceived body as its own."

14. A disciple asked, "As I haven't resolved my doubt concerning birth and death, my life seems to be as meaningless as that of a mayfly, and the world seems to be in vain. What should I do about this?" The Master said, "In an ancient writing you find a passage: 'From the viewpoint of change, heaven and earth do not remain unchanged even a moment; but from the viewpoint of immutability, all things including myself never come to an end.' Inquire into the meaning of this passage."[185]

15. The Master said, "All sentient and insentient beings in the world are endowed with the element of life. There is not a being that is completely annihilated; things transform into different forms. For example, a decomposing human corpse makes the soil rich, and the spot will be thick with grass, which, being mowed, can be made into compost. When this is used as fertilizer, the crop will absorb it, yielding grains, which become blood and flesh in human beings, helping maintain human life and actions. From this point of view, nothing in the universe

---

183. *Kṣaṇa* (S), lit., as instant.
184. *Antarābhāva* (S), the intermediate existence between death and reincarnation, a stage varying from seven to forty-nine days.
185. Unidentified.

is completely annihilated; even a straw can manifest ten billion transformation bodies (*nirmanakāya*) of the Buddha, exhibiting various creative transformations and powers. Therefore, inquire into such a principle as this and get enlightened to the truth that all things in the universe live eternal lives in the truth of no arising and no ceasing."

16. At a New Year's Day ceremony, the Master said to an assembly, "Although yesterday was one day and today is another without there being anything special about either day, the year up to yesterday is called 'last year' and the year starting today is called 'this year.' Likewise, although the spirit remains the same whether one is alive or dead, the world where one is alive is called 'this world' and the world where one goes after death is called 'the other world.' Though there is birth and death to the body, which is made from earth, water, fire, and air and, hence, difference between this world and the other world, there is no birth or death to the spirit, since it is immortal. Therefore, to the enlightened, the birth, old age, illness, and death of a human being is like the change of spring, summer, autumn, and winter, and the difference between the other world and this world is like that between last year and this year."

17. The Master said, "No matter how much money and grain you amass during life, you can't take that wealth with you when you die. So how can you regard that wealth as an eternal possession? Instead, you should do charitable work as much as you can without abiding in the idea of doing so, thereby sowing the seeds of pure blessedness and virtue.[186] The truly eternal possession is the vow toward the correct dharma and the spiritual power one attains as the result of practicing it. Hence, one can be the owner of wisdom and blessedness in the infinite world only if one exerts oneself to the practice with the ever-renewed great vow."

18. The Master addressed an assembly at a Zen monastery: "Do you know what the world of *yama* and the messenger from Hades are?[187] The *yama*'s world is right within the fence of your own house, and the messenger from Hades is none other than your own family members. Let me explain why. Because of the attachment to family members that has been forged during one's lifetime, one's spirit cannot soar high when one's body dies, falling again within the fence of one's house; and, if there is no opportunity for it to be incarnated into a human being, it will be reincarnated into a domestic animal or even an insect. That's

---

186. Or "nonleaking" (S. *anāsrava*) merit.
187. In the Vedas the god of the dead, with whom the spirits of the departed dwell. In Buddhist mythology, the regent of the *nārakas* (hell), residing south of Jambudvipa, outside of the Cakravālas, in a place of copper and iron.

why all buddhas and patriarchs from ancient times have taught that one should act without attachment and leave without attachment to anything, lest one fall into the evil path."

19. The Master said, "One should daily cultivate one's mind in order to be free from attachment; for one who has a strong attachment to wealth, sex, fame, and profit, or to one's own spouse and children, clothes, food, and shelter, suffers from agony and worry far more than those whose attachment is not so strong when they disappear. Such a one will experience a hell in this very world and, when that person dies, he or she will be driven into the sea of misery, dragged by attachment, losing freedom. How could we be careless about this matter?"

20. The Master said, "Recently, some people have chosen their grave sites and made a firm resolution to be buried there. The numinous consciousness of such a one will go to the grave site as soon as the person dies, and, if there is no opportunity for it to be incarnated into a human being, it will unawares fall into the evil path, moving farther away from the path of human reincarnation. How can one be so careless?"

21. One of the disciples acted obstinately against what the Master ordered him to do. The Master said, "If you stick to your opinion on a trivial matter, you will do the same on matters of grave importance. Then, you will stick to your way for all things, failing to be delivered by me. If you do not receive the deliverance, my effort to save you will be to no avail."

22. The Master addressed an assembly at a Zen monastery: "If you, severing the worldly attachment of love and vehement desire, purify your mind and keep attaining the power of spiritual cultivation by listening daily to the dharma words, you achieve not only your own deliverance; your dharma power[188] will fill the empty dharma realm so that even the microbes and insects in that region can be delivered. The dharma power can be compared to the power of the sun. The sunbeam does not intend to thaw snow and ice, but they are thawed by it naturally. Likewise, the screens of past karma of ordinary people and other sentient beings are sometimes thawed by the dharma power of the practitioners of the Way who have cut off evil dispositions and worldly thoughts."

23. The Master said, "There are heavenly people and there are earthly people. Heavenly people have mild desire and noble thoughts, so clear energy ascends from them; earthly people have burning desire and base thoughts, so turbid energy descends from them. This is the crossroads of the good path and the evil path. Reflecting on one's mind,

---

188. The power of Buddha-truth to do away with calamity and subdue evil.

one will know to what kind of people one belongs and what will become of oneself in the future."

24. The Master said, "The bright moon can shine upon all things only if the clouds in the sky are dispelled, and the moon of wisdom will rise and shine upon all sentient beings as a mirror only if the clouds of vehement desire are dispelled from the mental sky of the practitioner. Only then can the practitioner be a great dharma master who can deliver sentient beings suffering in the evil path."

25. The Master said, "One morning I was looking toward Mt. Pyŏn and saw a clear aura in the middle of the empty sky. Later I went there to find an assembly of Buddhist practitioners who had started a Zen retreat at Wŏlmyŏngam. If one's mind is purified through spiritual concentration, the base and turbid elements of one's mind will be eradicated, and clear and numinous energy will soar into the highest heavens, so that the triple world in ten directions will be influenced by that energy and the beings in the six realms of existence and the four forms of birth will be wrapped in that dharma power, being redeemed in the world of the Buddha and delivered after death."

26. The Master attended a regular evening dharma meeting and, looking one by one at the participants under the lantern, said, "The aurae that rise above each of you is different one from another. From some whose turbid energy has subsided through extensive practice for a long period, only the pure aura arises; some have more clear aura than turbid aura; some have half clear and half turbid aura; some have more turbid than clear aura; and some have only turbid aura." He said further, "The greedier one is, the more turbid one's spirit becomes so that it cannot rise high. When such a one dies, he or she cannot receive a human body, being reborn as a beast or an insect. One who, though mild in desire, exerts him- or herself to the extension of knowledge only, neglecting good affinities and the accumulation of virtuous merits to other people, may rise high but is liable to be born in the realm of asuras or birds. Therefore, if the cultivator of the Way is enlightened to his or her original nature, cultivates it, and acts correctly, distinguishing right from wrong, then eventually, that person will attain an adamantine spirit (*yŏngdan*),[189] with which he or she can freely choose his or her reincarnation without being dragged by the wheel of the six realms of existence. Such a one can also attain the ability to devote him- or herself to spiritual cultivation, touring the empty dharma realm with only the adamantine spirit leaving the body behind."

27. The Master said, "If one always exerts oneself with utmost sincerity to keep one's mind-ground from being disturbed, to keep one's

189. The Chinese original, *ling-tan*, means an elixir of immortality; here it simply means an unbreakable unit of spirit.

mind-ground free from being deluded, and to keep one's mind-ground free from being defiled, one will be endowed with great spiritual ability to deliver the sentient beings suffering in hells. An act of helping someone have faith in the true dharma of the Buddha becomes a good seed of attaining buddhahood for eternity."

28. When Kim Kwang-sŏn died, the Master, shedding tears, said to the assembly of his followers, "To speak of P'al-san,[190] we have grown fond of each other while we shared suffering and happiness for more than twenty years. Though there is no change of arising and ceasing or ups and downs in the dharma body, his physical body has left us for good, and we cannot see his countenance any more. How can I not be sorrowful? For the sake of his spirit, I will say a few dharma words concerning the principles of birth and death, going and coming, and extinction of karmic retribution. Listen to me carefully for consolation on our loss of him. If you have an awakening at these words, it will be a great benefit not only for you but also for P'al-san.

In the words of the ancient Buddha, it is said that the karmic retribution for many previous rebirths can be extinguished if you pursue the practice in the dharma after being enlightened to the great truth of neither birth nor death, neither going nor coming. Now, the method of extinguishing the karmic retribution will be like this. If someone causes pain and loss to you, you should regard it as paying off an old debt and take it calmly, without resenting, hating, or confronting that person. If you lose your turn to requite it, the cycle of karmic retribution will stop for good. Or, you can become enlightened to the realm where birth and death and suffering and happiness are all void, and let your mind rest there. Neither birth and death nor karmic retribution can occur in that realm. If one has reached that realm, then it can be said that one has completely extinguished the sufferings of birth and death and karmic retribution."

29. Pak Che-bong asked, "How is the spirit of the deceased benefited by the service for the dead on every seventh day for forty-nine days and the memorial service?"[191] The Master answered, "One of the mysterious principles in the universe is that things respond to the influence of other things. For instance, fertilization of the soil after sowing seeds makes considerable difference in the quantity of crops one harvests although the earth, seeds, and fertilizer are all insentient. If the insentient grains can be influenced by other insentient things, why shouldn't

---

190. Kim Kwang-sŏn's dharma title.
191. During the period of forty-nine days the deceased is in the intermediate state (*antarābhāva*); at the end of forty-nine days, judgment having been made, one enters upon one's next state. By observing the proper rites, one's family may aid one in overcoming one's perils and attaining a happy destiny.

the spirit of the deceased, the most numinous of all, be influenced by the sincere devotion of other people? If, for the sake of the spirit of the deceased, many people offer silent prayers, make donations, and have a high priest give sermons, then the spirit of the deceased is affected by the minds of the people concerned and the spirit of the people concerned, so that the spirit can be delivered immediately; even if the deceased has fallen into the evil path, his or her spirit can gradually be promoted toward the good path; or even if one had heavy debt in his or her lifetime, it can be taken off if the donation on that person's behalf is used for the public service, and merits can be accumulated if one had no debt during his or her lifetime. The principle of mutual responses is comparable to that of electrical currents."

30. One of the disciples asked, "From ancient times there has been a custom of holding a Buddhist service for the spirit of the deceased. In the service, sons, daughters, relatives, and friends make offerings to the buddha statue or have the priests of high virtue give sermons and recite Buddhist scriptures for the sake of the spirit. How could this service affect the spirit? What difference would the degree of sincerity and the dharma power of the priest make on the spirit?" The Master said, "To show one's sincerity to the spirit of the deceased one holds prayers and makes offerings to the Buddha statue. An old saying goes, 'Sincerity can move heaven.' Thus, the effect of prayers and making offerings to the Buddha statue will be proportional to the degree of sincerity; and the sermon and recitation of the scriptures will have an effect on the spirit proportional to the dharma power of the priest. As a result some spirits can, unaware, enter the good path after paying off all evil karma of the past; some can get rid of the evil karma, directly returning to the good path; some can be helped to find the right path for the next life though they were lost in the intermediate existence between death and reincarnation; some can be released from momentary attachment, becoming free and enjoying blessedness in the human and heavenly realms. If, however, the sincerity of the family of the deceased is not outstanding and if the dharma power of the priest is deficient, the means so used may not have any effect on the root of the spirit. This is because the spirit of the deceased will not be affected unless the sincerity of the family of the deceased is utmost, just as a farmer cannot expect a great crop unless he exerts his sincerity and other necessary works to raise the crop."

31. Sŏ Tae-wŏn asked, "Can the spirit of the deceased hear and understand the deliverance sermon?" The Master answered, "Some spirits do and some do not hear or understand it; however, the spirit understands the sermon not because it is awakened, but because the power of merits, affecting the spirit, becomes the cause of deliverance. Just as a fly, which cannot fly a long distance by itself but can go a long

distance if it is attached to a horse that runs a thousand *ri* [400 km], the spirit can gradually return to the world of the Buddha through the deliverance service."

32. Kim Tae-gŏ asked, "Today, the forty-ninth day deliverance service was held for the spirit of a two-year-old infant. Even the spirit of an adult may not understand the details of the deliverance service. How could such an infant spirit hear and understand them and be delivered?" The Master said, "There is no difference between an adult and an infant in the spirit. The way the spirit of the deceased is delivered by the deliverance service is comparable to fertilizing a plant or to metal pieces being attached to a magnet. Since all sentient beings live with the roots of their spirits in the empty dharma realm, services held through the empty dharma realm become effective fertilizer for the root of the spirit."

33. Tae-gŏ asked further, "If the memorial service is held in this way, can one's evil karma accumulated in one's lifetime, light or heavy, be extinguished at once for one to be delivered?" The Master said, "Whether one's karma can be extinguished depends on the heaviness and lightness of one's karma, the sincerity of those who are in charge of the service, and the dharma power of the priest. Just as ice can be thawed by the sun's heat, the karma can be thawed at once or over quite a long time. However, the merits of holding the memorial service will never be lost; the service will help the spirit find good affinities."

34. Tae-gŏ asked further, "Why have you decided upon the forty-ninth day as the day for the deliverance service?" The Master answered, "The spirit of the deceased stays in the intermediate state generally for forty-nine days before receiving a new body in accordance with karmic affinity. Thus, the deliverance service is held on that day, following the words of the Buddha, in order to make the deceased collect the pure unitary thought once more. However, many spirits get their next bodies in accordance with their attachments as soon as they leave their old bodies."

35. Tae-gŏ asked further, "In the Nirvāṇa Sūtra it is said, 'If one wants to know matters of one's previous life, one must see what one has received in one's present life; if one wishes to know matters of one's next life, one must only see what one has done in the present life.'[192] If we examine the way people are blessed or punished in their present lives, however, we find that some people who deserve punishment are blessed in a rich family while other people who deserve blessedness suffer miseries in a poor household. How can we say that the karmic law of retribution is correct?" The Master answered, "That's why all buddhas and patriarchs warned people to hold a pure thought at their

---

192. Unidentified.

last breaths. One who enjoys prosperity in spite of evil mentality is one who produced good karma in the earlier part of his or her previous life but became depraved in the last part and breathed the last breath with a wicked thought. One who is good-natured but suffers miseries in the present life is one who unawares produced evil karma in the early years of his or her previous life but turned his or her mind from evil to good upon repentance in his or her later years. Thus, the one thought of one's last moment becomes the first thought of one's next life."

36. Tae-gŏ asked further, "At death one leaves this world for the other world. Can the numinous consciousness freely come and go between the two worlds as if it were in this world?" The Master answered, "There is no difference in the perceptive mind before and after one's death; but there is a difference, in going and coming, between the spirit that is dragged by greed, anger, and delusions and the one that has subjugated them. The spirit that is bound by greed, anger, and delusions, being tied to attachment, is not free in going and coming at the time of death, and, being covered by karmic power, is illuminated only by the realm of attachment, to which it is dragged. When it receives its new body, it has inverted and absurd visions so that the world of beasts and insects looks beautiful to the spirit. Consequently, it unawares enters the womb with sexual desires as if it were in dreams. When it chooses human parents, the spirit enters the womb with sexual desire. If one has an aspiration for a fixed karma but fails to receive a human body, the spirit receives in the realm of beasts and insects what is similar to the fixed karma so desired. Thus, the spirit bound by greed, anger, and delusions is not free from birth and death, suffering limitless miseries in the six realms of existence and being dragged through the cycle of twelvefold dependent origination. The spirit that has subjugated greed, anger, and delusions, however, is free in going and coming at the time of death because it is not bound by attachment. It can see and think right; it is not dragged by karma because it distinguishes right places from wrong places. When it is reincarnated, it, being imperturbable, receives the new body correctly. When it enters the womb, it is conceived by meeting the new parents in terms of a debt of gratitude. Whatever one aspired to establish will be realized as fixed karma. Thus, the spirit is free from birth and death and turns the wheel of the twelvefold dependent origination without being attracted to the cycle of the six realms of existence."

37. Tae-gŏ asked further, "What is the cause of one being closely related to another?" The Master answered, "Ordinary sentient beings come into close relations with others in terms of friendliness and love or in terms of hatred while buddhas and bodhisattvas come into relations with all sentient beings in terms of compassion in order to deliver them."

38. Tae-gŏ asked further, "Can one be delivered only after death?" The Master answered, "Since one can be delivered while living or after death, it will be more effective for one to deliver oneself before death than for someone else to deliver one's spirit after death. Hence, one should always tame one's mind to be bright, clean, and right so that the six consciousnesses should not be tainted or defiled while passing through the six dusts.[193] One who attains to this stage will acquire the great ability to deliver others, and will have finished the deliverance of his or her own self. However, few have attained this stage. That's why all the cultivators of the Way of the three time periods exerted themselves in ascetic religious practice."

## X. On Faith and Devotion

1. The Master said, "When a mentor meets someone who wishes to be his or her disciple, the mentor tests that person's faith first. If the follower has a sincere faith, the master's dharma can be transmitted to him or her, and the disciple will accomplish something of great merit. If the follower's faith is weak, the mentor's dharma cannot be transmitted to him or her, and the follower will not accomplish anything meritorious. What then is faith? First of all, the disciple should not harbor any doubt about the dharma master. Even if many people slander the dharma master in many ways, one's faith in him or her should not be shaken thereby, and one should not harbor any doubts. Secondly, one should follow the guidance of the mentor without asserting one's own opinion or being stubborn. Thirdly, no matter how strict the mentor may be in teaching or how severely the disciple is reproved, or even if the mentor exposes the faults of the disciple in public, or even if the disciple is ordered to do hard work, the disciple should submit to all of them without any complaints. Fourthly, the disciple should not hide his or her faults from the mentor but instead report everything truthfully. If a disciple can satisfy these four criteria of faith, he or she will be equipped with the vessel of dharma for buddhahood and patriarchs."

2. The Master said, "Although there are thousands and tens of thousands of different layers among the capacities of the practitioners, they are broadly divided into three levels: high, intermediate, and low.

---

193. Six qualities (S. *guna*) produced by the objects and organs of sense, i.e., sight, sound, smell, taste, touch, and mental object; the organs are the six roots, and the six perceptions or discernments are the six consciousnesses. The six qualities or dusts are therefore the cause of all impurity. Cf. Hui-neng, *Liu-tsu t'an ching* (*T*, 2008.48.351a–b): "We should purify the mind so that the six aspects of consciousness, namely, sight, sound, smell, taste, touch, and mentation, in passing through their six sense gates will neither be defiled nor attached to their six sense objects. When our mind works freely without any hindrance and is at liberty 'to come' and 'to go,' then we have attained the intuitive insight of prajñā, which is emancipation."

Those of high capacity carry out the practice with confidence because they recognize the correct dharma and have faith in it as soon as they see and hear it. Those of intermediate capacity, neither having a thorough comprehension of the dharma nor being totally ignorant of it, are suspicious of the dharma and the teacher, constantly putting them on their scales. Those of low capacity accept the mentor's directions without discriminating right from wrong and without calculating and doubting the mentor and dharma. Of these three capacities, those with high capacity are the most valuable and desired in the order of religious teaching because they make progress in their practice without delay and contribute greatly to the expansion of the task of the order. Those of low capacity, in spite of lacking self-ability, can succeed in achieving the goal because they value the dharma, have firm faith in the mentor, and exert endless effort. Of the three, those of intermediate capacity are capricious and the most difficult to teach; they are apt to belittle the dharma and to slight the mentor. Because they lack a firm aspiration and sincerity, they can hardly succeed in religious practice or public service. Therefore, those of intermediate capacity must exert themselves to surmount their difficulties. Among those of low capacity, we find some who leap to the level of high capacity; however, if they go through the intermediate capacity, they face dangerous routes, and hence they must be very cautious."

3. A disciple asked, "I am not only dull but have a short period of training behind me; thus the day of success seems to be far away. What should I do?" The Master said, "Natural endowment and the length of time one spends for training in the dharma are not decisive factors for succeeding in the cultivation of the Way. Success in the cultivation of the Way depends mainly on whether or not one exerts oneself with faith, zeal, doubt (ǔi), and sincerity.[194] Anyone who exerts oneself with faith, zeal, doubt, and sincerity will surely succeed in the cultivation of the Way within a definite period of time."

4. The Master said, "When a particular condition inspires ordinary people to practice in the dharma, their faith seems to pierce heaven at some times, only to fade away over time. Faith sometimes fluctuates depending on such changes as gaining or losing power and having domestic discord or recovering domestic peace. One will succeed in attaining to high excellence in the cultivation of dharma only if one keeps the aim constant in those circumstances by checking one's faith, changing adverse conditions into agreeable ones, and keeping agreeable ones from turning to wicked and excessive ones."

5. The Master said, "Anyone with a high position, power, wealth, or extensive learning in the world finds it difficult to have faith in and enter

---

194. See above, *Canon*, pt. 2, chap. 5, sec. 1, for the meaning of these four articles.

the great Way. If such a one develops aspirations for the religious practice and devotes oneself to a religious order, it is due to the great vows that person made in his or her past life."

6. The Master said, "There are some who, in spite of being my followers, have not established a firm faith in me, trying to do as they please in accordance with their talents and their points of view. What, then, could be the use of being my disciple? If one who cultivates the Way with great aspirations and vow has consecrated a firm faith in me, he or she will have no doubt or complaint no matter what I say or what I ask one to do. Only when such a firm faith is established will his or her mind and my mind become one mind so that his or her effort and my effort will not be in vain."

7. The Master said, "The reason for checking the faith of an aspirant in the Way is threefold: faith is the vessel to contain the dharma, the motive power of solving all *ŭidus*, and the basis of observing all precepts. Practice without faith is like applying fertilizer to a dead tree; all the effort will be in vain. Therefore, you will be unable to deliver yourselves unless you have a firm faith. The highest merit in guiding others lies thus in helping them develop faith in their hearts."

8. The Master said, "In having faith in the three precious ones,[195] there are two ways of doing so, namely, by the other-power[196] and by the self-power. To have faith in the other-power is to believe in and revere the actual Buddha, dharma, and the order; to have faith in the self-power is to discover Buddha, dharma, and the order in one's own nature and have faith in them and practice therewith. Since these two are the bases of each other, one must practice them together. At the final stage of the practice, however, all things in the universe and the empty dharma realm transform into the three precious ones without any distinction between the other-power and the self-power."

9. The Master asked his disciples, "How much did you miss me when you didn't see me for a long time?" The disciples replied, "We missed you very much." The Master said, "I am sure you did. However, no matter how earnestly the child may observe its filial duty, it cannot match the love the parents have for their children. Likewise, no matter how much a disciple may revere the teacher, it cannot match the care the mentor has for the disciple. If the disciple's faith and reverence for the mentor measure up to only half of the mentor's love and care for the disciple, the dharma can be transmitted from the mentor to the disciple."

10. The Master said, "When one, as a disciple, receives the dharma

---

195. Buddha, dharma, and sangha, i.e., Buddha, the doctrine, and the order.
196. Another's strength, especially that of a buddha or bodhisattva obtained through faith in Mahāyāna salvation. Those who have this faith and trust to salvation by faith are contrasted with those who seek salvation by works or by their own strength.

from the mentor, one cannot receive the dharma completely if one does not give one's heart and sincerity to the mentor. Take Zen master Kujŏng for illustration.[197] When he first became a Buddhist monk, it was on a very cold day in winter that he was ordered by his mentor to install a cauldron, and he installed it nine times until dawn the next day. As he had no complaints in his heart for all that, he received the title Kujŏng and became a monk. Thereafter he did not receive any special instruction from his master for several decades while he was serving his mentor with unwavering faith and trust. As his mentor's illness became serious, he devoted himself to attend his mentor. During this time he was suddenly awakened and realized that to be enlightened for oneself is none other than receiving the dharma. Anyone who searches for the dharma must have as much faith as this to receive the dharma completely."

11. The Master said, "Although the spring breeze blows without partiality, only the living trees can receive its energy to grow. Sages expound the dharma equally and without partiality for all; however, only the faithful ones can receive them."

12. Upon returning from a sightseeing tour to Mt. Kŭmgang, the Master said, "The owner of the inn in Mt. Kŭmgang where I stayed this time was a Christian and was living a happy life with a firm faith. So I asked him for his background. During thirty years of his religious faith, he said, he had been buffeted by the waves of adversity. While confronting such difficulties in life, however, he thanked God for his love if fortunate things came around to his door and thanked God for warning against his faults if unfortunate things did. Thus his faith in God was strengthened in both favorable and adverse conditions, and he was able to live a happy life. Now, take a moment to check the level of your faith. The owner of the inn has a limited faith only in the other-power without comprehending the fundamental source of truth, and yet he is able to lead a happy life. If you, having faith both in the other-power and the self-power, were to have your faith weakened by the vicissitudes of life, how could you say that your faith and sincerity are genuine? Since you have found the source of a perfect and truthful religious faith, you, constantly checking your faith, should control your mental spheres with the power of faith but should not have your faith shaken by circumstances, lest you should be a foolish person."

---

197. Kujŏng (nine cauldron) was a monk during the Silla period; no name is known except "Nine Cauldron." While he was carrying hemp fabric on the A-frame on his back, he met Zen master Muyŏm (799–888) of the Sŏngju-san sect. Since Kujŏng wanted to become Muyŏm's disciple, Muyŏm tested his faith and devotion by making him install a cauldron nine times throughout a freezing night; Kujŏng carried out the order with no complaint. For Muyŏm, see Han Ki-tu, *Han'guk sŏnsasang yŏn'gu*, pp. 136–137.

13. When the Master was staying at Sŏktu-am, Chang Chŏk-cho, Ku Nam-su, and Yi Man-gap, being frail women, used to walk a hundred *ri* [40 km] to pay homage to the Master. The Master, thinking their faith laudable, said to them, "Your faith is extraordinary, but would you even eat feces if I told you to?" Hearing this, the three went out of the room and brought feces. The Master said, "Sit down. From what you are doing, I can see that your faith in me is so sincere that you would even eat something worse than feces if I asked you to. At present, this order is small and simple, so I can often pay attention to you. When the order expands, however, I may not even be aware of your coming and going. Now, check and see whether your faith in me will be as unwavering as today in such times. Keep today's faith and sincerity throughout eternal kalpas."

14. Once when the Master was giving a sermon, Kim Chŏng-gak was dozing in the first row. Seeing this, the Master scolded her saying, "Chŏng-gak dozing in the front row is as ugly as a water buffalo." Chŏng-gak, hearing this, immediately rose to her feet and, smiling, bowed down four times to the Master. Seeing this, the Master said, "I have often scolded her so harshly that she could have been disgusted at me. However, her faith in me has never weakened for all that. She is a person who will follow me in life and in death." The Master continued, "If there is something the mentor cannot say to the disciple and there is something the disciple cannot say to the mentor, then their mentor-disciple relationship is not genuine."

15. The Master said, "While I was sitting in the head dharma master's room, I saw the face of Ro Tŏksongok clearly appearing in front of my eyes, where it stayed for a while. As she has faith that can pierce heaven, her most faithful mind thus reached me though we are separated by mountains and rivers of more than a hundred *ri*."

16. Chŏng Sŏk-hyŏn said to the Master, "Although my circumstances are full of adverse conditions that can cause me suffering, I find pleasure in my life through prayers to Dharmakāya Buddha." The Master said, "I am not sure whether Sŏk-hyŏn has found pleasure in prayers to Dharmakāya Buddha with a sound knowledge of their virtue and power. However, such prayers are a way of finding happiness in misery. If one lives in this way, one can be happy in miserable circumstances. While I was at Mt. Pongnae, a few people following me suffered from extreme hardships, with poor shelter and food and hard labor in that remote mountainous region. However, they found great joy only in learning the dharma and attending me. To give another example, the first nine disciples,[198] with no experience of hard labor, went through extreme hardships to reclaim the tidal land in Yŏnggwang

---

198. See above, *SS*, I:6.

during the harsh, snowy winter. However, they, having no complaints or discontent, turned all the hardships into pleasure as they realized the significance of founding a new religious order and followed with pleasure whatever order I gave them. Though it might have appeared to others that they suffered extreme hardship, they realized heavenly beatitude with intense pleasures in this mundane world. Now that you have made up your mind to pursue the practice and public service in this order, you should be able to transcend all kinds of hardships with firm faith and far-reaching aspiration, turning all adverse conditions into pleasures. Only then will you be able to continue realizing a paradise in eternity."

17. One of his disciples chopped off his left hand as a token of his consecration of faith,[199] but the Master severely reproved him for doing so, saying, "Your body is the indispensable asset for carrying out practice and public service. How can you think you show your faith by destroying such an important asset? Moreover, true faith and devotion reside in the mind, not in the body; hence no one should ever commit such an act." The Master continued, "No matter how outstanding one's learning and writing may be and how highly one may be revered by the public for an extraordinary feat, it alone is not sufficient for one to succeed to the supreme lineage of this order; only one who dedicates him- or herself to practice and public service in this order with faith and devotion that does not diminish even at the risk of his or her life can succeed."

18. Mun Chŏng-kyu asked, "Song Kyu, Song To-song, and Sŏ Tae-wŏn are now young. Which of the three do you think has more promise for the future?" As the Master kept silent for quite a while, Chŏng-kyu continued, "It is difficult for me to judge as they each have different merits and demerits." The Master said, "Song Kyu is not a person you can measure with your own intellectual capacity. Ever since I met Song Kyu and his brother To-song, I have never been worried about them; there has not been a single thing they did not do when I asked them to do it or a single occasion on which I had to repeat an order for them to carry out. Thus, my mind became their minds and their minds became my mind."

19. The Master said, "The principal sages who will preside over the world come with the special providence of heaven and earth. Hence, if sentient beings dedicate themselves to them and their order, their wishes will come true quickly. If, however, they disrespect or interfere with them, severe punishment may come their way. Furthermore, anyone whose mind functions identically with those of the principal sages can exercise the same power."

---

199. It was Sŏ Tae-wŏn. See Appendix II.

## XI. Aphorisms

1. The Master said, "All scientific learning has limits to its use; however, the training for the right function of one's mind, once completed, has no limits to its use as it is constantly applied in all circumstances. Therefore, the moral training of the mind is basic to all other learning."

2. The Master said, "What the practitioner seeks is to know the essence of mind in order to attain freedom of mind, to know the principle of birth and death in order to transcend them, and to comprehend the principle of transgressions and blessings in order to control them at will."

3. The Master said, "If one's mind is good, whatever one does is good; if one's mind is evil, whatever one does is evil. Therefore, one's mind is the fundamental source of good and evil."

4. The Master said, "If a crook has much money, knowledge, or power, these become the cause for committing evil acts. Only when one's mind is upright can money, knowledge, and power be the conditions of eternal blessings."

5. The Master said, "Good is preferable to evil; however, one can fail to do a major good if one is bound by a minor good. Wisdom is preferable to delusions; however, great wisdom can be hindered if one is stuck with small wisdom. Hence, one can attain greatness provided only that one trains oneself not to be bound by what is small."

6. The Master said, "If one knows of one's own delusion, one will attain wisdom; if one believes oneself to be wise, failing to realize lack of wisdom, one, even if wise for the time being, gradually becomes deluded."

7. The Master said, "One who cultivates the great Way must pursue both concentration and wisdom; however, one should attain true wisdom by grounding it in concentration. A man of enterprise must develop both virtue and talent; however, his talent becomes true talent only when it is based on virtue."

8. The Master said, "A dauntless one is liable to meet a formidable enemy; a talented one is liable to err."

9. The Master said, "A deluded one tries hard to get rid of anxiety and worry when suffering from them but busies him- or herself to produce them when free of them; thus, there is no end to anxiety and worry in the deluded life."

10. The Master said, "One who aspires to attain to the great Way should not expect to attain it in a short time. One cannot go a long distance at a quick pace; one cannot attain the great way if one is impatient. The huge tree is the result of a tiny bud's growth of many years; the attainments of buddhas and bodhisattvas are the results of the devoted efforts they made over long periods without diminishing their initial aspirations and vows."

11. The Master said, "Two *māra* hindrances obstruct one from attaining the great Way: keeping oneself from making progress by giving oneself up without knowing one's own capacity, and keeping oneself from making progress by being complacent and thinking too highly of oneself. One will never attain the great Way unless one shakes off these two *māra* hindrances."

12. The Master said, "A hopeless person is physically alive but spiritually dead. A villain who commits murder, robbery, and adultery can be a buddha or bodhisattva once that person changes his or her mind; however, one in despair has no ability before that person's hope comes around. Therefore, buddhas and bodhisattvas made a vow to give hope to all sentient beings and exert themselves to arouse hope in them throughout endless worlds."

13. The Master said, "There is no real talisman-pearl. If you can get rid of the greed of your mind and can be free from what you desire to do and from what you abhor to do, then you have got the very talisman-pearl."

14. The Master said, "If you want to correct others, you must correct yourself first; if you want to teach others, you must learn first; and if you want to receive favors from others, you must offer favors to others first. If you do so, you will be able to get all you want and cooperate with others in harmony."

15. The Master said, "We may call one strong who overcomes others, but we may call one stronger who overcomes oneself; for the power to overcome everyone under heaven accrues to the one who can ably overcome him- or herself."

16. The Master said, "There are two kinds of deluded people. First is the one who, unable to control his or her own mind, tries to control someone else's mind. Second is the one who, unable to manage his or her own business, tries to meddle with someone else's business and suffers from being involved in the quarrels of other people."

17. The Master said, "There are proper ways one ought to follow when one seeks after something. Since deluded people seek after what they wish without knowing the proper way, the more they seek, the farther what they seek after runs away. As buddhas and bodhisattvas seek after what they wish in accordance with the proper way, what they wish comes their way naturally even though they do not seek after it."

18. The Master said, "One who works first and then eats later is a person of virtue; one who eats first and works later is a mean person."

19. The Master said, "Deluded are those who love to be blessed but hate to strive after virtue, who hate to meet with calamity but love to do evil. This is because the deluded do not know the sources of fortune and misfortune and, even if they know them, they do not act in accordance with what they know."

20. The Master said, "One who amply bestows spiritual, physical, and material favors on others will be blessed in the future; one who feels at ease with his or her place in any circumstance will be peaceful; and one who is content with his or her lot is the wealthiest."

21. The Master said, "Though deluded beings appear to be busy with their own interest, they eventually suffer loss. Though buddhas and bodhisattvas appear foolish to be concerned only with someone else's interest, they eventually benefit themselves."

22. The Master said, "Wise is the one who is faithful to the assigned work without being concerned with his or her position being high or low, for the achievement will shine splendidly as time passes. Deluded is the one who seeks fame and credits without being faithful to the assigned work, for the fame and credits of such a one are eventually brought to nought."

23. The Master said, "One who thinks highly of him- or herself will be humbled, and one who is eager to defeat others will eventually be defeated."

24. The Master said, "The more one's good deed is exposed, the less its merit becomes; and the more one's vice is concealed, the deeper its roots spread. Therefore, the merit of a good deed is augmented when it is concealed, and the treachery of an evil one is diminished when it is exposed.

25. The Master said, "Assistance rendered in secret is a greater virtue [than assistance known to the beneficiary]; and doing harm to someone secretly is a worse evil [than harm known to the victim in advance]."

26. The Master said, "If one is resentful when his or her good deed gets no recognition from other people, the bud of evil grows out of the good deed; the bud of good grows out of an evil deed if one repents after committing it. Therefore, one should not be complacent upon doing a good deed as it can obstruct one's further progress, nor should one be desperate and degraded upon committing an evil."

27. The Master said, "The deluded love to receive things free but do not know that they can be the cause of loss several times greater than what they receive. The wise not only do not love to receive things free but, if things come their way free, they do not keep them to themselves but distribute them to proper places, thus preventing any calamity from coming their way."

28. The Master said, "Since a truthful one harbors no falsehood in his or her mind, whatever that person does turns out to be truthful. Since a sage harbors no antagonism in mind, whatever the sage does turns out to be virtuous. Thus, the truthful one has a mind that is always upright and, hence, free from wickedness; the sage has a mind that is always peaceful and free from suffering."

29. The Master said, "Do not make empty promises that you will give someone something nor exaggerate what you have given to others. Those empty promises and exaggerations become your debt and damage your virtue. Do not make empty vows through the dharma realm; the empty vows with which one cheats the dharma realm become the cause of dreadful suffering."

30. The Master said, "One who has eradicated malice and spite from his or her mind can dissolve malice and spite in someone else's mind."

31. The Master said, "Enmity is the fundamental source of calamity; and amity is the fundamental source of blessedness."

32. The Master said, "One who once committed an evil can have a bright future open as the vicious aura around that person's body dissolves if he or she is truly penitent and accumulates merits and virtues. A dismal future will await one who did good in the past if that person harbors resentments or grudges, which produce a malicious aura around one's body against others."

33. The Master said, "A deluded being turns a benefactor into an object of resentment if the benefactor fails to render a favor just once after rendering it ten times. The cultivator of the Way, however, is grateful to one who has done good just once after doing evil ten times. Thus, deluded beings find harm in favor, bringing forth discord and destruction, while the cultivators of the Way discover favors in harm, bringing forth peace and comfort."

34. The Master said, "A good person teaches the world with good and a vicious person awakens the world with vice; thus, their merits for teaching and awakening are equal. A good person works for the world and is blessed for that, while a vicious person works for the world while committing evil deeds. Hence, we should take pity on a vicious person instead of hating that person."

35. The Master said, "There is nothing to discard under heaven if you know how to make use of it."

36. The Master said, "Saying a few words or writing a line, one can bring hope and peace or despair and misgivings to others. Thus, it is not only because of one's evil temperament that one commits evil, but because of ignorance of the cause of good and evil that one often commits evil without being aware of doing so."

37. The Master said, "To violate the precepts that prohibit one from killing, stealing, and sexual misconduct is to commit a grave offense; however, it is an even worse evil to cause one to lose faith in the correct dharma and thereby close the path toward the eternal future. To give money, clothes, and food in abundance to charity is to do good; however, it is a greater good to help others aspire to have faith in the correct dharma and thereby help open the path for many kalpas of reincarnation."

38. The Master said, "Three kinds of people are past salvation. First is the one who reveres no one as his or her superior. Second is the one who does all things shamelessly. Third is the one who is dead to all sense of shame after committing an evil."

39. The Master said, "A member of an organization who violates its rules destroys it; and one who ignores the public's opinion of the organization violates the will of heaven."

40. The Master said, "Of a special personality is the one who continues being common among the multitude without doing any particular good or demonstrating any particular skill but exerts him- or herself toward realizing the great Way. Such a one will eventually bring forth a great success."

41. The Master said, "The thread of life of a religious order depends for its existence not on establishments or wealth but on the continuous transmission of the wisdom of the dharma."

42. The Master said, "One can attain true liberty only by refraining from self-indulgence, and one can gain a great profit only by ridding oneself of selfish desire. Therefore, one who wants true liberty observes precepts[200] well; and one who seeks a great profit cultivates public spirit."

43. The Master said, "Deluded beings adopt buddhas and bodhisattvas as their field of blessings, and buddhas and bodhisattvas adopt deluded sentient beings as their field of blessings."

44. The Master said, "If one, as a human being, does not understand the vast world of the six realms of existence and four forms of birth, one knows only one side of the world. If one does not understand the principle of promotion and demotion through the six realms of existence and four forms of birth, one knows only what is before one's eyes."

45. The Master said, "One who has not an iota of self in his or her mind owns the triple world in the ten directions."

## XII. Exemplary Practice

1. Once the Master was on his way by sea from the port of Pŏpsŏng to Pongnae Cloister at Puan. There came an unexpected storm, and the vessel was rocking turbulently with the waves. The passengers as well as the sailors were out of their senses, some crying, some vomiting, and some collapsing, thus causing a commotion in the boat. Witnessing this, the Master said with a calm but serious look, "Even in a perilous situation like this, you can be saved by means of the will of heaven if you repent your past evil deeds and pledge to do good in the future. Collect yourselves!" Influenced by his virtue and power, the passengers

---

200. See above, *Canon*, pt. 3, chap. 11, for the precepts.

managed to collect themselves, and after a while, the wind died down and the waves subsided. Seeing his calm and magnanimous air and compassionate and bright posture, they continued to revere the Master.

2. One day the Master visited Silsang-sa, where two old monks, upon bitterly scolding a young novice for not taking their advice for Zen practice, said to the Master, "A person like him cannot be delivered even if a thousand buddhas were to come at the same time; he is a lost spirit." The Master, smiling, said, "Reverends! You did mean to take good care of him, however, it is you that keep him from practicing Zen forever." One of the old monks said, "Why do you say that it is we who keep him from practicing Zen forever?" The Master said, "If you force one to do what that person does not want to do, he or she will hate to do it altogether. If I tell you that there is gold in the rock on the mountain over there and that, therefore, you ought to break the rock to take the gold out of it, would you believe in me and start mining the rock right away?" The old monk, pondering for a while, said, "I would not start mining it simply on the basis of your words." The Master said, "What would you do if I forced you to do it when you have no faith in my words? You would regard my words as much less trustworthy. Likewise, that novice who has neither interest in nor aspiration to Zen practice will have a false idea of it if you force him to do it and, if he does, he will never practice it. Thus, what you are doing is not a skillful means of delivering people." The old monk asked, "What, then, is a skillful means to deliver him?" The Master answered, "If you are sure of there being gold in the rock, you should mine the gold for yourself and make use of it. Then, people may want to know how you became so rich. If you tell them, checking how sincerely they want to know, how gratefully will they try to mine the gold? I think this is a skillful means for delivering people." The old monks, straightening up their postures, said, "What a boundless skillful means you have!"

3. One day at Pongnae Cloister, the Master was not eating the supper being served. His attendants, Kim Nam-ch'ŏn and Song Chŏk-pyŏk, asked the reason. The Master said, "During my stay here, I have been greatly indebted to you both. However, you are going to quarrel with each other tonight and leave here before sunrise; hence I refuse to have supper." The two said, "We are intimate friends. We may get upset for some reason; however, we would not be so upset as to leave here. So, please, have your supper." A few hours later, the two got involved in a quarrel and, losing their tempers, started packing up. Nam-ch'ŏn, remembering the Master's warning, remained in the order observing the Master's teaching the rest of his life, but Chŏk-pyŏk left the next morning.

4. When the headquarters was first built in Iksan county in the ninth year of this order (A.D. 1924), a small taffy business was run for a while

as a means of earning the order's living. The Master always said to his disciples, "In today's world, people's minds are not all well-balanced, so you should lock the gates and take goods into safekeeping lest they be stolen. If they are stolen, we not only suffer the loss but let others commit evil. So, be careful." The Master even provided them with a lock; but the disciples, from lack of experience, did not take sufficient precautions, and the taffy together with the containers was all stolen one night. The disciples were so awe-stricken and worried that they did not know what to do. Seeing this, the Master said, "Don't worry. The one who came to our place last night is a great teacher to you. Though you have faith in me as the most esteemed mentor, you were not sufficiently warned by what I said the other day. From now on you will be careful without my warning. So regard the minor material loss of last night as the tuition for the teacher."

5. One of the disciples, his character and conduct being rude and violent, could not wean himself from the vicious habits of his past even after several years in the order. So some of the disciples said to the Master, "Since it does not seem likely that he will make any improvement even if you keep him under your guidance for one hundred years, he should be sent back home as soon as possible so that the morals of this religious place can be kept pure." The Master said, "How can you say things like that? If he is like that even in this precinct of the order, what would become of him in the secular world? Furthermore, to view this order differently from the secular society is to have a narrow-minded, Hīnayānistic, and self-righteous view. From a broader point of view, social injustice is the very injustice of this order, and the injustice of this order is the very injustice in the secular world. How could it be right for one to try to remove injustice from a Buddhist order into the secular world? The main purpose of Buddha-dharma is to train people toward goodness by all available skillful means. Thus, we will fail to do our duty if we associate ourselves only with good people. Therefore, even if someone cannot easily be changed for the better by your guidance, you should do your best to the last without abandoning him in hatred. Unless he is not fit for this practice and hence chooses to leave, you, as the followers of Buddha-dharma, should not sever the common affinity among those who aspire to attain to buddhahood."

6. One of the disciples violated an article of the order's regulations, so the members of the order met to decide on his expulsion. Seeing this, the Master said, "I wonder how you dared to make such a decision. It is not my intention to expel him. My people are not limited to tens of thousands of followers around me, and this order is not limited to the several acres of establishments; all people in the world are my people, and all the establishments in the world are the precinct of this order. Any one of my followers may leave me, but I will not desert him

or her." Thereafter, the Master called the disciple to him, sometimes scolding him and sometimes admonishing him for his faults. Thus, the Master guided him eventually to reform himself for the better.

7. When the Master was staying at Yŏngsan, a few prostitutes became his followers, occasionally visiting the temple. People around the Master, annoyed by them, said to him, "If those women attend this pure and clean place for dharma practice, other people will laugh at us, and the development of this order will definitely be hindered. We will be better off if you stop them from coming." The Master said with a smile, "You'd better stop such idle talk! The main purpose of Buddha-dharma lies in delivering all sentient beings by means of the spirit of infinite compassion and mercy. Why should they alone be excluded from the general purpose? The gate of deliverance is rather open for such people suffering in misery. Hence, it is our duty to welcome such deluded beings wholeheartedly and help them realize the vice of their lives and feel ashamed of it so that they can discard it themselves. Now, how could we neglect our own duty for fear of other people's ridicule? Some people are high and some low in social standing, and certain occupations are noble and others humble; however, all sentient beings are endowed with the identical Buddha-nature. Anyone, being ignorant of this truth, who dislikes to learn together with such women is more difficult to save than they."

8. After the revolt of the Korean people against Japanese oppression in 1919, public feelings grew sharper, and the surveillance of the Japanese officials upon the Master grew more intense every day. While the Master was staying at Kŭmsan-sa, he was taken to the Kimje police station, where he had to undergo a severe interrogation. While he was staying at Yŏngsan, he was taken to the Yŏnggwang police station, where he had to undergo interrogations for several days. In addition to these, the Master experienced various oppression and restraints in his life. However, he treated his oppressors gracefully, without disliking or hating them. The Master said to his followers, "They are just doing their duty and we have only to do our duty. If what we are doing is right, no one will be able to harm or stop us in the end."

9. A Japanese policeman addressed the Master disrespectfully by his name without the proper honorific form. Seeing this, O Ch'ang-gŏn, feeling indignant at the policeman's disrespect, scolded him bitterly and sent him away. The Master said to Ch'ang-kŏn, "He behaves like that because he does not know me. What is the use of scolding him? One who wishes to transform others by teaching should exert him- or herself to influence them by holding them in hearty obedience. If one knows when to accept defeat, there will be a day to win; if one defeats others where one should not, there will be a day for one to be defeated eventually."

10. Because one of his disciples had disturbing political thoughts,[201] the Master was interrogated by a Japanese policeman for a whole day and was urged to take an oath that he would take care that none of his disciples cause any further trouble. The Master said, "Though parents want to discipline all of their children for the better, they cannot always succeed in doing so because they are different from one another in character and conduct. Though the leaders of a nation desire to better their people, they cannot do so because of the different wishes and thoughts of the people. Likewise, although I exert myself to better my followers, I cannot change them for the better overnight. Therefore, although I will do my best to better them, I cannot take an oath that I shall not have anyone like him from now on." Upon returning, the Master said to an assembly, "For a long time, the strong and the weak have developed antagonism against each other, and there have been severe discriminations among people, so that countless people have built up grudges and resentments against oppression and humiliation. As a result, a great war will break out, and, thereafter, human intelligence will gradually advance so that individuals and nations will help each other, become friends and understand each other; they will not infringe on each other's sovereignty."

11. A man asked the Master, "Could there be one who has seen into his or her original nature in a degenerate world like this?" The Master said, "There should be more sages who have seen their original natures especially in a world like this, shouldn't there?" The man asked further, "Sir, have you really seen into the original nature and attained buddhahood?" The Master said, smiling, "Seeing into one's own nature and attaining buddhahood is not something you do with words, nor can you understand it when it is explained to you in words. Unless you have attained to that realm, you can never comprehend it. One's religious and moral achievement will be attested by all people of later generations under heaven in the future."

12. A police detective was assigned by the Japanese police authority to stay at the headquarters of the order for surveillance of the Master and the order. He stayed for several years. The Master treated him in the same way as he loved and took care of his own beloved disciples. One of his disciples said, "Aren't you doing too much for him?" The Master replied, "Your thought is different from mine. What's wrong with saving him by influencing him for good?" The Master was always concerned about him whether or not he was present and, eventually, he was influenced by the compassionate Master so much that he was led to conversion. Thereafter he rendered various help to the order and was given the dharma name Hwang I-ch'ŏn.

---

201. See Song Pyŏk-cho.

13. When the Master was at Yŏngsan, a policeman of the district police station sent for the Master from a neighboring village, and the Master was about to leave to see him. Seeing this, the disciples around him were indignant at the policeman's insolence, pleading with the Master not to go. The Master said, "Why do you think I should not go and see him?" One of the disciples said, "Although this is indeed the degenerate age when the great sage is not recognized, how could a petty policeman dare to order the great man who guides several hundred disciples to come or go? If you follow his directive, not only will your dignity as the leader be tarnished, but it will be a considerable disgrace to the order." The Master said, "Although what you say makes sense, you need not worry about this matter. I have my own thoughts about it." So saying, the Master went to see the policeman. Upon returning, the Master said to his disciples, "He was awed and satisfied that I answered his summons. Consequently, his desire to oppress has been lessened considerably. If I had not been there, however, he would have felt like oppressing us even more, and the consequence would have been much worse. As you know, the Japanese aggressors are trying to crush any Korean organization. Therefore, it is best to handle a case like this as I did. In general, if you wish to be treated well by others, you must first establish positive achievement worthy of recognition by the world. Then, in proportion to the achievement, you will be received cordially by the public. However, in the mental states of buddhas and bodhisattvas who have attained the honorable position, the idea of such high position does not remain."

14. Some of the new indigenous religious orders in Korea attracted the attention of the government authority and society for improper financial matters and sex scandals. Thus, all religious orders suffered frequent interference and inspections by [Japanese] government authorities. Seeing that there was not even a minor error in our order, they returned saying, "The system, plan, and practice of the Society for the Study of Buddha-dharma[202] are such that they can ably handle even the whole nation if entrusted." Hearing this, the Master said, "Since a truthful religious order has a doctrine that is to help individuals, families, the nation, and the whole world live well, there is no reason why we could not run even the whole world."

15. When the Master was at Seoul Temple, he weeded the garden himself and said, "There are two meanings to my weeding today. One is to set an example to those who are in charge of the temple that they should always put the precinct of the temple in trim order; and the other is to teach that if one does not examine one's mind frequently, worldly thoughts will occupy the mind just as weeds grow thick if an

---

202. The name of this order until 1947, when the name was changed to Won Buddhism.

area is neglected for even a few days. Thus, my action is to show that practice is analogous to weeding the precinct and that one should check one's practice while weeding the precinct and weed the precinct as a way of practice, purifying both the precinct and one's mind. Please, bear these two meanings in mind so that my original purpose should not be forgotten."

16. The Master always kept his belongings neatly arranged so that he could grope for them even in the dark. He kept the area very clean and did not allow dust to collect anywhere it should not, saying, "If the belongings one uses are disorderly, it shows that one's mind is distracted; and if one's area is not clean, it shows that the field of one's mind is coarse. If the mind is coarse and lazy, nothing can be managed properly. How can this matter be regarded as trivial and neglected?"

17. Whenever the Master was leaving his room even for a moment, he locked his stationery case. One of his disciples asked for the reason, and the Master replied, "Since my place of residence is frequented by men and women, young and old, who are immature in moral training as well as people from outside, I am doing this lest they should be tempted to commit evil."

18. The Master did not throw away even a little piece of paper, a pencil stub, or a piece of string, and said, "No matter how plentiful certain things are, one will suffer the karmic retribution of poverty if one wastes them. For instance, one will be reincarnated in a place where water is scarce and suffer from lack of water if one wastes water, even though water is abundant."

19. The Master was never at a loss when he confronted any urgent matter since he always looked ahead and prepared at his leisure for what was going to happen. And since he did not throw away useless articles rashly, having their future use in mind, they were like new and used later in many cases.

20. The Master always warned against luxury beyond one's means in food, clothing, and shelter, and said, "If one gives oneself to extravagance beyond one's means in food, clothing, and shelter, one can ruin both oneself and one's family. Even if one is wealthy, one should not give oneself to luxury because, if one does, wicked thoughts will boil in one's mind, hindering one's religious practice. Therefore, those who are engaged in the religious practice should always choose plainness and simplicity in food, clothing, and shelter."

21. Once the Master got out of the headquarters together with a few disciples through the main gate and a few children playing there all bowed to him except the youngest one. The Master, patting it on its head, said, "If you bow to me, I will give a candy." The child made a bow, and the Master, smiling, continued walking for a while. Then the

Master said suddenly, "Wait here for me just a few minutes; I forgot something." The Master went back to his room and returned with some candies for the child. Giving them to the child, he resumed his walking. Thus, he was always faithful even on a trivial matter.

22. While the Master was ill in bed, a disciple suggested, "A follower in the neighborhood has a comfortable chair. I will bring it for you." The Master said, "Never mind! When the owner is not at home, how would I let you bring it for my own comfort? It is better not to use someone else's belongings, except in circumstances that make it unavoidable, without the owner's spontaneous offer or permission, even if the owner is intimately related to you."

23. When the Master received letters, he always read them and made replies right away. Afterward, he carefully saved some and burned others at a clean place, saying, "Since a letter carries the sincerity of the writer, it is improper to place it carelessly."

24. One day the Master scolded one of his disciples quite severely. When the disciple came back to the Master after a while, the Master received him with the sage countenance of compassion. Seeing this, a disciple beside him asked for the reason. The Master said, "A while ago I scolded him in order to destroy the vicious thought in his mind; now I am trying to strengthen his rectified mind."

25. Yang Ha-un, the Master's wife, took full charge of the private household of the Master before he founded the new religious order, undergoing all kinds of hardships and even more hardships thereafter, toiling and moiling at rice fields and upland fields. His lay followers, feeling sorry for her, were planning to release her from such hard toil by collecting donations from every sector of the order. Hearing of this, the Master said, "Although your opinions sound morally plausible, stop the plan. Now that she is not a personage who can make a direct contribution to the founding of a grand religious order like this, she should not receive help from the general public. Unless she lacks the ability to support herself, she will find it honorable and happy to live by her own ability."

26. Yi Ch'ŏng-ch'un was greatly disillusioned when she happened to see a pair of male and female pigs copulating. Liquidating her worldly belongings, she entered the religious order for practice. While she was devoting herself to practice, she expressed her resolution to offer all of her land to the order. Hearing the offer, the Master said, "Your intention is truly laudable; however, you should think it over since the human mind can change." Although the Master refused the offer several times, Ch'ŏng-ch'un pleaded with him to accept because her original intention had not changed and she was moved by the Master's several refusals. The Master, finally granting her wish, said, "When you

give in charity, cultivate virtue like heaven and earth, which do not abide in the idea of favoring others, so that the merit of your virtuous deed may remain pure in eternity."

27. When the Master visited Maryŏng Temple, O Song-am came to him and said, "My daughters Chong-sun and Chong-t'ae have refused to get married since they became your disciples. Although their refusals displease me, I leave them alone since I cannot alter their minds. Hence, I request that you assume the responsibility for their future." The Master said, "Unlike the traditional Buddhist system, marriage is not prohibited by law in the system of this order. However, how can I be indifferent to those who, with an unusual vow, aspire to pursue the religious practice and public service with the purity of their minds and bodies? Yet their future depends more on their minds than on their parents or their mentor. Therefore, let us do our best to guide them correctly, leaving the final responsibility to them." Song-am stood up and bowed down upon his knees, giving a willing consent to his two daughters' plan to be devotees of this order.

28. When the Master made a trip to Pusan, Im Ch'ilbohwa came to see him and said, "I would very much like to invite you to my house." The Master said, "Although your faith is admirable, would your husband, who is not yet a follower, not mind my visit?" Ch'ilbohwa said, "When I told him of my intention to invite you to dinner and asked whether he would like it, he said, 'Although I am not yet a formal follower as I do not practice the dharma thoroughly, it would be a great honor for us if such a great master would visit us.'" The Master, presuming his affinity with them in former lives, gladly accepted the invitation.

29. A man came to the Master and begged to be accepted as his disciple. The Master said, "Why don't you come once or twice more before you make a decision?" The man said, "My determination is firm. Please, give me your permission right away." The Master, after thinking for a while, gave him the dharma name Ilchi.[203] The man came out of the Master's room and said to the others, "Our affinity in our former lives must have been very special for us all to become disciples of the same master." Upon saying so, the man, announcing that he had good medical pills, urged the disciples to buy and use the pills without any suspicion. When no one bought them, Ilchi said in an angry tone, "How could you treat a fellow disciple so?" He was gone before the sunset.

30. One of the disciples was thatching the roof of a house in the precinct of the order. Since he left the straw thatch without tying it down with straw rope to the roof, the Master asked him, "Won't your

203. Ilchi means "before the sunset" or "only one day."

work come to naught if there is a strong wind overnight?" The disciple, however, left the thatching without tying it, saying, "The wind is not so severe in this area." That night a strong wind arose quite unexpectedly, and the thatch was completely blown off the roof. The disciple was at a loss for what to do, saying, "This disaster is due to my stupidity in going against the warning the Master gave with the precognition of his paranormal power." The Master said, "I only told you the safe and right thing to do, but you did not follow my advice. You are to be blamed more for making a being of divine skill of me. If you think of me as such a being, you will only be looking for mysterious traces in me instead of learning the great truth and correct doctrine. If you do so, you will be lost into a wicked way. I urge you to correct your thoughts and follow only the safe and right course of action."

31. Once when Yi Un-oe was seriously ill, someone from her family came running to the Master and asked for a cure. The Master said, "Send for a doctor right away and let him treat her for her illness." When she was recovered from illness after a few days, the Master said, "When Un-oe was ill a few days ago, it was not right for you to ask me first for the treatment. I am a mentor to cure you of your spiritual illness; my knowledge is primarily of the Way and its virtue. There are medical doctors specializing in each physical illness. From now on, you may consult with me about the cure of spiritual illness; however, you should consult with a medical doctor about the treatment of physical illness. To do so is to know the correct path."

32. When his second son, Kwang-ryŏng, became ill, the Master had someone in the family take good care of him. When he died prematurely, the Master said, "We can only do our best; what is beyond the control of human ability is destiny." And his handling of the order's business and preaching were as usual.

33. When Yi Tong-an died, the Master stood in silent tribute for a minute and tears ran down his cheeks. Seeing this, his disciples comforted him by saying, "Please, don't grieve too much over his death." The Master said, "Though I may not be hurt, I cannot but grieve over his leaving us. From the very beginning of this order, he has given his full support to my intentions and plans with a firm faith in me, and he never minded whether he was put in a high or low position while he was devoting himself to the task of this order."

34. A young dog raised in the precinct of the headquarters was bitten fatally by a huge dog in the neighboring village. As it was giving cries of pain at the point of death, the Master heard it and said with his countenance full of compassion, "To human beings and beasts alike, life is dear and death is feared." When it breathed its last, the Master ordered the one in charge of rituals to observe the seven deliverance services for the spirit of the dog and provided for the expenses.

35. Even though the Master may be kind to everyone, a person might dare not to be cordial; even though he may scold his disciples' misbehavior, none of them would be resentful; and even though he may know that someone is good for nothing, he would not give up on that person.

36. Though the Master warned some of his disciples against talking glibly without practicing, he did not prohibit the disciples from talking. Though he warned them about being talented without being virtuous, he never disregarded the talent.

37. While leading his followers, the Master had four strict prohibitive rules: first, turning a public property into a private use; second, staying home for a long time without justifiable reason after leaving one's own home and entering the order, or running a private business; third, not cooperating with others in public affairs but instead taking one's ease; and fourth, devoting oneself to quiet illumination (spiritual cultivation) in the hope of attaining thereby a paranormal power instead of pursuing the great Way of the threefold practice.[204]

38. The Master had a fivefold standing rule in praising and criticizing his followers in accord with their capacity. The first was to omit praising or criticizing those who do everything correctly; the second was to apply criticism only to those who made minor errors occasionally while doing things right most of the time in order to eliminate even the minor flaws; the third was to apply both praise and criticism to those who did things right or wrong half of the time; the fourth was to apply only praise to those who did things right only occasionally while doing things wrong most of the time, so that their good minds could be acknowledged and encouraged; the fifth was to omit both praising and criticizing those who did things wrong all the time, to wait and see for a while.

39. The Master used to scold those good disciples with firm faith more than necessary for even a minor error; and he scolded those ill-natured with little faith less than necessary and praised them more than necessary even for minor praiseworthy deeds. One of the disciples asked why. The Master said, "One who does nine out of ten actions right but errs once should be helped to correct even the minor error so that his or her moral character can be as pure as pure gold or jade. One who does nine out of ten actions wrong but does one right should be helped to foster the seed of goodness in his or her character."

40. When the Master was about to appoint a person to a post, he used to inquire of the person's faith, public spirit, and practice first, and then knowledge and talent.

---

204. See above, *Canon*, pt. 2, chap. 4.

41. The Master occasionally showed his appreciation for Korean traditional music. When he listened to such operas as *Ch'unhyangjŏn*, *Simch'ŏngjŏn*, and *Hŭngbujŏn*, he praised the grandeur of the heroine's chastity in *Ch'unhyangjŏn*, of the filial piety in *Simch'ŏngjŏn*, and of the brotherly love in *Hŭngbujŏn*. He emphasized the importance of constancy and harmony among people, saying, "The moral principles of loyalty, chastity, filial piety, and brotherly love should be practiced in any era though they may be applied in different forms in different times."

42. If any matter of concern happened in the order, the Master exerted himself with his disciples if it was a matter of work, shared pleasures with them if it was a joyous matter, worried together with them if it was a troublesome matter, and shared sorrow with them if it was a matter of sorrow. While doing so, he did not do anything inhumane, take anything beyond his means, or rely on chance.

43. When the members in the headquarters were called out to labor on a project, the Master was always with them to direct the project, and said, "For you not to neglect the three necessary things for the body [food, clothes, and shelter] as well as the three necessary things for the mind [spiritual cultivation, inquiry into facts and principles, and mindful choice in karmic action], you are called out to labor like this." If anyone was absent without justifiable excuse or anyone was idle at the project, the Master scolded them severely.

44. A man who had traveled widely in the country met the Master and said in admiration, "Of the mountains and rivers I have seen, Mt. Kŭmgang was the most beautiful, and of so many people I have met, I have never seen anyone as great as you, the Master!" The Master said, "Why do you mention only mountains and people? Don't you know that a religious order unprecedented in history under heaven is being established in this country?"

45. When An Ch'ang-ho, better known by his title Tosan, visited the headquarters of this order, the Master welcomed him and acknowledged his patriotic service to the nation. Tosan said, "What I am doing is narrow in scale and short in skill, rendering little benefit to the nation; some compatriots have been persecuted because of me. What you are doing is vast in scale and proficient in skill, contributing greatly to the good cause without putting anyone under restraint or persecution. How great your ability is!"

46. The Master said, "As for talent I lack even a manual skill; as for knowledge, I lack even elementary learning. Why do you believe in and follow me?" However, though he seemed to have no ability, there was nothing he was unable to do, and there was nothing he could not know though he seemed to know little. In transforming sentient beings for the better, his virtue was superior to that of heaven and earth; and in pen-

etrating facts and principles,[205] his wisdom was brighter than the sun and moon.

47. Kim Kwang-sŏn said with a sigh, "Living under his guidance in the order for the past twenty years, I have esteemed and tried to model myself after whatever the Master said and did. I realized, however, that I cannot do one in a thousand. Among so many things I wish I could learn, there are especially three things I am unable to match. First is his pure public spirit; second is his constant sincerity; and third is his magnanimity to tolerate both good and evil. According to my observation, the Master's thoughts and acts, whatever he says and does, reveal only his public spirit and nothing of selfishness. His thoughts, words, and acts are all for the establishment of this order and for nothing else. This is what I deeply admire and wish to learn. To observe the way the Master devotes himself to establish this order, besides his natural endowments being outstanding, the sincerity with which he directed us nine disciples to reclaim the tidal land at Kilyong-ni[206] has not diminished a bit after so many years, and today his sincerity seems to be increasing rather than diminishing. This is what I deeply admire and wish to learn. According to my observation of the Master's guidance of his followers, he admonishes with even more love those who behave detestably, saying, 'Who can't get along well with a good-natured person? To treat with love those who behave detestably is an act of great mercy and the great compassion of the Buddha.' This is what I admire and wish to learn."

## XIII. On the Order

1. The Master said, "The camaraderie between a mentor and a disciple should be as intimate as that between father and son in order for teaching and learning to be effectual. Fellow religious practitioners will not hesitate to give advice and encouragement to each other if the camaraderie between them is as close as that between brothers. Only then can moral sentiment be communicated between them and the practice of using the mind like a buddha or bodhisattva can be shared, so that a powerful team spirit can be formed for one another's religious practice and for public service."

2. At the ceremony for the twelfth anniversary of the order's founding, the Master addressed the assembly: "You have just heard the reports on the achievement of public service and the results of practice in this order for the past twelve years. Now, you may each express what you feel about them." Many disciples came to the front and one after another expressed their thoughts. After listening to all of them, the

---

205. See above, *Canon*, pt. 2, chap. 4, sec. 2.
206. See above, *SS* I:6, 8, for "nine disciples" and the reclamation.

Master said, "Although your remarks are proper in general, there is one important point you have failed to recognize. I will tell you that point. Some of you have associated with me here for many years, others for only a few years. Thus, there arises the difference between senior members and junior members. The point you failed to recognize at this anniversary is that senior members and junior members should be aware of indebtedness to each other, and, therefore, grateful to each other. Ever since they joined the order, the junior members have been able to pursue their practice with the preestablished doctrine at pre-established facilities for which they did not toil because of the merits of the senior members who exerted themselves to establish the facilities with single-hearted devotion. Thus, what could the juniors learn and on what could they depend but for the senior members? Therefore, the junior members should always be grateful to the seniors and pay respect to them. Although the senior members have established the doctrine and facilities with sincere devotion ever since the beginning of the order, what would become of all the efforts of so many years if the junior members did not come to make use of these facilities, revere the doctrine, and manage all the organizations? And how could this order and doctrine be transmitted to the eternal future and how could the endless merits of the devotion be appreciated in the endless world, but for the endless junior members? Therefore, the senior members should welcome and feel grateful to the junior members. If the junior members and senior members always feel this way toward each other, our order will doubtlessly become prosperous without limit and your merits will be transmitted endlessly."

3. When the Master was once in Seoul, several disciples came to see him and said, "We, fellow disciples, are very happy to be born in the same district at the same era and to pursue the practice under the same enlightened master. This is due to a good karmic affinity in our past lives and this affinity will keep us forever from separation." Listening to this, the Master said, "What you have just said makes me pleased on the one hand and worried on the other. It is my pleasure to see that you are getting along well and are happy in my presence. What worries me, however, is that, although you are happy to be together according to a good karmic affinity, a bad karmic affinity could be produced out of this good one." One of the disciples asked, "How could a bad karmic affinity be produced out of such a good one as this?" The Master said, "A bad karmic affinity is created more in a close relationship—such as that between father and son, brothers, spouses, and friends—than in a remote one. In intimate relationships and because of intimacy, one can become careless and fail to observe common courtesy and etiquette, so that the good intention to take care of someone produces resentment and the good intention to teach leaves one open to misunderstanding.

Eventually, the intimate relationship can become worse than that among strangers." One of the disciples asked, "What should be done to prevent anything wrong from arising and to keep our good affinity in eternity?" The Master said, "Do not force others to do what they do not wish to do. Do not think yourself to be superior to others or persist in trying to get the better of your opponent. Learn from the right or wrong actions of others and reflect them in your actions, but never speak of another's faults. Do not try to enjoy the monopoly of the Master's love. Be more respectful to each other as you become closer friends and do not fail to observe due etiquette. If you follow these rules, good affinity will be maintained and the pleasure you share will not change for a long time."

4. The Master said, "If you make contact with people of diverse backgrounds, you will find that each one has a distinctive character. For instance, each individual's uniqueness is formed by the particular doctrine one understands from among many doctrines, by what one has learned from long-term experience, by a particular conception one has formed of a doctrine based on one's viewpoint, or by the particular habit one is born with. If one stands by one's own idiosyncratic character without trying to understand other people's idiosyncrasies, even close friends can offend each other and get into conflicts. One does so because a person with different habits and knowledge may reject, despise, or even hate the other if, first, the other does not know what one knows; second, the other has different customs from one's own; third, there is a generation gap; or, fourth, whatever one has learned in this or past lives is different from that of the other. In short, this happens when one does not know how to tolerate the idiosyncratic characteristics of other people from a broader point of view. Thus, one can be spoken ill of by others even if one is not faulty. For example, though it is said that Devadatta found eighty-four thousand faults with the Buddha, it was not because the Buddha was faulty, but because he could not understand the Buddha because his learning and training were different from those of the Buddha. Such being the case, each of you, being a member of the assembly gathered from various districts with different learning and knowledge, must understand and tolerate the different idiosyncrasies of your fellow practitioners lest you offend each other. Only then can you get along with each other."

5. The Master said to his disciples, "No noise is produced by people or things when they are separated from each other. However, a certain sound is produced when they come close and make contact with each other. Metallic sound is produced when metals contact metals, and a stone sound is produced when rocks hit each other. Likewise, the voice of justice will be heard when righteous people make contact with each other, while a vicious voice will be heard when wicked people get

together. Look! The voices of merciful and compassionate sages of ancient times are still ringing in the ears of all sentient beings although thousands of years have passed since they founded their orders. Too, the voices of the wicked are still infecting the minds of millions of people. As a certain sound is sure to be produced by you who are gathered here to work together, be careful to produce only good sound in eternity. If so, it will not only be a great fortune for you but an auspicious event for the whole world."

6. The Master said, "The value of one's activity in the world is proportional to the magnitude of the work undertaken with a given personality and effort. Depending on the scope of the work, the life of its undertaking continues in the history of humankind. To speak of the magnitude of public service, one's service could be extended to one's private household, to one's nation or country, or to the whole world. To speak of the life of public service, some efforts can last several decades, some several hundred years, some for thousands of years, and some for eternity. Thus, the magnitude and length of public service depend on the condition of the undertaking. Now, the greatest undertaking in magnitude and longevity is the religious mission, for a religious mission has no national boundary or term of service. When the Buddha Śākyamuni with his twelve hundred disciples begged alms from door to door, when Confucius traveled around from state to state without being hired by any king, and when Jesus walked about with the twelve apostles, their influence was trifling. Today, however, their doctrines have spread all over the world, shining more and more brilliantly as time passes. Since you have entered this order as devotees, I want you to be the leaders of the greatest and longest-lasting undertaking by understanding the value of the religious mission and exerting endless effort for it."

7. The Master said, "A devotee (chŏnmu ch'ulsin) in this order is one who has consecrated his or her mind and body for the public well-being, and, hence, it is a devotee's obligation to exert him- or herself to public service, ignoring personal fame, privilege, and avarice. It is regrettable to observe, however, that some of you, having forgotten the devotee's original resolution and being given to faultfinding, bear grudges against others, and doubt the teacher and the correct doctrine of the order; and your original altruistic resolution is gradually changing into egoistic thoughts. Your initial vow was to do good for pure blessedness and to cultivate the deeds of a bodhisattva among deluded beings; however, some of you commit evil where you are supposed to do good for blessedness and let delusions grow while cultivating the way of the bodhisattva. If so, the evil karma will be much worse than that in the secular world. How could this not be dreaded? You should always examine your mind against what I have just said to see whether you are a devotee to serve others or a devotee who expects others to serve you.

If you are a devotee serving others, continue the good work; if you are a devotee expecting others to serve you, then you ought to change your mind; if you cannot, you had better return to your home lest the dreadful karma be piled up on you."

8. Noticing that Chŏng Yang-sŏn and others were emaciated as a result of devotion to hard work in the kitchen, the Master said, "You must be getting emaciated as a result of toilsome work. The way you do toilsome work for the religious practice and public service in this order, working at a factory, in a kitchen, or a production department, can be compared to refining iron at a smithy, where various useful tools are made after the iron is refined of impure material. You can attain bodhisattvahood, as pure as pure gold with all the impure elements gone, only if you attain the three great powers[207] in such a difficult condition. Since an outstanding personality cannot be attained without training in difficult conditions, just as pure wrought iron cannot be made without the heat of the forge, you should understand this point and thereby live in peace and bliss."

9. One of the disciples asked, "There is a saying that those who will be reincarnated into yellowish-brown serpents will be found more among the priests of the degenerate age than among the laity. Why will that be?" The Master said, "A vice committed by a layperson generally affects an individual or a family, but the vice of a priest who does not lead the laity right can ruin their lives for many reincarnations. The suit and bowl of rice a priest takes are the result of a peasant's blood and a woman weaver's sweat. If a priest lives an idle life without doing what he or she is supposed to do, therefore, it will be the same as sucking all the juice from the life's blood of the people. Furthermore, if the priest, being aware of indebtedness to the fourfold beneficence,[208] does not recompense for its sources, he will be the one who is ungrateful to one's family, society, nation, and the world. This may sound unreasonable to some; however, what I have just said is not unreasonable. Therefore, you should often examine yourselves against your initial aspiration and exert yourselves in order to safeguard against failure."

10. The Master said, "We should never become 'demons of sweat and blood.' Those are called 'demons of sweat and blood' who, using their position and power or trickery, squeeze the property out of the people of lower position without paying the due price, the property they earned by toiling and moiling. Those are also called 'demons of sweat and blood' who attempt to live comfortably by depending on relatives or friends for food and clothing. Hence, we should always examine our

---

207. The powers of spiritual cultivation, inquiry into facts and principles, and mindful choice in karmic action. See above, *Canon*, pt. 2, chap. 4, for details.
208. See above, *Canon*, pt. 2, chap. 2, for details.

lives to see how much public service we render daily to deserve this livelihood. We may feel easy if we have rendered sufficient public service to deserve this livelihood. If we attempt to live a comfortable life under the pretense of public service, we will be getting into heavy debt for eternity and will be unable to avoid being 'demons of sweat and blood.' We should awaken ourselves to this."

11. Once at Seoul Temple, the Master asked Yi Wan-ch'ŏl to carry a load on an A-frame on his back to the Seoul railway station, but Wan-ch'ŏl said, "I feel awkward about doing this because it will damage my dignity as the dharma master of this temple and as the supervisor of a dozen laborers hired for repair work on the temple building." So the Master had O Ch'ang-gŏn carry it to the station. Upon returning from the station, the Master asked Wan-ch'ŏl, "What do you think of your handling of the matter a while back?" Wan-ch'ŏl said, "I don't think there was anything terribly wrong about it." The Master said, "You should. If you, being ashamed of carrying a load on your back, dare to disobey your mentor's order, and you do not think of it as a grave mistake, how can you claim to be a devotee and how can one expect you to be a dharma master to deliver all sentient beings? If you cannot do away with such delusive thought, you had better return to your home." As the Master reproved Wan-ch'ŏl in these words, Wan-ch'ŏl apologized for his mistakes and thereafter exerted himself to the religious practice without concern for his dignity.

12. A disciple in charge of the vegetable field belonging to the order caught a great many white grubs at the vegetable field; these he dried and sold to an herbal medicine shop for a sizable sum of money. Another disciple, his supervisor, reported this matter to the Master, saying, "Since this is extra income and since he is in need of clothes, would it be all right if I buy him some clothes with the money?" The Master said, "Although it is extra income, it should be returned to the public fund since it was earned while he was working in the public service. Furthermore, since the money was made by taking so many lives, the karmic retribution will be harsh if you buy him clothes with the money although the killing was not without justification." The Master granted a suit of Korean clothes for him, saying, "Use the money for the benefit of the general public so that he can be free from evil karmic retribution."

13. A disciple responsible for taking care of an orchard belonging to the order had to kill myriad insects with insecticide. As he felt very uneasy about it, he expressed his worry to the Master. The Master said, "You can exert yourself for the public service without fearing the karmic retribution a bit; it will not fall on you. However, if you satisfy your selfish interest out of this work even a little bit, you will be unable to escape the harsh karmic retribution."

14. When one of the disciples living in the vicinity of the headquarters of the order took such trivial things as twigs of firewood to his home, the Master said, "The household of the order, no matter how poor it may be, will not be affected by a few twigs of wood or a few nails. However, if you appropriate the public property that many people have donated to the order, you will suffer from unexpected calamity, losing many times more than what you take. I am warning you in advance against such calamity."

15. The Master asked, "What do you think of the idea that the order establish a system to help devotees whose households suffer from poverty so that such people can devote themselves to the public work without being distracted by concern for their own household? Chŏn Ŭm-gwang replied, "I think that such a system should be established." The Master asked again, "If, at this time when such a system has not been established, a devotee's household has reached a level of destitution such that we cannot bear to witness the misery, what should be done?" Sŏ Tae-wŏn replied, "If the devotee is an ordinary staff member, he or she may be sent back home for a limited period of time to take care of the household. If the devotee holds an important position in the order, it seems desirable that the order decide to help his or her household temporarily." The Master asked further, "What should be done if the number of devotees who need help increases in the future when such a system becomes effective?" Yu Hŏ-il replied, "To solve such problems, there should be established in the headquarters an organization to guide and help the devotees' households." The Master said, "The things you three have said are all good, and we may try to establish and apply such a system gradually. However, at the moment, when the order cannot afford to do so, there shall not be any devotee in active service who should be attending to his or her own household even if the organization of the order may be expanded only on a limited scale."

16. The Master said, "Under the system of devotees in this order, one can pursue the religious practice and public service either as a married person or as a celibate person, male or female, with special aspirations and vows discarding worldly desires. Thus, the order accepts devotees in accordance with the order's regulations and the wishes of the applicants. If, however, one, without special aspirations and vows, leads a celibate life either because one is forced by particular circumstances or because one desires to be free from the burdens of worldly life, while envying the pleasure of the worldly life, it is a great loss to that person, to the order, and to the world. Moreover, in one's next rebirth, one will be born a good-looking person, but will be made an object of ridicule. Therefore, if one is not confident of celibacy, one should make a right decision again. And if one is on the way with a firm

conviction, one should keep one's integrity unsullied in order to realize one's original aspiration to purify the mundane world and open the gates of wisdom and blessedness for all sentient beings."

17. The Master often took care of the male and female celibate disciples, saying, "If you live just this one life with pure heart for the order and the world, discarding desires for wealth, sex, fame, and gain, it will be much greater in value than many lives you might live for your household in the mundane world. You will gain pure blessedness and honor in many reincarnations for the merits of this one life, eventually attaining the great result of buddhahood. If you live the celibate life only in name without accomplishing true merits, your life will be in vain. Be intent on your religious practice."

18. The Master said, "When one submits an application to become a devotee, one should think about it very carefully. If, after taking a vow in front of the empty dharma realm and the public that one would consecrate oneself to the religious practice and public service in this order, one changes one's mind halfway and goes into private business and hedonism, this amounts to deceiving heaven and earth and, hence, one will not be forgiven by Truth, and one's way will be blocked. One should be careful when one stands in a position to guide people. If one misleads the general public by claiming falsely that one has attained the great enlightenment, this also amounts to deceiving the Truth and, thus, one will not escape from falling into the evil path [of beasts, hungry ghosts, and hells]."

19. The Master said to his disciples, "What we do is like what the wild geese do. Just as the wild geese flock together and move to north or south to open a place to roost in accordance with different seasons, we gather together from the east or the west, answering the call of the times, in accordance with our affinities from our past lives. If any goose goes astray from the line led by the leader or becomes careless in the line, however, it can be caught in a net or shot dead by a bullet. The net and bullet, to one who cultivates the Way and transforms people for the better with religious truth, are the conditions of wealth and sex."

20. The Master said, "The intrepid lion or tiger can be killed by such a trifle as mange if it spreads over their bodies. Likewise, one who pursues the religious practice with a great aspiration can have his or her life plan spoiled by a few minor spiritual ills that, like mange, block that person's initial aspirations. Hence, one who pursues the religious practice should always guard against the spiritual mange before it starts infesting one's moral life. Now, let me give you some examples of mental mange. One develops spiritual mange if, first, one feels regretful to hear one's mentor's public admonition, thinking that the admonition was especially directed to oneself; second, one forgets one's purpose of joining the order and seeks in the order the warm treatment one can

expect at home; third, one acts against friends' advice, let alone finding a paragon therein, and confronts with hostility whomever one meets, even thinking the advisor to be one's foe; fourth, as one wins higher position and public confidence, pride gradually swells in one's mind; fifth, one seeks favors from everybody in the public and tries to make oneself comfortable at the expense of others; sixth, one is resentful of the leader and fellows for being unsympathetic, while one's own mind and words are careless; and seventh, the more one is cared for by others, the less one is satisfied, thus acquiring a bad habit. Though none of these mental ills is an atrocious evil, it can be a mental mange that can disturb the zeal of the religious practitioner. Mind that no such mental mange hide in you."

21. When one of the disciples, being appointed a *kyomu*, was leaving for a branch temple of this order, the Master said, "I feel that I have so far left you alone without taking as much care of you as others. I hope you don't feel that I have neglected you. In general, to get a good crop, a farmer pays much more attention to a dry field that is poor in soil but weedy than to one that has rich soil and no weeds. Likewise, some people should be given admonitions and advice quite often, while some others need not be admonished or advised so often. So, don't feel that you have been neglected."

22. Upon returning to Pongnae Cloister from Yŏngsan, the Master said to his disciples, "On my way back, I happened to take a look around a market. In the morning, an earthenware dealer was coming to the market with a load of earthenware on an A-frame on his back while another man was coming with an empty A-frame on his back. When they were returning home, the earthenware dealer, having sold his wares, was going with an empty A-frame on his back, while the man who had come with an empty A-frame on his back was going with earthenware he bought. Now, I could tell from their looks that both men were contented. When the two men came to the market, neither of them came for the sake of the other, and yet both were happy as they obtained what they each wanted. From this I found a principle that we humans depend on one another and each becomes the ground of the other for existence. I also saw a man who got angry at a storekeeper's arrogance and returned without buying what he needed, and the people there laughed at him, saying that he came to the store for warm reception from the storekeeper rather than for shopping. Another man just bought what he needed, ignoring the storekeeper's manner, and the people there praised him for being a man who takes pudding rather than praise. While I was watching these scenes, the communal life you lead in the order came to my mind in comparison with what I saw and heard, making me smile and sigh. I want you to comprehend what this story implies."

23. The Master said, "It is fortunate that you have found this religious order. However, as this is an assembly of people with diverse habits and learning and since only a great person can understand another great person, there are a few who leave the order when they unsuccessfully confront a minor trial. Such a person is like a blind person who gets hold of the doorknob by sheer luck but turns away in anger when he or she stumbles over the threshold, thus getting into the way of those wandering by. A blind one takes all the necessary precautions against odds because that person knows about blindness. One whose mind's eye is blind, however, falls into a deep pit because such a one does not know that he or she is mentally blind. Thus, it is dangerous to be mentally blind."

24. The Master said, "It has been many years since I opened a wholesale store and started business. However, I have gained little profit because I have given goods to many retailers on credit. Only a few retailers sold the goods and paid me back, making considerable profits for themselves. Most of the retailers did not sell the goods, storing them in their houses and then bringing them back after a while. Many retailers lost the goods and did not pay me back for them. Thus, I have suffered a great loss. From now on, however, I will commend, and supply with more goods, only those who sell the goods well, making profits for themselves and paying me back for the goods. I will scold those who bring the goods back and take to the court of law those who lose the goods and do not pay for the loss." The Master then asked, "Do you understand what I mean by this analogy?" One of the disciples said, "By the analogy of opening a new store you mean that you have founded a new religious order. By saying that the retailer pays you back and makes considerable profit, you mean that your disciples, upon listening to your dharma teachings, propagate your teachings well and get great benefit by practicing them. By saying that some retailers return the goods, you mean that some of your disciples do not practice what they have learned though they have not forgotten them. By saying that some retailers have lost the goods and do not pay for the goods, you mean that some of your disciples, upon learning your teachings, never propagate the teachings, never practice them, and even forget all the teachings. By saying that you will have the court of law take care of the matter, you mean that, since some of your disciples, upon listening to your teachings, never practice and even forget all the teachings, they will certainly commit wrongdoing and suffer the consequences." The Master said, "You have got it right."

25. On a New Year's Day, the Master said to an assembly, "In my dream last night, I met a man of unusual ability and he was saying, 'This order will no doubt grow in great prosperity but it worries me that, as the order expands its power, its members may look down upon

other people and other organizations. So, you should warn your followers in advance.' Although dreams are unreliable, my dream last night seems to have a message especially because it was so clear and it happened on a New Year's Eve. Hence, never lose the sense of respect no matter whom you meet and never be contemptuous of anyone since a person of the humblest station has the power to render help to the growth of this order or to do damage to it. In this way you should handle all situations. This will have a great effect on the future of this order."

26. A newspaper carried an article in which this order was commended, and members of the order all rejoiced over the good news. Seeing this, the Master said, "When there are people who commend, there are also people who slander. As the order grows in prosperity and fame, there will be people who become jealous of us. Being aware of this point in advance, you should keep doing carefully what is right without being moved by commendation or slander."

27. The Master said, "One who intends to accomplish something great in the world will face hardships and troubles proportionate to the scale of the task. Buddhas, bodhisattvas, sages, and other great figures through all ages underwent all sorts of hardships before they succeeded in their tasks. The Buddha Śākyamuni, discarding all the glories of a prince, left the royal palace for a mendicant life and underwent six years of ascetic practice and self-mortification until his great enlightenment. Even after the establishment of his order, he experienced all sorts of difficulties; one of his disciples was persecuted by the heretics. The great teachings of the Buddha, however, have been transmitted through his disciples until today, and he and his teachings are worshiped by numberless sentient beings. Confucius suffered all sorts of hardships while he was wandering from state to state to establish in those states the moral principles he rectified in the *Ch'un-ch'iu*.[209] Once he was called 'a dog in a funeral house.' He suffered the disturbance of Chen Tsai. Through his disciples' continuous endeavors, however, the Confucian morality and law and order were firmly established, and Confucius is respected today as a great sage of the world. Jesus, too, had to suffer all sorts of persecutions and false incrimination while he was spreading his gospel, eventually being crucified. However, his teaching has spread all over the world through the hard work of his disciples. Since we have to work to realize our goal in a stormy world like this, how could we expect to be free from criticism and trouble? So far we have been free from any severe censure or oppression; however, it is possible that the order's reputation may be damaged by some members'

---

209. The book attributed to Confucius—the *Spring and Autumn Annals* or the *Annals of the State of Lu* (722–484 B.C.).

mistakes as the order gradually grows in number of followers and amount of work to be done. If the purpose of our order is truly to benefit the world and if our mission is necessary for delivering sentient beings and curing the world of moral illness, however, our order will not be damaged by the mistakes of a few members or by the failure of a few tasks. Even if the order were to suffer from calumny and persecutions, the true nature of this order will eventually be revealed. This can be compared to a mountain that, though hidden behind the fog for a while, appears even more clearly when the fog clears. Therefore, if you exert yourselves with clear conscience to the achievement of our goal without being distracted by any hardships and troubles, it is my firm belief that our great task will be accomplished perfectly."

28. The Master said, "There are three causes of failure in any enterprise. The first is to wish a quick, great success without exerting effort to the undertaking. The second is to handle the task rashly without knowing the roots and branches or what is first and what is second. The third is to adhere to trivial failure or profit before the completion of the undertaking, thus undermining the ground of success. Anyone who manages an undertaking should always be careful about these three points."

29. The industrial center of the order was engaged in chicken raising with the support of the county authority. One day the water heater in the pen broke and many chickens were killed. The one in charge of the chickens was alarmed and reported the accident to the county authority right away. Hearing the report, the official in charge said, "If you wish to succeed in chicken raising in the future, you should be prepared to face much greater accidents than this one. When you do chicken raising on a large scale, you sometimes suffer a great loss from an unexpected accident and calamity; and there are numerous ways to revive the chickens. Unless you experience failure on a small scale, you may not be able to prevent failure on a large scale. Thus, a minor loss at this time will be a living lesson for you to prevent a great loss in the future. So, don't be discouraged, and keep up your good work." The disciple, returning from the county office, reported to the Master, who said, "The words of the official in charge are a sermon. Besides the old saying, 'Experience is a good teacher,' this minor failure will be a model for great success in the future. This is not merely a lesson for chicken raising. While you pursue the religious practice and public service in our order, you must check to examine the causes of success and failure whenever a task is well accomplished or ends in failure. We must watch the movements of other religions to learn when they are accepted and when they are rejected by the world. We must learn further how they make their orders shine eternally in the history of humankind and how they become notorious, leaving stains there. If we continue doing only

what is right, reflecting on and correcting ourselves, we will be able to benefit individuals, families, societies, and the nation so that our order will be an exemplary one welcomed by all. If, however, we do not check ourselves, managing matters rashly, all sorts of faults will be committed, and our order will be rejected by the word. How can we afford to be careless?"

30. The Master said, "It is a natural law that nothing grows great unless it grows out of something small. Thus, anything great in the world must have grown out of something small. If we examine the histories of all great religions, their influences were weak at their initial stages. Their influences gradually grew as time passed on, and they became today's great religions. All other great enterprises, too, are nothing but accumulations of small things and powers. If we exert our selfless efforts to the foundation and development of this order following the principle that to accomplish something great one must start with something small, then, eventually, this order will be a great influence in the world even when the order does little. The same principle applies to the religious practice. If you patiently follows the correct steps of practice in accordance with the mentor's directions, you will eventually succeed in attaining the great Way. If, on the other hand, you plot for a rapid expansion of the order or if you try to attain great power of the Way by a partial intensive cultivation in a short time, it is nothing but a deluded desire and contrary to reason. You will be wasting your time and energy, no matter how hard you may try. Thus, I hope that you achieve your goal in the religious practice, in public service, or in any other undertaking, following the principle that to accomplish something great one must start with something small, and without being distracted by the desire to accomplish it overnight or by vanity."

31. The Master said, "There is a principle that, when one is to be charged with a great task, one is first tested by heaven. If one is to be hired for a day's work or for a whole year, one's qualification and credibility are examined; how much more should one be tested when heaven is to charge one with the greatest task under heaven? Hence, one who wishes to accomplish a great task should take care to pass this test."

32. The Master said, "When a great religious order is to be established, it is necessary for the founder to find someone with talent, knowledge, and wealth. However, such a person can only play the role of the fence of a house. It is more important to find someone who is a true person of sincerity and devotion even if dull and ignorant. Such a person will be a truly devoted leader of the order and successful in all things he or she does."

33. At a regular dharma meeting, the Master addressed the assembly: "Today I will distinguish between a founder and a subversive of this

order. So listen carefully. The founder of the order is one who exerts efforts with mind and body, or makes donations with material things, to this order; makes indirect contribution to the development of the order by attending the dharma meeting regularly and thereby becoming an exemplar to others; participates in the regular-term training sincerely; makes use of the dharma in daily life with a thorough knowledge of the doctrine and system of the order, which one attains through the diligent study of the scriptures at home. A subversive of the order is one who causes much damage to the order spiritually, physically, or materially; interferes with the development of the order and hurts the order's reputation by acting as he or she pleases; does harm to him- or herself and others without doing anything beneficial; violates the precepts rashly because of his or her inability to correct old habits as the result of having little interest in the dharma meeting and in the regular-term training. You should exert yourselves to accumulate the merits of the honorable and eternal founder by clearly understanding the difference between a founder and a subversive. Never be a subversive element."

34. The Master said, "Though there can be many ways by which one can contribute to the founding of this order, I am listing the following eleven essential points, by which all the founding merits shall be assessed. The first is to devote one's mind and body totally to the order. The second is to donate material abundantly. The third is to be constant in one's religious faith from the time of initiation. The fourth is to add explanatory notes to the scriptures and record sermons to a great extent. The fifth is to observe the regulations and precepts of the order well. The sixth is to make fellow members of the order happy by all good means so that they may make progress in the religious practice and public service. The seventh is to do all one can to develop this order. The eighth is to advocate public spirit. The ninth is not to abide in the idea of having done good to others. The tenth is to rectify oneself, especially if one is notorious for vice, upon becoming a follower of the order and thereby become an exemplar to caution and encourage others. The eleventh, which applies especially to one with reputation in the world, is to become a follower of the order whereby others are encouraged, making this order visible to the world."

35. Hwang Chŏngsinhaeng asked, "The Buddha taught that one should give to charity without abiding in the idea of giving,[210] and Jesus taught that one should not let the left hand know what the right hand gives. Since you record the merit of public service of all followers in

---

210. See *Chin-kang po-jo po-lo-ching*, *T*, 235.8.749a: Subhuti, thus a bodhisattva should give charity without a mind abiding in false notions of form. Why? Because if a bodhisattva's mind does not abide in forms when practicing charity, his merit will be inconceivable and immeasurable.

accord with the criteria of merit you have established, won't this be the cause of scheming in the minds of those who render public service?" The Master replied, "Although those who pursue public service should do so without abiding in the idea of doing so for the accumulation of pure merit, those who should honor and commend acts of charity must evaluate correctly."

36. The Master said to his disciples, "Be the owners of public affairs! It has been a traditional practice for one to leave one's private household or business to one's children. The public establishments and enterprises are to be inherited by one who works only for the public well-being with public spirit. If you, understanding this principle, foster public spirit, you will be the owner of all the establishments, institutions, and honors of this order. Since this order is public property, which should be managed by people of high virtue and public spirit, you should exert yourselves to be the masters of public spirit."

37. The Master delivered a precautionary instruction to the assembly of *kyomu*: "You should be aware of and grateful to the greatness and importance of the fourfold beneficence[211] in this turbulent period and should guide the followers of this order to have a sound and faithful spirit by helping them understand it. Recently, some religious orders in this country [Korea] have often squeezed properties out of their followers, letting them neglect their households and thereby having a bad influence on society. As a consequence, they were so severely censured by the public that they could not survive. You should guide our adherents to attend to their occupations in such a way that they can improve their lives through faith in and practice of the teachings of this order. As the strict wall between men and women has long been fallen in accordance with the changing current of the world, there is no need to erect it again; however, the comradeship should be maintained with extreme care so that the dignity of the order is not damaged. The destiny of our order will depend on whether these three conditions are satisfied or not. So, bear in mind what I have said."

38. The Master delivered a precautionary instruction to the assembly of *kyomu*: "One who is to preach and convert people ought to be honest and clean-handed in giving and taking monies; be exact and prompt in settling the accounts of the public fund; be unmoved by any groundless rumors; abstain from commenting rashly on the political conditions of the times; abstain from speaking ill of other religions and the objects of their worship; abstain from revealing the faults of the followers; harmonize with all followers by avoiding conceit and excessive condescension; be particularly careful about male and female relations; be gener-

---

211. See above, *Canon*, pt. 2, chap. 2, for the details of fourfold beneficence.

ous in revealing the merits of others and never exaggerating one's own merit; abstain from directing the follower's faith exclusively to oneself; be careful to keep the spirit of public service from being limited to a district; and bear in mind that a *kyomu* at a branch temple represents the head dharma master of the order and, hence, fulfill one's duty with full qualification thereof."

39. At the end of a fiscal year, the Master used to order Cho Kap-chong and others to submit a correct statement of the accounts for the year and the budget for the new fiscal year and audit it, saying, "If the income and expenditure of a household, an organization, or a nation are not balanced, the household, the organization, or the nation cannot prosper. In the past, one was not supposed to be a truly religious person if one argued about property. As the spirit and flesh in the new world should be perfectly balanced, so, at each branch temple as well as at the headquarters of the order, the income and expenditures should be checked in an account book so that neither spiritual nor physical life may be defective. To carry out this goal effectively, it is made part of the order's system that the grading scale is set for evaluating not only the progress of the religious practice but also the amount of the public service."

40. The Master said to the assembly of *kyomu*; "When you preach or write on behalf of sentient beings, do not say or write, aiming at winning their favors, an empty theory that cannot be practiced in daily life or difficult words of exaggeration, sophistication, and mystery or words that will cause them to do partial practice. Such words can neither be useful to the world nor effective in helping to produce enlightened beings of the Way."

41. The Master said, "One who guides the mass of people should always check the direction of their spirit thoroughly. If there appears any sign of decay in the public morals, the guide should inquire how to correct it, exerting him- or herself to rectify it either by preaching or by deeds as may be necessary. If the general public reveals a reluctance to labor, for instance, the guide should turn the tendency by engaging in labor. To a person who is conceited and constantly strives after fame and riches, the guide must demonstrate modesty and humility in deeds so that such a conceited person may feel ashamed of his or her conceit. Thus, prevention in advance and rectification afterward are the skillful means of a bodhisattva to transform sentient beings by teaching."

42. The Master said, "To establish a new religious order in any age, it is important to have a doctrine and system superior to those of the previous ones; however, it cannot succeed in being firmly established if it cannot find like-minded comrades who will apply the doctrine and system widely. Thus, in the order of the Buddha in ancient times, the

ten chief disciples[212] of Śākyamuni, among twelve hundred followers, each played the role of exemplar according to his particular powers or gifts. When the Buddha delivered a sermon, it was the ten disciples who first put the teaching into practice and encouraged others so that the great masses were gradually influenced by their exemplary conduct, eventually establishing the great order at Gṛdrakūṭa. To give an example of how the ten disciples transformed others by exemplary conduct: When one of the disciples committed an evil deed and a direct accusation seemed to bring about a countereffect, a few of the ten disciples discussed an indirect approach. One of the few committed the same evil as the one committed by the culprit, and the other summoned him and gave him a severe admonition; the latter confessed the guilt in the presence of the culprit and pledged not to commit the wrong again. Eventually, the wrongdoer was influenced to repent and to rectify his life. This was one of the skillful means the ten disciples used to edify others with the Buddha's teachings. To guide the masses, they sometimes pretended not to know what they knew and to have done wrong though they did right. Sometimes, they, though never greedy, pretended to have changed themselves from selfish to unselfish persons; sometimes, they, free from love and lust, pretended to be slaves to love and lust and then to change themselves to be free from them. Thus, overtly and covertly, as parents raise their children or a hen broods her eggs, the ten disciples did all sorts of merciful and compassionate deeds so that they saved the Buddha a great deal of trouble and the great masses were able to be transformed for the better by the teachings of the Buddha. How great their compassion was and how vast their merits were! Now, you, too, should model yourselves after what the ten disciples did so that you can be the leaders and the central figures in establishing this order."

## XIV. Prospects

1. The Master said, "When the world enters into the degenerate and troublesome era, a great savior sage with a truthful doctrine potent enough to rule the world appears of necessity, rectifies the world, and harmonizes the spirit of humankind by redirecting the energy of heaven and earth."

2. Upon the great enlightenment on April 28, 1916, the Master composed numerous odes and poems in Chinese characters, which he

---

212. Each of them was master of one power or gift: Śāriputra of wisdom, Maudgalyāyana of supernatural powers, Mahākāśyapa of discipline, Aniruddha of deva vision, Subhūti of explaining the void, Pūrṇa of expounding the law, Kātyāyana of its fundamental principles, Upāli of maintaining rules, Rāhula of the esoteric, and Ānanda of hearing and remembering.

collected in a booklet and called *Pŏbŭi taejŏn* [A complete work of the interpretation of the doctrine]. Though the purport was too profound and mysterious for an ordinary intelligence to comprehend, the gist of the work was that the vein of true dharma, which had disappeared for a while, was appearing again; and that the general trend of the world is such that when unreasonable times are gone, reasonable times are sure to follow. He also wrote of how he would establish a new religious order. Afterward, he burned the book himself to keep it from being handed down to posterity. However, the first phrase of the introduction and the following eleven stanzas have come down in recitation.

> The fundamental truth, which has been since the opening of
> heaven and earth by T'ai-chi, descends upon the mind of one
> who abandons the yin (dark) era, which is gone, and takes
> over the yang (bright) era, which is approaching.
>
> Having trodden ten thousand valleys and a thousand
>           mountain peaks,
> I have met a host devoid of any trace of worldliness.
>
> As wild grass grows on the beneficence of rain and dew,
> The returning fortune of heaven and earth awaits one with
>           rectified mind.
>
> When an arrow pierces the bright sun in the heaven,
> Five colored clouds burst from the hole, surrounding one's
>           body.
>
> For a hermit riding on a cloud who was looking for an
>           enchanted land,
> The world of universal harmony and serenity was the best.
>
> The river ten thousand *ri* long is filled with the meaning of
>           the world;
> Mountains and rivers, yin and yang, are harmonized with
>           their origin in the Tao.
>
> What kind of place is the district of Honam?
> It is the best of the beautiful lands under heaven.
>
> The angles of heaven and earth are measured with a ruler,
> And those measurements dispatched cloth to humanity.
>
> All things in the universe mature in its womb;
> The presence of the sun and the moon harmonize day and
>           night.
>
> Heaven and earth tremble as a wind is blown into the empty
>           sky;

All countries become brightened as the moon hangs in the
    east.

When rain and wind, snow and frost have passed,
Flowers bloom at a time and spring stays for ever.

By training in the Way, the mind is as graceful as the moon
    above a thousand peaks;
By cultivating virtue, the body is as rich as a ship loaded with
    ten thousand bags.[213]

3. Because one of the disciples was holding only the Chinese language in esteem, the Master warned, "The attainment of moral perfection does not require of one a mastery of any particular language. Hence, you should let go of that false conviction. From now on, all the scriptures should be written in a language that the general public can understand. In the near future, people all over the world will translate the scriptures written in Korean into their languages and learn the teaching of this order. Thus, do not hold in esteem only the Chinese language, which is difficult to learn."

4. When the Master first constructed a few thatched houses for the

---

213. These lines can be understood as verses Sot'aesan composed rejoicing in the truth of Irwŏnsang to which he had been enlightened after eighteen years of ascetic practice and having a view of the great order to be founded with a view to deliver all sentient beings suffering in the seas of misery. The import of the verses is as follows.

After he underwent all sorts of difficulties in search of truth for so many years, he was finally enlightened to the ultimate truth of the universe.

Now he sees that all living beings depend on the fourfold beneficence for sustenance of their lives and that the great fortune of heaven and earth returns to the one who has rectified his or her mind.

When he looks at the world with a mind that transcends everything in the world, everything is the manifestation of the truth.

When one makes a vow and practices with devotion, one is endowed with the great power of truth.

The world is full of work to be done, and all living beings come to the world and grow in accordance with the creative transformation of the Way (Tao).

The district of Honam is the land where a new grand order is to be founded.

Moral laws deriving from the principles of noumenon and phenomenon and existence and nonexistence should be elucidated for human beings to follow.

All things in the universe are of unitary origin of the truth of Irwŏn, and the creative transformation of change is based on the truth of Irwŏn.

As he reflects the truth on heaven and earth, heaven and earth favorably respond to him. As he opens the gate of a grand order in this Oriental land, the whole world is to be brightened.

As the dark age is replaced with a new and fresh world with a new law to govern it, the world will become a peaceful paradise.

If one attains the three great powers (of emancipation, enlightenment, and the Mean) by cultivating virtue through the threefold practice and lives a life of gratitude, one's virtue will influence the whole world.

Iksan headquarters, he asked a small number of his disciples, "What can our order be compared to at this stage?" Kwon Tae-ho replied, "It is like a seed-bed for rice farming." The Master asked again, "Why is that so?" Tae-ho replied, "Although our order is so small at present that only scores of followers learn and rejoice in your teaching, the whole world will eventually be full of your teaching as a result of what we are doing here and now." The Master said, "You are right. Just as the rice farming in the vast fields originates in the small seed-bed, we shall be regarded as the ancestors of a great worldwide order in the future. Some may laugh at us hearing what I say, but after the first generation (thirty-six years) there will be increasing numbers of people who hunger after this teaching. Several decades after that, this teaching will be demanded everywhere in this country [Korea], and by the world in several hundred years. When this order is established as a world religion, there will be numberless people who regret not to have seen me; and not only you who are among the first hundred followers, but those who participated in this order within the first generation will be envied and venerated."

5. Upon returning from his sightseeing trip to Mt. Kŭmgang, the Master wrote a verse for his disciples:

> As Mt. Kŭmgang becomes known to the world,
> Chosŏn [Korea] will become Chosŏn again.

Then he said, "Mt. Kŭmgang is one of the most splendid mountains in the world; it will be designated as an international park in the near future and decorated resplendently by each country. Thereafter, people from all over the world will be looking for the owner of the mountain. If the owner has nothing prepared, with what can he treat the guests?"

6. On an anniversary of the founding of this order, the Master addressed an assembly: "There is a great treasure for us, and it is Mt. Kŭmgang. This country will become famous to the world because of Mt. Kŭmgang, and the latter will glitter because of its owner. Thus, this country and Mt. Kŭmgang and its owner, being closely tied together, will be the light of the world. Accordingly, you should exert yourselves to possess the qualification for the ownership of Mt. Kŭmgang instead of having a pessimistic view of our current situation.[214] The owner of Mt. Kŭmgang should cultivate a personality like Mt. Kŭmgang; you will attain its light if you cultivate and are enlightened to your original nature. To be like Mt. Kŭmgang, you should maintain your original nature, which is as pure and guileless as Mt. Kŭmgang; devote yourselves to your duty as respectfully as Mt. Kŭmgang; and be as adaman-

---

214. Korea under Japanese occupation.

tine as Mt. Kŭmgang, not weakening in your faith and devotion. Then the mountain will be the substance and you the function; the substance remains in quiescence while the function is in motion. Though the mountain fulfills its role as substance while it remains as it is, you must act right in order to fulfill the role as function. Hence, train yourselves in the supreme and great way of the Buddha so that you may be welcomed in the world just as Mt. Kŭmgang is known to the world and develop the order as an exemple for all other orders. If so, the country and the people will both shine brilliantly."[215]

7. When the Master visited Chŏnju, he said to Mun Chŏng-gyu and Pak Ho-jang, who came to pay homage to him, "On my way to Chŏnju, I saw many ludicrous things. When I was passing by a place in the morning, some were in deep sleep even though things were noisy outside, the day already having broken. Another was spreading seeds in cold wind and ice. Still another was shivering in summer clothes in the unbearable cold." Chŏng-gyu, comprehending the implication, asked, "How long will it take until people who sleep in the broad daylight will wake up, and those who sow seeds in ice and those who wear summer clothes in winter come to realize the right time to work?" The Master said, "The one who is unaware of the bright day outside and is in deep sleep will wake up as the outdoor movements become noisier and, once awakened, will open the door to see the day's having broken and eventually will start to work. The one who sows seeds in ice and the one who wears summer clothes in winter will of necessity fail as they engage in business at the wrong time. Only after suffering enormously from failure and hardships will they learn from the way others with knowledge of the right time engage in business; thus they will gradually mature to know the right time."

8. Kim Ki-ch'ŏn asked, "In recent years, quite a number of people have organized factions, each assuming the air of righteousness and claiming that they are teachers. In examining what they do, I do not find anything good for which they may be called teachers. Can they still be called teachers?" The Master answered, "They are true teachers." Ki-ch'ŏn asked again, "Why do you call them true teachers?" The Master answered, "Since you have learned to distinguish truth from falsehood from them, can't they be called teachers?" Ki-ch'ŏn asked further, "Yes, they can be called my teachers in that sense. However, when will they qualify themselves as true teachers?" The Master answered, "When fabrication is exposed, authenticity returns, and truth is revealed when falsehood is recognized. Hence, a feigned teacher will

---

215. This should be understood as encouraging words for the Korean people, whose situation looked hopeless because they had lost their national identity to Japanese aggressors at that time.

be transformed into a genuine one by the method of trial and error through the experience of being fake or genuine, false or true."

9. The Master said, "In these days, the world is full of those who wish to be enlightened to the Way without the necessary practice, those who wish success without effort, those who wait for the time without preparation, those who mock at the great Way with sorcery, and those who slander righteous people with tricky propaganda. They each feign to have unusual abilities, making a great fuss; they are nothing but goblins haunting in broad daylight. As the world is entering the era of further enlightenment, however, such people will find no place to stand, and only the correct doctrine essential for humanity and justice will prevail in the world. The world so enlightened is called 'the world of bright daylight.'"

10. One day when the Master was taking a walk in Nam-san Park in Seoul, a few youths, having noticed his extraordinary, majestic appearance, approached him and, greeting him, gave their name cards to him, so he also gave them his card. The youths, quoting a newspaper article wherein a new religious order that had raised a big scandal was criticized, said, "The leaders of this religion have committed vicious deeds; hence, we, the youth association, will censure them and annihilate them." The Master asked, "What exactly are the vicious deeds they committed?" One of the youths said, "By teaching superstition they delude the world and deceive the people, squeezing property out of miserable peasants. That's why we will exterminate them from society." The Master said, "I can understand your intentions. If one makes desperate efforts to pursue something one would have at the risk of one's life, one will never be dissuaded from doing it. How are you going to stop them?" The young man asked, "Do you mean then that that religion will continue forever?" The Master replied, "What I mean is not whether that religion will last long or not but that you cannot force one to quit what one wants at the risk of his or her life. As everyone loves what is beneficial and hates what is harmful, people will make friends when they are beneficial for each other and abhor each other when they are harmed by each other. A truthful teaching may seem to give no benefit at the beginning but will be beneficial to the world eventually while a wicked teaching may look beneficial at the beginning but will eventually cause a great harm to the world. Therefore, if that religion is a path of righteousness, it will never be annihilated by any blow; and if it is a wicked path, it will vanish even if it is left alone."

11. The young man asked again, "If so, by what method do you think the world will be transformed for the better?" The Master replied, "Although there is not any particular method, I will answer your question by an analogy. Suppose a farmer who is well versed in agricultural affairs works hard and gathers a great harvest. Then other farmers will

model themselves after him. If, however, a farmer whose farming is not good tries to teach other farmers how to farm, they will not follow his advice. Thus, I hold the view that if one wishes to transform others by teaching, one must first practice what one teaches." The young man responded, "I can see that you edify others by such a masterful method. Since the religious order in question drives innocent people into misery, however, shouldn't it be extinguished from the world?" The Master said, "That religion is making a contribution to the well-being of the world just as you are." The young man asked, "How is that religion contributing to the world?" The Master said, "That religion can be compared to a chaser, without whom a hunter cannot get what he wants. This is an era when the old world should be reformed into a fresh new one. When the world is still in deep sleep without realizing the situation, religious orders of various kinds arise in various places, awakening people from sleep and stirring up their minds. Only then, after experiencing all sorts of things, genuine or fake, true or false, and having tried to cheat and having been cheated, will men of talent and ability come to learn whether a thing is genuine or fake or an act is right or wrong. Then, they will eventually discover a truthful and righteous religious order and its true leaders, accomplishing with them something honorable for the world. Now, this is partly owing to those religious cults playing the role of chasers. How, then, can you say that they haven't made an important contribution to the world?" The young man asked further, "By the way, how can we also be working for the sake of the world?" The Master said, "You scrutinize the religious orders in order to bring before the public their admirable deeds and to censure their wrongdoings. Whoever is criticized will feel vexatious and will try to be free from such criticisms, by straightening themselves up. Thus, you render help to those who do right and press for self-examination those who are supposed to work for the world but do wrong. Since they may not get the power to make progress but for your scrutiny, your merit is also great." The young men, all deeply impressed by the Master's awesome presence, bowed, saying, "Your words have illumined all directions."

12. A visitor asked, "I trust that the doctrine of your order is right and pertinent to the times, but I wonder what will happen to the order with your successors since the order has only a short history and a shallow foundation." The Master said, "If you are convinced that this is a truthful religion, then you need not worry whether this religious order will expand or not with my successors. Look! Robbery, being vicious, is prohibited by criminal law and ostracized by society. However, this crime, instead of being eradicated, keeps bothering us, because there are some people who are so poor that they need to commit a robbery. If so, how much more should the truthful teaching for human jus-

tice necessary for all humankind be needed? Let me give you another example. When people make use of various goods and technologies in their daily lives, they do so not for the sake of the inventors, but for their own convenience. Just as they will keep using them even if they are told not to, people will keep to their faith in the religious teaching even if they are forced not to, once they are benefited by their faith in the teaching. And if there are many people who believe in this religious teaching, this religious order will expand, won't it?"

13. A visitor asked, "Both in the Orient and in the Occident, numerous religions for thousands of years closed their doors against each other, quarreling with each other. In recent years, there have arisen several new religions in various places, each asserting its own identity and rejecting the others, thus adding to the existing uneasiness. What will be of the future of the religious world?" The Master answered, "Suppose someone, married in Seoul, lived with his children and then traveled alone through many countries of the world. In a few of those countries he begot several children; several years later he returned to Seoul. Suppose further that those children, grown up in their respective countries, got together at one place to meet with their father. It may not be easy for them to be friendly and kind to one another since they have different facial complexions, languages, customs, and manners. As they grow mature with passing the years and understand how they are related, becoming familiar with different customs, they will then be awakened to the brotherhood of their own bone and flesh and eventually live in peace. In this way all religions have become different from one another although their origin is unitary. When human intelligence becomes far more advanced and when the light of truth reaches everywhere, all religions will form a family and maintain harmony and peace."

14. When Cho Song-gwang came to see the Master for the first time, the Master said, "You look different from others. Do you have a religious faith?" Song-gwang said, "I have been believing in God for several decades and now I am an elder at a Presbyterian church." The Master asked, "As you say you have believed in God for many years, I wonder whether you can tell me where God is." Song-gwang said, "It is said that God is omniscient, omnipotent, and omnipresent." The Master asked, "Then, have you seen God, heard his words, and received his instructions?" Song-gwang said, "So far I haven't seen him or talked with him." The Master asked, "Then you haven't yet become an intimate disciple of Jesus, have you?" Song-gwang asked, "What should I do so that I may see Jesus and receive his instructions?" The Master said, "If you become one of his true and intimate disciples by exceptional practice, you can see him." Song-gwang said, "In the Bible it is said that Jesus will come and go like a thief at the end of the world and

there will be some signs of his presence. Will he really come?" The Master said, "Since sages tell no lies, you will know Jesus' coming and going if you are awakened to your own numinous awareness by serious practice." Song-gwang said, "For a long time, I have been waiting for a great mentor who will guide me. Seeing you today, I feel like following you as a disciple right away. However, I have qualms of conscience as if I were an apostate." The Master said, "A true disciple of Jesus in Christianity will know what I am doing, and a true and intimate disciple of mine in this order will also know what Jesus did. One who does not see the truth feels like an apostate, estranged from each religion and hostile to other religions. Those who are enlightened to the truth know that all religions are of one household although they have different names in accordance with the different times and districts of their foundations. Hence, I leave it to your own discretion whether you come or go." Song-gwang, arising from his seat and bowing down upon his knees, implored to be his disciple. The Master, granting his wish, said, "You cannot be a true disciple of mine unless your faith in God becomes deeper even after you decide to follow me."

15. The Master said, "One day I was reading a Buddhist scripture and found the following tale. One of the Buddha's disciples asked, 'When we see you and listen to your teaching, we are filled with deep respect and infinite joy; however, there are some people who speak ill of you and some who slander you, even interfering with our coming to see you. Inasmuch as the Buddha always teaches with compassion and mercy, I do not understand why they are against you.' The Buddha answered, 'When the sun rises in the east, its light shines first upon the summit of Mt. Sumeru, the highest mountain, and then it shines on the plateaus, and finally it shines on the lowest fields. It is not because the sun has a sense of discrimination that it shines on the highest mountain first and the lowest field last; it is because of the difference in heights of the mountain and fields that there is the difference of the first and the last, though the sun shines indifferently. So it is with the Buddha's preaching. Although the light of his infinite wisdom shines in all directions without discrimination, some comprehend earlier than others depending on their intellectual capacities. When they listen to the Buddha's sermon at the same place, bodhisattvas understand it first, then *pratyekabuddhas*, *śrāvaka*s,[216] and those whose good roots (*kuśala-*

---

216. A *pratyekabuddha* (S) is one who seeks enlightenment for him- or herself, a believer who is diligent and zealous in seeking wisdom, who loves loneliness and seclusion. A *śrā-vaka* (S) is a hearer, a term applied to the personal disciples of the Buddha; its general connotation relates it to Hīnayāna disciples who understand the four dogmas, rid themselves of the unreality of the phenomenal, and enter nirvāṇa.

*mūla*) are determined (*niścaya*);[217] finally, those sentient beings who had no affinity with the Buddha will gradually receive the light of the Buddha's wisdom. However, the deluded sentient beings who defame the Buddha's teaching while living in the light of his wisdom are like blind people who deny the beneficence of the sunlight while living in it, as they cannot see it. Hence, you had better mind your own business without hating those deluded sentient beings or being discouraged or dejected. How can we expect that all human beings will have the same high intellectual capacity?' Now, you should take this tale as a model for your spiritual journey. Be indifferent to the faults of others and to the others' having disregard for you. The vicissitudes of the world are like the change of day and night, so that, when the dark age is replaced by a bright one, all the sentient beings will be aware of the beneficence of the Buddha and exert themselves to recompense the Buddha for his beneficence."

16. Ch'oe To-hwa asked, "Now that there are many people who are anxiously waiting for the coming of Maitreya and the establishment of his order under the dragon-flower tree,[218] what kind of a Buddha is Maitreya and what kind of an order is the Dragon-Flower order?" The Master said, "By Maitreya Buddha is meant that the truth of Dharma-kāya Buddha[219] is prominently known to the world; and by the Dragon-Flower order is meant that the teaching 'Everywhere is the Buddha manifested; hence, do all things as making an offering to the Buddha'[220] is widely practiced." Chang Chŏk-cho asked, "When will such a world be realized?" The Master replied, "It is now gradually being realized." Chŏng Se-wŏl asked, "There should be a first master of such a world, shouldn't there?" The Master replied, "Whoever is enlightened to one truth after another of the great Way is the master."

17. Pak Sasihwa asked, "Some Buddhist sects each claim that Maitreya Buddha has already come and is now establishing the Dragon-Flower order. Which sect will be the true Dragon-Flower order?" The Master said, "The Dragon-Flower order will not be established by mere words. The Dragon-Flower order will naturally be established by those who, without making such claims, are enlightened to the true meaning of Maitreya Buddha and do what the Maitreya Buddha should do. They will even directly meet with Maitreya Buddha."

---

217. Those whose good seeds are sown by a good life to be reaped later.
218. *Nāga-puṣa* (S) the dragon-flower tree, which will be the bodhi-tree of Maitreya, the Buddhist messiah, when he comes to earth; his assembly will gather under it and preach the Buddha-truth.
219. See above, *SS* II:9, 11, for Dharmakāya Buddha.
220. See above, *Canon*, "Mottoes of the Order."

18. Sŏ Tae-wŏn asked, "What will the world be like when Maitreya Buddha's era comes and the Dragon-Flower order is generally completed?" The Master said, "In that era, human intelligence will be far advanced, so that there will be no antagonism or conflicts in the human world. People will distinguish the real from the unreal and truth from falsehood so that they will gradually abolish the old practice of worshiping the statue of the Buddha for longevity and blessedness; they will sow seeds of riches, honor, and longevity, taking all things of the universe and the empty dharma realm as the fields of blessings. People will help each other to become living buddhas and deliver sentient beings. They will mutually recognize the power of the Buddha in each other, and buddhas will reside in each house. They will find their temples wherever they go. The grandeur of such a world will be beyond description. In that world, Buddha-dharma will be followed everywhere under Heaven so that the difference between priest and laity will be gone, state and church will not hinder each other, and practice and daily mundane life will not hinder each other, benefiting all sentient beings."

19. The Master said, "In recent years, there have been some people who hold the view that since this is the end of the world there remains nothing but the complete destruction of the world. I do not think that it will happen. This is, no doubt, a degenerate age: the traces of the ancient sages have become remote and their teachings on justice and morality have been dimmed. However, this world will never be ruined. The world to come will be a truly civilized and highly moral world. Thus, now is the end of the old world and the beginning of a new one. It is difficult for the general public to foresee the future; however, why shouldn't one who can measure the civilization of the new world feel secure and happy?"

20. The Master continued saying, "The hearts of the people in the coming world will be as follows. Whereas people today regret when they cannot take another's property by force, defeat, or hurt others, people in the coming world will regret when they cannot give to others, lose to others, or help others. While people today lament when they cannot pursue their own interests or rise in the world and win fame and power, people in the coming world will be worried when they cannot work for the benefit of the public and when they lose the leisure for spiritual cultivation by taking advantage of the opportunity to rise in the world and win fame and power. Whereas many people today love to do evil, people in the coming world will hate to do evil. Whereas today's individuals, families, societies, and nations defend themselves by erecting fences and walls, there will be harmony without limitation among individuals, families, societies, and nations in the coming world.

Whereas people today are ruled by material civilization, people in the coming world will control material civilization with the strengthened spiritual culture, as they will have a highly advanced morality. Material civilization will be of help to the advancement of morality. In the near future, people will enjoy the truly civilized world where there will be no thieves in the mountains and no one will pick up a lost item on the road."

21. The Master said, "The level of advancement of today's world is comparable to the dawn, the moment when the dark night is almost gone and the bright sun is about to rise in the east. That the West is civilized first is like the light brightening the mountain tops in the west first when the sun rises in the east. When the sun reaches the zenith of the sky, its light shines upon the whole world equally. At that time people will realize the world of great morality and true civilization."

22. The Master said, "As the world in the past was immature and dark, those who had power and knowledge could live by exploiting the weak and innocent people. Since the people in the coming world are bright and intelligent, no one of high or low rank will be able to exploit other people. Consequently, vicious and dishonest people will become poorer while upright and truthful people will become richer."

23. The Master said, "Although Koreans have made a notable improvement in their style of living and their stubbornness of thinking has considerably changed for the better, there remain areas of deficiency, which are to be gradually improved. However, Korea will be the leader of all countries in the world as far as morality is concerned. This country is like a fish that is transforming into a dragon."[221]

24. The Master continued, "There will be some people in the coming world who will love nature's beauty. Some people will make parks on the tops of high mountains, planting various trees and flowering plants or digging ponds for breeding fish, with curious rocks and old trees nicely arranged around them. Below the parks will be built houses where the inhabitants take in the sunlight during the day and turn on electric lights during the night. They will live lustrous lives, wanting nothing. When they come out of the houses, they will enjoy the luxuriant woods above their houses. Climbing to the top, they will find exquisite birds and insects singing and dancing among beautiful flowers and plants. In such famous mountains as Mt. Kŭmgang and Mt. Chiri in this country [Korea] only the men of power will be able to have their houses built. Some will even make artificial mountains on which to build their houses. When they build their houses, they will use natural

---

221. "From fish to dragon" means something like "from rags to riches" or "from a log cabin to the White House."

rocks instead of artificial sculptures. Thus, the people in general in the coming world will love the beauty of nature and prefer it to artificial beauty."

25. The Master continued, saying, "Wealthy religious organizations will have stations on the tops of huge mountains and parks where magnificent shrines of portraits will be built to enshrine the portraits and chronicles of those who dedicated their lives to the public well-being. Spectators from everywhere will visit them, and even dignitaries of high rank will observe them with adoration. Renowned dharma masters, while leading a monastic life at a scenic monastery or nunnery, will go to temples in urban areas to deliver sermons, and the people's shout of joyous welcome will shake the mountains. The laity then will escort the dharma master and his or her company into the temple, where they will offer food to the dharma master and request a sermon. The dharma master will elucidate the necessary wisdom for human life, the principles of the causal laws of karmic retribution, or the profound principles of human original nature. After the sermon, the audience will make handsome gifts, which the dharma master will leave at the temple. The dharma master then will visit other temples where he or she will be received in this way."

26. The Master said, "In every town and every village there will be not only schools but public halls where people will regularly gather for dharma meetings, and such ceremonies as coming of age, marriage, funeral, and ancestral worship will be conveniently carried out. Whereas religious people today are not much trusted because the religious orders today do not train their followers sufficiently, in the coming world the followers of each religious order will receive considerable training so that their personalities will be considerably different from those of nonbelievers. Consequently, religious believers will be sought when government offices and other societal positions are to be filled by men of talent."

27. The Master continued, saying, "Even today there are employment agencies in big cities; in the coming world, there will be considerably more employment agencies everywhere serving those looking for jobs. There will be matrimonial agencies for suitors, nursery schools, and day-care centers for the mothers who must go to work. For helpless old people there will be asylums for the aged provided by the government and social agencies or charitable workers so that those helpless old people can live comfortably. It is inconvenient in many ways to live in a poor and remote village today; however, in the future those poor villages will be provided with all sorts of facilities for convenient living. There will be cafeteria and fast-food restaurants so that people can have their meals without cooking at home all the time. There will be many

tailors and self-service laundries so that busy people will have no difficulty in having their clothes tailored or washed."

28. The Master said, "It was customary in the past that one's property, much or little, was inherited by one's own children only or an adopted son if one had no child of one's own; and the descendants took for granted that they would inherit their parents' property. In the future, however, many people will use only part of their property for the education and livelihood of their children and the remaining for the missionary, educational, and charitable works of the general public. While people today try to make a profit by harming others, people in the coming world will regard benefiting others as profit because, in accordance with the advancement of human intelligence, they will experience the principle that one is harmed as much as one harms others and one is benefited as much as one benefits others."

29. When the Master delivered a sermon, it sometimes seemed as if the great chilicosm was subdued and all beings in the six realms of existence and the four forms of birth were rejoicing together in his majestic and virtuous air. Whenever this happened, Pak Sasihwa, Mun Chŏng-gyu, and Kim Nam-ch'ŏn danced, their gray hair streaming, while Chŏn Sam-sam, Ch'oe To-hwa, and Ro Tŏksongok rose to their feet and bowed down toward the Master repeatedly. As they were stirring excitement in the dharma hall and animating the joy in the dharma, the Master, with a smile on his holy countenance, said, "When a great order is to unfold, bodhisattvas call a meeting in the yin-realm to decide their roles in the opening order. They are bodhisattvas who have come to this order with the responsibilities to dance and bow. At present it is only a few of us who rejoice in the dharma; however, in the future, all beings in the six realms of existence and four forms of birth in the triple world in the ten directions will rejoice in this dharma together."

30. One of the disciples asked, "I can surmise that our order has been established with a great destiny; however, I would like to know how many thousands of years it will last." The Master answered, "Unlike the religious orders of the past, this order is not one that comes into being often. Since this is the one that appears at the beginning of the cycle of the great chilicosm, the destiny of this order will be endless."

## XV. Entrusting

1. The Master said to many of his disciples, "When I see you, I feel deeply kindhearted because it is only you who, ahead of so many other people, sought our special dharma affinity and this teaching with special aspiration. Sometimes I am saddened, however, to see that some of you

lessen your devotion to cultivation of the Way, let selfish motives grow in your hearts, and do not follow my guidance as you should. What are you going to do if I leave for good on a long journey of rest, cutting off all affinities, while you forget your original intention and fail to recognize my intention? It will not be easy to find me, then, no matter how hard you may try to do so. So, be awakened again so that I may not think this way. An emancipated one has a frame of mind that ordinary people can never understand. When such a one does something in this world, it looks as though that person would not leave the place for millions of years; however, such a one will leave no trace of him- or herself, like an empty sky, once he or she decides to let go of the mind."

2. In January of the twenty-sixth year of this order (1941), the Master expressed the gāthā of the dharma transmission[222] and said, "It was customary for the masters in the past to deliver the gāthā of the dharma transmission in a hurry at the moment of death to a few secretly; however, I deliver it to you in advance and to everybody equally. Whether you will receive the dharma completely or not depends on the status of your religious practice. Hence, exert yourselves to the religious practice lest you lament later."

3. One year (1942) before his entrance into nirvāṇa, the Master often had the disciples he had appointed hasten the compilation of the *Pulgyo chŏngjŏn*[223] and often sat up until midnight supervising the compilation. When the manuscript was completed, he had it sent for printing, and said to his disciples, "As I don't have much time left, I am forced to have this work printed even though I feel it is not perfect. However, the essentials of my lifetime ambition and planning are expressed in this one volume. Hence, accept this and let the dharma contained therein be transmitted through tens of thousands of generations by learning it in words, practicing it with your bodies, and awakening to it in your hearts. In the near future there will be innumerable people all over the world who will recognize and revere the dharma as they will be deeply moved thereby."

4. A few months before entering into nirvāṇa, the Master often gave a charge to those assembled or to individuals: "I am about to leave for a remote and deep place to rest. Examine yourselves and make a firm resolution not to regress in my absence. As this is the time of trial, those with shallow faith will wither away while those with firm faith will produce good fruit. I have transmitted my teaching in such a way that anyone with faith and public spirit can receive it; hence, take the true

222. See above, *Canon*, pt. 2, chap. 1, sec. 6, for "Verse on Irwŏnsang"; and *SS* VII:31 above for comments.
223. *Pulgyo chŏngjŏn* [Correct canon of Buddhism], comp. by Kim T'ae-hŭp (Seoul: Pulgyo Sibosa, 1943).

dharma for the blood and flesh of your spiritual life as soon as possible lest you later regret not having received it."

5. One day, the Master said to Song Kyu, "Until today, ever since you met me, you have only carried out whatever I asked you to do and never insisted on your own opinion. You have done so because your faith in me has been unlimited. But what are you going to do if I leave you all of a sudden? From now on, try to formulate your own opinions and to lead the order for yourself." He continued, "As the [Japanese] government authorities are fastening their eyes on me more and more sternly, it looks unlikely that I can stay here any longer. There will be some who will harass you, and it will be difficult to get through the difficult moments. However, take it easy since there will be nothing critical."

6. The Master said, "If you continue making progress with the initial aspirations you had in following me, no one will fail to succeed. When one changes from low to medium intellectual capacity or when one cannot overcome the critical moment of the medium capacity with which one is born, one is afflicted by all sorts of spiritual illness, thus failing to attain the high capacity. Thus, you should exert yourselves to overcome the critical moment of the medium capacity. The symptoms of illness of the medium capacity are as follows. First, one feels weary of practice and bored by everything, having worse thoughts and words than those of the people in the secular world. Second, although one is not completely enlightened to the truth, one is not totally ignorant either, so that when one says or writes something that is admired by those who are impressed thereby, one feels that one is superior to all. Such a person, being self-confident, forgives his or her own faults and criticizes his or her senior teachers rashly, sticking obstinately to his or her own views while casting doubt on the mentor and the dharma. One with this symptom is liable to bring all his or her efforts to naught, ruining the great task for eternal kalpas. That's why the buddhas and patriarchs in the past also warned against oscillation and doubt about the mentor and the dharma. Now, there are quite a few among you who are seized with this disease. Examine yourselves to get rid of it, or you will not only ruin yourselves but be the cause of trouble for the order. Thus, you ought to exert yourselves to overcome the critical moment of the medium capacity. To rid oneself of this disease easily, one must give one's mind to one's mentor completely, reflect on one's initial vows, and recollect often the danger of the medium capacity. Once you rid yourselves of this danger, your journey toward the buddha stage will be as fast as if you fly a jet plane."

7. In January of the twenty-eighth year of this order (1943), the Master released the doctrinal chart and said, "The quintessence of my teaching lies herein; but how many can understand the true essence of

my intention? It seems likely that only a few among you can receive the true essence of my teaching completely. It is because, first, the spirit is inclined to wealth and sex, and second, it is inclined to fame and vanity so that you fail to have a complete mental concentration on the dharma. You must make a decision to choose either this or that way but not both; you can succeed only if you take one way."

8. The Master asked the assembly at a Zen monastery, "Who, throughout the whole world from ancient times to the present, has attained the greatest skillful means and thereby served as the vessel to deliver all sentient beings suffering in the sea of misery? By what practice did the sage attain the ability? And what kind of ability have you decided to acquire through the practice in this order?" After a few disciples answered, Song To-sŏng said, "Those who acquire the greatest skillful means and serve as the vessel to deliver all sentient beings are all buddhas of the three periods of the time. What we aspire to attain more than anything else is the Buddha's ability. Hence, without being attracted to wicked ways or trivial learning through millions of kalpas, we will exert ourselves to attain the Buddha's wisdom and ability to solve the problem of old age, illness, and death and to deliver the sentient beings suffering in the sea of misery." The Master said, "Recently, however, there are some who have joined this order but revere learning other than this dharma and some who even leave this order to acquire knowledge other than this dharma. It is regrettable. Hence, make a new oath, each of you, renewing your original vows, that you will exert yourselves for the religious practice in this dharma." Each of those in the assembly submitted a written oath in compliance with the Master's order and continued his or her exertion.

9. The Master said, "For the past twenty-eight years since the opening of this order, my teaching has been mainly in the interpretation of the dharma and, as a result, those with medium or low capacity, becoming old foxes, are prone to take the dharma lightly and cannot attain to the true Way, though those with superior capacity have no problem. This is a matter of great concern. From now on, therefore, the teaching should be focused on an integrated discipline with the threefold practice[224] without being one-sided toward interpretation of the dharma."

10. The Master said, "I have established many religious orders through many aeons; however, this is the largest in scale. Therefore, starting with the nine disciples[225] when this order was first founded, innumerable followers will devote themselves to this order, which they will regard as their own lives."

---

224. See above, *Canon*, pt .2, chap. 4, for the details of the threefold practice.
225. See above, *SS* I:6, 8.

11. The Master said, "I have taught you for a long time and have observed three regrettable things. First, while there are many who can talk about the profound truth, there are few who are enlightened to the pure realm of truth and who reveal in conduct what they are enlightened to. Second, there are many people who see with the naked eye, but few who can see with the mind's eye. Third, there are many who have seen the incarnated Buddha (*nirmāṇakāya*), but few who have clearly seen the essential body (*dharmakāya*) of the Buddha."

12. The Master said, "There are three difficulties in this religious order. First, it is difficult to be enlightened to the ultimate realm of Irwŏn.[226] Second, it is difficult to put the truth of Irwŏn into practice and thereby maintain the True Thusness of one's own original nature in motion and at rest. Third, it is difficult to explain the truth of Irwŏn in clear and simple terms for the general public to be enlightened to it. If the cultivator of the Way makes up his or her mind and exerts him- or herself sincerely to attain it, even the most difficult task will turn out to be rather an easy one while the easiest thing will turn out to be the most difficult task to the one who is unwilling to do it or the one who discontinues it in the middle of the way."

13. The Master said, "Deluded people are not aware of the beneficence of heaven and earth's rain and dew; and ordinary people are not aware of the sage's virtue. People realize the beneficence of the rain only after a drought, and the world realizes the beneficence of the teaching only after the sage has left."

14. At a regular dharma meeting on the sixteenth of May 1943 (28 W.E.), the Master gave a sermon to the assembly, saying "On my way to this enlightenment hall, I saw several children playing in the grove beside the way. Upon seeing me, one of them shouted a watchword and all of them, standing up, bowed to me. Their behavior was seemly; and I think it is the sign of their gradually becoming mature. When very young, one lives without understanding the relationship with one's parents and brethren, let alone the degrees of kinship, but one comes to know them as one gradually becomes mature. Likewise, the cultivator of the Way, when deluded, spends time without knowing how a person can become a buddha or a bodhisattva, how a person is related with heaven and earth and all things therein, or how a person comes into and leaves the world; but one comes to know them as one matures in the religious practice. Thus, we can say that our progress in the comprehension of the Way is comparable to the children's gradually maturing. As an infant grows to be an adult, an ordinary human being becomes a buddha by enlightenment, and a disciple becomes a teacher

---

226. See above, *Canon*, pt. 2, chap. 1, sec. 1; *SS* II:7, for the meaning of Irwŏn.

by learning, you, too, acquire true ability, become teachers of your juniors and proper guides of the great task of delivering sentient beings and curing the world of illness. It is said in the *Yin-fu ching*, 'Birth is the source of death; death is the source of birth.' Birth and death are like the cycle of the four seasons or the repetition of day and night. This is the principle whereby all things in the universe are being operated and the truth whereby heaven and earth circulate. Buddhas and bodhisattvas are free and not deluded when they come and go, while ordinary human beings and other sentient beings are bound and deluded when they go through birth and death. But there is no difference between the former and the latter as far as their physical birth and death are concerned. Thus, by having faith in the dharma as well as the mentor, you should exert yourselves to attain the ability to be free from and not deluded by the process of birth and death. The dharma meeting we are having now is comparable to a marketplace where people gather for shopping. Once you have come to a marketplace, you should sell your goods and buy others' goods for your needs, which will be useful for your living. Likewise, you may share your ideas with the public if they are of benefit to others, get the doubtful points explained by others, and take the words of others as a model, so that you may not come and go for nothing. Grave is the matter of birth and death and swift is impermanence. This is something one should not take lightly."

15. The Master said, "Since the goal of our task is religious edification, education, and charity, we will succeed only if these three areas of work are completely carried out in balance."

16. The Master said, "In the doctrine I have formulated, the fundamental principles of the doctrine with Irwŏn as the essence, viz., threefold practice, eight articles, and fourfold beneficence,[227] shall not be altered in any country and at any time. However, the remaining sections and systems may be changed to fit the times and the country."

17. The Master said, "In the past, religious orders, government, and private organizations all guided the general public on the principle of discrimination. In the coming world, however, the public will not be harmonized by the principle of partiality and discrimination. Therefore, in our order, anyone who attains the great enlightenment, whether a priest, a lay person, a man or woman, old or young, shall be held in reverence as the Tathāgata of supreme enlightenment.[228] On the occasion of birthdays, memorial days, and other ceremonies, celebration or mourning, as the case may be, should be offered to all those who devoted themselves to the foundation of this order rather than to any particular individual."

---

227. See above, *Canon*, pt. 2, chaps. 1, 2, and 4.
228. See above, *Canon*, pt. 3, chap. 17, no. 6.

18. The Master said, "It is important for you to put down in ink and talk about my teaching to transmit it to our posterity; however, it is more important for you to put it into practice and thereby be enlightened to it so that the line of this dharma may not be cut in the future. If you do so, the merit will be incalculable."

19. The Master said, "A master's creation of a new dharma, the disciples' reception and transmission of the dharma to their posterity, and the general public's reception and practice of the dharma with pleasure in the future form a trinity; their merits are equal."

# Appendix I

## Translator's Notes on Restoration of the Text

I would like to explain here why those crucial points of the doctrine in the old *Canon* (1943 edition) that were altered in the new *Canon* (1962 edition) have been restored in this translation. There are five places in this translation of the *Canon* where I have restored the crucial tenets of Sot'aesan's original teaching in the old *Canon* that should have been left intact when the new *Canon* was redacted: (1) the doctrinal chart, (2) the practice of Irwŏnsang, (3) repentance, (4) the ailing family and its remedy, and (5) the four fundamental principles.

1. Sot'aesan said (*SS* XV:7) that the quintessence of his teaching is epitomized in the doctrinal chart. The quintessence lies in the faith in and the practice of the truth of Irwŏnsang, Dharmakāya Buddha, which is the fundamental source of the fourfold beneficence (heaven and earth, parents, brethren, laws) and the Buddha-nature of all sentient beings. The essence of the way of faith is the awareness and requital of beneficence; the essence of the way of practice lies in correct enlightenment and right practice. It can readily be shown that whatever is in the doctrine of Won Buddhism turns around the realization of these two goals.

The artery of faith lies in the essential principles of beneficence requital of the fourfold beneficence: harboring no false thought after rendering favors to others, protecting the helpless, acting for mutual benefit, and doing justice and forsaking injustice. As laid out by Sot'aesan, the heart of Won Buddhist religious faith has been cut out and replaced with the four essentials for social reform (cultivation of self-ability, the wise as the standard, education of the children of others, veneration of those dedicated to public service), the performance of which does not religiously relate one to the source of one's life, the fourfold beneficence. The insertion of the latter cuts the artery of the Won Buddhist religious faith, making it impossible for anyone to have faith in Won Buddhism who cannot, for instance, "educate the children of others" as is required by one of the essentials. Furthermore, the removal of the essential principles of beneficence requital cuts the artery of the Won Buddhist religious faith since worship of Dharmakāya Buddha lies in requiting beneficence as making an offering to Buddha.

Thus, the essential principles of beneficence requital should be restored as Sot'aesan originally intended, deleting the four essentials.

The way of practice lies in correct enlightenment and right practice of the truth of Irwŏnsang, Dharmakāya Buddha, the three aspects of which are concentration/calmness (samādhi), wisdom (prajñā), and morality (śīla). These three terms have been deleted from the chart, thereby severing the artery of the practice of the truth of Dharmakāya Buddha, for, as Hui-neng said, one's own *dharmakāya* consists in them; by deleting them the bridge connecting to Dharmakāya Buddha is removed. Thus, I have restored them in this translation. Another significant alteration in the way of practice is incessant Zen in motion and at rest, which together with the essential principles of beneficence requital in the way of faith highlights the unique and salient feature of Sot'aesan's new Buddha-dharma.

2. In the section "Practice of Irwŏnsang" of the old *Canon*, one is advised to take an unwavering faith in the truth of Irwŏnsang as the compass needle for practice, for the destination is not in view unless one is enlightened into one's own Buddha-nature. Hence, correct practice can start only if one is enlightened to the truth of Irwŏnsang; otherwise one cannot know, nourish, or use one's own mind, which is as perfect, complete, utterly fair, and selfless as Irwŏn, namely, prajñā-wisdom. In the redacted new *Canon* (1962 edition) the truth of Irwŏnsang itself is made to play the role of the model of practice; there is no requirement of "being enlightened to the truth of Irwŏnsang"; the all-important term "prajñā-wisdom" has been deleted; and one is advised to know, nourish, and use one's mind as perfect, complete, utterly fair, and selfless as Irwŏnsang, the circular symbol, which Sot'aesan said (*SS* II:6) is like a finger pointing at the moon. Now it can readily be shown that it makes little sense to take the truth of Irwŏnsang as the model of practice. As Chinul taught, all practice prior to enlightenment is defiled practice. No mind is perfect, complete, utterly fair, and selfless unless it is prajñā-wisdom; one cannot hammer out one's mind as round as a circular form Irwŏnsang; a finger should not be mistaken for the moon.

3. In part 3, chapter 8, in the new *Canon* ("Discourse on Repentance"), "Verse on Repentance" is missing. To delete the verse is like deleting the mantra from the Heart Sūtra; the Discourse explains the principles and necessity of repentance, which is supposed to be accomplished while reciting or chanting the verse by the illocutionary force of the chanting. The deletion is comparable to tearing off the prescription for a certain disease upon explaining reasons for taking certain medicine. Since it is recited or chanted as part of certain rituals in Won Buddhism anyway, it should be restored as in the old *Canon*.

4. The title of chapter 15 in the Korean original of the new *Canon* (1962) is "Ailing Society and Its Remedy," which is an alteration of the title "Ailing Family and Its Remedy" in the old *Canon*. And "the leader of a society" in the new *Canon* has replaced "the head of a household" in the old *Canon*, leaving intact the text of the chapter that is meant to be a prescription for remedying the morally ailing family. This alteration made the chapter useless for curing the ills of a society whose cells are families. Thus, ever since the publication of the 1962 *Canon*, the chapter, which was otherwise a very important tenet of a new religion, has been useless, for no head of a Won Buddhist family would have been so presumptuous as to fancy himself a social leader. Who could play the role of a social leader—the president, the king, chief justice, pope? Do they not wish to cure their societies of moral ills? Just as a living organism is made of cells, a society is made of families; you cannot save a living organism if its cells are dying, and you cannot cure the ills of the society unless all the families are morally sound. And Sot'aesan and Chŏngsan (the "mother of dharma") were wise enough to see this, prescribing "Ailing Family and Its Remedy." Thus, the original title should be restored. See *SS* IV:43, for Sot'aesan's original intentions.

5. Part 1, chapter 1 ("The Four Fundamental Principles") of the old *Canon* has been inserted with considerable revisions as chapter 7 in the new *Canon* as if the four principles were the conclusion of the whole doctrine. This chapter should be entered as a chapter of part 1, "General Introduction," for the following reasons.

These are not themselves any tenet of the doctrine though they are included in chapter 1, part 2 ("Doctrine"), in the old *Canon*; they state four main objectives of the order. The first platform, "Correct Enlightenment and Right Practice," requires one to be enlightened to the truth of Irwŏnsang and follow the threefold practice, which are the central tenets of the doctrine. The third platform, "Practical Application of Buddha-dharma," which suggests that one should learn and make practical application of Buddha-dharma, is not a matter of doctrine. This chapter is chapter 1 of part 2 ("Doctrine") in the old *Canon*; however, it should be noticed that its part 1 is "A Treatise on the Renovation of Korean Buddhism," which is replaced with "General Introduction" in the new *Canon*. The chapter in question should logically have been included in part 1 since it is not itself a tenet of the doctrine.

The apparently fuzzy relationship with the Buddhist order can be cleared up by perusing the doctrinal chart that precedes the "General Introduction," for the question "What is Won Buddhism?" can be best answered by explaining the import of the order's four fundamental principles or platforms. It can be made clear that Sot'aesan opened a

new religious order by a critical synthesis of the three religious doctrines with it, still taking Buddha-dharma as the central tenet, as a means to the realization of the four fundamental principles or objectives. Of course, these are the ways to be followed if Sot'aesan's dual goals of "saving sentient beings" and "curing the world of illness" are to be realized.

It can readily be shown that the tenets of Irwŏnsang and the threefold practice are formulated as a means to the realization of the objective "correct enlightenment and right practice"; the tenet of fourfold beneficence for the realization of the objective "awareness and requital of beneficence"; and the tenet of four essentials for the realization of the objective "selfless service for the public."

My translation project with these problematic issues was presented to the leadership of the order in 1992. The leadership eventually established a commission for correct translation of the scriptures of Won Buddhism, which should produce a translation with no "smell" or "color" of Buddhism. To the Supreme Council of the Order of Won Buddhism I formally submitted a plea that the restorations in question be permitted; the council decided that not a single word in the *Canon* should be restored. It should be noted here that Chŏngsan advised that the 1943 edition, *The Correct Canon of Buddhism* (*Pulgyo chŏngjŏn*) should be preserved permanently (*KC*, VI:288). A careful, comparative study of the two versions will prove that the restorations in question are absolutely necessary for the soundness of its doctrine. The errors should be corrected not only in the translated version but in the Korean original, the errors having been made not by Sot'aesan or Chŏngsan, but by the redaction committee assigned by Chŏngsan.

# Appendix II

## *Individuals in* The Scripture of Sot'aesan

The following biographical notes on Sot'aesan's disciples and others are excerpts drawn from Song In-gŏl (宋仁傑), *Taejonggyŏng soge naonŭn saramdŭl* 대종경속에나오는삶들 (Individuals in *The Scripture of Sot'aesan*).

An Ch'ang-ho (安昌浩, 1878–1938): An eminent patriot known by his cognomen Tosan (島山); born in Kangsŏ, P'yŏngan province; went to the United States in 1900 and returned in 1906 to Korea, where he organized Shinminhoe (新民會); went in 1908 to the United States, where he organized Hŭngsadan (興士團); secretary-general of internal affairs of the Shanghai Temporary Government after the March 1 (1919) independence movement; arrested by the Japanese authority in 1932 and served three years in prison; arrested again in 1937; died in 1938 from illness contracted during imprisonment. Appears in XII:45.

Chang Chŏk-cho (張寂照, dt. It'awŏn 二陀圓, 1878–1960): Born in T'ongyŏng, South Kyŏngsang province; originally a follower of Kang Il-sun; converted to Sot'aesan during his stay at Pongnae Cloister in Mt. Pyŏn; respected as one of the order's three heroines for her outstanding conversion activity together with Ch'oe To-hwa and Pak Sasihwa during the incipient stage of the order. Appears in X:13; XIV:16.

Cho Chŏn-gwŏn (曺專權, dt. Kongt'awŏn 空陀圓, 1909–1976): Born in Kimje-gun, North Chŏlla province; Cho Song-kwang's daughter; originally a devout Christian like her father, converted to Sot'aesan in 1923 (8 w.e.); the first celibate devotee; the first female *chongsa* (宗師); a master preacher; one of the few great leaders of the order. Appears in IV:8; VI:12.

Cho Kap-chong (趙甲鐘, dt. Ŭisan 義山, 1905–1971): Born in Imsil-gun, North Chŏlla province; converted to Sot'aesan in 1924 (9 w.e.); devoted himself to the growth of the order for forty-seven years; appointed a member of the order's Supreme Council. Appears in XIII:39.

Cho Song-gwang (曺頌廣, dt. Kyŏngsan 慶山, 1876–1957): Born in Chŏngju, North Chŏlla province; participated in the Tonghak

Rebellion at age eighteen; with its failure hid himself studying Chinese medicine, becoming very proficient; at twenty-seven converted to Christianity, founding a Church in Kubong in five years, becoming an elder at forty-three; in 1924 (9 w.e.) met Sot'aesan and converted to him on the spot, becoming an official member of the order the next year; elected chairman of the order (Society for the Study of Buddha-dharma) in 1931 (16 w.e.); let three of his daughters (Man-sik, Chŏn-gwŏn, Il-gwan) become celibate devotees. Appears in III:39; VIII:20; XIV:14.

Cho Wŏn-sŏn (曹元善, dt. Hoesan 回山, 1896–1950): Born in Yŏng-gwang, South Chŏlla province; one of Sot'aesan's disciples during the construction of the Iksan headquarters of the order. Appears in VI:29.

Ch'oe Che-u (崔濟愚, 1824–1864). Founder of Ch'ŏndogyo (天道教). Appears in VI:31.

Ch'oe Nae-sŏn (崔內善, dt. Changt'awŏn 丈陀圓, 1895–1964): Born in Wanju-gun, North Chŏlla province; became a devout lay follower around the thirteenth year of the order. Appears in V:29.

Ch'oe Suinhwa (崔修仁華, dt. Kyŏngt'awŏn 慶陀圓, 1889–1980): Born in Imsil-gun, North Chŏlla province; originally a Ch'ŏndogyo follower; converted to Sot'aesan in 1934 (19 w.e.) at age forty-six; became a devotee in 1936, making a considerable contribution to the order. Appears in VI:30.

Ch'oe Suun (崔水雲). See Ch'oe Che-u (崔濟愚).

Ch'oe To-hwa (崔道華, dt. Samt'awŏn 三陀圓, 1883–1954): Born in Chinan-gun, North Chŏlla province; converted to Sot'aesan during the Zen retreat in Mt. Mandŏk; respected as one of the three heroines of the order for her outstanding conversion activity during the incipient stage of the order. Appears in XIV:16, 29.

Chŏn Sam-sam (田參參, dt. Sŏngt'awŏn 成陀圓, 1870–1948): Born in Chinan-gun, North Chŏlla province; one of Sot'aesan's disciples during his Zen retreat at Mt. Mandŏk. Appears in XIV:14.

Chŏn Ŭm-gwang (全飲光, dt. Hyesan 惠山, 1909–1960): Born in Chinan-gun, North Chŏlla province; converted to Sot'aesan during his Zen retreat at Mt. Mandŏk. Appears in III:11; VIII:20; XIII:15.

Chŏng Il-sŏng (鄭一成, 1879–1941): Born in Kwangsan-gun, South Chŏlla province; became a lay member in 1927 (12 w.e.); worked as devotee for a while but returned home. Appears in IX:12.

Chŏng Kong-ch'il (鄭公七, no biographical information available). A faithful but poor follower. Appears in V:18.

Chŏng Se-wŏl (鄭世月, dt. Ch'ilt'awŏn 七陀圓, 1896–1977): Born in Kimje, North Chŏlla province; met Sot'aesan in 1923 (8 w.e.) during his stay at Pongnae Cloister in Mt. Pyŏn; in the seventeenth

year, entered the order to devote herself to the order's mission. Appears in XIV:16.

Chŏng Sŏk-hyŏn (鄭石現, 1879–1947): Born in Iksan-gun, North Chŏlla province; met Sot'aesan in 1924 (9 w.e.) and converted to him; made one of her two daughters become a celibate devotee. Appears in X:16.

Chŏng Yang-sŏn (丁良善, dt. Tŏkt'awŏn 德陀圓, 1914–1986): Born in Yŏnggwang-gun, South Chŏlla province; became a female celibate devotee in 1934 (19 w.e.); her father, two sisters, and a brother all became devotees in the order. Appears in XIII:8.

Chŏngsan. *See* Song Kyu.

Hwang Chŏngsinhaeng (黃淨信行, dt. P'alt'awŏn 八陀圓, 1903– ): Born at Yŏnan, Hwanghae province; met Sot'aesan in Seoul in 1938 (23 w.e.); made a huge donation to the order; a member of the first female Supreme Council of the order. Appears in XIII:35.

Hwang I-ch'ŏn (黃二天, dt. Pungsan 鵬山, 1910–1990): Born in Wanju-gun, North Chŏlla province; a policeman appointed by the Japanese government to conduct surveillance on the order; converted to Sot'aesan, protecting the order from the harsh surveillance. Appears in XII:12.

Im Ch'ilbpohwa (林七寶華, dt. Yŏngt'awŏn 永陀圓, 1896–1972): Born in Masan, South Kyŏngsang province; converted to Sot'aesan in 1934 (19 w.e.); made a significant contribution to the founding of Ch'oyang and Masan temples. Appears in XII:28.

Kang Chŭngsan (姜甑山): *See* Kang Il-sun. "Kang" is his family name and "Chŭngsan" his cognomen.

Kang Il-sun (姜一淳, 1871–1909): The founder of Chŭngsan'gyo (甑山教). Appears in VI:31.

Kim Chŏng-gak (金正覺, dt. Sŏnt'awŏn 善陀圓, 1874–1952): Born in Chŏnju, North Chŏlla province; initially a follower of Chŭngsangyo (甑山教); converted to Sot'aesan and became a devotee in 1925 (10 w.e.). Appears in X:14.

Kim Ki-ch'ŏn (金幾千, dt. Samsan 三山, 1890–1935): Born in Yŏnggwang-gun, South Chŏlla province; one of Sot'aesan's first nine disciples; participated in the embankment project and the authentication prayer; the first disciple who received the approval of "seeing into the nature" (見性認可) from Sot'aesan; died while serving as *kyomu* at a branch temple. Appears in IV:9; V:21; VI:32, 34, 35, 36, 37, 38; VII:22; XIV:8.

Kim Kwang-sŏn (金光旋, dt. P'alsan 八山, 1879–1939): Born in Yŏnggwang-gun, South Cholla province; one of Sot'aesan's first nine disciples; participated in the embankment project and the authentication prayer; devoted himself to the establishment of the order until his death. Appears in I:6; IV:54; VII:20; IX:28; XII:47.

Kim Nam-ch'ŏn (金南天, dt. Kaksan 角山, 1869–1941): Born in Chŏnju, North Chŏlla province; waited on Sot'aesan during the latter's stay at Pongnae Cloister in Mt. Pyŏn. Appears in III:26, 54; IV:36; XII:3; XIV:29.

Kim Sammaehwa (金三昧華, dt. Nakt'awŏn 洛陀圓, 1890–1944: Born in Seoul; converted to Sot'aesan during the Zen retreat at Mt. Mandŏk. Appears in V:32.

Kim Tae-gŏ (金大舉, dt. Taesan 大山, 1914–1998): Born in Chinan-gun, North Chŏlla province; succeeded Chŏngsan as the third head dharma master of the order in 1962 and retired in 1994; helped expand the order to a great extent, with more than four hundred branch temples established in Korea and thirty overseas. Appears in III:63; IX:32, 33, 34, 35, 36, 37, 38.

Kim Yŏng-shin (金永信, dt. Yungt'awŏn 融陀圓, 1908–1984): Born in Seoul; met Sot'aesan in 1924 (9 w.e.); one of his disciples during his construction of Iksan headquarters; one of the first two celibate devotees with Cho Chŏn-gwŏn; the first female *kyomu*. Appears in III:16, 28.

Ku Nam-su (具南守, dt. Ch'et'awŏn 體陀圓, 1870–1939): Born in Chŏngŭp-gun, North Chŏlla province; one of Sot'aesan's disciples during his stay at Pongnae Cloister in Mt. Pyŏn. Appears in X:13.

Kwŏn Tae-ho (權大鎬, 1910–1931): Born in Changsu-gun, North Chŏlla province; Kwŏn Tong-hwa's younger brother; became a devotee at nineteen. Appears in XIV:4.

Kwŏn Tong-hwa (權動華, dt. Tongt'awŏn 東陀圓, 1904– ): Born in Changsu-gun, North Chŏlla province; attended the order's first summer Zen retreat in 1926 (10 w.e.); a lay follower. Appears in III:13.

Min Chayŏnhwa (閔自然華, dt. Nakt'awŏn 樂陀圓, 1859–1932): Born in Seoul; a devout Buddhist for fifteen years before meeting Sot'aesan in 1924 (9 w.e.), when she was sixty-five; Yi Kong-chu's mother. Appears in VI:16.

Mun Chŏng-gyu (文正奎, dt. Tongsan 冬山, 1863–1936): Born in Koksŏng-gun, South Chŏlla province; met Sot'aesan in 1920 (5 w.e.) at Pongnae Cloister at age fifty-eight, becoming a devout disciple. Appears in III:33; IV:36; VII:14, 22; X:18; XIV:7, 29.

No Tŏksongok (盧德頌玉, dt. Hyŏnt'awŏn 賢陀圓, 1859–1933): Born in Namwŏn, North Chŏlla province; converted to Sot'aesan during his Zen retreat at Mt. Mandŏk; introduced her grandson Kim Tae-gŏ to Sot'aesan. Appears in X:15; XIV:29.

O Ch'ang-gŏn (吳昌建, dt. Sasan 四山, 1887–1953): Born in Yŏng-gwang-gun, Sout Chŏlla province; one of Sot'aesan's first nine disciples; participated in the embankment project and the authen-

tication prayer; exerted a great effort to help establish the order. Appears in I:6; IV:55; XII:9; XIII:11.

O Chong-t'ae (吳宗泰, dt. Hyŏngtawŏn 亨陀圓, 1913–1976): Born in Chinan-gun, North Chŏlla province; a celibate female devotee, appointed abbot of the order's Yŏngsan Monastery. Appears in XII:27 together with her father and her twin sister.

O Song-am (吳松庵, dt. Huisan 輝山, 1886–1948): Born in Chinan-gun, North Chŏlla province; met Sot'aesan in 1934 (9 w.e.) to entrust his two twin daughters (Chong-sun and Chong-t'ae) to Sot'aesan's care. Appears in XII:27.

Paek Hang-myŏng (白鶴鳴, 1867–1929): Born in Yŏnggwang-gun, South Chŏlla province; entered the Buddhist order upon the death of both parents; restored Naejangsa, where he taught "half farming and half Zen" to the sangha; moved to Wŏlmyŏng-am, where he discussed the future of Korean Buddhism with Sot'aesan. Appears in VII:18, 19.

Pak Che-bong (朴濟奉, dt. Chesan 霽山, 1888–1957): Born in Ulsan, South Kyŏngsang province; converted to Sot'aesan in 1936 (21 w.e.) and became a devotee, serving as kyomu at several temples. Appears in IX:29.

Pak Ho-jang (朴戶張, ?–1929): Met Sot'aesan in 1920 (5 w.e.) at Pongnae Cloister and became his follower; made considerable contribution during the inchoate stage of the order. Appears in XIV:7.

Pak Kwang-jŏn (朴光田, dt. Sungsan 崇山, 1915–1986): Born in Yŏnggwang-gun, South Chŏlla province; Sot'aesan's son; made a great contribution to establishing and expanding Won'gwang University (圓光大學校) as its first president; a member of the Supreme Council. Appears in II:3, 4, 5, 6.

Pak Sasihwa (朴四時華, dt. Ilt'awŏn 一陀圓, 1867–1946): Born in Namwŏn, North Chŏlla province; converted to Sot'aesan in 1924 (9 w.e.), becoming one of his first nine female disciples; respected as one of the three heroines (with Chang Chŏk-cho and Ch'oe To-hwa) of the order for her outstanding conversion activity during the order's incipient stage. Appears in XIV:17, 29.

Pak Se-ch'ŏl (朴世喆, dt. Osan 五山, 1879–1926): One of Sot'aesan's first nine disciples; participated in the embankment project and the authentication prayer. Appears in I:6.

Pak Tae-wan (朴大完, dt. Yŏngsan 靈山, 1885–1958): Born in Yŏch'ŏn-gun, South Chŏlla province; met Sot'aesan in 1927 (12 w.e.) at age forty-three; in 1935 (20 w.e.) appointed kyomu of Osaka temple in Japan and returned after a year's mission because of the Japanese government's severe oppression. Appears in III:39.

Pak Tong-guk (朴東局, dt. Yuksan 六山, 1897–1950): Born in Yŏnggwang-gun, South Chŏlla province; Sot'aesan's younger brother

and one of his first nine disciples; participated in the embankment project and the authentication prayer. Appears in I:6; IV:49.

P'alsan. *See* Kim Kwang-sŏn.

Samsan. *See* Kim Ki-ch'ŏn.

Sŏ Chung-an (徐中安, dt. Ch'usan 秋山, 1881–1930): Born in Kimje-gun, North Chŏlla province; met Sot'aesan at Pongnae Cloister in 1923 (8 w.e.) at age forty-two, suggesting that he leave the mountain valley for a rural or an urban area to open the gate of a new religious order; played the major role in the construction of Iksan headquarters by providing the land; first president of the Society for the Study of Buddha-dharma. Appears in VII:17.

Sŏ Tae-wŏn (徐大圓, dt. Wŏnsan 圓山, 1910–1945): Born in Yŏng-gwang-gun, South Chŏlla province; Sot'aesan's nephew; converted to Sot'aesan in 1929 (14 w.e.); a celibate devotee, appointed a member of the order's Supreme Council at age thirty-two; made an important contribution to the compilation of the *Pulgyo chŏngjŏn* (佛教正典; Correct canon of Buddhism) with his sound knowledge of Buddhist scriptures; cut his left hand to show the depth of his faith in Sot'aesan just as Huiko (慧可, 487–593) had. Appears in VI:4, 5, 6, 7, 8, 9; IX:31; X:18; XIII:15; XIV:18.

Song Chŏk-pyŏk (宋赤壁, dt. Hasan 夏山, 1874–1939): Born in Ch'ungch'ŏng province (county unknown); originally a follower of Kang Il-sun (姜一淳, 1871–1909), the founder of Chŭngsan'gyo; introduced to Sot'aesan by Song Kyu and waited on Sot'aesan during the latter's stay at Pongnae Cloister in Mt. Pyŏn. Appears in IV:55; XII:3.

Song Kyu (宋奎, dt. Chŏngsan 鼎山, 1900–1962): Born in Sŏngju-gun, North Kyŏngsang province; Sot'aesan's best disciple; succeeded him as head dharma master of the Order of Won Buddhism and led the order from 1943 to 1962; received by Sot'aesan as the "mother of the dharma" of the new religious order; laid the foundation of the order in the three areas of the order's projects: edification, education, and charity; renamed the order Wŏnbulgyo (圓佛教) in 1947; analects codified as one of the two holy scriptures of the order, titled *Chŏngsan chongsa pŏbŏ* (鼎山宗師法語; Master Chŏngsan's dharma words). Appears in III:9, 21, 26; VII:22; X:18; XV:5.

Song Man-gyŏng (宋萬京, dt. Mosan 慕山, 1876–1931): Born in Kimje-gun, North Chŏlla province; met Sot'aesan in 1924 (9 w.e.) at Naejangsa; made a significant contribution to the construction of Iksan headquarters; worked for five years as a devotee. Appears in III:39.

Song Pyŏk-cho (宋碧照, dt. Kusan 久山, 1876–1951): Born in Sŏngju-gun, North Kyŏngsang province; father of Song Kyu and Song

To-sŏng; *kyomu*; served one year in prison for writing a letter of criticism of the Japanese emperor in 1939. Appears in III:6; 40.

Sŏng Sŏng-wŏn (成聖願, dt. Chŏngt'awŏn 正陀圓, 1905–1984): Born in Imsil-gun, North Chŏlla province; met Sot'aesan at her house in Seoul in 1924 (9 w.e.) and converted to him; made a considerable contribution to the foundation of Seoul Temple. Appears in IX:4.

Song To-sŏng (宋道性, dt. Chusan 主山, 1907–1946): Born in Sŏngju-gun, North Kyŏngsang province; Song Kyu's younger brother and Sot'aesan's son-in-law; one of the latter's eminent disciples; died while carrying out the order's relief project for war refugees from Manchuria and Japan. Appears in II:24; III:20; VI:32; VII:30; X:18; XV:8.

Yang Ha-un (梁夏雲, dt. Sipt'awon 十陀圓, 1890–1973): Born in Yŏnggwang-gun, South Chŏlla province; Sot'aesan's wife; took care of his household affairs. Appears in XII:25.

Yang To-shin (梁道信, dt. Hunt'awŏn 薰陀圓, 1918– ): Born in Pusan, South Kyŏngsang province; met Sot'aesan in 1931 (16 w.e.) in Pusan; became a celibate devotee in 1932; appointed a member of the order's Supreme Council. Appears in III:17.

Yi Chae-ch'ŏl (李載喆, dt. Ilsan 一山, 1891–1943): Born in Yŏnggwang-gun, South Chŏlla province; one of Sot'aesan's nine disciples who participated in the embankment project and the authentication prayer; obtained a copy of the Diamond Sūtra (*Kŭmganggyŏng* [金剛經]) for Sot'aesan's perusal. Appears in IV:15.

Yi Ch'ŏng-ch'un (李青春, dt. Ot'awŏn 五陀圓, 1886–1955): Converted to Sot'aesan in 1923 (8 w.e.) as a retired courtesan; donated most of her property (land) to the order when the order was financially in need of help; a member of the Supreme Council. Appears in III:21; XII:26.

Yi Ch'ŏng-p'ung (李清風, no biographical information available): Waited on Sot'aesan during his stay at Pongnae Cloister in Mt. Pyŏn. Appears in VII:18.

Yi Chŏng-wŏn (李正圓, dt. Hŭit'awŏn 喜陀圓, 1871–1933): Born in Kosŏng, South Kyŏngsang province; converted to Sot'aesan in 1925 (10 w.e.). Appears in IV:18.

Yi Ch'un-p'ung (李春風, dt. Hunsan 薰山, 1876–1930): Born in Kŭmnŭng-gun, North Kyŏngsang province; a devotee for five years. Appears in I:10; III:34; IV:55; VI:20.

Yi Ho-ch'un (李昊春, dt. Hangsan 恒山, 1902–1966): Born in Yŏnggwang-gun, South Chŏlla province; one of Sot'aesan's disciples during the construction of Iksan headquarters. Appears in VI:32.

Yi Inŭihwa (李仁義華, dt. Taet'awŏn 大陀圓, 1879–1963): Born in Chŏnju, North Chŏlla province; met Sot'aesan when she was fifty-seven after several miseries; the first lay follower promoted to the

dharma stage of subjugation of *mara* by dharma power while living during the first generation of the order. Appears in III:27.

Yi Kong-ju (李共珠, dt. Kut'awŏn 九陀圓, 1896–1991): Born in Seoul; first met Sot'aesan in 1924 (9 w.e.) in Seoul; dictated Sot'aesan's sermons more than any other disciples, thus the nickname "Dharma Pouch"; poured her wealth into the order during the early years of the order and continued to make huge donations to the order throughout her career in the order; a member of the first Supreme Council of the order. Appears in IV:17; VI:1; IX:4.

Yi Man-gap (李萬甲, dt. Want'awŏn 完陀圓, 1879–1960): Born in Chŏnju, North Chŏlla province; one of Sot'aesan's disciples during his stay at Pongnae Cloister in Mt. Pyŏn. Appears in X:13.

Yi Sun-sun (李旬旬, dt. Isan 二山, 1879–1941): Born in Yŏnggwang-gun, South Cholla province; one of Sot'aesan's nine disciples who participated in the embankment project and the authentication prayer; stayed a lay disciple thereafter. Appears in III:19.

Yi Tong-an (李東安, dt. Tosan 道山, 1892–1941): Born in Yŏnggwang-gun, South Chŏlla province; one of Sot'aesan's disciples during the construction of Iksan headquarters, becoming a devotee at thirty-one. Appears in IV:27; XII:33.

Yi Tongjinhwa (李東震華, dt. Yukt'awŏn 六陀圓, 1893–1968): Born in Hamyang-gun, South Kyŏngsang province; converted to Sot'aesan in 1924 (9 w.e.); appointed a member of the Supreme Council; donated her property to the establishment of Seoul Temple; respected as "the mother in the order." Appears in IV:6.

Yi Un-oe (李雲外, dt. Chunt'awŏn 準陀圓, 1872–1967): Born in Kŭmnŭng-gun, North Kyŏngsan province; Song Pyŏk-cho's wife; mother of Song Kyu and Song To-sŏng. Appears in XII:31.

Yi Wan-ch'ŏl (李完喆, dt. Ŭngsan, 1897–1965): Born in Yŏnggwang-gun, South Chŏlla province; met Sot'aesan in 1921 (6 w.e.) and became a devotee in 1930 during the construction of Iksan head-quarters; devoted himself for the growth of the order until his death in 1965. Appears in XIII:11.

Yi Wŏn-hwa (李願華, dt. Satawŏn 四陀圓, 1884–1964): Born in Naju-gun, South Chŏlla province; waited on Sot'aesan during his ascetic practice before the great enlightenment; devoted herself to the spreading of the dharma. Appears in VI:2.

Yu Hŏ-il (柳虛一, dt. Yusan 柳山, 1882–1958): Born in Yŏnggwang-gun, South Chŏlla province; a Confucian elite; met Sot'aesan in 1932 (17 w.e.); became a devotee at age fifty-two. Appears in IV:53; XIII:15.

Yu Kŏn (劉巾, dt. Ch'ilsan 七山, 1880–1963): Born in Yŏnggwang-gun, South Chŏlla province; one of Sot'aesan's first nine disciples; participated in the embankment project and the authentication prayer. Appears in I:6.

# Chinese Character Glossary

*chagŏp ch'wisa* 作業取捨
Chasuwŏn 慈壽院
Chayugwŏn 慈育院
*chen-yen* 真言
Cheng-hao 程顥
*Cheng-tao ko* 證道歌
*chi* 智
*chieh* 桀
*chigi* 至氣
*Chin-kang ching* 金剛經
*chin-kung miao-yu* 真空妙有
Chinmuk 震默
*Chinŏn* 真言
Chinp'yo 真表
*Chinsim chiksŏl* 真心直說
Chinul 知訥
Chiri-san 智異山
*Chogye* 曹溪
*Chogyejong* 曹溪宗
Chŏlla 全羅
*chŏng* 正
Chŏng Toryŏng 鄭道令
*chongbŏpsa* 宗法師
*Chŏnggwanp'yŏng* 貞觀坪
*chonggyo* 宗教
*Chŏngjŏn* 正典
Chŏngjong 定宗
Chŏngsan 鼎山
*chŏngsin suyang* 精神修養
Chŏngŭp 井邑
Chŏnju 全州
*chŏnmu ch'ulsin* 專務出身
Chosŏn 朝鮮
*Chosŏn pulgyo hyŏksillon* 朝鮮佛教革新論
Chou 紂
*Choung chŏn* 趙雄傳
Chu Hsi 朱熹

Chu Ko-liang 諸葛亮
Chuang-tzu 莊子
*Chung-yung* 中庸
Chungjong 中宗
*Chŭngsan chongdan kaeron* 甑山宗團概論
*Chŭngsando* 甑山道
*Chŭngsan'gyo* 甑山教
Chungwŏn 重遠
Ch'a Kyŏng-sŏk 車京石
Ch'an 禪
Ch'ing 清
Ch'oe Che-u 崔濟愚
Ch'oe Si-hyŏng 崔時亨
Ch'ŏndogyo 天道教
Ch'ŏngnyŏnam 青蓮庵
*ch'ŏnjiŭn* 天地恩
*ch'ŏnju* 天主
*ch'ulgawi* 出家位
*ch'un-ch'iu* 春秋
*Ch'unhyang chŏn* 春香傳
Dogen 道元
*fei* 非
Haeinsa 海印寺
Hamyŏl 咸悅
*Han'guk minjok chonggyo* 韓國民族宗教
Ho-tse Shen-hui 荷澤神會
*Hoebo* 會報
*Hoegyu* 會規
Honam 湖南
Hong Wŏlcho 洪月初
*hsiang* 相
*Hsiao ching* 孝經
*Hsien-tsung chi* 顯宗記
*hsin* 信
*Hsin-hsin ming* 信心銘
*hsing* 性

*Hsü-hsü-an tso-chan-wen* 休休庵坐
　禪文
*Hua-yen* 華嚴
*Hui-ch'ung* 慧忠
*Hui-neng* 惠能
*hŭisawi* 喜事位
*Hŭngbu chŏn* 興夫傳
*Hŭngdŏksa* 興德寺
*hwadu* 話頭
Hwahaeri 花海里
Hwangdŭng 黃登
Hyujŏng 休靜
*i* 義
*I ching* 易經
*i-hsin san-mei* 一心三昧
*i-yüan-hsiang* 一圓相
Iksan 益山
*Imjejong* 臨濟宗
Insuwŏn 仁壽院
*ip'ansŭng* 理判僧
*irhaeng sammae* 一行三昧
Iri 裡里
Irwŏnsang 一圓相
*jen* 仁
*Jōdoshū* 淨土宗
Kakhwangsa 覺皇寺
*Kaksae chin'gyŏng* 覺世真經
Kang Il-sun 姜一淳
*kanhwa Sŏn* 看話禪
*kanna Zen* 看話禪
*kapcha* 甲子
Kilyongni 吉龍里
Kim Hae-un 金海雲
Kim Sŏng-sŏp 金成燮
Kim Tae-gŏ 金大舉
Kim T'ae-hŭp 金泰洽
Kimje 金堤
*kōan* 公案
Kobu 古阜
Koguryŏ 高句麗
*kong* 空
*kongan* 公案
*kongjŏk yŏngji* 空寂靈知
Koryŏ 高麗
Kosubu 高首婦
*Kuei-yang* 潙仰
Kujŏng 九鼎
Kŭmgang-ni 金剛里

Kŭmsan-sa 金山寺
*kungan* 公案
*kunggung ŭrŭl* 弓弓乙乙
Kunsŏ-myŏn 郡西面
Kusu-san 九首山
Kyeryong-san 鷄龍山
*kyo* 教
*kyodan* 教團
*Kyojŏn* 教典
*kyomu* 教務
*kyŏng* 敬
Kyŏngsang 慶尙
*kyosa* 教史
*li* 禮
Lin-chi 臨濟
*Liu-tsu t'an-ching* 六曹壇經
*Lun-yü* 論語
Mansŏng-ni 萬石里
Maryŏng 馬靈
Maŭm-ni 馬邑里
*Meng-tsu* 孟子
*minjung* 民眾
Mirŭk-sa 彌勒寺
Moak-san 母岳山
*moktak* 木鐸
*mokugyo* 木魚
*mugŭk* 無極
*mugŭk taedo* 無極大道
Muhak Chach'o 無學自超
Munjŏng 文定
*munyŏm* 無念
Myŏngjin hakkyo 明進學校
Myŏngjong 明宗
Naejangsa 內藏寺
Nam-san 南山
*Nan-hua ching* 南華經
Nan-yang Hui-chung 南陽慧忠
Nan-yüeh Huai-jang 南岳懷讓
Nichiren 日蓮
Ongnyŏbong 玉女峰
Pae-san 盃山
Paek Hang-myŏng 白鶴鳴
Pak Chung-bin 朴重彬
Pak Kong-u 朴公又
*Pak T'ae-bu chŏn* 朴太傅傳
*pŏbŭi taejŏn* 法義大典
Poch'ŏngyo 普天教
Pogwang-sa 普光寺

*pŏmnyurŭn* 法律恩
Pongnae 蓬萊
Pongsŏ-sa 鳳棲寺
*pŏpsa* 法師
Pŏpsŏng-p'o 法聖浦
Pou 普愚
*poŭnmi* 報恩米
Puan 扶安
*Pulbŏp yŏn'guhoe* 佛法研究會
*Pulcho yogyŏng* 佛祖要經
Pulgap-sa 佛甲寺
*Pulgyo* 佛教
*Pulgyo chŏngjŏn* 佛教正典
Pulgyo Sibosa 佛教時報社
*Pulgyo taejŏn* 佛教大典
*Pulgyo yŏn'guhoe* 佛教研究會
*pumoŭn* 父母恩
Pyŏn-san 邊山
P'alsan 八山
*P'alsang chŏn* 八相傳
Rinzai 臨濟
*Samhak* 三學
Samsan 三山
*Sangje* 上帝
*Sap'ansŭng* 事判僧
*sari yŏn'gu* 事理研究
*saŭn* 四恩
Sejo 世祖
*Sejŏn* 世典
Sejong 世宗
Shang 商
Shen-nung 神農
*Shih-ching* 詩經
*shingon* 真言
*shinmi* 辛未
*Shōbōgenzō* 政法眼藏
*Shu ching* 書經
Shun 舜
Silsang-sa 實相寺
*Simch'ŏng chŏn* 沈清傳
*simdan* 心丹
Sinhŭng 新興
Sŏktu-am 石頭庵
*sŏn* 禪
Son Pyŏng-hŭi 孫秉熙
Sŏndogyo 仙道教
*sŏng* 誠
Song Kyu 宋奎

Song To-gun 宋道君
*sŏngga* 聖歌
Songgwang-sa 松廣寺
Songhang-ni 松鶴里
Sŏngjong 成宗
Sŏngju-san 聖住山
*sŏnjŏng* 禪定
*Sŏnyo* 禪要
Sot'aesan 少太山
*sunanjang* 受難章
Sunch'ang 淳昌
Sunji 順之
*Susim kyŏl* 修心訣
Suun 水雲
*Suyang yŏ'ngu yoron* 修養研究要論
*Ta-hsüeh* 大學
*Ta-sheng chi-hsin lun* 大乘起信論
*Ta-sheng chi-kuan fa-men* 大乘止觀 法門
Taegakchŏn 大覺殿
Taehan 大韓
*Taejonggyŏng* 大宗經
*Taesun chŏn'gyŏng* 大巡典經
Taewŏn-sa 大院寺
Tan'gun 檀君
*tanjŏn* 丹田
*Tao-chieh* 盜拓
*tao-te* 道德
*Togyŏl* 道訣
Tongdae-mun 東大門
*Tonggyŏng taeŏn* 東經大典
Tonghak 東學
*tongp'oŭn* 同胞恩
Tosan 道山
*Tsao-tung tsung* 曹洞宗
*Tsu-t'ang chi* 祖堂集
Tsung-mi 宗密
Tung-shan Liang-chieh 洞山良价
T'aego-sa 太古寺
*t'aegŭk* 太極
T'aein 泰仁
*T'aeŭlchu* 太乙呪
*T'aeŭlgyo* 太乙教
*T'ai-chi* 太極
*to* 道
*todŏk* 道德
*tŏk* 德
*ŭidu* 疑頭

*ŭn* 恩
*undo* 運度
Wang Yang-ming 王陽明
*wŏlbo* 月報
*Wŏlmal t'ongsin* 月末通信
Wŏlmyŏng-am 月明庵
*wŏn* 圓
Wŏnbulgyo 圓佛教
*Wŏnbulgyo chŏnsŏ* 圓佛教全書
*Wŏnjong* 圓宗
*wŏnsang* 圓相
Wŏn'gak-sa 圓覺寺
*wŏn'gwang* 圓光
*wu-chi* 無極
*Wu-chiao chang* 五教章
*yama* 閻羅
Yang-shan Hui-chi 仰山慧寂
*yangban* 兩班
Yao 堯

Yi Hoe-gwang 李晦光
Yi Podam 李寶潭
Yi T'aejo 李太祖
*Yin-fu ching* 陰符經
yin-yang 陰陽
*Yŏmsongjip* 念誦集
*Yongdam yusa* 龍潭遺詞
*yŏngdan* 靈團
*yŏngga* 靈駕
Yŏnggwang-gun 靈光郡
Yŏngsan 靈山
*yŏn'gu* 研究
Yŏnsan'gun 燕山君
Yu Hŏ-il 柳虛一
*Yü-shu ching* 玉樞經
Yuil Hagwŏn 唯一學院
Yujŏng 維靜
*yunyŏm* 有念

# Glossary of Terms

**Amitābha** (S.) [阿彌陀佛]: The buddha of Measureless Light, boundless life, and enlightenment.

**asura** (S.) [阿修羅]: Fallen gods or demons, beings in one of the six realms of existence [六道].

**beneficence** [恩]: The benefits produced by things. The term "grace" is avoided in this translation because its meaning implies mercy (like divine grace), clemency, lenity, and charity, which have little to do with the favors done to one by the fourfold beneficence (of heaven and earth, parents, brethren, and laws).

**bodhisattva** (S.) [菩薩]: One who aspires to the attainment of buddhahood and devotes himself or herself to altruistic deeds, especially deeds that cause others to attain enlightenment.

*chagŏp* (K.) [作業]: Production of karma. Since the Sanskrit term "karma" means "action" or "deed," "karma production" means "production of action." Thus threefold karma [三業] should mean acting with body, mouth, and volition. However, production of karma means more than just acting; it implies that one sows the good or evil seeds the fruits of which one cannot but reap in accordance with the law of karma. Karma, good or evil, follows one like a debt until it is paid off. Sot'aesan has used this crucial term in this sense throughout the *Pulgyo chŏngjŏn* [佛教正典] and *Wŏnbulgyo kyojŏn* [원불교교전].

*chagŏp ch'wisa* (K.) [作業取捨]: Literally, "taking what is right and forsaking what is wrong while producing karma." For brevity this is translated as "mindful choice in karmic action."

*chongbŏpsa* (K.) [宗法師]: Head dharma master, the highest priest elected by the Supreme Council in the Won Buddhist order (like the pope in the Catholic church).

*chŏngjŏn* (K.) [正典]: "Correct Canon"; in the canon of Won Buddhism, book 1 of *The Scriptures of Won Buddhism*.

*chŏngsin* (K.) [精神]: The spiritual and moral life in general as used in the founding motto of Won Buddhism; unfolding the spirit [精神開闢]. When used in the context of Zen meditation, it means the mental state that is clear and calm, with no discrimination or attachment.

*chŏnmu ch'ulsin* (K.) [專務出身]: A devotee who has left his or her home to devote his or her life to the mission of the Won Buddhist order.

**Ch'ŏndogyo** (K.) [天道教]: The religion founded by Ch'oe Che-u [崔濟愚; 1824–1864], teaching the unity of heaven and humankind.

*ch'ŏnjiŭn* (K.) [天地恩]: The favors or beneficence of heaven and earth, without which one cannot exist.

**Chŭngsan'gyo** (K.) [甑山教]: A Korean indigenous religion founded by Kang Il-sun [姜一淳; 1871–1909].

*ch'ulga* (K.) [出家]: Literally, "leaving home"; transcending the boundary of concern for one's own self, family, clan, and state, and taking all sentient beings as one's own body and the whole universe as one's own home. In Won Buddhism *ch'ulgawui* [出家位] is the dharma stage where one has reached such a moral perfection.

**compassion** [慈悲; S. *karuṇā*]: A Buddhist technical term meaning sympathy of the Buddha for sentient beings who suffer and the will to end their suffering.

**consciousness** [識; S. *vijñāna*]: The eight consciousnesses include visual, auditory, olfactory, gustatory, tactile, mental, governing, and storehouse consciousness.

**defilement** [煩惱; S. *kleśa*]: The passions and ignorance that cause one to wander in saṁsāra and keep one from reaching enlightenment.

**delusion** [痴; S. *moha*]: Ignorance, stupidity, or blindness.

**dependent origination**: *See* "twelvefold dependent origination."

**dharma** (S.) [法]: The teaching given by the Buddha; the moral principles; the truth; the all-encompassing principle that governs all manifestations of things and events; transcendental reality. In plural form, "dharmas" denotes things, phenomena, events, attributes, or beings. The expression "Buddha-dharma" in this work means the teachings of the Buddha as Sot'aesan originally intended to mean.

**dharma realm** [法界]: See *dharmadhātu*.

*dharmadhātu* (S.) [法界]: Literally, "the realm of dharmas"; the nature or essence of dharmas, which is the unifying, underlying reality as the ground of all things, both noumenal and phenomenal.

**dharmakāya** (S.) [法身]: The dharma-body, or the body of reality, which is formless, unchanging, transcendental, and inconceivable; synonymous with "suchness"; the cosmic body of the Buddha; the essence of all beings. In Won Buddhism, Dharmakāya Buddha is the object of religious worship; a circular symbol, Irwŏnsang, is used as its sign.

**dhyāna** (S.) [禪那]: meditation, abstraction, trance.

**doubt** [疑]: A technical term in Zen Buddhism used to signify the unremitting inquiry into a *hwadu/ŭidu* for an awakening. This has nothing to do with the skeptical mental state.

**dragon**: A mythical snakelike being (S. *nāga*), usually said to be living in the ocean; used as a symbol of calmness in Zen meditation.

*duḥkha* (S.) [苦]: Bitterness, unhappiness, suffering, pain, distress, or difficulty. The two types of suffering are internal—i.e., physical and mental—and external—i.e., attacks from without. The four types of *duḥkha* are birth, aging, illness, and death. The eight types are these previous four along with the pain of parting from that which is loved; of meeting with that which is hated; of failing in one's aims; and that caused by the five *skandha*s (the five fundamental aggregates of a living being: form, feeling, perception, volitional action, consciousness).

***dveṣa*** (S.) [瞋]: Anger, hate, dislike; one of the three poisons, along with greed and delusion.

**emptiness** [空; S. *śūnyatā*]: The void or insubstantial nature of everything—the central teaching of Buddhism. Through realization of emptiness one attains liberation and the perfection of buddhahood. Emptiness is not a nihilistic void, but a wondrous state wherein dynamic events can take place. True realization of emptiness is a state free of all types of clinging, a state encompassing all and unifying all.

**evil**: In Won Buddhism, transgression or violation of any of the thirty precepts by body, mouth, or mind.

**evil path** [惡道]: The three evil paths of transmigration: hells, hungry ghosts, beasts.

**facts and principles** [事理]: See *sariyŏn'gu*.

**four forms of birth** [四生]: Viviparous, as with Mammalia; oviparous, as with birds; moisture- or water-born, as with worms and fishes; metamorphic, as with moths from chrysalis, or with devas, or in hells, or the first beings in a newly evolved world.

**four kalpas** (S.) [四劫]: *Vivarta kalpa*, consisting of twenty small kalpas during which worlds and the beings on them are formed; *vivarta-siddha kalpa*, kalpa of abiding or existence, sun and moon rise, differentiation of sexes, rise of heroes, formation of the four castes, evolution of social life; *samvarta kalpa*, kalpa of destruction, consisting of sixty-four small kalpas when fire, water, and wind destroy everything except the fourth *dhyāna*; *samvarta-siddha kalpa*, kalpa of annihilation.

**gāthā** (S.) [偈頌]: A stanza, a set of verses. In Won Buddhism, Sot'aesan's enlightenment is expressed in a panegyric verse frequently called the verse of Irwŏnsang.

**hell** [地獄]: A place or state of torment; in Buddhism, more akin to Christian purgatory, being not permanent. Although the duration of life in hell may be long, depending on the gravity of one's karmic offenses, eventually it will be terminated, and the hell dweller will once more be born in higher planes of existence.

***hŭisawi*** (K.) [喜捨位]: "Donator" or "benefactor." In Won Buddhism, an honorific term for anyone whose son or daughter has ascended to the dharma rank of subjugation of *māra* by the power of dharma.

**hungry ghost** [餓鬼; S. *preta*]: A denizen of one of the miserable planes of existence. Some hungry ghosts have human stomachs that burn with hunger, but tiny throats through which food cannot pass. An extremely greedy person may be reborn in this state.

***hwadu*** (K.) [話頭]: The essential point in a *kongan* story (given to a Zen student as a topic of meditation).

***hyŏksillon*** (K.) [革新論]: A treatise on renovation.

***irwŏn*** (K.) [一圓]: Unitary circle without circumference, thus invisible, referring to Dharmakāya Buddha, the noumenal essence of all things in the universe, the original nature of all buddhas and enlightened beings, the Buddha-nature of all sentient beings, nirvāṇa, and original enlightenment. In Won Buddhism, it refers also to the noumenal essence of the fourfold beneficence (heaven and earth, parents, brethren, laws).

***irwŏnsang*** (K.) [一圓相]: Literally, "the form of the unitary circle." A sign of the unitary circle (*irwŏn*), thus visible. Like a finger pointing at the moon, it plays the role of a sign signifying Dharmakāya Buddha, which is called Irwŏn in Won Buddhism. Irwŏnsang is enshrined in the temples of Won Buddhism as the object of religious worship and as the standard of practice.

**kalpa** (S.) [劫]: A Sanskrit term meaning "aeon." A day of Brahmā; a period of 432 million years of mortals.

***kanhwa sŏn*** (K.) [看話禪]: Meditation practiced with the mind concentrated on a *hwadu*.

**karma** (S.) [業]: Literally, "action" or "deed"; the effect of a deed, which survives death and contributes to the formation of one's next life. The law of karma asserts that virtuous or evil deeds of body, mouth (speech), and mind (volition) will inevitably bring corresponding results to the doer, in this or a future life.

***kongan*** (K.) [公案]: Literally, "public document"; a conundrum used in Zen as a meditation practice. Of the seventeen hundred, only twenty are used in Won Buddhism. The *Pi yen lu* [碧巖錄; Blue Cliff record] contains a hundred, and the *Wu-men kuan* [無門關; Gateless barrier], forty-eight.

***kongbu*** (K.) [工夫]: Originally, exertion in practice, especially with Zen conundrums like sitting in Zen meditation with such *hwadu* as Everything returns to the one; where does the one return? In Won Buddhism, the term means exertion in moral and religious practice toward the realization of buddhahood through the threefold practice [三學; spiritual cultivation; inquiry into facts and principles; mindful choice in karmic action.] *Kongbu* also means study done by a student. In this work, the word "study" is reserved for studying scriptures.

***kyojŏn*** (K.) [教典]: The scripture of the order. See *Wŏnbulgyo kyojŏn*.

***kyomu*** (K.) [教務]: Literally, "devoted to edification" in Won Buddhism, thus one who exerts him- or herself to the spreading of the Won Buddhist dharma. The term "*kyomu*" is used to refer to a Won Buddhist priest.

**Maitreya** (S.) [彌勒]: Literally, "the kind one"; a great bodhisattva, the future Buddha after Śākyamuni Buddha, who will come to this world to teach the dharma.

***māra*** (S.) [魔]: The personification of any defilement or negative tendency that hinders one from practicing the dharma. The destroyer, evil one, devil; he sends his daughters or assumes monstrous forms or inspires wicked men to seduce or frighten the sage. In Won Buddhism, *māra* consists of the three poisons, viz., greed (for wealth, sex, fame, and gain), anger (hatred, detestation, ill will), and delusions (stupidity, foolishness, jealousy, conceit, and false thought).

**mindful choice** [取捨]: Literally, "taking and forsaking"; taking what is right and forsaking what is wrong. For the sake of brevity "mindful choice" is used in this translation.

***moha*** (S.) [痴]: Illusion and delusion, infatuation, foolishness, ignorance, stupidity.

**Mount Sumeru** (S.) [須彌山]: The mythical mountain of ancient Indian cosmology, located at the center of each world.

***mugŭk*** (K.) [無極]: The Korean reading of the Chinese *wu-chi* [無極], meaning the ultimate of nonbeing, which is the ontological basis of *tai-chi* [太極], the great ultimate.

***munyŏm*** (K.) [無念]: Literally, "no thought"; used in the sense of harboring no false thought, e.g., if you do not abide in the idea of having rendered a favor to someone after rendering it, you practice the virtue of no thought.

***namo amitābha*** (S.) [南無阿彌陀佛]: Homage to (*namo*) the boundless, infinite, or immeasurable (*amitā*). "*Amitābha*" means "boundless light," referring to the presiding Buddha in the Western Paradise, whose mercy and wisdom are perfect. In Won Buddhism, Amitābha is identical with one's own original nature, which is eternal light and enlightenment. In Won Buddhism, "*namo amitābha*" means taking refuge in the eternal light and enlightenment of one's own Buddha-nature. This implies that in Won Buddhism there is no Western Paradise outside of one's own Buddha-nature.

**nature** [性]: Normally used with "self," i.e., "self-nature" [自性], which is a translation of the Sanskrit term "*svabhāva*" meaning "the essence or substance of a thing," the unchanging, noumenal essence of all things contrasted with their phenomenal characteristics.

***nirmāṇakāya*** (S.) [化身]: The incarnated body of the Buddha. To benefit certain sentient beings, a buddha incarnates himself into an appropriate visible body, such as that of Śākyamuni Buddha.

**nirvāṇa** (S.) [涅槃]: In Won Buddhism, release, liberation, bliss, or tranquil extinction after death.

**nonregression** [不退轉]: A stage of spiritual achievement in which a bodhisattva will never fall away from the stage of a bodhisattva and become a *śravaka*, *pratyekabuddha*, or ordinary person. In Won Buddhism, one must ascend to the stage of *ch'ulga* [出家] or transcendence to attain this stage.

**noumenon**: The realm of reality; contrasted with the phenomenal realm of appearance and disappearance. In the truth of Irwŏnsang, "great" [大] and "small" [小] are used to refer to these two realms respectively; by "great" is meant the essence of all things in the universe and by "small" the phenomenal world of diversity. However, in Buddhist metaphysics, the essence is identified with "true emptiness."

***pŏmnyurŭn*** (K.) [法律恩]: Literally, "the beneficence of laws." The beneficence of civil, penal, moral, and religious laws and injunctions to which one owes one's life.

***pŏpsa*** (K.) [法師]: Dharma master. In Won Buddhism, anyone who is promoted to the dharma stage of subjugation of *māra* by the power of dharma is acknowledged as a dharma master.

**practice**: See *kongbu*.

**public service**: What one gives in terms of spiritual, corporeal, and material contributions to the public (the order); an English translation of *saŏp* [事業; literally, "an enterprise or a business"]; one of the dual tasks of the religious life in Won Buddhism, the other being the religious practice [工夫].

**Pulgyo** (K.) [佛教]: Buddhism.

***Pulgyo chŏngjŏn*** (K.) [佛教正典]: *The Correct Canon of Buddhism*, the 1943 edition of the canon of Won Buddhism put out by the Society for the Study

of Buddha-dharma; the official canon of Won Buddhism from 1943 to 1962.

*pumoŭn* (K.) [父母恩]: The beneficence of parents, the beneficent parental source of one's existence.

*rāga* (S.) [貪慾]: Greed, vehement longing, or excessive desire; one of the three poisons; tainted by and in bondage to the five desires arising from the objects of the five senses: things seen, heard, smelled, tasted, or touched; the five desires of wealth, sex, food and drink, fame, and sleep.

**reciprocal destruction** [相剋]: Literally, "mutual opposition" as used in the yin-yang [陰陽] philosophy. One of the dual principles of yin and yang philosophy.

**reciprocal production** [相生]: Literally, "mutual harmony" or mutually letting the other live. One of the dual principles of yin and yang philosophy.

**samādhi** (S.) [定]: Concentration; composing the mind; intent contemplation; perfect absorption of thought into the one object of meditation.

**saṃsāra** (S.) [娑婆]: The world of birth and death; the phenomenal world.

*sariyŏn'gu* (K.) [事理研究]: Inquiry into facts [事] and principles [理]. By facts are meant rightness and wrongness, and gain and loss in human affairs; by principles are meant the universal principles of noumenon and phenomenon and the being and nonbeing of all things in the universe. By being and nonbeing are meant the cycle of the four seasons; such atmospheric phenomena as wind, cloud, rain, dew, frost, and snow; the birth, aging, illness, and death of all things; and the transformation of rise and fall and prosperity and decline.

**self-nature** [自性]: *See* nature.

*śīla* (S.) [戒]: Precepts; morality.

**silent confession** [心告]: Prayer offered silently to Dharmakāya Buddha, the source of the fourfold beneficence.

*simji* (K.) [心地]: The mind-ground or, simply, mind, from which all things spring.

**six realms of existence** [六道]: The realms of hells, hungry ghosts, animals, malevolent spirits, human existence, and deva existence.

*solsŏng* (K.) [率性]: Following or leading the nature. Sot'aesan has used this term in the sense of leading or commanding the nature. In the *Chung-yung* [中庸; Doctrine of the Mean] this term is used in the sense of following the nature; the nature mandated by Heaven is not something that one can lead or command, but follow.

*Sŏn* (K.) [禪]: The Korean reading of the Chinese character *ch'an* [禪; J. Zen].

*Sŏnjŏng* (K.) [禪定]: The Korean reading of the Chinese *ch'an-ting*, being the Chinese rendering of the Sanskrit *dhyāna*. Sŏn covers the whole ground of meditation, concentration, reaching the ultimate beyond emotion or thinking.

**Sot'aesan** (K.) [少太山]: The dharma title of Pak Chung-bin [朴重彬], the founder of Won Buddhism.

**suchness**. Buddha-nature, Dharmakāya, *dharmadhātu*, ineffable reality (S. *tathatā*).

*tathāgata* (S.) [如來]: Literally, "the thus-come one." An epithet of the Buddha; one who has attained full realization of suchness (*tathatā*), and who thus neither comes nor goes anywhere.

**ten directions** [十方]: The whole universe: east, west, south, north, southeast, northeast, southwest, northeast, zenith, nadir.

**threefold practice** [三學]: The triple discipline in Won Buddhism: spiritual cultivation, inquiry into facts and principles, mindful choice in karmic action; samādhi, prajñā, *śīla*; nourishing the nature, seeing the nature, following the nature.

*todŏk* (K.) [道德]: The way and its virtue; "*to*" signifies the normative principle all things ought to follow, "*dŏk*," the virtue brought about when they are followed. When the Won Buddhist order is referred to as the order of *todŏk* [道德會上], it means the religious order that teaches it.

*tonghak* (K.) [東學]: Literally, Eastern learning; an indigenous religious movement founded by Choe Che-u [崔濟愚; 1824–1864], renamed Ch'ŏndogyo [天道教; teaching of the heavenly way].

*tongp'oŭn* (K.) [同胞恩]: Beneficence of brethren or fellow beings; the favors of compatriots, people, animals, plants, without which one cannot exist.

**triple world** [三界; S. *trilokadhātu*]: The three realms of a world: a realm of sensuous desire, a realm of pure form, and a formless realm.

**true thusness** [真如; S. *bhūtatathatā*]: Reality as contrasted with unreality or appearance; unchanging or immutable as contrasted with form and phenomena; also called self-existent pure mind, Buddha-nature, Dharmakāya, and dharma-nature.

**true void cum marvelous existence: A translation of** *chin'gong myoyu* [真空妙有], which means that the true void is mysteriously existing; truly void, or immaterial, yet transcendentally existing; the dual aspects of Dharmakāya Buddha.

*tuṣita* (S.) [兜率天]: The heaven in the realm of desire from which each buddha descends to earth; the "heaven of contentment"; the present dwelling place of Maitreya, the next buddha of our world.

**twelvefold dependent origination** [十二緣起; S. *dvādaśanga-pratītya-samutpāda*]: The interlinked factors of saṃsāra: ignorance, action, consciousness, name and form, the six sense organs, contact, feeling, craving, grasping, becoming, birth, and old age and death.

*ŭidu* (K.) [疑頭]: A topic of doubt, normally a problem set by Zen masters, upon which thought is concentrated as a means to attain inner unity and illumination.

*ŭn* (K.) [恩]: Literally, "favor, beneficence, grace," of which "beneficence" is preferable to "grace" because in the Won Buddhist tenet of the fourfold *ŭn* there is no connotation of "divine grace." In Won Buddhism, this technical term is used to signify the source of one's existence, which R. Niehbur calls "the universal beneficence of nature." Just as fish in the ocean owe their life to the seawater, humans owe their existence to the fourfold beneficence: heaven and earth, parents, brethren, and laws.

*undo* (K.) [運度]: In Chŭngsan'gyo, the preestablished schedule of the universe.

**Way** (K. *to*) [道]: Truth, ultimate principle, or universal law.

**Wŏnbulgyo** (K.) [圓佛教]: Won Buddhism; the name of the Won Buddhist religious order.

**yin-yang** (C.) [陰陽]: The cosmic dual principle: positive and negative; male and female.

*yunyŏm* (K.) [有念]: Carefulness; mindfulness.

# Selected Bibliography

## Won Buddhist Canonical Works

*Chŏngsan chongsa pŏbŏ* 鼎山宗師法語 (The religious discourses of Master Chŏngsan). Iri: Wŏnbulgyo Chŏnghwasa, 1972.

*Chosŏn pulgyo hyŏksillon* 朝鮮佛教革新論 (A treatise on the renovation of Korean Buddhism). Iri: Pulbŏp Yŏn'guhoe, 1935.

*Hoewŏn suji* 會員須知 (What the members of the order should know). Iri: Pulbŏp Yŏn'guhoe, 1921.

*Kŭmgangsan ŭi chuin* 金剛山의主人 (The owner of Mt. Kŭmgang). Iri: Wŏlgan Wŏn'gwangsa, 1990.

*Kŭnhaengbŏp* 勤行法 (The method of diligent practice). Iri: Pulbŏp Yŏn'guhoe, 1943.

*Pogyŏng samdae yoryŏng* 寶經三大要領 (Three essential principles of treasury scripture). Iri: Pulbŏp Yŏn'guhoe, 1934.

*Pogyŏng yuktae yoryŏng* 寶經六大要領 (Six essential principles of the treasury scripture). Iri: Pulbŏp Yŏn'guhoe, 1932.

*Pulbŏp yŏn'guhoe kŭnhaengbŏp* 佛法研究會勤行法 (The Method of Dilligent Practice of the Society for the Study of Buddha-dharma). Iri: Pulbŏp Yŏn'guhoe, 1939.

*Pulbŏp yŏn'guhoe kyuyak* 佛法研究會規約 (Regulations of the Society for the Study of Buddha-dharma). Iri: Pulbŏp Yŏn'guhoe, 1927.

*Pulbŏp yŏn'guhoe sangjobu kyuyak* 佛法研究會相助部規約 (Regulations of the Department of Mutual Help, the Society for the Study of Buddha-dharma). Iri: Pulbŏp Yŏn'guhoe, 1935.

*Pulbŏp yŏn'guhoe t'ongch'i chodan kyuyak* 佛法研究會統治組團規約 (Regulations for ruling the units, the Society for the Study of Buddha-dharma). Iri: Pulbŏp Yŏn'guhoe, 1931.

*Pulbŏp yŏn'guhoe yoram* 佛法研究會要覽 (A brochure of the Society for the Study of Buddha-dharma). Iri: Pulbŏp Yŏn'guhoe, 1945.

*Pulcho yogyŏng* 佛祖要經 (The essential scriptures of the Buddha and patriarchs). Iri: Wŏnbulgyo Chŏnghwasa, 1965.

*Pulgyo chŏngjŏn* 佛教正典 (Correct canon of Buddhism). Comp. Kim T'ae-hŭp. Seoul: Pulgyo Sibosa, 1943.

*Suyang yŏn'gu yoron* 修養研究要論 (Essentials of cultivation and inquiry). Iri: Pulbŏp Yŏn'guhoe, 1927.

*Taejonggyŏng sŏnoerok* 大宗經選外錄 (What is left out of selection for the *Scripture of Sot'aesan*). Iri: Wŏnbulgyo Ch'ulp'ansa, 1982.

*Wŏnbulgyo chŏnsŏ* 圓佛教全書 (Collected works of Won Buddhism). Iri: Wŏnbulgyo Ch'ulp'ansa, 1977.

*Wŏnbulgyo kyojŏn* 원불교교전 (The scriptures of Won Buddhism). Iri: Wŏnbulgyo Ch'ulp'ansa, 1962.

*Wŏnbulgyo kyosa* 圓佛教教史 (A doctrinal history of Won Buddhism). Iri: Wŏnbulgyo Chŏnghwasa, 1975.

*Yejŏn* 禮典 (The canon of rites). Iri: Pulbŏp Yŏn'guhoe, 1935.

*Yejŏn sŏngga* 禮典聖歌 (The Won Buddhist book of rites and hymns). Iri: Wŏnbulgyo Chŏnghwasa, 1968.

**Buddhist Classical Works**

*Chin-kang po-jo po-lo-mi ching* 金剛般若波羅密經. *T,* 235.8.748c–752c.

*Ching-te ch'uan-teng lu* 景德傳燈錄. *T,* 2076.51.196b–467a.

*Chinsim chiksŏl* 真心直說. *T,* 48.2019.999a–1004a.

*Chung-lun* 中論. *T,* 1564.30.1a–39b.

*Fo wei shou-chia-chang-che shuo yeh-pao-ch'a-pieh ching* 佛爲首迦長者說業報差別經. *T,* 80.1.891–895.

*Fo-hsing lun* 佛性論. *T,* 1610.31.787a.

*Fo-shuo hsien-che wu-fu-te ching* 佛說賢者五福德經. *T,* 777.17.714.

*Hsin-hsin ming* 信心銘. *T,* 2010.48.376b–377a.

*Hua-yen ching i-hai po-men* 華嚴經義海百門. *T,* 1875.45.627a–636c.

*Koryŏguk pojosŏnsa susimgyŏl* 高麗國普照禪師修心訣. *T,* 2020.48.1003c–1021b.

*Kŭmgang sammaegyŏng* 金剛三昧經. *T,* 273.9.365b–374b.

*Liu-tzu ta-shih fa-pao tan-ching* 六祖大師法寶壇經. *T,* 2008.48.347c–362b.

*Miao-fa lien-hua ching* 妙法蓮華經. *T,* 262.9.1a–62b.

*Mo-ho chih-kuan* 摩訶止觀 *T,* 1911.46.1a–140c.

*Mo-ho po-jo po-lo-mi-to hsin ching* 摩訶般若波羅密多心經. *T,* 251.8.848c.

*Pi-yen lu* 碧巖錄. *T,* 2003.48.140a–225c.

*Shih-ti ching* 十地經. *T,* 286.10.497c–535a.

*Ssu-shih-erh chang ching* 四十二章經. *T,* 784.17.722–724.

*Ta-fang-kuang fo hua-yen ching* 大方廣佛華嚴經. *T,* 278.9.395a–788b.

*Ta pan-nie-p'an ching* 大般涅槃經. *T,* 374.12.365c–603c.

*Ta-sheng chi-kuan fa-men* 大乘止觀法門. *T,* 1924.46.641c–6424a.

*Ta-sheng chi-shin lun* 大乘起信論. *T,* 1666.32.575b–591c.

*Taishō shinshū daizōkyō* 大正新修大藏經. Tokyo, 1914–1922.

*Wei-mo-chieh so-shuo ching* 維摩詰所說經. *T,* 475.14.537a–557b.

*Wu-men-kuan* 無門關. *T,* 2005.48.292a–299c.

**Works in Asian Languages**

Chang Pyŏng-gil 張秉吉. *Chŭngsan chonggyo sasang* 甑山宗教思想 (The religious thought of Chŭngsan'gyo). Seoul: Seoul Taehakkyo Chulp'anbu, 1976.

Chi Kyo-hŏn 池教憲. "Han'guk sirhak sasang kwa Sot'aesan sasang" 韓國實學思想과少太山思想 (Korean practical learning and Sot'aesan's thought). In *IMWS,* pp. 539–565.

*Chinsan Han Ki-du paksa hwagap kinyŏm: Han'guk chonggyo sasang ŭi chae cho-myŏng* 震山韓基斗博士華甲紀念: 韓國宗教思想의再照明 (Dr. Han Ki-du festschrift: Reexamination of Korean religious thought). Iri: Wŏn'gwang Taehakkyo Ch'ulp'an'guk 圓光大學校出版局, 1993.

Cho Chŏng-je 趙正濟. "Wŏnbulgyo ŭi kyŏngje kwan" 圓佛教의經濟觀 (The Won Buddhist view of economics). In *IMWS,* pp. 1255–1266.

Chŏng Pong-gil 鄭奉吉. "Wŏnbulgyo wa kwahak" 圓佛教와科學 (Won Buddhism and science). In *WBS* 6 (1982): 131–154.

Chŏng Sun-il 鄭舜日. "Silch'ŏnjŏk inyŏmhwa ŭi panghyang esŏ pon Sadaegangnyŏng 實踐的理念化의方向에서본四大綱領 (The Four platforms viewed from the idealization for practice). In *HMWS*, pp. 793–812.

———. "Sot'aesan taejongsa ŭi pŏpsŏl yŏn'gu" 少太山大宗師의法說研究 (A study of Great Master Sot'aesan's sermons). In *HCSC*, pp. 1445–1474.

———. "Ŭn sasang ŭi pŏpkye yŏn'gi chŏk chomyŏng" 恩思想의法界緣起的照明 (Reflections on the thought of beneficience from the viewpoint of dharmadhātu causation). In *IMWS*, pp. 463–477.

———. "Wŏnbulgyo ŭi samgyo wŏnyung sasang" 圓佛教의三教圓融思想 (The Won Buddhist thought on the mutual adaptability of the three religions). *WBS* 18 (1994): 551–578.

Chŏng Yŏng-gyu 丁永奎. *Taesun chŏnggyŏng haesŏl* 大巡典經解說 (An exegesis of the *Taesun chŏngyŏng*). Kimje: Chŭngsan'gyo Ponbu, 1984.

Chu Ch'il-sŏng 朱七星. "Wŏnbulgyo sasang kwa sirhak sasang" 圓佛教思想과實學思想 (Won Buddhist thought and the thought of practical learning. In *IMWS*, pp. 567–584.

*Chŭngsando tojŏn* 甑山道道典 (The scripture of Chŭngsando). Taejŏn: Chŭngsangdo, 1997.

Ch'oe Tong-hŭi 崔東熙. "Sot'aesan ŭi ponch'e kwan" 少太山의本體觀 (Sot'aesan's view on noumenon). In *IMWS*, pp. 1241–1254.

*Ch'ŏndogyo kyŏngjŏn* 天道教經典 (The scripture of Chŏndogyo). Seoul: Ch'ŏndogyo Chungang Ch'ongbu, 1981.

Han Chong-man 韓鍾萬. "Irwŏnsang chilli ŭi sangjŭksŏng" 一圓相真理의相卽性 (The nature of mutual identity in the truth of Irwŏnsang). *WBS* 1 (1975): 9–21.

———. "Irwŏnsang sinang chang ŭi yŏn'gu" 一圓相信仰章의研究 (A study of the chapter: The faith in Irwŏnsang). In *WBS* 10, 11 (1987): 17–36.

———. "Sot'aesan Taejongsa ŭi minjung chonggyo sasang" 少太山大宗師의民衆宗教思想 (The Great Master Sot'aesan's thought on popular religion). In *IMWS*, pp. 639–661.

———. "Sot'aesan Taejongsa ŭi saengae wa sasang" 少太山大宗師의生涯와思想 (The life and thought of Great Master Sot'aesan). In *IMWS*, pp. 11–35.

———. "Taejongsa wa Chŏngsan Chongsa ŭi Kyorich'egye Pigyo" (A comparison of the doctrinal systems of the Great Master [Sot'aesan] and Master Chŏngsan]. *WBS* 23 (2000): 9–34.

———. "Wŏnbulgyo kyori ŭi hyŏngsŏng kwajŏng kwa kŭ kibon sŏnggyŏk" 圓佛教教理의形成過程과그基本性格 (The formative process of the Won Buddhist doctrine and its essential characteristics). In *HC* 1 (1971): 79–99.

———. "Wŏnbulgyo samhak suhaeng kwa korak ŭi munje" 圓佛教三學修行과苦樂의問題 (The Won Buddhist threefold practice and the issue of suffering and happiness). *WBS* 18 (1994): 365–392.

———. *Wŏnbulgyo sinangnon* 圓佛教信仰論 (A treatise on Won Buddhist faith). Iksan: Wŏnbulgyo Ch'ulp'ansa, 1995.

———. "Wŏnbulgyo ŭi hoet'ong sasang" 圓佛教의會通思想 (Won Buddhist thought of mutual adaptability). In *HKCS*, pp. 1155–1179.

———. "Wŏnbulgyo ŭi sinang non" 圓佛教의信仰論 (A treatise on Won Buddhist faith). In *KM*, pp. 123–169.

*Han'guk chonggyo* 韓國宗教 (Korean religions), vols. 1–23. Wŏn'gwang Taehakkyo Ch'ulp'an'guk 圓光大學校出版局.

Han Ki-du 韓基斗. "Chŏngsan ŭi sasang" 鼎山의思想 (Chŏngsan's thought). In *HKCS*, pp. 1229–1258.

———. "Han'guk sasangsa esŏ pon Sot'aesan sasang" 韓國思想에서본少太山思想 (Sot'aesan's thought from the viewpoint of the ideological history of Korea). In *IMWS*, pp. 397–414.

———. *Han'guk sŏnsasang yŏn'gu* 韓國禪思想研究 (A study of Korean Zen thought). Seoul: Ilchisa, 1991.

———. "Irwŏnsang kwa Wŏnbulgyo" 一圓相과圓佛教 (Irwŏnsang and Won Buddhism). In *WBS* 10, 11 (1987): 95–138.

———. "Irwŏnsang pŏbŏ ŭi kich'o yŏn'gu" 一圓相法語의基礎研究 (A study of the foundation of the Irwŏnsang dharma words). In *ICCY*, pp. 621–660.

———. "Musisŏn ŭi ponjil" 無時禪의本質 (The essence of timeless Zen). *WBS* 1 (1975): 141–180.

———. *Sŏn kwa musisŏn ŭi yŏn'gu* 禪과無時禪의研究 (A study of Zen and timeless Zen). Iri: Wŏn'gwang taehakkyo ch'ulp'an'guk, 1985.

———. "Sot'aesan Taejongsa ŭi suhaeng kwan" 少太山大宗師의修行觀 (On Sot'aesan's view of practice). In *IMWS*, pp. 235–258.

———. "Sot'aesan ŭi saengae wa sasang" 少太山의生涯와思想 (Sot'aesan's life and thought). In *IMWS*, pp. 12–35.

———. *Wŏnbulgyo chŏngjŏn yŏn'gu* 圓佛教正典研究 (A study of the canon of Won Buddhism). Iksan: Wŏn'gwang Taehakkyo Ch'ulp'an'guk 圓光大學校出版局, 1994.

———. "Wŏnbulgyo kyogang-e nat'anan samhak ŭi sasangjŏk wŏnch'ŏn" 圓佛教教綱에나타난三學의思想的源泉 (The ideological provenance of the threefold practice in the doctrine of Won Buddhism). In *HSS*, pp. 1197–1214.

———. "Wŏnbulgyo sŏn ŭi ŭimi esŏ pon kongbu" 圓佛教禪의意味에서본工夫 (Practice viewed in the sense of Won Buddhist Zen). *WBS* 18 (1994): 393–434.

———. "Wŏnbulgyo suhaengnon" 圓佛教修行論 (A treatise on Won Buddhist practice). In *KM*, pp. 171–222.

———. "Wŏnbulgyo ŭi sae pulgyo kaech'ang panghyang" 圓佛教의새佛教改創方向 (Won Buddhist directions for opening a new Buddhism). In *HCCS*, pp. 1089–1102.

Han Nae-yŏng 韓乃影. "Sot'aesan ŭi sahoe sasang" 少太山의社會思想 (Sot'aesan's thought on society). *WBS* 18 (1994): 241–260.

Han Sang-ryŏn 韓相璉. "Wŏnbulgyo ŭi ch'orakchŏk koch'al" 圓佛教의哲學的考察 (A philosophical investigation of Won Buddhism). In *KM*, pp. 363–378.

Han Sŭng-jo 韓昇助. "Han'guk chŏngsinsa ŭi maengnak esŏ pon Wŏnbulgyo" 韓國精神史의脈絡에서본圓佛教 (Won Buddhism viewed in the context of the ideological history of Korea). In *WBS* 4 (1980): 40–66.

Hong Pŏm-ch'o 洪凡草 *Chŭngsan'gyo kaesŏl* 甑山教概設 (A survey of Chŭng-san'gyo). Seoul: Changmunsa, 1982.

Hong Yun-sik 洪潤植. "Han'guk bulgyosa sangŭi Wŏnbulgyo" 韓國佛教史上의圓佛教 (Won Buddhism in the context of the history of Korean Buddhism). In *IMWS*, pp. 447–462.

———. "Han'guksa ŭi maengnak esŏ pon Wŏnbulgyo" 韓國史의脈絡에서본圓佛教 (Won Buddhism viewed from the historical context of Korea). In *HMWS*, pp. 103–122.

Kim Hong-ch'ŏl 金洪喆. "Han'guk shin chonggyo sasang kwa Sot'aesan sasang" 韓國新宗教思想과少太山思想 (The thought of new religions in Korea and Sot'aesan's thought). In *IMWS*, pp. 663–691.

———. *Han'guk sinhŭng chonggyo ŭi hyŏnhaeng.* 韓國新興宗教의現行 (Contemporary status of the newly risen religions in Korea). In *HC* 23: 443–515.

———. "Sot'aesan ŭi in'gan sang" 少太山의人間像 (A personal profile of Sot'aesan). *WBS* 18 (1994): 287–310.

———. "Wŏnbulgyo kyodan hyŏngsŏngsa" 圓佛教教團形成史 (A historical sketch of the formation of the Won Buddhist order). In *HKCS*, pp. 1061–1081.

———. *Wŏnbulgyo sasang non'go* 圓佛教思想論考 (A study of Won Buddhist thought). Iri: Wŏn'gwang taehakkyo ch'ulp'an'guk, 1980.

———. "Wŏnbulgyo sasang-e nat'anan sahoe pyŏndong yoin-e kwanhan yŏn'gu" 圓佛教思想에나타난社會變動要因에關한研究 (A study of the causes of social change as reflected in Won Buddhist thought). In *HMWS*, pp. 1013–1035.

———. "Wŏnbulgyo ŭi huch'ŏn kaebyŏk sasang." 圓佛教의後天開闢思想 (Won Buddhist thought on the unfolding of the later heaven). In *WBS* 4 (1980): 67–95.

Kim In-ch'ŏl 金仁喆. "Sot'aesan sasang ŭi kibon kujo" 少太山思想의基本構造 (The fundamental structure of Sot'aesan's thought). In *IMWS*, pp. 143–161.

Kim Kui-sŏng 金貴聲. "Sot'aesan ŭi p'yonghwa kyoyuk sasang" 少太山의平和教育思想 (Sot'aesan's thought on peace education). *WBS* 17, 18 (1994): 131–156.

Kim Nak-p'il 金洛必. "Chŏngshin kaenyŏm ŭi yŏnwŏn kwa t'ŭksŏng" 精神概念의淵源과特性 (The origin and characteristics of the concept of spirit). In *HMWS*, pp. 813–826.

———. "Ch'ogi kyodan ŭi togyo sasang suyong" 初期教團의道教思想受容 (Adoption of Taoist thought during the early years of the order). In *WBS* 10, 11 (1987): 701–724.

Kim P'al-gon 金扒坤. "Sot'aesan ŭi p'yŏnghwa kwan" 少太山의平和觀 (Sot'aesan's view of peace). *WBS* 17, 18 (1994): 109–130.

Kim Pyŏng-su 金炳洙. "Kyori hyŏngsŏng kwajŏng esŏ pon tanjŏnju ŭi wisang" 教理形成過程에서본丹田住禪의位相 (The phase of the elixir-field-concentration Zen in the process of the formation of the doctrine). *WBS* 18 (1994): 435–470.

Kim Sam-nyong 金三龍. "Sot'aesan Taejongsa ŭi in'gansang" 少太山大宗師의人間像 (A personal profile of Great Master Sot'aesan). In *IMWS*, pp. 117–131.

Kim Sŏng-gon 金星坤. "Wŏnbulgyo ŭi chayŏn hwan'gyŏnggwan" 圓佛教의 自然環境觀 (The Won Buddhist view of the natural environment). In *HCSC*, pp. 1491–1500.

Kim Sŏng-gwan 金聖觀. "Sangjing kwa simsŏng" 象徵과心性 (Symbolism and the nature of mind). In *HMWS*, pp. 971–1000.

———. "Wŏnbulgyo ŭi simsŏnggwan" 圓佛教의心性觀 (The Won Buddhist view of mind and nature). In *HKCS*, pp. 1181–1202.

Kim Sŏng-jang 金成長. "Sot'aesan ŭi kyohwa sangdam wŏlli wa silche" 少太山의教化相談原理와實際 (Sot'aesan's theory and practice of edification and counseling). *WBS* 18 (1994): 261–286.

———. "Wŏnbulgyo ŭirye ŭi sŏnggyŏk" 圓佛教儀禮의性格 (The nature of Won Buddhist rites). In *HKCS*, pp. 1203–1228.

Kim Sun-im 金順任. "Sot'aesan Taejongsa ŭi yulligwan" 少太山大宗師의 倫理觀 (The Great Master Sot'aesan's view of ethics). In *IMWS*, pp. 321–345.

———. "Wŏnbulgyo musisŏn sasangsŏnjŏk ŭi chomyŏng" 圓佛教無時禪의 事上禪的照明 (A reflection on Won Buddhist timeless Zen against practical Zen). In *HCSC*, pp. 1529–1546.

———. "Wŏnbulgyo todŏk sasang ŭi il koch'al" 圓佛教道德思想의一考察 (An inquiry concerning the moral thought of Won Buddhism). In *HMWS*, pp. 853–895.

———. "Wŏnbulgyo wa C. G. Jung ŭi simsŏng kujosŏl pigyo" 圓佛教와 C. G. Jung 의心性構造說比較 (A comparison of Won Buddhist and C. G. Jung's theories on the structure of mind and nature). In *HSS*, pp. 1271–1304.

Kim Sŭng-dong 金勝東. "Han'guk ch'ŏrhaksa-e issŏsŏ ŭi Sot'aesan sasang" 韓國哲學史에있어서의少太山思想 (Sot'aesan's thought in the history of Korean philosophy). In *IMWS*, pp. 415–433.

Kim Sŭng-hwan 金承煥. "Han'guk sasangsa rŭl t'onghae pon Wŏnbulgyo" 韓國思想史를通해본圓佛教 (Won Buddhism from the viewpoint of Korean ideological history). In *KM*, pp. 693–698.

Kim To-jong 金道宗. "Song Chŏng-san ŭi chŏngch'i ch'ŏrhak" 宋鼎山의 政治哲學 (Chŏng-san Song Kyu's political philosophy). In *HCSC*, pp. 1635–1646.

Kim Tu-hon 金斗憲. "Sŏngni ŭi yŏn'gu" 性理의研究 (A study of the principle of human nature). In *KM*, pp. 343–361.

Kim T'ak 金鐸. "Wŏnbulgyo sayo kyori ŭi ch'egyehwa kwajŏng" 圓佛教의 四要教理의體系化過程 (The tenet of four essentials in the doctrine of Won Buddhism: The course of its systematization). In *IMWS*, pp. 259–287.

Kim Un-hak 金雲學, trans. and ed. *Shinyŏk Kŭmganggyŏng ogahae* 新譯金剛 經五家解 (A new translation of the five masters' interpretations of the Diamond Sūtra). Seoul: Hyŏnam-sa 玄岩社, 1980.

Kim Yŏng-du 金永斗. "Sot'aesan taejongsa ŭi sŏn sasang" 少太山大宗師의 禪思想 (The Great Master Sot'aesan's Zen thought). In *IMWS*, pp. 347–372.

———. "Wŏnbulgyo tanjŏnju sŏnbŏp ŭi t'ŭkching ko" 圓佛教丹田注禪法의 特徵考 (A study of the distinctive features of Won Buddhist Zen with concentration at the elixir-field). In *WBS* 6 (1982): 97–116.

————. "Wŏnbulgyo ŭi Sŏn sasang" 圓佛教의禪思想 (Zen thought in Won Buddhism). In *HKCS*, pp. 1117–1136.

————. "Wŏnbulgyo ŭi tono chŏmsu kwan" 圓佛教의頓悟漸修觀 (The Won Buddhist view of sudden enlightenment and gradual cultivation). In *HMWS*, pp. 827–852.

Kim Yong-ch'ŏn 金用天 and Ch'oe Tong-hŭi 崔東熙. *Ch'ŏndogyo* 天道教. Iri: Wŏn'gwang Taehakkyo Ch'ulp'an'guk, 1976.

*Kinyŏm munch'ong* 紀念文叢 (Collection of commemorative essays). Wŏnbulgyo Ch'ulp'ansa 圓佛教出版社, 1971.

Ko Yun-sŏk 高允錫. "Wŏnbulgyo saŭn sasang ŭi kwahakchŏk chomyŏng" 圓佛教四恩思想의科學的照明 (A scientific reflection on the fourfold beneficence of Won Buddhism). *WBS* 18 (1994): 351–364.

————. "Wŏnbulgyo wa hyŏndae kwahak" 圓佛教와現代科學 (Won Buddhism and modern science). In *IMWS*, pp. 1201–1224.

Kŭm Chang-t'ae 琴章泰. "Han'guk yugyo sasang kwa Sot'aesan sasang" 韓國儒教思想과少太山思想 (Korean Confucianist thought and Sot'aesan's thought). In *IMWS*, pp. 479–492.

Mochizuki Shinkō 望月信亨. *Bukkyō daijiten* 佛教大辭典 (Encyclopedia of Buddhism). 10 vols. Tokyo: Bukkyō jitten kankōsho, 1931–1935.

Mubi Sŭnim 無比스님. *Kŭmganggyŏng ogahae* 金剛經五家解 (A translation of the five masters' interpretations of the Diamond Sūtra). Seoul: Pulgwang Ch'ulp'anbu 佛光出版部, 1992.

*Munsan Kim Samnyong paksa hwagap kinyŏm: Han'guk munhwa wa wŏnbulgyo sasang* 文山金三龍博士華甲紀念韓國文化와圓佛教思想 (Dr. Kim Samnyong festschrift: Korean culture and Won Buddhist thought). Iri: Wŏn'gwang Taehakkyo Ch'ulp'an'guk 圓光大學校出版局.

No Kwŏn-yong 魯權用. "Kisillon ŭi ilsim samdae sasang ŭl t'onghae pon Irwŏnsang sinang sogo" 起信論의一心三大思想을通해본一圓相信仰小考 (A minor study of faith in Irwŏnsang from the viewpoint of one mind and its three greatness in the *Awakening of faith*). In *WBS* 6 (1982): 155–178.

————. "Saŭn ŭi sinangjŏk ŭimi-e kwanhan chaeinsik" 四恩의信仰的意味에關한再認識 (Reappraisal of the religious significance of the fourfold beneficence). In *HMWS*, pp. 773–792.

O Chi-yŏng 吳知泳. *Tonghak sa* 東學史 (A history of Tonghak). Seoul: Pakyŏngsa, 1982.

Pak Chŏng-hun 朴正薰, comp. *Hanuran hanich'i-e* 한울안한이치에 (In unitary principle within one fence). Iri: Wŏnbulgyo Ch'ulp'ansa, 1982.

Pak Hŏn-muk 朴憲默. "Wŏnbulgyo ŭi miraesang" 圓佛教의未來像 (The Won Buddhist view of the future). *WBS* 18 (1994): 579–598.

Pak Hun 朴勳. "Irwŏnsang sangjing ŭi yŏn'gu" 一圓相象徵의研究 (A study of the symbolism of Irwŏnsang). In *ICCY*, pp. 101–148.

Pak Kil-chin 朴吉眞. "Irwŏnsang yŏn'gu" 一圓相研究 (A study of Irwŏnsang). In *ICCY*, pp. 1–58.

Pak Kwang-jŏn 朴光田. "Irwŏnsang-e taehayŏ" 一圓相에대하여 (On Irwŏnsang). In *KM*, pp. 11–18.

Pak Maeng-su 朴孟洙. "Ch'ogi kyosa yŏn'gusang ŭi che munje: Pulbŏp yŏn'guhoe ch'anggŏnsa-rŭl chungsim ŭro 初期教史研究上의諸問題: 佛法

研究會創建史를中心으로 (Various problems in the study of the early history of the order, focusing on the history of founding the Society for the Study of Buddha-dharma). *WBS* 10, 11 (1987).

———. "Wŏnbulgyo ch'ogi kyosa ŭi shin yŏn'gu" 圓佛教初期教史의新研究 (A new study of the early history of Won Buddhism). In *IMWS*, pp. 67–98.

Pak Sang-kwŏn 朴相權. "Sot'aesan ŭi haesŏkhak-e taehan yŏn'gu" 少太山의解釋學에대한研究 (An inquiry concerning Sot'aesan's hermeneutics). *WBS* 17, 18 (1994): 157–178.

———. "Wŏnbulgyo kŭnbon chilli ŭi kujojŏk t'ŭkching" 圓佛教根本真理의構造的特徵 (The structural characteristics of the fundamental truth of Won Buddhism). In *HMWS*, pp. 759–772.

———. "Wŏnbulgyo sinangnon" 圓佛教信仰論 (A theory of Won Buddhist faith). In *IMWS*, pp. 219–234.

Pojo Chŏnsŏ 普照全書 (Complete works of Pojo). Comp. Pojo sasang yŏn'guwŏn. Sŭngju: Puril ch'ulpansa, 1989.

Pyŏn Sŏn-hwan 邊鮮煥. "Irwŏnsang ŭi chilli wa chonjae sinbijuŭi" 一圓象의真理와存在神秘主義 (The truth of Irwŏnsang and the existential mysticism). In *ICCY*, pp. 459–472.

Shin Sun-ch'ŏl 申淳鐵. "Pulbŏp yŏn'gu hoe ch'anggŏnsa ŭi sŏnggyŏk" 佛法研究會創建史의性格 (The nature of a history of founding the Society for the Study of Buddha-dharma). In *HMWS*, pp. 897–912.

Shin To-hyŏng 辛道亨. *Kyojŏn kongbu* 教典工夫 (A study of the scriptures of Won Buddhism). Iri: Wŏnbulgyo Ch'ulp'ansa, 1974.

Sim Tae-sŏp 沈大燮. Sot'aesan ŭi sahoe kaejo pŏp (Sot'aesan's method of social reform). *WBS* 18 (1994): 203–240.

Sŏ Kyŏng-jŏn 徐慶田. "Irwŏnsang sangjing kwa chechonggyo sangjing ŭi pigyo koch'al" 一圓相象徵과諸宗教象徵의比較研究 (A comparative study of the symbolism of Irwŏnsang and that of various religions). In *WBS* 5 (1981): 1–43.

———. "Kyohwa hak ŭi chŏnmang kwa kwaje" 教化學의展望과課題 (Prospects and tasks of the science of edification). In *HMWS*, p. 913.

———. "Sot'aesan Taejongsa ŭi miraegwan" 少太山大宗師의未來觀 (The Great Master Sot'aesan's view of the future). In *IMWS*, pp. 373–393.

———. "Sot'aesan ŭi kyohwa kwan" 少太山의教化觀 (Sot'aesan's view of edification). In *HSS*, pp. 1241–1270.

———. "Sot'aesan ŭi yŏksa ch'angjo ŭisik 少太山의歷史創造意識 (Sot'aesan's idea of creating a new history). *WBS* 17, 18 (1994): 89–108.

———. "Yongsu ŭi kong sasang kwa Sot'aesan ŭi wŏn sasang-ŭi pigyo yŏn'gu" 龍樹의空思想과少太山의圓思想의比較研究 (A comparative study of Nāgārjuña's *śūnyavāda* and Sot'aesan's thought of Irwŏnsang). In *ICCY*, pp. 915–945.

*Sŏksan Han Chong-man paksa hwagap kinyŏm: Han'guk sasangsa* 釋山韓鍾萬博士華甲紀念: 韓國思想史. Iri: Wŏn'gwang Taehakkyo Ch'ulp'an'guk 圓光大學校出版局, 1991.

Son Chŏng-yun 孫正允. *Sot'aesan Taejongsa* 少太山大宗師 (Great Master Sot'aesan). Iri: Wŏnbulgyo Ch'ulp'ansa, 1991.

———. *Wŏnbulgyo yongŏ sajŏn* 圓佛教用語事典 (A dictionary of Won Buddhist terms). Iri: Wŏnbulgyo Ch'ulp'ansa, 1993.

Song Ch'ŏn-ŭn 宋天恩. *Chonggyo wa Wŏnbulgyo* 宗教와圓佛教 (Religion and Won Buddhism). Iri: Wŏn'gwang taehakkyo ch'ulp'an'guk 圓光大學校 出版局, 1979.

———. "Hyŏndae munmyŏng kwa Wŏnbulgyo ŭi sasang chŏk taeŭng" 現代文明과圓佛教의思想的對應 (Modern civilization and Won Buddhist ideological response). In *IMWS*, pp. 1183–1200.

———. *Irwŏn munhwa san'go* 一圓文化散考 (Various thoughts of the Won Buddhist culture). Iksan: Wŏnbulgyo Ch'ulp'ansa, 1994.

———. "Sot'aesan Pak Chung-bin taejongsa ŭi chonggyo kwan" 少太山 朴重彬大宗師의宗教觀 (Great Master Sot'aesan Pak Chung-bin's view of religion). In *HCSC*, pp. 1429–1444.

———. "Sot'aesan Taejongsa mannyŏn-ŭi kyohwa wa pŏmmun ko" 少太 山大宗師晚年의教化와法門考 (A study of Great Master Sot'aesan's edi- fication and sermons during his last years). In *IMWS*, pp. 37–66.

———. "Sot'aesan ŭi Irwŏnsang chilli" 少太山의一圓相真理 (Sot'aesan's truth of Irwŏnsang). In *HKCS*, pp. 1083–1096.

———. "Wŏnbulgyo kyojo ŭi yŏn'gu" 圓佛教教祖의研究 (A study of the founder of Won Buddhism). In *KM*, pp. 19–69.

———. "Wŏnbulgyo kyori ŭi Sirhak chŏk sŏnggyŏk" 圓佛教教理의實學的 性格 (The characteristics of practical learning in the doctrine of Won Buddhism). In *HMWS*, pp. 943–969.

———. "Wŏnbulgyo sasang ŭi yŏn'gu" 圓佛教思想의研究 (A study of Won Buddhist thought). In *WBS* 1 (1975): 77–140.

———. "Wŏnbulgyo ŭi sŏngni insik" 圓佛教의性理認識 (Understanding the principle of human nature in Won Buddhism). In *HCCS*, pp. 1127–1142.

Song In-gŏl 宋仁傑. *Taejonggyŏng soge naonŭn saramdŭl* 대종경속에나오는 사람들 (Individuals in the scripture of Sot'aesan). Iksan: Wŏlgan Wŏn'g- wangsa, 1996.

Song Kyu 宋奎. "Irwŏnsang e Taehayŏ" 一圓相에대하여 (On Irwŏnsang). *HH*, pp. 212–219.

———. "Pulbŏp yŏn'guhoe ch'anggŏnsa" 佛法研究會創建史 (History of founding the Society for the Study of Buddha-dharma). In *HH*, pp. 229– 318.

Sŏsan Hyujŏng 西山休靜. *Sŏn'ga kwigam* (Paragon of Zen tradition). Seoul: Poyŏn'gak, 1978.

*Sot'aesan taejongsa t'ansaeng paekchunyŏn kinyŏm nonmunjip: Illyu munmyŏng kwa wŏnbulgyo sasang* 少太山大宗師誕生百週年紀念論文集: 人類文明과圓佛 教思想 (The commemorative essays for Sot'aesan centennial: Human civi- lization and Won Buddhist thought). Iri: Wŏnbulgyo Ch'ulp'ansa 圓佛 教出版社, 1991.

*Sungsan pak kil-chin paksa kohi kinyŏm: Han'guk kŭndae chonggyo sasangsa* 崇山朴吉真博士古稀紀念韓國近代宗教思想史 (Dr. Pak Kil-chin festschrift for his seventieth birthday: A history of religious thought in recent Korea). Iri: Wŏn'gwang Taehakkyo Ch'ulp'an'guk 圓光大學校出版局, 1984.

*Taesun chŏn'gyŏng* 大巡典經 (The scripture of the great itinerancy). Kimje: Chŭngsan'gyo Ponbu, 1979.

*Taesun chŏn'gyŏng haesŏl* 大巡典經解說 (An explanation of the *Taesun chŏn'gyong*). Kimje: Chŭngsan'gyo Ponbu, 1984.

Terada Toru and Mizuno Yaoko, ed. *Dōgen* 道元. 2 vols. Tokyo: Iwanami shoten, 1970.

*Tonggyŏng taejŏn* 東經大典 (Great canon of Tonghak). Seoul: Ŭryu Munhwasa,
1973.

Ueda Chiaki 上田千秋. "Enbukkyo no shakai fukushi katsudō" 圓佛教と社會
福祉活動 (Won Buddhism and social welfare work). In *HMWS*, pp. 1037–
1070.

Ui Hyakuju 宇井伯壽. *Bukkyō shisō kenkyu* 佛教思想研究 (A study of Buddhist
thought). Tokyo: Iwanami shoten, 1940.

———. *Zenshūshi kenkyū* 禪宗史研究 (A study of the history of Zen Buddhism).
3 vols. Tokyo: Iwanami shoten, 1939–1943.

Ŭiam Sŏngsa 義庵聖師. *Kakse chin'gyŏng* 覺世真經 (True scripture for enlightening the world). Seoul: Ch'ŏndogyo Chungang Ch'ongbu, 1906.

Wŏn Sŏk-cho 元奭朝. "Munhwa chich'e wa chŏngshin kaebyok" 文化遲滯
와精神開闢 (The cultural arrears and the spiritual unfolding). In *HMWS*,
pp. 1001–1012.

*Wŏnbulgyo kyogo ch'onggan* 圓佛教教故叢刊 (Comprehensive collection of
the early publications of Won Buddhism). 6 vols. Iri: Wŏnbulgyo Chŏnghwasa 圓佛教正化社, 1968–1974.

*Wŏnbulgyo sajŏn* 圓佛教事典 (An encyclopedia of Won Buddhism). Iri:
Wŏn'gwang Taehakkyo Ch'ulp'an'guk, 1974.

*Wŏnbulgyo sasang* 圓佛教思想 (Won Buddhist thought). Vols. 1–18. Iri:
Wŏn'gwang Taehakkyo Ch'ulp'an'guk 圓光大學校出版局, 1973–1994.

Yang Ŭn-yong 梁銀容. "Han'guk chonggyo sasang esŏ bon shin chonggyo"
韓國宗教思想에서본新宗教 (New religions viewed in the context of the
history of Korean religions). In *HC* 23:164.

———. "Han'guk togyo wa Sot'aesan sasang" 韓國道教와少太山思想 (Korean
Taoism and Sot'aesan's thought). In *IMWS*, pp. 585–606.

———. "Sot'aesan taejongsa kwan ŭi chŏn'gae" 少太山大宗師觀의展開
(Unfolding the view on the Great Master Sot'aesan). *WBS* 18 (1994):
311–350.

Yi Chŏng-nip 李正立. *Chŭngsangyo sa* 甑山教史 (A history of Chŭngsangyo).
Kimje: Headquarters of Chŭngsangyo, 1977.

———. *Taesun ch'ŏrhak* 大巡哲學 (Philosophy of great itinerancy). Kimje:
Chŭngsangyo Ponbu, 1947, 1984.

Yi Hang-nyŏng 李恒寧. "Wŏnbulgyo ŭi munhwasa chŏk ŭi 圓佛教의文化史的
意義 (The significance of Won Buddhism in cultural history). In *KM*, pp.
379–386.

Yi Hye-hwa 李惠和. *Sot'aesan Pak Chung-bin ŭi munhak segye* 少太山朴重
彬의文學世界 (The literary realm of Sot'aesan Pak Chung-bin). Seoul:
Kip'ŭnsaem, 1991.

Yi Hyŏn-hŭi 李炫熙. "Sot'aesan kwa Han'guk kŭndae sasang" 少太山과韓
國近代思想 (Sot'aesan and the modern ideology of Korea). In *IMWS*, pp.
625–638.

———. "Sot'aesan Sasang ŭi kŭndaesa chŏk chomyŏng 少太山思想의近代史
的照明 (Reflections on Sot'aesan's thought against modern history). *WBS*
17, 18 (1994): 21–46.

Yi  Hyŏn  t'aek  李鉉澤.  "Wŏnbulgyo  ŭi  ŭn  sasang"  圓佛教의恩思想  (The
thought of beneficence in Won Buddhism). In *HKCS*, pp. 1097–1116.

Yi  Kŏn-in  李建仁.  "Wŏnbulgyo  ŭi  in'gan  kyoyuk  non"  圓佛教의人間教育論
(The Won Buddhist theory of human education). *WBS* 18 (1994): 599–622.

Yi  Kong-jŏn  李空田.  "Sot'aesan  Taejongsa  ŭi  in'gansang"  少太山大宗師의
人間相 (A personal profile of Great Master Sot'aesan). In *IMWS*, pp. 133–
142.

Yi  Kwang-jŏng  李廣淨.  "P'yoŏ-e  nat'anan  Sot'aesan  sasang"  標語에나타난
少太山思想  (Sot'aesan's  thought  expressed  in  mottoes).  In  *IMWS*,  pp.
163–186.

Yi  Sŏng-t'aek  李成澤.  "Ŭn  sasang  kwa  minjok  munje"  恩思想과民族問題  (The
thought of beneficence and the problem of [Korean] race). In *HCSC*, pp.
1475–1490.

Yi  Ton-hwa  李敦化.  *Ch'ŏndogyo  ch'anggŏnsa*  天道教創建史  (A  history  of  the
foundation  of  Ch'ŏndogyo).  Seoul:  Ch'ŏndogyo  Chungang  Chongriwŏn,
1982.

Yi  Ŭl-ho  李乙浩.  "Han'guk  koyu  sasang  kwa  Sot'aesan  sasang"  韓國固有
思想과少太山思想  (Korean  native  thoughts  and  Sot'aesan's  thought).
In *IMWS*, pp. 435–446.

———.  "Irwŏnsang  ŭi  sangjing  hakchŏk  ihae"  一圓相의象徵學的理解  (Sym-
bolical understanding of Irwŏnsang). In *HCCS*, pp. 1103–1112.

*Yŏsan Yu Pyŏng-dŏk paksa hwagap kinyŏm: Han'guk ch'orhak chonggyo sa-
sang* 如山柳炳德博士華甲紀念: 韓國哲學宗教思想 (Festschrift for Dr. Yu
Pyŏngdŏk's  sixtieth  birthday:  The  thought  of  Korean  philosophy  and  religion). Iri: Wŏn'gwang Taehakkyo Ch'ulp'an'guk 圓光大學校出版局, 1990.

Yu  Myŏng-jong  劉明鍾.  "Sot'aesan  ŭi  kesong  kwa  sŏngnihak"  少太山의偈
頌과性理學  (Sot'aesan's  gāthā  and  the  philosophy  of  human  nature).  In
*IMWS*, pp. 513–519.

———.  "Wŏnbulgyo  ŭi  sŏngnisŏl"  圓佛教의性理說  (The  Won  Buddhist  theory
of human nature). *WBS* 18 (1994): 539–550.

Yu  Pyŏng-dŏk.  柳炳德.  "Han'guk  chonggyo  maengnak  esŏ  pon  Wŏnbulgyo
sasang"  韓國宗教脈絡에서본圓佛教思想  (Won  Buddhist  thought  viewed
from the Korean religious context). In *HMWS*, pp. 27–84.

———.  *Han'guk  minjung  chonggyo  sasangnon*  韓國民衆宗教思想論  (An  essay
concerning Korean folk religions). Seoul: Siinsa, 1985.

———.  *Han'guk  sasang  kwa  Wŏnbulgyo*  韓國思想과圓佛教  (Korean  thought
and Won Buddhism). Seoul: Kyomunsa, 1989.

———.  *Han'guk  shinhŭng  chonggyo*  韓國新興宗教  (New  religions  of  Korea).  Iri:
Wŏn'gwang Taehakkyo Ch'ulp'an'guk, 1974, 1992.

———.  "Ilche  Sidae  ŭi  Pulgyo"  日帝時代의佛教  (Buddhism  during  the  Japanese occupation). In *PKC*, pp. 1159–1187.

———.  "Irwŏnsang  chilli  ŭi  yŏn'gu"  一圓相真理의研究  (A  study  of  the  truth  of
Irwŏnsang).  Ph.D.  diss.,  Wŏn  Kwang  University,  1974.  In  *ICCY*,  pp.  149–
326.

———.  "Sot'aesan  taechongsa  ŭi  chilli  chŏk  chonggyo  kwan"  少太山大宗師의
真理的宗教觀  (Great  Master  Sot'aesan's  view  of  truthful  religion).  *WBS*
17, 18 (1994): 47–88.

————. "Sot'aesan ŭi silch'ŏn sirhak" 少太山의實踐實學 (Sot'aesan's practical learning for practice). In *HSS*, pp. 1215–1240.

————. *T'al chongyo sidae ŭi chonggyo* 脫宗教時代의宗教 (Religion in the era of religious alienation). Iri (Cholla Pukto): Wŏn'gwang taehakkyo ch'ulp'an'guk, 1982.

————. *Tonghak-Ch'ŏndogyo* 東學天道教 (Eastern learning and the religion of heavenly way). Seoul: Kyomun-sa, 1976.

————. "Wŏnbulgyo ŭi chilli kwan" 圓佛教의真理觀 (The Won Buddhist view of truth). In *KM*, pp. 71–122.

————. "Wŏnbulgyo ŭi Pulgyo kwan" 圓佛教의佛教觀 (Won Buddhist view of Buddhism). In *HKCS*, pp. 1137–1154.

————. *Wŏnbulgyo wa Han'guk sahoe.* 圓佛教와韓國社會 (Won Buddhism and Korean society). Seoul: Siinsa, 1977, 1986.

————. "Wŏnsasang non" 圓相論 (A view on the thought of the circular symbol). In *WBS* 1 (1975): 22–77.

————, ed. *Irwŏnsang chilli ŭi che yŏn'gu* 一圓相真理의諸研究 (Various studies of the truth of Irwŏnsang). Iri: Wŏn'gwang Taehakkyo Ch'ulp'an'guk 圓光大學校出版局, 1989.

————, ed. *Wŏnbulgyo sasang ŭi chŏn'gae* 圓佛教思想의展開 (The development of Won Buddhist thought). Seoul: Kyomunsa, 1990.

Yu Sŏng-t'ae 柳聖泰. "Taegŭk tosŏl esŏ pon Irwŏnsang chilli" 太極圖說에서본一圓相真理 (The truth of Irwŏnsang viewed from the standpoint of T'ai-chi tu shuo). In *IMWS*, pp. 493–512.

————. *Wŏnbulgyo wa Tongyang sasang* 圓佛教와東洋思想 (Won Buddhism and eastern thought). Iksan: Wŏngwang Taehakkyo Ch'ulp'anguk, 1995.

Yun E-heum (I-hŭm) 尹以欽. "Han'guk minjok chonggyo ŭi yŏksajŏk silt'ae" 韓國民族宗教의歷史的實態 (The historical reality of Korean folk religion). In *HC* 23:87–120.

### Works in European Languages

Abe, Masao. *Zen and Western Thought.* Ed. William R. LaFleur. Honolulu: University of Hawai'i Press, 1985.

Aitken, Robert. *The Gateless Barrier.* San Francisco: North Point Press, 1990.

Bechert, Heinz, and Richard Gombrich, eds. *The World of Buddhism.* London: Thames and Hudson, 1984.

Bielefelt, Carl. *Dōgen's Manuals of Zen Meditation.* Berkeley: University of California Press, 1988.

Blofeld, John, trans. *The Zen Teaching of Huang Po on the Transmission of Mind.* New York: Grove Press, 1958.

————, trans. *The Zen Teaching of Hui Hai.* New York: Samuel Wiser, 1972.

Blyth, R. B. *Zen and Zen Classics.* Vol. 4: *Mumonkan.* Tokyo: Hokuseido Press, 1966.

Buswell, Robert E., Jr. "Buddhism in Korea." In Joseph Kitagawa and Mark D. Cummings, eds., *Buddhism and Asian History.* New York: Macmillan, 1987.

————. "Ch'an Hemeneutics: Korean View." In Donald S. Lopez, Jr., ed., *Buddhist Hermeneutics.* Honolulu: University of Hawai'i Press, 1988.

——— "Chinul's Alternative Vision of Kanhwa Sŏn and Its Implications for Sudden Awakening/Sudden Cultivation." In *Pojo sasang* (The thought of Pojo) 4:425–447. Seoul: Puril ch'ulpansa, 1990.

———. "The Debate Concerning Moderate and Radical Subitism in Korean Sŏn Buddhism." In *HCSC*, 489–519.

———. *The Formation of Ch'an Ideology in China and Korea*. Princeton, N.J.: Princeton University Press, 1989.

———. *The Korean Approach to Zen*. Honolulu: University of Hawai'i Press, 1983.

———. *The Zen Monastic Experience*. Princeton, N.J.: Princeton University Press, 1992.

Buswell, Robert E., Jr., and Robert M. Gimello, eds. *Paths to Liberation: The Mārga and Its Transformations in Buddhist Thought*. Honolulu: University of Hawai'i Press, 1992.

Chan, Wing-tsit, trans. *Instructions for Practical Living*. New York: Columbia University Press, 1963.

———, trans. *The Platform Scripture*. New York: St. John's University Press, 1963.

———, trans. *Reflections on Things at Hand: Compiled by Chu Hsi and Lü Tsu-ch'ien*. New York: Columbia University Press, 1967.

———, trans. and comp. *A Sourcebook in Chinese Philosophy*. Princeton, N.J.: Princeton Unviersity Press, 1963.

Chang, Chug-yuan, trans. and ed. *Original Teachings of Ch'an Buddhism: Selected from the Transmission of Lamp*. New York: Grove Press, 1969.

Chang, Garma C. C., ed. *The Buddhist Teaching of Totality: The Philosophy of Hwa Yen Buddhism*. Univeristy Park and London: Pennsylvania State University Press, 1971.

———. *A Treasury of Mahāyāna Sūtras: Selections from the Mahāratnakūṭa Sūtra*. Trans. the Buddhist Association of the United States. University Park and London: Pennsylvania State University Press, 1983.

Chen, Kenneth K. S. *Buddhism in China: A Historical Survey*. Princeton, N.J.: Princeton University Press, 1973.

Choi, Joon-Sik (Ch'oe Chun-sik). "The Concept of Peace in Korean Thought: A Study of the Concept Seen in the Thoughts of the Three New Religious Thinkers of Nineteenth-Century Korea." *KJ* 32, 1 (1992): 5–26.

Chon, Pal-khn (Chŏn P'al-gŭn). *The Scripture of Wŏn Buddhism*. Iri: Wŏn Kwang Publishing Co., 1988.

Chong, Key-ray. *Wŏn Buddhism: A History and Theology of Korea's New Religion*. Lewiston, N.Y.: Mellen Press, 1997.

Chung, Bongkil. "Appearance and Reality in the Truth of Irwŏnsang." In *HSS*, pp. 1461–1472.

———. "Beneficence as the Moral Foundation in Wŏn Buddhism." *JCP* 23 (1996): 193–211.

———. "The Concept of Dharmakāya in Wŏn Buddhism: Metaphysical and Religious Dimensions." *KJ* 27, 1 (1987): 4–15.

———. "The Ethics of Wŏn Buddhism: A Conceptual Analysis of the Moral System of Wŏn Buddhism." Ph.D. diss., Michigan State University, 1979.

————. "Human Nature and Morality in Won Buddhism." In *HC* 11, 12 (1987): 67–78.

————. *An Introduction to Won Buddhism*. Iri: Wŏnbulgyo, 1993.

————. "Moral Perfection and the Ethics of Grace in Won Buddhism." In *HMWS*, pp. 1071–1198.

————. "A Philosophical Analysis of the Truth of Irwŏnsang." *Won Buddhist Studies* 1 (1996): 1–25.

————. "Psychotherapeutic Implication in Won Buddhism." In *WBS* 10, 11 (1987): 573–588.

————. "The Relevance of Confucian Ethics." *JCP* 18, 2 (1991): 143–159.

————. "Ultimate Reality and Meaning in Sot'aesan's Irwŏnism." *Ultimate Reality and Meaning* 15, 1 (1992): 36–47.

————. "What Is Won Buddhism?" *KJ* 24, 5 (May 1984): 18–32.

————. "Won Buddhism: A Synthesis of the Moral System of Buddhism and Confucianism." *JCP* 15, 4 (1988): 425–448.

————. "Won Buddhism and Contemporary Society." In *HC* 14 (1989): 135–150.

Cleary, Thomas, and J. C. Cleary, trans. *The Blue Cliff Record*. Boulder and London: Shambala, 1977.

————, trans. *Entry into the Inconceivable*. Honolulu: University of Hawai'i Press, 1983.

————, trans. *The Flower Ornament Scripture*. 3 vols. Boston and London: Shambala, 1984.

————, trans. *The Sutra of Hui-neng Grand Master of Zen with Hui-neng's Commentary on the Diamond Sutra*. Boston and London: Shambala, 1998.

Conze, Edward. *Buddhism: Its Essence and Development*. New York: Harper and Row, 1975.

————. *Buddhist Studies 1934–1972*. London: Bruno Cassirer, 1967.

————. *Buddhist Texts through the Ages*. Ed. with I. B. Horner et al. New York: Harper and Row, 1964.

————. *Buddhist Thought in India*. Ann Arbor: University of Michigan Press, 1967.

————, trans. and ed. *The Large Sutra on Perfect Wisdom with the Divisions of the Abhisamayālaṅkāra*. Berkeley: University of California Press, 1975.

————, trans. *Perfect Wisdom: The Short Prajñāparamitā Texts*. London: Buddhist Publishing Group, 1973.

————, trans. *The Perfection of Wisdom in Eight Thousand Lines and Its Verse Summary*. San Francisco: Four Seasons Foundation, 1973.

Cozin, Mark. "Won Buddhism: The Origin and Growth of a New Korean Religion." In *Religion and Ritual in Korean Society*, ed. Laurel Kendall and Griffin Dix. Berkeley: Institute of East Asian Studies, University of California, 1987.

De Bary, William Th., ed. *The Buddhist Tradition in India, China and Japan*. New York: Vintage, 1972.

De Bary, William Th., and others, eds. *Sources of Chinese Tradition*. New York: Columbia University Press, 1960.

Donner, Neal, and Daniel B. Stevenson, trans. *The Great Calming and Contemplation: A Study and Annotated Translation of the First Chapter of Chih-i's*

Mo-ho Chih-kuan. Kuroda Institute for the Study of Buddhism and Human Values. Honolulu: University of Hawai'i Press, 1993.

Dumoulin, Heinrich. *Understanding Buddhism: Key Terms*. Trans. Joseph S. O'Leary. New York and Tokyo: Weatherhill, 1994.

———. *Zen Buddhism—A History: India and China*. New York and London: Macmillan, 1988.

———. *Zen Enlightenment: Origins and Meaning*. Trans. John C. Maraldo. New York and Tokyo: Weatherhill, 1979.

———, ed. *Buddhism in the Modern World*. New York: Collier Books, 1976.

Dumoulin, Heinrich, and Ruth Fuller Sasaki. *The Development of Chinese Zen*. New York: First Zen Institute of America, 1953.

Fromm, E., D. T. Suzuki, and Richard De Martino. *Zen Buddhism and Psychoanalysis*. New York: Grove Press, 1963.

Fung, Yu-lan. *A History of Chinese Philosophy*. 2 vols. Trans. Derk Bodde. Princeton, N.J.: Princeton University Press, 1952.

Garfield, Jay, trans. and commentary. *The Fundamental Wisdom of the Middle Way: Nāgārjuna's Mūlamadhyamakakārikā*. New York: Oxford University Press, 1995.

Gimello, Robert M. "Sudden Enlightenment and Gradual Practice: A Problematic Theme in the Sŏn Buddhism of Pojo Chinul and in the Ch'an Buddhism of Sung China." *Pojo sasang* (The thought of Pojo), 4:165–203.

Gómez, Luis O., trans. *The Land of Bliss: The Paradise of the Buddha of Measureless Light*. Honolulu: University of Hawai'i Press, 1996.

Gregory, Peter. *Inquiry into the Origin of Humanity: An Annotated Translation of Tsung-mi's Yüan jen lun with a Modern Commentary*. Kuroda Institute for the Study of Buddhism and Human Values. Honolulu: University of Hawai'i Press, 1995.

———, ed. *Studies in Ch'an and Hua-yen*. Kuroda Institute for the Study of Buddhism and Human Values. Honolulu: University of Hawai'i Press, 1983.

———. *Sudden and Gradual: Approaches to Enlightenment in Chinese Thought*. Kuroda Institute for the Study of Buddhdism and Human Values. Honolulu: University of Hawai'i Press, 1987.

———. *Traditions of Meditation in Chinese Buddhism*. Honolulu: University of Hawai'i Press, 1986.

Hakeda, Yoshito, trans. *The Awakening of Faith*. New York and London: Columbia University Press, 1967.

Hamilton, F., and Cairns, H., eds. *The Collected Dialogues of Plato*. New York: Bollingen Foundation, 1961.

Han, Woo-keun. *The History of Korea*. Trans. Lee Kyung-shik. Honolulu: East-West Center Press, 1970.

Heidegger, Martin. *Being and Time*. Trans. J. Macquarrie and E. Robinson. New York: Harper and Row, 1962.

———. *An Introduction to Metaphysics*. Trans. R. Manheim. New Haven, Conn.: Yale University Press, 1959.

Hurvitz, Leon. *Chih-i (538–597): An Introduction to the Life and Ideas of a Chinese Buddhist Monk*. Mélanges Chinois et Bouddhiques, vol. 12: 1960–1962. Bruxelles: Institute Belge des Hautes Études Chinoises, 1980.

————, trans. *Scripture of the Lotus Blossom of the Fine Dharma*. New York: Columbia University Press, 1976.

Inada, Kenneth. *Nāgārjuna: A Translation of His* Mūlamadhyamakakārikā *with an Introductory Essay*. Tokyo: Hokuseido Press, 1970.

Jayatilleke, K. N. *Early Buddhist Theory of Knowledge*. London: Allen and Unwin, 1963.

Kalupahana, David J. *Causality: The Central Philosophy of Buddhism*. Honolulu: University of Hawai'i Press, 1975.

————. *A History of Buddhist Philosophy*. Honolulu: University of Hawai'i Press, 1992.

————. *Nāgārjuna: The Philosophy of the Middle Way*. Albany: State University of New York Press, 1986.

Kang, Wi-Jo. "Meeting between Western and Eastern Religions." In *IMWS*, 1623–1632.

————. "Won Buddhism as a Reforming Element of Korean Buddhism." In *KM*, 795–802.

Kant, Immanuel. *Critique of Pure Reason*. Trans. Norman Kemp Smith. London: Macmillan, 1968.

————. *Groundwork of the Metaphysics of Morals*. Trans. H. J. Paton. New York: Harper and Row, 1964.

Keel, Hee Sung. *Chinul: The Foundation of the Korean Sŏn Tradition*. Berkeley and Seoul: Berkeley Buddhist Series, 1984.

Kim, Bok-in. "Sot'aesan's View of Religious Ecumenism." In *HCCS*, 1197–1224.

————. "A Theological Foundation of United Religious Movement in Won Buddhism." In *HCSC*, 1766–1786.

Kim, Hee-jin. *Dōgen Kigen: Mystical Realist*. Tuscon: Univeristy of Arizona Press, 1987.

Kim, Sunggon. "Religious Pluralism and the Unity of Religions." In *IMWS*, 1877–1890.

Kim, Yong Joon. *The Ch'ondogyo Concept of Man*. Seoul: Pan Korea Book Corporation, 1978.

Kitagawa, Joseph, and Mark D. Commings, eds. *Buddhism and Asian History*. New York: Macmillan, 1987.

Kranewitter, Rudolf. "Gegenwart und Zukunft der Weltreligionen." In *IMWS*, 1891–1914.

LaFleur, William R., ed. *Dōgen Studies*. Kuroda Institute for the Study of Buddhism and Human Values. Honolulu: University of Hawai'i Press, 1985.

Lamotte, Étienne. *History of Indian Buddhism*. Trans. Sara Webb-Boin. Louvain-Paris: Peters Press, 1988.

————. "The Buddha, His Teachings and His Sangha." In Heinez Bechert and Richard Gombrich, eds., *The World of Buddhism*. New York: Thames and Hudson, 1984.

Lancaster, Lewis. "Buddhism and the Collective Perceptions of our Time." In *IMWS*, 1713–1734.

Lee, Ki-baik. *A New History of Korea*. Trans. Edward W. Wagner with Edward J. Shultz. Cambridge, MA: Harvard University Press, 1984.

Legge, James, trans. *Confucius: Confucian Analects, The Great Learning and The Doctrine of the Mean.* Oxford: Clarendon Press, 1893.

————. *The I Ching.* The Sacred Books of the East. Vol. 16, pt. 2: *The Yi King.* Oxford: Clarendon Press, 1899.

————, trans. *The Works of Mencius.* Vol. 2 in The Chinese Classics. Oxford: Clarendon Press, 1895.

Lopez, Jr., Donald S., ed. *Buddhist Hermeneutics.* Kuroda Institute for the Study of Buddhism and Human Values. Honolulu: University of Hawai'i Press, 1988.

————. *Elaboration of Emptiness: Uses of the Heart Sūtra.* Princeton, N.J.: Princeton University Press, 1996.

Lu, K'uan Yü (Charles Luk). *Ch'an and Zen Teaching.* 3 vols. York Beach: Samuel Wiser, 1970.

————, trans. *The Vimalakirti Nirdesa Sūtra.* Berkeley and London: Shambala, 1972.

Makra, Mary Lelia, trans. *The Hsiao Ching.* New York: St. John's University Press, 1961.

Masunaga, Reihō. *A Primer of Sōtō Zen.* Honolulu: University of Hawai'i Press, 1971.

McRae, John R. *The Northern School and the Formation of Early Ch'an Buddhism.* Kuroda Institute for the Study of Buddhism and Human Values. Honolulu: University of Hawai'i Press, 1986.

Murti, T. R. V. *The Central Philosophy of Buddhism.* London: George Allen and Unwin, 1955.

Neville, Robert. "World Community and Religion." In *IMWS*, 1561–1588.

Park, Kwang Soo. *The Won Buddhism (Wŏnbulgyo) of Sot'aesan.* Bethesda, Md.: International Scholars Publications, 1997.

Park, Sung Bae. *Buddhist Faith and Sudden Enlightenment.* Albany: State University of New York Press, 1985.

Pine, Red, trans. *The Zen Teaching of Bodhidharma.* Berkeley: North Point Press, 1987.

Plato. *The Collected Dialogues of Plato.* Trans. and ed. F. Hamilton and H. Cairns. New York: Bollingen Foundation, 1961.

Powel, William F., trans. *The Record of Tung-shan.* Kuroda Institute for the Study of Buddhism and Human Values Honolulu: University of Hawai'i Press, 1986.

Radhakrishnan, Sarvepalli, and Charles A. Moore. *A Sourcebook in Indian Philosophy.* Princeton, N.J.: Princeton University Press, 1957.

Ramanan, K. Venkata. *Nāgārjuna's Philosophy.* Delhi: Motilal Banarsidas, 1966.

Robertson, Roland. *The Sociological Introduction of Religion.* New York: Schocken Books, 1970.

Robinson, Richard H. *Early Mādhyamika in India and China.* New York: Samuel Weiser; reprint by Motilal Banarsidass, Delhi, 1976.

Sangharakshita. *A Survey of Buddhism.* Bangalore, India: Indian Institute of World Culture, 1957.

Sekida, Katsuki, trans. *Two Zen Classics: Mumonkan and Hegiganroku.* New York and Tokyo: Weatherhill, 1977.

Shim, Jae Ryong. "The Philosophical Foundation of Korean Zen Tradition: The Integration of Sŏn and Kyo by Chinul (1158–1210)." Ph.D. diss. University of Hawai'i, 1979.

Smart, Ninian. "Modern Civilization and World Community." In *IMWS*, 1589–1622.

Seo, Kyong-bo. "A Study of Korean Zen Buddhism Approached through the Chodangjip." Ph.D. diss. Temple University, 1969.

Soothill, William Edward, *A Dictionary of Chinese Buddhist Terms*. London: Kegan Paul, Trench, Turner, 1934.

Stcherbatsky, Th. *Buddhist Logic*. 2 vols. New York: Dover Publications, 1962.

———. *The Central Conception of Buddhism and the Meaning of the Word "Dharma."* London: Royal Asiatic Society, 1924.

———. *The Conception of Buddhist Nirvana*. The Hague: Mouton and Co., 1965.

Streng, Frederick J. *Emptiness: A Study in Religious Meaning*. Nashville, Tenn., and New York: Abingdon Press, 1967.

Suzuki, Daisetz Teitaro. *Essays in Zen Buddhism*. 3 vols. London: Rider & Co., 1949–1953.

———, trans. *The Laṅkāvatāra Sūtra*. Boulder, Colo.: Prajñā Press, 1978.

———. *Manual of Zen Buddhism*. Evergreen ed. New York: Grove Press, 1960.

———. *Studies in Laṅkāvatāra Sūtra*. London and Boston: Routledge and Kegan Paul, 1930.

———. *Studies in Zen*. London: Rider, 1955.

———. *The Training of the Buddhist Zen Monk*. Kyoto: Eastern Buddhist Society, 1934.

———. *Zen and Japanese Culture*. New York: Pantheon Books, 1959.

Takahashi, Hatada. *A History of Korea*. Trans. Warren W. Smith and Benjamin H. Hazard. Santa Barbara Calif.: A.B.C. Clio, 1969.

Takakusu, Junjirō. *The Essentials of Buddhist Philosophy*. Westport, Conn.: Greenwood Press, 1973.

Taylor, John B. "Prospects and Problems of Cooperation among Religions." In *IMWS*, 1633–1672.

*Teachings of Jeungsando, The*. Taejŏn: Chŭngsando Ponbu, 1999.

Thurman, Robert A., trans. *The Holy Teaching of Vimalakīrti*. University Park and London: Pennsylvania State University Press, 1981.

Watson, Burton, trans. *The Lotus Sutra*. New York: Columbia University Press, 1993.

———. *The Zen Teachings of Master Lin-chi*. Boston and London: Shambala, 1993.

Williams, Paul. *Mahāyāna Buddhism*. London and New York: Routledge, 1989.

Wittgenstein, Ludwig. *Philosophical Investigations*. Trans. G. E. M. Anscombe. Oxford: Basil Blackwell, 1953.

———. *Tractatus Logico-Philosophicus*. London: Routledge and Kegan Paul, 1922.

Wu, John C. H., trans. *Tao Tĕ Ching*. New York: St. John's University Press, 1961.

Yampolsky, Philip B. *The Platform Sutra of the Sixth Patriarch*. New York: Columbia University Press, 1967.

———, trans. *The Zen Master Hakuin*. New York: Columbia University Press, 1971.

Yokoi, Yūhō, trans. *Zen Master Dōgen: An Introduction with Selected Writings*. Tokyo: Weatherhill, 1976.

# Index

Printed in the United States
By Bookmasters